D0911596

"Superb investigative disciplines . . . and so readable." —Norman Mailer

"Tough-minded . . . comprehensive." —*Chicago Tribune*

"Careful and disquieting analysis of the mysteries of Dallas." —Arthur Schlesinger Jr., two-time Pulitzer Prize and National Book Award winner and former Special Assistant to President Kennedy

"This authoritative book opens a box of secrets. It offers disquieting, even terrifying, answers to the questions we have all been asking." —Len Deighton

"Of all the books written about the Kennedy assassination, this is the first one that has convinced me there is a plausible trail of evidence leading to a conspiracy." —William Attwood, former Ambassador and Special Assistant to the U.S. delegation at the U.N.

"So lucidly arranged and so forcefully mounted that I now feel compelled to believe that there was a conspiracy to kill President Kennedy." —Robert MacNeil, former Executive Editor of the *MacNeil/Lehrer Newshour*

"A thoughtful and responsible book." —Former Congressman Judge Richardson Preyer, House Select Committee on Assassinations

"Deserves to be read and taken seriously by all those who care about truth or justice." —G. Robert Blakey, former Chief Counsel, House Select Committee on Assassinations

"Right on the button . . . a choice book for the budding student of America's crime of the century." —*The Atlanta Journal-Constitution*

Not in Your Lifetime

Also by Anthony Summers

The Eleventh Day: The Full Story of 9/11 and Osama bin Laden
(with Robbyn Swan)

Sinatra: The Life
(with Robbyn Swan)

The Arrogance of Power: The Secret World of Richard Nixon
(with Robbyn Swan)

Official and Confidential: The Secret Life of J. Edgar Hoover

Honeytrap: The Secret Worlds of Stephen Ward
(with Stephen Dorril)

Goddess: The Secret Lives of Marilyn Monroe

The File on the Tsar (with Tom Mangold)

Not in Your Lifetime

The Defining Book on the
JFK Assassination

ANTHONY SUMMERS

OPEN ROAD

INTEGRATED MEDIA
NEW YORK

Cover design by Andrea C. Uva

ISBN 978-1-4804-3548-3

This edition published in 2013 by Open Road Integrated Media, Inc.
345 Hudson Street
New York, NY 10014
www.openroadmedia.com

for Colm, Fionn, and Lara

Contents

CONTENTS

Preface

After fifty years, does the assassination of President Kennedy still matter? It is now as far from us in time as the assassination of Abraham Lincoln was for people living during World War I. Nevertheless, the murder still haunts America and the wider world. For those who were adults at the time, the killing of President Kennedy is a generational milestone. For those much younger, what happened in Dallas persists as a spectral presence even in this new century.

There are multiple reasons why the assassination lingers in the public mind. No other death of a single individual—and one so young, embodying the hopes of a new generation—so traumatized an era. It stays with us in part because John F. Kennedy was killed during the Cold War, at a time when nuclear war seemed a real and constant threat; and in part, too, because November 22, 1963, signaled an end to the sense of cozy security of the previous decade, the waning of public trust in authority. Above all, though, the assassination stays with us because of a perception by millions around the world that there is a mystery—that the full truth of what happened remains unknown.

The idea that the murder of the 35th President of the United States was the result of a conspiracy, not the act of a lone assassin, was there from the start. Who might have been behind such a plot depended on a person's political view, on what they read, on what broadcast made an impression at any given time. Had one or both of America's Communist foes, the Soviet Union or its upstart protégé Cuba, had a hand in the assassination? Had anti-Castro exiles killed Kennedy? Or the Mafia? Or the CIA, or the "military industrial complex"? Or two or more of the above combined?

What the polls have consistently shown is that millions do not believe what the official inquiry that followed the assassination, the Warren Commission, told them happened—that a loner named Lee Harvey Oswald, who had no known motive, killed the President. 74 percent of those Americans polled in a January 2013 study believed—to the contrary—that there had been a conspiracy. A 2009 CBS poll put the figure as high as 76 percent. 74 percent of respondents, according to the same poll, believed there had been "an official cover-up to keep the public from learning the truth about the assassination." The vast majority, 77 percent, thought the full truth would never be known.

This book was first published three decades ago as *Conspiracy*, a title deriving not from any fixed view of mine but because a new probe, by the House Assassinations Committee, had found there had "probably" been a plot. Four editions later, when I updated the book in 1998, a new publisher agreed to the title it now carries—*Not in Your Lifetime*. I should explain.

In early 1964, as the Commission began its work, Chief Justice Earl Warren was asked if all the investigation's information would be made public. He replied, "Yes, there will come a time. *But it might not be in your lifetime* [author's emphasis]. I am not referring to anything especially, but there may be some things that would involve security. This would be preserved but not made public." Warren was thinking of alleged assassin Oswald's visits to the Soviet Union and Mexico, he explained later, and there may indeed have been national security ramifications at that time.

The Soviet, Mexican, and Cuban aspects of the case certainly were hypersensitive at the time—and in some respects may have implications today.[1] Step by step down the years, however, and to the chagrin of some federal agencies, millions of pages of documents have been released. The JFK Act of 1992—more properly the President John F. Kennedy Assassinations Records Collection Act—brought an avalanche of material into the public domain.

Fifty years on, however, we do not have it all. Some Army Intelligence and Secret Service records have been destroyed. There are questions about the whereabouts of some Naval Intelligence material. In 2012, the National Archives stated that rather less than its 1 percent of assassination-related records— out of a total of some five million pages—will not be made public until 2017. It is not clear, and the Archives administration has not counted, just how many documents are actually involved. It is known, though, that the Central Intelligence Agency has withheld 1,171 documents as "national security classified." Some of them, we know, are records that researchers very much want to see—in particular, documents relating to former CIA officers whose activities have aroused justifiable suspicion.

Researchers have reacted with outrage. Professor Robert Blakey, who was Chief Counsel for Congress' assassination investigation in the late 1970s, criticized the National Archives for using "bureaucratic jargon to obfuscate its failure to vindicate the public interest in transparency." He laid the blame, though, not on the Archives so much as the CIA. "I think," he wrote as this book went to press, "the Agency is playing the Archives."

Remaining documents will be released in 2017, the Archives

administration has promised, "unless the President personally certifies on a document by document basis that continued postponement is necessary." Full releases or no full releases, however, the lack of a real official will to investigate—long ago—means that outstanding mysteries about the assassination will never be resolved. This new edition of my book has been heavily rewritten, shorn of items that now seem redundant, and updated in light of information now available. Its title remains, however, *Not in Your Lifetime*.

Anthony Summers
Connecticut and Ireland
2013

Main Characters

The author personally spoke with forty-eight of the principal characters listed below—along with many more interviewed for this book.

John F. Kennedy: the 35th President of the United States

The Oswald family

Lee Harvey Oswald: the lone assassin, according to the first official inquiry. A later finding by a congressional committee suggested he had at least one accomplice.

Marguerite Oswald: Oswald's mother

Marina Oswald (née Nikolaevna Prusakova): Oswald's wife. They were married in the Soviet Union and she accompanied him back to the United States.

Robert Oswald: Oswald's elder brother

Charles "Dutz" Murret: Oswald's uncle in New Orleans, connected to organized crime

Lillian Murret: Charles Murret's wife

Significant individuals

William Alexander: Assistant District Attorney in Dallas

Guy Banister: former senior FBI agent, allegedly involved with Oswald in New Orleans

Comer Clarke: British reporter who claimed Fidel Castro told him that Oswald spoke of killing Kennedy while in Mexico City

John Connally: Governor of Texas, seriously wounded in shooting that killed the President

Oscar Contreras: Mexican leftist student who said he met a man who identified himself as Oswald but who may have been an impostor

Jesse Curry: Dallas police chief

Nelson Delgado: marine who served with Oswald

George de Mohrenschildt: Russian émigré, linked to U.S. intelligence, who associated with Oswald on his return from the Soviet Union

David Ferrie: former airline pilot with links to Oswald, the anti-Castro movement, and organized crime

Captain Will Fritz: headed the Dallas police Homicide unit and questioned Lee Harvey Oswald

Jim Garrison: New Orleans District Attorney who opened a local assassination investigation in 1967

"Alek Hidell": pseudonym Oswald used, probably derived from the name of John Heindel, a marine who had served with him. This name was used to purchase the rifle found at the Texas School Book Depository.

Marie Hyde: American tourist who, in the company of her acquaintances Monica Kramer and Rita Naman, twice encountered Oswald in the Soviet Union

Lyndon B. Johnson: Vice President who became President on the death of President Kennedy

Robert F. Kennedy: President's brother and Attorney General of the United States

Monica Kramer: U.S. tourist in the Soviet Union who twice

encountered Oswald in the company of her friend Rita Naman and their acquaintance Marie Hyde

Clare Booth Luce: former U.S. diplomat and financial supporter of anti-Castro exiles, married to Henry Luce, the publisher of *Time* and *Life* magazines

Thomas Mann: U.S. Ambassador in Mexico City

John McVickar: U.S. consular official at the Moscow Embassy who dealt with Oswald

Yuri Merezhinsky: Soviet citizen present when Oswald met his future wife, Marina

Yuri Nosenko: KGB officer who defected to the United States after the assassination, claiming detailed knowledge of the Soviet handling of Oswald

Ruth Paine: friend of Marina Oswald in Texas. Oswald stayed at her home on the eve of the assassination.

Delphine Roberts: New Orleans right-wing activist and secretary to Guy Banister (her daughter was also called Delphine)

Jack Ruby (née Rubenstein): Dallas nightclub owner, with lifelong links to organized crime, who shot and killed Oswald on November 24

Richard Snyder: Consul at U.S. Embassy in Moscow who handled Oswald, had worked for the CIA

J. D. Tippit: the Dallas policeman shot within hours of the President's murder. Oswald was identified as his killer.

Edward Voebel: New Orleans schoolfriend of Oswald who was in the Civil Air Patrol with him

Major General Edwin Walker: right-wing agitator and victim of an assassination attempt—apparently by Lee Harvey Oswald—in April 1963

Abraham Zapruder: amateur cameraman who shot a film of the assassination that became key evidence

Individuals associated with U.S. intelligence

James Angleton: CIA Counterintelligence chief whose department collected information on Oswald before the assassination. He liaised with the Warren Commission, and—in 1971—ordered material on Oswald to be removed from the home of CIA station chief in Mexico City

"Maurice Bishop": cover name reportedly used by a U.S. intelligence officer alleged to have met with Oswald before the assassination and to have tried to fabricate evidence linking him to Cuban intelligence. Controversy has swirled around the possibility that he may have been one and the same as the late David Phillips, a senior CIA officer involved in anti-Castro operations.

Captain Alexis Davison: Assistant Air Attaché who doubled as doctor at the U.S. Embassy in Moscow. He had intelligence connections and met Oswald

Allen Dulles: Director of the CIA until late 1961, later member of Warren Commission

Desmond FitzGerald: head of the CIA's Cuba operations who led plans to topple Fidel Castro and personally met with supposed Castro traitor Rolando Cubela

William Gaudet: editor who worked for the CIA and whose name appeared next to Oswald's on Mexico City visa list.

William Harvey: senior CIA official who coordinated CIA-Mafia plots to kill Castro

Richard Helms: CIA Deputy Director for Plans who headed covert operations in November 1963 and later became CIA Director

Howard Hunt: senior CIA officer who was involved with anti-Castro operations

George Joannides: CIA officer who controlled the DRE, the anti-Castro group that—for propaganda reasons—exploited Oswald's pro-Castro activity. House Assassinations Committee Chief Counsel Robert Blakey condemned Joannides' later role as CIA liaison to the Committee as having been "criminal."

Lieutenant Colonel Robert E. Jones : Operations Officer, U.S. Army 112th Military Intelligence Group. Said that the Army had a file on Oswald.

Robert Maheu: former Chicago FBI agent and liaison between the CIA and the Mafia

John McCone: CIA Director at time of the assassination

J. Walton Moore: CIA Domestic Contact Division officer in Dallas

Otto Otepka: chief security officer at the State Department whose study of defectors included Oswald

David Phillips: senior CIA officer running anti-Castro operations with an emphasis on propaganda—later headed Western Hemisphere Division. Phillips was in Mexico City at the time of Oswald's visit in the autumn of 1963. It has been suggested that he used the cover name "Bishop." *See entry above.*

Winston Scott: CIA station chief in Mexico City in 1963. On his death, a draft manuscript with information on Oswald's visit to Mexico—and tape recordings labeled "Oswald"—were removed from his home by the CIA and taken to Washington, DC.

FBI

Warren De Brueys: New Orleans special agent alleged to have been seen with Oswald

Charles Flynn: Dallas agent who met Jack Ruby as a "potential criminal informant" in 1959

J. Edgar Hoover: FBI Director

James Hosty: Dallas agent who handled the Oswald case before assassination

John Quigley: New Orleans agent who responded when Oswald asked to see an agent in New Orleans in summer 1963

Gordon Shanklin: Special Agent in Charge in Dallas at the time of the assassination. Agent Hosty said he ordered the destruction of a note from Oswald.

James Wood: agent who questioned George de Mohrenschildt in Haiti after the assassination

Individuals involved with Oswald and Cuba

Gilberto Alvarado: Nicaraguan intelligence agent whose allegation linked Oswald to Cuban diplomats in Mexico City

"Angel" or "Angelo": Hispanic said to have visited Silvia Odio in the company of a man introduced as "Leon Oswald"

Manuel Artime: key figure at CIA's Bay of Pigs invasion who claimed President Kennedy approved Castro assassination plan

William Attwood: Special Adviser to U.S. delegation at the United Nations, who led secret contacts with Havana before the assassination

Eusebio Azcue: outgoing Cuban Consul in Mexico City, who met a visitor who used the name Oswald and said he came to believe he was an impostor

Carlos Bringuier: New Orleans representative of the Directorio Revolucionario Estudiantil (DRE), involved in suspect street fracas with Oswald

Fidel Castro: Cuban Prime Minister in 1963—he later became President

Rolando Cubela (CIA cryptonym AMLASH): Castro aide who, the CIA came to believe, had turned traitor and intended to kill the Cuban leader. He may in fact have remained loyal to Castro.

Jean Daniel: French journalist for *L'Express* whom Kennedy used to sound out Castro—was with the Cuban leader on November 22

Manuel Antonio de Varona: vice president, then leader, of exiles' Cuban Revolutionary Council

Hermínio Díaz García: Cuban anti-Castro fighter and associate of Mafia boss Santo Trafficante. He reportedly told his comrade Tony Cuesta, leader of the group Commandos L, that he personally took part in the President's assassination. Died in a raid on Cuba in 1966.

Sylvia Durán: secretary to Cuban Consul in Mexico City who processed Oswald's visa request

Loran Hall: worked with anti-Castro groups and the CIA and was linked to Santo Trafficante. His claim to have visited Silvia Odio sidelined a key indication of conspiracy.

Daniel Harker: Associated Press reporter in Havana who cited a remark by Castro that appeared be a threat to U.S. leaders

Lisa Howard: ABC-TV reporter who met Castro and later acted as go-between in contacts with Havana before November 22

Carlos Lechuga: Cuban Ambassador to the United Nations, involved with the United States in backchannel peace feelers before the assassination

"Leopoldo": Hispanic who led the three men who visited Silvia Odio, introducing one of the group as "Leon Oswald"

Reinaldo Martinez: Cuban exile, said he learned in 1966 that his close friend Herminio Díaz had admitted having taken part in the President's assassination

Alfredo Mirabal: the incoming Cuban Consul in Mexico City, also intelligence officer, briefly saw individual who said he was Oswald

Silvia and Annie Odio: daughters of wealthy Cuban activist Amador Odio, who told of a visit before the assassination of two Hispanics accompanied by a man introduced as "Leon Oswald"—who had supposedly spoken of killing either Castro or Kennedy

Orest Pena: anti-Castro exile in New Orleans who claimed he saw Lee Harvey Oswald with FBI Agent De Brueys

Carlos Quiroga: anti-Castro exile and associate of Carlos Bringuier who visited Oswald in New Orleans

Dr. Rene Vallejo: Castro aide who acted as liaison in U.S.–Cuba contacts before the assassination

Antonio Veciana: leader of the anti-Castro group Alpha 66. Claimed that his U.S. intelligence contact, "Maurice Bishop," met with Oswald before the assassination, and later tried to fabricate information linking Oswald to the Cuban Embassy in Mexico.

Individuals related to Jack Ruby or to organized crime aspects of the case

José Alemán: son of former Cuban government minister who quoted Mafia boss Santo Trafficante as saying President Kennedy was "going to be hit"

Robert "Barney" Baker: Hoffa thug who had two phone conversations with Jack Ruby shortly before the assassination

Edward Becker: casino employee, later investigator, who claimed

that Carlos Marcello discussed having the President killed
and setting up a "nut" to take the blame

Emile Bruneau: associate of Marcello aide who helped Oswald
get bail after a street dispute in New Orleans

Judith Campbell (later Exner): woman who had a sexual relationship with President Kennedy and later with Mafia boss Sam
Giancana

Joseph Campisi: owner of a Dallas restaurant who visited Jack
Ruby in jail

Joseph Civello: man who reportedly represented Mafia boss Carlos Marcello in Dallas

William Hawk Daniels: federal investigator, later judge, who
listened in on a phone conversation between Jimmy Hoffa
and an aide in which there was discussion of killing Robert
Kennedy

Sergeant Patrick Dean: officer in charge of the police basement
security operation at the time Jack Ruby killed Oswald

Sam Giancana: Chicago Mafia boss and coordinator of CIA-
Mafia plans to kill Fidel Castro

Jimmy Hoffa: Teamsters Union boss who was close to Santo Trafficante and reportedly wanted both President Kennedy and
Robert Kennedy dead

Tom Howard: Jack Ruby's first lawyer

Liverde: last name of Marcello aide named as having been at
meeting at which assassination of the President was discussed

Carlos Marcello (born Calogero Minacore): Mafia boss in New
Orleans and the southeastern United States, said to have
discussed a plan to assassinate the President using a "nut"
to take the blame and to have admitted the crime in old age

John Martino: linked to organized crime, U.S. intelligence, and the anti-Castro movement—his widow said he knew the assassination was about to occur. Reportedly said Oswald was "put together" by the "anti-Castro people."

Lewis McWillie: friend of Jack Ruby and manager of Tropicana nightclub in Havana, in which Santo Trafficante had a major interest

Murray "Dusty" Miller: aide to Jimmy Hoffa whom Ruby called two weeks before the assassination

Edward Partin: Teamsters official in Louisiana who said Jimmy Hoffa wanted both President Kennedy and Robert Kennedy dead

Nofio Pecora: associate of Carlos Marcello who knew Oswald's uncle Charles Murret. Jack Ruby called his office number less than a month before the assassination.

Carl Roppolo: oil geologist who, according to Edward Becker, was present when Carlos Marcello discussed a plan to murder President Kennedy

John Roselli: top mobster and go-between in the CIA-Mafia plots to assassinate Fidel Castro

Sam Termine: Marcello henchman who knew Oswald's mother

Jack Todd: associate of Santo Trafficante whose phone number was found in Jack Ruby's car after the murder of Lee Harvey Oswald

Santo Trafficante: Florida Mafia boss linked to CIA-Mafia plots to assassinate Fidel Castro. He was reportedly visited by Jack Ruby in Cuba in 1959—allegedly said before the assassination that President Kennedy was "going to be hit."

Jack Van Laningham: inmate imprisoned with Mafia boss Carlos Marcello, who claimed Marcello admitted having had a role in the assassination.

Irwin Weiner: financial adviser to Jimmy Hoffa who offered conflicting explanations of a phone conversation he had with Ruby less than a month before the assassination

John Wilson: detainee in a camp in Cuba along with Santo Trafficante in 1959. Reported after the assassination that a "gangster type named Ruby" had visited "Santos" in the prison.

Not in Your Lifetime

Read not to contradict and confute, nor to believe and take for granted . . . but to weigh and consider.

—Francis Bacon

CHAPTER I

Ambush

It may be he shall take my hand
And lead me into his dark land
And close my eyes and quench my breath...
But I've a rendezvous with Death

— battle poem by Alan Seeger, quoted by John F. Kennedy

In his office at the White House, President Kennedy looked gloomily across the desk at his press secretary. "I wish I weren't going to Dallas," he said. The secretary replied, "Don't worry about it. It's going to be a great trip."

It was November 20, 1963. The President had received warnings about Dallas from all sides. Senator William Fulbright had told him, "Dallas is a very dangerous place. I wouldn't go there. Don't you go." That morning, Senator Hubert Humphrey and Congressman Hale Boggs had advised him not to go, the congressman saying, "Mr. President, you're going into a hornet's nest."

The President knew he had to go. Dallas, a thousand miles away, had voted overwhelmingly for Richard Nixon in the last presidential election. This time around, the state of Texas as a whole was sure to be tough territory for the Democrats, and Kennedy was determined to take the initiative.

Yet Texas was a menace. Dallas, sweltering in its interminable summer, was dangerously overheated in a different way. It was a mecca for the radical right. Leading lights of the community included a racist former Army general, a mayor who reportedly sympathized with the city's flourishing and furiously right-wing John Birch Society, and a vociferous millionaire obsessed with the Communist menace. Men of their ilk cried "treason" at Kennedy's talk of racial integration, his nuclear test ban treaty, and the possibility of accommodation with the Communist world. It was only a year since the Cuban Missile Crisis, and the President was now showered with accusations that he had gone soft on Fidel Castro. Right-wing extremism was the boil on the face of American politics, and Dallas the point where it might burst. But Kennedy had set his mind on going.

On November 21, the President flew south from Washington, DC, to San Antonio, his first stop on the Texas tour. All went well there, and Kennedy made a speech about the space age. "We stand on the edge of a great new era. . . ." He went on to Houston and talked about the space program again. "Where there is no vision, the people perish. . . ." Before the President arrived in Fort Worth, at midnight, he had traveled safely in four motorcades.

November 22 began with a speech in the rain and a political breakfast. Then, back in his hotel room, Kennedy read the newspapers. In the *Dallas Morning News*, he saw an advertisement placed by "The American Fact-Finding Committee." Headlined "Welcome, Mr. Kennedy, to Dallas," it inquired, "Why do you say we have built a 'wall of freedom' around Cuba when there is no freedom in Cuba today? Because of your policy, thousands of Cubans have been imprisoned . . . the entire population of 7,000,000 Cubans are living in slavery. . . ." The advertisement, whose leading sponsors included a local organizer of the John Birch Society and the son of H. L. Hunt, the Dallas oil millionaire, prompted the President to turn to his wife and murmur, "You know, we're heading into nut country today."

Four days earlier, when the President visited Miami, there had apparently been a security flap. A motorcade was reportedly canceled following concern about disaffected Cuban exiles. The Secret Service had information that a right-wing extremist had spoken of a plan to shoot the President "from an office building with a high-powered rifle." Perhaps his personal escort had mentioned it to Kennedy, for now—in Fort Worth—he murmured to an aide, "Last night would have been a hell of a night to assassinate a president. . . . Anyone perched above the crowd with a rifle could do it." John F. Kennedy even crouched down and mimed how an assassin might take aim.

Just before noon, the President arrived in Dallas. There were welcoming crowds at the airport, and then he was traveling to the city center in an open limousine. As Kennedy passed, one spectator said to her husband, "The President ought to be awarded the Purple Heart just for coming to Dallas."

At 12:29 p.m., the motorcade was amidst cheering crowds, moving slowly through the metal-and-glass canyons of central Dallas.

For a while, there had been no talking in the President's car. Then, with the passing crowd a kaleidoscope of welcome, the wife of the Governor of Texas, Nellie Connally, turned to smile at the President and said, "Mr. Kennedy, you can't say Dallas doesn't love you." The President, sitting behind her and to her right, replied, "That is very obvious." With his wife, Jacqueline, beside him, he continued waving to the people.

Ponderously, at eleven miles an hour, the procession moved onto Elm Street and into an open space. This was Dealey Plaza, a wide expanse of grass stretching away to the left of the cars. To the right of the President towered the Texas School Book Depository, a warehouse, the last high building in this part of the city. Its far end marked the end of the urban ugliness and the end of likely danger to the President during the motorcade. Here there was a grassy slope, topped by an ornamental colonnade. In the lead car, an officer looked ahead at a railway tunnel and said to a colleague, "We've almost got it made." It was twelve seconds past 12:30 p.m.

The several shots rang out in rapid succession. According to a Secret Service agent in the car, the President said, "My God, I'm hit."[1] He lurched in his seat, both hands clawing toward his throat. As Jacqueline Kennedy remembered it just a week later—in an interview partially suppressed at the time:

> "You know when he was shot. He had such a wonderful expression on his face. . . . [Then] he looked puzzled . . . he had his hand out, I could see a piece of his skull coming off; it was flesh-colored not white. He was holding out his hand—and I can see this perfectly clean piece detaching itself from his head. . . ."

Directly in front of the President, Governor Connally had heard one shot and was then hit himself. He screamed. For five seconds, the car actually slowed down. Then had come more gunfire. The President had fallen violently backward and to his left, his head exploding in a halo of brain tissue, blood, and bone. To Mrs. Connally, it "was like buckshot falling all over us."

As the car finally gathered speed, Mrs. Kennedy believed she cried:

> "I love you, Jack . . . I kept saying, 'Jack, Jack, Jack' . . . All the ride to the hospital, I kept bending over him saying, 'Jack, Jack, can you hear me? I love you, Jack.' I kept holding the top of his head down trying to keep the . . ."

She was unable to finish the sentence.

From the front seat the Governor's wife heard the President's wife exclaim, "Jack . . . they've killed my husband." Then: "I have his brains in my hand." This last Mrs. Kennedy repeated time and time again.

Half an hour later, in an emergency room at nearby Parkland Hospital, a doctor told the President's wife what she already knew: "The President is gone." Governor Connally, though seriously wounded, survived.

The dying of President Kennedy was brutally brief. Yet it took some time and care to write this summary of the shooting with integrity. Fifty years on, much has changed about our perception of the Kennedy era. Many no longer see the brothers as innocent martyrs of an idealized time called Camelot. A mass of persuasive information links their names to election tampering, to philandering that may have risked more than their reputations, to compromising contacts with the Mafia, and—by black irony—to assassination plots. A public that once revered the Federal Bureau of Investigation and trusted the Central Intelligence Agency has been made cynical by revelations of sins ranging from incompetence to unconstitutional malfeasance—in the CIA's case, too, a sordid history of murder plots.

With the passing of half a century, much remains unclear about what happened in Dealey Plaza. Few murders in history had such a massive audience or were caught in the act by the camera, yet for millions the case remains unsolved. No assassination has been analyzed and documented so laboriously by public officials and private citizens. Yet the public has remained understandably skeptical.

Skeptical when, after one official probe proclaimed the assassination was the work of a lone gunman, another declared it the result of a conspiracy—"probably." Skeptical after a welter of media coverage and books, when much of the media work has proven inaccurate or biased, and when supposedly authoritative books have been unmasked as inept, or naïve, or cynical propaganda. The 1991 movie *JFK*, directed by Oliver Stone, misled a whole new generation of filmgoers with a hodgepodge of half-truth and excess masquerading as revelation about conspiracy. A heavily promoted tome called *Case Closed*, by Gerald Posner, hoodwinked its readers with its packaging of the opposite message—that there could be no real doubt that the assassination had been the uncomplicated act of a lone gunman.

Above all, perhaps, the public attitude to the Kennedy assassination has been tempered by all the scandals, all the exposés that over the years have eroded belief in government. Far from starting with the premise that the authorities tell the truth, a depressingly large number of people now accept as a given that the government constantly lies. If it does not actively lie, many are persuaded, it conceals the truth. Much of the material in this book was pried out of reluctant agencies thanks to the Freedom of Information Act—albeit a law long since seriously emasculated—and to the JFK Records Act, passed into law in 1992 specifically to enforce release of assassination-related records. Yet some records remain unreleased, many under the rubric of "national security," the justification used by Chief Justice Earl Warren to explain why some material would not be released in the lifetime of his audience. Hence the title of this book: *Not in Your Lifetime*. What sort of national security concerns prevent us seeing all there is to see about the Kennedy assassination, a supposed random act by a lone nut, all these years later? It is a question to ponder while reading this book.

For all of these reasons, thinking people remain uncertain who was behind the killing of President Kennedy. Why the murder was committed, only the arrogant or the opinionated can pretend to know for sure. And weary though we may be after decades of controversy and nitpicking, any serious inquiry has to begin where life ended for John F. Kennedy—the moment the shots were fired in Dealey Plaza.

I

DALLAS
The Open-and-Shut Case

The Evidence Before You

"Detection is, or ought to be, an exact science, and should be treated in the same cold and unemotional manner."

—Sherlock Holmes, in *The Sign of the Four*

In any fatal shooting inquiry, the primary factors are ballistics and wounds. Human testimony, though often crucial, must be weighed against the picture presented by hard evidence. In the Kennedy assassination, they are the raw material for the answers to key questions. How many gunmen fired how many bullets, and from what position? If gunfire came from more than one vantage point, there obviously must have been more than one assassin. Similarly, if more shots came from one position than could be fired by one gunman in the available time, it follows that accomplices were at work.

Evidence there was in profusion, and much of it was poorly handled in the first investigation. This is what we are left with—leaving aside for the moment the question of assigning guilt for the shooting.

Dealey Plaza provided a field day for the ballistics experts. Soon after the assassination, a policeman found three spent cartridge cases lying near an open window on the sixth floor of the Texas School Book Depository, the large warehouse to the right rear of President Kennedy's car at the time of the attack. Within an hour, another policeman spotted a bolt-action rifle,[1] the now infamous 6.5-mm Mannlicher-Carcano, stashed behind a pile of boxes and also on the sixth floor.

A number of bullet fragments were recovered—from the wounds suffered by the President and Governor Connally, and in the presidential limousine. One bullet,[2] which looked almost undamaged to the inexpert eye, turned up on a stretcher at Parkland Hospital, where the victims had been treated. Suffice it to say, at this point, that firearms experts have firmly linked the cartridge cases to the rifle; they are sure the whole bullet and the bullet fragments came from the same gun.

Bullet damage was also noticed on the inside of the windshield of the presidential car and on a section of the curb in Dealey Plaza. No other gun or missiles were recovered immediately after the assassination.[3] The catalog of ballistics evidence is at least clear-cut, but the accounting of the wounds is a different matter.

The autopsy on President Kennedy, one of the most important autopsies in twentieth-century history, was seriously flawed. Had it not been, much wearisome doubt could have been avoided.

An hour and a half after the shooting of the President, there was a struggle over his corpse. At the hospital, as the Secret Service team prepared to take the body to Washington, DC, Dr. Earl Rose, the Dallas County Medical Examiner, backed by a Justice of the Peace, barred their way. The doctor said that, under Texas law, the body of a murder victim may not be removed until an autopsy has been performed. Justice of the Peace Theran Ward, declared the President's death, "just another homicide as far as I'm concerned."

Kenneth O'Donnell, special assistant to the dead President, replied, "Go screw yourself." The Secret Service agents put the doctor and the judge up against the wall at gunpoint and swept out of the hospital with the President's body. They were wrong in law, and with hindsight denied their President an efficient autopsy. That evening, at eight o'clock, three doctors at Bethesda Naval Hospital began the examination to determine precisely how the President had died.

Incredibly, according to the expert study commissioned by the House Select Committee on Assassinations in the 1970s, the doctors "had insufficient training and experience to evaluate a death from gunshot wounds." Not one of them was a full-time forensic pathologist, an expert in determining the cause of death in criminal cases.

The late Medical Examiner for New York City, Dr. Milton Helpern, said of the President's autopsy, "It's like sending a seven-year-old boy who has taken three lessons on the violin over to the New York Philharmonic and expecting him to perform a Tchaikovsky symphony. He knows how to hold the violin and bow, but he has a long way to go before he can make music."

Cruel words, yet some of the autopsy's shortcomings are glaring even to the layman. Although the President's fatal injuries were to his head, and although the location of such wounds is crucial information, routine procedures were not followed. The doctors failed to shave Kennedy's head to lay bare the skull damage, apparently because the Kennedy family wanted him to look good should the casket be left open. And, although the damaged brain was removed and fixed in formaldehyde, the doctors omitted to section it to track the path of the bullet or bullets. As discussed later, the brain itself later disappeared.

The chairman of the medical panel for the House Assassinations Committee, Dr. Michael Baden, was to declare in 1978 that the autopsy had been deficient in "the qualification of the pathologists . . . the failure to inspect the clothing . . . the inadequate documentation of injuries, lack of proper preservation of evidence, and incompleteness of the autopsy."

The autopsy doctors had been handicapped by instructions relayed by phone from the President's brother Robert, huddled with the widow in a VIP suite upstairs. A 1992 report in the *Journal of the American Medical Association* confirmed that the family, concerned in particular that the world would learn that Kennedy suffered from a progressive disease of the adrenal glands, wanted to prevent several routine procedures. The organs of the neck were not examined.

To this day, the precise nature of the President's injuries remains unclear. The autopsy doctors described four wounds: a small wound at the back of the skull; a massive defect in the right side of the skull; a small hole near the base of the neck, slightly to the right of the spine; and a hole in the throat.

The throat wound had been obscured by the Dallas doctors when they performed a tracheotomy to insert an airway, during the hopeless bid to save the President's life. Unnecessary confusion reigns over the injury supposedly located near the back of the neck. The Autopsy Descriptive Sheet placed it five and a half inches below the tip of the right mastoid process, a bump at the base of the skull. The autopsists' working sketch, the death certificate, a report by FBI agents present at the autopsy, the statements of several Secret Service agents, and the holes in Kennedy's jacket and shirt are consistent with a wound some six inches lower than reported.

The doctors failed to dissect this wound, an elementary procedure that might have established the path of the bullet. The hole was merely probed, not opened up and tracked to its destination. Documents suggest that photographs and X-rays were taken during the probing attempt. If so, however, the current location of those images remains unknown.

There is also confusion about the fatal injuries to Kennedy's head. With the body long buried, forensic scientists in later years have had to base their findings on the extensive surviving X-rays and photographs—access to them is restricted to experts and doctors approved by the Kennedy family. They were examined in 1966 by the original autopsy doctors—astonishingly for the first time. They had never until then seen the pictures of the postmortem they had themselves supervised. The same material, and the President's clothing, has since been much scrutinized— by an Attorney General's medical panel in 1968, the Rockefeller Commission panel, pathologists for the Assassinations Committee in the 1970s, and by some of the Dallas doctors and other interested physicians.

The autopsy doctors located the small wound at the back of the skull as being two and a half centimeters to the right and slightly above the protuberance at the back of the skull. Other medical panels, working with the X-rays and photographs, decided that this had been a serious mistake, that the small wound was in fact four inches higher than described. Dr. Michael Baden, head of the Assassinations Committee panel, said that it could be seen in the photographs, above the hairline. It is unclear how such a conflict arose, unless—perhaps—from misinterpretation of the photographs (see Photo 7).

There has been lasting disagreement as to the true location of even the fatal wound, the massive defect described by the autopsy doctors as a hole thirteen centimeters wide, extending both forward and back, on the right side of the head. Some of the autopsy photographs became available to the public in spite of the restrictions,[4] and one of them (see Photo 8) shows a large flap of scalp and bone laid open, like a hatch cover, beside a terrible hole directly above the dead man's right ear. This conflicts with the majority of the human testimony on the location of the wound.

Seventeen of the medical staff who observed the President in Dallas were to describe the massive defect as having been more at the *back* of the head than at the side. A large bone fragment, found in Dealey Plaza after the assassination, was identified at the time as belonging to the back of the skull.

The Secret Service agent who climbed into the President's limousine as the shooting ended, Clint Hill, said, "I noticed a portion of the President's head on the right rear side was missing. . . . Part of his brain was gone. I saw a part of his skull with hair on it lying in the seat. . . . The right rear portion of his head was missing. It was lying in the rear seat of the car." Two other Secret Service agents gave similar descriptions.

Jacqueline Kennedy came to one of the doctors in the emergency room, her hands cupped one over the other. She was holding her husband's brain matter in her hands. "From the front, there was nothing," she later said of the wounds. "But from the back you could see, you know, you were trying to hold his hair and his skull on."

Dr. Robert McClelland, a general surgeon on the team that attended the dying President, was one of those best qualified to describe the head wound from memory. "I took the position at the head of the table," McClelland told the Warren Commission, "I was in such a position that I could closely examine the head wound, and I noted that the right posterior portion of the skull had been blasted. It had been shattered, apparently, by the force of the shot so that the parietal bone was protruded up through the scalp and seen to be fractured almost along its posterior half, as well as some of the occipital bone being fractured in its lateral half, and this sprung open the bones that I mentioned, in such a way that you could actually look down into the skull cavity itself and see that probably a third or so, at least, of the brain tissue, posterior cerebral tissue and some of the cerebellar tissue had been blasted out." The wound McClelland described would look like the drawing below, a drawing that he approved for publication during the 1960s.

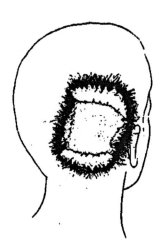

The only neurosurgeon present at the President's deathbed, Dr. Kemp Clark, described the wound as a "large, gaping loss of tissue" located at the "back of the head . . . toward the right side." No less than eleven other Parkland doctors, and four nurses—including the supervising nurse—have described this gaping wound at the back of the head. The same interpretation has been put on the description of the wound by twenty people who saw it at Bethesda Hospital in Washington, DC. Two of the technicians who X-rayed the President's body during the autopsy recalled a posterior wound. One of them, Jerrol Custer, said it was enormous. "I could put both my hands in the wound." The head of the Secret Service team, Roy Kellerman, who was assigned to the President that day and who attended the autopsy; two FBI agents assigned to the autopsy; and a mortician who prepared the body for burial, also recalled a wound at the back of the head.

Drawings of the large head wound were made from memory for the Assassinations Committee by the FBI's observers, James Sibert and Francis O'Neill, and by the mortician, Thomas Robinson. While they vary in locating the height of the wound, they place it at the rear or right rear of the head, not at the side.

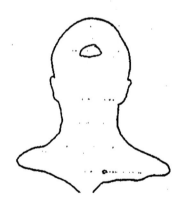

Wound position according to FBI Agent James Sibert

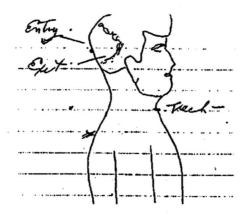

Wound position according to FBI Agent Francis O'Neill

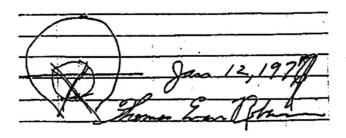

Wound position according to mortician Thomas Robinson

Not one of the Parkland or Bethesda witnesses have described a wound like the one in the autopsy picture, which shows a great hole above the right ear, and the rear of the head virtually unmarked (see Photo 8).

What, then, to make of that photograph? After studying it,

several of the Dallas medical staff expressed consternation. One, Dr. Fouad Bashour, insisted the photograph was wrong. "Why do they cover it up?" he said. "This is not the way it was!"

In an interview with the author, the Dallas surgeon Robert McClelland offered an explanation. When he saw the President in the emergency room, he said, a great flap of scalp and hair had been "split and thrown backwards, so we had looked down into the hole." In Photo 8, however, McClelland believes the scalp is being pulled forward, back to its normal position, to show what looks like a small entrance wound near the top of the skull. This is not visible in Photo 8. "I don't think they were trying to cover up the fact that there was a large hole," said McClelland, "but that's what they were doing. . . . They were covering up that great defect in the back and lateral part of the head by pulling that loose scalp flap up. You can see the hand pulling the scalp forward."[5]

Dr. McClelland said the "great defect in the back" is visible on some photographs among the set of some fifty pictures he saw at the National Archives—pictures in which the torn scalp has been allowed to fall back on the President's neck, pictures the public has never seen. His explanation may go a long way to resolve the apparent discrepancy. It certainly demonstrates that no outside researcher should form judgments on the basis of a set of photographs that may or may not be complete.

According to the pathologist who directed the autopsy, Dr. Humes, his colleague Dr. Pierre Finck, and the former director of photography at the Naval Medical School, who was the principal cameraman at the autopsy, not even the "official" set of autopsy photographs at the National Archives is complete. Pictures they remembered being taken, or thought should have been taken, are not in the collection. Photographs of the interior chest are not there. Nor, according to Dr. Finck, are certain photographs of the skull injuries.

With some pictures missing or possibly missing, and some showing injuries as witnesses do not recall having seen them, some have suspected forgery—notwithstanding a finding by a majority of the Assassinations Committee photographic panel that the pictures are authentic.[6]

Such doubts were encouraged by the comments of Floyd Reibe, a former Bethesda technician who himself took some of the autopsy photographs. He claimed that some of the photographs in the National Archives are "phony and not the photographs we took."

In 1994, the Assassination Records Review Board stated that a second set of autopsy photographs may have survived, photographs apparently made from the original negatives and thus presumably authentic. If so, they would be key evidence, but the matter was left unresolved.

There are other problems with the autopsy record, not least the bizarre fact that the President's brain is missing. Sometime after the assassination, it was sent to President Kennedy's former secretary, along with the photographs and X-rays, for safekeeping. Safe it was not—at least not from the point of view of future investigators. In 1966, after the materials passed into the care of the National Archives, it was discovered that the brain was no longer with the photographs and X-rays. Also absent were tissue sections, blood smears, and a number of slides.

The Assassinations Committee, which could find no trace of the missing material, favored the theory that Robert Kennedy, the President's brother, disposed of it to avoid tasteless display in the future. A vial containing a part of the brain was destroyed by the Secret Service some six years after the assassination. Whatever the full facts, the result was to hamper the work of later forensic pathologists.

The autopsy X-rays also feature in the catalog of mismanagement. Dr. McClelland, the surgeon who worked on the dying President in Dallas, reviewed the set of X-rays at the National Archives in 1989. He was quoted afterward as saying that they showed head injuries different from those he saw in the emergency room in 1963. Jerrol Custer, a former Bethesda technician who made some of the autopsy X-rays in 1963, claimed—as did his colleague of the autopsy photos—that some of the X-rays were "fake."

A physicist and radiation therapist at the Eisenhower Medical Center, Dr. David Mantik, submitted the X-rays to a technique called optical densitometry. "This data," he told the author, "provides powerful and quantitative evidence of alteration to some of the skull X-rays. They appear to me to be composites."

It is not for this author to judge whether such suspicions are justified. What is clear, however, is that the best evidence, the President's wounded body, was squandered. The deficiencies of the autopsy, and the mismanagement of the record, added fuel to the lasting controversy.[7]

Aside from the evidence of body and bullets, there is one further invaluable aid to any analysis of the assassination. This is the short but infinitely shocking film made by an amateur cameraman in the crowd, Abraham Zapruder. Having initially left his camera at home, Zapruder had hurried home to fetch it at the last moment. So it was that he came to make the eighteen seconds of truly apocalyptic film that has remained the subject of diverse interpretation. The most famous amateur movie in the world was shot from a vantage point on a low concrete wall to the right front of the approaching President. For all its fame, and although no description can replace actual viewing of the Zapruder film, its contents must be summarized here.

As the motorcade turns to come straight toward his lens, Zapruder catches the last uneventful seconds, with the President and his wife smiling and waving in the sun. Then the limousine vanishes for a moment behind a street sign. When it emerges, the President is clearly reacting to a shot—his hands clenched and coming up to his throat. Governor Connally turns around to his right, peering into the backseat. He begins to turn back, goes rigid, and shows signs that he, too, has been hit. Jacqueline Kennedy looks toward her husband, who is leaning forward and to his left. There is an almost imperceptible forward movement of the President's head, and then, abruptly, his skull visibly explodes in a spray of blood and brain matter. He is propelled violently back into the rear seat of the car, then bounces forward and slides to the left into Mrs. Kennedy's arms. The savage backward lurch by the President occurs, to the eye, at the instant of the fatal wound to the head. Then, as Mrs. Kennedy apparently reaches for a fragment of her husband's skull on the back of the car, a Secret Service agent jumps aboard from behind, and the limousine finally accelerates away.

Abraham Zapruder sold his film to *Life* magazine for a quarter of a million dollars. The magazine later published still frames from the material, but the moving footage was not shown on television until March 1975. The film was a key tool for both official investigations, not least because it provides a near-precise time frame for the assassination.

In 1978, however, it took on new importance, for its use in conjunction with a hitherto neglected item of evidence, one that was greeted as the most momentous single breakthrough in the case since 1964. It followed news that the sounds in Dealey Plaza had apparently been recorded—and included identifiable gunshots.

This evidence, if evidence it is, had been ignored for sixteen years. It was a battered blue "Dictabelt," a routine recording of police radio traffic that had been made, just as on any ordinary day, on the day of the President's murder. To the layman it is a mishmash of barely comprehensible conversation between policemen in the field and their dispatch office at headquarters. The gaps between speech seem a meaningless blur of distorted sound and static. That certainly is what was assumed by the Dallas police and the Warren Commission, who used the recording only to establish police movement and messages. The Dictabelt long lay abandoned in a filing cabinet at Dallas police headquarters, until a director of the police Intelligence Division took it home. There it might have stayed, were it not for the keen archival mind of a private researcher named Mary Ferrell. Long aware of the recording, she drew the attention of the Assassinations Committee to its possible significance.

Recovered in 1978, the Dictabelt was submitted to Dr. James Barger, chief acoustical scientist for the firm of Bolt, Beranek and Newman. The company specialized in acoustical analysis, working not only on such projects as underwater detection devices for the U.S. Navy, but also on studies of matters of national importance. In 1973, during the investigation of Watergate, the firm advised on the famous gap in the White House tapes. Its expertise had been used, too, in the prosecution of National Guardsmen involved in the shooting of students at Kent State University.

Nobody expected very much from the crackly Dallas police recording submitted to Dr. Barger. His work, though, along with a further study performed by two scientists at the City University of New York, turned out to be pivotal to the deliberations of the Assassinations Committee. Technical processes, including the use of equipment not available in 1963, enabled Barger to produce a visual presentation of the sound-wave forms on a part of the tape that—his initial findings indicated—had great significance.

With his New York associates, Professor Mark Weiss and Ernest Aschkenasy, Dr. Barger then designed an acoustical reconstruction in Dealey Plaza. Early one morning in 1978, guns boomed once again at the scene of President Kennedy's murder. The results showed that impulses on the police recording matched sound patterns unique to the scene of the crime. Certain impulses, the scientists theorized, were indeed gunshots. They declared that the sounds had been picked up by a microphone moving along at about eleven miles per hour at the time of the assassination. They surmised that this was mounted on the motorcycle of a police outrider in the presidential motorcade, and that the recording had been made because the microphone button was stuck open at the time. Working from photographic evidence and testimony, Assassinations Committee staff decided that the motorcycle had been one ridden by Officer H. B. McLain. It appeared that the scientists and the investigators had achieved a tour de force of detection.

The Committee's experts concluded that gunfire had come from in front of the President as well as from behind him. At least two gunmen were therefore involved in the assassination. Aware that acoustics today has a rightful place in forensic science, that it has been admitted into evidence in court, the Assassinations Committee was forced into a dramatic reassessment. The acoustics finding formed a major plank of its official finding that President Kennedy was "probably" murdered as the result of a conspiracy.

Soon, however, came dissenting expert opinion. First from the FBI, with a skimpy report declaring the two-gunman theory "invalid." Even a lay reading revealed this critique to be hopelessly flawed, and it deserves no public airing here. The first serious blow to the acoustical evidence came in a 1982 report by the National Academy of Sciences. A panel of distinguished scientists concluded that the Committee's studies "do not demonstrate that there was a grassy-knoll shot." At the core of the finding lay not some abstruse scientific deduction, but the curiosity of a drummer in Ohio, Steve Barber.

Barber came to the controversy thanks to a girlie magazine. In the summer of 1979, *Gallery* offered its readers, among the nudes, a record of the section of the police Dictabelt that includes the noises said to be gunshots. Barber, who played it again and again, detected something the experts had missed. What had been thought to be unintelligible "crosstalk"—conversation coming in from another radio channel—Barber's ear identified as the voice of Sheriff Bill Decker, in the lead car of the motorcade. The sheriff's voice occurs at the same point on the recording as the sound impulses that the Committee's experts said were gunshots. What he is saying is, "Move all men available out of my department back into the railroad yards there . . . to try to determine just what and where it happened down there. And hold everything secure until the homicide and other investigators can get there." Clearly, Decker did not issue his orders till *after* the shooting.

Undeterred, acoustical scientist James Barger said this apparent anomaly could have been caused in several ways. Was it possible that the Dictabelt needle jumped back—as was said to occur sometimes with that old-fashioned system? Or did the process of copying the original police recording cause the illusion of "crosstalk"?

Dr. Barger stood by his original findings. "The number of detections we made in our tests, and the speed of the detections—the odds that that could happen by chance are about one in twenty. That's just as plain as the nose on your face."

In the fullness of time, however, it has become evident to others that the findings are far from proven. Barber's discovery triggered an onslaught on the acoustics evidence. Because of the timing, the Academy of Sciences was to conclude the sounds on the recording had to be something *other* than gunshots, static perhaps, but not gunshots.

Fifty years on, a significant number of responsible researchers indeed think that a conspiracy finding based on the acoustics is untenable. A 2001 study by researcher Michael O'Dell suggested that the impulses on the Dictabelt "happen too late to be the assassination gunshots," and that "there is no statistical significance of 95% or higher for a shot from the grassy knoll."

On the other hand, one of those who has specialized in the acoustics evidence asserted in a 2010 book that there was indeed a shot from the knoll, and that it was the fatal headshot. Only for O'Dell, author of the 2001 study, to produce a further analysis refuting the Committee's findings, as this book was going to press.

It is evident that science—whether forensic, acoustic, or ballistic—has produced no certainties, and will not resolve the questions surrounding the Kennedy assassination.

House Assassinations Committee Chief Counsel Robert Blakey, though shaken by the negative studies of the acoustics evidence, nevertheless held to his view. "I think our conclusion was correct," he has said. "On balance, I say there were two shooters in the Plaza, and not just because of the acoustics. . . ." Blakey remained persuaded by "all the other evidence and testimony," not least the human testimony about the day of the assassination. "I find on balance," Blakey added, "that the earwitness and eyewitness testimony is credible."

CHAPTER 3

How Many Shots?
Where From?

*"The great tragedy of Science—the slaying of a
beautiful hypothesis by an ugly fact."*

—Thomas H. Huxley, evolutionist,
nineteenth century

Much of the testimony of those present when President Kennedy was shot may seem old hat to readers with long memories.
Yet it remains vitally relevant to any serious account of the assassination.

Of 178 people in Dealey Plaza—according to an Assassinations Committee survey—no less than 132 later came to believe that only three shots had been fired. Three spent cartridges were found near the window of the Texas School Book Depository. Initially, therefore, a count of three shots seemed rational, if not conclusive. Most witnesses' statements, though, were given hours—in some cases weeks—later, when the generally published version of the assassination had already put the total of shots at three. A few people, including Mrs. Kennedy and a Secret Service agent in the follow-up car, thought they had heard as few as two shots. O thers, though, thought they had heard more than three, some speaking of as many as six or seven.

Ballistics and acoustics specialists have looked at how and why people become mixed up in their memories of gunfire. The sound of a first shot comes upon a witness when he does not expect it, subsequent shots compound the surprise, and muddle ensues. Further confusion may be caused by the fact that a rifle shot actually makes three minutely separated sounds—the muzzle blast, the sound of a bullet breaking the sound barrier, and finally the impact on the target. On the other hand, say the experts, those listening in the immediate target area probably receive the least distorted impression of gunfire.

Oddly, and inexcusably, the first inquiry produced no statement of any kind from the two police outriders traveling to the right rear of the President. Twelve people in the target area did go on record. All but one of the five surviving in the car itself, and two other outriders, spoke of three shots. Their predicament, however, was hardly conducive to rational recall. Mrs. Kennedy understandably said she was "very confused." Governor Connally was himself severely injured during the shooting, and Mrs. Connally was preoccupied trying to help him. The two outriders to the President's left rear were shocked by being spattered with the President's blood and brain matter.

The two Secret Service agents in the car, one of them the driver, had to make vital decisions. Both, however, did have interesting comments on the shots. Agent Kellerman said later that the last sound he recalled was "like a double bang—*bang! bang! . . .* like a plane going through the sound barrier." Agent Greer, the driver, also said the last shot cracked out "just right behind" its predecessor. This could conceivably mean the two agents heard a single bullet breaking the sound barrier, or that they heard two shots very close together indeed—far closer together than one man could achieve with a bolt-operated rifle. Agent Kellerman thought that, based on what he heard and the wounds he observed later at the autopsy, "there have got to be more than three shots."

In spite of being himself shot in the hail of gunfire, Governor Connally—an experienced hunter—remembered that because of the "rapidity" of the shots, "the thought immediately passed through my mind that there were two or three people involved, or more, in this; or that someone was shooting with an automatic rifle."

As for the bystanders nearest to the off side of the President's car, one, Mary Moorman, made estimates ranging from two to four shots. Like those in the car, she was first preoccupied, and then in such a panic, that she was distracted. (She was taking a photograph as the limousine approached, then threw herself to the ground, shrieking, "Get down! They're shooting!") Near her, Charles Brehm thought he heard three shots.

Gayle Newman, standing on the curb on the near side of the President's car, thought there could have been four shots. Then there was Maurice Orr, who also stood on the nearside pavement and was one of those closest to the President. Orr, questioned a few minutes after the tragedy, thought there could have been as many as five shots.

The Warren Report favored the silent testimony of the three cartridges lying near the sixth-floor window, combined with its reading of the autopsy details and the Zapruder film. It said there had been three shots, one of which missed, all fired from behind and above Kennedy.

Then, in 1978, came the acoustic study of the Dictabelt that appeared to cast real doubt on the Warren lone-gunman finding and suggested—as summarized by the Assassinations Committee's Robert Blakey—that there had been "four shots . . . The first, second, and fourth came from the Depository; the third came from the grassy knoll." Four shots, including one from the raised ground to the right front of the President, posited at least two assassins.

The acoustics study of the Dictabelt appeared to provide a time frame for the shooting. Taking zero as the time of the first shot, the second would have been fired 1.66 seconds later, the third at 7.49 seconds, and the fourth at 8.31 seconds (allowing for an error of about 5% in the Dictabelt's running speed). The brevity of the pause between the first and second shots, both fired from the rear, raised questions as to whether one lone gunman could possibly have fired both. That issue will be dealt with later, along with the question as to whether more than one assassin fired from the rear.

A fractional pause between the third shot, from the knoll, and the fourth, from the rear—acoustics study or no acoustics study—could explain a great deal. With less than a second between them, the two shots could have sounded like one to those who believed only three were fired altogether. It would also make sense of the comments of two of those in the target area and best placed to hear the gunfire. It would explain Governor Connally's impression that someone was shooting with an automatic rifle, Agent Greer's observation that the last shot was "just right behind" its predecessor, and Agent Kellerman's recall of a "double bang"—like the sound barrier being broken. Kellerman may have been right in his belief that there were more than three shots.

The acoustics work suggested that all but the third shot originated "in the vicinity of the sixth-floor southeast corner window of the Texas School Book Depository." The experts wondered though, whether further tests might indicate that some of the shooting had come from the Daltex Building next door.

The most refined study was reserved for the third shot, because the Committee was acutely aware of the need to resolve whether there had really been a sniper on the knoll. The acoustics study concluded that the third shot was "fired from a point along the east-west line of the wooden stockade fence on the grassy knoll, about eight feet west of the corner of the fence" (see Photos 5, 6). Professor Weiss and his colleagues suggested it was certain the shot had come from behind the fence—allowing for a margin of error of five feet in either direction. A mass of evidence seemed, at last, to fall into place.

Onetime Congressman, later President, Gerald Ford served on the Warren Commission and wrote afterward, "There is no evidence of a second man, of other shots, or other guns." That was not so, even in 1964.

Of the 178 witnesses whose statements were available to the Warren Commission, 49 believed the shots came from the Texas School Book Depository, 78 had no opinion, and 30 came up with answers that do not mesh with the rest of the evidence; 21, though, believed the shots had come from the grassy knoll. Another sample of the statements suggests 61 witnesses believed that at least some of the gunfire originated in front of the motorcade. A number of others said as much in statements to newspapers or private researchers.[1] Few of these witnesses were called to testify.

Here are the opinions of the fifteen people in the immediate target area, where the experts say sound impressions are least distorted. Of those in the car, Mrs. Kennedy had no opinion on where the shots came from. Governor Connally—injured before the fatal shot—thought he heard shooting behind him. His wife said on one occasion that she believed all shots came from the rear, on another, "I had no thought of whether they were high or low or where. They just came from the right." Agent Greer, the driver, said the shots "sounded like they were behind me." Agent Kellerman said only that his main impression was of sound to the right—perhaps to the rear. Two police outriders to the left rear of the car, the two splattered with blood and brain, had no idea where the shooting originated. Those at the eye of the storm were hardly well placed for rational recall.

The two policemen to the President's right rear, very close to him, were excellently placed. One of them, Officer James Chaney, closest to the President, thought some of the shooting came from "back over my right shoulder." He also said, however, that "when the second shot came, I looked back in time to see the President struck in the face by the second bullet."

Kennedy's close aide, Kenneth O'Donnell, was traveling in the car immediately behind the presidential limousine. He testified that he thought, "in part" based on "reconstruction," that the shooting had come from the rear. "In part"? O'Donnell later told a friend, House Speaker Tip O'Neill, that he had been pressured by the FBI not to say what he firmly believed, that gunfire had come from in front of the motorcade.

Mary Moorman, to the passenger side of the limousine, and busy taking pictures, could not tell where the shots came from. Maurice Orr, opposite her, was also too confused. Charles Brehm, not far away, said in a formal statement that shots came from behind him. On the day of the assassination, however, he was reported as saying he thought "the shots came from in front of or beside the President." On the other side of the street, standing on the grass with their children, were William and Gayle Newman. Mr. Newman's affidavit, sworn just after the assassination, said, "I was looking directly at him when he was hit in the side of the head. . . . I thought the shot had come from the garden directly behind me, that was on an elevation from where I was right on the curb. Then we fell down on the grass as it seemed we were in the direct path of fire." The Commission omitted both Newman statements from its "Witnesses" section.

Sixteen people in or outside the Book Depository, behind the President, suggested that some shooting came from the knoll. They included the Depository manager, the superintendent, and two company vice presidents. Secret Service Agent Forrest Sorrels, traveling in the lead car and nearing the end of the knoll at the moment of the fatal shot, stared instinctively at the knoll. He first reported, "I looked toward the top of the terrace to my right as the sound of the shots seemed to come from that direction." Only later, in his Commission testimony, did Sorrels go along with the conventional wisdom that the source of the gunfire was exclusively to the President's rear.

Secret Service agent Paul Landis, in the car behind the President, made an interesting distinction. He said, "I heard what sounded like the report of a high-powered rifle from behind me." Landis drew his gun, and then, "I heard a second report and saw the President's head split open and pieces of flesh and blood flying through the air. My reaction at this time was that the shot came from somewhere toward the front . . . and looked along the right-hand side of the road." Landis was not called to testify before the Warren Commission.

Several police officers also thought the shots came from the knoll area. The reaction of Dallas County Sheriff Bill Decker, riding in front of the President, was to bark into the radio, "Notify station 5 to move all available men out of my department back into the railroad yards." The railroad yards were just behind the fence—where the Committee acoustics experts placed a gunman.

Loosely speaking, the "grassy knoll" refers to the whole area the President's limousine passed after leaving the Book Depository to its rear (see page 24). It is easiest to describe it as three sectors. First a narrow slope topped by trees and bushes. Then a much longer slope up to a semicircular colonnade, with access steps and a retaining wall. Beyond that, the slope continued beside the road, topped by more vegetation and a fence. The fence made a right angle, which, in 1963, faced directly toward the oncoming motorcade. By the last stage of the shooting the President's limousine was a mere thirty-five yards from the point on the fence where Committee acoustics experts placed a gunman.

About a dozen people were on the grassy knoll when the President was shot, and almost all believed some of the gunfire came from behind them, high up on the knoll itself. For several, there could be no talk of illusions or echoes. The shooting was frighteningly close. Their stories, for the most part, never heard by the first official inquiry, are jolting even after fifty years.

Gordon Arnold, a young soldier of twenty-two, was home on leave on November 22. Armed with his movie camera, he was to claim, he walked to the top of the grassy knoll just before the President arrived, looking for a good vantage point. He went behind the fence, looking for a way to get to the railroad bridge that crossed the road directly in front of the motorcade route. From there, his view would be perfect. Arnold was moving along the fence—on the side hidden from the road—when ". . . this guy just walked towards me and said that I shouldn't be up there. He showed me a badge and said he was with the Secret Service and that he didn't want anybody up there." It sounded sensible enough, and Arnold retreated to the next best spot—beside a tree on the road side of the fence, high on the grassy slope beyond the colonnade. Then the motorcade arrived.

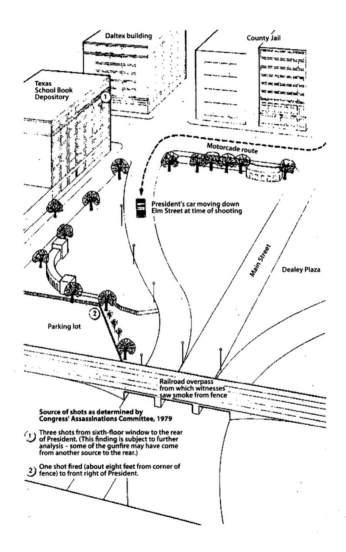

Dealey Plaza, November 22, 1963

Arnold maintained, "The shot came from behind me, only inches over my left shoulder. I had just got out of basic training. In my mind, live ammunition was being fired. It was being fired over my head. And I hit the dirt." The shooting that he remembered as being to his rear was so close, Arnold claimed, that he heard "the *whiz* over my shoulder. I say a *whiz*—you don't exactly hear the *whiz* of a bullet, you hear just like a shock wave. You *feel* it . . . you feel something and then a report comes just behind it."

Arnold's dramatic story was not published until 1978—he could have concocted it on the basis of earlier reports. Yet his account found some support. Texas Senator Ralph Yarborough, who had ridden in the motorcade two cars behind the President in 1963, recalled having seen a man in Arnold's position. Yarborough said, "Immediately on the firing of the first shot I saw the man . . . throw himself on the ground . . . he was down within a second, and I thought to myself, 'There's a combat veteran who knows how to act when weapons start firing.' "

A railroad supervisor on the bridge, Sam Holland, observed a man he described as a "plainclothes detective or FBI agent or something like that" before the shooting. Something, moreover, led policemen to run up the grassy slope immediately afterward.

Mary Woodward, Maggie Brown, Aurelia Lorenzo, and Ann Donaldson all worked at the *Dallas Morning News*. They spoke of "a horrible, ear-shattering noise coming from behind us and a little to the right." What they said was in the press the very next day, yet all four witnesses went unmentioned and unquestioned by the Warren Commission.

John Chism said, "I looked behind me, to see if it was a fireworks display." His wife, Mary, said, "It came from what I thought was behind us." The Chisms were not called by the Warren Commission.

A. J. Millican, who had been standing in front of the colonnade, said of the final gunfire, "I heard two more shots come from the arcade between the bookstore and the underpass, and then three more shots came from the same direction, only farther back. Then everybody started running up the hill." Mr. Millican was not called by the Warren Commission.

Jean Newman stood halfway along the grassy knoll and said her first impression was that "the shots came from my right." Ms. Newman was not called by the Warren Commission.

Abraham Zapruder, of film fame, was using the concrete wall on the grassy knoll as a vantage point. A Secret Service report of an interview with him reads: "According to Mr. Zapruder, the position of the assassin was behind Mr. Zapruder." In testimony to the Warren Commission, Zapruder recalled that one shot reverberated all around him, louder than all the others. This would be consistent with a shot fired on the knoll itself, much closer to Zapruder than gunfire from the Book Depository.

Sam Holland, the railroad supervisor at the parapet of the railway bridge over the road, directly faced the President's car as it approached (see diagram, page 24). Holland also had an excellent view of the fence on the knoll. He told police immediately after the assassination that there had been four shots and that he had seen "a puff of smoke come from the trees."

Holland persisted in maintaining that at least some of the firing "sounded like it came from behind the wooden fence. . . . I looked over to where the shots came from, and I saw a puff of smoke still lingering underneath the trees in front of the wooden fence." Pressed as to where the shots had come from, Holland replied, "Behind that picket fence—close to the little plaza—there's no doubt whatsoever in my mind" (see Photo 6).

The Warren Commission heard Holland's testimony but

ignored it. Skeptical suggestions that he saw smoke or steam from a locomotive make no sense. The railway line itself is far from the fence on the knoll. Rifles, on the other hand, sometimes do emit smoke.

Holland's account was supported—with variations as to the precise location of the smoke—by eight witnesses, most of them fellow railroad workers, who stood on the same bridge. Others saw the same phenomenon from other vantage points—one of them a man in a better position than anyone to observe suspicious activity by the fence on the knoll. Railroad worker Lee Bowers, perched in a signal box that commanded a unique view of the area behind the fence, said he noticed two men standing near the fence shortly before the shots were fired. One was "middle-aged" and "fairly heavyset," wearing a white shirt and dark trousers. The other was "mid-twenties in either a plaid shirt or plaid coat . . . these men were the only two strangers in the area. The others were workers that I knew."

Bowers said, too, that when the shots were fired at the President "in the vicinity of where the two men I have described were, there was a flash of light, something I could not identify, but there was something which occurred which caught my eye in this immediate area on the embankment . . . a flash of light or smoke or something which caused me to feel that something out of the ordinary had occurred there."

Lee Bowers was questioned by the Warren Commission but cut off in mid-sentence when he began describing the "something out of the ordinary" he had seen. The interrogating lawyer changed the subject.

Six witnesses, all of them either distinguished public figures or qualified to know what they were talking about, claimed to have smelled gunpowder in the air. Three witnesses who had traveled in the motorcade—the Mayor's wife, Mrs. Cabell; Senator Ralph Yarborough; and Congressman Ray Roberts—later mentioned such a smell. Unlikely, surely, that the odor could have reached them from a sixth-floor window high above. Surprising, too, that they could have smelled it from the grassy knoll, yet it seems they were in that general area when they did notice it. Police Officer Earle Brown, on duty at the railway bridge, and Mrs. Donald Baker, at the other end of the knoll, reported the same acrid smell.

Another policeman, Patrolman Joe Smith, was holding up traffic across the road from the Book Depository when the motorcade passed by. On hearing the gunfire—and a woman cry out, "They're shooting the President from the bushes!"—Smith ran to the grassy knoll, the only bushy place in the area. In 1978, he still remembered what he reported shortly after the assassination, that in the parking lot, "around the hedges, there was the smell, the lingering smell of gunpowder."

The Assassinations Committee photographic panel would examine a Polaroid photograph taken by bystander Mary Moorman at the moment of the fatal shot. A shape—some believe it is a man's head—can be seen in the fenced area on the knoll (see Photo 5). The shape is no longer there in subsequent photographs.

In 1978, amid the excitement over the Assassination Committee's conclusion that two guns were fired at President Kennedy, rather less attention was given to the Committee's decisions on a secondary but equally vital question. Which of the shots actually hit the President?

If the only comprehensive visual record of the Kennedy assassination had been shown on television on November 22, 1963, most people in the United States would have gone to bed that night certain that their President had been shot from the front and only perhaps—by an earlier shot—from behind. The general public was not shown the full Zapruder film until more than a decade later. They were, within days, given a verbal description of the footage on CBS television. The narrator was Dan Rather, then a junior television correspondent, who had been permitted to view the film. Rather said that at the fatal headshot the President "fell *forward* with considerable violence [author's emphasis]." He omitted to say what is in fact mercilessly obvious from any alert viewing of the film. It is manifestly clear that the President jerked *backward* at the moment of the shot that visibly exploded his head.

Members and staff of the Warren Commission did see the Zapruder film, yet nowhere in its report is the backward motion mentioned. Still frames from the film were published in the Warren Commission volumes, but with the two frames following the headshot printed in reverse order—supposedly the result of a printing error at the FBI—which did nothing for clarity. The first impression of the ordinary person viewing the film today, however, is that the President was knocked backward by a bullet originating in front of him, from the direction of a sniper on the grassy knoll.

The pros and cons on the evidence for a shot from the front have long been argued to and fro. Some noted gory details, which seemed to reinforce the thesis of a hit from the front. Both motorcycle officers riding to the left *rear* of the President were splattered with blood and brain coming toward them. Officer Hargis, only a few feet from Mrs. Kennedy, said later that he had been struck with such force by the brain matter that for a moment he thought he himself had been hit. Officer B. J. Martin, who rode to Hargis's left, later testified that he found blood and flesh on his motorcycle windshield, on the left side of his helmet, and on the left shoulder of his uniform jacket.

A student, Billy Harper, was later to pick up a large piece of the President's skull in the street, at a point more than ten feet to the *rear* of the car's position at the time of the fatal shot. The evidence is that the human debris, including other skull fragments, was driven backward. Some researchers, making light of the fact that people in the front of the car were also "covered with brain tissue," see this as further evidence of a hit by a knoll gunman.

In 1979, the Assassinations Committee said this was not so. On all the evidence, it thought that only two of the four shots—almost certainly fired by a gun in the sixth-floor corner window of the Book Depository, to the rear—found their human targets. The two other shots, one from the Depository, the other from the grassy knoll, missed.

How to account then for the President's lurch backward in the Zapruder film? A wound ballistics expert told the Committee he thought it reflected "a neuromuscular reaction . . . mechanical stimulation of the motor nerves of the President." The Committee's medical panel, with one doctor dissenting, supported the thesis that the backward movement was either "a neurological response to the massive brain damage" or a "propulsive" phenomenon, sometimes known as "the jet effect."

Studies of the X-rays and photographs convinced the doctors that the bullet had entered in the upper part of the skull and exited from the right front. They agreed that the rear wound was "a typical entrance wound." In spite of the fact that the brain had not been fully sectioned, as the panel would have preferred, existing pictures of it may be thought to support the notion that the headshot was fired from behind.

The Committee was further convinced by new tests on the bullet specimens. Dr. Vincent Guinn, a chemist and forensic scientist, broke new ground with his "neutron activation" tests—a process in which the specimens were bombarded with neutrons in a nuclear reactor. The results appeared to many to resolve fundamental areas of controversy.

Dr. Guinn was supplied with all the surviving bullet specimens, the several pieces from the car, tiny fragments removed from the wounds of both the President and Governor Connally, and the full-size bullet found on the stretcher at Parkland Hospital.[2] He concluded that these represented only two bullets and that it was "highly probable" that both were of Mannlicher-Carcano manufacture—the ammunition designed for the rifle found in the Book Depository.

Guinn was equally confident about a third conclusion, one that—in conjunction with the ballistics evidence—supported the thesis that the fatal headshot was fired from behind. Guinn's tests indicated that fragments from the President's brain matched the three testable fragments found in the car and that they, in turn, came from the same bullet. Since ballistics experts concluded that the fragments in the car were fired by the gun in the Book Depository, it seemed certain that a shot from the Depository did hit the President in the head. The Committee decided this was the fourth shot and that it was fatal.

Over the objections of staffers who felt Guinn's work was inherently flawed—the fragments had been handled in a slipshod fashion over the years, and some appeared to be missing—the Committee accepted the findings. The fourth shot, it accepted, had not come from the knoll.

Dr. Guinn's study also influenced what the Committee eventually decided about an issue that went to the very heart of the debate between the lone assassin theorists and those who believe more than one shooter was involved—and still does. It was an issue that had initially stumped the Warren Commission.

Back in 1964, Warren investigators analyzing the Zapruder film concluded that a lone assassin would not have had time to fire his rifle again between the moment the President was first seen to be hit and the time Governor Connally appeared to react to his wounds. It had seemed, however, that the only alternative was that *two* gunmen had fired almost simultaneously.[3]

The Warren Commission's staff found a way to dispose of that disquieting notion—eventually producing what became known as the "magic bullet theory." According to the theory, a single bullet—the one found on a stretcher at Parkland Hospital—had coursed right through President Kennedy, inflicting the wounds to his back and throat, and gone on to cause the multiple injuries to Governor Connally's torso, wrist, and thigh.

That is what the Warren Commission asked the world to believe, and what over the years was to cause more skepticism than anything else about the physical evidence. The most persistent objection arose from the remarkable state of preservation of the bullet found at the hospital. It remained almost intact (see Photo 15). Consider, though, what—according to the Warren theory—the bullet is supposed to have done.

As it theoretically progressed, it purportedly pierced the President in the back; coursed through his upper chest; came out through the front of his neck; went on to strike the Governor in the back; pierced a lung; severed a vein, artery, and nerve; broke the right fifth rib, destroying five inches of the bone; emerged from the Governor's right chest; plunged on into the back of the Governor's right forearm; broke a thick bone, the distal end of the radius; came out of the other side of the wrist; and finally ended up in the left thigh. It then supposedly fell out of the thigh, to be recovered on the stretcher at the hospital.

From 1964 on, doctors with long experience of bullet wounds had great difficulty in accepting that a bullet could cause such damage, especially to bones, and still emerge almost unscathed. Typical of such doubters was Dr. Milton Helpern, former Chief Medical Examiner of New York City, once described by the *New York Times* as knowing "more about violent death than anyone else in the world." Dr. Helpern, who had conducted two thousand autopsies on victims of gunshot wounds, said of the magic bullet:

> The original, pristine weight of this bullet before it was fired was approximately 160–161 grains. The weight of the bullet recovered on the stretcher in Parkland Hospital was reported by the Commission at 158.6.[4] I cannot accept the premise that this bullet thrashed around in all that bony tissue and lost only 1.4 to 2.4 grains of its original weight. I cannot believe either that this bullet is going to emerge miraculously unscathed, without any deformity, and with its lands and grooves intact. . . . You must remember that next to bone, the skin offers greater resistance to a bullet in its course through the body than any other kind of tissue. . . .
>
> This single-bullet theory asks us to believe that this bullet went through seven layers of skin, tough, elastic, resistant skin. In addition . . . this bullet passed through other layers of soft tissue; and then shattered bones! I just can't believe that this bullet had the force to do what [the Commission has] demanded of it. . . .

Dr. Robert Shaw, professor of thoracic surgery at the University of Texas, the doctor who treated Governor Connally's chest wounds, was never satisfied that the magic bullet caused all his patient's injuries.

Three of the seven members of the Warren Commission doubted the magic-bullet theory, even though it appeared in their own report. The commissioners wrangled about it up to the moment their findings went to press. John McCloy had difficulty accepting it. Congressman Hale Boggs had "strong doubts." Senator Sherman Cooper told the author in 1978 that he was "unconvinced."

Senator Richard Russell did not want to sign a report that said definitely that both men were hit by the same bullet. He wanted a footnote added that noted his dissent, but Warren failed to put one in. On a audiotape held at the Lyndon B. Johnson Library, Russell is heard telling President Johnson, "I don't believe it." And Johnson responds, "I don't either."

Was all this doubt unjustified? The House Assassinations Committee thought so—and proceeded to endorse the magic bullet theory.

The majority of the Committee's forensic pathology panel, for their part, decided that the medical evidence was consistent with the one bullet having wounded both victims. They thought, moreover, that the photographic exhibits, and the Zapruder film, in particular, showed that the President and the Governor were lined up in a way "consistent with the trajectory of one bullet." They listened to the opinion of a ballistics witness, who said that a Mannlicher-Carcano bullet could indeed emerge only minimally deformed after striking bone. The ballistics experts were satisfied, meanwhile, that the magic bullet had been fired from the Mannlicher-Carcano rifle.

Finally, for the first time, the controversial bullet was linked to the wound in Governor Connally's wrist. Dr. Guinn's neutron activation tests indicated that the makeup of the bullet was indistinguishable from fragments found in the Governor's wrist. Guinn believed it "extremely unlikely" that they came from different bullets.

In light of all that support and even though—unlike the Warren Commission—it believed a second assassin had fired from the knoll in front of the President, the Assassinations Committee fell into line on the matter of the almost intact "magic bullet." Here is the sequence of the shots fired on November 22, as the Committee saw it:

Shot 1   (from the Depository) missed.
Shot 2   (from the Depository)—the almost intact bullet—caused perhaps survivable wounds to both Kennedy and Connally.
Shot 3   (from the grassy knoll) missed.
Shot 4   (from the Depository) hit Kennedy in the head, killing him.

Tests done later—one of them reported in the *Journal of the American College of Surgeons* in 1994—appeared to validate the notion that a bullet could cause serious damage without losing any more of its metal content than did the magic bullet.[5] For a number of reasons, though, the magic bullet controversy has not gone away.

First, there is doubt as to whether the bullet in question was really found on Governor Connally's stretcher. While tests appear to link the magic bullet to fragments removed from Connally's arm, moreover, no fragments survived from his chest—or indeed from the President's throat wound. Statements by a former Parkland Hospital operating-room supervisor, and by a policeman who guarded the Governor's room, refer to the retrieval of more fragments than could possibly have come from the magic bullet.[6]

Nurse Audrey Bell, the supervisor, said she handled "four or five bullet fragments" after their removal, placed them in a "foreign body envelope," and handed them over to the authorities. Contemporary reports confirm that she did hand over fragments. Bell, meanwhile, said that "the smallest was the size of the striking end of a match and the largest at least twice that big. I have seen the picture of the magic bullet, and I can't see how it could be the bullet from which the fragments I saw came."

In the wake of Bell's comments came another from a patrolman who guarded Connally's room, Charles Harbison. He stated that on November 25 or 26, when the Governor was being moved, somebody—he thought it was a doctor—gave him fragments. Since he recalled "more than three," and since he and Bell refer to different incidents, could they all have come from the magic bullet?

Dr. Pierre Finck, one of the doctors who performed the autopsy on the President—otherwise a staunch defender of the Warren Commission findings—expressed doubt on this one. "There are," he testified, "too many fragments."

X-rays, moreover, show that one fragment remained buried in Connally's thigh. His doctors had chosen to leave it there. In 1993, when he died, the FBI saw merit in the suggestion that the fragment be removed from his body. Connally's grieving family objected, however, and the fragment was buried with him. Modern tests might have gone far to resolve doubts about the magic bullet.

A more thorough and efficient autopsy might have established whether—as official probes have found—the bullet did indeed go through the President's back and upper chest before exiting his throat. As reported earlier, photographs taken of the interior chest at autopsy could not be found.

A statement by former Bethesda laboratory technician James Jenkins, who was at the autopsy, raised further doubt. "What sticks out in my mind," he recalled years later, "is the fact that Commander Humes [the presiding surgeon] put his little finger in [the back wound] and, you know, said that . . . he could probe the bottom of it with his finger, which would mean to me it was very shallow."

Later, when the surgeons had opened the President's chest, Jenkins watched as they tried to track the wound again, using a metal probe. "I remember looking inside the chest cavity and I could see the probe . . . through the pleura [the lining of the chest cavity]. . . . You could actually see where it was making an indentation . . . where it was pushing the skin up. . . . There was no entry into the chest cavity. . . . No way that could have exited in the front because it was then low in the chest cavity . . . somewhere around the junction of the descending aorta [the main artery carrying blood from the heart] or the bronchus in the lungs. . . ."

As for the throat wound, numerous Dallas doctors and nurses who saw it before a tracheotomy incision obscured it, believed it to be a wound of entry—not of exit, as official reports have suggested. They have described it as very small, no bigger than a pencil. Some of them wondered whether a bullet had entered there and lodged in the chest. At autopsy, Humes found a bloody bruise at the top of the right lung, but no bullet. The throat-wound area was merely probed with a finger, not sectioned. In sum, all opinion on the throat wound—and the back wound for that matter—is based not on evidence but on guesswork.

Having reviewed the X-rays and photographs in 1988, and recalling his experience as a surgeon on the team that attended the dying President, Dr. Robert McClelland was forthright. "I think he was shot from the front. . . . I think that the rifle bullet hit him in the side of the head and blew out the back of his head. . . . I certainly think that's what happened, and that probably somewhere in the front part of the head, in the front part of the scalp, there probably was an entry wound, which—among all the blood and the laceration there and everything—was not seen, by us or anybody else perhaps, and it blew out the back part of his head. . . ."

Mortician Thomas Robinson did tell Assassinations Committee staff that he recalled seeing a small wound "about a quarter of an inch . . . at the temples [sic] in the hairline to the right side of the head."

Another member of the Dallas medical team, Dr. Charles Crenshaw, claimed in a 1992 book that the wounds he saw indicated gunfire from the front.

Others thought the massive damage to the President's skull was perhaps the result of not one headshot but of two impacting almost simultaneously. Kennedy's personal physician, Admiral George Burkley, attended the autopsy and was to tell the Assassinations Committee that he "conceded the possibility" of two such shots. Dr. Baden, head of the Committee's medical panel, acknowledged the "remote" possibility that the fatal head wounds "could have been caused by a shot from the grassy knoll, and that medical evidence of it has been destroyed by a shot from the rear a fraction of a second later."

The Committee itself decided that notion was contrary to trajectory data and the time frame it had constructed from the Zapruder film and its acoustics findings. But the argument did not deter independent medical observers who studied the X-ray evidence in 1994.

Dr. Mantik, the Eisenhower Medical Center radiation therapist who expressed suspicion that some of the X-rays had been tampered with, thought the fakery was designed to divert attention from evidence indicating a shot from the front.

Dr. Joseph Riley, an expert in neuroanatomy, concentrated on two key X-rays. He deemed them authentic, but felt they had been misinterpreted. "The autopsy evidence," said Riley, "demonstrates conclusively that John Kennedy was struck in the head by two bullets, one from the rear and one from the right front."

As recently as 2006, moreover, a lengthy study performed in part by the Livermore National Laboratory under the auspices of the U.S. Department of Energy, challenged key evidence that had persuaded the Assassinations Committee that the single bullet theory was valid. Their findings, published in the *Journal of Forensic Sciences*—the periodical of record of the American Academy of Forensic Sciences—pointed to "inconsistencies" in the data used by Dr. Guinn, who tested bullet specimens for the Committee.

The new calculations, the 2006 study reported, "considerably weaken support for the single-bullet theory." Rather, the study suggested, "the extant evidence is consistent with any number between two and five rounds [not merely the four posited by the Committee] fired in Dealey Plaza."[7]

These have been voices from a forensic and scientific tower of Babel. All this study of the evidence, and all the theorizing, may have been in vain. So poorly were the wounds reported by the autopsy surgeons, so shoddy was the handling of the brain and the collection of bullet fragments, so elusive is the truth about the nature and the location of the X-ray and photographic materials, so controversial is the acoustics evidence, that no one—however expert—can say the evidence proves anything beyond a reasonable doubt.

Theories about the meaning of the physical evidence are just that—speculation that compels belief in neither a lone assassin nor a conspiracy.

But then there is the human testimony.

CHAPTER 4

Other Gunmen?

*"The physical evidence and eyewitness accounts do
not clearly indicate what took place on the sixth floor
of the Texas School Book Depository at the time John
F. Kennedy was assassinated."*

—Dallas Police Chief Jesse Curry, 1969

The last the people of Dallas saw of President Kennedy was his
slumped figure. Then a Secret Service agent leaped into the
backseat of the limousine as another—in the follow-up car—
impotently brandished an automatic rifle. Then confusion
reigned in Dealey Plaza, and it was the grassy knoll that seemed
to attract most attention at first. Spectators and police seemed to
think it was a key place to look for assassins.

Rosemary, daughter of amateur photographer Phillip Willis, had been running alongside the President's car as it passed
the knoll. As she ran, she caught a glimpse of someone standing behind the corner of a concrete retaining wall. He appeared
"conspicuous" to her, and seemed to "disappear the next instant."
As we have seen, photographs bear out her story.

From his perch on top of a nearby high building, Jesse Price
found his attention drawn to something behind the fence on the

knoll. A man, about twenty-five and wearing a white shirt with khaki trousers, ran off "toward the passenger cars on the railroad siding."

The man seemed to be carrying something. Lee Bowers, the railway towerman who had seen two strangers behind the fence just before the assassination, had partially lost sight of them in foliage. At the time of the shooting, however, he had observed some sort of commotion behind the fence.

Then policemen began pouring into the area, one of the first of them Patrolman Joe Smith. He rushed into the parking lot behind the fence because a woman said the shots had come "from the bushes." It was there, as we noted, that Smith smelled gunpowder, there that he had a very odd encounter.

The patrolman, who had drawn his pistol as he ran, was starting to feel "damn silly" when he came upon a man standing beside a car. On seeing Smith and an accompanying deputy, the man reacted swiftly. As Smith remembered it, "This character produces credentials from his hip pocket, which showed him to be Secret Service. I have seen those credentials before, and they satisfied me and the deputy sheriff. So I immediately accepted that and let him go and continued our search around the cars." It was a decision Officer Smith later bitterly regretted, for there were no authentic Secret Service agents on the grassy knoll.[1]

All Secret Service men in Dallas that day have been accounted for by official reports. There were none stationed in Dealey Plaza, and those in the motorcade are said officially to have stayed with their cars. No genuine agents are known to have been in the grassy knoll parking lot.

A Secret Service agent, in 1963, was the essence of the crew-cut, besuited American young man. The man encountered in the parking lot was not like that. As Officer Smith put it, "He looked like an auto mechanic. He had on a sport shirt and sport pants. But he had dirty fingernails, it looked like, and hands that looked like an auto mechanic's hands. And afterwards it didn't ring true for the Secret Service."

The policeman recalled wryly, "At the time, we were so pressed for time, and we were searching. And he had produced correct identification, and we just overlooked the thing. I should have checked that man closer, but at the time I didn't snap on it. . . ."

Smith and the deputy sheriff were not alone in their sighting of the "Secret Service man." Gordon Arnold, the soldier who claimed he found himself virtually in the line of fire during the shooting, said he, too, encountered a "Secret Service agent" just before the assassination. Another Dallas witness, Malcolm Summers, spoke of seeing a man with a gun when he approached the knoll after the shooting.

Former Dallas Police Chief Jesse Curry said in 1977 that he thought the "Secret Service agent" on the knoll "must have been bogus . . . Certainly, the suspicion would point to the man as being involved, some way or other, in the shooting, since he was in an area immediately adjacent to where the shots were— and the fact that he had a badge that purported him to be Secret Service would make it seem all the more suspicious."

Within minutes of the assassination, an off-duty Dallas policeman, Tom Tilson, happened to be driving with his daughter on the road beyond the railway tracks. From there, just after hearing first word of the shooting on the car radio, he saw a man "slipping and sliding" down the railway embankment. Tilson said in 1978 that the man "came down that grassy slope on the west side of the triple underpass . . . had a car parked there, a black car. He threw something in the backseat and went around the front hurriedly and got in the car and took off. I saw all of this and I said, 'That doesn't make sense, everybody running to the scene and one person running from it.' "

Officer Tilson said his seventeen years of police experience, coupled with the news by then pouring over the radio, prompted him to give chase. He lost his quarry after a while, but—as his daughter confirmed—managed to get the license number of the car. He reported the incident, and the number, to Dallas Police Homicide that afternoon.

Officer Tilson's account appears to have been passed over in the chaos of the hours that followed, and there is no record of the car number he noted. There were other reports in Dallas that afternoon about speeding cars, one of them carrying stolen Georgia plates.

In Dealey Plaza, within minutes of the shooting, the focus had shifted from the grassy knoll. Before and during the shooting, people in the crowd had noticed a man, or a man with a gun, in a window of the sixth floor of the Texas School Book Depository. Some said they saw two men.

Fifteen minutes before the assassination, a bystander named Arnold Rowland asked his wife if she would like to see a Secret Service agent and pointed to a window on the sixth floor. He had noticed, he said, "a man back from the window—he was standing and holding a rifle . . . we thought momentarily that maybe we should tell someone, but then the thought came to us that it [was] a security agent."

Rowland testified that he had seen the rifle clearly enough to make out the telescopic sight and realize it was a high-powered weapon. The man he saw was not in the famous window, at the right-hand end of the sixth floor, but in the far *left*-hand window. Rowland also said that, at the same time, he spotted a second figure, at the famous right-hand window (see Photo 4).The second man was dark-complexioned, leading Rowland to think he was black.

The Warren inquiry rejected Rowland's comments about a second man, even though a deputy sheriff confirmed that the witness had mentioned the man right after the shooting. When he told FBI agents about the second man, Rowland said, "They told me it didn't have any bearing or such on the case right then. In fact, they just the same as told me to 'forget it now.' . . . They didn't seem interested at all. They didn't pursue this point. They didn't take it down in the notation as such."

The Warren Commission Report ignored and omitted altogether statements the FBI took from two other witnesses. These also referred to two men, and the first of them seems to corroborate what Rowland said.

Shortly before the assassination, bystander Ruby Henderson saw two men standing back from a window on one of the upper floors of the Book Depository. Like Rowland, she particularly noticed that one of the men "had dark hair . . . a darker complexion than the other." He might have been Mexican, she thought. Henderson had the impression the men were looking out as if "in anticipation of the motorcade."

Henderson recalled having seen the two men after an ambulance removed a man who had been taken ill. An ambulance had indeed been close by, and the time was routinely logged. The sighting of the two men can therefore be placed as having occurred less than six minutes before the assassination.

The report of another witness, who also observed two men just before the assassination, is even more disquieting. Carolyn Walther noticed two men with a gun in an open window at the extreme right-hand end of the Depository. Though she was unsure that the window was on the sixth floor, photographs and the location of innocent employees in fifth-floor windows establish that she must have been looking at the infamous sniper's perch. Mrs. Walther said:

> I saw this man in a window, and he had a gun in his hands, pointed downwards. The man evidently was in a kneeling position, because his forearms were resting on the windowsill. There was another man standing beside him, but I only saw a portion of his body because he was standing partly up against the window, you know, only halfway in the window; and the window was dirty and I couldn't see his face, up above, because the window was pushed up. It startled me, then I thought, 'Well, they probably have guards, possibly in all the buildings,' so I didn't say anything.

If Mrs. Walther had sounded the alarm, it would probably have been too late. She had barely noticed the second man when the President's motorcade swept into view.

No one appears to have bothered to interview another witness, one who had an ideal vantage point from which to observe the sixth-floor window on November 22. John Powell was one of many inmates housed on the sixth floor of the Dallas County Jail, spending three days in custody on minor charges. In the minutes before the assassination, he told friends and family members, he and cellmates saw two men with a gun in the window opposite. So clearly could he see them, he said, that he recalled them "fooling with the scope" on the gun. "Quite a few of us saw them. Everybody was trying to watch the parade. . . . We were looking across the street because it was directly straight across. The first thing I thought is, it was security guards. . . ."

Like Ruby Henderson and Arnold Rowland, Powell recalled spontaneously that one of the men appeared to have dark skin.

Though some inmates of the county jail were apparently questioned after the assassination, it is not clear that any official ever spoke with Powell at the time. His story emerged only years later, after a friend contacted a Dallas area newspaper.

The testimonies that referred to two men acting suspiciously were either to be judged mistaken or ignored by the Warren Commission.

There never was serious interest in the possibility that two assassins or more might have lain in wait for the President. For the focus of official interest became, less than five minutes after the shooting, a hunt for just one man.

Two other bystanders, clerks from the county building, noticed a man in the sixth floor just before the shooting. He looked "uncomfortable" as though he was "hiding or something." To the clerks, he seemed to be looking toward the grassy knoll rather than in the direction from which the President would be arriving.

Then there was Howard Brennan, later to become a star witness for the Warren Commission. He had stood across the road from the Depository and reported having seen a man at the right-hand sixth-floor window both before and during the shooting. After the second shot, said Brennan, "This man I saw previous was aiming for his last shot." He then drew back "and maybe paused for another second as though to assure himself that he had hit his mark," before disappearing.

Close by Brennan, a fifteen-year-old schoolboy named Amos Euins also saw a rifle being fired from the famous window. "I could see his hand," he said later, "and I could see his other hand on the trigger, and one hand on the barrel thing." Another youth in the crowd, James Worrell, said he looked up after the first shot and saw "six inches" of a rifle barrel sticking out of the window.

Three people traveling in the motorcade, the Mayor's wife and two photographers, saw part of a rifle protruding from the window—though neither photographer reacted fast enough to take a picture.

Less than five minutes after the shooting, a policeman called in over the radio to say, "A passerby states the shots came from the Texas School Book Depository." Three employees at the Depository came forward about the same time to say that, while watching the motorcade from a fifth-floor window, they had heard suspicious sounds above them—a clatter like a rifle bolt being operated and what sounded like shells being ejected onto the floor. The police operation gradually became more organized, the Depository was sealed off and a floor-by-floor search begun.

As early as 12:44 p.m., the police radio put out a first description of a suspect in the assassination:

"Attention all squads. The suspect in the shooting at Elm and Houston is supposed to be an unknown white male approximately thirty, 165 pounds, slender build, armed with what is thought to be a 30-30 rifle . . . no further description at this time."

The Warren Commission never did establish the source of this description. Its best guess was that it derived from a policeman's exchange with Brennan, one of the witnesses who reported having seen a man with a gun in the sixth-floor window. Whatever the source, policemen in Dallas now had a lead, however vague, a rough description of somebody to be on the lookout for.

At 1:16 p.m., forty-five minutes after the assassination, operators at Dallas police headquarters were startled by a civilian's voice breaking into official radio traffic. A citizen was relaying news of fresh drama and a second murder:

Citizen: Hello, Police Operator?
Operator: Go ahead, go ahead, Citizen using police radio.
Citizen: We've had a shooting out here.
Operator: Where is it at?
Citizen: On Tenth Street.
Operator: What location on Tenth Street?
Citizen: Between Marsalis and Beckley. It's a police officer. Somebody shot him.

A couple of miles from Dealey Plaza, on a leafy street in the Oak Cliff district, a police officer had indeed been shot. He was patrol-car driver J. D. Tippit, and he was dead. Within four minues, drawing on what witnesses at the scene said, the police broadcast a description of a suspect in this second murder: "A white male approximately thirty, five-eight, slender build, has black hair, a white jacket, a white shirt, and dark trousers."

As police cars raced to join the hunt for the killer of a fellow officer, two more citizens decided they had something to report. On hearing police sirens wailing, shoe-shop manager Johnny Brewer had looked up to see a young man walk into the entranceway of his shop. "His hair was sort of messed up," Brewer would recall, "looked like he'd been running." When the police cars went away, so did the young man.

Brewer left the shop and walked a few doors away to speak to the ticket seller at a movie house, the Texas Theater. The mysterious young man, they figured, had entered the theater without buying a ticket. They telephoned the police, and fifteen officers arrived within minutes. Patrolman Nick McDonald, who was one of the officers, went around to the theater's rear entrance.

When the lights came up in the auditorium, shoe-shop manager Brewer pointed to a man sitting near the back. McDonald advanced cautiously through the almost-empty theater, checked a couple of other customers on the way, but kept an eye on the man at the back. When he reached the fellow, a nervous-looking young man, he ordered him to his feet. The man started to rise, brought his hands half up and punched McDonald between the eyes. Then, McDonald told the author, the suspect went for a pistol in his waistband. During a brief scuffle, the gun misfired. Then more officers arrived, and the Dallas police had their prisoner.

A slim young man of twenty-four, he was hustled out of the theater, through a hostile crowd, and into a police car destined for headquarters. Minutes earlier, during the scuffle with McDonald, he had cried, "Well, it's all over now."

In so many ways, as America knows to its cost, it was by no means all over. The prisoner was Lee Harvey Oswald.

CHAPTER 5

Did Oswald Do It?

"He didn't think there would be any more work done that day."

—Oswald's ostensible reason for leaving the scene
of the crime, quoted by Captain Will Fritz,
Dallas Chief of Homicide

The suspected assassin was to be questioned by the Dallas police, the FBI, and the Secret Service for nearly two days—two days in which he steadfastly denied any part in the murder of either President Kennedy or Officer Tippit. As to learning the detail of what he said, the Warren inquiry would rely on retrospective reports written by the chief of the Homicide Bureau, Captain Will Fritz, and the other officers who talked to Oswald.[1]

Oswald was quite open about his basic background, the out-line of a life now well known around the world. He had been born in 1939 in New Orleans, joined the U.S. Marine Corps at the age of seventeen, and then, in 1959, traveled to the Soviet Union.

Behaving like a defector who wanted to become a Soviet citizen, Oswald had stayed in Russia for two and a half years. After marriage to a Soviet wife and the birth of a baby daughter,

NOT IN YOUR LIFETIME

Oswald returned to the United States and to Texas, where his mother lived.

During 1963, Oswald told the police, he spent several months in New Orleans, where he began to take an active interest in Cuban politics. He admitted having demonstrated in favor of Fidel Castro, and—for his part in an ensuing street incident—having been arrested by New Orleans police. This, said Oswald, was the only time he had been in trouble with the police, and a check proved him right.

The interrogators asked Oswald if he was a Communist, and he replied that he was a Marxist but not a Marxist-Leninist. That was a little too sophisticated for Dallas law-enforcement officers, and Oswald said that would take too long to explain. Of his recent activity, Oswald described how he had looked for work in Dallas and eventually taken a laboring job at the Texas School Book Depository.

On several occasions, as he was escorted around the police station, Oswald faced a barrage of questions from the world's press. Radio and television microphones recorded his strenuous denial of any involvement in the Kennedy assassination. Asked point-blank, "Did you kill the President?" Oswald replied, "I didn't shoot anybody, no, sir." He told the press this more than once. On the last occasion, as he was being dragged away through the seething crowd of reporters, Oswald said, "No, they're taking me in because of the fact that I lived in the Soviet Union." As he was hustled away, he almost shrieked, "I'm a patsy!"

If Oswald really was just a fall guy, he had been bewilderingly well framed. Even before his arrest, police were finding evidence that was to prove damning, evidence black enough and copious enough to give any prosecutor a good case. Consider now the

67

facts that would have been used against Oswald if he had come to trial.

Half an hour after the assassination, near the famous sixth-floor Depository window, a sheriff's deputy had noticed a stack of book cartons. They were stacked high enough to hide a crouching man should a casual observer approach from behind him. There, on the floor, in the narrow space between the boxes and the window, were three empty cartridge cases. A rifle was found soon afterward, by two other officers searching the other end of the sixth floor. From the prosecutor's point of view, it was to provide the clinching evidence against Oswald.

The gun was a bolt-action rifle with a sling and telescopic sight and was stamped with the serial number C-2766. It was a 6.5-mm Mannlicher-Carcano, a hitherto undistinguished Italian rifle of World War II vintage. There was a live round in the breech ready for firing. The weapon was examined for fingerprints at Dallas police headquarters, then flown to FBI headquarters in Washington. Experts there found some traces of fingerprints on the metal near the trigger, but they were reportedly too incomplete to be identified. Then, four days later, Lieutenant Day of the Dallas police sent the FBI a palm print, which, he said, he had "lifted" from the barrel of the rifle before sending it to Washington, DC. The palm print was firmly identified as that of the right hand of Lee Harvey Oswald.

At dawn on November 23, as Oswald ended his first night in custody, came a discovery that incriminated him even further. In Chicago, the staff of Klein's Sporting Goods Company, searching through their files at the request of the FBI, came upon the records for the rifle with serial number C-2766. Klein's, who did a large mail-order business, had sent such a gun on March 20—eight months before the assassination—to a customer called A.

Hidell, at P.O. Box 2915, Dallas, Texas. The order form, which Klein's had received a week earlier, was signed "A. Hidell," in handwriting.

For the early investigators, the case now seemed effectively broken. The serial number at Klein's matched the number on the gun found at the Depository, and that gun had borne Oswald's palm print. The signature "A. Hidell" and the hand-printed part of the order form were firmly identified by government document examiners as Oswald's handwriting. Dallas police said that Oswald, when arrested, had been carrying a forged identity card, as well as documents in his own name. The forged card bore the name "Alek J. Hidell," yet the photograph attached was Oswald's. Dallas P.O. Box 2915 turned out to belong to Lee Oswald.

Nor was that all. In a crevice on the butt of the rifle was a tuft of cotton fibers. These were examined microscopically at the FBI laboratory, which judged them compatible with fibers in the shirt Oswald was wearing when arrested.

Oswald's wife, Marina, was to testify months later that her husband had owned a rifle. She had seen it, she was to say, in late September, at the house near Dallas where she was then staying. Oswald and his wife were living apart, seeing each other only occasionally, in the months before the assassination. Marina, with her two children, was staying at the house of a friend named Ruth Paine. Many of Oswald's possessions had been stored in the Paine garage, and it was there that Marina said she had last seen the rifle, wrapped in a blanket. Police saw the blanket during a search of the garage after the assassination. By then there was no rifle, but an FBI examination suggested the blanket had been stretched by hard, protruding objects.

The evidence that the rifle had been stored in the Paine garage, however, was thin. "The fact is," wrote Commission lawyer Wesley

Liebeler in a memo requesting changes to the draft of the Warren Commission Report, "that not one person alive ever saw that rifle in the . . . garage in such a way that it could be identified as that rifle." He was ignored.

On the eve of the assassination, Oswald had asked a fellow employee, Buell Frazier, to drive him to Mrs. Paine's house. Frazier quoted him as saying, "I'm going home to get some curtain rods . . . to put in an apartment." Oswald had then stayed the night with his wife and left the next morning before she was up, at 7:15 a.m. He then walked over to Frazier's house, just a few doors away, to get a lift to work. Frazier's sister noticed that Oswald was now carrying a heavy brown bag, and Frazier asked about it as the two men drove into the city. Oswald said something about "curtain rods," and Frazier remembered he had mentioned rods the night before. At the Texas School Book Depository, Oswald walked ahead into the building, holding the package tucked under his right armpit.

After the assassination, during their search of the sixth floor, police found a brown paper bag large enough to have contained the Mannlicher-Carcano rifle. It appeared to be homemade. The FBI later found a palm print and fingerprint on the bag, and these matched Oswald's right palm and his left index finger. Fibers found on the paper were very similar to fibers on the blanket in the Paine garage.

The day after the assassination, again in the garage, police made further dramatic finds. They came up with two photographs, both of Oswald apparently holding a rifle in one hand, two left-wing newspapers in the other, and with a pistol on his hip (see Photo 16). The Warren Commission was to decide that the photograph was authentic. Oswald's wife, indeed, was to say that she had photographed her husband in this odd pose the previous spring. The background in the pictures was the back-yard of the house where the couple had lived at that time. An FBI photographic expert determined that the photographs had been taken with an Imperial Reflex camera believed to have belonged to Oswald. On top of all that, there was the ballistics evidence.

As we have already seen, expert opinion was that the "magic bullet," found on the afternoon of the assassination at Parkland Hospital, was fired in the Mannlicher-Carcano to the exclusion of all other weapons. The three cartridge cases found at the Depository were also firmly linked with the rifle. The ballistics evidence involved in the policeman's shooting seemed damning, too. Cases found near the scene of the killing had been fired in the pistol that Oswald had with him when arrested.

Long before this catalog of evidence had been prepared, the Dallas authorities expressed great confidence in the case against Oswald. At 7:10 p.m. on the evening of the assassination, Oswald was charged with the killing of Police Officer Tippit. Later that night, Assistant District Attorney William Alexander and Captain Fritz of Homicide decided there were also grounds to charge Oswald with the President's murder. In 1978, Alexander told the author that Oswald's departure from the Depository after the assassination, coupled with the "curtain rods" story and the communist literature found among Oswald's effects, was enough to justify the second charge. According to Police Chief Curry, Oswald was brought from his cell sometime after 1:30 a.m. and charged by Judge David Johnson that he "did voluntarily and with malice aforethought kill John F. Kennedy by shooting him with a gun."[2]

The former police chief, the late Jesse Curry, commented that Oswald's reaction was "typical." He said, "I don't know what you're talking about. What's the idea of this? What are you doing this for?" Judge Johnston said, "Oswald was very conceited. He said sarcastically, 'I guess this is the trial,' and denied everything."

All of Oswald's denials were later to be dismissed as outright lies, and some of them certainly were. Yet wholesale rejection of Oswald's statements may be ill judged. A reexamination of what he said may provide clues to his real role in the assassination story.

Oswald and the Mannlicher-Carcano Rifle

From the start, Oswald told his interrogators that he had never possessed a rifle of his own. In later interviews, after the FBI had traced the order for the rifle at the mail-order firm in Chicago, and asked Oswald directly whether he had bought the weapon, he denied it outright. He volunteered the fact, however, that he had indeed rented Dallas P.O. Box 2915, and had been using it at the time the rifle was allegedly sent to that box number. It was never established that it was he who picked up the package containing the rifle at the post office.[3]

Oswald did admit to having used the name "Hidell"—the name in which the rifle had been ordered—saying he "had picked up that name in New Orleans while working in the Fair Play for Cuba organization." At one stage, though, Oswald seemed to contradict himself, saying that he "had never used the name, didn't know anybody by this name, and had never heard of the name before." This, though, was probably truculent weariness, for he then snapped, "I've told you all I'm going to about that card. You took notes, just read them for yourself if you want to refresh your memory." Why exactly was Oswald reluctant to discuss the fake I.D. card? As it turns out, his use of the name Hidell is intriguing.

The Warren Report contained a statement on the subject that was untrue. It declared, "Investigations were conducted with regard to persons using the name 'Hidell' or names similar to it. . . . Diligent search has failed to reveal any person in Dallas or New Orleans by that name." In fact, the Commission's own files contain a statement by a John Rene Heindel. He said, "While in the Marine Corps, I was often referred to as 'Hidell'—pronounced so as to rhyme with 'Rydell.' . . . This was a nickname and not merely a mispronunciation." Heindel revealed, moreover, that he had served in the U.S. Marines with the alleged assassin. They had both been stationed at Atsugi Base in Japan. Finally, Heindel lived in New Orleans, where Oswald was born, spent part of his youth, and lived during the summer of 1963. All this, for the investigator, has potential significance.

Any serious study of the Kennedy case must consider the possibility—many would say the probability—that Oswald had some connection with either the CIA or some other branch of U.S. Intelligence. If there was such a connection, it could perhaps have begun at Atsugi, where Oswald and Heindel both served and which was an operational base for the CIA. This period will be covered at length later in this book. We shall also see that, if Oswald was drawn into an assassination conspiracy by others— or framed—the process probably began during his New Orleans stay in 1963. These factors make it all the more disturbing that the Warren Report omitted altogether to mention that there was a real "Hidell"—and even untruthfully stated the contrary.

None of the thousands of Warren Commission documents reflects serious inquiry into whether or not there was any

Heindel-Oswald association after the Japan period. Heindel himself was never called to testify before the Warren Commission. The evidence gathered by the House Assassinations Committee, as published in 1979, shows no investigation of Heindel. This is the more remarkable given the role played by U.S. Army Intelligence on the day of the assassination, and specifically concerning the Hidell alias.

There were, from the start, curiosities about the way the name Hidell emerged after the assassination. According to later police testimony, a U.S. Army draft card in Hidell's name was found in Oswald's wallet immediately after his arrest. One of the first two detectives to question Oswald reported that Oswald actually pretended his name was Hidell at first. Yet, although the immediate rash of police press statements on the case included a mass of incriminating detail, the name Hidell did not come up publicly until the next afternoon, following the discovery of a mail order in that name for the rifle.[4] The name "O. H. Lee," an inversion of Oswald's real name, in which he was registered at his Dallas rooming house, was provided to reporters within hours of the assassination. Hidell was not. Behind the scenes, however, official communication lines hummed with references to the name within a few hours of the assassination. It now appears that the police and the FBI were only fully alerted to the Hidell alias after contact with a third force—part of the U.S. intelligence apparatus.

Army Intelligence agents were in Dallas on the day of the assassination, backing up the Secret Service in security operations for President Kennedy's visit. At San Antonio, to the north of the Texas border with Mexico, Lieutenant Colonel Robert Jones was operations officer for the 112th Military Intelligence Group. As soon as he heard about the assassination, Jones said, he urgently requested information from his men at the scene of the crime. By early afternoon, he had received a phone call "advising that an A. J. Hidell had been arrested." (Oddly, published information suggests that the call did not mention the name Oswald, although both names were on documents in Oswald's wallet.) Jones said he quickly located the name Hidell in Army Intelligence files. It cross-referenced, Jones claimed, with "a file on Lee Harvey Oswald, also known by the name A. J. Hidell." This, in turn, contained information about Oswald's past, including his time spent in the Soviet Union and the fact that he had recently been involved in pro-Castro activities in New Orleans.

Indeed, according to the Assassinations Committee summary of Jones' testimony, the file had been opened in mid-1963, "under the names Lee Harvey Oswald and A. J. Hidell," following a New Orleans police report of Oswald's activities in support of Castro. With the file in front of him, said Lieutenant Colonel Jones, he promptly got on the telephone to tell the FBI in Dallas about the contents of the Oswald file. One person he spoke to was Agent in Charge Gordon Shanklin. That, Jones has testified, was the end of his role in the matter, apart from writing a report summarizing the day's developments.

It seems important to know everything possible about Oswald's use of the name Hidell—not least because it was a mail order in that name which linked him in so damning a fashion to the Mannlicher-Carcano rifle. The Warren Commission asked to see any Army documents that might be relevant to Oswald, but was never shown the file Jones described on oath. For years, independent researchers asked for them, only to be told they could not be found.

In 1978, the Assassinations Committee was informed that the Army's Oswald file had been destroyed in 1973—as a matter of "routine." In a masterpiece of understatement, the Assassinations Committee report said it found the destruction of the Army Intelligence file "extremely troublesome, especially when viewed in the light of the Department of Defense's failure to make this file available to the Warren Commission." The Committee said it found Lieutenant Colonel Jones' testimony "credible."

It is apparent that Oswald used the name Hidell only on his pro-Castro propaganda leaflets, at one stage of his stay in New Orleans in the summer of 1963, and on mail-order forms when he sent for the rifle alleged to have been used in the President's murder and the pistol allegedly used to shoot Officer Tippit. If Jones' testimony is correct, Army Intelligence had its own independent information about some use of the name Hidell by Oswald.[5] Document releases show this was the case, at least in New Orleans. There is no sign, however, that Army Intelligence advised the Warren Commission of the fact.

When the Assassinations Committee complained about the U.S. Army's destruction of its Oswald file, it noted that "without access to this file, the question of Oswald's possible affiliation with Army Intelligence could not be fully resolved." The suspicion that the alleged assassin had been somehow affiliated to an intelligence agency will be examined in depth in this book. The role of Army Intelligence in the early hours of the investigation remains obscure and poorly documented.

One other source mentioned by Lieutenant Colonel Jones might have been able to throw more light on official knowledge of Oswald before the assassination. This was Dallas FBI Agent in Charge Shanklin, with whom Jones said he spoke on the afternoon of the murder. As will be discussed later, Shanklin has been widely held responsible for ordering the destruction of correspondence written by Oswald. A letter from Oswald to the FBI was deliberately destroyed after the assassination, when it should have been preserved as evidence. The Assassinations Committee called this "a serious impeachment" of Shanklin's credibility.

Oswald's use of an alias—any alias—to buy a gun, remains perplexing. If this was an attempt to conceal his real identity, as protection against taking blame for future crimes involving the rifle, Oswald was indeed a foolish fellow. Hard though it may be for a European to comprehend, in Texas it is still as normal to own a gun as not. In 1963, a man could buy a rifle across the counter in dozens of stores with few or no questions asked. Oswald could have done so and risked nothing more than a future shaky visual identification by some shop assistant.

As it is, Oswald not only gave his own post-office box number on the order for the gun, and committed his handwriting to paper, but also invited exposure—so we are told—by going out to murder the President with a Hidell identity card in his pocket and a Hidell-purchased rifle under his arm. One of the two policemen who first questioned him said Oswald gave his name as "Hidell."

It is said that criminal cunning is invariably flawed by stupidity, but other evidence suggests Oswald was far from stupid. School records show that in several subjects he was three years ahead of his class, and his intelligence was noted by his officers in the Marine Corps. How, then, to explain this next anomaly? While "frantically" denying any part in the assassination, it was Oswald who sent the police straight to some of the most incriminating evidence of all.

On the morning of the day following the assassination, Oswald provided details of where he had stayed in Dallas and where his belongings were kept. Although some of his possessions were kept at his lodgings, Oswald volunteered the fact that he stored many items in the garage of the Paine house, where his wife was staying. Officers armed with a search warrant were soon on their way back to the Paine address, which had already been searched once the previous day. According to the police account, the officers returned triumphantly to headquarters with the enormously incriminating photographs of Oswald holding a rifle and with a pistol at his hip[6]

At 6:00 p.m. that evening, when Oswald was confronted with an enlargement of one of the pictures, his reaction was confident. According to Captain Fritz, head of Homicide:

He said the picture was not his; that the face was his face, but that this picture was not him at all, and he had never seen the picture before. When I told him that the picture was recovered from Mrs. Paine's garage, he said that picture had never been in his possession. . . . He denied ever seeing that picture and said that he knew all about photography, that he had done a lot of work in photography himself, that the picture had been made by some person unknown to him. He further stated that since he had been photographed here at the City Hall and that people had been taking his picture while being transferred from my office to the jail door, that someone had been able to get a picture of his face and that, with that, they had made the picture. He told me that he understood photography real well, and that in time, he would be able to show that it was not his picture, and that it had been made by someone else.

Oswald's claim that the photographs were faked could reasonably be written off as desperate prevarication. Expert testimony that the pictures were taken with a camera believed to have been Oswald's, and his widow's statement that she took them for her husband, have been persuasive evidence that this was so. It may be no coincidence that one of the left-wing newspapers held by Oswald contained, in its correspondence column, a letter from Dallas signed "L. H." The pictures of Oswald with the suspect rifle are probably what they appear to be. That probability, however, does not end the puzzle surrounding the photographs—why and when were they taken, and with what purpose in mind?

Marina Oswald, the reader will recall, first claimed she remembered taking only one photograph of Oswald with the rifle, in the backyard. Then, when there turned out to be two different poses, she said she might have taken two. Later, in 1978, she said she could not remember how many had been taken, and that seems to be her safest tack. Oswald's mother Marguerite referred in her testimony to seeing another photograph, in which Oswald held the rifle over his head with both hands. That picture, said Marguerite, was destroyed by her and Marina just after the assassination to protect Oswald. Marina was never asked by the Warren Commission about this third photograph, though it made her claim to have "forgotten" taking more than one photograph less plausible. In fact, there was a fourth photograph.

In 1976, when the Senate Intelligence Committee was probing the role of the intelligence agencies in investigating the assassination, it found another pose in the same series of pictures. This was in the possession of a Dallas policeman's widow, the former Mrs. Roscoe White. She said her husband had told her it would be very valuable one day. As the polite prose of the Assassinations Committee was to put it later, Policeman White had "acquired" the picture in the course of his duties after the assassination. A fellow officer has mentioned having made "numerous" copies of the Oswald pictures for his colleagues. However, even if this particular print was intended merely as a keepsake, why was there no copy of it in the evidence assembled for the official inquiry? It reflects, at best, sloppy handling of evidence. Several officers must have known about this version of the photograph in 1963, for it shows Oswald in a stance that was copied in police reenactment experiments. Perhaps, indeed, they once knew of more copies. The last act of this comedy of police work did nothing to still the suspicions of those who suspected hanky-panky with the rifle poses.

Oswald's outburst suggesting that the Dallas police were trying to frame him with the photograph remains just that—an accusation. Yet there is the nagging possibility that there was some sort of cover-up—not necessarily involving the police but other, possibly unknown, Oswald associates.

The backyard photographs raise the ambivalent role of Oswald's Russian-born wife, Marina. In 1977, her authorized biography suggested that the deliberate destruction of copies of the pictures was the act of a loyal wife misguidedly trying to protect her husband—not knowing whether he had really killed the President or not.

Before burning the pictures, however, Marina did tell the police that Oswald owned a rifle. As the weeks went by, she was to be responsible for a mass of testimony incriminating her husband.[7] As Oswald's wife, of course, she was potentially in an excellent position to supply information about him. As a frightened foreigner caught in the eye of the cyclone of America's tragedy, she may have felt bound to cooperate in every way possible.

Nevertheless, while the Warren Commission used her testimony to help convict her husband in the public mind, its staff did not trust her. They felt, sometimes knew, that Marina had on occasion deceived them. One Commission lawyer wrote in a memorandum, "Marina Oswald has lied to the Secret Service, the FBI, and this Commission repeatedly on matters which are of vital concern to the people of this country and the world." As late as 1979, the Assassinations Committee wrote caustically of her professed ignorance of Oswald's activities. It referred to her past testimony as "incomplete and inconsistent" and noted that it had not relied on her during its investigation. Marina tended to have lapses of memory on the most improbable subjects. Asked if her husband liked photography, Marina said she did not think so. Asked whether he owned a camera, she said she could not remember.

Asked if Oswald once did a job involving photography, she pleaded ignorance. That was odd, given that Oswald did possess cameras and had had employment that involved photographic equipment. On account of that job, Oswald provided yet another tantalizing thought about those rifle pictures.

In March 1963, when the rifle photographs were allegedly taken, Oswald was working in the photographic department of Jaggars-Chiles-Stovall, a Dallas graphic-arts company that did work for the U.S. Army. According to a former colleague, "About one month after he started . . . he seemed interested in whether the company would allow him to reproduce his own pictures, and I told him that while they didn't sanction that sort of thing, people do it now and then." With that in mind, it has even been suggested that Oswald *himself*—perhaps with assistance—doctored his own incriminating pictures. Then, if caught committing mayhem with his newly acquired gun, he would be able to show that the photographs were fakes. It would thus appear that he had been framed—just as Oswald claimed at the police station—and he would be on the way to escaping a murder charge. A scenario worthy of Agatha Christie—though she might have deemed it too far-fetched.

The Assassinations Committee, of course, would have none of this. Its photographic panel decided the pictures were genuine and appealed to common sense. Why, it asked, would a forger treble the risk by making several different versions of his forgery?

There is, in fact, another way of interpreting the pictures. It permits them to be authentic images of Oswald yet makes them false in a quite different way. It may provide a clue to their purpose.

All the photographs purport to show Oswald proudly displaying two recognizable left-wing newspapers, *The Worker* and *The Militant*. In that fact lies an apparent contradiction. *The Worker* was the newspaper of the Communist Party of the United States, which was generally aligned toward Moscow. *The Militant* was the organ of the Trotskyite Socialist Workers' Party, which regularly expressed views diametrically opposed to those of *The Worker* and Moscow. The two publications differed violently in terms of ideology, and no genuine self-respecting Socialist would have advertised himself holding both at once. By 1963, Oswald, whatever his failings, was familiar with these very basic contradictions. Yet, the photographs aside, Oswald had been corresponding with both Communist factions.

This could suggest, some believe, that Oswald was now merely masquerading as a Marxist while working to some other secret purpose. In that case, if the pictures were genuine, they may have been a private joke to be shared with some unknown second party.[8] Alternatively, the pictures may be evidence of a clumsy operation designed to discredit the vocal left as a whole.

Those possibilities, as the unfolding story will show, lie at the very heart of the assassination mystery. Meanwhile, photographic specialists disagreed, police inefficiency was apparent, and Marina's true knowledge of the backyard pictures remained obscure. The controversy over the photographs sputtered on.

Of the material evidence concerning Oswald and the rifle, some points to Oswald having handled the rifle, such as the fibers caught in the rifle butt and the blanket in which the weapon had allegedly been wrapped at the Paine house. These items were circumstantially persuasive, but the FBI did not claim they were forensically conclusive.

There is a point to make about the fibers found on the rifle butt, which the FBI felt "could have come" from the shirt Oswald was wearing when arrested. Oswald himself remarked while in custody, and long before the forensic import of the shirt was known, that he had changed his shirt at his rooming house after the assassination. If that was true, then the fibers tend to link Oswald to the rifle through a shirt he was not wearing at the time of the murder. They may indicate that he had previously handled the rifle, while perhaps making it less probable that he used it in the Book Depository. The same applies to the partial fingerprints and the palm print allegedly found on the gun.

The partial prints found near the trigger-guard of the rifle were too vestigial to be linked firmly to Oswald. It is not true, as was suggested on national television in 1993, that an independent analysis made it "very likely" they were Oswald's. Experts disagree, again, and we are left with the 1963 verdict of the FBI laboratory, which said the partial prints were useless for identification purposes.

The palm print allegedly found on the underside of the rifle was positively identified as Oswald's. It could not be detected on the rifle, however, when it reached FBI headquarters. It was produced only days later, by Lieutenant Carl Day, the officer who first processed the weapon in Dallas, as a "lift" he said he had made on the night of the assassination.[9]

In terms of evidence, the most significant feature of the palm print is its location. According to Day, it was on the bottom side of the metal barrel—at a place accessible only when the wooden stock was removed. In other words, the print had been impressed on the rifle when the weapon was disassembled. What is more, it was an old print. "I would say," Day recalled, "that this print had been on the gun several weeks or months." If the print was authentic, it indicated only that Oswald had handled the rifle at some time. It was not proof that he used it to shoot the President.

What, then, of the allegation that Oswald carried the Mannlicher-Carcano to the Depository on November 22?

The "Curtain Rods" Story

Oswald did admit to having brought a package of some sort to work with him on the morning of the assassination, but strenuously denied it contained a rifle. He claimed it was merely a bag containing his lunch, made up of a cheese sandwich and an apple. When asked the size of the package, Oswald replied, "Oh, I don't recall. It may have been a small sack or a large sack. You don't always find one that just fits your sandwiches." When he gave this evasive answer, the prisoner was well aware the police had already heard the ominous story about curtain rods from Buell Frazier, the workmate who had driven Oswald to his wife's place the night before the assassination, then back to work the next morning.

The Commission would dismiss the curtain rods factor as a fabrication, quoting Oswald's landlady as saying his apartment needed neither curtains nor rods and saying that no rods had been found at the Depository. Yet photographs of curtain rods have turned up in the Dallas police files on the assassination. A press photographer, Gene Daniels of the Black Star agency, moreover, recalled that Oswald's landlady asked him not to take photos in Oswald's room until she had "the curtains back up." In fact, he took pictures as curtain rods were being hammered into position over the uncurtained windows. This was within twenty-four hours of the assassination.

The curtain rods story, then, may not have been a total fiction. In custody, however, Oswald denied having told Frazier he intended fetching rods for his rented room—even insisted that he had not carried a long package, nor placed it on the backseat of Frazier's car, on the morning of the murder. Both denials are implausible, because there is no reason to doubt the word of either Frazier or that of his sister, who also saw Oswald with the long package. Ironically, it was Frazier and his sister who created a slight doubt that Oswald had, in fact, been carrying the murder weapon rather than his "curtain rods."

Both insisted Oswald's parcel had been a good eight inches shorter than the disassembled Mannlicher-Carcano. Frazier demonstrated this by showing that Oswald could not physically have carried a 35-inch rifle tucked into his armpit with the base cupped in his hand, as Frazier remembered. He could have done so only if the package was shorter. Yet the Commission thought Frazier and his sister were mistaken. To bolster the notion that Oswald did carry the rifle to the Depository, they had the 38-inch paper bag that had been found by the window on the sixth floor. The bag was firmly linked to Oswald by a fingerprint and a palm print, although it was free from scratches or oil—odd, as the rifle had been oiled when found.

All the same, the preponderance of the evidence strongly suggests that Oswald owned the Mannlicher-Carcano and did bring it to work on the day of the assassination. But did he, using that rifle, fire three shots at the President on November 22, 1963?

The Cartridge Cases on the Sixth Floor

Few have disputed the fact that three used cartridge cases were found near the famous sixth-floor window, and one live round in the breech of the rifle. Rarely, however, has anyone raised the troublesome fact that *only* these were found—anywhere. Not a single spare bullet for the Mannlicher-Carcano was found on Oswald's person, at his rooming house, or among his effects stored at the house where his wife was living. No prints were found on the spent shells nor on the live round remaining in the chamber.

Intensive inquiry traced only two stores in the area where a man could buy ammunition suitable for the rifle.[10] One of these was well outside Dallas itself, and both gun shops were sure they had never had Oswald as a customer. In any case, ammunition is normally sold in hundreds or dozens of bullets, not by the handful.

The conventional account of the assassination thus assumes improbably that Oswald had previously exhausted his supply of ammunition—all save the four bullets accounted for at the Book Depository. It suggests, too, that he set off to shoot the President of the United States confident that he would use only those bullets that day. The four lonely exhibits on the sixth floor justify more thought than they have been given. For some, they nourish the suspicion that they were planted to incriminate Oswald.

All the technical evidence shows that the three used cartridge cases had been fired from the Mannlicher-Carcano. It is reasonable to suppose, then, that the rifle on the sixth floor was used to fire two shots at the President. The presence of a third cartridge, however, does not, necessarily mean that the rifle was used for a third shot at the motorcade.

The reason for doubt was spotted by Assassinations Committee Congressman Christopher Dodd, struggling to interpret the acoustics evidence that seemed to suggest how rapidly the Depository shots had been fired. Dodd realized that there was an apparent contradiction. In his view, the brevity of the pause between the first and second shots meant a likelihood that *two* rifles were at work to the rear of the President that day. Since scientific evidence indicated that the second shot hit both the President and the Governor and was fired from the Mannlicher-Carcano, Dodd reasoned that the first shot must have been fired by his hypothetical second gun. On that basis, Dodd could attribute only two of the recovered cartridge cases to shots fired in the assassination—the one credited with hitting the President and the Governor and the one presumed to have caused the fatal wound to the President's head.

What, then, to make of the third used cartridge case on the sixth floor? Congressman Dodd noted that the ballistics evidence showed merely that the cartridge cases were fired in the rifle at some point in time. Any or all of them could have been fired at some previous date. In this case, Dodd suggested, the third cartridge case could have been left in the breech after a firing previous to the assassination and ejected on the sixth floor only to make way for the bullets actually used in the murder. It is a tortuous thought, but, as Dodd explained it, logical enough. If his theory is right, the ballistics evidence in the case against Oswald is reduced—but only by one bullet. The fact remains that an apparently damning chain of evidence still appears to link him to the crime.

It is time to recap: The remnants of two bullets came from a rifle ordered in the name of Hidell but in handwriting attributed to Oswald. Fingerprint evidence showed that Oswald had handled that rifle, at least when disassembled. He brought a package to work on the day of the assassination, and a paper bag bearing his prints was found near the sixth-floor window. It is easy to conclude that it was Oswald—whoever and however many his accomplices—who fired the two shots that killed the President and wounded Governor Connally. Pause, however, once more.

There has been controversy down the years about Oswald's proficiency as a marksman. The official inquiry noted that Oswald's Marine Corps shooting record revealed him—at different times—as a "fairly good shot" and a "rather poor shot." The Warren Report omitted entirely, however, the recollection of Oswald's marksmanship by one of his former marine comrades that "we were on line together, the same time, not firing at the same position, but at the same time, and I remember seeing his shooting. It was a pretty big joke because he got a lot of 'Maggie's drawers'—you know, a lot of misses, but he didn't give a darn." There is no evidence that Oswald's marksmanship improved dramatically between his career in the U.S. Marines and the time of the assassination.

The answer to the question "Could Oswald have done it with the Mannlicher-Carcano?" is short and unsatisfying. It is: "Maybe or maybe not."

There is a more important question, of great relevance to a judgment about Oswald's guilt. Was Oswald actually on the sixth floor and in a position to shoot at the President at 12:30 p.m. on November 22? In 1979, new evidence increased the uncertainty.

Oswald—Sniping at the President or Eating His Lunch Downstairs?

Predictably enough, Oswald told his interrogators he was nowhere near the sixth floor when the President was shot. As the head of the Dallas Police Homicide Bureau reported: "I asked him what part of the building he was in at the time the President was shot, and he said that he was having lunch about that time on the first floor."* His snack, said Oswald, also took him to the second-floor lunchroom, but he claimed he had been on the first floor at the moment the President passed by. Unlike some of Oswald's denials, this cannot be dismissed out of hand.

The official inquiry found it impossible to prove anything about Oswald's whereabouts at the time of the shooting. Three of Oswald's prints were found on book cartons found near the suspect window, but that proved nothing. Oswald had legitimately worked on the sixth floor, and his were not the only prints found on the cartons. One identifiable palm print was found, but never linked to any individual. It did not belong to any of the employees known to have worked with the boxes, nor to official investigators who handled them after the assassination.[11] It remains possible that the prints belonged to an unknown assassin who did fire from the sixth floor. A chemical test on Oswald's right cheek, to identify possible deposits resulting from firing a rifle, proved negative.[12]

In the end, the Warren Report gave weight to a flimsy claim that Oswald was still on the sixth floor at 11:55 a.m., a full thirty-five minutes before the assassination. This assertion was based on the 1964 testimony of Charles Givens, a Depository worker who said he returned from lunch to fetch cigarettes from the sixth floor and saw Oswald then and spoke with him. It has since emerged from Warren Commission documents, however, that

---

* References to specific floors of the Texas School Book Depository are rendered in the American style. The American first floor is equivalent to the British ground floor. British readers should subtract one floor to understand to which location reference is made.

Givens was sought by the police after the assassination because he had a police record—involving narcotics—and was missing from the Depository.

When picked up and questioned, he mentioned nothing about having seen Oswald upstairs after everyone else had left. On the contrary, he said he "observed Lee reading a newspaper in the domino room where the employees eat lunch about 11:50 a.m." The "domino room" was on the *first* floor of the Depository. Even if what he said later is true—about seeing Oswald just five minutes later on the sixth floor—it would signify little that Oswald was upstairs more than half an hour before the assassination.

Other evidence suggests that Oswald not only declared his intention of going downstairs to lunch, but actually did so. It is evidence which, with disregard for the facts, official inquiries have either probed little or ignored.

When Oswald's coworkers left the sixth floor for their lunch break around 11:45 a.m., they left behind them an Oswald vocally impatient to come down and join them. Two, Bonnie Ray Williams and Billie Lovelady, remembered Oswald shouting to them as they went down in the elevator, "Guys! How about an elevator?" and adding words to the effect: "Close the gate on the elevator" or "Send one of the elevators back up." Sometime after this, around noon, Bonnie Ray Williams went back to the sixth floor to eat his own lunch in peace and quiet. Later, his lunch bag, chicken bones, and empty pop bottle were found there to prove it. Williams stayed on the sixth floor until at least 12:15 p.m., perhaps until 12:20. He saw nobody, certainly not Oswald.

Under interrogation, Oswald insisted he had followed his workmates down to eat. He said he ate a snack in the first-floor lunchroom alone, but thought he remembered two black employees walking through the room while he was there. Oswald believed one of them was a colleague known as Junior, and said he would recognize the other man but could not recall his name. He said the second man was short.

There were two rooms in the Book Depository where workers had lunch, the "domino room" on the first floor and the lunchroom proper on the second floor. There was indeed a worker called Junior Jarman, and he spent his lunch break largely in the company of another black man called Harold Norman. Norman, who was indeed short, said later he ate in the domino room between 12:00 and 12:15 p.m., and indeed thought "there was someone else in there" at the time, though he couldn't remember who. At about 12:15, Jarman walked over to the domino room, and together the two black men left the building for a few minutes. Between 12:20 and 12:25—just before the assassination—they strolled through the first floor once more, on the way upstairs to watch the motorcade from a window. If Oswald was not in fact on the first floor at some stage, it is noteworthy that he described two men—out of a staff of seventy-five—who actually were there. This information is nowhere noted in the Warren Report.[13]

The Report said no employee saw Oswald after 11:55 a.m., when he was still on the sixth floor. That ignored two items of evidence. Bill Shelley, a foreman, said he saw Oswald near the telephone on the first floor as early as ten or fifteen minutes before noon. An employee called Eddie Piper said he actually spoke to Oswald "just at twelve o'clock, down on the first floor." The Warren Commission had these statements but omitted them.

Within hours of the assassination, Oswald told interrogators that he left the first floor for the second-floor lunchroom to get

a Coca-Cola from the dispensing machine there. Oswald's statement was again supported by Eddie Piper, who said Oswald told
him: "I'm going up to eat." It has also been corroborated by a
witness who was never questioned by the Commission.

In 1963, Carolyn Arnold was secretary to the vice president
of the Book Depository.[14] An FBI report, omitted from the Warren Commission Report, said Arnold was standing in front of
the Depository waiting for the motorcade when she "thought
she caught a fleeting glimpse of Lee Harvey Oswald standing in
the hallway . . . on the first floor." When the author contacted
Arnold in 1978 to get a firsthand account, she was surprised
to hear how she had been reported by the FBI. Her spontaneous reaction, that the FBI had misquoted her, came *before* the
author explained to her the importance of Oswald's whereabouts
at given moments. Arnold's recollection of what she observed
was clear—having spotted Oswald had been her one personal
contribution to the record of that memorable day. As secretary
to the company vice president she knew Oswald; he had been in
the habit of coming to her for change. What she claimed she told
the FBI is very different from the Bureau report of her comments.

"About a quarter of an hour before the assassination," she said
in 1978, "I went into the lunchroom on the second floor for a
moment. . . . Oswald was sitting in one of the booth seats on the
right-hand side of the room as you go in. He was alone as usual
and appeared to be having lunch. I did not speak to him, but I
recognized him clearly."

Arnold had some reason to remember having gone into the
lunchroom. She was pregnant at the time and had a craving for
a glass of water. She also recalled, in 1978, that this was "about
12:15. It may have been slightly later."[15]

Should we believe Arnold's 1978 recollection or the FBI

account of what she told them back in 1963? Memories do blur, not least when much time has passed. One might think the FBI's contemporary report more trustworthy than Arnold's. FBI agents, however, are as fallible as other mortals. Mistakes in their reports, seen during research for the author's biography of J. Edgar Hoover, ranged from spelling errors to outright distortions.

Agents in Dallas after the assassination, we know, worked under intolerable time. "Hoover's obsession with speed," former Assistant Director Courtney Evans recalled, "made impossible demands on the field. I can't help but feel that had he let the agents out there do their work, let things take their normal investigative course, something other than the simple Oswald theory might have been developed. But Hoover's demand was 'Do it fast!' That was not necessarily a prescription for getting the whole truth."

Other former FBI agents recall having been virtually ordered to avoid leads that might indicate a possible conspiracy, to follow only those that would prove Oswald was the lone assassin.

Let us, then, allow for the possibility that Carolyn Arnold's 1978 memory is correct, that she did see Oswald downstairs at 12:15 p.m. or later. It is, of course, possible that Oswald scurried upstairs to shoot the President after Arnold saw him in the second-floor lunchroom. Yet, as we have seen, bystander Arnold Rowland said he saw two men in sixth-floor windows, one of them holding a rifle across his chest, at 12:15. Rowland's wife confirmed that her husband drew her attention to the man, whom he assumed to be a Secret Service agent. There was, of course, no such agent, and no other employees were on the sixth floor at that time.

The time detail—12:15—is the vital point here. It can be fixed so exactly because Rowland recalled having seen the man with the rifle just as a nearby police radio squawked out the news that the approaching motorcade had reached Cedar Springs Road. The police log shows that the President passed that point between 12:15 and 12:16.

Carolyn Arnold's given time for leaving her office—12:15 or later—is corroborated by contemporary statements made by her and office colleagues. She told the FBI she finally left the building, after visiting the lunchroom, as late as 12:25 p.m. If Arnold saw Oswald in the lunchroom at 12:15 or after, who were the two men, one of them a gunman, whom Rowland said he saw in the sixth-floor windows?

There never was any reliable eyewitness identification of Oswald in the sixth-floor window after he was seen downstairs. The Commission, however, set store by the evidence of Howard Brennan, a spectator in the street who stood directly opposite the Depository. He said he saw a man moving around at the famous "sniper's perch" window between 12:22 and 12:24 and that, at the moment of the assassination, he looked up to see the man fire his final shot. Later that day, Brennan was taken to a police identity lineup that included Oswald. He failed to make a positive identification of Oswald as the man he had seen in the window—even though he had seen Oswald's picture on television before attending the lineup.

A month later, however, Brennan told the FBI he was sure the man he had seen was Oswald. Three weeks on, he was saying he couldn't be sure. And many months later, Brennan told the official inquiry that he could have identified Oswald at the lineup but had feared reprisals from the Communists.

Brennan's testimony was replete with contradiction and confusion. He claimed to have been watching as the last shot was fired, yet saw neither flash, smoke, nor recoil. Testimony showed that, in the immediate aftermath of the tragedy, he did not at once draw attention to what he claimed to have seen in the Book Depository, but joined others hurrying toward the grassy knoll. Questioning suggested that Brennan at first stated he had seen smoke in the area of the knoll. The Commission was able to conclude only that "Brennan believes the man he saw [in the Depository] was in fact Lee Harvey Oswald."

In 1979, the Assassinations Committee Report did not use Brennan's testimony at all. Brennan was less consistent than many a witness discredited or totally ignored by the official inquiry. He may have seen a gun, or a man with a gun, but his testimony does not put Oswald in the sixth-floor window.

Nor does the physical evidence support that notion. When caught, Oswald was wearing a long-sleeved rust-brown shirt with a white T-shirt beneath it. He said he had changed his clothing since the assassination and that he had worn a long-sleeved "reddish-colored shirt" at work that day. This may have been true. A policeman who saw Oswald after the assassination, but before he left the Depository, said on seeing him under arrest that "he looked like he did not have the same clothes on." The policeman explained that the shirt Oswald had on at work had been "a little darker."

Whether Oswald changed or not, neither shirt fits with the clothing described by those who noticed a gunman on the sixth floor between 12:15 and 12:30 p.m.[16] Rowland, who made the earliest sighting, remembered a "very light colored shirt, white or a light blue . . . open at the collar . . . unbuttoned about halfway" with a "regular T-shirt, a polo shirt" beneath it. Even Brennan, the man who inconsistently claimed to be able to recognize Oswald as having been a gunman, described the man he saw in the window as having worn "light-colored clothes, more a khaki color." The two clerks from the county building, who also noticed a man in the sixth-floor window, spoke of an "open neck . . . sport shirt or a T-shirt . . . light in color, probably white" and of a "sport shirt . . . yellow."

Mrs. Walther, who saw two men in the window only moments before the assassination, said, "The man behind the partly opened window had a dark brown suit, and the other man had a whitish-looking shirt or jacket, dressed more like a workman that did manual labor. *It was the man with the gun that wore white* [author's emphasis]." None of these statements about light-colored clothing fit either the rust-brown shirt Oswald was wearing when arrested or the red shirt he said he had been wearing at the time of the assassination.

The fact is that Oswald could not be placed on the sixth floor either at the time of the shooting or during the half hour before it. The last time he was seen before the assassination was apparently by Carolyn Arnold—in the second-floor lunchroom. The next time Oswald was firmly identified was immediately after the assassination—again in the second-floor lunchroom.

When the shots rang out in Dealey Plaza, one motorcycle policeman, Marrion Baker, thought they came from high in the Book Depository. He drove straight to the building, dismounted, and pushed his way to the entrance. Joined by the building superintendent, whom he met in the doorway, he hurried up the stairs to the second floor. Just as he reached it, Baker caught a glimpse of someone through a glass window in a door. Pistol in hand, the policeman pushed through the door, across a small vestibule, and saw a man walking away from him. At the policeman's order, "Come here," the man turned and walked back.

Baker noticed the man did not appear to be out of breath or even startled. He seemed calm and said nothing. Though reports conflict, it seems he may have been carrying a bottle of Coca-Cola.[17]

At that moment, as Baker was about to start asking questions, the Depository superintendent arrived and identified the man as an employee. He was, of course, Lee Oswald, and the room was the second-floor lunchroom, exactly where Oswald had been last seen—at most, fifteen minutes before the assassination. Baker let Oswald go, and hurried on upstairs.

The Warren Report reckoned the policeman confronted Oswald one and a half minutes after having heard the shots. It calculated that Oswald, as the gunman on the sixth floor, took slightly less than that to reach the lunchroom door. Other apparently competent reconstructions have suggested that Baker took less time and that Oswald, if he was a sixth-floor gunman, would have taken longer to clear up and get downstairs.

The Warren Report just succeeds in getting Oswald downstairs in time to be confronted by Patrolman Baker. After making its own tests at the scene, the Assassinations Committee in 1979 said merely that the available testimony "does not preclude a finding that Oswald was on the sixth floor at the time the shots were fired." Alternative, independent calculations say that, had Oswald really been a gunman, he could not have reached the lunchroom in time for the meeting with the policeman. The best evidence seems to be that Oswald was down in the lunchroom fifteen minutes before the assassination, and just two minutes afterward.

The fresh look at Oswald's whereabouts becomes even more significant in the knowledge that the President was late for his appointment with death. He was due to arrive at his first Dallas appointment at 12:30, and that was about five minutes' drive beyond the Book Depository. Had the motorcade been on time, it would have passed beneath the windows of the Depository at 12:25 p.m. This was clear from from the President's published schedule for the day, and would have come into the calculations of any would-be assassin. A killer planning the assassination would hardly have been sitting around downstairs after 12:15 p.m., as the evidence about Oswald suggests, if he expected to open fire as early as 12:25.

It may be argued that the alleged assassin was merely trying to assure himself of an alibi. If so, it was a curious and unreliable way to go about it, and the lunchroom an odd spot to choose. That room was deserted at all relevant times, and Lee Oswald was seen there only by chance observers. On the other hand, it is hard to understand why Oswald, known to be interested in politics and politicians, would stay in the lunchroom when he knew the President was about to pass by. We know he was aware of the President's visit, because earlier that morning he had asked a workmate why the crowd was gathering outside. Told the President was coming and which way he was coming, Oswald had said merely, "Oh, I see." Supporters of the official story say, of course, that this was another attempt to establish an alibi, by professing ignorance of the very fact that President Kennedy was in town. Oswald's wide-eyed question does not ring true.

The evidence does cast enormous suspicion on Oswald. Aside from the evidence linking him to the rifle, his own statements— above all, the implausible "curtain rod" tale—leave him looking guilty of something. The evidence does not, though, put him behind a gun in the sixth-floor window. Some information, indeed, suggests that others manned the sniper's perch. "We don't have any proof that Oswald fired the rifle," former Police Chief Curry said in 1969. "No one has been able to put him in that building with a rifle in his hand."

If Oswald was as he claimed "just a patsy," it looks as though he realized his predicament the moment the hue and cry started in Dealey Plaza. It was from then on that the Oswald who had behaved so coolly in the encounter with the policeman gradually began to behave like a man in a panic.

Oswald's account of leaving the scene of the crime goes like this: He told his interrogators how he had gotten his Coca-Cola in the second-floor lunchroom, how he had met the policeman and then gone downstairs. In the uproar, said Oswald, he heard a foreman say there would be no more work that day, so decided to leave—by the front door. Outside the Depository, he encountered a crew-cut young man whom he took to be a Secret Service agent because he flashed an identity card. Oswald had directed the "agent" to a telephone, then traveled home to his lodgings by bus and taxi.

All this is rather well supported by other witnesses. A clerical supervisor returning to her second-floor office said she saw Oswald, Coca-Cola bottle in hand, within a couple of minutes of the assassination: "I had no thoughts or anything of him having any connection with it all because he was very calm." The foreman in question was indeed on the ground floor. The "Secret Service agent" Oswald directed to a phone was probably one of two reporters who rushed in looking for a phone on which to call their newsrooms—and recalled being pointed to one by a young man.[18] Oswald's story of how he got home is corroborated by the bus ticket found in his pocket when he was arrested, and by a Dallas taxi driver.

Would a wholly innocent man have gone home within minutes of the assassination of the President of the United States just because he "didn't think there would be any more work done that day"? Would not the natural thing, for a politically aware person like Oswald, have been to linger awhile in the excited atmosphere outside the Depository? Moreover, the decision to take a taxi home, which Oswald himself admitted he had never done before, also suggests flight. Once he did reach his lodgings, much became mysterious—not least the shooting of a policeman that led to his arrest.

CHAPTER 6

The Other Murder

*"There is still a real possibility that Oswald was on his
way to meet an accomplice at the time of the Tippit
murder. I led the Dallas investigation of that aspect of
the case and was never satisfied on that point."*
—Assistant District Attorney William Alexander, 1977

It was just before one o'clock, half an hour after the assassination, when Earlene Roberts, the housekeeper at Oswald's
rooming house in the Oak Cliff district, answered the telephone.
A friend was calling to tell her what had happened, and Mrs.
Roberts turned on the television to catch the news. Just then—
at 1:00 p.m.—her lodger Lee Oswald came bustling in. Roberts
said, "Oh, you're in a hurry," and went on watching TV. Oswald
went to his room and, as he himself later acknowledged, changed
his clothes and armed himself with a .38 revolver. He was out of
the house again within five minutes, and Roberts—who recalled
looking out of the window—last saw him standing at a bus stop.
In those five minutes, Roberts was to say, she had noticed something else, something that seemed inexplicable.

While Oswald was in his bedroom, she said, she had seen a
Dallas police car come slowly by the house and pull up. As it did

so, its horn sounded several times. Mrs. Roberts later described
the incident under oath.

Commission Lawyer: Where was it parked?
Mrs. Roberts: It was parked in front of the house . . .
                   directly in front of my house.
Lawyer: Where was Oswald when this happened?
Mrs. Roberts: In his room. . . .
Lawyer: Were there two uniformed policeman in
                   the car?
Mrs. Roberts: Oh yes.
Lawyer: And one of the officers sounded the horn?
Mrs. Roberts: Just kind of *tit-tit*—twice.

After the police car's horn sounded twice, the housekeeper
said, the vehicle moved slowly away. She did not remember
clearly the police number on the side of the vehicle. In statements in the days to come, however, she would repeat that she
had seen the car stop and heard what sounded like a signal on the
horn. This was a problem for the official inquiry, as checks with
the police suggested there was no patrol car at that point at one
o'clock. There was, moreover, no known reason for any police
car to visit Oswald's address so early in the case. He had not yet
been missed from the Book Depository. The official breakdown
of the day's events shows that Oswald's name did not crop up at
all until just before 2:00 p.m.

According to the record, nobody in authority knew about his
rented room until *after* two o'clock, when he volunteered it at
the police station. The Warren Report dealt with the mystery
the way it often did when the evidence failed to fit—by bury-
ing the police car horn-sounding incident in an obscure section

of the Report and implying that Mrs. Roberts was mistaken. The matter of the signaling car, however, may be pertinent to Oswald's movements in the ten minutes after 1:00 p.m., ten minutes that were to end in the murder of a policeman about a mile away.

The police radio log showed that at 12:45 p.m. patrol car driver J. D. Tippit was ordered into the Oak Cliff area. At 12:54 p.m., when he reported that he was in the area, he was instructed to "be at large for any emergency." At 1:00 p.m., as Oswald reached his rooming house, police headquarters called Tippit on the radio, and he did not reply. At 1:08 p.m., Tippit did call headquarters again, and this time the dispatcher failed to reply. The officer never called in again. Instead, eight minutes later, at 1:16 p.m., came the call from a member of the public using Tippit's car radio: "We've had a shooting here . . . it's a police officer, somebody shot him."

J. D. Tippit—just J.D. to his friends—was lying dead in a puddle of blood beside his patrol car. He had been gunned down on East Tenth, a quiet, tree-lined street about a mile from Oswald's lodgings.

The Warren Report decided on the following probable scenario. Tippit, cruising slowly along East Tenth, it was thought, had come upon Oswald walking on his own. The policeman pulled up and spoke to him, probably because he looked something like the broadcast description of the suspect in the President's assassination. After a brief exchange through the car window, Tippit got out and began walking around the vehicle to approach Oswald. Oswald then suddenly pulled a revolver and fired four times, killing the policeman instantly. He ran off, noticed by a dozen witnesses, scattering shell cases as he went.

Later, after the hue and cry led to Oswald's arrest in a nearby movie theater, five of the witnesses would identify Oswald at police lineups. Crisply summarized in the Warren Report, it all sounded straightforward.

The Warren Commission had shown little interest in fully investigating the Tippit shooting. Only a handful of relevant witnesses testified to the Commission, and contradictions in the evidence were papered over.

The star witness to the murder itself was a Dallas waitress named Helen Markham, supposedly the only person to have seen the shooting in its entirety. The official version, which accepted her testimony as "reliable," credited Markham with having watched the initial confrontation between Tippit and his murderer and with having peeped fearfully through her fingers as the murderer loped away—thus becoming competent to identify Oswald at a police lineup.

This "reliable" witness, however, made more nonsensical statements than can be cataloged here. She said she talked to the dying Tippit, who understood her until he was loaded into an ambulance. All the medical evidence, and other witnesses, indicate that Tippit died instantly from the head wound. Another witness who saw the shooting from his pickup truck and got out to help the policeman, put it graphically: "He was lying there and he had—looked like a big clot of blood coming out of his head, and his eyes were sunk back in his head. . . . The policeman, I believe, was dead when he hit the ground."

Markham said twenty minutes passed until others gathered at the scene of the crime. Nonsense. Men were in Tippit's car almost at once calling for help on the police radio, and a small crowd was there by the time an ambulance arrived three minutes later, at 1:10 p.m.

Markham was credited with having recognized Oswald within three hours at the police station. So hysterical was she at the station, however, that she was able to enter the lineup room only after the administration of ammonia. Before the Commission, Markham repeatedly said she had not been able to recognize anyone at the lineup—then changed her tune only after pressure from counsel.[1]

The quality of the star witness in the Tippit shooting was described by Joseph Ball, a senior counsel to the Warren Commission itself. Speaking at a public debate in 1964, he said Markham's testimony had been "full of mistakes." She had been an "utter screwball . . . utterly unreliable."

Other witnesses would paint a very different picture of events when Tippit was killed. Some of their statements, however, were also controversial. Acquilla Clemons, who ran out from the porch of a house close to the spot where Tippit was killed, told independent investigators that she had seen not one but two men near the policeman's car just before the shooting. Here is part of the transcript of a filmed interview with Clemons:

Interviewer:	Was there another man there?
Mrs. Clemons:	Yes, there was one, other side of the street. All I know is, he tells him to go on.
Interviewer:	Mrs. Clemons, the man who had the gun. Did he make any motion at all to the other man across the street?
Mrs. Clemons:	No more than tell him to go.
Interviewer:	He waved his hand and said, "Go on."
Mrs. Clemons:	Yes, said, "Go on."

According to Clemons, the man with the gun went off in one direction, the second man in another. She described the man with the gun as "short and kind of heavy," wearing "khaki and a white shirt"—a description that does not fit Oswald. The second man, she said, was "thin" and tall rather than short, a description that could perhaps refer to Oswald.

According to reporters who visited Clemons several years later, she—and her family—still spoke of having seen two men at the scene of the shooting of Officer Tippit. Another witness, Frank Wright, added a further odd detail. Having heard the shots as he sat in his living room, he told researchers, he went to his front door in time to see the stricken policeman roll over once and then lie still. "I saw a man standing in front of the car," he said. "He was looking toward the man on the ground." This man, Wright said, "ran as fast as he could go and he got into his car. His car was a little gray old coupé. It was about a 1950–1951, maybe a Plymouth. . . . He got in the car and he drove away as quick as you could see."

What Frank Wright and Acquilla Clemons had to say became ammunition for independent researchers who believed others—unknown—had played a role in the Tippit shooting.

More than three decades later, the work of a veteran broadcast journalist named Dale Myers brought a degree of clarity where confusion and rumor had reigned. Myers' 1998 book, devoted solely to the Tippit murder, impresses as being the most thorough study of the case. His analysis of a mass of testimony and the ballistics evidence dispels much of the doubt as to Oswald's guilt in the Tippit murder.[2]

Myers noted that Mrs. Clemons' statements about having seen two accomplices—rather than a lone gunman—are unsupported by any other testimony, even though Clemons was only one of a number of witnesses at or near the scene at the time. Wright's account, with its claim that he saw the apparent gunman drive away in a car, was also his and his alone—and was disputed by others well placed to observe events.

The best evidence in the Tippit case, meanwhile, was the forensic evidence. Four revolver cartridge cases were produced as having been recovered at the scene, and Oswald had been carrying a .38 Smith & Wesson revolver at the time of his arrest. He admitted later that the gun was indeed his, and offered a feeble excuse for having had it with him when arrested. "You know how boys do when they have a gun. They just carry it."

Sloppy police work, though, gave openings to skeptics who thought two gunmen had been involved in the Tippit shooting. Careless talk brought confusion as to whether the firearm that killed Tippit was a revolver, like Oswald's weapon, or an automatic. Two of the cartridge cases produced in evidence were of one make, two of another. A vital record in any firearm case, the chain of possession—the record as to who retrieved which cartridges, where and when—was inadequate.

In the overall picture, these points are of little importance. Given that Oswald had both types of ammunition in his revolver when caught, the discrepancy in the make of the cartridges becomes insignificant. The sloppiness over the chain of possession appears to reflect not deception but inefficiency.

Firearms experts said unanimously that all four bullets removed from Tippit's body had characteristics consistent with those of Oswald's weapon. Two of the four cartridge cases recovered, which had a good chain of possession, definitely came from Oswald's gun. The bulk of the evidence—and common sense—suggest that Oswald killed Officer Tippit on his own.

Even so, questions remain, questions that troubled official investigators after the assassination and remain unresolved today. Could Oswald have traveled the nine tenths of a mile from his lodgings to the scene of the Tippit shooting on foot, unaided, in the time available?

Even by using the shortest possible time frame—and ignoring factors that militated against it, the Warren Commission fudged the issue. So did the Assassinations Committee, years later. Did Oswald have transport to get to the site of the policeman's murder on East Tenth, and if so, who provided it? And why was he there? Where was he headed?

The official who directed the initial investigation of the Tippit shooting, former Assistant District Attorney William Alexander, voiced his suspicions in an interview with the author fifteen years after the assassination. "Along with the police," he said, "we measured the route, all the conceivable routes he could have taken to that place; we interrogated bus drivers, we checked the cab-company records, but we still do not know how he got to where he was, or why he was where he was. . . . Was he supposed to meet someone? Was he trying to make a getaway? Did he miss a connection? Was there a connection? If you look at Oswald's behavior, he made very few nonpurposeful motions, very seldom did he do anything that did not serve a purpose to him. People who've studied his behavior feel there was a purpose in his being where he was. I, for one, would like to know what that was."

As he drove the author along the route Oswald is supposed to have taken to the Tippit murder, the former Assistant District Attorney slapped the dashboard and repeated, "Oswald's movements did not add up. . . . No way. Certainly he may have had accomplices."[3]

There are further outstanding questions. If the account of the housekeeper at the rooming house was true, if she really did see a police cruiser outside the house just after 1:00 p.m. and hear it sounding its horn, was Tippit the driver? It's conceivable—Tippit did not respond to the police dispatcher at 1:00 p.m. Could it be that Tippit drove Oswald to the spot where the policeman was murdered?

Were there things about Tippit that never came out? Shortly before his death, several witnesses claimed, Tippit spent some ten minutes sitting in his patrol car at a service station not far from where he would be killed. He then drove off at high speed. There was also a claim that, shortly before he was murdered, Tippit hurried into a record shop near the site of the killing, used the store's telephone, dialed a number, then rushed out again.

Another unresolved lead was the statement of a garage mechanic who said he saw a man behaving suspiciously on the afternoon of the assassination—he appeared to be trying to hide himself—in a car parked near the scene of the Tippit shooting. That night, the mechanic recognized Lee Oswald, from his pictures on television, as the man he had seen in the car. He had taken the number of the car, and it turned out to belong to a friend of Tippit.[4]

"It may be," said Andy Purdy, former senior staff counsel on the Assassinations Committee, "that Officer Tippit, by himself or with others, was involved in a conspiracy to silence Oswald. And when the attempt to kill Oswald by Tippit failed, then Jack Ruby* was a fallback."

Long after the assassination, there would be claims—one of them from an associate of a Mafia boss suspected of involvement in

---

* Jack Ruby—infamous as the Mob-connected club owner who was to kill Oswald two days after President Kennedy's assassination—an act that will be dealt with at length in a later chapter.

the assassination—that Oswald had been on his way to a planned rendez-vous at the time Tippit was shot. As this book will show, the alleged assassin was involved in a weird world of intrigue. He had blundered into a quicksand of intelligence agents, Cuban exile plotters, and thugs, and it may be that he was in over his head.[5]

CHAPTER 7

A Sphinx for Texas

"Constitutional scrutiny of Intelligence services is largely an illusory concept. If they're good, they fool the outsiders—and if they're bad they fool themselves."

—John le Carré

Fifteen years on, standing in the sixth-floor window of the Texas School Book Depository, Jesse Curry stared out over Dealey Plaza and remembered the oddest prisoner he ever had: "One would think Oswald had been trained in interrogation techniques and resisting interrogation techniques," said the retired Dallas police chief. Curry's puzzlement was echoed by Assistant District Attorney Alexander, who told the author, "I was amazed that a person so young would have had the self-control he had. It was almost as if he had been rehearsed, or programmed, to meet the situation that he found himself in."

"Rehearsed? Rehearsed by whom?" I asked Alexander. He could only shake his head and murmur, "Who knows?"

Lee Oswald was an enigma, and not only for Texas law enforcement officials. In the summer of 1964, when the Warren Report was being drafted, the alleged assassin's elder brother, Robert, received a call from a Commission lawyer holed up in a cabin in Vermont, working on the chapter that would deal with the question of *why* Oswald might have killed President Kennedy. Robert Oswald was "flabbergasted," he would recall, that the Commission had yet to find a motive for the man it had pegged as the lone assassin.

Motive is a basic ingredient that any investigator seeks in any crime, but the Commission never found one for Oswald. Its Report stated, "No one will ever know what passed through Oswald's mind during the week before November 22, 1963," and made do with guesses about "hostility to environment," "hatred for American society," and the like. There has never, moreover, been any evidence that the alleged assassin was insane.

In 1979, the Assassinations Committee could come up only with talk about Oswald's "conception of political action, rooted in his twisted ideological view of himself and the world around him." Were the same conclusion to be drawn about all young people of Oswald's addled left-wing politics, we should expect presidents to be assassinated all the time. The Committee admitted that it picked on that explanation only "in the absence of other more compelling evidence"—a phrase perhaps suggesting that its section on motivation was written before the science and other evidence forced a finding that there had been more than one assassin.

Where the Committee identified likely sinister hands behind the assassination, they were those of Mafia bosses or anti-Castro activists. It avoided the question of how Oswald's left-wing stance might fit into such scenarios, and dwelled hardly at all on the possibility that—*because* of that very stance—he may have seemed ripe for a setup. Whatever the truth about that, Oswald's lack of motive has mitigated in his favor. In his police questioning, indeed, the alleged assassin gave his captors the impression that he had rather *liked* President Kennedy.

"I am not a malcontent; nothing irritated me about the President," Oswald replied mildly when asked after the assassination what he had thought of Kennedy. He said, too, "I have no views on the President. My wife and I like the President's family. They are interesting people. I have my own views on the President's national policy." In this instance, Oswald's version was corroborated almost unanimously by those who knew him. The accused's wife, Marina, whose testimony was to damn him in so many other ways, told of Oswald's enthusiasm for Kennedy. She said of her husband, "He always spoke very complimentary about the President. He was very happy when John Kennedy was elected. . . . Whatever he said about President Kennedy, it was only good, always."

Kennedy was voted into office while the Oswalds were living in Russia, and Marina said of Lee, "He was very proud of the new President of his country." She said Oswald called Kennedy "a good leader" and usually gave the impression that "he liked him very well." Acquaintances and relatives told the official inquiry much the same thing, and Oswald's attitude apparently remained consistent in the months before the assassination. In August, when the Oswalds were in New Orleans, the American press was full of the latest Kennedy family tragedy, when the President's newborn son died two days after birth. Then, like many people in America, Oswald followed bulletins on the baby's progress with concern. He hoped the child would survive, worried when its condition went downhill.

More dispassionate was the opinion of a policeman who interviewed Oswald at that very same period, following an incident on a New Orleans street between Oswald and anti-Castro exiles. Lieutenant Francis Martello also formed the impression that Oswald liked President Kennedy. Martello thought Oswald was: "Not in any way, shape or form violent. . . . [A]s far as ever dreaming or thinking that Oswald would do what it is alleged that he has done, I would set my head on a chopping block that he wouldn't do it." In a conversation about civil rights a month before the assassination, Oswald said he thought Kennedy was doing "a real fine job, a real good job."[1]

It frequently occurs, of course, that people commit crimes that seem out of character. The night before the assassination, there had perhaps been a sign that something was brewing in Oswald regarding the President. When Marina brought up the subject of Kennedy's impending visit, she was to say, her husband avoided talking about it. According to Marina, Oswald was preoccupied that night with personal worries, pressing Marina to live with him once again, talking a lot of making a fresh start by moving the family into an apartment together. It was hardly the talk of a man planning a crime that might, as it indeed turned out, spell his own imminent death.

In custody, aside from his "frantic" denials that he had murdered the President and his shout of "I'm just a patsy!" to the press, Oswald did drop a hint that he would have more to say. He would tell none of it, though, until he could get legal advice. When allowed a visit by the president of the Dallas Bar Association, Oswald spoke of wanting to find a lawyer "who believes in anything I believe in, and believes as I believe, and believes in my innocence as much as he can, I might let him represent me."

According to a Secret Service agent present, Oswald "wanted to contact a Mr. Abt, a New York lawyer whom he did not know but who had defended the Smith Act 'victims' in 1949 or 1950 in connection with a conspiracy against the government." An attorney known for his leftist activism—he had joined the Communist Party in the 1930s—Abt was away from home during the weekend of the assassination. Oswald, who never did reach him, also talked of asking the American Civil Liberties Union to find him a lawyer. Nothing came of it. Oswald was a mystery, and he knew it.

When his brother, Robert, visited him in custody, Oswald warned him: "Do not form any opinion on this so-called evidence." Robert wrote later in his diary: ". . . I searched his eyes for any sign of guilt or whatever you call it. There was nothing there—no guilt, no shame, no nothing. Lee finally [sic] aware of my looking into his eyes, he stated: 'You will not find anything there.' " The years of endless investigation, of groping toward an understanding of Oswald's real role, have given us no firm answers.

We now have fragments, however, of a picture of Oswald that was denied to the public in the wake of the assassination. Ironically, it was President Lyndon Johnson—the man who succeeded Kennedy and appointed the Warren Commission—who eventually dropped the heaviest official hint that Lee Oswald was more than he appeared to be. In a 1969 interview for CBS Television, Johnson remarked: "I don't think that [the Warren Commission] or me or anyone else is always absolutely sure of everything that might have motivated Oswald or others that could have been involved. But he was quite a mysterious fellow, and he did have connections that bore examination." That was an understatement, but the former president felt he had said too much. He asked CBS to withhold that section of his interview on grounds of "national security." CBS obliged by suppressing Johnson's remarks until 1975.

It was that word "security" again. As mentioned in the preface, Chief Justice Warren had used it in 1964 in answer to a question as to whether Warren Commission documentation would be made public. "Yes," he had replied, "there will come a time. But it might not be in your lifetime. I am not referring to anything especially, but there may be some things that would involve security. This would be preserved but not made public."

At the time, no one in the media raised objections about document withholdings that involved security—even if withholdings were a little difficult to square with the official verdict that the President had been killed by a single misguided young man acting alone. Oswald had previously lived in the Soviet Union, after all, and this was the height of the Cold War era. Withholdings justified by security seemed harder to accept, however, once the Assassinations Committee found that Oswald had probably *not* acted alone but as part of a plot involving the Mafia and anti-Castro operatives.

A perennial explanation, of course, has been that secret intelligence agencies have to protect their information-gathering systems and the identities of personnel. On its face, that is acceptable—but only if that is the genuine reason for withholding documents. The concern has been that U.S. Intelligence agencies have continued to use the "national security" excuse for retentions that are unjustified.

In 1977, when the FBI went through the motions of releasing a hundred thousand pages from its Kennedy assassination files, the U.S. media uttered an uncritical cheer. At the press conference to mark the event, reporters seemed uninterested or ill-equipped to ask probing questions. The author found himself virtually alone in pressing the FBI spokesman into an admission that "up to 10 percent of the [Kennedy] file will not be released." One reason for retaining records, the spokesman said, was to protect individuals' privacy. The other was the familiar one, "national security." Even after the passage of the JFK Records Act in 1992, which mandated the release of all Kennedy assassination material unless a real case could be made for retention, the FBI continued to resist full disclosure.

The Central Iintelligence Agency, for its part, over the years released assassination-related documents only when under intense pressure, at the insistence of congressional committees, or—in more recent years—when obliged to comply with the Records Act. Sometimes, "released" documents have turned out to be censored virtually out of existence.

The Warren Commission, scholars now know, did not see a multitude of documents that are today deemed assassination-related. Senior Assassinations Committee staff, empowered to investigate the President's murder with the authority of the House of Representatives, ended their probe still stymied by CIA procrastination and evasiveness.

Much of this book will be given over to assembling the pieces we do have of the documentary jigsaw. Sometimes the emerging picture will seem to point to a sinister Communist conspiracy—a specter that President Johnson, just after the assassination, feared "could conceivably lead the country into a war which could cost forty million lives." What was the truth about the many months Oswald the defector spent in the Soviet Union? What had his contacts been with Soviet Intelligence? Marina, the wife Oswald had brought home from Russia, remained something of a mystery in her own right. Even before the assassination, the CIA had pondered whether she might be a Soviet plant, sent to the United States with a phony identity. The Agency's questions to the Russians about Marina failed to extract satisfactory answers.

In 1964, when the Warren Commission considered the possibility that Marina might be a Soviet agent, Senator Russell commented almost casually, "That will blow the lid if she testifies to that." She did not, of course, but there is little indication that the Commission were very keen to peer under the lid. Some leads, which raised questions not merely about the Soviets but about the activity of U.S. intelligence, were left unpursued.

One of Oswald's Dallas acquaintances, Teofil Meller, told police after the assassination that—in 1962—he had taken precautions before continuing to associate with the recently returned defector. He had checked with the FBI, he said, and agents had said Oswald was "all right." What did that mean?

Another Dallas resident, George de Mohrenschildt, befriended Oswald after his return from Russia. Like Meller, he later claimed he had felt the need to check up on Oswald, in his case by seeing J. Walton Moore, an agent with the CIA's Domestic Contacts Division. According to de Mohrenschildt, the agent replied without hesitation: "Yes, he is okay. He is just a harmless lunatic." What would a CIA man in Dallas have known about Oswald, as early as 1962, to be able to give assurances without even checking CIA files? (The de Mohrenschildt connection will be discussed later.)

Long after the assassination, while researching a book about Jack Ruby, the Scripps-Howard correspondent Seth Kantor realized that a call he had made in the early evening of November 22 had intriguing potential significance. Kantor, who had covered the Kennedy visit to Dallas, looked again at notes of calls he had made in the afternoon and early evening of the day of the assassination. His managing editor, the notes reminded him, had urged him to phone the Florida number of Hal Hendrix, a journalist who also worked for the Scripps-Howard chain. Hendrix, the editor told Kantor, "had some background on Oswald" for him.

Kantor's notes showed that—as early as 6:00 p.m. on the day

of the assassination—Hendrix supplied details of Oswald's past, his defection to Russia, and his recent pro-Castro activities. Now, in retrospect, Kantor pondered the fact that Hendrix had seemed knowledgeable about the alleged assassin.

Hendrix was no run-of-the-mill journalist. Earlier in 1963, he had won a Pulitzer Prize for his coverage of the Cuban Missile Crisis. Then he excelled himself again. In an article published on September 24, he cited observers saying that an "ouster" of the pro-Kennedy President Bosch of the Dominican Republic could occur "overnight." Bosch was overthrown in a coup the very next day.

Whatever his skills as a newsman, Hendrix reportedly had the advantage of having access to a CIA source at Homestead Air Force Base, south of Miami. In the months and years to come, he would become known to his Washington colleagues as "The Spook"—because, in Kantor's words, "of the handouts he reputedly took from the CIA." In 1976, Hendrix would plead guilty to having withheld information from a Senate committee probe into multinational corporations and the CIA. He had lied to the committee with the collusion of the CIA, and had concealed his access to CIA information. This was the man who "had some background" on Lee Oswald to give Kantor in the early evening of November 22, 1963.

As previously mentioned in the context of Oswald's "Hidell" alias, U.S. Army Intelligence had a file on Oswald before the assassination. As a result, a colonel was feeding information to the FBI within an hour of Oswald's arrival at the police station. It would be good to satisfy oneself that this was just an example of the efficiency of Army Intelligence. That, however, became impossible when the Army applied the ultimate censorship and destroyed its Kennedy files.

Soon after the Assassinations Committee learned the military records had been shredded, Congressman Richardson Preyer told the author: "There have been instances of files being, I guess you could say, maliciously withheld or even destroyed. . . . We don't know what the motive is."

It is hugely improbable that any U.S. agency—or top leadership of an agency—had any part in the assassination. The Assassinations Committee concluded in 1979 that neither the Secret Service, nor the FBI, nor the CIA, were involved as organizations. On the other hand, the Committee considered evidence indicating that individual members of agencies might have had prior covert associations with Oswald and might have even played a role in the assassination. One particularly serious allegation remains, as the Committee's Chief Counsel put it, "undiscredited."[2] Yet the shifty behavior of the intelligence organizations may conceal—inefficiency aside—an embarrassing truth less heinous than actual involvement in the assassination.

The Warren Report stated, "Close scrutiny of the records of the federal agencies involved and the testimony of the responsible officials of the U.S. government establish that there was absolutely no type of informant or undercover relationship between an agency of the U.S. government and Lee Harvey Oswald at any time." Today, with Watergate and a string of CIA scandals behind us, we know such all-embracing trust was naïve—the Warren Commission staff did not see all the records in 1964. In 1979, the House Assassinations Committee was careful not to express confidence that no agency had any type of relationship with Oswald.

The transcript of one Warren Commission executive session, throws an interesting light on the CIA's attitude to the ethics of disclosure in the early 1960s. Commission member Allen Dulles, himself a former CIA Director, briefed colleagues on how a CIA official would deal with inquiries about an agent he had recruited.

Dulles:	He wouldn't tell.
Chief Justice Warren:	Wouldn't he tell it under oath?
Dulles:	I wouldn't think he would tell it under oath, no.
Chairman:	Why?
Dulles:	He ought not to tell it under oath. Maybe not tell it to his own government, but wouldn't tell it any other way [sic].
Chairman:	Wouldn't he tell it to his own chief?
Dulles:	He might or he might not.

Whatever Lee Oswald might eventually have revealed about himself and U.S. intelligence was lost to history forever two days after his arrest. In the late morning of November 24, the Dallas police chief decided to move his prisoner to the county jail. In the basement of City Hall, as Oswald was being led to a police car, a bystander with a revolver lunged forward to fire a single lethal bullet into Oswald's stomach (see Photo 44). Jack Ruby, a local club owner with Mafia connections, had silenced Oswald once and for all. The last words the accused assassin had heard before being shot were a newsman's shouted question: "Have you anything to say in your defense?"

Oswald was conscious for a few minutes after being shot. Police officers laid him down on the front floor of a nearby office, and one tried to talk to him. Detective Billy Combest told the author of Oswald's dying response to questioning about the assassination: "At that time, I thought he was seriously injured, so I got right down on the floor with him, just literally on my hands and knees. And I asked him if he would like to make any confession, any statement in connection with the assassination of the President. . . . Several times he responded to me by shaking his head in a definite manner. . . . It wasn't from the pain or anything—he had just decided he wasn't going to correspond with me, he wasn't going to say anything."[3]

Before Oswald was carried to an ambulance, someone applied artificial respiration—the worst possible treatment for an abdominal wound because it multiplies the chances of severe internal bleeding. At Parkland Hospital, the doctors who two days earlier had tried to save the President's life now worked in vain over Oswald.

The corpse was taken to a mortuary, where an FBI team photographed Oswald and took his fingerprints for the last time. Late on November 25, the same afternoon that President Kennedy was laid to rest in Arlington, the alleged assassin was buried in a cemetery outside Dallas, in a moleskin-covered coffin, within a sealed concrete vault, beneath a black slab bearing only the word OSWALD. No details, not even dates of birth and death.

Today, we still have only glimpses of who he really was in life.

II

OSWALD
Maverick or Puppet?

CHAPTER 8

Red Faces

*"Ask me, and I will tell you I fight
for Communism."*

—Lee Harvey Oswald, in a letter from Russia, 1959

The reaction in Dallas to the capture of Oswald could aptly be described as Pavlovian. The moment local officials realized he had been in Russia, and discovered armfuls of Communist propaganda amongst his belongings, they began sounding off about an international Communist conspiracy to kill the President.

Far away in Washington and Moscow, a different breed of official reacted with more sophistication. CIA and the KGB officers knew full well the questions that would soon be asked: Was Oswald an agent? Was he one of ours or one of theirs? These questions still await satisfactory answers; those that have been given are riddles in the sand.

In a 1975 memorandum, then CIA Director William Colby recalled how in November 1963 he had hurriedly consulted the files because "we were extremely concerned at the time that Oswald, as an American returning from the USSR, might have been routinely debriefed by DCD [Domestic Contacts Division]."

None of the subsequent traces, Colby wrote, revealed Agency contact with Oswald.

In February 1964, a Soviet intelligence officer defecting to the United States gave a glib account of Moscow's reaction to the assassination. This was Yuri Nosenko, who claimed that within hours of the news he had himself been ordered to investigate the Soviet end of the Oswald case. A special plane had been dispatched to Minsk, where Oswald had lived, to collect all official papers on the alleged assassin's stay in Russia. The results, Nosenko insisted, had been negative, because the KGB had "decided that Oswald was of no interest." "I can unhesitatingly sign off," he claimed, "to the fact that the Soviet Union cannot be tied into this in any way."

Neither the CIA nor the Soviet disclaimers convinced the Senate Intelligence Committee when, in 1975, it looked into the performance of intelligence agencies at the time of the Kennedy assassination. Senator Richard Schweiker, who was prominent in that inquiry and had access to many classified U.S. intelligence files, said of Oswald in an interview: "Either we trained and sent him to Russia, and they went along and pretended they didn't know—to fake us out—or in fact, they inculcated him and sent him back here and were trying to fake us out that way."

Oswald did move in a mysterious way. And, in the effort to bring his shadowy profile into focus, the outsider labors under an enormous handicap. His main sources are people for whom untruth is a way of life—officials of the intelligence community.

The author Edward Epstein caused a stir in 1978 with a book suggesting that Oswald may have been recruited by the KGB, though not with assassination in mind. Epstein drew heavily on interviews with former CIA Counterintelligence chief James Angleton—long unrivaled as an interpreter of Soviet skullduggery and also, famously, a master of deception and disinformation.

In 1975, at a Senate Intelligence Committee hearing, Angleton was asked to verify a quotation of something he had reportedly said earlier. Angleton responded in characteristically opaque style: "Well, if it is accurate, it should not have been said."

By the time Oswald defected to the Soviet Union in 1959, Angleton was already embarked on the course that would define the rest of his career—and in a sense the Agency's ability to operate effectively—the obsessive hunt for a mole. Angleton believed that an agent who answered to the Soviets had penetrated the CIA, and specifically the Soviet Russia Division. He was obsessed with the notion, an obsession that effected his every response to the defection to Russia of an insignificant young man called Oswald, and, in the long run, to the assassination itself.

Our look at the world as seen by Angleton first follows the proposal that the youthful former marine Oswald was recruited by the Communists—bearing in mind always that he may also have been the tool of others with very different loyalties and purposes.

The fledging Oswald was a contradiction. At sixteen, in New Orleans, he was reportedly devouring communist literature from the library and apparently writing to the Socialist Party of America for information.[1] According to one high school friend, he began spouting about Socialism, declaring that he was "looking for a communist cell in town," that "communism was the only way of life for the worker."

Another contemporary said that reports that the young Oswald had been "studying communism" were nonsense, that Oswald had a funny way of showing that communism was the only course for him. For he was simultaneously trying to join the U.S. Marine Corps, a potent symbol of American "imperialism"—if you happened to be on Oswald's professed side of the political fence.

Oswald tried to cheat his way into the Marine Corps while still under enlistment age and—when he failed—began devouring his elder brother's Marine Corps manual as avidly as he had reportedly been studying Marxist tracts. According to his mother, Oswald learned the handbook until he "knew it by heart" and finally succeeded in joining up six days after his seventeenth birthday. The shapes in the fog around Oswald will suggest, though, that his zeal to become a U.S. marine, like his socialist bent, may have been less than spontaneous.

During basic training, recruit Oswald declared an interest in aircraft maintenance and repair, and spring 1957 saw him learning radar and air-traffic control. These and further assignments called for a security check, which Oswald passed. According to the official record, he was granted clearance at a "Confidential" level. Over these months, Oswald emerged as a loner who kept apart from his marine buddies. He did not always run with the pack when the unit was allowed out of camp, and some of his actions seem to have been a little mysterious. While at Keesler Air Force Base, friends thought Oswald used his weekend passes to go "home" to New Orleans, a hundred miles away. As we now know, however, his mother had moved to Texas. Other relatives, who did live in New Orleans, said Oswald did not come visiting.

Marine Oswald did rather well. He finished seventh in a class of thirty and qualified as an Aviation Electronics Operator—an assignment designed for those credited with above-average intelligence. This led to a foreign posting with MACS-1, Marine Air Control Squadron One in Atsugi, Japan. In 1957, Atsugi was a base for the now famous U-2 spy plane, and Oswald was entering a world of military secrets. In the controversy over the alleged assassin's true colors, this period is pivotal.

Atsugi Air Base, a few miles southeast of Tokyo, had been inherited by the Americans from Japan's World War II air force. When Oswald arrived, it had become a jump-off point for U.S. Marine Corps fighter jets and Navy Constellations equipped for detecting enemy radar. Atsugi was also the site of a radar "bubble" responsible for surveillance of a vast sector of air space. Its function, according to the Warren Report, was "to direct aircraft to their targets by radar, communicating with the pilots by radio." The squadron also scouted for incoming foreign aircraft, mostly Russian or Chinese planes that had strayed.

Oswald worked in the radar bubble, gazing for hours at a time at the blips on the screen, plotting aircraft courses. The newcomer proved so good at his job that one officer wrote, "I would desire to have him work for me at any time. . . . He minds his business and he does his job well." Sometimes, as the senior enlisted man, Oswald served as crew chief. One of the leading marines in Oswald's group was to say of him, "He had the sort of intelligence where you could show him how to do something once and he'd know how to do it, even if it was pretty complicated."

While Oswald worked in the radar room, he witnessed a phenomenon that mystified almost everyone. Sometimes, out of the ether, a pilot's voice would request weather information for an altitude of ninety thousand feet. In 1957, no one had heard of a plane that flew that high. The mystery lasted only until the marines discovered they were living at close quarters with a newfangled aircraft called the U-2. The officers called it a "utility plane," but the U-2 was a spy in the sky, perhaps the West's most important single military intelligence asset.

As the weeks passed, Oswald and his friends saw the U-2 in action as it was wheeled out of a special hangar, as it rocketed aloft at astonishing speed, and as it returned from distant missions. Long and pencil-thin, the U-2 looked like something out of science fiction. There were no spy satellites then, and it was invaluable to the United States for penetrating Soviet and Chinese air space to return laden with telltale photographs. Army and air bases, seaports and factories, all were vulnerable to the high-altitude eyes of the U-2.

The beauty of it, for Western intelligence, was that the Communists were powerless to intercept the U-2. The superplane flew so high that no ground-to-air missiles or conventional aircraft could touch it. Its precise operational altitudes were top secret, as was any technical data that would teach the Russians how to knock the U-2 out of the sky. Oswald and his friends were left in no doubt about the secrecy. The hangar where the planes were kept was ringed by guards with submachine guns, and the marines were under orders to say nothing about what they saw and heard on the airfield and in the radar room.

It is probable that Atsugi also held another secret almost as sensitive as the U-2 project—a stockpile of nuclear weapons. According to the American agreement with Japan, no nuclear armament should have been stored on American bases, but personnel at Atsugi suspected the pact was violated.

One officer, Lieutenant Charles Rhodes, recalled having been taken by a colonel to a vast underground complex "at least three stories below ground." On either side of a central thoroughfare, in deep alcoves, Rhodes observed huge armaments that he identified as bombs. The colonel did not say what they were and did not invite questions.[2]

The aura of military secrecy at Atsugi was fascinating for

everyone, down to the lowliest marine, and some have suggested that for Oswald it was more than that. Lieutenant Charles
Donovan, the officer in charge of Oswald's radar team, said he
remembered a day when Oswald discussed the U-2's radar blips
with him. One marine friend recalled Oswald wandering around
Atsugi with a camera taking pictures. He later served at another
U-2 installation, in the Philippines, where his duties included
standing guard at a hangar that housed the airplane.

If Oswald's photographs were of radar installations or of the
U-2 in action, they would have been manna from heaven for
Soviet intelligence. Some believe Oswald made sinister contacts
who were just that—spies.

Just as he had once gone off alone on trips to New Orleans,
Oswald now went on two-day trips to Tokyo. He confided to a
friend that he was having an affair with a Japanese nightclub
hostess. That on its own would have been normal enough,
but Oswald seemed to be living above his station. The hostess
worked at the Queen Bee, one of the smartest clubs in the city.
Its clientele were American officers rather than enlisted men,
and a night with one of the hostesses cost more than Oswald
earned in a month.[3]

Oswald and the hostess were sometimes seen together, and
his mates marveled that a woman of her style and beauty had
time for Oswald. Perhaps they simply underestimated Oswald's
amatory talents, but some have suspected that the Queen Bee
hostess pumped Oswald for classified information. Loose talk in
the Tokyo clubs, like soldiers' bar talk anywhere, was known to
cause security leaks, and the use of sex as bait for intelligence
information is as old as spying itself.

Whatever the nature of the liaison, Oswald reacted miserably
to news that his unit was to be transferred to the Philippines.

ANTHONY SUMMERS

It was then, in October 1957, that his early image as a model U.S. marine began to look tarnished. According to the record, Oswald shot himself in the arm, inflicting a minor wound, before the unit was due to leave Atsugi. He allegedly did so with a pistol he had purchased privately and kept in his locker. For possession of an unregistered weapon against service regulations, Oswald was fined and sentenced to twenty days' hard labor.

If he had been trying to dodge transfer to the Philippines, he failed. Oswald was discharged from the hospital in time to leave Japan with his unit and did not return to Atsugi for several months. When he did get back, he got into trouble again, this time reportedly because he picked a quarrel at a party. A second court-martial acquitted him of deliberately having poured a drink over a sergeant, but found him guilty of using "provoking words."

This time, Oswald spent eighteen days in the cells. From then on, former friends said, he spoke bitterly against the Marine Corps, which reinforced his reputation as a loner. He avoided marine associates and was again seen with Japanese acquaintances, both male and female.

In autumn 1958, during a crisis sparked by fighting between Communist and Nationalist Chinese forces, Oswald's radar unit apparently moved to Taiwan. Oswald reportedly again drew attention to himself by loosing off four or five shots into the darkness, then claiming he had fired at "men in the woods" who had failed to answer a challenge. He was transferred shortly afterward back to Atsugi—once again to be seen with a striking woman—this time a Eurasian. Oswald told a friend she was half Russian.[4]

In December 1958, Oswald's tour of duty in the Pacific ended, when he was transferred back to the United States, to the El Toro Air Station in Santa Ana, California. His unit's function there, according to Lieutenant Donovan, was "to surveil for air-craft, but basically to train both enlisted men and officers for later assignment overseas." Like other officers, Donovan found Oswald "a good crew chief," "very competent," "brighter than most people." The lieutenant took Oswald on at chess and found him "very good" at the game. He noted, too, that the young marine "was particularly capable in the field of world affairs." Oswald had a special interest—it became clear that he was pre-occupied with things Russian.

At El Toro, Oswald applied to take a Marines proficiency examination in written and spoken Russian. He failed, but showed a knowledge of the basics of the language. He was observed in weeks to come to be laboring hour after hour over his Russian books, and to have begun reading a Russian-language periodical. He played Russian records, so loudly they could be heard outside the barrack block, and began addressing people in Russian whether they understood it or not. Oswald even had his name written in Russian on one of his jackets.

Marine friends nicknamed him "Comrade Oswaldskovich," and young Lee thought that as funny as they did. Fellow marine Kerry Thornley, noted later, "He often joked about Communism. I remember one time a master sergeant got up on the tailgate of a truck for a lecture of some type. Oswald put on a Russian accent to exclaim, "Ah! Another collectivist farm lecture."

Oswald openly showed himself interested in socialist ideology and in Soviet politics in particular. He once again subscribed to the *People's World*, the socialist newspaper he had first read as a youth in New Orleans. Marine Thornley, who discussed politics with Oswald, gained the impression that he thought "Marxist morality was the most rational morality to follow," Communism "the best system in the world."

With another marine, Nelson Delgado from Puerto Rico, Oswald also held animated discussions about Cuba, where Fidel Castro had just seized power. Both young men said they supported the Castro revolution and discussed traveling to Havana together one day. Delgado suggested that Oswald write to the Cuban Embassy in Washington, DC, and Oswald later said he had made contact with Cuban diplomats. Delgado noticed that his friend started getting more letters than usual, some of which bore the Cuban official seal.

On trips into Los Angeles, with Delgado, Oswald would say he was on his way to "visit the Cuban Consulate." One night, when an outsider asked for him at the camp entrance, Oswald was allowed to stand down from guard duty to see the visitor. He went to the gate, where Delgado saw him deep in a long conversation with a man he thought was Cuban.

"Delgado's testimony has the cast of credibility," a senior aide to the CIA's James Angleton commented years later in a memorandum, "[and] says a lot more of possible operational significance than is reflected by the language of the Warren Report, and its implications do not appear to have been run down or developed by investigation." After the Kennedy assassination, the aide observed, Soviet and Cuban cooperation with the American inquiry was minimal, "designed to cover up an admission of knowledge of, or connection with, Oswald."

Who was the stranger who had reportedly visited Oswald at El Toro, Angleton's aide wondered. And "was there reporting from Los Angeles to Washington and Havana that could, in effect, represent the opening of a Cuban file on Oswald?"[5]

Shortly before the end of his Marine Corps service, Oswald asked Delgado to take a duffel bag to a bus-station locker in Los Angeles. Along with personal property, according to Delgado and another marine, it contained photographs taken from various angles that showed a fighter aircraft. Oswald could have obtained the pictures legitimately, during training, but Delgado wondered later why he had kept them. Meanwhile, whatever his allegiance, Oswald was getting ready for a dramatic move.

Earlier, in spring 1959, Oswald had applied to study philosophy at the Albert Schweitzer College in Switzerland, and the college had accepted him. In a letter home to his brother, Oswald had written, "Pretty soon I'll be getting out of the Corps and I know what I want to be and how I'm going to be it." Now, in August, he behaved as though he were impatient to leave the Marine Corps. He asked for an early release on the ground that his mother, who had been injured at work some time earlier, needed him. He applied for a passport, openly stating in the application that he intended to travel to Russia and Cuba. This hardly squared with his pretense of going home to look after his mother, but there is no sign that the Marine Corps raised any query. The passport was forthcoming, and on September 11, 1959, Oswald was out of the U.S. Marines and on his way to Texas.

Twenty years later, in a superficial review of Oswald's service record, the Assassinations Committee found nothing very out of the ordinary about this. There is no sign that the Committee talked extensively with Oswald's former marine comrades. Nor, apparently, did it ponder the Marine Corps' tolerance for his Russophilia or the lack of reaction to his plans for travel to the Soviet Union.

Once in Texas, Oswald told his brother he was going to New Orleans to "work for an export firm." It was not true. Having reached New Orleans, he boarded a ship bound for Europe, disembarked at the British port of Southampton on October 9, then moved on rapidly. By midnight the next day, he was checking into a hotel in Finland's capital, Helsinki. Oswald was on the last lap of his journey to Moscow, and things continued to go smoothly.

Within two days, having had no advance notice that has ever emerged, the Soviet Consul in Helsinki granted Oswald a six-day tourist visa to enter the Soviet Union. His trip there, by train, was to be on the most expensive ticket available—"De Luxe," an odd choice for a young man on a tight budget. Later, we shall consider whether he could have afforded the trip at all.

Oswald's easy access to the Soviet Union has encouraged the suspicion that the Russians were expecting him. It is prompted by a claim that Swedish intelligence detected a flying visit by Oswald to Stockholm, where he may have visited the Soviet Embassy.[6] Normal practice, CIA and State Department studies showed, was to keep visa applicants waiting for at least a week—and often as many as two.

The Soviet Consul in Helsinki at the time was believed to be an undercover KGB officer, and U.S. intelligence learned he could issue a visa in minutes if convinced the would-be traveler was "all right." Oswald apparently came up to scratch. He arrived in Moscow by train on October 16, 1959, to be met by an Intourist representative and shepherded to the Hotel Berlin. He registered on check-in as a student.

After two weeks, and a series of contacts with Soviet officials, Oswald walked into the U.S. Embassy in Moscow. There, according to the consular officials who received him—Consul Richard Snyder and Vice-Consul John McVickar—Oswald declared his wish to renounce his American citizenship. He slapped his passport down on the table, along with a formal letter that ended, "I affirm that my allegiance is to the Union of Soviet Socialist Republics."

Oswald declared that he had "voluntarily told Soviet officials that he would make known to them all information concerning the Marine Corps and his speciality therein, radar operation, as he possessed." He added, too, "that he might know something of special interest." On the face of it, Oswald was now not only a defector, but also a self-declared traitor to his country.

Was it as simple as that? One of the American consular officials, John McVickar, felt that Oswald was "following a pattern of behavior in which he had been tutored by a person or persons unknown . . . seemed to be using words he had learned, but did not fully understand . . . in short, it seemed to me there was a possibility that he had been in contact with others before or during his Marine Corps tour who had guided him and encouraged him in his actions."

As late as 1978, former Vice-Consul McVickar told the author he still had the nagging feeling that Oswald's performance at the Embassy had not been spontaneous. If he was right, what "person or persons unknown" had coached Oswald?

Had Oswald been in contact with Communist agents in Japan or the United States, and perhaps defected at their urging? It would be said following the assassination—by a person with links to U.S. intelligence—that Oswald had himself had said he associated with Communists in Tokyo.[7] If Oswald indeed had contact with Communist agents, however, they may not have been his only connection with the secret world.

Take a second look, and the picture blurs.

CHAPTER 9

Cracks in the Canvas

"We have not been told the truth about Oswald."

—Senator Richard Russell, former Warren Commission member, 1970

Back on the Marine air station in California, Oswald's roommate had been puzzled. Nelson Delgado had heard his friend talk of being in contact with Cuban officials—and knew he had been receiving a Russian newspaper. He had asked Oswald incredulously, "They let you get away with this in the Marine Corps, in a site like this?"

It was a good question. Oswald was openly dabbling with revolution while working in a sensitive area on an American military base at the height of the Cold War. Yet the nearest anyone came to blowing the whistle had been when mailroom workers reported the "leftist" nature of Oswald's mail. An officer, Captain Block, raised the matter briefly with Oswald, who reportedly explained that he was "trying to indoctrinate himself in Russian theory in conformance with Marine Corps policy." That was as far as it went, and Oswald went on playing Russian records, reading Russian books, generally flaunting his preoccupation with things Soviet. This failed, apparently, to trigger any official concern.

Another Oswald acquaintance at the California base, Kerry Thornley, had also been doing his share of youthful talking about Communism. "Looking back," he said long afterward: "I feel that both Oswald and I must have been put under surveillance by the Office of Naval Intelligence during our periods of active duty in the Marine Corps. The Cold War was raging then. He was widely regarded as a Communist."

Thornley had a point; it is odd that Oswald's indiscretions do not crop up in any Navy file—at least none that the public has been permitted to see. Omissions from official records sometimes turn out to be more significant than what is included.

Was no one alert enough to bother with Oswald's socialist protestations? Did Naval Intelligence hear about Oswald but fail to take the matter seriously? Should we merely apply the human-error theory of history to the Oswald case?

Perhaps. If so, however, it was the start of an extraordinary chain of anomalies and official oversights, a chain that would last virtually without interruption until the day President Kennedy was assassinated. So many inconsistencies that even cautious researchers have come to suspect that—somewhere along the line—Oswald the youthful Socialist became a tiny cog in the machinery of American intelligence.

To pursue that thesis involves fumbling in the historical dark, persistent perusal of the documentary record, and an awareness that some documents may still be withheld or have long since been destroyed.

Those at the serious core of the critical community have lurched from theory to theory. In the end, though, they are left with these questions: Was Oswald diverted from his Marxist course and used for what some intelligence department construed as patriotic duty? Was he identified as a left-winger and then unwittingly exploited by American intelligence? Was he recruited by Soviet or Cuban intelligence? Or was he, as official reports have insisted, just the confused disciple of the Left he appeared to be, controlled by nobody and no country, a scrap of flotsam on the political tide?

If Oswald was some sort of pawn on the intelligence chessboard, a logical place to start looking for oddities is in the record of his military service.

The Warren Report skated quickly over the details of Oswald's progress in learning Russian, saying only that—in a test he took after being transferred from Japan to California—he rated "poor." In fact, Oswald scored +4 in Russian reading, meaning that he got four more answers right than wrong. He scored +3 in written Russian, and −5—indeed a low result—in understanding spoken Russian. Though qualified as "poor," the results show that Oswald had grasped the basic principles. They indicate that he had been working on his Russian before leaving Japan.

Marine Dan Powers, one of his comrades, saw Oswald outside the base in the company of a Eurasian woman. He gathered that she was half-Russian and was teaching Oswald the Russian language. We know nothing of the woman's political allegiances.

What may also be significant, something the Warren Report skipped quickly past, is that Oswald somehow made remarkable progress in Russian between late February 1959, when he failed the U.S. Marine Corps test, and the summer of that year in California. A friend, knowing of Oswald's interest in Russian, arranged for him to meet his aunt, who was studying Russian for a State Department examination. Oswald and the aunt, Rosaleen Quinn, had supper together in Santa Ana, and he conversed with her in Russian for about two hours. According to Quinn, Oswald spoke Russian better, and with much more assurance, than she did after working with a teacher for more than a year. Oswald explained his progress by saying he had been listening to Radio Moscow.

This was the man who only months earlier had achieved a miserable −5 in understanding spoken Russian, let alone speaking it. The Warren Report skipped past the inconsistency, but there is a morsel of information that may explain it—and open a Pandora's box of further questions.

Two months after the assassination, at a closed executive session of the Warren Commission, Chief Counsel Lee Rankin outlined areas of the case that required further investigation. He said: "We are trying to run that down, *to find out what he studied at the Monterey School of the Army in the way of languages* [author's emphasis]."

The Army Language School in Monterey, California, now the Defense Language Institute, has long provided highly sophisticated crash courses in languages ranging from European languages to the most obscure dialects. It was, and is, used by U.S. government and military agencies to familiarize personnel with languages ranging from Swahili to Mandarin Chinese. The School was functioning and teaching foreign languages to members of the military in 1959, when Oswald was based in California. The official record makes no mention of Oswald ever receiving instruction in Russian, or any language, during his Marines service, at Monterey or anywhere else. Yet the Rankin reference to finding out *"what he studied* [author's emphasis] at the Monterey School of the Army" suggests that, at one stage anyway, Commission staff thought Oswald had studied at the School.

Other episodes during Oswald's service as a marine deserve reflection. There may be something strange about the incident at Atsugi when Oswald is said to have shot himself in the arm. Some marines present at the time did say Oswald was slightly wounded. Two others who were also there, Thomas Bagshaw and Pete Connor, recalled that the bullet missed Oswald and hit the ceiling. None of the three unit doctors who would have been involved, meanwhile, remembered treating a marine who had suffered a self-inflicted wound in the arm. Is it a little odd that all three medics failed to recall the bizarre incident?

Another curious detail of Oswald's tour of duty in the Far East relates to the stint he and his unit did on Taiwan in fall 1958. Lieutenant Charles Rhodes recalled that, during that phase, Oswald was suddenly flown from Taiwan to Atsugi. The explanation in the record is that he was transferred for "medical treatment"—the nature of which raises a further question mark.

Oswald supposedly had urethritis, a mild venereal ailment incurred—the Marine Corps file comically tell us—"in line of duty, not due to own misconduct."

One of the doctors on record as having treated Oswald, interviewed by the author, did not recall the episode. The "line of duty" notation had probably been a routine device, he said, used to avoid jeopardizing Oswald's pay. (A similar note had been entered in the record in connection with Oswald's supposed self-inflicted bullet wound.)

What does seem strange is that urethritis, the mildest of the venereal illnesses, should have been judged sufficient cause to fly Oswald to another base far across the China Sea. Urethritis can be a nuisance, but thousands suffer from it while going on with their everyday lives.

Given the various imponderables, and given the saga to come, could the bullet wound the doctors cannot remember, and the minor ailment that required transoceanic travel, have been a pretext to cover the removal of Oswald from circulation for some other purpose?

While doing research for another book, the author puzzled over a contradiction between the official record and the personal history—available only much later—of an officer in Britain's Royal Navy in World War I. The contemporary record had the officer in a Navy hospital on the island of Malta when his later recollections had him running around bursting with health on the Russian mainland. The author later discovered the officer had at the time been an ace British intelligence operative. The hospital record had been merely a cover, fabricated to hide his part in a sensitive operation.

The sickness ploy, it turns out, is a fairly common intelligence technique. Without for a moment comparing young Oswald to a top World War I agent, is it possible that he, too, had ailments of expediency?

Since his arrival in Japan, Oswald had lived literally in the shadow of American intelligence operations. At Atsugi, where he witnessed the U-2 spy flights, there had been a cluster of some two dozen buildings bearing innocent-looking signboards that read "Joint Technical Advisory Group." This was the euphemistic title used for one of the CIA's largest bases in the world, one that oversaw covert operations in Asia.

The official account asserts only that Oswald, like other marines working in the Atsugi radar room, had a "Confidential" clearance. Lieutenant Donovan, who commanded Oswald's radar team in California, was to say, however, that Oswald gained a higher rating. "He must have had 'Secret' clearance to work in the radar center," Donovan insisted, "because that was a minimum requirement for all of us." Oswald's comrade Nelson Delgado said,

"We all had access to classified information. I believe it was classified 'Secret.'"

While some enlisted men who served with Oswald did have only "Confidential" ratings, another of his closest associates said he heard a "rumor" at the time that Oswald was an exception. "Oswald, I believe, had a higher clearance," said Kerry Thornley, who served with Oswald in California, "I believe that he at one time worked in the security files; it is the S and C files, somewhere at LTA or at El Toro . . . probably a 'Secret' clearance would be required."

A report by the Marine Corps Director of Personnel, written after the assassination, appears to say Oswald may have had a "Secret" clearance when carrying out certain duties.

Whatever his precise status, there is no sign that the Marines command doubted Oswald's reliability—in spite of two court-martial offenses—or questioned his loyalty when he started openly flaunting Marxist convictions and Russophilia. The future alleged assassin kept his security clearance.

The next puzzle is a financial one. As a lowly enlisted man, could Oswald have saved enough money from his pay as a marine to make the roundabout trip to Moscow that followed? The record suggests not, for his only bank account, which he emptied on leaving, contained a paltry $203.[1]

There is a logistical hiccup, meanwhile, in the conventional account of Oswald's journey to Moscow, one that floored Commission staff. The Warren Report stated that Oswald arrived in England on October 9, 1959, and, "the same day, flew to Helsinki, Finland, where he registered at the Torni Hotel." This ignored the apparent problem of a British date stamp in Oswald's passport, a stamp indicating that—though Oswald did arrive at Southampton on October 9—he did not leave until the *next day*.

The record of exit, stamped by an immigration officer at London Airport, reads, "Embarked 10 Oct 1959."

That raises a question, for the only direct flight from London to Helsinki on October 10, Flight 852, did not get on to the ground at the airport for the Finnish capital until 11:33 p.m.—hardly allowing Oswald time to check in at Helsinki's Torni Hotel by midnight, as recorded in the hotel's registration book.[2]

The day after arriving in Helsinki, for no apparent reason, Oswald checked out of the Hotel Torni—a first-class, downtown hotel—and into the Hotel Klaus Kurki, also downtown and also first class.

Do the oddities and anomalies noted in this chapter suggest that young Oswald was used as some sort of tool of U.S. intelligence, wittingly or unwittingly?[3]

The CIA, of course, consistently denied any involvement with him. In 1964, its then Director, Kennedy appointee John McCone, testified that: "My examination has resulted in the conclusion that Lee Harvey Oswald was not an agent, employee, or informant of the CIA. The Agency never contacted him, interviewed him, talked with him, or received or solicited any reports or information from him, or communicated with him directly or in any other manner."

The Assassinations Committee received similar assurances from CIA chiefs in 1979—including Richard Helms, who in 1963 had been Deputy Director for Plans responsible for activity involving agents and informers. Helms had sworn as early as the year after the assassination that there was "no material in the Central Intelligence Agency, either in the records or in the mind of any of the individuals, that there was any contact had or even contemplated with him [Oswald]." He also assured the

Commission that a member of its staff had been welcomed at CIA headquarters and given access to "the entire file."

Assurances given by Helms, however, may today seem less than convincing. In 1975, when the Senate Intelligence Committee investigated CIA plotting to murder Cuban leader Fidel Castro, Helms was pressed as to why he had not told even Director McCone about the assassination schemes. He responded lamely. "I guess I must have thought to myself, 'Well this is going to look peculiar to him. . . .' This was, you know, not a very savory effort." In 1964, when McCone had assured the Warren Commission that the Agency had no links to Oswald, he did so on the basis of a briefing provided by Helms.

The most charitable interpretation of Helms' statements to official inquiries may have been encapsulated by Helms himself, in this exchange with the Senate Intelligence Committee:

Senator Morgan: You were charged with furnishing the Warren Commission information from the CIA, information that you thought relevant?

Helms: No, sir, I was instructed to reply to inquiries from the Warren Commission for information from the Agency. I was not asked to initiate any particular thing.

Senator Morgan: . . . in other words, if you weren't asked for it, you didn't give it.

Helms: That's right, sir.

A few years later Helms, pressed by the House Assassinations Committee to explain why the Warren Commission had not been told about CIA efforts to murder Fidel Castro, Helms shrugged off the omission. "I am sorry," he said, "It is an untidy world."

Some of Helms' "untidiness" had by that time become very apparent. In 1977, having pleaded nolo contendere to charges concerning testimony to another Senate committee, he had been fined and handed a two-year suspended jail sentence for making misleading statements on oath about the CIA's operations against President Allende of Chile. Helms said he had merely been obeying the higher authority of his Intelligence loyalty oath. In his only public speech as CIA Director, he said the nation "must to a degree take it on faith that we, too, are honorable men."

CIA Chief of Counterintelligence James Angleton, documents show, offered the FBI Assistant Director William Sullivan advice as to how the Bureau should deal with the Warren Commission. The Commission, he wrote, would likely put the same questions to both the CIA and the FBI. Two, he foresaw, would be:

1. Was Oswald ever an agent of the CIA?
2. Does the CIA have any evidence showing that a conspiracy existed to assassinate President Kennedy?

He proposed the concise replies:

1.) No

and

2.) No.

Angleton, who had primary responsibility for CIA dealings with the Warren Commission, would testify that he "informally" discussed the assassination with Commissioner—and former CIA Director—Allen Dulles. Dulles, for his part, privately coached CIA officers on how best to field the question as to whether Oswald had been an agent.

According to a CIA internal memorandum, Dulles "thought language which made it clear that Lee Harvey Oswald was never an employee or agent of CIA would suffice. . . . Mr. Dulles did not think it would be a good idea to cite CIA procedures for agent assessment and handling for Oswald to have been chosen as a CIA agent to enter Russia. There are always exceptions to every rule." The CIA memo's author agreed, noting that "a *carefully phrased denial* [author's emphasis] of the charges of involvement with Oswald seemed most appropriate." Did the Agency have special reasons to be careful in the phrasing of its denial?

The Agency readily acknowledged having held a "201" file on Lee Oswald—"201" being the generic description for a file opened on anyone in whom the CIA had taken an interest. Oswald's 201 was the "principal repository" for documents on the alleged assassin. The fact that there was one did not mean he was an agent—nor that he was not.

The CIA said it had 1,196 documents on Oswald, some hundreds of pages long, almost all of which have since been declassified. How the 201 file was handled before the assassination, what was put in it and what was not, and when, may tell us more than the contents of the documents themselves.

The file was opened on December 9, 1960, more than a year after Oswald's defection—a delay that rang alarm bells in the minds of Assassinations Committee staff. The Agency, staffers reasoned, would have become interested in Oswald a year earlier, the moment it learned he was in Moscow declaring his readiness to give the Soviets radar information of "special interest." His defection had been reported in the *New York Times*, in the *Washington Post*, and across the country

Why would the CIA not have opened a 201 file at once?

Another factor fueled the Committee's suspicions. As at all or most diplomatic missions, U.S. embassies around the world were then as now peppered with intelligence officers, just as Moscow's embassies were filled with "Secretaries" and "Attachés" working for Soviet intelligence. The record said that Consul Richard Snyder, one of the two officials who interviewed Oswald at the U.S. Embassy, had worked for the CIA in the past—for a year, much earlier. The Assassinations Committee found, however, that his CIA file had been "red-flagged because of a 'DCI [Director of Central Intelligence] statement and a matter of cover.' " The reference to cover, the Assassinations Committee felt, remained unexplained and "extremely troubling."

Today, there is something else. The official account had it that Oswald went to the American Embassy in Moscow just once at the time of his defection, and that he visited only the consular office on the ground floor. Joan Hallett, who worked as a receptionist at the Embassy—she was married to the then Assistant Naval Attaché—recalled years later that Oswald went to the Embassy "several times." She said, too, that Consul Snyder and the security officer "took [Oswald] upstairs to the working floors, a secure area where the Ambassador and the political, economic, and military officers were. A visitor would never, ever get up there unless he was on official business, I was never up there."

The full picture of the CIA's interest in Oswald may not be in his 201 file at all. "Agency files," the Assassinations Committee noted, "would not always indicate whether an individual was associated with the Agency in any capacity. . . ."

Intelligence agencies regularly use false names in documents—on occasion to mislead enemy agents, at other times to protect the secrets of one department from another. Sometimes, while the name on a file may be real, its contents have been falsified to divert attention from the subject's real activity.

A set of notes on "cover," prepared by senior CIA official William Harvey, reflected his wish that subjects "should have phony 201 in LRG [Central Registry] to backstop this, documents therein forged and backdated."[4]

The following exchange took place between former CIA Director Allen Dulles and Congressman Hale Boggs during an executive session of the Warren Commission:

Dulles: There is a hard thing to disprove, you know. How do you disprove a fellow was not your agent? How do you disprove it?

Boggs: You could disprove it, couldn't you?

Dulles: No. . . . I never knew how to disprove it.

Boggs: Did you have agents about whom you had no record whatsoever?

Dulles: The record may not be on paper. *But on paper, you would have hieroglyphics that only two people know what they meant, and nobody outside of the agency would know* [author's emphasis]; and you could say this meant the agent, and somebody else could say it meant another agent.

Asked whether, if Oswald was an agent, a CIA chief would know who had hired him, Dulles replied, "Someone might have done it *without authority* [author's emphasis]." His response opens the door to another possibility, that Oswald could have been hired at low level, without formal backing, in a way that left no identifiable trace.

Confronted with these possibilities, some Committee staff continued to suspect the CIA was hiding something about its handling of the Oswald matter. Distrust of the CIA, though, may have diverted attention from another possibility—that Owald was used by another intelligence agency altogether.

There are oddities about the U.S. Navy's response to his defection. At one level, the Marine Corps reacted as one might expect.[5] In California, where Oswald last served, aircraft call signs, codes, and radio and radar frequencies were changed within weeks. Oswald's former associates recalled being questioned about him by visiting officials in civilian clothes.

In another respect, however, the Oswald defection was not handled in the same way as those of other military enlisted men. "A net damage assessment, indicating the possible access Oswald had to classified information," said Colonel Thomas Fox, former head of counterintelligence at the Defense Intelligence Agency, "would have to be undertaken."

Damage assessments were conducted following the defections of the only two enlisted men known to have gone over to Communist nations before the Oswald episode—and of two others who defected soon after him. In spite of the fact that Oswald had worked on highly secret bases, however, the Navy admitted that—in his case—no "formal damage assessment was conducted."

Some hypothesized that Oswald was part of a covert program to slip individuals into the Soviet Union in the guise of defectors, "sleepers" who could gather information of use to U.S. intelligence. There had been a sudden rash of turncoats in the eighteen months up to 1960, two former Navy men, five Army personnel stationed in West Germany, and two employees of the U.S. National Security Agency—the top-secret agency charged with breaking foreign codes and ciphers. Of civilians who went to the Soviet Union, one had—like Oswald—previously served as an enlisted man in the U.S. Navy.[6]

For all the speculation, however, the callow twenty-year-old that was Oswald was surely an improbable candidate to be sent on a mission behind the Iron Curtain. Could it be, though, that at a time of concern about the increased number of U.S. defectors, he was seen as a source of information on how the Soviets handled military defectors? Was Oswald an unwitting tool, a genuine leftist whose movements and communications could be monitored and in time—potentially—debriefed? Was he, perhaps unwittingly, primed with false information designed to deceive his Soviet hosts?

The concept of Oswald as agent is not merely the far-fetched notion of conspiracy theorists. A former Chief Security Officer at the State Department, Otto Otepka, said that in 1963 his office engaged in a study of American "defectors" that included Oswald. Five months before the Kennedy assassination, according to Otepka, the State Department was still uncertain whether Oswald was or had been "one of ours or one of theirs."

Whether or not he was the lone renegade of the official account, Oswald certainly became a focus of interest for Soviet and American intelligence when he arrived in the USSR. The protestations of both nations' intelligence services, made in the years that followed, only raise further doubt.

CHAPTER 10

Mischief from Moscow

"A Communist must be prepared to . . . resort to all sorts of schemes and stratagems, employ illegitimate methods, conceal the truth . . ."

—Lenin

Five days after his arrival in Moscow in fall 1959, Oswald tried to commit suicide—or acted as though he wished to kill himself. Here is his melodramatic account of the episode—complete with evidence of Oswald's mild dyslexia—taken from an "Historic Diary" found in his effects years later:

Oct. 21

Eve. 6:00 Recive word from police offial. I must leave country tonight at 8.0 p.m. as visa expirs. I am shocked!! My dreams! I retire to my room. I have $100 left. I have waited for 2 year to be accepted. My fondes dreams are shattered because of a petty official; because of bad planning I planned to much!

7.0 p.m. I decide to end it. Soak rist in cold water to numb the pain. Than slash my left wrist. Then plaug wrist into bathtub of hot water. I think 'when Rimma comes at 8. to find me dead it will be a great shock.' somewhere a violin plays, as I wacth my life whirl away.

This entry in Oswald's journal, apparently written long afterward, records his reaction when told that the Russians did not, at first—ostensibly—want him to stay in the country.[1] The "Diary," and Soviet hospital records, say Oswald was found bleeding in his hotel room by his Intourist guide Rimma Shirokova and rushed to the Botkin Hospital, where he spent a week recovering.

Some version of this episode evidently did occur. The "Diary" and relevant Soviet documents, however, contain clues indicating deception by both the Soviets and Oswald.[2]

The Botkin Hospital records, as released by Moscow after the assassination, state: "The patient does not speak Russian. One could judge only by his gestures and facial expression that he had no complaints."

Oswald's guide Shirokova, interviewed by this author, also said he could barely manage to say "Good morning" or "Thank you" in Russian. This does not sound like the Oswald who, months earlier in California, could converse in passable Russian for two hours.[3]

Also interviewed by the author, Dr. Lydia Mikhailina, a former Botkin Hospital psychiatrist whose name appears in the Soviet hospital file, recalled thinking at the time that Oswald did understand Russian—but *acted* as though he could not speak it.

Dr. Mikhailina, who had been in charge of Oswald's case, said her patient had superficial cuts to his wrists. She did not, however, believe he had really attempted suicide. She described his psychiatric condition as "absolutely normal."

Shown the hospital record as it was shared with the U.S. government, Dr. Mikhailina became first puzzled, then annoyed.

Her own medical notes on Oswald had been omitted, and other entries appeared to her to have been forged—not to have been written by a medical professional. There were signatures by a "doctor" whose name meant nothing to Mikhailina, even though she had worked at the hospital for thirty years.

The Oswald "Diary," to the extent it covered the period, merely sketched out his time in Russia. The intention, perhaps, had been to cover the ground in the barest possible terms—omitting anything that might reveal the involvement of Soviet intelligence.

Oswald's first Soviet contacts, his Intourist guides, were typically sources of information for the KGB, the main Soviet intelligence agency. Other foreigners' experiences, meanwhile, showed that hospitalization was on occasion used to cover a period during which the KGB questioned the new arrival. In Oswald's case, we have no details as to where Oswald was or how he was handled for the six weeks after the end of November, when it became evident that he had left his hotel room.[4]

The Soviets decided in January 1960—in Oswald's words, "after a certain time, after the Russians had assured themselves I was really the naïve American"—to move him out of Moscow. Though technically still an American citizen, he was issued with a stateless person's identity card, given funds by the "Red Cross"—a euphemism at the time for a section of the MVD, the internal security organization—and dispatched by train to the city of Minsk, 450 miles away.

In Minsk, he began what was probably the most luxurious period of his life before or afterward. From the "Diary," from witnesses interviewed in later years, and from photographs, we know Oswald was lodged in accommodation that, by 1960 standards, was beyond a lowly Soviet worker's wildest dreams—a roomy apartment with balconies overlooking the river.

He was given employment on the assembly line of the nearby Byelorussian radio and television factory as an assembler, and paid wages that—combined with a continuing "Red Cross" allowance—provided Oswald with more money than he could spend. He spent many evenings at the movies, the theater, or the opera, often with a girl on his arm. He had dalliances of one sort or another with five young women. Oswald was, he wrote in the "Diary," "living big."

The last of the young women Oswald met in Minsk was to become his wife and would cause lasting concern after the assassination. In mid-March 1961, after just over a year in the city, he met Marina Prusakova, the woman he would marry just a few weeks later and take back to the United States with him, and who would bear his two children. Her story remains to this day a mass of contradictions.

Marina gave the Warren Commission the following sketch of her life. She had been a war baby, born in 1941, who never knew her father and whose mother died while she was still a student in Leningrad—today's Saint Petersburg. At eighteen, in 1959, she had qualified as a pharmacist and moved to live with an uncle and aunt in Minsk. By 1961, she said, she was settled into a job in the pharmacy of a Minsk hospital and was enjoying a busy social life.

According to Marina, and by Oswald's written account, the first encounter with the young American defector occurred by chance at a trade union dance. There was a further meeting a week later, again at a dance, and romance blossomed. When Oswald was admitted to the hospital in which she worked—to have his adenoids removed—Marina visited and brought little gifts. Oswald, on the rebound from his most recent affair, asked her to marry him even before his hospital stay ended. The registry office marriage took place on April 30, less than two months after the meeting at the dance.

The Warren Commission would have little choice but to accept this account of the whirlwind courtship. The record as released, however, shows the Commissioners and staff had serious doubts about Marina—on all fronts.

Though Marina has provided some of the most damning evidence against her husband, she has been hopelessly inconsistent. She won initial public sympathy with her comment in broken English: "Lee good man. Lee not shoot anyone." Then she moved from saying he had been a good husband to claiming he had been violent toward her. She identified the Mannlicher-Carcano rifle as her husband's "fateful rifle," only to say later she was not sure that it had belonged to him.

Marina would identify her husband as having been—the President's assassination aside—the would-be killer who had earlier fired at and missed Major General Edwin Walker, a right-wing extremist. She told a story, too, of Oswald having put a pistol in his belt when former Vice President Nixon came to Dallas. She had stopped him going out, she claimed, by locking him in the bathroom—an allegation that crumbled when it was found the bathroom door locked only from the inside. Nixon had not been in Dallas, moreover, at the relevant time.

From having given the impression that she thought her husband shot Kennedy, Marina would switch in later years to protesting his innocence. "I think he is not guilty," she said in 1993, "he liked Kennedy . . . after his arrest he insisted that he did not shoot anybody. . . . I believe he spoke the truth."

Marina's reaction to difficult questions, Warren Commissioner Senator Russell commented, tended be along the lines,

"Don't know what you're talking about." Commission atttorney Norman Redlich, a future dean of New York University School of Law, formally recorded his concern that she had "repeatedly lied."

Marina's memory was foggy on points a woman could be expected to remember—like who had first introduced her to Oswald. On the basis of Marina's early testimony and the Oswald "Diary," Commission staff decided the Soviet Cupid was Yuri Merezhinsky, a student at the local medical institute. Years later, questioned by the Assassinations Committee, Marina said she remembered no one of that name, then that she did recall the name, then that she did not after all.

Ernst Titovets, a former medical student in Minsk who would rise to become a professor of neurology, well remembered the night Oswald and Marina met. As a friend of the alleged future assassin, he recalled in a 2010 memoir, they had gone together to the soirée at the Trade Union Palace of Culture. First there was a talk by Professor Lydia Cherkasova, a Party member with entrée to the elite. Her son Yuri Merezhinsky, who apparently featured in Oswald's first encounter with Marina, was indeed there that evening.

Watching Marina and Merezhinsky with his friend, Titovets had thought even then that there was "something funny about the whole situation," something "fishy." Years later, after talking with both Merezhinsky and his mother, he came to the conclusion that the KGB had engineered Oswald's meeting with Marina. "Oswald," he was to write, "was unattached at the time. To get him deeply involved with a pretty girl that the KGB must have had control over was a potential way to obtain a string to pull. . . . It might serve as a way of obtaining valuable information."

The CIA had multiple concerns about Marina's background. That uncle of hers in Minsk was not just any uncle but a lieutenant-colonel in the MVD, the Soviet internal security organization. There was a question mark, too, over the final stage of her life in Leningrad before leaving for Minsk.

The CIA doubted information that—fresh out of her training as a pharmacist in Leningrad—Marina had quit her very first job after just one day, then taken a supposed vacation that lasted several months. One of those months, she acknowledged, had been spent at a government "rest home."

There was intense interest, too, in a name and Leningrad address found in Marina's address book. The Russian name, she said, was of someone she had met at the "rest home." A CIA computer trace on the address came up with a match to an apartment block where another American defector had stayed.[5]

A claim made years later by Yuri Merezhinsky, the key figure in the first Oswald-Marina meeting, may explain a good deal. Asked whether Marina would not have been afraid to meet a foreigner, he replied: "She had nothing to lose. She knew foreigners in Leningrad, from *where she had been deported for prostitution* [author's emphasis]."

Merezhinsky learned this, he said in a taped interview, from both associates in Leningrad and from Marina herself. He made the same claim in an 1993 interview with the author Norman Mailer. If it is true, Soviet intelligence may indeed have had a hold on Marina—and may have hoped through her to learn more about Oswald.

Lee Oswald himself had shown he knew, or thought he knew, that he remained a KGB target. One evening in Minsk, Ernst

Titovets remembered, Oswald "said he believed his place was bugged." He spent time checking power points, a vent in the floor, and voicing the thought that there might be a device concealed in the ceiling.

The suspicion was well founded, vindicated after the fall of Soviet Communism by a Russian press report that the KGB had indeed bugged Oswald's apartment. After men in plain clothes told the residents on the floor above to go away for a few days, microphones had been installed in the ceiling of the apartment below.

A Fairy Story from the KGB

After President Kennedy's assassination, the Soviets were to admit none of this. Then something extraordinary occurred. Two months later, when the Warren Commission investigation was under way, a KGB agent defected to the United States and made claims that made the USSR seem all innocence.

The defector, Yuri Nosenko, said the KGB had considered Oswald "unstable" and not bothered to question him in depth. His Soviet colleagues, Nosenko insisted, never grilled Oswald about his knowledge of U.S. radar in the Far East, about the U-2's spy missions, or about other military information he might have.

Thirty-six-year-old Nosenko, in the prime of his career at the time he defected, said he had been deputy chief of the American-British section of the KGB's Second Chief Directorate, the department that handled counterintelligence. It had fallen to him, he said, to supervize the Oswald case. The KGB had initially known nothing of the young American's military background, he maintained, and would not have been interested anyway.

In Minsk, according to Nosenko, agents merely maintained "a discreet check" on Oswald, in light of the possibility that he might be some sort of U.S. "sleeper agent." In November 1963, on news of the assassination, Nosenko said, the file on Oswald had been flown from Minsk to Moscow for close analysis.

CIA inquisitors tried for years to break Nosenko, and in some ways his story did start to fall apart. He was to admit he had exaggerated his KGB rank to make himself seem more attractive to the Agency. Another KGB defector, moreover, said Nosenko had not held the positions he claimed.[6]

Senior CIA officers came to believe, nevertheless, that they were dealing with more than a defector's ploys to ingratiate himself—he was, they suspected, a deliberate Soviet plant. The consequences would have been "staggering," as Richard Helms put it in retrospect, "if Nosenko had been hurriedly briefed and dispatched to mislead us about any Soviet connection with the assassination."

The issue never was resolved. The Warren Commission failed to mention Nosenko at all in its Report. Years later, even after questioning the defector and catching him in further apparent inconsistencies, the Assassinations Committee could not decide what had motivated him.[7]

Nosenko's account defied belief, CIA veterans agreed. The Soviets had gone to great lengths all over the world, former officer Harry Rositzke wrote, to get information out of lowly American personnel who might be "unsophisticated and lonely"—including not least "enlisted men in the armed forces." "Marines," said Newton Miler, former head of the CIA section responsible for counterintelligence against the KGB, had been "prime KGB targets"—even if they merely served as guards at embassies.

In retirement, Richard Helms was to characterize Nosenko's claims as to what the KGB had supposedly *not* done about Oswald as "odd," "highly unlikely." The former deputy chief of the CIA's Soviet Bloc Division told the Assassinations Committee it was "absolutely unthinkable" that Oswald would not have been questioned.

As a marine who had served on a base for the CIA's U-2 spy plane, Oswald would have been of special interest—and that may be the key to Soviet deception about him.

On May 1, 1960, a U-2 spy plane under CIA control had crashed near the Soviet city of Sverdlovsk, an event that led to heightened tension between America and the USSR.[8] The plane's pilot, Gary Powers, was captured alive and flown rapidly to Moscow. Equipment in the wreckage left no doubt that his mission had been espionage.

Even today, the full truth about the U-2's downing has not been fully established. Later, after his release, Powers voiced the suspicion that Oswald may have given the Soviets technical data that helped target the airplane. Whether or not he did so, the Soviets may have thought—after Powers' capture—that the young Marines defector could be helpful.

Powers recalled the Soviets having questioned him intensively about operations at the U-2's base in Atsugi, Japan. To his interrogators, it may have seemed logical to bring in another American familiar with Atsugi to comment on the captive's responses. Did Oswald play such a role?[9]

In a letter home after the U-2 shootdown, Oswald wrote: "He seemed to be a nice bright American-type fellow when I saw him in Moscow." Powers, for his part, recalled spotting a peephole through which he was observed during his incarceration. The Oswald "Diary," however—for what it is worth—places him far

from Moscow, at a May Day party in Minsk, on the day Powers was shot down. Nevertheless, an acquaintance who knew
Oswald later back in the States quoted him as having said he
"was in Moscow for the May Day parade at one time." Of the
three such national holidays Oswald spent in Russia, the only
one unaccounted for is the May Day on which Powers was shot
down.[10]

All this aside, some would suggest in years to come that the
Soviets were behind the assassination of President Kennedy.
The Warren Commission, and later the Assassinations Committee, found no evidence for such a notion. All responsible
analysts have said as much. There is no reason to suppose that
Soviet leaders ever considered such folly, or that the removal
of President Kennedy would have served Soviet political ends.
Nevertheless, the questions about the KGB's handling of Oswald
remain.

In a 1993 interview, the man who headed the agency while
Oswald was in Russia, Vladimir Semichastny, offered fresh
information—though almost certainly less than the truth. The
former KGB chief guardedly conceded, for the first time, that
Oswald had been interrogated. "There were conversations," he
said, but Oswald had "outdated information . . . not the kind of
information that would interest such a high-level organization
like ours."

Credibly enough, Semichastny said Oswald was seen as poor
potential agent material. His counterintelligence and intelligence departments "looked him over to see what he was capable
of, but unfortunately neither could find any ability at all." The
KGB chief said, too, that the Russians "concluded he was not

working for American intelligence." As for Marina having been planted on Oswald, Semichastny flat out denied it.

The denial, however, runs contrary to the credible information summarized in this chapter. Semichastny's lofty dismissal of the idea that Oswald was of much serious interest to the Soviets, moreover, can now be discounted.

The Assassination Records Review Board, which in 1996 was at last granted access to the contemporaneous Minsk KGB file, reported that the dossier "details over two years of extensive surveillance and analysis by the KGB of Lee Harvey Oswald."

It is unlikely that the full reality of how the Soviets handled Oswald has yet surfaced. The same, however, remains true of the role of U.S. Intelligence. All these years later, a whole world of Intelligence has stayed the way its masters wished—through the looking glass.

An "Intelligence Matter"

"Intelligence-gathering activities . . . have a special
and secret character. . . . These activities have their
own rules and methods of concealment which seek to
mislead and obscure."

—President Dwight D. Eisenhower, 1960

In Washington, DC, on January 20, 1961, John F. Kennedy took the oath of office. Hatless and coatless in the biting cold, he made the stirring speech that marked the start of his presidency: "We observe today not a victory of party but a celebration of freedom. . . . Let every nation know, whether it wishes us well or ill, that we shall pay any price, bear any burden, meet any hardship, support any friend, oppose any foe, in order to assure the survival and success of liberty."

In early February, on the other side of the world, Lee Harvey Oswald began the move that was eventually to link Kennedy's savage fate with his own. "I desire," he wrote in a letter to the American Embassy in Moscow, "to return to the United States."[1]

Oswald was launched on more than a year of bureaucratic exchanges that were to culminate in U.S. and Soviet authorities approving his return to the United States with his wife, Marina, and their first child. On a trip to the U.S. Embassy, Oswald said he had "learned a hard lesson" and now better appreciated the United States and its freedoms. He was anxious, as well he should have been, that he might be prosecuted and jailed on return to America. As though to preempt that, he claimed that he had not after all—as he had initially asserted—shared with the Soviets information acquired during his Marine Corps stint.

Oswald's passport would be renewed and returned to him by Consul Snyder, the official with a CIA background who had seen him at the time of his defection. The public record, as it appears in the Warren Report, seems as normal as an unusual process could be—obscuring another of the inconsistencies that so dog the Oswald saga.

The U.S. Passport Office should have posted a "lookout card" on Oswald following his defection, a flag to alert officials should he apply for fresh documentation at any American Embassy in the world. In his case, and because the government was paying the expense of getting him home, a lookout card should have been mandatory until such time as the loan was repaid. No such card was placed in the file—an omission the State Department has explained away as human error.[2]

If such laxness were common, this might seem a trivial detail. During the period of Oswald's time in the USSR, however, the State Department kept close tabs on American travelers with apparent Communist sympathies, catching quite innocuous people in the net. How did a person like Oswald escape the net? There are clues that may indicate what went on beneath the surface.

In 1959, following Oswald's defection, U.S. Vice-Consul McVickar had suggested to an American journalist, Priscilla Johnson, that she go to his hotel to interview him—telling her, as he did so, that "there was a thin line between her duty as a correspondent and as an American." Johnson, who was in Moscow for the North American News Agency (NANA), was not the average reporter. Seven years earlier, she had applied to join the CIA and—though she had not gotten the job—the Agency maintained interest and repeated contact with her for years.

In testimony to the Warren Commission after the assassination, Johnson would say that—in the interview with her—Oswald said he "hoped his experience as a radar operator would make him more desirable" to the Soviets. This was clearly news, yet Johnson's published story, when it appeared in the *Washington Evening Star*, made no mention of it at all. "I think," a CIA official would note three years later, "that Miss Johnson can be encouraged to write pretty much the articles we want."

By the 1970s, Priscilla Johnson would be listed in CIA documents as a "Witting Collaborator 01 code A1." An FBI document had cited a State Department security officer as saying her 1959 contact with Oswald had been "official business."[3]

On November 5, 1959, within a week of Oswald's defection, U.S. Navy headquarters sent Moscow a message asking for updates on any developments "in view of *continuing interest* [author's emphasis] of HQ, Marine Corps and U.S. intelligence agencies." This, the document stated in capital letters, was an "INTELLIGENCE MATTER."

Did a U.S. agency take a look at or make contact with Oswald in the later stages of his stay in the Soviet Union? Photographs of Oswald, standing beside a British-registered car, in Minsk's Central Square, may point to that (see Photo 10). The Warren Report noted that two photos had been "taken by American tourists" in August 1961—a few months after Oswald's marriage to Marina. The tourists, according to the Report, "did not know

Oswald, nor did they speak with him; they remembered only that several men gathered near their car." The Commission had been supplied with the photographs by the CIA.

Background documents and interviews enlarge on the Warren account. Three American women, on a motoring tour, had exchanged "small talk" with Oswald while taking the photographs. On their return, according to the CIA, the three were contacted in line with a then-common Agency custom of contacting Americans fresh home from Iron Curtain countries. Of more than 150 photographs borrowed from the women by the CIA, just five were copied and filed. CIA staff supposedly realized only after the assassination that Oswald featured in one of them. One of the women later supplied another photo in which he appeared.

The way the Oswald photo just happened to have been culled in the original selection—out of 150 available—strains belief. One CIA employee said the choice was made because an Intourist guide appeared in the shot, another that it "showed a crane in the background." One of the three former tourists, contacted by the author, cast a whole new light on the episode.

Rita Naman, who is of British origin, said that while she and a friend, Monica Kramer, were touring the Soviet Union by car—a rare expedition in those Cold War years—they encountered Oswald not once but twice. First in Moscow, in early August, when he alarmed their Intourist guide by addressing them through the open window of the car. Later, in the square in Minsk, he had again approached the car, and been photographed. Is it likely that the two meetings, in the space of ten days and in cities more than four hundred miles apart, happened merely by chance?[4]

The identity and role of the third of the woman tourists turns out to be intriguing. She was Marie Hyde, an older American who struck up an acquaintance with Naman and Kramer at their hotel in Moscow. Hyde, Naman recalled, was not the average tourist. She seemed familiar with Russia, knew her way around the Moscow subway and, in general, came over as "a very sharp cookie." Kramer, Naman told the author, remarked early on, not too seriously, that Hyde could be some sort of American agent.

The author could not trace Hyde or find out anything much about her background. Naman, however, added curious details of how she came to be with them on their tour in the first place. Hyde had approached them in Moscow, saying she was "separated from her tourist group" and wanted to join them on the trip to Minsk, then—through Poland—back to the West. Such a deviation from the prearranged schedule was very much out of the ordinary in the Soviet Union of those Cold War days. Hyde managed it, though, and in Minsk—when they encountered Oswald in the square—it was very much at her initiative that photographs were taken. Hyde took one photograph herself, using Kramer's camera, then gave her own camera to Naman to get a second shot.[5]

Naman and Kramer appeared to the author to have been ordinary tourists, but was Marie Hyde? Were the two meetings with Oswald, in cities far apart, both fortuitous? Was it merely a whim that prompted Hyde to have the photographs taken in the square? Or was she prompted to do so by a branch of U.S. intelligence?[6]

"We had no contact with Mr. Oswald," William Colby, CIA Director in the 1970s, would insist in an interview with CBS' Dan Rather. "No contact with him before he went to the Soviet

Union, and no contact with him after he returned from the Soviet Union. No contact with him while he was in the Soviet Union." Pressed by Rather, Colby maintained that—prior to 1963—all the CIA had on Oswald was an FBI report on his defection, a report from the U.S. Navy, and "some material from the Embassy in Moscow."

If Colby was economical with the truth, fragments of information may give us a glimpse of how Oswald may have been handled. In late May 1962, while in Moscow completing the formalities involved in leaving the Soviet Union—and getting clearance for his wife and baby to accompany him—Oswald again visited the U.S. Embassy. One of those he saw there, Dr. Alexis Davison, was the Embassy physician—and somewhat more than that. The following year, Davison, who was also Assistant Air Attaché, would be expelled from the Soviet Union for his role in the CIA's handling—in an operation directed by James Angleton—of the Soviet traitor Colonel Oleg Penkovsky.

The U.S. phone number and address of Davison's mother would be found in Oswald's address book after the assassination (see facsimile on facing page). Asked about the entry years later by the Assassinations Committee, the former diplomat said he "assumed" he had supplied the Oswalds with his mother's address as a kindness. His mother was Russian-born, he explained, always hospitable toward fellow Russians coming to the United States for the first time—as was Marina. To volunteer the address, he claimed, was "not unusual." Given that Davison was a diplomat linked to highly sensitive intelligence activity, given that Oswald was at very least a suspect character, and given that the episode occurred at the height of the Cold War, it is not unreasonable to question that statement.[7]

The Oswalds and their baby began their return to the United States on June 1, 1962, starting with a wearisome forty-three hour train journey that took them from Moscow, through Poland and divided Germany, to the port city of Rotterdam in Holland (see Photo 11). Oswald's address book, and the notes he made in it, again offers a puzzling detail.

It has been supposed that Lee and Marina both entered the West through the strictly monitored checkpoint at Helmstedt, then a key crossing point between Communist East Germany and West Germany. Though Marina's passport was stamped at the checkpoint, Oswald's was not—perhaps because he had an American passport. There is, though, the hint of a possibility that his movements were not as long assumed.

Amid the jumble of notes in his little book is a hand-drawn map (see facsimile on next page) of a portion of the then divided city of Berlin, which is more than a hundred miles east of Helmstedt. On this rough map, prominently marked, was the train station that—for travelers alighting from long-distance trains running east to west—was the main access point to West Berlin.

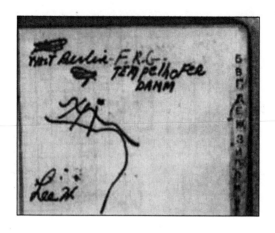

What need did Oswald have for information on that access point? It seems highly improbable, on the known data, that Oswald broke his journey for any significant amount of time in West Berlin—unless, remote possibility, he continued west by other means. Did he have time, though, for a meeting with someone during a Berlin stopover? Had there perhaps been a plan for a meeting there, a plan that was later abandoned? During the Cold War, West Berlin was a hive of intelligence activity.

In Holland, before leaving for the United States, the Oswalds stayed in the city of Rotterdam. Not at a hotel but in accommodation recommended—and according to Marina Oswald arranged for—by the U.S. Embassy in Moscow. Marina was to describe it variously, after the assassination, as a "private apartment" or "boardinghouse." The documentary record of the Oswalds' journey shows a stay in Holland of only one night. Marina, for her part, said the stay lasted two or three days.

The Rotterdam stay worried Warren Commission Chief Counsel Lee Rankin, who said at an executive session, ". . . it is unexplained why they happened to go there and stay, and got a place to live, some little apartment, and what they were doing." Clues in Oswald's notes may again throw light on the matter.

Scribbled on one page (see facsimile below) is the jotting: "Holl—TRAM n. 11, Left to Right, Mathenesserlaan 250." Research in Holland established that this was a lodging house, Huize Avila, and that—according to its former landlord—he would not have rented a room for just one day or even for a few days. The Huize Avila, or Avila House, catered for monthly rentals. If the advance arrangements for the Oswalds' stay were made by the U.S. authorities, was this a place the Americans rented on a long-term basis—a place suitable for a debriefing session?

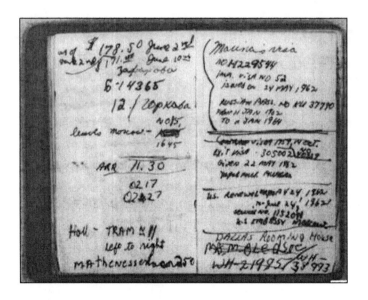

The Oswalds apparently crossed the Atlantic by sea aboard the liner SS *Maasdam*, arriving at Hoboken, New Jersey, on June 13.[8] Defector and self-declared traitor though Oswald supposedly was, no representative of a U.S. intelligence agency was on the pier to meet him. Instead, the couple were met and assisted by Spas Raikin, described in the Warren Report as "a representative of the Traveler's Aid Society, which had been contacted by the Department of State." That was something of a simplification.

Raikin was also secretary-general of the American Friends of the Anti-Bolshevik Bloc of Nations, an émigré group in direct touch with the FBI and U.S. Army Intelligence. The group also had contacts with anti-Communist activists in New Orleans, headquartered in the very building where, in months to come, Oswald's name was to be linked with CIA-backed anti-Castro activists.

Oswald traveled on to Texas, to the Dallas-Fort Worth area, paying the airfare with money advanced by his brother, Robert. There followed the difficult process of adjusting to life in American society, a process made more uncomfortable by Oswald's mother meddling in her son's affairs. The couple soon found a place to themselves, a rented bungalow in Fort Worth, and Oswald took a job as a manual worker at a metal factory. This was a mundane phase of his life—but for the glaring apparent omissions that have bothered, and still bother, virtually everyone interested in the case. The way the American military and intelligence authorities treated his return, or claimed they did, remains inexplicable.

There is no known evidence to indicate that the U.S. Navy considered prosecuting Oswald, a Marine Corps reservist who was by his own account a traitor. The form Oswald signed on leaving active duty had said clearly that personnel could "be recalled to duty . . . for trial by court-martial for unlawful disclosure of information" and listed the penalties for doing so. Oswald's defection, and his talk of having given the Soviets radar data, had supposedly caused the American military to expedite changes in its secret codes. Even so, the Marine Corps record reflects no interest in even talking with the prodigal on his return from Russia, let alone putting him on trial. The Office of Naval Intelligence contemplated no action against Oswald, it told the FBI. It merely asked instead to be informed of the results of a Bureau interview with him.

The FBI, for its part, had not placed Oswald on the list of the thousands of people categorized by the Bureau as potentially disloyal. It had opened a "security case" on him in light of his defection to Russia, and FBI agents in Texas did seek him out on his return. They asked Oswald whether he had been approached by Soviet intelligence while in the USSR, and Oswald said he had not. When he declined to take a lie-detector test, that, effectively, was that. The Oswald "security case" was closed shortly afterward.[9]

Yet in March 1961, as soon as he showed signs of wanting to return to the United States, a senior State Department official had written that any risk involved in returning Oswald's passport "would be more than offset by the opportunity provided the United States to obtain information from Mr. Oswald concerning his activities in the Soviet Union." It makes no sense that, according to the record, Oswald was never comprehensively debriefed.

Thomas Fox, former Chief of Counterintelligence at the Defense Intelligence Agency, found it "inconceivable," he told an interviewer, that U.S. intelligence would not have wanted to ask Oswald how he had been handled by the KGB. Some former defectors were interviewed by the CIA on their return. Robert Webster, a former Rand Development Corporation employee who defected at the same time as Oswald, had been brought to Washington and debriefed by CIA officers and U.S. Air Force personnel for two weeks. Notwithstanding official denials that Oswald faced similar questioning, tantalizing leads suggest that he did.[10]

One CIA memorandum indicates that CIA officials at least discussed "the laying on of interviews" with Oswald on his return to the States. Its author, Thomas Casasin, who had been a senior member of the Soviet Russia Division department responsible for "research related to clandestine operations" in the USSR, recalled having discussed Oswald with two senior colleagues in 1962. In his memo, written three days after the assassination, Casasin wrote:

1. It makes little difference now, but REDWOOD had at one time an OI interest in Oswald. As soon as I had heard Oswald's name, I recalled that as Chief of the 6 Branch I had discussed . . . the laying on of interview(s) through KUJUMP or other suitable channels. At the moment I don't recall if this was discussed while Oswald and his family were en route to our country or if it was after their arrival.

2. . . . We were particularly interested in the OI Oswald might provide on the Minsk factory in which he had been employed, on certain sections of the city itself, and of course we sought the usual BI that might help develop target personality dossiers.

"REDWOOD," we now know, was a CIA cryptonym for "action indicator for information" for the CIA's Soviet Russia Division. "KUJUMP" was the cryptonym for the Agency's "Domestic Contact Division." "OI," which occurred twice, stood for "Operational Intelligence."[11]

The recollections of another former CIA officer indicate—if truthful—that Oswald was indeed debriefed after coming home. Donald Deneselya, who in 1962 worked in the Soviet branch of the Directorate of Intelligence, was fired by the CIA in 1964— and is thus a controversial figure. According to Deneselya, as reported by the Assassinations Committee, he "reviewed a contact report from representatives of a CIA field office who had interviewed a former U.S. marine who had worked at the Minsk radio plant following his defection to the USSR." The marine, who Deneselya thought may have been Oswald, had been living with his family in Minsk. The contact report he saw, he said, had been four or five pages long.

Deneselya's claim does not stand entirely alone. A Washington psychiatrist once employed by the CIA recalled having been asked to meet a young American just back from Russia. This had been in mid-1962, and the subject was married to a Soviet wife. The psychiatrist thought, after the assassination, that he recognized photographs of Oswald as the man he had questioned for the CIA.[12]

Donald Deneselya, for his part, added a further potential clue. In a 1993 interview with the Public Broadcasting System's *Frontline* program, Deneselya said that the debriefing report he saw had been "signed off to by a CIA officer by the name of Anderson." Other former officers questioned by *Frontline* said they remembered a colleague—known by the name of "Major Andy Anderson"—who conducted debriefings for the Domestic Contact Division.

Months later, while working on newly released files, a *Frontline* consultant came upon a handwritten notation in Oswald's 201 file that read "Anderson OO on Oswald." "OO" was the CIA's numerical code for the Domestic Contact Division.[13] Finally, a former Deputy Chief of the Domestic Contact Division, speaking on condition that he not be identified, told *Frontline* that the CIA did indeed debrief Oswald.

John Newman, the former U.S. Army intelligence officer who located the Anderson document, noted that questioning Oswald would have been a perfectly normal thing for the CIA to have done. The Agency's denial of interest in Oswald, Newman thought, was "a big billboard saying there's something else. . . . There's an unexplained anomaly, and among the questions it poses is whether or not the Agency had an association with Oswald." The Anderson notation and the apparent debriefing, Newman said, was on a memorandum from CI/SIG—the Counterintelligence Special Investigation Group—run by James Angleton.

In Dallas in 1962, the CIA's Domestic Contact Division was represented by an officer named J. Walton Moore. He was reportedly to say—apparently with knowledge—that the young man just back from Russia was "perfectly all right."

CHAPTER 12

Oswald and the Baron

"He checked with J. Walton Moore about Oswald."
—Jeanne de Mohrenschildt, 1977

In June 1962, less than a week after arriving in Texas, Oswald made a telephone call to a Russian exile living in Fort Worth. What he wanted, apparently, was a letter of reference vouching for his competence in spoken Russian. What came of the call, made to Peter Gregory, an engineer in the oil business, was an entrée to the world of Russian and East European émigrés who lived in Dallas. In the weeks that followed, Lee Oswald and his wife regaled a bevy of exiles with their accounts of current everyday life in the Soviet Union. The couple seemed shabby, incongruous in the smart drawing rooms of their affluent new friends.

In this improbable milieu, Oswald met a man who would soon become his confidant. Fifty-one-year-old oil geologist George de Mohrenschildt was, in the Warren Commission's notable understatement, a "highly individualistic person of varied interests." The man who took the Marxist defector under his wing had been born before World War I into a Russian aristocratic family and technically had the right to call himself "Baron."[1] By 1962, he had been in the United States for more than two decades, held a master's degree in petroleum geology, and was on his fourth wife. He was the archetype of the prosperous White Russian exile of the period, a well-traveled sophisticate with entrée to affluent society (see Photo 12).

Along the way, the Baron had acquired connections to the world of intelligence that remain blurred to this day. During World War II, by his account, he had cooperated with French intelligence "collect[ing] facts on people involved in pro-German activity." In 1942, records show, he had expressed a desire to work for the Office of Strategic Services, the forerunner of the CIA. In Washington, DC, that year, he lived in the same house as a British intelligence officer and a senior American naval officer. In the 1950s, at New York's exclusive Racquet Club, de Mohrenschildt was often seen with Jake Cogswell, who would reportedly become a CIA operative. Later, back in the States from a stay in Yugoslavia during which he was accused of making drawings of military fortifications, the CIA debriefed him. Over several meetings, the subsequent report said, the CIA debriefer "obtained foreign intelligence which was promptly disseminated to other federal agencies in ten separate reports."

From late 1960 until autumn 1961, following travel in Central America and the Caribbean with his fourth wife Jeanne, de Mohrenschildt offered the State Department a written record of the journey. The couple had been in Guatemala, a major jumping-off point for CIA-backed Cuban exiles, during the Bay of Pigs invasion. Following his association in Dallas with Lee Harvey Oswald, de Mohrenschildt was to be involved in activity in the Caribbean that—his CIA file shows—involved both Agency and Army Intelligence personnel.

These connections did not escape those who knew de Mohrenschildt in Dallas. One acquaintance gathered he did something for the State Department. His attorney and friend, Patrick Russell, told the author he got the feeling de Mohrenschildt might himself have been a CIA agent.[2] He knew, he said, that his client would "undergo debriefing" each time he returned to the States from abroad. Russell felt de Mohrenschildt's association with Oswald "went a little deeper than friendship."

The de Mohrenschildts were to claim they encountered the Oswalds by chance, in the fall of 1962, as the result of a casual introduction by friends in the Russian community. One early account had it that they were taken to see the couple by a Dallas businessman of Russian extraction, Colonel Lawrence Orlov. Orlov, though, told an interviewer that it was obvious at the meeting that the Oswalds and the de Mohrenschildts had met before. De Mohrenschildt was to tell the FBI that they had been introduced by the doyen of the affluent Russian colony in Dallas, George Bouhe. Bouhe said it did not happen that way. De Mohrenschildt's widow Jeanne told the author: "My husband and I heard from the Russian community of an American marine that defected to Russia and returned bringing a young wife and daughter. . . . He needed a job and she needed help with the child. So we decided to take them under our wing."

The de Mohrenschildt-Oswald friendship that ensued has raised a major question because of something de Mohrenschildt said during his Warren Commission testimony. He asked a couple of people, he said, whether it was "safe"—given the young man's background as a former defector—for him and his wife to associate with Oswald. One of the people, he said rather vaguely, could have been "Mr. Moore, Walton Moore . . . He is a government man—either FBI or Central Intelligence. . . . We saw each other from time to time, had lunch . . . a very interesting person."[3]

J. Walton Moore was indeed with the CIA. He was employed by the CIA's Domestic Contact Division in Dallas, charged with making contact with people who had information on foreign matters. Moore's supposed response, when asked by de Mohrenschildt about Oswald, has sensational implications.

In her interviews with the author, de Mohrenschildt's widow Jeanne said she had been present during the exchange with the CIA man. When Oswald's name was brought up, she said, Moore "seemed to be aware of Oswald. He knew who we were talking about. He said the CIA had absolutely no trace on him, that he was perfectly all right and clear. The CIA had nothing on him in the records."[4]

If Moore did say that, de Mohrenschildt's CIA friend was spinning a line. Agency files did, of course, contain information on Oswald's defection to the Soviet Union. An even more discordant note is Jeanne's allegation that Moore was at once familiar with the Oswald case when the subject was brought up. If the CIA had nothing on Oswald, how was its employee in Dallas qualified to comment without even checking?

The reference to Moore in de Mohrenschildt's testimony, and the fact that Moore was with the CIA, remained unnoticed for years. When it did surface, in the 1970s, the CIA said it was "no commenting" the matter. Moore himself fobbed off a reporter, declaring airily, "To the best of my recollection, I hadn't seen de Mohrenschildt for a couple of years before the assassination. I don't know where George got the idea that I cleared Oswald for him. I never met Oswald. I never heard his name before the assassination."

Questioned by the Assassinations Committee as to when he had last seen de Mohrenschildt before the murder of the President, Moore was more careful about his "best recollection." While still denying that Oswald was discussed, Moore indicated that from 1957 on he "had 'periodic' contact with de Mohrenschildt for 'debriefing' purposes over the years." Jeanne de Mohrenschildt responded to that assertion with scorn. At the relevant time, she told the author, the CIA man was so close an associate that he and his wife were dining with the de Mohrenschildts once a fortnight.

The truth about the alleged exchange about Oswald between J. Walton Moore and George de Mohrenschildt remains unclear—another of those question marks hanging over the Agency's role in the case. De Mohrenschildt's association with Oswald, meanwhile, plays a significant part in this history.

They made a strange pair. De Mohrenschildt, thirty years older than Lee Oswald, was swashbuckling, sophisticated. Oswald, by contrast, was introverted, consumed with idealistic notions, grindingly poor. Yet just as George de Mohrenschildt played the Germanophile during the war, infuriating friends with sardonic *"Heil Hitler"* salutes while privately working for the Allies, so now was he well equipped to cultivate Oswald. He was a maverick among his Dallas friends, an articulate champion of minority causes, a liberal who loved to flout convention. He had no trouble building a bridge to Oswald and seems genuinely to have liked him. "Oswald was a delightful guy," he would say years later. "They make a moron out of him, but he was smart as hell. Ahead of his time really, a kind of hippie of those days."

The Soviet episode aside, the Baron and the "hippie" covered a lot of ground together. In an unfinished manuscript de Mohrenschildt wrote before he died, he portrayed Oswald as a young man whose ideas would today raise few eyebrows. Oswald shared with de Mohrenschildt a sense of outrage over racial dis-crimination in the United States—he spoke admiringly of Martin Luther King. Most poignant of all are Oswald's comments to him about President Kennedy. As reported by de Mohrenschildt, Oswald repeatedly praised the President for his efforts both to improve the racial situation and to reach an understanding with the Communist nations. De Mohrenschildt quoted Oswald, who within a year would be accused of killing Kennedy, as saying of him, "How handsome he looks, what open and sincere features he has! How different he looks from the other politicians! . . . If he succeeds he will be the greatest president in the history of this country."

The two new friends talked hour after hour about Oswald's experiences in the Soviet Union. When Oswald arrived in the United States, he had started collecting notes on his stay in Rus-sia and had spoken briefly of getting them published. He now handed the notes to de Mohrenschildt, respectfully asking for his opinion. According to de Mohrenschildt's son-in-law Gary Taylor, Oswald became putty in de Mohrenschildt's hands, "Whatever his suggestions were, Lee grabbed them and took them."

In October 1962, when de Mohrenschildt and Russian friends visited the Oswalds at their run-down apartment in Fort Worth, he suggested Oswald would have better work opportunities in Dallas, thirty miles away, and that Marina would be better off staying with one of the émigré families for a while. There was evident tension between Oswald and Marina, and some thought Oswald had been beating his wife. De Mohrenschildt's proposal was accepted. Later, some of those present would say de Mohren-schildt had seemed oddly clear about Oswald's job prospects in Dallas, that he was possibly supplying Oswald with money.[5]

The day after the meeting at his apartment, Oswald followed de Mohrenschildt's advice, quit his job in Fort Worth without notice, and made his way to Dallas. Apart from a few days at the city YMCA, it is not known where Oswald stayed for the best part of the next month.

He rented a post-office box, a system that—assuming no official surveillance—ensured the receipt of mail with absolute privacy. Oswald used a post-office box wherever he went from then on. He did land a new job, meanwhile, one that paid within a few cents exactly the same as his old job in Fort Worth. George de Mohrenschildt's wife and daughter would both say that, though technically Oswald got the work through the Texas Employment Commission, it was de Mohrenschildt who fixed it for him. The job involved photography, a skill Oswald was keen to learn. The firm he joined was an odd setting for a former defector to the Soviet Union who had, by his own account, given away U.S. military secrets.

Oswald's new employment was with a graphic-arts company called Jaggars-Chiles-Stovall which, along with advertisements for newspapers and trade catalogs, handled contracts for the U.S. Army Map Service. Much of the work involved material obtained by the very U-2 planes Marine Oswald had once watched in Japan, and only employees with a special security clearance were supposed to see it. In practice, the staff worked in cramped conditions that made secrecy impossible. Oswald worked side by side with a fellow employee, Dennis Ofstein, who had previously worked in the Army Security Agency. Though closemouthed at first, Oswald loosened up a little when he realized Ofstein knew some Russian.

Ofstein would recall the surprisingly professional way his new colleague discussed matters of Soviet military interest. Oswald mentioned "the dispersement of military units, saying they didn't intermingle their armored divisions and infantry divisions and various units the way we do in the United States, and they would have all of their aircraft in one geographical location and their infantry in another." Once, when Ofstein helped Oswald enlarge a picture, he said it had been taken in Russia and showed "some military headquarters and that the guards stationed there were armed with weapons and ammunition and had orders to shoot any trespassers."

Over six months at Jaggars-Chiles-Stovall, Oswald became acquainted with sophisticated camera techniques. He also acquired items of photographic equipment that seemed unlikely possessions for a youngster living on a pittance. When police seized Oswald's effects after the assassination, they were to say, they found a Minox camera—the sort usually referred to as a "spy camera."[6] The police also seized three other cameras, a 15-power telescope, two pairs of field glasses, a compass, even a pedometer. The total cost of all this equipment must have been substantial.

Oswald's address book, also confiscated after the assassination, contained the words *micro dots*, written alongside the entry for the Jaggars-Chiles-Stovall company.[7] The microdot technique is a system of photographic reduction that conceals a mass of written material in a minute spot the size of a punctuation mark—a technique that has little use outside espionage. Taken together, Oswald's activities, possessions, and associations jar with his public image of a hard-up workingman.

In the weeks before Christmas 1962, Lee and Marina lurched from crisis to crisis in their married life. The Russian exile colony buzzed with rumors that Oswald was physically abusing his wife. Oswald, for his part, complained that Marina had her faults—including gossiping to others about their sex life. Many local Russians backed away from the marital strife, but George and Jeanne de Mohrenschildt continued to spend time with the couple. As the year 1963 began, Oswald moved into a new phase of his short life—the phase that would end with his arrest as the alleged assassin of President Kennedy.

Hunter of the fascists

The New Year's card for 1963 arrived early at the Soviet Embassy in Washington, DC, wishing the employees "health, success, and all the best" and signed "Marina and Lee Oswald." Oswald the Marxist was at it again—in truth, he had never really stopped. In spite of his expressed disappointment about life in the Soviet Union, Oswald had been sending off for socialist literature since soon after his return to the United States. He subscribed to *The Worker*, the newspaper of the American Communist Party, and to *The Militant*, a news sheet produced by the Socialist Workers' Party. Those who knew him would remember him reading Marx and Lenin, and in the first weeks of 1963, he fired off more letters asking for leftist propaganda. At the same time, he also read H. G. Wells, biographies of Hitler and Nikita Khrushchev—and a book on President Kennedy—and subscribed to that capitalist publication *Time* magazine.

Around this time, according to Marina, her husband came up with his idea of a solution to their marital problems, suggesting she and their child return to the Soviet Union. Marina even wrote to the Soviet Embassy asking for assistance in returning to Russia. Then she became pregnant again, news that delighted Oswald and apparently ended talk of his wife soon going back to Russia. It was at this point, the documentary record shows, that Oswald started buying guns.

In March 1963, mail-order forms and company records establish, a Mannlicher-Carcano 6.5-mm rifle and a Smith & Wesson .38 revolver were shipped to Dallas. The rifle was the weapon that would be found in the Texas School Book Depository after President Kennedy's murder, and the revolver would be linked to the shooting of Officer Tippit, allegedly killed by Oswald after the assassination. The rifle cost only $21.45, including postage, the revolver $29.95. The weapons were sent to Oswald's post-office box in Dallas, and document examiners identified the handwriting on the order forms as his (see Photos 13, 14).

There is, though, a puzzle. The weapons were ordered in the name of "Hidell," the nickname given to one of Oswald's former comrades in the Marine Corps. Oswald is not known to have used the name as an alias at any time other than when purchasing the guns. Yet, as we have seen, a senior U.S. Army Intelligence officer was to say his unit had a "Hidell" file before the assassination—before the guns were of any known interest—because, the officer said, it was an Oswald alias. Why would Army Intelligence have become aware of the gun purchases at the time Oswald made them?

Oswald would first use the rifle seven weeks before the President's assassination, official reports were to conclude, in a failed attempt to kill a prominent former U.S. Army officer living in Dallas, Major General Edwin Walker. The House Assassinations Committee would find that the evidence strongly suggested Oswald was involved. Whether or not that was so, the attempt on the general is an important and neglected part of the saga.

By the time the attempt on his life occurred, General Walker was notorious as leader of the ultraconservative right, opposed to accommodation with the Soviet Union, opposed to racial desegregation, opposed to anything that smacked remotely of liberalism. Two years earlier, as commander of the U.S. Army's 24th Division in West Germany, he had been relieved of his command for foisting political propaganda on his troops. In high dudgeon, he resigned from the Army and launched himself into politics on an extreme right platform.

In late 1962, General Walker played a leading role in an episode that led to a Mob trying to prevent a black man from enrolling as a student at the University of Mississippi. The episode led to two deaths and many injuries, and the General was temporarily confined to a mental institution. By early 1963, however, he was back in Dallas, stirring up more trouble as a leading light of the local John Birch Society. For the "Marxist and liberal idealist" Oswald, living in Dallas as he was, General Walker was an obvious political bogeyman.

General Walker came up in both Oswald's conversations with George de Mohrenschildt, who himself fulminated about General "Fokker" Walker and—at a de Mohrenschildt dinner party in early 1963—with oilman Volkmar Schmidt, who compared Walker to Adolf Hitler. Oswald, for his part, said he thought America was "moving toward fascism." For what happened next, the Warren Report would rely on the testimony of Marina, and on persuasive evidence found among Oswald's effects.

At a new and larger apartment the couple took, Oswald turned one room into a study where he could write and work on his photographic hobby—a hobby with an apparently murderous purpose. Months later, the police would seize five photographs, taken with a camera they linked to Oswald, that showed the rear of General Walker's home and nearby railway tracks. Details in one photograph indicated it had been taken on March 10, two days before the mail order went off to purchase the Mannlicher-Carcano rifle. The weapon was shipped to Dallas on March 20.

Shortly afterward, according to Marina's testimony, Oswald had the rifle and said he was going to use it for hunting. Marina's statements as to what she knew of her husband's use of the gun, however, were to be ludicrously inconsistent. She would tell the FBI two weeks after the assassination that she "had never seen Oswald practice with his rifle or any other firearm and he had never told her he was going to practice." She would repeat that on four further occasions. Then months later, she would refer to a day in January 1963 when she had seen her husband cleaning the rifle after practicing with it—this two months before, as the order forms establish, the gun had even been purchased! By 1978, when Marina testified to the Assassinations Committee, she would say Oswald often went out to practice and cleaned the gun each week.

If Oswald cleaned the Mannlicher-Carcano, he had to have rifle maintenance equipment—pull-through cord, oil, and the like. Just as no ammunition was to be found among Oswald's effects, however, no such cleaning equipment would be found after the assassination.

At the end of March, allegedly, Oswald had his wife take photographs of him, revolver on hip, holding the rifle in one hand and two leftist newspapers in the other. While the author believes these are probably genuine photographs, some have claimed—as discussed earlier—that they were faked (see Chapter 5).

In the first week of April, Oswald stopped working at Jaggars-Chiles-Stovall. He began spending entire days away from home, Marina was to say, never fully explaining what he was doing with the time. On April 12, when according to Marina he stayed out very late, someone tried to shoot General Walker.

At 9:00 p.m. that evening, General Walker would say, he was working at a desk in a downstairs room opposite an un-curtained window. He was seated there when, after a single loud bang, a bullet smashed into the wall of the room. It missed his head by inches. The police were summoned, but no one was ever caught. The case remained unsolved until after the assassination of President Kennedy, when the Warren Commission was to decide that Oswald—and Oswald alone—had been the culprit.

The ballistics evidence in the Walker shooting is unclear. The bullet recovered from General Walker's home had been severely distorted by the impact on a window frame and the wall, and a firearms panel could not say whether it had been fired from the Mannlicher-Carcano. A contemporary police report described the bullet as "steel-jacketed, of unknown caliber," and press reports after the shooting quoted the police as identifying the bullet not as 6.5 but 30.06 caliber.[8] If the bullet evidence was inconclusive, however, other evidence indicated that Oswald was at least involved.

When he went out on the night of the attack on General Walker, Marina was to say, he left her a note—a note she thought she remembered finding before he got home. Ten days after the assassination of the President, a note that was to be identified as being in Oswald's handwriting did turn up inside a book among Oswald's effects. It told Marina how to get to the city jail "if I am alive and taken prisoner," and asked her to tell "the Embassy"— the Soviet Embassy?—what had happened.

According to Marina, Oswald had rushed home in a panic at 11:30 p.m., blurting out that he had fired his rifle at General Walker but did not know whether he had killed him. He showed her notes he had made and photographs he had taken while planning the shooting. He had buried his rifle near the General's house, he said, and would go back days later to retrieve it. He promised he would never do such a thing again. Marina told no one of the incident at the time, she said, because the murder attempt had failed.

The weekend after the incident, when George and Jeanne de Mohrenschildt visited the Oswalds, something truly remarkable occurred. According to Jeanne, she saw Oswald's rifle in a cupboard during the visit and mentioned it to her husband, prompting George, "with his sense of humor," to say jokingly to Oswald, "How is it that you missed General Walker?" This was just a jest, Jeanne said, made not out of knowledge but because the attempt on Walker was in the news and because George recalled the conversations he and Oswald had had about the General. According to George, Oswald's reaction to the intended joke was that he "sort of shriveled . . . made a peculiar face . . . became almost speechless." Someone changed the subject, and no more was said.

Told like that, the story sounds conclusive. Like so much else about the case, however, it is shot through with contradiction. Marina's statements suggested that Jeanne de Mohrenschildt saw the rifle in a cupboard at the apartment days *before* the attempt on General Walker. Is it probable, though, that after the attempt on Walker, when she and her husband were supposedly striving to cover up Oswald's role, Marina would have readily opened a cupboard door and allowed Jeanne to see the rifle?

On the matter of when the rifle was seen, the de Mohrenschildts' accounts were also skewed. After the assassination, in an interview with officials, the couple was to say Jeanne had spotted the gun as early as the autumn of the previous *year*. Another Jeanne account would suggest she saw the weapon on a day that, according to Marina, it was still buried near General Walker's house. Had the Walker case ever come to court, a defense counsel would have played up such flaws in the testimony, and a slew of other oddities.

In 1967, more than three years after the Kennedy assassination, George de Mohrenschildt would say he had come upon fresh and "very interesting information." While sorting luggage retrieved from storage, he said, he had come across another copy of the by then famous photograph of Oswald holding his guns and leftist magazines. On the back of this copy of the photograph there were two inscriptions. One, which Assassinations Committee examiners found to be in Oswald's handwriting, read, "To my friend George from Lee Oswald," along with a date— "5/IV/63." Given the time frame involved, this must refer to 5 April 1963, though it is written not in the order Americans write the date—month/day/year—but day first, European-style. Nor would Americans use the Roman numeral IV for the numeral 4. A check of the dozens of letters and documents written by Oswald produces not one example of a date written like the one on the back of the photograph.

The second inscription, which is written in Russian Cyrillic script, translates as "Hunter of fascists ha-ha-ha!!!" (see Photo 17). Expert testimony to the Assassinations Committee was that the ironic slogan—clearly directed at Oswald—had been written and then rewritten in pencil—but not, document examiners said, by either Oswald, Marina, or George de Mohrenschildt. Nor, by implication, by Jeanne—whose parents had been Russian—since the experts said it was written by someone unfamiliar with Cyrillic script. Wise here, perhaps, to note that document examiners are not infallible, as they themselves readily admit.[9] The writer was most likely one of the Oswalds or one of the de Mohrenschildts. Which of them it was remains another unsolved riddle.

On the subject of the rifle, the rifle that was to be a key item of evidence after the President's assassination, there is yet another puzzle. How had Oswald come by the money to buy the

Mannlicher-Carcano—and indeed his handgun? His finances for the period were meager at best—all who knew him said he was living at poverty level, scraping by—and his known income has been carefully documented. Two large sums he owed following his return from the USSR—large, for the ordinary worker, by 1962 standards—were $200 to his brother and $435 to the State Department, for their contribution to his travel costs. He at first repaid the money, as one might expect, in dribs and drabs, ten dollars at a time. Then, all of a sudden, within less than seven weeks, he was able to pay off what remained of the State Department debt of $396.[10] This in a period during which he earned only $490.

How did Oswald pay the rent and keep his family for those seven weeks on a balance of just $94? The rent alone took $68, ostensibly leaving Oswald the princely sum of less than four dollars a week to provide for his family and pay the bills. Nonsense, clearly. Yet on March 12, within days of paying off his State Department loan, a money order form for $21.45 was sent off to buy the Mannlicher-Carcano.[11] On the known evidence, it seems possible that Oswald received an influx of funds, funds that enabled him to pay off his debts and purchase the rifle, from a source that was never identified.

As for the shot fired at General Walker, there was from the beginning testimony that suggested more than one person was involved, testimony the House Assassinations Committee took seriously. For General Walker was not the only person startled by the loud report of the shot that almost killed him. Walter Coleman, a fourteen-year-old boy, heard the shot while standing in a doorway of a nearby house—and at once peered over the fence to see what was going on. What he saw, he said, was a suspicious scene involving not one but at least two men.

Young Coleman, the Assassinations Committee noted, "saw some men speeding down the alley in a light green or light blue Ford, either a 1959 or 1960 model. He said he also saw another car, a 1958 Chevrolet, black with white down the side, in a church parking lot adjacent to General Walker's house. The car door was open, and a man was bending over the backseat as though he was placing something on the floor of the car."[12]

When the Walker case was reopened following the President's assassination, Coleman said he had gotten a look at the men he had seen drive away. Neither of them had resembled Oswald. Oswald did not own a car and only began learning to drive many months later.

General Walker had known he might be in danger. Aides accompanied him everywhere he went and acted as security guards at his house. Four nights before the shooting incident one aide, Robert Surrey, had spotted two men prowling around the house, "peeking in windows and so forth." General Walker had deemed the information serious enough to report to the police the next morning. Several days before the shooting, said Max Claunch, another aide, he several times noticed a "Cuban or dark-complected man in a 1957 Chevrolet" drive slowly around the General's house.

The Assassinations Committee would report that it had conducted only a "limited," abortive investigation into the evidence that suggests more than one person was involved in the Walker shooting. It was a regrettable omission. The Committee, though committed to the belief that Oswald took part in the assassination, stated that it was "not necessary to believe all of what Marina said about the [Walker] incident, nor to believe that Oswald told her all there was to know, since either of them might have been concealing the involvement of others . . . it is possible that associates of Oswald in the Kennedy assassination had been involved with him in earlier activities. . . . If it could be shown that Oswald had associates in the attempt on General Walker, they would be likely candidates as the grassy-knoll gunman."

In one of the coincidences that run through this case, a 1957 Chevrolet—a description similar to that of one of the suspicious cars seen near General Walker's home—would be sought by Dallas police on the day of the Kennedy assassination. Police radio transcripts show that two hours after the President had been killed, when Oswald was already in custody, headquarters put out a description of a 1957 Chevrolet sedan suspected of carrying weapons. The car had last been seen near the scene of the shooting of Officer Tippit, the Dallas policeman killed after the President's assassination.

A detail in the report of a 1957 model Chevrolet in the vicinity of General Walker's house may conceivably have offered a clue—the statement by one of the General's aides that the cruising vehicle was driven by a "Cuban or dark-complected man." Cuba and Cuban politics were of importance to both General Walker and Lee Oswald.

By 1963, Cuba was Walker's favorite rabble-rousing topic, another reason to vilify President Kennedy. He and others on the extreme right blamed the President personally for the fact that Fidel Castro was still in power, still ruling a Communist enclave off the coast of the United States. In the months before the assassination, General Walker would be at meetings of Cuban exiles, in the words of one witness, "trying to arouse the feelings of the Cuban refugees in Dallas against the Kennedy administration." It was one of the General's aides, Robert Surrey, who was to produce the "Wanted for Treason" leaflet distributed in Dallas before Kennedy's visit that November.

The jingoism typified by General Walker found a significant following, and the President himself took the outcry seriously. When he learned that a film was to be made based on the book *Seven Days in May*—a fictional account of a plot by right-wing generals to overthrow an American president because of his "appeasement of the Communists"—Kennedy offered the White House as a shooting location.

Cuba and the U.S. posture toward Cuba is key to the disentangling of the Kennedy assassination story. Cuba, and the continuing questions about the shadowy activity of U.S. intelligence.

George de Mohrenschildt apparently left Dallas nine days after the attempt on General Walker's life, to spend the months that followed involved in oil exploration on the Caribbean island of Haiti. A change of address postcard from Oswald aside, the improbable relationship had ended as abruptly as it had begun. George de Mohrenschildt's name, however, would crop up in CIA and U.S. Army Intelligence files in the months that followed. One former CIA official, Nicholas Anikeeff, acknowledged that he had known de Mohrenschildt for years and "believed" he saw him in the spring of 1963. "I talked with de Mohrenschildt," he said, "and may have spoken with him about Oswald." Anikeeff was reportedly a branch chief in the CIA's Soviet Russia Division in the early 1960s.

A CIA document written years later, meanwhile, refers obliquely to correspondence between Anikeeff and de Mohrenschildt. It was filed by Raymond Rocca, deputy to CIA Counterintelligence chief James Angleton. As analysis of available information shows, Angleton's department monitored Oswald's progress from the time of his defection until the assassination. He was perhaps seen as potentially useful, perhaps to be manipulated in some way—as the developing story will suggest.

Lee Oswald was to spend the summer of 1963 in New Orleans, a time frame and a city that are central to the Assassinations Committee's thesis that anti-Castro exiles and elements of the Mafia may have been involved in the Kennedy assassination. From that point on, in public, Oswald would become known for leftist posturing in support of Fidel Castro. Other information, though, suggests that he also had links to *anti*-Castro activity.

Who was playing what game? For in a scenario where much is obscure, there certainly was a game. The backdrop was Cuba.

III

CONSPIRACIES
Cuba and the Mob

CHAPTER 13

The Company
and the Crooks

"Anti-Castro activists and organizations . . .
acquired the means, motive and opportunity to assas-
sinate the President."

—Staff report to the House Select Committee on
Assassinations, 1979

Cuba was President Kennedy's albatross, but it had hung in the rigging of the American ship of state for decades. Washington had perceived it as just another poverty-stricken island in the sun, an American puppet that would hopefully stay that way. So it had, mostly under the rule of a former Army sergeant named Fulgencio Batista, an old-fashioned dictator whose priority was to line his own pockets. He was able to do so above all because of the patronage of American organized-crime bosses, who turned Havana into a mecca for gambling and prostitution. That was fine for everyone but the vast majority of the Cuban people, who remained miserably poor.

On New Year's Day, 1959, Cuba had rallied to the liberation call of a rebel named Fidel Castro, and Batista fled. In Washington, DC, as in America's citadels of organized crime, the government of President Eisenhower watched and waited to see what sort of revolution Castro wrought. Few in the outside world suspected its true Marxist colors, but the Central Intelligence Agency had for years watched Castro with foreboding. Within months of his coming to power, it was clear that Cuba was to be a Communist state, raising the specter of a Soviet outpost on America's doorstep. The United States reacted with instinctive outrage, nowhere more strongly than at the CIA and in the Eisenhower White House.

The Agency began encouraging the activities of the many thousands of anti-Castro exiles who had flooded into the United States, mostly to Florida and the South. Under the direction of a CIA officer named Howard Hunt, later to become notorious for his role in Watergate, the refugee leaders formed a united front organization—which eventually became the Cuban Revolutionary Council. With the assistance of the CIA, known to insiders as "The Company," young Cubans were recruited for armed struggle against Castro. At camps in Florida and Panama, and later in Guatemala and Nicaragua, U.S. Army officers trained the exiles for an invasion of their homeland. Hunt had a recommendation. "Assassinate Castro," he proposed, "*before* or coincident with the invasion (a task for Cuban patriots). Discard any thought of a popular uprising against Castro until the issue has already been militarily decided."

In the White House, Richard Nixon was Vice President. With President Eisenhower in poor health and seeing out the last days of his administration, Nixon had a more active role than most deputy leaders. He was close to many of the wealthy Americans and Cubans who had most interest in the fall of Castro, and was by his own account the "strongest and most persistent advocate" of efforts to bring it about. Nixon willingly became the White House action man on the Cuban project, reportedly favoring the extreme rightists among the Cuban exiles.

On one of the tapes that were to destroy his presidency, Nixon brooded about what could come out given the involvement of several Cuban exiles in Watergate: "You open that scab, there's a hell of a lot of things and we just feel that it would be very detrimental to have this thing go any further. . . ." And, later the same day: "If it gets out that this is all involved, the Cuban thing, it would be a fiasco."

In November 1960, at the height of preparations for an exile invasion, John F. Kennedy was elected President. The plans he inherited from the CIA and the previous administration led him into a situation worse than fiasco. Kennedy loyalists and their opponents would long argue about where fault lay for what occurred on April 17, 1961, when a force of Cuban exiles was put ashore at the Bay of Pigs on Cuba's south coast. Sifting through the multiple accounts, it seems that the new President had been inadequately briefed by the CIA and received bad military advice.

The idea was that the exiles would establish a beachhead, then capture and hold an area that could be claimed as the territory of the provisional government. Against all the evidence, it was blithely hoped a general uprising against Castro would follow, leading to Castro's fall from power. In fact, the motley band of fifteen hundred Cuban exiles went ashore into terrain bristling with well-prepared Castro defenders. They floundered in treacherous salt marshes, ran out of ammunition when Castro's airplanes sunk their supply ships, and were ignominiously routed. Many were killed and more than a thousand rounded up and marched off to prison.

In public, President Kennedy accepted full responsibility, but the Bay of Pigs fiasco became the cause of lasting acrimony. In the CIA and in some military circles, the President was accused of vacillation. He had refused permission for air strikes and intervention by U.S. armed forces, on the grounds that such action was politically indefensible. The CIA's Howard Hunt told the author how, as news of the debacle came in, he and colleagues reacted with dismay and scorn: "At CIA headquarters, in our war room . . . we thought, as the indications came in, that the administration would feel more and more an obligation to unleash some United States power to equalize the situation. We kept receiving the administration's refusals with incredulity. I felt a sense of hollowness . . . somewhere along the way we lost a good part of our national will to prevail. I think it was a failure of nerve."

Hunt's comments suggest the Agency knew in advance that the operation could not succeed without U.S. military support, that it had banked on being able to pressure the President into direct intervention. Worst of all, perhaps, CIA Director Dulles had encouraged the President to believe the landing would be followed by a mass popular uprising—a prospect that CIA intelligence reports indicated was wholly improbable.

There were also indications that the CIA had become a law unto itself. Contrary to the President's express orders, CIA officers had landed on the beach with the exiles. Agents had earlier told their Cuban protégés to press ahead with the invasion even were the President to call off the landing at the last moment. This, Robert Kennedy later commented, was "virtually treason." His elder brother said privately that he would like "to splinter the CIA into a thousand pieces and scatter it to the winds."

The President did not do quite that, but the ensuing shake-up led to the resignation of Director Dulles and of Deputy Director Richard Bissell, who had been responsible for the Bay of Pigs planning. Dulles, in a great irony, was eventually to serve on the Warren Commission probe of the President's assassination— a Commission that would gloss over the failings of American intelligence agencies. In the lower ranks of the CIA, the President had stirred lasting anger and resentment. For some officers, involvement with the Cuban exile movement had become a passionate commitment.

The President's brother Robert took over the responsibility of overseeing Cuban matters. Hunt, who thought him "an abrasive little man," recalled especially a significant clash between the younger Kennedy and William Harvey, a swashbuckling senior agent who played a leading role after the Bay of Pigs. In a less-than-subtle reference to the Bay of Pigs disaster, Harvey liked to display behind his desk a lurid poster that read "The tree of liberty is watered with the blood of patriots." Robert Kennedy found it and its owner objectionable, and Harvey was eventually moved sideways.

If the Kennedys had alienated many at the CIA, they roused even stronger passions among the hot-blooded Hispanic exiles. "The failure of the Bay of Pigs had a disastrous effect," Hunt said. "They were outraged that a country so powerful as the United States, only ninety miles away from their homeland, could have permitted a disaster such as the Bay of Pigs to have taken place. . . . The more knowledgeable, the more sophisticated people in the Cuban community, did blame the President personally."

For many, the catchword for the Bay of Pigs became the "Betrayal." The Cuban who had led the exiles onto the beaches, Pepe San Román, recalled that he afterward "hated the United

States. . . . Every day it became worse, and then I was getting madder and madder and I wanted to get a rifle and come and fight against the U.S. . . . For me, the government of the United States [had been] the utmost of everything—bigger than my father, than my mother, than God . . . it was so low, so low a blow to us with so many plans and so many hopes . . . they knew before they sent us, in my mind, that they were not going to go ahead with it."

San Román's comments were too gentle for some extremists, who placed the blame firmly on the American leadership. Mario Kohly Jr. quoted his late father, who claimed the Cuban presidency in exile, as saying, "John Kennedy sold out the American people. John Kennedy was a traitor . . . he was a Communist." The President had made enemies early in his tenure, and the ambiguity of his Cuba policy over the two years that followed increased the animosity.

The Bay of Pigs had stiffened the President's determination to resolve the Cuban problem aggressively. He went along with the precept that "there can be no long-term living with Castro as a neighbor," and pressed on with plans to get rid of him. The CIA, theoretically now more tightly controlled by the President's brother, set up an extraordinary new center of operations. Code-named "JM/WAVE," and situated in Miami, it was in effect the headquarters for a very public "secret war" against Cuba. This, the Agency's most ambitious project ever, came to involve seven hundred CIA personnel and co-opted Army officers recruiting, training, and supplying thousands of Cuban exiles.

The aim this time was to wage a war of attrition, to harass Castro with hit-and-run raids against industrial and military targets, and incite guerrilla warfare by anti-Castro groups operating inside Cuba. Robert Kennedy urged that "no time, money, effort—or manpower—be spared," and threw himself into the fray with boundless energy.

The nerve center of the new struggle was set up in Miami, where the vast majority of the exiles were concentrated. In woods on the campus of the University of Miami, the CIA established a front operation in the shape of an electronics company named Zenith Technological Services. At the height of its activity, in 1962, the JM/WAVE station controlled as many as six hundred Americans, mostly CIA officers, and up to three thousand contract agents. It spawned front operations—boat shops, detective and travel agencies, and gun stores. There were hundreds of "safe houses"—and accommodations ranging from apartments to opulent townhouses.

Of the quarter of a million Cuban refugees in the United States, many were content to settle into new lives. Others, including numerous brave young men, clutched at the new straw of hope the Americans held out. Night after night, launches slipped out of the Florida waterways on missions of sabotage and propaganda. The exiles built up huge arms caches, many of them concealed in the CIA's "safe houses." They trained with CIA facilities and U.S. military instructors. Few, however, appear to have given serious thought to the main flaw in the plans, that Fidel Castro remained a popular leader. The exiles' operations were to achieve little in the long run, except to confirm Castro's accusation that the United States was guilty of aggression.

The President and his brother had meanwhile committed themselves to bringing back the hundreds of exiles who had been captured at the Bay of Pigs, and resolved to get the men home by the end of 1962. A ransom was agreed, and the last of the Bay of Pigs captives were back by New Year's. At a rally in a Miami sports stadium, President Kennedy made a stirring speech of welcome—in which he not only railed against Castro and Communism, but appeared to promise much more. "I can assure you," Kennedy cried, having been presented with the flag of the force that had gone ashore at the Bay of Pigs, "that this flag will be returned to this brigade in a free Havana."

The speech in the Miami stadium was made only weeks after the final conclusion of the Cuban Missile Crisis. Through the month of October, the world had trembled as the leaders of the United States and Russia traded threats of war. The immediate cause had been the arrival in Cuba of Soviet missiles capable of bombarding the United States, and the outcome—to Castro's noisy fury—had been a Soviet agreement to withdraw them. The United States, for its part, had given indirect assurances that there would be no invasion of Cuba by the United States.

It was a commitment, Kennedy knew, that would earn him no honors among his political opponents. The Republicans would say, he reflected, that "we had a chance to get rid of Castro, and instead of doing so ended up by guaranteeing him." That was certainly what many in the CIA and the Cuban exile community thought. A measure of the gulf between Kennedy and such critics is the fact that some of them claimed the Soviet missiles were not in fact removed from Cuba.

"It has never been established that any missiles were ever removed from the island," Howard Hunt would still be telling the author in the late 1970s, "Mr. Khrushchev agreed that photo surveillance could be conducted of the departing Soviet ships, but there have been no satellite scanners or aircraft cameras developed yet that can peer inside a wooden crate or through a tarpaulin. [The President] did not insist upon on-site inspection or on boarding the Soviet ships as they departed. Hopefully the missiles were taken out, but nobody dares say that they were."

In the view of one Cuban exile the author interviewed, the outcome of the Missile Crisis was "a beautifully planned theatrical hoax."[1] The exile leadership did present a flag to the President at the rally in late December 1962, but—according to Hunt—"the Brigade feeling against Kennedy was so great that the presentation nearly did not take place at all." The exiles' distrust of the President, moreover, soon began to seem well founded.

In 1963, Kennedy began to clamp down on unauthorized exile military activity on U.S. territory. Things came to a head in mid-March after one of the most combative anti-Castro groups, Alpha 66, carried out a series of unauthorized attacks on Soviet ships in Cuban ports. Coming just months after the Missile Crisis, the raids were dangerously provocative—intentionally so, as this story will show. To dissociate the United States from the attacks, Kennedy acted firmly. The government announced that same month that it would "take every step necessary to make certain that American soil is not used as a base for refugee raids on Cuban and Soviet shipping." U.S. authorities matched words with action, seizing an exile vessel in Florida and using administration influence to abort another operation being mounted from the British-administered Bahamas.

The powerful American apparatus that had aided and abetted the exiles now had orders to obstruct them. The U.S. Customs and Immigration authorities, the Coast Guard, the Navy, and the FBI, all began frustrating the efforts of Cuban raiders. This clampdown on raids, some have claimed, served to mask other, more secret, plans to have Castro killed and overthrow the Cuban regime. At the time, however, reining in the exiles served to ease the tension with the Soviet Union. For its part, the Soviets began to withdraw thousands of military "advisers" from Cuba, a process that would continue.

The seemingly less aggressive posture on Cuba met with vociferous opposition within the United States. Richard Nixon made speeches urging its reversal, calling for action to force the Communist regime from power—overtly supporting the exiles. The exile militants and some of their CIA mentors, for their part, were enraged by the President's actions. They felt, as Howard Hunt put it, that U.S. assistance to the exiles was "a fraud, a fraud perpetrated on the Cuban people, and on the American people."

As part of the new policy, meanwhile, the President struck directly at the Cuban Revolutionary Council, the government-in-exile that had grown out of the anti-Castro front created by the CIA two years earlier, by cutting off financial support. Its leader, José Miró Cardona, resigned in fury, accusing Kennedy of breaking his pledges.

In the wake of the clampdown on exile activities, the head of the Miami Police Intelligence Unit, Charles Sapp, had begun receiving alarming information from his sources. What he learned on April 4, 1963, moved him to alert his superiors. "Since President Kennedy made the news release that the U.S. government would stop all raiding parties going against the Castro government," he wrote, "the Cuban people feel that the U.S. government has turned against them. . . . Violence hitherto directed toward Castro's Cuba will now be directed toward various governmental agencies in the United States."

From then on, Sapp told the author, his unit and the Miami Secret Service felt that public officials were under threat, the President especially. The inflamed temper of the exiles aside, the Florida authorities saw signs of danger from the lunatic fringe of the American Right. Just after the clampdown, a sinister hand-out appeared in mailboxes around Miami. It advised the exile community that only one development would now make it pos-sible for "Cuban patriots" to return to their homeland: ". . . if an inspired Act of God should place in the White House within weeks a Texan known to be a friend of all Latin Americans." It is hard to interpret this as anything but a call for the death of President Kennedy and his replacement by Lyndon Johnson. The handbill, which had the hallmarks of the John Birch Soci-ety, was signed, "A Texan who resents the Oriental influence that has come to control, to degrade, to pollute and enslave his own people."

If the sulfurous mix of violent exiles, recalcitrant CIA opera-tives, and political extremists were not enough, the President was faced with threats from a different quarter. CIA folly, com-bined with Kennedy zeal, had inflamed another foe—the Mob.

Sixteen weeks before Kennedy had become President, four immaculately suited gentlemen had chatted over cocktails in the Boom-Boom Room of Miami's Fontainebleau Hotel. They might have been businessmen discussing a deal, or politicians plan-ning strategy. In fact, two of the distinguished-looking men were Mafia hoodlums, and—with a go-between—they were meeting with a representative of the CIA. The topic on the agenda was the proposed assassination of Fidel Castro, the latest and most dangerous in a series of CIA schemes. Some fifteen years later, the plots would become known following an investigation by the Senate Intelligence Committee.

The CIA already had a unit with responsibility for kidnapping and murder, and the advent of Fidel Castro had been tailor-made for its attention. Top CIA officers had within a year been writ-ing memoranda recommending that "thorough consideration be given to the elimination of Fidel Castro," and by summer 1960, it was clear they meant it. Cables between Washington headquarters and the Havana CIA station discussed the "removal of top three leaders" and—in the case of Castro's brother Raúl, who in effect leads Cuba today—a plan for "an accident to neutralize this leader's influence."

The plots hatched against Castro himself would defy belief were it not that they have long since been documented. The wizards of the CIA's Technical Services Division, at first, fooled with the notion of impregnating Castro's shoes with chemicals that would cause all his hair to fall out—including the trademark beard. Without it, went the theory, Castro would lose his appeal to the masses. It was a small conceptual step from Castro beard to Castro cigars, to a plan to slip the leader of the revolution a spiked cigar—in the hope he would go berserk during one of his famous speech marathons. Some genius proposed trying for the same result by spraying Castro's broadcasting studio with a form of the drug LSD.

The CIA moved from silly schemes to murderous toys, and then to the real thing. By autumn 1960, the Technical Services Division had prepared cigars treated with a lethal poison. Castro, it was hoped, would die within moments of placing it in his mouth. In the months that followed, there would be a fungus-dusted diving suit impregnated with a strain of tuberculosis, and an exploding seashell to be planted in Castro's favorite skin-diving spot. Attempts were made to have the Agency's little surprises delivered by agents inside Cuba. In such an atmosphere, it should perhaps not be surprising that high officials eventually recruited criminals to help.

The dalliance between American intelligence and the Mafia had begun in World War II. Then, the Office of Naval

Intelligence had obtained the help of Lucky Luciano, at the time the "don of dons," in preventing German sabotage in U.S. dockyards. Through Meyer Lansky, his close associate, Luciano had mobilized his network of waterfront thugs accordingly and been rewarded by leniency for his own crimes. In Europe, the crime boss's Sicilian brothers helped Allied operations in the Mediterranean. All this is well documented, not least in the War Report of the Office of Strategic Services, the forerunner of the CIA.

Meyer Lansky, a financial wizard, went on to use the old-fashioned methods—murder and corruption—to adapt the structure of the Mob to the modern world, a process that led to what came to be known as "organized crime." The rival gangs now operated within a nationwide syndicate that Lansky himself reportedly described as "bigger than U.S. Steel." The difference was that the income came from the exploitation of human beings, the discipline from torture and killing, and the proceeds were salted away in legal investments.

It is now clear that a loose working relationship between organized crime and the CIA existed at least until the Vietnam War years, when Mob heroin-trafficking and CIA counter-insurgency found mutually convenient hunting grounds in Southeast Asia. There was an even clearer coincidence of interest during the secret war against Fidel Castro.

Castro's predecessor, Batista, had been a puppet on strings pulled by U.S. intelligence and the Mafia. In 1944, when the United States feared trouble from the Cuban left, Lansky reportedly leaned on Batista to step down for a while. He returned in 1952 after the then incumbent, Carlos Prío Socarrás, had been persuaded to resign—a departure reportedly eased by a massive bribe and a major stake in the casino business. It was then that the gambling operation in Cuba became a full-scale bonanza for the Mafia.

The gangster bosses established a glittering nexus of casinos and hotels that attracted American spenders like moths to a flame. The gaming tables and the nightlife—including prostitution on the grand scale—made Havana more lucrative for the syndicate than even Las Vegas. As a bonus there were rich pickings from narcotics, with Havana the crossroads of international trafficking. Estimates suggest the Mafia's Havana operation netted more than a hundred million in 1950s dollars a year—that translates as almost nine hundred million a year today.

When the Batista regime began to crumble, the Mob hedged its political bets by courting Fidel Castro. Many of the guns that helped him to power in 1959 had arrived courtesy of Mafia gunrunners, but the favor was not reciprocated. Lansky, who saw disaster coming, flew out of Havana the day Castro marched in. For a while, the casinos were allowed to continue operating under government control. Then Castro ordered the arrest of Lansky's associate Santo Trafficante who is believed—his casino interests aside—to have been responsible for moving European heroin shipments through Havana to the United States. Then, with the casinos closed down once and for all, Trafficante and other remaining casino operators were packed off to Florida. There, brooding mightily over the loss of their Havana goldmine, dreaming of return, the mafiosi were tailor-made coconspirators for the CIA's plans to kill Castro.

Lansky, the CIA learned, was offering a million-dollar bounty for Castro's murder. Other mobsters were already trying to kill him—by using a woman to slip poison into Castro's food—and may have come close to succeeding. An Assassinations Committee report noted that Castro suffered a serious "sickness" in the summer of 1960. The CIA decided it was time to join forces with the Mob, and an extraordinary operation began.

Top-level CIA conferences on teaming up with the Mafia to kill Castro included the Agency's Director Allen Dulles—a fact he would not reveal three years later as a member of the Warren Commission. With Dulles' and Deputy Director Richard Bissell's approval, the CIA's Office of Security went into action. A first step was to appoint a go-between, someone trusted by the CIA but sufficiently independent to protect the Agency in case of exposure. Robert Maheu, a former FBI agent with the FBI in Chicago, fit the bill.

So it was that Maheu and three other men convened for the fall 1960 meeting in the tawdry splendor of Miami's Fontainebleau Hotel. Two of them, both gangsters, used the names of "Sam Gold" and "John Rawlston." "Gold" was Chicago's crime boss Sam Giancana, who had had a piece of the Cuban rackets. "Rawlston" was Johnny Roselli, who had risen from humble beginnings running liquor for Al Capone in Illinois to the top of organized crime in Las Vegas. A decade earlier, the Kefauver Committee had identified him as a leading racketeer with close links to Meyer Lansky. The fourth man present, Joe Shimon, was a former Washington police inspector whom Giancana trusted.

It was Shimon who, during initial research for this book, explained to the author how the Mob side of the conspiracy worked. "Johnny called Sam and told Sam what he needed," Shimon said, "You had to have some individual who knew a lot of Cubans and knew the type of Cubans that could be prevailed upon to get into such a plot. They would have to be lawbreakers, but you had to have somebody who really knew the Cubans." The man who "really knew the Cubans," Shimon said, was Santo Trafficante.

Trafficante—whom the House Assassinations Committee was one day to suspect of involvement in the killing of President Kennedy—had a suitably dishonorable heritage. His father, who had come to the United States in the early twentieth century, had established a Florida power base that would never be seriously challenged. The young Trafficante inherited the Florida rackets and the Sans Souci Casino in Havana. The extent of his power had been recognized since 1957, when Albert Anastasia, at that time regarded as the most efficient and vicious gang leader in America, died riddled with bullets while sitting in a barber's chair. Anastasia had been attempting to move in on the Trafficante interests in Cuba.

Shortly after the first meeting at the Fontainebleau, Giancana came with Trafficante—who used the name Joe Pecora—to a second meeting with a CIA "support chief." The assassination of Fidel Castro was again discussed, and Trafficante made obliging noises. He, in his turn, introduced CIA officers to Antonio de Varona—a former Cuban prime minister who was soon to become vice president of the exiles' Cuban Revolutionary Council—and he was supplied with poison. The plan was for the poison to be slipped into Castro's food by an employee at his favorite restaurant. It never happened, supposedly because Castro gave up frequenting the restaurant. Had the plan worked, Castro would have died at the time of the Bay of Pigs invasion in April 1961—soon after President Kennedy took the reins of power.

After a year-long lull in assassination plans, the CIA's William Harvey supervised another episode involving poison pills and, as established by the Senate probe, "explosives, detonators, rifles, handguns, radios and boat radar." These devices were delivered to the same Cuban contact at a meeting in a Miami parking lot.

Again nothing happened. The House Assassinations Committee was to speculate that the Mafia bosses had by that time soured on the notion that the Cuban revolution could be reversed simply by killing Castro. After 1962, so far as is known, CIA attempts to murder Fidel Castro did not involve the Mob.

There has been prolonged polemic over whether and when President Kennedy learned of the plots against Castro, and whether he supported them. That he knew something of the plots by late 1961 is not in doubt. While being interviewed by the *New York Times'* Latin America correspondent, Tad Szulc, Kennedy suddenly leaned forward in his rocking chair and asked, "What would you think if I ordered Castro to be assassinated?"

Szulc replied that political assassination was wrong in principle and in any case would do nothing to solve the Cuba problem. Kennedy, Szulc wrote later, explained that "he was under great pressure from advisers in the intelligence community (whom he did not name) to have Castro killed, but that he himself violently opposed it on the grounds that for moral reasons the United States should never be a party to political assassinations."

Senator George Smathers, himself a passionate opponent of Castro, also had a conversation with the President on the subject. Smathers would recall that Kennedy expressed himself "horrified" at the idea of assassination. "I remember him saying," Smathers said, "that the CIA frequently did things he didn't know about, and he was unhappy about it. He complained that the CIA was almost autonomous."

CIA officials, for their part, were to say that, while it was not proper to discuss such things with the President, they assumed he was aware of and approved of the assassination plots. As for Attorney General Robert Kennedy, one reading of the record suggests he was furious when he learned of the Mafia role in the plots. This occurred when, in early 1962, he discovered the CIA was trying to protect Sam Giancana from prosecution, insisted on finding out why, and was then briefed on Giancana's part in the early murder plans by CIA attorney Lawrence Houston.

According to Houston, the information upset Robert Kennedy, who expressed "strong anger." "I trust," he said, "that if you ever try to do business with organized crime again—with gangsters—you will let the Attorney General know." Houston testified, "If you have ever seen Mr. Kennedy's eyes get steely and his jaw set and his voice get low and precise, you get a definite feeling of unhappiness."

Much later, in a discussion about the Castro assassination plots with two aides, Robert Kennedy claimed, "I stopped it. . . . I found out that some people were going to try an attempt on Castro's life and I turned it off."

It may be, though, that the Kennedys voiced disapproval only to create a smokescreen. In his biography of CIA Director Richard Helms, Thomas Powers argued that senior CIA officials refrained from saying on the record that President Kennedy approved such schemes—either because they had no proof, or because it was traditional for a secret service to "take the heat."

In his autobiography, written just before his death in 2002, Helms recalled the key role of the "Special Group," the term for a group of top presidential advisers first used during the Eisenhower administration. A key role of the Group, he wrote, aside from providing authorization for CIA covert action, was "to establish a screen, protecting the President from having to assume personal responsibility for every risky covert operation." When during the Kennedy administration the Group became the focal point for decision of Cuba activity, Helms noted drily, "Robert Kennedy, the Attorney General, added himself to the roster."

"There were ways we would speak about assassination off the record," former CIA Deputy Director Richard Bissell said in 1994, "ways we would speak about it without using the word. We had to protect the President," he added drily.

William Harvey, head of the Cuba task force in 1962 and early 1963, told the Agency's Inspector General that plans to kill Castro were an integral part of the CIA's contingency plan for murder in general—which "was developed in response to White House urgings." A former officer at JM/WAVE, the CIA's Florida headquarters, claimed Harvey was removed from the project in part because he "wasn't having Castro killed fast enough."

George Smathers, former U.S. Senator from Florida and the President's close friend, was to expand on his previous statements on the subject. "Jack," he said in 1994, "would be all the time, 'If somebody knocks this guy off, that'd be fine.' . . . But Kennedy obviously had to say he could not be a party to that sort of thing with the damn Mafia."

Did Robert Kennedy know, too? "Sure," Smathers said.

And then there are the claims of Judith Campbell, the California woman who was one of President Kennedy's lovers between 1960 and the late summer of 1962.[2] Campbell claimed that John Kennedy's personal relations with members of organized crime ran in direct conflict with his brother Robert's crusade to break the Mafia. In 1960, according to Campbell, there were secret contacts between Kennedy and Mob boss Sam Giancana to discuss Mafia support for his election campaign. There were also later contacts, she said, during the presidency, that "had to do with the elimination of Fidel Castro."

Campbell's account was specific in dates and details and supported by travel documents, by her annotated appointment book, and by official logs recording three of her visits to the White House. A credible source said Campbell told him the gist of her story soon after the events in question.

Finally, there was Robert Kennedy, monitoring anti-Castro operations on his brother's behalf after the failure at the Bay of Pigs. According to Sam Halpern, a former senior CIA official who worked the Cuba desk, the younger Kennedy ordered the Agency to have a case officer meet with Mafia figures. According to Halpern, Kennedy himself supplied the Mafia contacts.

President Kennedy was playing a horrendously dangerous game. For, throughout the presidency, his brother was vigorously pursuing his investigation of the Mafia—not least of Sam Giancana. As a quid pro quo for support during the election that brought Kennedy to power, Giancana and other top mobsters had evidently hoped for leniency under a Kennedy administration. By early 1962, however, Giancana would be overheard on an FBI wiretap saying, "The President will get what he wants out of you . . . but you won't get anything out of him."

If top Mafia bosses felt double-crossed, their law—the law of the Mob—might demand vengeance.

CHAPTER 14

The Mob Loses Patience

*"Mark my word, this man Kennedy is in trouble,
and he will get what is coming to him. . . . He is
going to be hit."*

—Mafia boss Santo Trafficante, late 1962

Publicly, the Kennedys' attitude toward organized crime had
been uncompromising. In 1956, Robert Kennedy, then only
thirty-one and counsel for the Senate Subcommittee on Investigations, began turning up evidence that gangsters had penetrated
the American labor movement. Some unions were already controlled by the Mob. Frightened informants told of massive sums
in union funds being diverted into private bank accounts, of
known gangsters acting as union officials, of murder and torture
inflicted on those who complained or tried to resist.

Typical of the horrors encountered was the following, taken
from Robert Kennedy's account of the inquiry:

There was the union organizer from Los Angeles who had
traveled to San Diego to organize jukebox operators. He was
told to stay out of San Diego or he would be killed. But he
returned to San Diego. He was knocked unconscious. When

he regained consciousness the next morning, he was covered with blood and had terrible pains in his stomach. The pains were so intense he was unable to drive back to his home in Los Angeles and stopped at a hospital. There was an emergency operation. The doctors removed from his backside a large cucumber. Later he was told that if he ever returned to San Diego it would be a watermelon. He never went back.

That victim was relatively lucky. Robert Kennedy's investigation was to turn up scores of killings—by multiple shooting in the face, by electrocution, by slow, excruciating torture.

Early on, the Kennedy inquiry led to the leadership of America's largest and most powerful union, the International Brotherhood of Teamsters. The Teamsters controlled the truck drivers and warehousemen nationwide, and exercised a direct influence on almost every industrial enterprise. The union was riddled with corruption, starting with its then president, Dave Beck. As the evidence piled up, a special Senate committee was assembled, with then Senator John Kennedy as a member and his brother as chief counsel. Its revelations destroyed Beck as a public figure and eventually saw him convicted and jailed for larceny and income-tax evasion. It was his successor James "Jimmy" Hoffa, though, who became the enduring focus of Kennedy prosecution and a dangerously vicious enemy.

Long before Hoffa became union president, Robert Kennedy was probing his crimes. Kennedy caught Hoffa red-handed giving a bribe to a Senate attorney, and a personal feud began. Hoffa wriggled out of the bribery case and two other charges, for perjury and wiretapping, and made no secret about how he did it. Dealing with a jury, he bragged, was "like shooting fish in a barrel." Robert Kennedy obsessed about Jimmy Hoffa, and their mutual hatred became a fact of public life. Among Hoffa's more printable descriptions of Robert Kennedy were "vicious bastard," "little monster," and "absolute spoiled brat." In the Senate Committee hearings, both Kennedy brothers clashed with Hoffa time and again, and one exchange exposed Hoffa's propensity for violence. Leaving one committee session, Hoffa was heard to mutter, "That S.O.B.—I'll break his back, the little son of a bitch." He was talking, very evidently, about Robert Kennedy.

In the 1960 Nixon-Kennedy election campaign, predictably enough, Hoffa threw his powerful union support behind Nixon. As the election approached, the Teamsters leader told a cheering audience of his members, "If it is a question, as Kennedy has said, that he will break Hoffa, then I say to him, he should live so long."

John Kennedy had appeared to share his brother's determination to cripple organized crime. Told that the Senate probe would likely implicate a powerful Democrat, Kennedy had replied, "Go back and build the best case against him that you can." His strenuous efforts in 1959 had helped push a new law governing union elections through both houses of Congress. It was bitterly attacked by union leaders, including Hoffa.

Robert Kennedy was aware from the evidence that he was up against not only union corruption but also the Mafia. He put it more carefully, referring to gangsters who "work in a highly organized fashion and are far more powerful than at any time in the history of the country. They control political figures and threaten whole communities. They have stretched their tentacles of corruption and fear into industries both large and small. They grow stronger every day."

Just before the 1960 election, the younger Kennedy's book *The Enemy Within*, his account of the struggle with Hoffa and the racketeers, became a bestseller. "No group," he wrote, "better fits the prototype of the old Al Capone syndicate than Jimmy Hoffa and some of his chief lieutenants in and out of the union. They have the look of Capone's men. . . . They have the smooth faces and cruel eyes of gangsters; they wear the same rich clothes, the diamond ring, the jeweled watch, the strong, sickly-sweet smelling perfume."

Among the names linked to Hoffa were Paul Dorfman and Barney Baker. Robert Kennedy referred to Baker as "Hoffa's ambassador of violence." Both, as this book will show, had links to Jack Ruby, the man who was to shoot Lee Oswald after the President's assassination, ensuring his silence. Robert Kennedy also spent months pursuing Sam Giancana and investigating the chain relationship that extended to Mafia bosses Meyer Lansky and Santo Trafficante.

In 1961, when his brother appointed him Attorney General, Robert Kennedy made clear that combating organized crime was to be a priority. It was, he said, a "private government . . . resting on a base of human suffering and moral corrosion." Until then, with FBI Director J. Edgar Hoover virtually denying the Mob's existence, Kennedy had been merely a thorn in the flesh of that private government. Now that he had power as the nation's top law-enforcement officer, he used it unrelentingly.

Jimmy Hoffa was a prime target. Within nine months of the election, thirteen grand juries, sixteen lawyers, and thirty FBI agents were concentrating on bringing the Teamsters leaders to justice. Kennedy's Justice Department became known as the "Get Hoffa Squad." Hoffa was indicted for taking payoffs from trucking companies, for conspiracy to defraud the trustees of the Teamsters' pension fund, and for taking illegal payments from an employer in Tennessee.

Hoffa used every trick he knew to get off the hook—including hunting for blackmail material. He would brag years later that he obtained "seamy" information that could have seriously damaged the Kennedys, and both brothers were vulnerable. Hoffa said he had compromising tape recordings of phone conversations between Robert and Marilyn Monroe, and may indeed have had such tapes. Persuasive testimony indicates that both brothers had affairs of one sort or another with the actress.[1]

It is likely that Hoffa also learned of John Kennedy's affair with Judith Campbell. At the very time she was seeing Kennedy, Campbell was being cultivated by both Mob boss Sam Giancana and by his henchman Johnny Roselli. Giancana, indeed, eventually became her lover for a while—after the relationship with Kennedy ended, she said. What was in it for Giancana, a man who had his pick of a bevy of women?

In July 1961, infuriated by the FBI surveillance ordered by the President's brother, Giancana lost his temper. "Fuck J. Edgar Hoover!" he shouted at a group of Chicago FBI agents. "Fuck your super boss, and your super super boss! You know who I mean. I mean the Kennedys! . . . I know all about the Kennedys . . . and one of these days we're going to tell all. Fuck you! One of these days it'll come out." For a top mafioso, intimacy with a mistress of the President offered potential access to information, and blackmail possibilities.

Giancana and Robert Kennedy had clashed long since, when the mobster appeared before the McClellan Committee. Thirty-three times, Giancana had pleaded the Fifth Amendment, the constitutional clause under which witnesses may refuse to give answers that might incriminate them. Kennedy had asked Giancana, "Would you tell us, if you have opposition from anybody, that you dispose of them by having them stuffed in a trunk? Is that what you do, Mr. Giancana?" Sam Giancana just pleaded the Fifth and giggled.

Brutal murder was a tool Giancana readily used. Federal investigators recorded him ordering the killing of opponents as casually as others might order a cup of coffee. The catalog of crimes linked to Giancana ranged from the old Mob method of dumping victims in rivers sealed in cement, to hanging a man on a meat hook for days until he succumbed to electric cattle prod, ice pick, and blowtorch. By this bloody path, Giancana had come to rule his own organized crime empire, an operation with an annual income reckoned at two billion dollars. By mid-1963, however, Robert Kennedy was making it difficult for Giancana to run that empire. He was the subject of blanket surveillance. FBI agents in cars sat outside his house twenty-four hours a day, every day. When Giancana went out golfing, the agents went, too.

In 1960, before the Kennedy presidency, there had been only thirty-five convictions for offenses connected with organized crime. In 1963, there were 288, a figure that doubled in the months that followed. Before the Kennedys came to power, Organized Crime Section lawyers spent 61 days in court and 660 days making investigations. In the final year of the Kennedy presidency, government lawyers fighting organized crime spent 1,081 days in court and 6,177 days in the field. "The end of an era had come," said Ralph Salerno, New York City's former chief organized crime investigator, "A tremendous financial empire was being very seriously threatened." Just how much the crime bosses and their lieutenants felt threatened is clear from wiretap surveillance transcripts.

"See what Kennedy done," Mob associate Willie Weisburg was tape-recorded saying in 1962 in a conversation with Philadelphia crime boss Angelo Bruno, "With Kennedy, a guy should take a knife, like one of them other guys, and stab and kill the fucker, where he is now. Somebody should kill the fucker. I mean it. This is true. But I tell you something. I hope I get a week's notice. I'll kill. Right in the fucking White House. Somebody's got to get rid of this fucker." That day, Bruno responded non-committally. A year later, though, he was talking of giving up and going back to his birthplace in Sicily. On another FBI tape, Bruno could be heard saying despondently, "It is all over for us; I am going to Italy, and you should go, too."

Others, of course, chose to fight rather than flee. "Organized crime had a practical motive to seek a quick end to the Kennedy administration," said Congressman—and professional historian— Floyd Fithian, following his service on the House Assassinations Committee. "The picture for organized crime was very bleak indeed. Bleak enough, in my opinion, for individual members of organized crime to seriously consider killing the President. For if John Kennedy no longer sat in the White House, it would only be a matter of time before his brother would leave the Justice Department. . . . Organized crime had the means to kill John Kennedy. It had a motive. And it had the opportunity."

The formal findings of the Assassinations Committee echo that assessment. That said, is there evidence that top criminals did plan to kill the President?

Jimmy Hoffa

By mid-1963, justice was catching up with Jimmy Hoffa. Though still managing to stay out of prison, he was now charged with conspiring to fix the jury in the Tennessee case over taking illegal payments from an employer. He would eventually be jailed, for the jury offense and for diverting a million dollars in union funds to his own use. By that time, though, Robert Kennedy would have had little taste for the victory—his brother the President would be dead. There is evidence, however, that—in 1962—Hoffa had planned to retaliate against the Kennedys with violence.

A prime witness in the Tennessee case was Edward Partin, a Teamsters official in Louisiana who gave federal investigators incriminating information on Hoffa. In the summer of 1962, Partin said, at a meeting in Hoffa's Washington office, the Teamsters leader talked of killing Robert Kennedy. According to Partin, Hoffa said: "Somebody needs to bump that son of a bitch off. . . . You know I've got a rundown on him . . . his house sits here like this [Hoffa drew with his fingers], and it's not guarded. . . . He drives about in a convertible and swims by himself. I've got a .270 rifle with a high-power scope on it that shoots a long way without dropping any. It would be easy to get him with that. But I'm leery of it; it's too obvious."

Hoffa's weapon of preference at the time, Partin said, was the bomb. "What I think should be done," he said, "if I can get hold of these plastic bombs, is to get somebody to throw one in his house and the place'll burn after it blows up. You know the S.O.B. doesn't stay up too late."

The evidence indicated he was telling the truth. According to Partin, who repeated his account to the author, Hoffa asked him to help obtain a suitable "plastic bomb" for the murder plan. Alerted by Partin, a federal investigator named Hawk Daniels listened in as Partin reported back to Hoffa in a telephone call. Daniels, who was later to become a Louisiana state judge, told the author, "Yes, there were two telephone calls, monitored by me. They originated with Partin and terminated with Hoffa on the other end of the line. Partin briefly brought up the subject of the plastic explosives and told Hoffa he had obtained the explosive Hoffa wanted. Hoffa then said, 'We'll talk about that later' and abruptly changed the subject. It was clear from the course of the conversation that he knew very well what Partin was talking about."

Daniels took Partin's warning seriously and informed the Justice Department, and law enforcement was apparently alerted to the danger. In early 1963, President Kennedy was to tell his friend Ben Bradlee, the future editor of the *Washington Post*, that a Hoffa "hoodlum" had been sent to Washington to shoot his brother. According to Partin in his interview with the author, however, the Teamsters leader "intended the death of the President as well as his brother." Other testimony suggests that Hoffa's friends in the Mafia shared his murderous intentions.

Santo Trafficante

Expulsion from Cuba and the CIA plots to kill Castro were not the only matters preoccupying Santo Trafficante. The Kennedys had dragged his name into public disrepute even before they came to power. As a result, the world had heard the director of the Miami Crime Commission define Trafficante as "the key figure in the Mafia circles of Tampa, Florida." Trafficante's Sicilian family had been discussed in the same breath as a score of gangland killings and narcotics operations. Trafficante saw his friends Hoffa and Giancana being pursued as never before. The writing was on the wall.

In 1962, according to testimony taken by the Assassinations Committee, Trafficante met at Miami's Scott-Bryant Hotel with a wealthy Cuban exile named José Alemán.[2] The subject for discussion was a million-dollar loan Trafficante was arranging, money that was to come from the Teamsters. The loan, he told Alemán, had "been cleared by Jimmy Hoffa himself."

According to Alemán, in an account he repeated at a 1978 meeting with the author, Trafficante said of the President, "Have you seen how his brother is hitting Hoffa, a man who is a worker, who is not a millionaire, a friend of the blue collars? He doesn't know that this kind of encounter is very delicate." (Hoffa was, in fact, a millionaire.) "It is not right what they are doing to Hoffa," Trafficante went on, "Hoffa is a hardworking man and does not deserve it."

In an apparent reference to the Mob's assistance in getting Kennedy elected in 1960, and the prosecutions that had followed notwithstanding, Trafficante went on to say the Kennedys were "not honest. They took graft and they did not keep a bargain. . . . Mark my word, this man Kennedy is in trouble, and he will get what is coming to him."

When Alemán disagreed, saying he thought the President was doing a good job and would be reelected to a second term, the Mafia boss replied very quietly. "You don't understand me," he said, "Kennedy's not going to make it to the election. He is going to be hit."

Trafficante, Alemán was to tell investigators, "made it clear [implicitly] that he was not guessing about the killing; rather he was giving the impression that he knew Kennedy was going to be killed." Alemán said he was "given the distinct impression that Hoffa was to be principally involved in the elimination of Kennedy."

It is clear how Alemán—at the time—interpreted Trafficante's remark that the President was "going to be hit." In his talks with investigators and in his interview with the author, it was understood that he believed "hit" meant "murder." In 1978, however, when Alemán was called to testify in public session before the Assassinations Committee, he proved hesitant and garbled his words. The words "going to be hit," he suggested at one point, could have meant merely that Trafficante thought the President was going to be defeated in the 1964 election.

Even almost two decades later, Alemán was a frightened man. The author was required to go through a complicated security routine before meeting with him. "I am very much concerned about my safety," he told the Assassinations Committee, "I sold my business. I been in my home because—I mean—Santo Trafficante can try to do anything at any moment." The Committee's Chief Counsel, Robert Blakey, said: "[We] have seen manifested in a witness that fear that is all too often characteristic of people called to testify in matters touching on organized crime. A fear that, frankly, must be recognized as justified."

At the time of his meeting with Trafficante, Alemán was already an FBI informant. He promptly reported the conversation to his Bureau contacts, he was to say, but they appeared to ignore him. In 1963, as he continued to meet with Trafficante, he told the FBI that he felt "something was going to happen. . . . I was telling them to be careful." Only when it was too late, according to Alemán, did the FBI take him seriously. On November 22, 1963, hours after the assassination of the President, agents rushed to see him.[3]

Carlos Marcello

In New Orleans, a diminutive Sicilian named Carlos Marcello had long had cause to rage against the Kennedys. Known as "the Little Man"—he was only 5'4" tall—Marcello was, with Trafficante, one of the two or three most sinister figures in the history of organized crime. Aaron Kohn, director of the New Orleans Metropolitan Crime Commission—a New Orleans citizen's group formed in response to the rampaging crime in the city—described Marcello to the author as "the most powerful single organized-crime figure in the southern United States . . . the head of the Mafia, or Costa Nostra, in this area."

During the 1930s and 1940s, Marcello had fought his way to the summit of the Mafia in his far-flung region. After an early narcotics conviction, he had always managed to place himself at several removes from crimes committed on his behalf. Unlike Santo Trafficante and Sam Giancana, he had not shown up at the 1957 Apalachin "convention," when many of his kind fell foul of law enforcement. He not only ruled his U.S. territory without serious challenge, but looked abroad for extra pickings. Before the advent of Castro, by one report, he had joined with Trafficante and Meyer Lansky in sharing the booty from Cuba.

Marcello had come to wield extraordinary influence. A list of those who actively sought clemency for him on the only federal offense for which he had in recent times been convicted—assaulting a federal agent—includes a sheriff, a former sheriff, a state legislator, two former state legislators, two former state police commanders, a president of a labor union, a bank president, two bank vice presidents, a former assistant district attorney, a chief probation officer, a former revenue agent, three insurance agents, five realtors, five doctors, a funeral director, and six clergymen. According to the Crime Commission's Aaron Kohn, Marcello had also corrupted "justices of the peace, mayors, governors . . . and at least one member of the Congress."

By the year of the Kennedy assassination, the Crime Commission estimated, the Marcello syndicate was raking in the stupendous sum of $1.114 billion annually. At today's rates, that would be around $8 billion. By one estimate, the syndicate was statistically the largest industry in the state of Louisiana, with Marcello its "midget Midas."

He, like Trafficante, was closely involved with Teamsters leader Jimmy Hoffa. When the pair got together at the height of the Kennedy-Nixon campaign, Marcello reportedly delivered $500,000 in cash for Nixon. Later, Marcello would be linked to an attempt to bribe the key prosecution witness in the Hoffa jury-tampering case.

Within three months of President Kennedy's inauguration, Marcello, too, fell victim to the Kennedy campaign against organized crime, in a way more dramatic than any other Justice Department target. For Marcello had an intractable problem, in spite of his power.

Though he had spent most of his life in the United States, Marcello had been born "Calogero Minacore"—to Sicilian parents—in Tunisia. Knowing that he faced possible deportation, he had arranged forged documentation that named his birthplace as Guatemala—at the time, a country likely to receive him kindly, and closer to his criminal empire than exile in North Africa or Europe. Nobody, however, really expected it would come to deportation.

With Robert Kennedy in the Justice Department, however, Marcello's clout counted for much less. On April 4, 1961, Marcello had been summarily arrested as he arrived to make a routine appearance at the New Orleans Immigration Department.[4] He was handcuffed, rushed to the airport, and flown to Guatemala—the solitary passenger aboard a special government jet. Later, he got back into the United States again, spirited in illegally either by boat or private plane and—with access once more to his army of lawyers and purchased favor—contrived to stay. From then on, however, Marcello remained locked in an endless legal wrangle with U.S. Immigration and with Robert Kennedy's Justice Department. Worst of all, he had been very publicly humiliated. To one of the world's top Mafia bosses, imbued with Sicilian pride, the experience had been intolerable. According to one compelling report, Marcello vowed revenge.

In autumn 1962, according to a former associate, the Mafia chief and three others convened on the mobster's three-thousand-acre estate outside New Orleans. For all his wealth, Marcello preferred on this occasion to talk in a ramshackle building that did occasional service as a hunting lodge. One of the men present was Edward Becker, whose background involved work in the casino business and undercover investigative work. Another was an oil geologist called Carl Roppolo, who hoped to bring the mobster in on a business deal. The third man there may have been a Marcello aide called Liverde. Becker is the source of the account that follows.

As the whiskey flowed, Becker said, the talk turned to Marcello's trials and tribulations under the Kennedy onslaught. As he talked of Robert Kennedy and the deportation episode, Marcello became enraged. Ranting on in his Sicilian-accented Southern drawl, he exclaimed that Robert Kennedy was "going to be taken care of."

Marcello referred to President Kennedy as a dog, Becker said, and his brother Robert was the tail. "The dog," he said, "will keep biting you if you only cut off its tail." If the dog's head were cut off, the biting would end. The meaning was clear. Were John F. Kennedy to be killed, his brother would cease to be attorney general and harassment of the Mafia would cease.

What he heard, Becker would tell the authorities repeatedly

over the years, left him in no doubt. Marcello had "clearly stated that he was going to arrange to have President Kennedy murdered in some way." The impression Becker got was that this was something Marcello had been considering for some time. On its own, the Marcello story might seem far-fetched. Taken together with the remarks attributed to his allies Trafficante and Hoffa, it is chilling. Like Alemán's account of the Trafficante threat, it, too, was reported to the FBI. Becker told his story to a former FBI agent he knew, Julian Blodgett, and Blodgett passed on the information to an FBI supervisor.

Four years after the Kennedy assassination, when Pulitzer Prize–winning author Ed Reid was researching a book on the Mafia, he, too, heard Becker's story—and the claim that he had seen to it that the information reached the FBI. When author Reid raised the matter with an FBI contact, the response was outrageous. At the personal direction of Director Hoover, the Bureau's only reaction was to cast aspersions not only on Becker's credibility, but on Reid's professional standards also.[5] The matter was dropped.

Witness Ed Becker's background was not lily white, but those who hold meetings with Mafia bosses tend not to be saints. On the credit side, it turns out that he was indeed in Louisiana at the relevant time and was apparently in business with his alleged companion, Roppolo.[6] Roppolo's family appear to have been close to Marcello, which made the alleged meeting with the Mafia leader plausible. Becker said, "Among people that came from the Old Country—Sicilians—and people that practiced the Machiavellian way of politics, it's quite common to talk about assassination, even of heads of state. I don't think it was beyond Marcello's grasp [to have the President killed]. He had the power. . . . He doesn't go around making idle statements. If he makes a statement, it's got to have some strength in it. . . . I'm saying he certainly was capable, and he certainly wanted it to happen."[7]

In 1979, the House Assassinations Committee took the account of Marcello's threat seriously. Noting the FBI's neglect in pursuing the matter, Chief Counsel Blakey declared that J. Edgar Hoover had violated his pledge to the Warren Commission that the Kennedy assassination case would remain open forever.

In considering Jimmy Hoffa's alleged menaces, the Committee noted that—not being a Mafia boss—he may not have had an apparatus capable of carrying out and covering up a crime of such enormity. Weighing the evidence of Marcello's reported threat, along with the similar reports about Hoffa and Trafficante, the Committee expressed puzzlement. Knowing Marcello's reputation for prudence and Trafficante's expertise in avoiding prosecution, it seemed odd that the Mafia bosses would have taken the risk of talking unguardedly well before the assassination.

The Committee found, however, that Trafficante and Marcello had "the motive, means, and opportunity to have President John F. Kennedy assassinated." As of 1979, Chief Counsel Blakey's personal opinion was that "the Mob did it. It is a historical truth."

As for the argument that Trafficante and Marcello put themselves at risk, the Committee noted that "any underworld attempts to assassinate the President would have indicated the use of some kind of cover, a shielding or disguise. . . . An assassination of the President by organized crime could not be allowed to appear what it was."

A further chilling element to Becker's account of the Marcello threat echoes exactly that speculation. In his very first account of the threat, he included a disturbing further detail. During the meeting on Marcello's estate, he said, the Mafia leader spoke of taking out "insurance" for the President's assassination. This he would achieve by "setting up a nut to take the blame." That, Becker has said, is "the way they do it all the time in Sicily."

The fiefdom of Carlos Marcello stretched from New Orleans and the cities of the Southeast as far inland as Dallas, in the heart of Texas. It was just months after Marcello's outburst that Lee Oswald, the man soon to earn infamy as the "lone nut" killer of President Kennedy, would arrive in New Orleans.

CHAPTER 15

Six Options for History

"My view is that there was, in fact, a relationship between the Cuban connection and the assassination . . . that more than one person was involved."

—Senator Richard Schweiker, following Senate Intelligence Committee probe, 1976

April 24, 1963. The assassination of President Kennedy was seven months away. The Texan vice president, Lyndon Johnson, had just been in Dallas predicting that the President would visit the state sometime soon. Now, on the evening of the twenty-fourth, amid the clatter of the Greyhound terminal in downtown Dallas, Lee Oswald boarded an overnight bus for New Orleans. He was returning to the city of his birth, and according to the earliest official findings, he would at once call relatives and go to stay temporarily at their home.

The details of Oswald's stay in New Orleans are important. The question around his movements at the start, for example, is underscored by the revelation that even the relatives with whom he stayed are of interest. Oswald's uncle, the Assassinations Committee established, had "worked for years in an underworld gambling syndicate affiliated with the Carlos Marcello crime family." It is a fact that will receive scrutiny later in this narrative. As the investigator picks his way through a minefield of clues, he must decide time and again whether he is dealing with coincidence or conspiracy.

The common denominator of Oswald's apparent activities and connections in the months before the assassination is Cuba. Oswald's is a shadowy image, now in focus in predictable pro-Castro colors, now flickering into sight in the improbable company of anti-Castro exiles and their allies in the ranks of both the Mafia and the world of intelligence. This multiple image of the alleged assassin leads us from New Orleans to the eve of President Kennedy's murder, leaving a trail of seeming contradictions.

There are six main lines of assassination theory.

1. Oswald did it on his own.

That was the Warren Commission version. For all the problems in the story, Oswald was a lone gunman with no clearly definable motive. He killed the President, the Commission suggested, because he hated American society, was a pro-Castro leftist, and sought a place for himself in history.

2. The Soviets did it.

This notion, based on virtually no evidence—and posited by only the odd eccentric—holds that Oswald was a cog in a plot conceived in Moscow. Though Oswald had surely been of interest to Soviet intelligence at the time of his 1959 defection, following his service in the Marine Corps, nothing at all suggests that the Soviets desired President Kennedy's death. Had they done so, the likely consequences, if detected, would have been deterrent enough. Neither the Warren Commission nor the Assassinations Committee thought Moscow had any part in the assassination.[1]

3. Castro's Cuba did it.

The theory that Communist Cuba was behind the tragedy has received serious attention over the years and still has adherents. The central reasoning behind the notion is that the assassination was a preemptive strike. Fidel Castro, or an element of Cuban intelligence, learned of CIA efforts to kill Castro and decided to strike first.

Kennedy's successor, President Johnson, for a time shared this suspicion, having learned of the CIA plots and in light of stories linking Oswald to Castro's agents. Johnson swung back and forth, however, between suspecting Castro, or some part of U.S. intelligence, or even a South Vietnamese faction.

There is nothing in the Warren Report about the U.S. plots to kill Castro.[2] The notion that Castro might have been responsible for the President's death was nevertheless taken seriously—so seriously that Chief Justice Warren dispatched counsel William Coleman on a secret mission. Coleman, who has spoken of the trip privately, was closemouthed when the author asked him about the assignment in 1994. "I can't talk," he said. "It was top secret." Asked to confirm or deny that he met Castro, he said: "No comment."

What Coleman did say is that the mission helped convince him that Castro had nothing to do with the President's death. The Warren Commission Report, and that of the House Assassinations Committee, took the same view.

One experienced investigative journalist, meanwhile, has

argued that Castro "had little to lose, and everything to gain, by pushing Oswald's buttons . . . by merely suggesting through underlings that Cuba's leader would appreciate his efforts." Another author, himself a former analyst on the CIA's Cuba desk, suggested in a 2012 book that—though he may have played no active role—Castro may have had advance knowledge of an intention by Oswald to kill the President, and simply let it happen.[3]

It seems to this author that for Castro to have risked provoking a devastating American revenge attack would have been suicidal folly. A greater insanity would have been to use a known pro-Castro activist like Oswald, whose involvement would point to Havana. Nevertheless, this book will report the allegations that Castro had a hand in killing the President.[4]

4. Anti-Castro elements did it, setting Oswald up.

This theory holds that Oswald was the confused leftist crank he appeared to be all along. He arrived in New Orleans and paraded his pro-Castro ideas, attracting the malign attention of anti-Castro militants linked to the Mafia—and to the CIA—in the struggle to overturn the Castro revolution. For such people, joined in their rage against the Kennedys—so goes the theory—the leftist Oswald was a perfect patsy. Wittingly or unwittingly, perhaps believing that he had found friends and allies for the first time in his life, Oswald was drawn into a plot to kill the President. In any version of this scenario, Oswald was set up to take solitary blame.

5. The Mafia did it.

The House Assassinations Committee Report said Mafia members may have been involved, and Chief Counsel Robert Blakey went further in a book published two years later. The evidence, he wrote, "established that organized crime was behind the plot to kill John F. Kennedy." While conceding that others may have worked alongside the mobsters, he did not waver in that view in the years that followed.[5]

In 2008, in a study written with access to information not earlier available, a historian and professor at the Naval War College, Dr. David Kaiser, agreed with Blakey. There was a conspiracy, he wrote, and the Mafia was involved.[6]

As will be shown in this narrative, one of the suspect Mafia bosses—Carlos Marcello of New Orleans—is alleged to have acknowledged his part in the assassination in old age.

6. An element of U.S. Intelligence was somehow involved.

This derives from the suspicion that Oswald became some sort of low-level tool of American intelligence at some point. Unable to credit the overt account of Oswald's improbable career as a Marxist marine, suspicious of the CIA's supposed lack of reaction to his Soviet odyssey, some have seen Oswald's leftist stance as merely a meticulously cultivated front. An alternative speculation is that—perhaps as an alternative to being prosecuted on his return to the United States—Oswald was pressured into allowing himself to be manipulated by American intelligence. Other variations of the speculation posit that he may not have known he was being manipulated. Or simply that, even if not complicit in the assassination, elements of U.S. intelligence were somehow compromised and—after the assassination— covered up.

These suspicions are not the unique preserve of paranoid minds. Representative Don Edwards, a former FBI agent, concluded in 1976—based on his work as chairman of the Constitutional Rights Subcommittee—that the FBI and the CIA were "somewhere behind this cover-up." Also in 1976, after more than a year of research, two U.S. senators came to troubling conclusions about Lee Oswald.

Democrat Gary Hart and Republican Richard Schweiker were assigned by the Senate Intelligence Committee to study CIA and FBI responses to the assassination. Following his privileged access to some classified files, and after the frustration of not being allowed to see others, Senator Hart expressed himself appalled. He commented bleakly, "I don't think you can see the things I have seen and sit on it . . . knowing what I know."

Hart rated the FBI and CIA investigation of Oswald's Cuba-related activity "C-minus." Then, referring directly to Oswald's time in New Orleans, the Senator raised questions more disturbing than mere inefficiency. He called for further investigation into "who Oswald really was—who did he know? What affiliation did he have in the Cuba network? Was his public identification with the Left a cover for a connection with the anti-Castro Right?" Finally, Hart declared his considered opinion that Lee Oswald was "sophisticated" enough to have acted as a "double agent."

Senator Schweiker was even more outspoken. In an interview with the author, he said, "the Warren Commission has collapsed like a house of cards. I believe that the Warren Commission was set up at the time to feed pabulum to the American people for reasons not yet known, and that one of the biggest cover-ups in the history of our country occurred at that time."

Of Oswald's role in New Orleans, Schweiker said, "I think that by playing a pro-Castro role on the one hand and associating with anti-Castro Cubans on the other, Oswald was playing

out an intelligence role. This gets back to him being an agent
or double agent. . . . I personally believe that he had a special
relationship with one of the Intelligence agencies. Which one,
I'm not certain. But all the fingerprints I found during my eighteen months on the Senate Select Committee on Intelligence
point to Oswald as being a product of, and interacting with, the
intelligence community."

It was the Hart/Schweiker inquiry that led to the establishment by Congress of the Assassinations Committee, which was
to startle America with its "probable conspiracy" verdict and
the credence it gave to a second gunman having been at work.
Its Final Report tentatively concluded that anti-Castro Cuba
groups were not—"as groups"—involved in the assassination.
On the other hand, individual group members may have been.

Some staffers on the Committee also ended their two-year
investigation convinced that Oswald was some sort of low-level
intelligence agent. The most vocal of them, Gaeton Fonzi, became
convinced that Oswald had an "association with the CIA" and
contacts "with a number of Agency assets." In a 1993 book, he
named a specific CIA officer, David Phillips, as having "played a
key role in the conspiracy to assassinate President Kennedy."[7]

Others have suspected that U.S. intelligence covered up something involving Oswald, without necessarily having had any part
in the assassination. "We can finally say with some authority,"
a former U.S. Army intelligence analyst wrote in 1995, "that
the CIA was spawning a web of deception about Oswald weeks
before the President's murder." Deception over some covert
operation unconnected to the assassination, or deception mask-
ing the hand of U.S. intelligence operatives in the murder? In
the former analyst's view, we do not yet have "enough of the
pieces" to answer that heaviest of questions.[8]

Another author, a former *Washington Post* journalist, came away from a study of the last weeks before the assassination suspecting that the CIA had indeed been running "a closely held operation involving Oswald." He is convinced that the available evidence shows that senior CIA officers were knowledgeable about Oswald's activity and state of mind, failed to flag him for special attention—which made them "criminally negligent"—then covered it up.[9]

The public was burdened with no such options in the aftermath of the Kennedy assassination. Lee Oswald was firmly labeled a disciple of the extreme Left who had acted alone. Was the verdict just, or were Oswald and his apparent heroes victims of a vicious double-cross by forces of the extreme Right? If an answer is to be found, it lies in the evidence of the months that immediately preceded the assassination, much of it omitted or underplayed by the Warren Commission. It was then grossly distorted by a fiasco of an investigation, and a circus of a trial, led by New Orleans District Attorney Jim Garrison in 1967.

The evidence survives thanks to decades of work by congressional committees and independent researchers, and was further illuminated by the release of more documentation in the 1990s. As the Assassinations Committee's Chief Counsel, Robert Blakey, put it, the Committee provided a road map that pointed to New Orleans as the point of departure for further investigation. It may fairly be called a labyrinth rather than a road map, a maze that leads to Dealey Plaza.

Somewhere, deep in the labyrinth, lies the truth about Lee Oswald.

CHAPTER 16

Viva Fidel?

"The fact that Oswald was a member of this organi-
zation . . . the Fair Play for Cuba Committee . . . is
a fact that can be viewed from many different ways."

—Wesley Liebeler, Warren Commission lawyer
assigned to Cuban aspects of the assassination

Cuba, of course, had first loomed as significant in Oswald's
life years earlier—before even his Soviet Russia period. There
had been his shared enthusiasm—with his Marine Corps comrade Nelson Delgado—for the Castro revolution, his comment
that he had made contact with Cuban diplomats, and the visit
he had from a man Delgado believed was Cuban. Cuba—and
whether Oswald's public posture was genuine or part of a false
front involving other schemers—is at the heart of the puzzles
surrounding Oswald's stay in New Orleans.

In the spring of 1963 in Dallas, days before leaving for
New Orleans, Lee Harvey Oswald wrote a letter to the Fair
Play for Cuba Committee (FPCC)—a pro-Castro organization headquartered in New York. In his unmistakable scrawl,
peppered as it often was with the evidence of his mild dyslexia, Oswald reported:

"I stood yesterday for the first time in my life, with a placare around my neck, passing out fair play for Cuba pamplets ect. . . . I was cursed as well as praised by some. My homemade placard said: Hands Off Cuba! Viva Fidel! I now ask for 40 or 50 more of the fine, basic pamplets."

Indeed, two Dallas policemen would remember having seen a man standing on Main Street wearing a pro-Castro sign and handing out leaflets. A 1962 envelope, found among Oswald's possessions after the assassination, would show that he had received correspondence from the FPCC since soon after his return from Russia. Documents, meanwhile, show that the FBI— which was intercepting the FPCC's mail—was aware of Oswald's letter to the group three days before he left for New Orleans. This may be very significant.

Once in New Orleans, Oswald took a job as maintenance man with a coffee production company, found an apartment, and summoned his wife, Marina, to come from Dallas to join him. Then, in late May, he embarked in earnest on the pro-Castro posturing that was to occupy the entire summer. In a new letter to the Fair Play for Cuba Committee, he said he was planning to set up a branch in New Orleans. He asked for advice on tactics, a bulk delivery of propaganda material, and application forms for the members he hoped to recruit. He confided, too, that he was "thinking about renting a small office at my own expense." That detail was to take on special significance.

The director of the FPCC replied promptly and politely, advising caution. In overwhelmingly conservative New Orleans, he pointed out, pro-Castro efforts faced serious obstacles. The director warned Oswald against provoking "unnecessary incidents which frighten away prospective sup-porters." Oswald was to ignore the advice. Pro-Castro agitation was so important and pressing for him, it seemed, that he did not even wait for the response from New York or for the lit-erature he had requested. He appeared to have his own plan and purpose.

Within days, according to the Warren Commission, he was at the Jones Printing Company near his place of work, ordering a thousand copies of a leaflet in support of Castro.[1] He used the name "Osborne" when placing the order, and again days later, at Mailer's Service Company, to order five hundred applica-tion forms for prospective FPCC members and three hundred membership cards. Copies of the leaflets were to survive their distribution. Some bore Oswald's own name and address and—on occasion—his post-office box number but a different name, "Hidell." There, too, in the space for "President" on one of the New Orleans FPCC cards, was the handwritten name "A. J. Hidell"—the name in which the infamous Mannlicher-Carcano had been ordered.[2] According to an officer who testified to the Assassinations Committee, an Army Intelligence file would be opened—while Oswald was in New Orleans—under the names Oswald and Hidell.

The FPCC "chapter" in New Orleans was entirely fictional. Lee Oswald was the sole member of a group that existed only on paper, but it was a role he exploited to the full. He wrote to *The Worker*, the Communist newspaper to which he had long subscribed, enclosing "honorary membership" cards for Gus Hall and Benjamin Davis, the leaders of the American Com-munist Party. Then he sallied forth to tout the Castro cause in public.

On June 16, Oswald was seen on the dock at the port of

New Orleans, handing out pro-Castro leaflets to sailors from an aircraft carrier, the USS *Wasp*. Like the previous propaganda distribution in Dallas, this effort quickly fizzled. Alerted by a passing naval officer, a policeman ordered Oswald to leave.

Then, for nearly two months it was as if his feverish preparations, the accumulation of a mass of propaganda, had all been for nothing, as though Lee Oswald had lost interest in Cuba. He read a lot, but books about communism were in a minority. A later FBI check on Oswald's library visits would show that he dabbled in everything from *Everyday Life in Ancient Rome* and *Hornblower and the Hotspur* to James Bond, Aldous Huxley, and science fiction. He also read *Profiles in Courage*, by John F. Kennedy, and a new book about Kennedy, *Portrait of a President*. The Kennedy books, however, were just two of twenty-seven books Oswald read that summer. He read no library books at all about Cuba.

In July, Oswald went with his uncle Charles Murret to a Jesuit seminary in Mobile, Alabama, where his cousin Eugene was studying. At the cousin's request, he gave a talk on his experiences in the Soviet Union in which he made clear that Soviet-style communism was in his view a dismal failure. Life in Russia, Oswald said, was not for him. Meanwhile, to others, he was asserting exactly the opposite.

Privately, both Oswald and his wife had been keeping up their correspondence with the Soviet Embassy in Washington, DC, supposedly still planning the return to Russia that had first been mooted in Dallas. Both asked for visas, although the correspondence suggests Oswald wanted Marina to go back to Russia by herself.

Oswald the Castro activist, meanwhile, had merely been put on ice. In August, three months before the Kennedy assassination, he again leaped purposefully into action. From this moment on, nobody could fail to remember Lee Oswald and his loyalty to Fidel Castro. What follows is the conventional account.

On August 5, Oswald ventured into what was supposedly the enemy camp. He paid a visit to a New Orleans store owned by Carlos Bringuier, a fanatically anti-Castro militant playing an active role in the struggle to remove Castro. According to Bringuier and his companions, Oswald came in unannounced, struck up a conversation, and posed as a friend of the exiles. He presented himself, they would allege later, as a Marine Corps veteran who had experience in guerrilla warfare and was willing to train exiles, even take part in the armed struggle against Castro.

The following day, the exiles' story goes, Oswald was back at the store again, still trumpeting the very opposite of his usual pro-Castro creed. This time, he left a Marine Corps manual as proof of his qualifications, and departed repeating his desire to fight Castro. Then, just three days later, he turned up in downtown New Orleans, coolly handing out *pro*-Castro leaflets (see Photos 18, 19).

Carlos Bringuier, supposedly tipped off by a friend, angrily accosted Oswald in the city center. The Cuban harangued passersby, telling them how Oswald the Communist had earlier deceitfully offered support to the exiles. A crowd gathered, and Bringuier made a great show of losing his temper with Oswald. Things appeared to turn ugly, and the police intervened. Oswald, along with Bringuier and two of his friends, was taken to a police station and charged with disturbing the peace.

The officers at the police station sensed something phony, and their comments are interesting. Lieutenant Francis Martello was to say of Oswald, "He seemed to have them set up to create an incident." Sergeant Horace Austin, for his part, said that Oswald "appeared as though he is being used by these people and [was] very uninformed." Who, though, was using whom?

A rational explanation is that Oswald deliberately provoked a dispute as part of a scheme to establish his credentials as a Castro supporter more firmly—and his subsequent actions were to support that idea. Oswald was now engaged in advertisements for himself.

The day after the clash with the exiles, Oswald approached the city editor of the *States-Item* newspaper, cajoling him to give more coverage to the FPCC campaign. Three days later, he reportedly went so far as to telephone a prominent New York radio journalist, Long John Nebel, offering to appear on Nebel's radio show at his own expense.

Then, exactly a week after the incident involving the exiles, Oswald contrived another scene in the street. On the morning of August 16, he went to the waiting room of a state employ- ment office and offered two dollars each to anyone who would help him hand out leaflets, "for a few minutes at noon." He found a recruit, a student named Charles Steele, and—along with another man who has never been identified—they duly passed out pro-Castro leaflets outside the International Trade Mart.

The leafleting lasted only a few minutes, but in that brief space of time, Oswald's demonstration was filmed by a unit from the local TV station WDSU. The pictures survive, haunting images of a slender, clean-cut young man, a hint of a smile on his lips, diffidently dispensing propaganda to passersby. Oswald's effort brought the publicity he was courting.

Within a day, a local radio station broadcast an interview with him about Cuba and the FPCC. A few days after that, he took part in a lengthy broadcast debate about Cuba. The debate was a spirited duel with Ed Butler, director of a virulently anti-communist organization called the Information Council of the Americas, and Carlos Bringuier, the anti-Castro exile who had been Oswald's principal opponent in the street fracas. Oswald handled himself well and was articulate. His opponents, though, had somehow found out about Oswald's defection to the Soviet Union, and the main effect of the program was to expose Oswald as a Communist.

Then Oswald's public pro-Castro activity ended again. He would never again venture out in support of the Castro regime. He did not need to, for now he was indelibly stamped as a Castro militant. Oswald had successfully carried out part of some sort of a plan. But what plan?

The Warren Commission was to offer one rationale. Oswald was preoccupied with hopes of getting to Cuba, the Commission thought, and his antics in New Orleans were perhaps aimed at acquiring ideological qualifications that would make him acceptable to Havana. On its face, the evidence available at the time seemed to support that conclusion. In the period between the New Orleans phase and the assassination, Oswald was—as we shall see—to go through the motions of trying to get clearance from the Cubans to go to Havana. First appearances, though may well deceive.

Telltale clues, few of them known to the first official inquiry, may suggest Oswald was part of a covert intelligence scheme that involved Cuba and was designed to *discredit* supporters of the Castro regime. Consider again the story of Oswald's New Orleans FPCC campaign.

*   *   *

On August 1, Oswald mailed a new letter to the FPCC in which he reported his energetic activity in aid of the Castro cause. In this progress report—complete with the customary spelling errors—Oswald wrote, "Through the efforts of some exial 'gusanos' [an abusive nickname for anti-Castro militants, meaning "worms"] a street demonstration was attacked and we were officially cautioned by police. This incident robbed me of what support I had leaving me alone. Nevertheless thousands of circulars were distrubed and many, many pamplets which your office supplied."

Oswald was telling the story of the incident in which he had clashed with his supposed natural rivals, the anti-Castro militants of New Orleans. There is just one problem. No such incident is known to have occurred until almost a week *after* Oswald reported it to the FPCC. Was the whole episode as phony as Oswald's prophetic letter?

The confrontation with the exiles sounds oddly stagy. By Carlos Bringuier's account, when he and his cronies cursed Oswald and threw some of his leaflets up in the air, Oswald's reaction was to smile. Bringuier was to say he then took off his glasses and prepared to hit Oswald. Oswald went on smiling and said, "Okay, Carlos, if you want to hit me, hit me." There was no fight. Later, after all the participants had been charged with disturbing the peace, the case came up in the municipal court. In a decision that may say something about the conservative attitudes of New Orleans in 1963, Oswald was fined ten dollars while charges against Bringuier and his associates, the people who had actually started the fracas, were dismissed.

That scenario is odd but possible. What sticks in the throat is Bringuier's account of Oswald's behavior a couple of days before the incident—his contradictory visit to offer his services as a military instructor to the anti-Castro side. Had this been a deliberate move to draw attention to himself, to provoke the exiles into attacking his impending street demonstration? This is really the only explanation that even begins to resolve the contradiction. In the end, however, it does not bear scrutiny.

Oswald could not have known the approach to the exiles would bear fruit, that one of their number would—just by luck—happen to notice his pro-Castro leafleting, call reinforcements, and make a counter-demonstration. The implausibility of the visit to Bringuier's store, coupled to the fact that Oswald apparently reported the incident to the FPCC before it occurred, suggests the whole affair may have been a charade. If so, what purpose did it serve?

The conventional explanation—that the incident was rigged to give Oswald impressive pro-Castro credentials—may be half the answer. The other half, usually ignored, is that the FPCC incident was a solid propaganda coup for the *anti*-Castro side. First there was the street encounter itself, when Bringuier was able to "expose" Oswald as a "traitor to this country," a man who had tried to double-cross the exiles. Then, with attention once attracted by the arrests and the subsequent court case, there was an excuse for the real propaganda show—the broadcasts on radio and television. Now, before a large audience, FPCC's New Orleans representative could be dramatically exposed as a Marxist convert who had defected to Russia. Bringuier, moreover, who was ever eager to resort to Congress' Committee on Un-American Activities, then called on his supporters to ask their congressmen for a full investigation of the treacherous Communist Lee Oswald.

As likely as not, Oswald's apparent clash with the exiles was a staged propaganda operation—the sort of seemingly harmless trick that could be pulled, with variations, all over the United States. By 1963 the FBI, the CIA, and U.S. Army Intelligence were engaged in precisely such clandestine operations against numerous left-wing organizations. In the FPCC's case, there had long been a sustained effort not merely to penetrate and spy on the group, but to damage and discredit it.

"We did everything we could to make sure it was not successful," Joseph Smith, a former CIA Clandestine Services officer, told the author, "to smear it, and I think to penetrate it."

Outsiders knew little of this until the Senate Intelligence Committee probe of 1976, and much may still remain hidden. One document the Senate published, an FBI memo written in September 1963, shows that such operations had been going on almost as long as the FPCC had existed. The memo concluded:

> We have in the past utilized techniques with respect to countering activities of mentioned organization in the U.S. During December 1961, [FBI] New York prepared an anonymous leaflet which was mailed to selected FPCC members throughout the country for the purpose of disrupting FPCC and causing split between FPCC and its Socialist Workers Party (SWP) supporters, which technique was very effective. Also during May 1961, a field survey was completed wherein available public source data of adverse nature regarding officers and leaders of FPCC was compiled and furnished [FBI executive] Mr. DeLoach for use in contacting his sources.

Other documents show that the CIA had penetrated the FPCC with its own agents, who supplied the Agency with photographs of documents and correspondence purloined from FPCC files. Army Intelligence, too, had "operational interest" in leftist groups, including the FPCC. The Intelligence Committee discovered at least one case in which a government informant had been "fronting" as a Castro supporter while remaining an approved source of Army Intelligence.

These were facts that the FBI, the CIA, and Army Intelligence would fail to share with the Warren Commission. The Army Intelligence role is especially troubling because of the revelation that the Defense Department, which once had a file on Oswald and Hidell, destroyed it. Congressman Preyer, a Committee member, told the author he thought the destruction of the file "malicious." The U.S. Army's action, the Assassinations Committee's Report noted, made it impossible to resolve from documentary evidence whether Oswald had an "affiliation with military intelligence."

In 1963, Army Intelligence controlled more agents, and was funded almost as well, as the CIA. As Congressman Preyer observed, it emerged in the 1970s that the Army had long been conducting surveillance and keeping files on thousands of private U.S. citizens. All this was done in the name of national security, and prime targets were dissident leftists of the kind Oswald publicly appeared to be. Once this invasion of privacy had been exposed, files hopefully were—as Congressman Preyer surmised—destroyed to protect the rights of the citizens who had been spied on. Probably, however, the same housecleaning operation also removed traces of how the Army's spying had been conducted and who had been doing it. Something of how the system worked had, however, gotten into the press as early as 1963.

One newspaper article, ironically published in Dallas,

Texas, had outlined exactly how somebody like Oswald could have been used. It stated that military intelligence teams from the U.S. Army, Navy, and Air Force—working in cities across America in liaison with the FBI and the police—were assigned to guard against "subversives seeking to harm the nation's security." One way of doing it, the article added, was to penetrate "subversive" groups. This was being done by undercover agents who had "actually joined these groups to get names, addresses, past activities, and future plans, or have established networks of informants to accomplish the same result. . . . Often one small tip from an individual has meant bringing the pieces together for some Intelligence agency."

This information appeared in the first week of August 1963, the very week that, in New Orleans, Lee Oswald, and Carlos Bringuier engaged in that unconvincing fracas over the FPCC. Other records show that Army Intelligence was deeply involved in monitoring domestic activity involving Cuba. Against that background, and with the knowledge that Army Intelligence destroyed its "Oswald-Hidell" records, it certainly seems possible that Oswald may have been part of an intelligence operation.

If so, was he being spied upon, or was he himself engaged in an intelligence game? The speculation is justified not least because—buried in the text of a congressional report, long ignored—lies a story and a personality remarkably similar to Oswald's.

In November 1963, just four days before the Kennedy assassination, a young man called John Glenn appeared before the House Committee on Un-American Activities. Questioning revealed that he had joined the Fair Play for Cuba Committee in autumn 1962 and had tried to visit Cuba, at first by traveling through Mexico. Then in summer 1963, at the very time Oswald was active in New Orleans, Glenn did reach Cuba, and—having outstayed his original visa—tried to travel on to Algeria, another citadel of the Left. The parallels with Oswald are numerous. Just as Oswald's fare home from Russia had once been paid by the State Department, so Glenn's was paid from Europe. Like Oswald, Glenn used a post-office box as a mailing address and subscribed to *The Militant*. Like Oswald, he had previously traveled to the Soviet Union and Eastern Europe, in his case supposedly as a guide for an American "travel agency."

It remains possible that Glenn was a genuine supporter of leftist causes, but his background is suggestive. He had abruptly interrupted his university career to join the U.S. Air Force, where he became an intelligence operative. He received a "Crypto" clearance and studied Russian. His career as a leftist began soon after he left Air Force Intelligence. The result of his foray to Cuba was an appearance before the House Un-American Activities Committee that smeared the FPCC as a Communist front organization.

Whether or not Glenn was an authentic leftist or a plant, a released document relating to an FBI informant in July 1963 makes it entirely clear that penetration operations were taking place. It reads:

> [T]he undersigned went to New York . . . to brief an FBI informant who is going to Cuba for two weeks. . . . He has been under FBI control for nearly [three] years penetrating the three pro-Castro organizations in NYC: the Fair Play for Cuba Committee (FPCC); the Casa Cuba, and the José Martí Club. . . . [I]n the last six months, he has become a

valuable penetration for the FBI. . . . He has the appearance and other attributes . . . for the role of pro-Castro revolutionary. The Cubans have expressed an interest in his moving to Cuba to work.

Once Oswald had been exposed as a former defector to Russia, anti-Castro militant Carlos Bringuier also issued a shrill call for a congressional inquiry into Oswald's activities, just as there had been into Glenn's. While we cannot draw firm conclusions, the similarities between Glenn and Oswald are very striking. Meanwhile, several pieces of information about the New Orleans affair—at one time unknown or unexplained—fit neatly into the scenario of deliberate subversion against the FPCC.

Bringuier was New Orleans delegate of the Directorio Revolucionario Estudiantil (DRE)—an exile group that had been deeply involved with the CIA since the Bay of Pigs, and would continue to be so involved until years after President Kennedy's assassination. Another former DRE leader, Isidor Borja, would tell the Assassinations Committee that he "recalled Bringuier's contact with Oswald and the fact that *the DRE relayed that information to the CIA at the time* [author's emphasis]."

The CIA's Howard Hunt, in testimony to the Assassinations Committee, said the DRE had been "run" for the Agency by David Phillips, a senior CIA officer who, for reasons that will become clear as the story unfolds, likely knew more about Oswald than he ever revealed.

The fingerprints of Intelligence activity mark every stage of the process by which Oswald was exposed as a Communist. Little about that, it seems, was spontaneous. First, Bringuier got the ball rolling with a call to William Stuckey, a young New Orleans reporter who had a weekly radio program on station WDSU. Stuckey recorded and broadcast his initial interview with Oswald—one that he was later to recall as having been oddly "deliberate"—then began to arrange the follow-up television debate.

What ensued was a classic case of media manipulation for political profit. Stuckey found himself showered with information guaranteed to smear Oswald. First, according to Stuckey, the Special Agent in Charge of the local FBI office, Harry Maynor, obligingly read out large extracts from Oswald's file to him over the phone. That, Stuckey was to say, was how he learned of Oswald's earlier defection to the Soviet Union. It was not the tight-lipped response a journalist might normally have expected from the Bureau, and Stuckey wondered later whether he had been set up.[3]

The DRE's Bringuier also eagerly pressed similar information on the reporter—information he had obtained, he said, by sending Carlos Quiroga, an exile associate posing as a Castro sympathizer, to see Oswald. Quiroga, a CIA memorandum shows, was "a candidate for the CIA Student Recruitment Program, designed to recruit Cuban students to return to Cuba as agents in place."

Finally, the same day, Stuckey received a call from Edward Butler, executive director of a right-wing propaganda organization called the Information Council of the Americas (INCA). He told Stuckey that, following his own calls to Washington, he had confirmed Oswald's Soviet connection with "someone at the House Un-American Activities Committee." CIA records show that the CIA had repeated contacts with Butler in the 1960s. A 1965 document would describe him as a "very cooperative source and seems to . . . welcome any opportunity to assist the CIA." His production manager at INCA in the summer of 1963, meanwhile, was a member of the Cuban Revolutionary Council, the anti-Castro government-in-exile the CIA had created.

The outcome of the Oswald radio debate was a foregone conclusion. Oswald, Communist and traitor, was duly ambushed on the air. After the assassination, the story of the exposé was laid out for the public in the Warren Report—without the details about how Stuckey had been primed and by whom. INCA's man Butler was never summoned to be asked about the "someone" in Washington who had told him of Oswald's defection to the Soviet Union. Nor was Carlos Quiroga.

The FBI record of its contact with Stuckey suggests that he gave the Bureau information about Oswald, rather than the other way around. This is one of a series of disquieting inconsistencies that raise questions about FBI probity—pointers, once again, that may suggest American intelligence agencies had some special knowledge that tempered their handling of the Oswald case.

First there is the contact between Oswald and the FBI of August 10, following the fracas with Carlos Bringuier. In custody at the New Orleans police station, Oswald had taken the initiative of asking to see someone from the FBI, an organization he supposedly detested. He asked and the FBI obliged. For an hour and a half, Special Agent John Quigley sat talking with Oswald in the New Orleans police station.

According to Quigley, he had gone to the police station unbriefed, with no knowledge of Oswald's history. "I did not know who this individual was at the time," he would testify to the Warren Commission. Yet in 1961, during Oswald's time as a defector to the Soviet Union, his U.S. Navy file had been reviewed by the FBI in New Orleans, the city of his birth—by Agent Quigley.

A contemporary report by Quigley may tell us why Oswald may have wanted to see an FBI agent after the clash with Bringuier. Quigley noted that he had been contacted by a police intelligence officer who "said that Oswald was desirous of see-ing an agent and *supplying to him information with regard to his activities with the FPCC in New Orleans* [author's emphasis]." Quigley's report of what Oswald told him was not included in any reports to FBI headquarters, field offices, or other agen-cies, for two months to come—until after Oswald had made the pre-assassination trip to Mexico that was in time to become so controversial.

The performance of the New Orleans FBI office was patchy in other ways. As the Senate Intelligence Committee noted with puzzlement, the FBI had closed its security case on Oswald in late 1962—even though mail intercepts had revealed his contacts with the newspaper *The Worker*. This was a communist contact, in FBI terms, and should have justified the prompt reopening of the file.[4] Likewise, the record suggests that in April 1963, when FBI intelligence revealed that Oswald was in touch with the Fair Play for Cuba Committee—a major target of both the FBI and the CIA—nobody at Bureau headquarters reacted.

In August, when Oswald made news with his New Orleans street activities, FBI headquarters did ask the New Orleans office to investigate and report in full. Yet no report was sent until more than two months later, and it would be oddly uninforma-tive. The paper record does not reflect the attention the FBI in fact paid to Oswald, according to witnesses interviewed by the author.

Oswald's landlady in New Orleans, Nina Garner, said FBI agent Milton Kaack questioned her about Oswald within three weeks of his arrival in New Orleans. FBI director Hoover would tell the Warren Commission that he had obtained affidavits from every agent who had been in contact with Oswald, or who might have had knowledge of an attempt to recruit Oswald as an informant. In fact, two agents who had been involved in pre-assassination inquiries into Oswald's activity signed no such affidavits. One of them was New Orleans' Milton Kaack.

When the author contacted Kaack in retirement years later, the agent became more apoplectic than any of the many law enforcement agents the author had previously interviewed . He cried, "No! No! . . . You won't get anything out of me," and hung up.[5]

A story that the alleged assassin was a paid informant, with a payroll number, had been one of the first problems faced by the Warren Commission. The Assassinations Committee, for its part, considered allegations that Oswald had had some sort of relationship with the FBI while in New Orleans.

There was the claim of Orest Pena, a New Orleans bar owner who in 1963 himself supplied occasional information to FBI agent Warren De Brueys.[6] Pena was to say he had seen Oswald with Agent De Brueys on "numerous occasions" and that De Brueys threatened him physically before his Warren Commission appearance, warning him to keep quiet. Former agent De Brueys repeatedly denied Pena's accusation, and the Assassinations Committee believed him. Though the author also found De Brueys credible, interviews with Pena gave the impression that he produced his accusation about the FBI contact to hide some different but relevant truth.

Pena was active in anti-Castro exile politics and deeply involved with the Cuban Revolutionary Council. When Carlos Bringuier was arrested after the fracas with Oswald, it was Orest Pena who secured his release. In that sense, he was well placed to have information on the Oswald's activity. In his interviews for this book, meanwhile, he insisted that he knew Oswald had been working "for a government agency" in the summer of 1963.[7]

In 1994, the author tracked down a former FBI informant—documented as such—who said he learned that Oswald was indeed used by the FBI in New Orleans.

Joseph Burton, who—at the time of the author's interview—was running a locksmith's business in Plant City, Florida, said he was employed by the FBI for two years in the early 1970s to pose as a Marxist and infiltrate radical groups. He was sometimes accompanied by a woman from New Orleans, also an FBI asset.

The Bureau has admitted that Burton was "a valuable and reliable source" and was paid for his services. A senior official confirmed to the *New York Times* that the woman, whose name was not revealed, performed missions abroad for the FBI.

"I did several trips with her," Burton told the author, "and she said she and her husband—they were both working for the Bureau—knew Oswald had been connected with the FBI in the New Orleans office. Her Bureau contact, she said, told her Oswald had been an informant. . . . I talked about Oswald with the agent I usually met with in New Orleans. And he said, 'Oh, we owned him,' or something to that effect. They always used that statement if they were paying someone to cooperate with them."

The totality of the information about Oswald's activity in New Orleans justifies real suspicion that Oswald was wittingly or unwittingly manipulated by a government agency. The information fits with the FBI's Counterintellingence Program (COINTELPRO), instituted a few years earlier specifically to discredit and disable groups that were seen as subversive.

High on the COINTELPRO target list, along with the Communist Party and—less predictably—the National Association for the Advancement of Colored People (NAACP) and the Committee for a Sane Nuclear Policy (SANE), was the Fair Play for Cuba Committee.

COINTELPRO tactics called for spreading adverse publicity about groups and their members—not least by feeding potential smear information to cooperative journalists—and by setting up phony chapters of targeted organizations. By late 1963, a senior FBI official would report that "aggressive FBI investigation of the organization, coupled with an effective campaign of exposure of subversive influences in the group by the public press," had been highly successful against the FPCC.

"The episode of Oswald's FPCC chapter," the historian David Kaiser wrote in 2012, "bears all the marks of a COINTELPRO operation. . . . The behavior of the New Orleans police and the FBI certainly suggested that they knew Oswald's chapter was bogus."

Down the years, speculation as to the role of U.S. intelligence has been the common denominator of the persistent doubts about the true role of Lee Oswald. Oswald trailed behind himself, from Japan in 1958 to New Orleans in 1963, the shadow of an undefined connection with the secret world. How one interprets it all ranges from the reasonable man's skepticism over the apparent lack of intelligence interest in Oswald on his return from Russia, to Orest Pena's shrill accusations against the FBI in New Orleans.

It is possible that FBI and CIA denials of their agencies' involvement with Oswald were truthful. As the Assassinations Committee pointed out, however, Oswald's "possible affiliation with military intelligence" was never resolved.[8]

It may be, too, that Oswald was—at least in the months before the assassination—one remove away from the formal structures of the intelligence community. In the world of intelligence, many operations are run through cutouts, buffer organizations, or individuals whose actions can never be laid at the door of any specific agency of government. It may have been thus with Oswald in New Orleans.

In 1978, the House Assassinations Committee pursued research into clues that no one has ever explained away. The first of them is a long-discarded document, and an address synonymous with subterfuge.

CHAPTER 17

Blind Man's Bluff
in New Orleans

"In the months leading up to the assassination, I think Oswald got in over his head. He was no longer quite sure who he was working for, or why. Somebody was using him, and they knew exactly how and why."

—Staff Investigator, House Assassinations Committee, 1979

When he wound up his talk with Oswald, FBI agent Quigley left the New Orleans police station carrying a bundle of papers with him. Whether the agent understood it or not, the young prisoner had done as he said he would when he promised the FBI information. As Quigley would write later, Oswald had "made available" several examples of his pro-Castro propaganda. Two were the yellow leaflets he had been handing out in the street. The third was a forty-page pamphlet entitled The Crime Against Cuba. At first sight, it seemed an unremarkable tract, two years out of date, a stern critique of American policy toward Cuba. Yet The Crime Against Cuba was an evidential time bomb. Tucked away inside the back cover, at the very end of the text, was a rubber-stamped address. It read (see Photo 33):

FPCC

544 CAMP ST.

NEW ORLEANS, LA

To the eye, 544 Camp Street was a nondescript building on a corner, a shabby, three-storied relic of the nineteenth century. On one side, its peeling facade looked on to a dusty square dominated by a statue of Benjamin Franklin and frequented by dozing drunks (see Photo 29). Yet the building did not fit in at all either with Fair Play for Cuba or with its supposed New Orleans representative, Lee Oswald. Recent tenants until the summer of 1963 had included the Cuban Revolutionary Council, the umbrella organization of the *anti*-Castro exiles. There, too, was Guy Banister Associates, a detective agency in a building that was a meeting place for Cuban exiles. The building was known as a haven for rightist extremists, and the local FBI knew its habitués very well indeed. When Agent Quigley noticed that address on Oswald's pamphlet, it must have struck him as a total contradiction. Yet he and his FBI colleagues appear to have been incurious.

It was not that the improbable address escaped their attention. A few days after Oswald gave the first pamphlet to Agent Quigley, a second copy arrived in the mail—to be filed, rationally enough, under the serial number for documents concerning *anti*-Castro activity. This second copy had been sent in by a regular FBI informant who had watched Oswald's pro-Castro demonstration and pocketed a handful of his literature. FBI records show that Quigley lost little time in asking New York for information on the author of this pamphlet, Corliss Lamont. Other details, like a post-office box number Oswald had given, were promptly checked. According to the record, however, no one initially deemed it necessary or even interesting to investigate—at the time—what should have been utterly perplexing, the address that did not fit.

At some point, perhaps following the assassination, somebody did draw attention to it. The pamphlet sent in by the informant, as released to the public only fifteen years later, bears the scrawled sentence, "Note inside back cover." There, the address is circled and the same hand has added what appears to be "ck out"—presumably "check out." A glance at the Warren Report, however, suggests that any check the FBI may have made went nowhere. Buried deep in a chronology of Oswald's life is this sentence: "While the legend 'FPCC, 544 Camp St., New Orleans, LA,' was stamped on some literature that Oswald had in his possession at the time of his arrest in New Orleans, extensive investigation was not able to connect Oswald with that address."

Investigation by the Assassinations Committee, conducted years later on a cold trail, concluded that the FBI's effort was "not thorough." The Committee developed evidence "pointing to a different result," and it buttresses suspicion that the alleged assassin was involved in some covert operation. The address at 544 Camp Street may provide solid clues to conspiracy in the assassination of President Kennedy.

FBI agents did follow up on the Camp Street lead three days after the President's assassination, but only with superficial inquiries. They interviewed the building's owner, Sam Newman, who said he had never rented office space to Fair Play for Cuba. He advised "that to the best of his knowledge he had no recollection of seeing Oswald in or around the building." On the basis of a few interviews like this, the FBI filed the reports on which the official inquiry was to rely. Their conclusion was: no FPCC office and no Oswald at Camp Street. End of story.

Nobody reacted to the fact that, in addition to the pamphlets recovered in New Orleans, a further twenty were found among Oswald's possessions in Dallas, and ten bore stamps with the 544 Camp Street address. On top of that, the official inquiry dismissed clues in letters written by Oswald in the summer of 1963. These indicated that he had used an office in New Orleans.

In May 1963, less than a month after his arrival in the city, Oswald had written to the head of the FPCC in New York: "Now that I live in New Orleans I have been thinking about renting a small office at my own expense for the purpose of forming an FPCC branch here." Although even a humble office would cost about thirty dollars a month, Oswald wrote, he was intent on finding one. Warned by FPCC headquarters against rushing into anything, Oswald promptly replied, "Against your advice, I have decided to take an office from the very beginning." This sounded much as though Oswald had already found premises or was on the brink of doing so.

Two months later, he was still writing about the office—this time to report its closure. On August 1, having received no reply to his last letter, Oswald wrote, "In regard to my efforts to start a branch office . . . I rented an office as I planned and was promptly closed three days later for some obscure reason by the renters, they said something about remodeling, etc., I'm sure you understand. . . ."

Oswald occasionally did adjust the facts to fit his plans. He used untruths for a purpose, and there apparently was a purpose behind the FPCC caper in New Orleans. The knowledge we have today, that American intelligence was plotting against the FPCC at that very time in 1963, makes it impossible to ignore the pamphlets stamped 544 Camp Street and the repeated references to an office. Take another look at the dates involved, and at the oddly vague replies the FBI and Secret Service agents received from the building's landlord, Sam Newman.

Oswald's August 1 letter, saying he had briefly used an office but that it had been closed down, came just before the clash in the street with the anti-Castro exiles. If there is any basis of fact to his story about having had an office, it is a fair guess that he used it sometime during the latter part of July. Newman, the landlord, was to recall several abortive attempts to rent space at 544 Camp Street in the summer of 1963. These included a very brief rental by a man who "told him that he worked as an electrician by day and desired to teach Spanish by night." The man made an initial rental payment, only to return a week later saying he "had been unable to get enough students to enroll." Money, apparently, was no problem. The man told Newman to keep the deposit money. As Newman told it to the Secret Service, this occurred at exactly the time Oswald indicated he had used an office.

Though the man, described as being in his thirties and olive-skinned, was clearly not Oswald, the record provides another clue that may explain the discrepancy. After the assassination the authorities received a tip-off that Ernesto Rodríguez, an anti-Castro militant who "operated a Spanish school . . . had tape recordings of Spanish conversations with Oswald." Rodríguez did run a language school, and his father was in the electrical business. Under cursory questioning in 1963, he denied having such a tape but admitted that Oswald had contacted him "concerning a Spanish language course." The date, it turns out, fits—sometime soon after July 24.

Interviewed again in 1979, Rodríguez admitted that he had indeed met Oswald, but the story about Spanish classes seemed to have slipped his memory. Now, like the DRE's Carlos Bringuier, he claimed Oswald had visited him to offer his services in training anti-Castro Cuban exiles in guerrilla techniques. Indeed, Rodríguez was to say, it was he who sent Oswald to see Bringuier. Further checks reveal that, in 1963, Ernesto Rodríguez was a leading activist in the New Orleans campaign against Castro. He was one of those who controlled the funds of the Crusade to Free Cuba Committee, the fund-raising group for the CIA-backed Cuban Revolutionary Council (CRC). In that capacity, he was almost certainly in touch with William Reily, Oswald's employer in New Orleans and a backer of the Crusade.[1]

Rodríguez also helped manage the Council's affairs in New Orleans—its second most important base in the United States. The CRC had theoretically ceased to use 544 Camp Street by the time Oswald got busy in New Orleans, but the reality was rather different. The CRC enjoyed a flexible business relationship with the landlord Sam Newman, who made no initial charge for the office space—on the basis that the CRC would pay if it raised enough money from fund-raising. Anti-Castro militants were still using 544 Camp Street after Oswald's arrival in New Orleans, and came and went at will throughout the summer of 1963.

The exiles found a welcome in the offices of Guy Banister, the man who headed the detective agency at 544, and so apparently did Oswald. Leads from his former staff appear to confirm that Oswald, too, used that unlikely address—and may explain the devious purpose behind Oswald's pro-Castro campaign that summer. The information suggests Oswald was drawn into a U.S. intelligence scheme aimed at compromising the FPCC—and that Banister was deeply involved.

Guy Banister was an old-fashioned American hero. He had

been a star agent for the FBI, a tough guy whose long career had covered some of the Bureau's most famous cases, including the capture and killing of 1930s murderer and bank robber John Dillinger. He had been commended by FBI Director Hoover and served as a Special Agent in Charge for almost twenty years. He had retired, at fifty-three, following major surgery and a warning that he would henceforth be prone to unpredictable, irrational conduct.

New Orleans, nevertheless, had accepted Banister as Deputy Chief of Police, an appointment that ended following an incident in New Orleans' Old Absinthe House—he was said to have threatened a waiter with a pistol. Banister was now, by all accounts, a choleric man and a heavy drinker. Instead of retiring, however, he started Guy Banister Associates, the nominal detective agency.

The former FBI's man's intelligence background, coupled with a vision of himself as a super-patriot, now led him into a personal crusade against Communism. Banister supported the John Birch Society, Louisiana's Committee on Un-American Activities, the paramilitary Minutemen, published a racist tract called the *Louisiana Intelligence Digest*, abhorred the United Nations and believed plans for racial integration were part of a Communist plot against the United States. New Orleans Crime Commission Director Aaron Kohn, who knew Banister well, characterized him as "a tragic case." By 1963, his public persona can only be described as that of a right-wing nut.

After Castro's revolution in Cuba, though, Banister's concept of the Red Menace was shared by many, and it was dangerously close to official U.S. policy. He had thrown himself feverishly into the CIA-backed exile campaign to topple Castro, helping to organize the Cuban Revolutionary Democratic Front and Friends of Democratic Cuba. In 1961, before the Bay of Pigs invasion, he served as a munitions supplier.

By 1963, former members of Banister's staff said, the offices of the "detective agency" were littered with guns of every distinction. It was no coincidence that the Cuban Revolutionary Council, the exiles' government in exile, made its New Orleans base in the same building as his office. For both Banister and his Cuban protégés, the building was well located, close to the local offices of both the CIA and the FBI. For the agencies, Banister's intelligence background and independent status likely made him a convenient buffer, a circuit breaker for operations with which officialdom could not be openly associated. Even if his political passions and alcoholism made for a dangerously inflammable mix, Banister had his uses.

Banister's former FBI colleagues did not seriously investigate him or his office after the Kennedy assassination, and he died of a reported heart attack a few months later. Had he been available, it is doubtful whether the Warren Commission would have seen any reason to question him. In the record, the New Orleans FBI obscured 544 Camp Street, Banister's address, by referring to it only as 531 Lafayette Street. That was, in fact, one of the halves of the building at 544 Camp Street, an address that just might have sparked interest in Washington.[2]

Some investigation of Guy Banister came three years later, when New Orleans District Attorney Jim Garrison began his probe—and the resulting unsuccessful prosecution of a suspect—into a supposed New Orleans conspiracy to assassinate President Kennedy.[3] As the world learned from a stream of garish headlines, the trial was a fiasco that served only to obscure the evidence in a key location. The Garrison episode did, however, bring attention to some significant areas of that evidence.

An important development came when Assistant District Attorney Andrew Sciambra interviewed Banister's widow. After her husband's death, she said, she had found among his effects a number of Fair Play for Cuba leaflets. Banister had kept extensive files at his office, and these were scattered after his death. Some, allegedly, had been removed by government agents. Later, however, the Louisiana police Intelligence unit retrieved a "half-filled" filing cabinet containing records on "Communist groups and subversive organizations," and investigators learned something about the contents from index cards and police interviews.

Banister's file titles included: "Central Intelligence Agency," "Ammunition and Arms," "Anti-Soviet Underground," and "Civil Rights Program of JFK." Sandwiched between "Dismantling of U.S. Defenses" and "U.S. Bases—Italy" was a now-familiar name—"Fair Play for Cuba Committee." It was followed by the classification number 23-7. According to a state police officer who saw this file, it contained basic information on Oswald's activities in New Orleans. As Assassinations Committee staff noted, this file had since, "unfortunately," been destroyed.

In his hunt for Reds under the bed, Banister used to hire young men as inquiry and infiltration agents. To help his Cuban exile contacts, for example, Banister would send young men to mingle with students at New Orleans colleges, primed to report on budding pro-Castro sympathizers. Two such recruits were Allen and Daniel Campbell, both—like Oswald—former marines, and they had very relevant information.

Shortly after Oswald's supposed street confrontation with Cuban exile Carlos Bringuier, Daniel Campbell told the author, a young man "with a marine haircut" came into his office at 544 Camp Street and used the desk phone for a few minutes. The next time Campbell saw his visitor, he told me, was on television after the assassination. He had been, Campbell said he was certain, Lee Oswald.

Allen Campbell, Daniel's brother, told the New Orleans authorities in 1969 that he had been at Camp Street on one of the two occasions on which Oswald passed out FPCC leaflets.[4] One might have expected his boss, Guy Banister, infamous for his enraged outbursts, to have reacted with fury when told of the pro-Castro leafleting. Instead, Allen Campbell said, Banister merely laughed. Other former employees, meanwhile, recalled something that did make Banister angry—the use of the 544 Camp Street address on some of Oswald's FPCC propaganda.

Banister's secretary at the time, Delphine Roberts, provided information that goes far toward explaining Banister's behavior. Roberts, described by a former FBI agent and Banister associate as the "number one" source on events at Camp Street, claimed that her boss knew Oswald personally. According to her, Banister encouraged him to mount his FPCC operation from Camp Street. The author interviewed her in 1978, before she had talked to the House Assassinations Committee, then again in 1993.

This was a woman who had made her own mark on extreme rightist politics in New Orleans. Well born and educated, she was proud to call herself a Daughter of the American Revolution and had been a vociferous candidate for a place on the city council. In that campaign, in 1962, Roberts had declared herself opposed to "anything of a Communistic tinge," which to her meant almost anything much of the population regarded as progress. She railed, for example, against "racial integration of any kind, shape, or form, because it is an integral part of the international Communist criminal conspiracy." Roberts fulminated against what she regarded as federal interference in state affairs and demanded American withdrawal from the United Nations.

Guy Banister had not failed to notice, and brought Roberts into his office as personal secretary and researcher. They also became lovers. She was with him throughout the summer of 1963 and at the time of the Kennedy assassination. After the assassination, she said, Banister told her to discuss nothing with the FBI, and not to come to the office until the immediate uproar had blown over. A few months later, when Banister died, she distanced herself from the people she had known at 544 Camp Street and avoided interviews. She stalled questions from the District Attorney's office in 1967 and tried to elude Assassinations Committee staff in 1978.

When the author first made contact with Roberts, she repeatedly denied having heard the name Lee Oswald until after the assassination. Then she quietly began talking. A surviving sign of her conservative outlook was her opinion that U.S. intelligence agencies—in the late 1970s, when the author first interviewed her—were "being destroyed by so much exposure." So much had by then been revealed, however, that Roberts said she saw little point in continuing to be secretive herself. If what she said in her interviews with the author was truthful, suspicions about Lee Oswald's true role have been fully justified.

According to Delphine Roberts, Oswald walked into her office sometime in 1963 and asked to fill in the forms for accreditation as one of Banister's "agents." Roberts told me: "Oswald introduced himself by name and said he was seeking an application form. I did not think that was really why he was there. During the course of the conversation, I gained the impression that he and Guy Banister already knew each other. After Oswald filled out the application form, Guy Banister called him into the office. The door was closed, and a lengthy conversation took place. Then the young man left. I presumed then, and now am certain, that the reason for Oswald being there was that he was required to act undercover."

The precise purpose of Oswald's "undercover" role remained obscure to Roberts, but she learned that it involved Cuba and some sort of charade that required deception. Roberts said: "Oswald came back a number of times. He seemed to be on familiar terms with Banister and with the office. As I understood it he had the use of an office on the second floor, above the main office where we worked. I was not greatly surprised when I learned he was going up and down, back and forth.

"Then, several times, Mr. Banister brought me upstairs, and in the office above I saw various writings stuck up on the wall pertaining to Cuba. There were various leaflets up there pertaining to Fair Play for Cuba. They were pro-Castro leaflets. Banister just didn't say anything about them one way or the other. But on several occasions, when some people who had been upstairs would bring some of that material down into the main office, Banister was very incensed about it. He did not want that material in his office."

One afternoon, Roberts said, she observed the end product of Oswald's preparations. As she was returning to the office, she saw "that young man passing out his pro-Castro leaflets in the street." In what appears to be corroboration of the incident that Allen Campbell recalled, she says she later mentioned what she had seen to Banister. His reaction was casual. "Don't worry about him. He's a nervous fellow, he's confused. He's with us, he's associated with the office."

Nothing Banister said indicated surprise or anger that somebody from his anti-Castro stable was out in the street openly demonstrating in favor of Fidel Castro. Delphine Roberts shrugged off the contradiction. "I knew that such things did take place, and when they did you just didn't question them. I knew there were such things as counterspies, spies and counterspies, and the importance of such things. So I just didn't question them."

What Delphine Roberts said was divulged with reluctance.[5] Other snippets of information, though, tend to support her account—and Daniel Campbell's claim—that Oswald visited 544 Camp Street. Her own daughter, also called Delphine, used another room upstairs at Camp Street for photographic work. She and a photographer friend, the daughter told me, also saw Lee Oswald occasionally.

Delphine— one could call her Delphine Jr.—said: "I knew he had his pamphlets and books and everything in a room along from where we were with our photographic equipment. He was quiet and mostly kept to himself, didn't associate with too many people. He would just tell us hello or good-bye when we saw him. I never saw him talking with Guy Banister, but I knew he worked in his office. I knew they were associated.

"I saw some other men who looked like Americans coming and going occasionally from the room Oswald used. From his attitude, and from my mother, and what I knew of Banister's work, I got the impression Oswald was doing something to make people believe he was something he wasn't. I am sure Guy Banister knew what Oswald was doing."

Banister's brother Ross told the Assassinations Committee that Guy "mentioned seeing Oswald hand out Fair Play for Cuba literature." Ivan Nitschke, a business associate of Banister's and a fellow former FBI agent, recalled that Banister became "interested in Oswald" in the summer of 1963. Adrian Alba, who ran the garage next door to Oswald's place of work, claimed to the Committee that he often saw Oswald in the restaurant on the ground floor of 544 Camp Street. That restaurant had a rear exit leading up to the office section of the building, and Banister was a regular patron.

Delphine Roberts, Sr., said she was sure that whatever the nature of Banister's "interest" in Oswald, it concerned anti-Castro schemes, plans that she felt certain had the support and encouragement of government Intelligence agencies. As she put it, "Mr. Banister had been a special agent for the FBI and was still working for them. There were quite a number of connections which he kept with the FBI and the CIA, too. I know he and the FBI traded information due to his former association." Banister's former employee, Daniel Campbell, also became convinced that his boss remained involved with the FBI.

An FBI report of an interview with Banister after the assassination indicates that he was asked questions about anti-Castro exiles but none at all about Oswald or use of the 544 Camp Street address on Oswald's propaganda. As for Banister and the CIA, an Assassinations Committee check revealed only that the Agency "considered using Guy Banister Associates for the collection of foreign intelligence" but decided against it. That, however, had been in 1960—three years before the Oswald episode.

Delphine Roberts told the author, "I think he received funds from the CIA—I know he had access to large funds at various times in 1963." She added that known intelligence agents and law-enforcement officers often visited Banister's office. She accepted the comings and goings as normal, because so far as she was concerned the visitors and her boss were "doing something to try to stop what was taking place, the danger that was facing this country because of Cuba."

It had been at Banister's instigation, in 1961, that the New Orleans branch of the Cuban Revolutionary Council had taken offices at 544 Camp Street. CIA records reveal that the Council's local representative "maintained extensive relations with the FBI. . . . Two of his regular FBI contacts were a Mr. de Bruce and . . . Guy Banister." Banister, who was long retired from the FBI, was referred to as an active FBI contact. As one associate of the Cuban Revolutionary Council representative put it, the office became a sort of "Grand Central Station" for the exiles.[6] The Mob, too, had its line into the Council—the exile group received an offer of a "substantial donation" from New Orleans Mafia boss Carlos Marcello.

The CRC also had a friend in a New Orleans advertising man called Ronnie Caire. Caire was a fervent supporter of the exile cause and had been a leading light in yet another anti-Castro organization, the Crusade to Free Cuba. The arm of coincidence was long indeed, it seems, in the New Orleans of 1963. After the assassination, Ronnie Caire would say he "seemed to recall" a visit from Oswald. He said Oswald had been "applying for a job."

The second CRC representative in New Orleans, Frank Bartes, turned up for the court case following the street fracas with the exiles, and indulged in a noisy argument with Oswald. He later said he warned the FBI that day that Oswald was dangerous. Yet a month later, in September, he told the Bureau Oswald "was unknown to him." Bartes was an informant for both the FBI and the CIA. CIA records show that he had been checked for use in a "contact and assessment" role as early as 1961, and he would be working for the Agency's Special Operations Division by 1965.

Unfailingly, in any study of Oswald in New Orleans, the connections seem to come full circle. The last of those connections is the one that links Oswald's name with that of David Ferrie.

David Ferrie was an oddity, more so even than Banister. He was a born flier, a skill that had earned him a career as a senior pilot with Eastern Airlines. For Ferrie that was not enough. His was a brilliant but erratic mind, which made for a tragically disordered life.[7] Ferrie dabbled in religion and ended up founding his own church. He dabbled in medicine and began a one-man search for the cause of cancer. He was a homosexual who compromised himself while at work. Eastern Airlines fired him. Ferrie might have remained an unknown eccentric, but then there was Cuba.

Ferrie was one of the mavericks who found a role for themselves in the efforts to topple Fidel Castro. His reputed ability to perform miracles with airplanes finally found an outlet. In 1961, before the Bay of Pigs invasion, Ferrie reputedly flew to Cuba dozens of times, sometimes on bombing missions, sometimes making daring landings to extract anti-Castro resistance fighters.

By the summer of 1962, at the age of forty-five, he was in New Orleans—dividing his time between a mix of liberal causes—he was for civil rights, anti-Castro activism, and a passion for young men. He was by now an outlandish figure, not least because he suffered from alopecia, an ailment that had left him not only bald-headed, but without eyebrows or body hair. Ferrie compensated by wearing a red toupee and sometimes grotesquely obvious false eyebrows. He would have been merely laughable, but his quirky intellect found him listeners in the world of political extremism.

As early as 1950, when he joined the U.S. Army Reserve, he had been stridently anti-Communist, writing in a letter to the commander of the U.S. First Air Force, "There is nothing I would enjoy better than blowing the hell out of every damn

Russian, Communist, Red, or what-have-you. . . . We can cook up a crew that will really bomb them to hell. . . . I want to train killers, however bad that sounds. It is what we need."

Ferrie was a rabble-rousing public speaker, with his favorite subject the festering Cuban confrontation, his principal whipping boy President Kennedy. After the 1961 catastrophe at the Bay of Pigs, in a speech on Cuba to the New Orleans chapter of the Military Order of World Wars, his attack on the President had been so offensive that Ferrie had eventually been asked to leave the podium. Detestation of the President became something of an obsession with him. Some, who heard Ferrie say angrily, "The President ought to be shot," would one day come to believe that in his case it had been no idle oratory. A favorite Ferrie theme was along the lines that "an electorate cannot be depended upon to pick the right man."

In some ways, he was politically compatible with Guy Banister, a man who would be remembered for an occasion on which he alarmed companions by pulling out a gun and shouting, "There comes a time when the world's problems can be better solved with the bullet than the ballot." Ferrie and Banister were joined, certainly, by fervent support for the anti-Castro cause. By the summer of 1963, reportedly, Ferrie had become a frequent visitor to 544 Camp Street.

Banister's secretary, Delphine Roberts, remembered Ferrie as "one of the agents. Many times when he came into the office, he used the private office behind Banister's, and I was told he was doing private work. I believed his work was somehow connected with the CIA rather than the FBI." Ferrie certainly was associated with Guy Banister and the Cuban exiles. On one of the days Oswald handed out pro-Castro leaflets in New Orleans, Ferrie led an anti-Castro demonstration a few blocks away. As with

Banister, moreover, there have been repeated allegations that Ferrie was involved with Oswald.

After the assassination, there was perfunctory inquiry into Oswald's membership, as a youth of nearly sixteen, in the Civil Air Patrol (CAP). Oswald, who had then been living in New Orleans with his mother, joined the Patrol as a cadet in 1955— when David Ferrie, already a skilled airman, was a leading light of the unit. After the assassination, one of Banister's employees said he thought he recalled seeing a photograph of Oswald, along with other onetime CAP members, in Ferrie's home. Asked about this on more than one occasion, Ferrie claimed he remembered nothing about Oswald and had had no relationship with him. Since he also denied knowing that the Cuban Revolutionary Council operated from 544 Camp Street, a fact he certainly did know, the denials should have raised suspicion.

The FBI, however, conducted only a nominal inquiry into Oswald's membership in the CAP, and the matter was dropped. There was no further action when one of Oswald's former schoolmates, Edward Voebel, first stated that he and Oswald had been in the Patrol "with Captain Dave Ferrie"—and then abruptly changed his mind. Suddenly, he "could not recall" the matter. The fact that Voebel had been scared, by a "crank-type telephone call" and a visit to his home by a strange man, left the FBI unphased.

Nor was the Bureau stung into action when another former cadet said Ferrie had scurried around to see him after the assassination to ask whether any old group photographs of Ferrie's squadron featured Oswald. Most of the squadron records, supposedly, had been "stolen in late 1960." Even in 1978, however, the House Assassinations Committee did better.

Investigators established that Ferrie's service with the Civil

Air Patrol fitted with that of Oswald. They identified six witnesses whose statements tended to confirm that Oswald had been present at patrol meetings attended by Ferrie. Compelling evidence, from records and witnesses, indicates that Oswald became a CAP cadet in summer 1955, when Ferrie was a volunteer instructor. Jerry Paradis, another former instructor, told the author, "I was a lieutenant coinciding with the months Oswald was a recruit. . . . I recall him as a very quiet, serious young man . . . David Ferrie was sort of the scoutmaster."[8]

In 1993, researchers for PBS's *Frontline* program discovered an old photograph that appears to settle the matter. Apparently taken in 1955, it shows CAP cadets at a cookout (see Photo 34). Former cadets, one of whom is himself in the picture, told *Frontline* they recognized both Oswald and Ferrie in the picture.

The Ferrie connection introduces another element into this baroque story—homosexuality. Ferrie's homosexuality, and his weakness for young males in particular, is a matter of record. Over the years, it repeatedly led him into trouble, and sometimes into police custody.[9] In the mid-1950s, Ferrie's misconduct with youths in the CAP led to scandal. There were reports of drunken orgies, of youngsters capering about in the nude, and in the end, it was this that ended Ferrie's tenure with the New Orleans unit. The Assassinations Committee noted that—homosexuality aside—Ferrie exerted "tremendous influence" through his close associations with his pupils in the Patrol.

Was Oswald so influenced, and did he—at the age of sixteen and on the threshold of adult sexual life—have a sexual encounter with Ferrie? While he later lived an active heterosexual life with his wife, Marina, there are straws in the wind on this subject. Oswald may have attended some of Ferrie's bacchanalia.

On one occasion while he was in the CAP, the then teenager worried his mother by staying out at a unit party until two in the morning.[10]

In the Marine Corps, some did wonder about Oswald's sexuality. He reportedly took friends to the Flamingo, a bar for homosexuals on the Mexican border that he appeared to have visited before. In Japan, he seemed comfortable in a "queer bar." One former Marines comrade, David Murray, said he kept his distance from Oswald because of a rumor that he was homosexual. "He had the profile of other homosexuals I'd known or come in contact with," former U.S. Marines Sergeant Dan Powers recalled, "The meekness, the gentleness—just that type of person. Having worked at YMCAs, etc., for me he just fitted into that category." The possible sexual connection aside, another lead may point to an Oswald-Ferrie link.

According to his mother, Marguerite, Oswald was first encouraged to join the Marines by a "recruiting officer" in uniform who "influenced [him] while he was with the Civil Air cadets." The man came to the Oswald apartment with Lee in tow, she said, to try to persuade her to let the boy join up while still underage. Her son, she said, "wanted me to sign a birth certificate saying that he was seventeen."

Is it likely that a genuine Marine Corps recruiting officer would have tried to persuade a cadet's mother to connive at breaking the law? An Assassinations Committee analysis notes that David Ferrie, for his part, "urged several boys to join the armed forces." Jack Martin, who worked for the Banister detective agency, would tell the FBI within three days of President Kennedy's assassination that Ferrie had helped Oswald get into the Marine Corps.

Ferrie, moreover, was no stranger to the fakery of personal documents—his own application form to join Eastern Airlines was but one example. Although a phony Oswald birth certificate was created, the Marines spotted the forgery. Oswald spent the next year studying the Marine Corps manual until "he knew it by heart," then joined up just days after his seventeenth birthday.

It was, of course, during this same period that Oswald started to manifest an interest in Marxism and far Left politics. The conventional view, ignoring the stream of anomalies in Oswald's career, has been to regard this as the start of an authentic lifelong commitment. With Ferrie's possible influence on Oswald in mind, consider the ambivalent approach Ferrie had to politics. He was "rabidly anti-Communist," yet sometimes described himself as a "liberal." Of Ferrie's position on Cuba, Delphine Roberts said, "Well, he had to act a part of being what many people would call wishy-washy, *one side and then the opposite side* [author's emphasis]. It was important for him to be that way. . . . He knew both sides."

Consider once again, then, Oswald's alleged teenage interest in socialism. The Warren Report failed to mention another comment by Oswald's former schoolfriend Edward Voebel. Reports that Oswald was already "studying Communism," according to Voebel, were "a lot of baloney." The comment recalls the plethora of incidents that have somehow rung false. How much of Oswald's parroted politics was also "baloney"?

We cannot know, but the potential influence of David Ferrie, looming darkly at a formative time in Oswald's life, is sobering. Whether or not Ferrie steered the mind and actions of Oswald the youth, some evidence suggests they were involved with each other in the summer of 1963.

Dean Andrews, a New Orleans lawyer, claimed after the assassination that Oswald came to his office several times to ask for help in appealing his undesirable discharge from the Marine Corps Reserve. Andrews, whose account was partially corroborated by office staff, said Oswald was accompanied on the first visit by some Mexican "gay kids," one of whom appeared to be Oswald's companion. Ferrie, the homosexual, had business links to Andrews.[11]

Ferrie had links, too, to the Louisiana Mafia boss who had spoken of assassinating President Kennedy, Carlos Marcello.

By the summer of 1963, two summers had passed since the Kennedy administration had unceremoniously deported Carlos Marcello from the United States. He had soon returned, in defiance of the Attorney General, and was seen openly around New Orleans, back in control of his crime empire. So far as Robert Kennedy was concerned, however, the battle was not over. On his personal order, the Justice Department stepped up the pressure against Mafia operations in the South and against Marcello personally. It was now war between the Kennedys and Marcello, just as there was war with Marcello's friend Hoffa.

Like Hoffa and Florida crime boss Santo Trafficante, Marcello is said to have confided—as noted in an earlier chapter—that he planned to have President Kennedy killed. In public, he fought renewed efforts to deport him—and two of those recruited to help were Guy Banister and David Ferrie.

The Marcello-Ferrie connection went back a long way, perhaps as far as 1961, when Marcello had sneaked back from exile in Guatemala. Of the several theories as to how exactly the Mafia boss came home, one long favored by investigators is that he was flown in by private plane. Although Marcello denied it, a contemporary Border Patrol report said the pilot of the aircraft had been David Ferrie.

From early 1962, by his own account, Ferrie had been employed as "investigator and law clerk" in the office of G. Wray Gill, one of Marcello's posse of attorneys. Ferrie also associated with Dean Andrews, another lawyer who provided his services to Marcello—and who was to claim he met Lee Harvey Oswald in 1963. In the three months leading up to the assassination, Ferrie was employed specifically to help Marcello fight the government's case of deportation. This involved at least one flight to Guatemala to gather evidence for the defense, work that one of Ferrie's associates described as that of "research librarian."

The research also involved weekend visits to two of Marcello's bases of operation, the Town and Country Motel in New Orleans and his estate outside the city, Churchill Farms, where Marcello had reportedly made his threat against President Kennedy's life. Hatred of the President was, we have seen, something Ferrie and Marcello had in common.

The high point of Ferrie's work on behalf of the Mafia leader came at exactly the period in 1963 that Ferrie was frequenting Guy Banister's office at 544 Camp Street. Banister, it seems, had reversed the zest for hunting gangsters that had once brought him distinction in the FBI. He, too, now lent his expertise to Marcello's cause, as the Assassinations Committee confirmed.

One secretary who worked in Banister's office during the crucial summer and autumn of 1963, Mary Brengel, recalled a day when, as she was taking dictation from Banister, he referred in a letter to his work in helping Marcello fight deportation. Brengel expressed surprise that her employer was involved with organized crime, and Banister responded curtly, "There are principles being violated, and if this goes on it could affect every citizen in the United States." He left no doubt that he was firmly on Marcello's side.

Then there was the family of the alleged assassin himself. We now know that key members of the Oswald family were touched by the Mafia—and specifically by the Marcello network. His father having died before he was born, Oswald had spent most of his childhood and formative years in the sole care of his mother, Marguerite. When he was fifteen, they had moved into an apartment at 126 Exchange Alley in New Orleans. The alley was in the French Quarter, amid the razzmatazz and sleaze synonymous with New Orleans. "Exchange Alley, specifically that little block that Oswald lived on," said New Orleans Metropolitan Crime Commission director Aaron Kohn, "was literally the hub of some of the most notorious underworld joints in the city."

The Oswalds had lived in substandard accommodation above a pool hall, a known hangout for gamblers. Not much is known of young Lee's teenage pursuits, but one episode suggests that the atmosphere of lawlessness was infectious. Edward Voebel, Oswald's schoolfriend, recalled having to dissuade his pal from a plan to break into a gun shop and steal a weapon. Boys in bad neighborhoods are prone to being rascals, but Oswald was more at risk than most. His mother had close connections to the gangster milieu.

A relative once said of Marguerite Oswald, "She's a woman with a lot of character and good morals, and I'm sure that what she was doing for her boys she thought was the best at the time. Now, whether it was or not is something else, I guess." Indeed, the touching portrait of Marguerite the embattled single parent is somewhat tarnished. The Assassinations Committee took a closer look at her known friends.

One was a New Orleans attorney named Clem Sehrt. He was, the Committee said, an "associate, lawyer, and financial adviser to a Louisiana banker associated with Carlos Marcello." Sehrt had himself been "long involved in a series of highly questionable undertakings, both business and political." Mrs. Oswald turned to Sehrt at the time her son Lee was trying to join the Marines, when underage, in the wake of his apparent association with the suspect David Ferrie. Sehrt was involved in the false birth certificate caper. After the assassination, according to information that reached the New Orleans Crime Commission, Sehrt was asked to represent Oswald. It is not known who asked him to do so.[12]

Marguerite's friendship with Sehrt was not a solitary brush with organized crime. She worked for some time for Raoul Sere, a lawyer who went on to become an assistant district attorney in New Orleans. According to former Crime Commission director Kohn, Sere was strongly suspected of being involved with "The Combine," a group of New Orleans figures who obstructed the course of justice with bribery and corruption. Kohn added, "The district attorney's office was then under the corrupt influence of the gambling syndicate—Carlos Marcello and others—to a very significant degree." Though reluctant to discuss the matter, Oswald's mother acknowledged having consulted Sere for advice after her son Lee went to the Soviet Union.

The Assassinations Committee found evidence, too, that Mrs. Oswald had been friendly with a man called Sam Termine. Termine was "a Louisiana crime figure who had served as a 'bodyguard' and chauffeur for Carlos Marcello." Investigation of Termine revealed that he was close to Oswald's uncle, Charles Murret. Murret, who was married to Marguerite's sister, Lillian, had a great deal of contact with Lee Oswald. He, too, it turns out, tracks back to the Mafia apparatus of Carlos Marcello.

Charles Murret was more than the "steamship clerk" he was painted by his family in testimony to the Warren Commission. His name had cropped up as early as 1944 in a survey of vice and corruption in New Orleans. An FBI report named him as being prominent in illegal bookmaking activities. Murret was for years an associate of a leader of organized crime in New Orleans, Sam Saia. The Internal Revenue Service identified Saia as one of the most powerful gambling figures in Louisiana. According to Crime Commission director Kohn, he "had the reputation of being very close to Carlos Marcello."

For the fatherless Oswald, Murret had been the nearest there was in his life to a father figure. He had actually lived with the Murrets for a while when he was three, and later often saw them on weekends. He had visited them while serving in the Marine Corps and, most significantly, saw a lot of his uncle in the New Orleans period before the assassination. He stayed with the Murrets for a while after his arrival in the city from Dallas, and Murret lent Oswald money.

When Oswald was arrested following the street fracas with Carlos Bringuier, it was the Murrets he called for help in getting bail. Only their daughter was at home when he got through on the telephone, but she contacted "a family friend," one Emile Bruneau. Bruneau, says an FBI report, in turn, contacted "some-one else" who duly arranged Oswald's release.

Bruneau, who reportedly admitted to the Assassinations Committee that he did indeed help, was described by Crime Commission director Kohn as "a big-time gambler." He was also, like Oswald's uncle Charles, an associate of one Nofio Pecora. Pecora, as we shall see, may have received a telephone call from

Oswald's killer, Jack Ruby, less than a month before the Kennedy assassination. Pecora, according to the Assassinations Committee Report, was "a longtime Marcello lieutenant."

Oswald's mother was sensitive about her family connections. During her Assassinations Committee interviews, she "declined to discuss her past activities at any length, refusing to respond to various questions." She would not say if she knew whether her brother-in-law Murret was acquainted with Marcello.

Nothing in Oswald's adult history suggests he felt empathy for Mafia criminals. Yet his family's connections, his apparent association with Marcello henchman David Ferrie, and the identity of those who arranged his release after the street fracas, cannot be ignored. The Mob, clearly, had every opportunity to become aware of Oswald, the posturing leftist. That becomes all the more ominous in light of the allegation that Carlos Marcello spoke of planning the President's murder, of "setting up a nut to take the blame."

None of this need detract from the suspicion that, while in New Orleans, Oswald was the tool of an anti-Castro intelligence operation. Former U.S. senator Richard Schweiker, whose Intelligence Committee investigation did the groundwork for the subsequent House Assassinations Committee probe, saw the information on New Orleans assembled for the first edition of this book—the material on 544 Camp Street in particular—as major progress. "It means," he said, "that for the first time in the whole Kennedy assassination investigation, we have evidence which places at 544 Camp Street intelligence agents, Lee Oswald, the Mob, and anti-Castro Cuban exiles. It puts all these elements together."

By the time New Orleans moved into the humid autumn of 1963, the disparate threads of assassination conspiracy did seem to come together. The days were slipping by toward tragedy in Dallas, and—to many of those who now saw President Kennedy as an obstacle, even an enemy—his words and overt actions only served to exacerbate a chronic grievance.

CHAPTER 18

The Cuban Conundrum

"Enmities between nations, as between individuals,
do not last forever."

—President Kennedy, June 10, 1963

The President stood in the open air, bareheaded as always, to address a throng of young people. It was graduation day at American University in Washington, DC, and the speech was the most significant he ever made on foreign policy. Kennedy told his listeners he intended to address the most important topic on Earth, "world peace," and his words indicated a major shift in the policy of head-on confrontation with Communism. "If we cannot now end our differences," the President said, "at least we can help make the world safe for diversity. For, in the final analysis, our most basic link is that we all inhabit this small planet. We all breathe the same air. We all cherish our children's future. And we are all mortal."

In the wake of the Cuban Missile Crisis, Kennedy was signaling that nuclear war must be made a remote possibility, the tensions of the Cold War eased. A month later, U.S. and British representatives signed an agreement with the Soviet Union that banned nuclear-bomb tests in the atmosphere, underwater, and in space. Announcing it, the President said: "Let us, if we can, get back from the shadows of war and seek out the way of peace. . . . Let history record that we, in this land, at this time, took the first step."

In 1963, to the forces of extreme conservatism in the United States, these words and actions seemed a dangerous deviation. To many Cuban exiles and their backers, it appeared to signal further betrayal of freedom's cause. For many years, the scenario painted by Kennedy hagiographers was of a president—determined to set the nation on a new course—opposed by plotters scheming to sabotage that policy and provoke confrontation with Havana and its Soviet patrons. Over the years, a more complex dynamic has emerged.

As of early spring 1963, things looked clear-cut enough. Alpha 66, one of the most aggressive of the exile groups, carried out a seaborne raid on a Cuban port and shot up a Soviet army installation and a Soviet freighter. Coming within months of the Missile Crisis, this was dangerously provocative. Then, in defiance of the President's demand to desist, the same group made two further attacks. With Moscow protesting vehemently, Kennedy moved to disassociate himself from the raids.

All along the Florida coast, U.S. authorities strove to interdict military activity by "freelance" groups like Alpha 66. The President did not say he was closing down all operations, only those not authorized by Washington. It seemed, though, that there no longer were many authorized missions. There were a few approved "pinprick" attacks in June, reportedly designed not so much to hurt Cuba as to warn Castro against interfering in other Latin American countries. Then, from mid-August, there was a steady tattoo of light airplane attacks, more commando raids, and sabotage. Castro stepped up his broadcast harangues, calling Kennedy "a ruffian . . . a horseman riding from error to error, from folly to folly."

Who ordered which raids is hard to disentangle without a full analysis of all the reports of the CIA, its auxiliaries in the armed forces, and the Special Group on Cuba overseen by Robert Kennedy.[1] The hagiographers' line has been that—though the Group did approve sabotage operations right up to and after the President's assassination—things were winding down, the will to overthrow Castro was evaporating. The truth may have been otherwise.

Throughout that summer, in camps on the Florida mainland and on islets and cays off the coast, exile fighters continued training for action under CIA control. According to a memoir by an Army officer seconded to the CIA as an instructor, Captain Bradley Ayers, the training was intensive and purposeful.[2] The authorities would never admit involvement, Ayers said. "One of the splinter, independent Cuban exile groups would publicly take credit for the raids."

By late summer 1963, according to Ayers, he was training above all small teams of commandos "to infiltrate Cuba, reach human targets, and assassinate them. Anyone in a senior position in government was fair game, and it reached down to the provincial heads, police chiefs and so on. But the principal target, we knew, was Castro—there was no secret about that amongst our people."

Ayers' account and a body of other information suggest that the President and his brother, the Attorney General, continued secretly to authorize far more activity—ruthless activity—than has ever been acknowledged. At the start of his assignment, in the spring of 1963, Ayers had been briefed at the CIA by General Victor Krulak, a personal friend of the President and a member of the Special Group. In the summer, according to Ayers, Robert Kennedy personally visited CIA personnel at their base in the Everglades. In the late fall, he flew by helicopter to one of the clandestine sites where assassination teams were trained.

Some exile leaders still talked that summer of "a new all-out drive" and the "ultimate invasion." Were they blowhards, deceived by empty assurances from Washington? Not so, thought one of the exiles Robert Kennedy took under his wing. Roberto San Román, brother of Pepe, the man who had led the exiles onto the beach at the Bay of Pigs, said in 1994, "We were never closer to liberation than we were in November 1963. . . . Even if it was just for their own ego, Kennedy and his brother—whom I knew well—wanted to get even with Castro."

Dean Rusk, who served as Secretary of State throughout the presidency, echoed that view in an interview with the author shortly before his death in 1994. "The Kennedys," Rusk said, "had an implacable hostility toward Castro, and they didn't let up."

No paper proof has ever surfaced showing that the President or his brother authorized the assassination of Fidel Castro. A document that surfaced in 2012—in the form of notes made by a secretary of a 1962 phone call to Secretary Rusk from CIA Director McCone—comes close. Both men had been at a meeting earlier in the day at which there had been agreement on unspecified strong measures to be taken against the Castro regime—a meeting that Robert Kennedy had attended.

McCone, a staunch Catholic who is known to have recoiled from involvement in murder, spoke elliptically. "M[cCone]," Rusk's secretary noted, "said the question came up this morning in connection with an individual that should not come up in m[eetin]gs. M[cCone] does not think we should countenance talking or thinking about that." The "individual," it is reasonable from the context to surmise, was Castro. "That," McCone surely knew Rusk would understand, was "assassination."[3] (See facsimile below.)

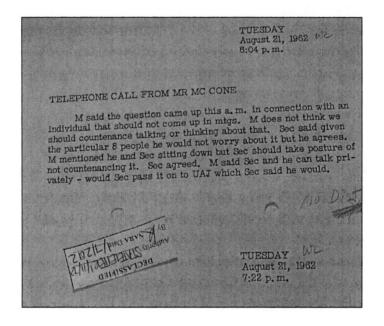

The notion that the Kennedys approved the concept of Castro's murder—for all Kennedy loyalists' denials—has been bolstered by books published in the past decade or so.[4]

Over many months, the CIA conducted a covert relationship with a senior Cuban who, the CIA believed, had turned traitor. This was Rolando Cubela, a hero of the revolution who had been in touch with the CIA on and off since early 1961. He had become disenchanted, he said, with increasing Soviet interference in Cuban affairs. There were some inconsistencies in Cubela's profile suggesting he might not be trustworthy, but the CIA nevertheless took him on as an "asset." By mid-1962, he was—according to the CIA account—telling his case officer that he favored "violent action . . . one master stroke" to overthrow Castro.

The orthodox thinking on the episode was for years that CIA officials—overstepping their authority—plotted Castro's assassination behind the backs of the President and his brother. If the brothers encouraged other assassination plots against Castro, though—as compelling information now suggests—why doubt they were likewise aware of the Cubela plot?[5]

There is something else. Many long accepted that Cubela may have been the traitor to Castro he appeared to be. A 2012 account of the episode by former senior CIA analyst Brian Latell, however, suggests persuasively that—as initially seemed possible—Cubela was a double agent all along. The "traitor," according to this thesis, reported every approach by the CIA back to Castro.

The possible implications are obvious, an encouragement to those who theorize that Castro—becoming aware at some point that the United States hoped to have him killed—struck first and had a hand in President Kennedy's assassination.

The totality of the evidence, though, is too tangled to justify that easy speculation.

With the exception of those privy to the continuing plans to overthrow Castro, Cuban exiles saw out the summer of 1963 filled with gloom and resentment. Passions ran highest among those the administration had discarded as extremists, whose operations were stymied by the Kennedy clampdown on unauthorized military activity.

A host of disparate exile groups had been trained and armed to the teeth, and admonitions from the White House only inflamed their determination to persist. One Bay of Pigs veteran said long afterward, "We used the tactics we learned from the CIA because we were trained by them to do everything."

The most militant groups, like Alpha 66—the group that incurred the President's wrath with its attacks on Soviet shipping—had no intention of going out of business. More worryingly, some of the CIA's protégés appear to have retained the loyalty and moral support of elements within the Agency itself. To such men, Kennedy's new policies were to be opposed and thwarted.

Over the years, the author talked many times with the founder of Alpha 66, Antonio Veciana, a man whose revelations were to lead to intensive congressional investigation. They appeared to identify an element, either of the CIA or of one of the tentacles of U.S. intelligence, as having been behind exile outrages—a shadowy presence that deliberately sought to sabotage the President's search for a modus vivendi with the Soviet Union.

When his group attacked Soviet ships in March 1963, Veciana claimed, it was on specific instructions from a man he knew as "Maurice Bishop"—the code name for his American intelligence handler. It was at Bishop's urging that Veciana and his colleagues bragged about their exploits at a Washington press conference. It was he who continued to press them to flout Kennedy orders and mount fresh actions. "It was my case officer," Veciana said, "who had the idea to attack the Soviet ships. The intention was to cause trouble between Kennedy and Russia. 'Bishop' believed that Kennedy and Khrushchev had made a secret agreement that the U.S.A. would do nothing more to help in the fight against

Castro. . . . He said you had to put Kennedy against the wall in order to force him to make decisions that would remove Castro's regime."

Veciana said he worked under the tutelage of "Maurice Bishop" from 1960, when the Cuban had been a leading accountant working in Havana, up to and beyond his flight from Cuba—for a total of nearly thirteen years. He had left Cuba following a botched assassination plot against Castro—the first but not the last that Bishop was to propose. His American patron also promoted armed landing operations and other skullduggery.

Ominously, Veciana asserted, Bishop told him in 1963 that "the best thing for this country was that Kennedy and his advisers should not be running it." Just months after Bishop uttered those sentiments, according to Veciana, he saw him in the company of Lee Oswald.

It was late August or the first days of September, Veciana recalled, when Bishop summoned him to a meeting in Dallas, Texas—a city where they often had rendezvous. On arrival in Dallas, Veciana was told to meet Bishop at a skyscraper business building in the downtown area. From the details Veciana provided, this has been identified as having been the Southland Center, headquarters of a major insurance group. It had a public area on the first floor. When Veciana arrived, a little ahead of schedule, Bishop was not alone.

In Veciana's words, "Maurice was accompanied by a young man who gave me the impression of being very quiet, rather strange and preoccupied. The three of us walked to a cafeteria. The young man was with us ten or fifteen minutes, until Maurice told him something like, 'All right, see you later,' and dismissed him." After the assassination, when Lee Oswald's face was plastered all over the newspapers and television screens, Veciana said, he at once recognized Oswald as the young man he had seen with Bishop in Dallas.

Veciana remained adamant that there was no mistake. An Assassinations Committee staff report noted: "There was absolutely no doubt in his mind that the man was Oswald, not just someone who resembled him." Veciana pointed out that he had been trained by Bishop and his associates to remember the physical characteristics of people. If it was not Oswald he saw with his handler, he said, it was his "exact double."

Oswald may indeed have visited Dallas at the date Veciana mentioned. Though he was based at the time in New Orleans, the alleged Bishop meeting occurred during a period for which his movements are sparsely documented. Oswald was unusually invisible between August 21 and September 17, making only one New Orleans appearance that was reported by witnesses. This was on Labor Day, September 2, when he reportedly visited Charles Murret—the uncle with Mafia connections.

Otherwise, Oswald's documented progress is marked by records of visits to the employment office, the cashing of unemployment checks, and the withdrawal of library books. These are not necessarily valid for charting Oswald's movements—the FBI could authenticate Oswald's signature on only a few of the unemployment documents. Of the seventeen firms where Oswald said he applied for work, thirteen denied it and four did not even exist. Even accepting the timetable the record suggests, moreover, there is one uninterrupted gap, between September 6 and 9.

A hint that Oswald may indeed have been out of New Orleans lies in the fact that three library books returned at the end of this period were overdue—a unique lapse in Oswald's usually meticulous library discipline over the months. On the evidence, there is no problem in accepting that there may have been an Oswald excursion to Dallas—five hundred miles away—within the Veciana time frame.[6]

"The Committee cannot be conclusive," Assassinations Committee Chief Counsel Robert Blakey told a public hearing, "but it can say that Veciana's allegations remain undiscredited." That careful statement reflected differences of opinion within the Committee about Veciana—differences colored by the possible implications of his claim.[7]

As detailed on a later page, the Committee found evidence that a person using the name Bishop did exist, and in the ranks of the CIA. This author, moreover, located a witness who had acted as cutout between Veciana and Bishop. The Committee established, too—though the available record is sparse—that the CIA did have contact with Veciana in the early 1960s. U.S. Army Intelligence also had an "operational interest," because of Veciana's role with Alpha 66. The CIA denied, however, having assigned a case officer to Veciana—a denial the Committee found hard to accept because he was the dominant figure in a major exile organization.

The Committee investigator who pursued the Veciana lead, Gaeton Fonzi, believed the Cuban's account of having seen Oswald with Bishop was truthful, that Bishop was indeed a CIA officer—and that he uncovered the real identity of the man behind the pseudonym. The issue will become pertinent as this story unfolds.

In June 1963, in Florida, federal agents enforcing the Kennedy clamp-down seized an aircraft and explosives intended for use in an exile bombing raid against the Shell Oil refinery in Cuba.

The Cuban and American veterans of the CIA's secret war they briefly detained, however, were not out of action for long. It was soon obvious that they were again active at camps near New Orleans, where Lee Oswald was by now involved in his own Cuban activities.

Anti-Castro exiles had been training for some time at Lacombe, a camp a few miles outside New Orleans where David Ferrie was by one account an instructor.[8] In late July, after an influx of guerilla trainees, federal agents raided a property in the area, seizing explosives, napalm, and bomb casings. The property was controlled by William McLaney who, with his brother, Mike, had operated out of Havana during the heyday of gambling before the Castro revolution.[9] After the raid, Carlos Bringuier, the exile who a few days later would be involved in the New Orleans fracas with Oswald, helped coordinate the dispersal of the exile trainees.

Among those detained or formally cautioned in the raid were a number of American advisers, including members of a group called Interpen—more grandly known as the Intercontinental Penetration Force. They included Alexander Rorke and Frank Sturgis, both of whom had persistently flouted government orders ever since the Missile Crisis. Rorke would die on a mission before the Kennedy assassination. Sturgis went on to gain notoriety years later as one of the Watergate burglars controlled by the exiles' CIA champion, Howard Hunt.

Sturgis' anti-Castro group reportedly received financing from the Mafia. Several of his associates arrested during the Kennedy clampdown were names that would later crop up in assassination-related evidence. One was Loran Hall, who had previously been in detention in Cuba along with Mafia boss Santo Trafficante—and will feature significantly at a later point in this book.

As so often in this labyrinthine tale, the names and the threads of evidence interconnect and merge under the common denominator of American intelligence and the Mafia. Here were some of the men most stung by the Kennedy clampdown on free-lance anti-Castro operations. "Those individuals sponsoring this activity," a 1970s Senate Intelligence Committee report was to note in masterly understatement, "were angered."

They must have been angriest at the message implied by the official statement that explained the government raids to the public. The raid on the Mafia-backed camp near New Orleans was described as designed to thwart "an effort to carry out a military operation against a country with which the United States is at peace."

The United States *at peace* with Castro's Cuba, true or not, was a notion the exiles and their backers would never accept.

Soon after the government closures of unauthorized training camps, and within a month of the alleged meeting between Oswald and the U.S. intelligence officer who used the name Bishop, the alleged assassin began the next and fateful phase of his Cuba-related activity. On September 17, 1963, Oswald walked into the Mexican Consulate in New Orleans and applied for a tourist card, the document necessary for entry to Mexico.

He had no difficulty in obtaining the card, for he was equipped with a copy of his birth certificate and a brand-new passport—the latest product of the former defector's improbably smooth relationship with the State Department. He had applied for the passport two months earlier, just before the start of his pro-Castro program in New Orleans, specifying on the application form—just as he had in 1959—that he intended to travel to the Soviet Union. He had even drawn attention to his inglorious past, acknowledging that his previous passport had been canceled.

Oswald's application went to the Passport Office of the State Department in Washington, DC, directed in those days by Frances Knight, a dragon of a bureaucrat famous for her stern restrictions on the movement of American leftists. On this occasion, however, the system seemed oddly paralyzed. No official queried the intentions of this self-declared Marxist who had once offered state secrets to the Soviets. Nobody was concerned, it seemed, about the possibility of a second defection. Oswald had his passport within twenty-four hours.

At the Mexican Consulate a few weeks later, he was promptly issued Tourist Card number 824085. It was a process that in due course would lead to a further—and baffling—CIA blip on the radar of the Oswald story.

Next to Oswald's name, at number 824084 on the list of all other people who applied for Mexican entry papers in New Orleans on September 17, was that of one William Gaudet. He had been a source for the CIA as far back as the late 1940s and, in the fall of 1963, was Mexico-bound at the same time as Oswald.

The author located Gaudet fifteen years later, living out his retirement at a seaside home in Mississippi. Pressed to explain how he came to be next to Lee Oswald on the list of applications for travel to Mexico, he said, "It is apparently because we both went into the Consulate one after the other. . . . It was pure coincidence and ah . . . because I certainly had not discussed it with him, because I hadn't talked to him. . . . I have no control over what the CIA did or did not do down in Mexico."

Gaudet's CIA file revealed only that he "provided foreign intelligence information" in the 1950s, and mentioned no contact after 1961. Gaudet, however, himself said he had contact with the CIA as late as 1969. He agreed that he was "just loaded down with coincidences" and that his appearance on the visa list was astonishing. On his September 1963 trip, he thought, he had merely passed through Mexico City in transit.

Gaudet said that, under cover of running a publication called the *Latin American Newsletter*, he worked for the CIA for more than twenty years. It was a secret connection, one that he confided to no one—not even his wife. Though retired, he was angry and suspicious about the way his name had been revealed—angry especially that his cover had been blown. "I am now convinced in my own mind," he said, "that those who are truly behind the conspiracy to kill Mr. Kennedy have done things purposely to draw attention to me."

While denying any involvement in the Oswald visit to Mexico, Gaudet said Oswald had been "known to him" in New Orleans. Then, adjusting the statement, he asserted that he had merely observed Oswald handing out leaflets in the street on several occasions. Gaudet had apparently observed him enough, nevertheless, to assess him as a "very nervous, frail, weak man."

After a few hours with William Gaudet, an interviewer came away, rightly or wrongly, with an impression of a man who knew more—perhaps only a little more—than he was prepared to discuss on the record. What he did say seemed intended to protect his own, probably innocent, role, out of indignation that his CIA cover had been blown.

During a second visit by the author, Gaudet let slip something that at the time meant little but in hindsight seemed more significant than his appearance on the Mexico visa list. It happened when the author became openly skeptical that Gaudet could have gained his obvious knowledge of Oswald purely from "coincidental" sightings in the streets of New Orleans. "I do know," Gaudet said then, "that I saw him one time with a former FBI agent by the name of Guy Banister. . . . What Guy's role in all of this was I . . . really don't know." Gaudet had paused briefly, but now said in a rush, "I did see Oswald discussing various things with Banister at the time, and I think Banister knew a whole lot of what was going on." He also said, "I suppose you are looking into Ferrie. He was with Oswald."[10]

Gaudet had seen Oswald with Banister, he volunteered, "near my office, which was at Camp Street and Common Street in New Orleans." This meant, of course, that Gaudet's office was a stone's throw from Banister's office at 544 Camp Street, the address that appears to link Oswald to anti-Castro activity—the very opposite of what he ostensibly stood for.[11]

The New Orleans connection is pivotal, whether one believes President Kennedy's murder was the work of Oswald alone, Cuban exiles, the Mafia, some element of American intelligence, or a synthesis of all three. Once again in this case, the leads come full circle.

Reasonably enough, Gaudet balked at the idea that the CIA as an agency had any involvement in the assassination. He thought, though, that there was a tie-in that would embarrass the CIA, that it was "extremely possible" that Oswald had been used by some element of American intelligence. Gaudet found nothing contradictory in the fact that the CIA has repeatedly denied any connection with Oswald. He said of his own CIA service, "They told me frankly when I did things for them that if something went awry they would never recognize me or admit who I was. If I made a mistake, that was just tough, and I knew it."

Gaudet did not believe Oswald killed the President. He said, "I think he was a patsy. I think he was set up on purpose." Asked to explain, he subsided into silence.

On September 16, 1963, just a day before Oswald applied for papers to travel to Mexico, a CIA officer briefed a senior Bureau counterpart on new plans for action against the Fair Play for Cuba Committee. "John Tilton, CIA," a senior FBI agent reported, "advised that his Agency is giving some consideration to countering the activities of [the Fair Play for Cuba Committee] in foreign countries . . . CIA is also giving some thought to planting *deceptive information which might embarrass the Committee* [author's emphasis] in areas where it does have some support. Pursuant to a discussion with the Liaison Agent, Tilton advised that his Agency will not take action without first consulting the Bureau, bearing in mind that we wish to make certain the CIA activity will not jeopardize any Bureau investigation."

As reported in these pages, U.S. intelligence had long been engaged in "countering activities," penetrating, discrediting, and smearing the FPCC. Mexico City was a place where the Committee was well supported, a fact that made its local chapter a target for the attention of American agents.

For a few days after obtaining his Mexican visa, Oswald busied himself writing a summary of his achievements as a Marxist activist in the service of socialism. The high point of the narrative, following a catalog of his diligent studies and sojourn in Russia, was his pro-Castro effort in New Orleans. As he had done in the past when he had urgent work to do on his own, Oswald got rid of his wife for a while. They would never again live together as husband and wife. Marina, burdened with one child and pregnant with a second, left to stay with her friend Ruth Paine in Texas.

Sometime on the evening of September 24, Oswald slipped away from his New Orleans apartment.

With two months to go until the assassination, then, the man who would be named as the assassin was at large, his true loyalties unclear—in an atmosphere of international uncertainty and— we now know—as conspiracy proliferated.

Nearly a year after the terrifying standoff between Washington and Moscow over Cuba, tension still simmered. Four years after Castro had triumphed, overt confrontation had been replaced by a lack of clarity and covert intrigue.

The Kennedy administration's Cuba policy was a dangerous mix of confrontation and hesitancy. Reining in exile military activity had rendered heavily armed activists venomously hostile. Elements of the CIA, meanwhile, remained embroiled in the secret war against Castro. It included plots to assassinate the Cuban leader—plots that may have been approved by Kennedy himself.

Key players in the murderous schemes had included not only exiles but U.S. Mafia bosses with their own reasons to see Castro gone. Those same Mafia chieftains, pursued and prosecuted to the point of desperation, loathed the Kennedy brothers.

U.S. intelligence agencies, meanwhile, were continuing— even stepping up—undercover efforts to counter pro-Castro organizations or individuals, penetrate groups with planted agents, read their mail, work secretly to besmirch the anti-Castro cause and thwart its efforts—even take the fight beyond the frontiers of the United States.

In that atmosphere, against that backdrop, Lee Oswald—the pro-Castro activist who was perhaps something more complex than that, a young man whose family was linked to the Mafia—began a weeklong visit to Mexico.

IV

ENDGAME
Deception and Tragedy

CHAPTER 19

Exits and Entrances in Mexico City

"Oswald's visit to Mexico City in
September–October 1963 remains one of the most
vexing sub-plots to the assassination story."

—Assassinations Records Review Board, Final Report,
1998

Fellow passengers would remember the young man who joined Continental Trailways bus number 5133 in the early hours of the morning of September 26, somewhere in southern Texas. He was somewhat unusual. During the journey to the Mexican border, and afterward on a Mexican bus, he positively advertised who he was and the reason for his journey.

He sought out two Australian women, Pamela Mumford and Patricia Winston, in seats at the back of the bus to regale them with stories of his service in the Marine Corps and in the Soviet Union. He pulled out his old 1959 passport to prove he really had been in Russia. He struck up a conversation with a British couple, Bryan and Meryl McFarland, and said he had been secretary of the Fair Play for Cuba Committee in New Orleans. He was traveling through Mexico, he confided, in order to get to Cuba where he hoped to see Fidel Castro. At a time of tension over Cuba, when Americans traveling there were liable to prosecution on their return, this man emphasized that his destination was Havana.[1]

Telling the two Australians that he had been to Mexico City before, the garrulous young man recommended the Hotel Cuba as a good place to stay.[2] Within an hour of the bus arriving, however, a hotel registration form was to show, a "Lee Harvey Oswald" checked into a different place altogether—the Hotel Comercio. He was allotted Room 18.

The young man on the bus and at the Comercio very likely was Lee Oswald. Bus and frontier records, later identification by fellow passengers, and handwriting in the hotel register, indicate strongly that Oswald did travel to Mexico City. It appears, too, that he returned to the United States six days later, again by bus.[3] The truth as to what Oswald did during his stay, though, remains the subject of doubt and speculation.

The Warren Commission was to decide that Oswald spent his leisure hours in Mexico alone, going to the movies, perhaps to a bullfight, and dining cheaply at a restaurant near his hotel. Its Report did not mention, however, the statement by another Hotel Comercio guest, who said he observed Oswald in the company of four Cubans, one of them from Florida. The hotel, it has since been reported, was a local haunt of anti-Castro Cuban exiles.

The truth behind the Oswald visit to Mexico hinges on Cuba. For someone—someone who may not have been the authentic Oswald—appears to have used the name "Oswald" in situations that would later seem highly compromising. Was an impostor at work, at least at some stages of the Oswald stay? Was the real Lee Harvey Oswald the victim of a sophisticated setup—one that did not necessarily have anything to with the assassination?

Far-fetched notion though that may seem, U.S. intelligence did practice impersonation in Mexico City at the relevant time—as this chapter will show. The Mexico episode is a labyrinth through which no one—official investigators included—has yet found a satisfactory way.

For Sylvia Durán—a young Mexican woman working in the consular section of the Cuban Embassy—Friday, September 27, had been a normal morning of processing visa applications. Then, shortly before lunchtime by her account, in came a young American. She would remember him as ungainly, hesitant, unsure of himself. He asked, "Do you speak English?" and was relieved to find she did. He was Lee Harvey Oswald, an American citizen, he said, and he wanted a transit visa. He wanted to travel to Cuba, stay for a couple of weeks, then fly on to the Soviet Union. The request was urgent, as he wanted to leave in three days' time.

As credentials, the visitor produced the documentary harvest of Oswald's time in the Soviet Union and New Orleans. Sylvia Durán was shown passports, old Soviet documents, correspondence with the American Communist Party, membership cards for the Fair Play for Cuba Committee, identification as president of the FPCC's New Orleans chapter, and a newspaper clipping about the demonstration that had ended in Oswald's arrest. There was even—Durán was to say—a photograph of Oswald in custody, a policeman on each arm. She would reflect later that it had looked phony, and indeed no such photograph is known to have been taken of Oswald prior to his arrest after the assassination.

Even at the time, Durán felt something was not right. The display of allegiance to the Cuban cause seemed strangely overdone. If the applicant was, as he claimed, a Communist Party member, why had he not arranged his visa the customary way, by applying in advance to the Communist Party in Cuba? In any case, Sylvia Durán was to point out, clearance for the onward journey to Russia was necessary before a Cuban transit visa could be issued. She would also need passport-size photographs to go with the visa application, she told the applicant, and suggested a place nearby to have some taken. Looking a little crestfallen, the visitor went off to obtain the photos.

When he returned, pictures in hand, Sylvia Durán accepted the visa application and told the man to call in about a week. He departed, protesting that he could stay in Mexico for only three days, only to return yet again later in the afternoon. The Consulate was by then closed to the public, but the man talked his way in and rushed back to Durán's office in a state of agitation. He said he had been to the Soviet Embassy—a visit that did occur, according to former Russian officials who spoke with the author years later—and was confident that the required visa for Russia would be granted. Could the Cubans now issue the visa to Havana?

When Durán checked with the Soviet Embassy by phone, however, the truth turned out to be otherwise. Though they knew about Oswald, they said, it could take as long as four months for Moscow to decide on his application to go to Russia. At that, the young stranger caused a scene that Durán said she would never forget. "He didn't want to listen," she told the author in 1978. "His face reddened, his eyes flashed, and he shouted, 'Impossible! I can't wait that long!' " Then the Consul himself, Eusebio Azcue, stepped in and reproved the fuming American. A person like him, he said, was "harming the Cuban revolution more than helping it."

Azcue and the man who would soon replace him him, Alfredo Mirabal, thought the supposed U.S. Communist Party membership card the applicant had produced looked suspect, strangely new and unused.[4] (Indeed, Oswald never had joined the Party.) When the American mocked Azcue and Durán as being mere "bureaucrats," the Consul angrily ordered him out of the building. That, Durán told the author, was the last she ever saw of him.[5]

The next day, Saturday, September 28—again according to the former Soviet diplomats—there was a second Oswald visit to the Soviet Embassy. If only the officials could be convinced to give him a Soviet visa, Oswald still seemed to hope, the Cubans would clear him to travel to Havana. The three Soviets who were to say they saw him that day were, in fact—as was and often is the case with "diplomats"—intelligence agents using cover. Interviewed by the author in Moscow in 1993, separately and without prior notice, the three former agents told a consistent story.

Oswald, they said, had arrived looking tense and nervous, begging to be given a visa at once. Impossible, they told him. As an American living in the United States, moreover, he should apply not in Mexico but to the Soviet Embassy in Washington, DC. Then the visitor told them he was sure he had been followed to the Embassy by American agents, and—perhaps to show how ready he was to confront his U.S. persecutors—tugged a handgun from his waistband. The burliest of the three agents, Valery Kostikov, gently relieved him of the weapon. Then, the conversation over and the gun returned to him—the former Soviet officials claimed—the downcast foreigner went on his way.

Months later, when Warren Commission lawyers probed the story of Oswald in Mexico, they had the benefit of only parts of the information summarized thus far. They did, though, have limited access—grudgingly provided—to top-secret information supplied by the CIA.[6] In Mexico City in 1963, from hiding places across the street from the Cuban and Soviet embassies, CIA agents routinely photographed visitors entering and leaving, bugged diplomats' offices with concealed microphones, and eavesdropped on telephone traffic—all with the collaboration of the Mexican intelligence service.

That the CIA did this is clear from the available record. In 1978 in Havana, moreover, intelligence officials showed the author some of the audio equipment they said they uncovered in 1964 at the Cuban mission. Every single telephone wall-socket, according to a Cuban electronics technician, contained a miniature microphone capable of transmitting conversations to CIA receiver points outside the building. The author was shown a device embedded in the arm of a chair, discovered—the Cubans said—in their Ambassador's office, as well as photographs of the building across the street where conversations were monitored and of the agents who manned it (see Photo 35).

Such CIA data as they were allowed to see, combined with other information, permitted the Warren Commission to build a scenario of an Oswald frantic to get to Cuba but rejected by the Communists he had expected to welcome him. The lawyers who wrote the Report were at a loss to see quite how that fitted into the overall picture of the case. Had there been serious investigation into the possibility that the assassination was not the work of a lone assassin, however, they might have read different signs in the evidence of New Orleans and Mexico. With the information available today—though there is clearly some that has still not surfaced—this tale of two cities raises serious questions.

What if Oswald had managed to get himself a Cuban visa, had traveled to Cuba, and had then gone on to be arrested for killing President Kennedy in Dallas weeks later? Even without having that in his record, as it turned out, Oswald's Fair Play for Cuba posturing in New Orleans, along with the apparent contacts with Communist diplomats in Mexico City, proved enormously provocative. The smoke of those contacts created immediate tension and apparently—for a dangerous moment— military alerts in both Washington and Moscow. There would be stories alleging that Oswald had been put up to the assassination by the Cubans.[7] In the fragile climate of November 1963, just over a year after the Missile Crisis, this was to be a moment of great peril.

There is reason to suspect that, during the Oswald episode in Mexico, others watched and schemed how to use his name and his activity to dark advantage—though not necessarily in connection with the assassination of the President. What can we really say that the authentic Oswald did in Mexico City?

When the troublesome American visited the Cuban mission, Consul Azcue had been working out the last weeks of his tour of duty in Mexico. He was back in Havana by the time the President was killed, and at first assumed—as did virtually everyone else—that the Oswald arrested in Dallas was one and the same as the man he had met. Then, two or three weeks later, Azcue watched a cinema newsreel that included scenes of Oswald under arrest for murder and being shot and killed by Jack Ruby. Those pictures of the alleged assassin, the former Consul told the House

Assassinations Committee in 1978, "in no way resembled" the man who had made a scene in his office.

Azcue remembered the man in his office as having been "maybe thirty-five years old," "of medium height," with features quite different from those of the authentic Oswald. The film, as Azcue said, shows a young man with a youthful, unlined face. It was, according to the Consul, "in radical contrast to the deeply lined face" of the man who—he said—came asking for a visa. The Lee Oswald arrested in Dallas was just twenty-four, 5'9½" tall, and very slim. Shown still photographs of the authentic Oswald, Azcue continued to say he believed "this gentleman was not, is not, the person or the individual who went to the Consulate."

The Consul's former colleague, Alfredo Mirabal, did not share Azcue's certainty but acknowledged that he saw the visitor only briefly when he peered out of his office to see what the fuss was about. Azcue, meanwhile, consistently maintained that he met someone other than the real Oswald. Was he mistaken? What of Sylvia Durán, who spent more time with the visa applicant than anyone else?

In her interviews with the author, Durán said that it never occurred to her in 1963 that the Dallas Oswald and the Oswald at the Consulate might have been different people. It had been not any visual image she initially saw but the name "Lee Oswald" in the newspaper after the assassination that made her think at once of the person who came to her office.[8] The brief news footage of Oswald being shot had not led her to think the victim was other than the man she had encountered.

In 1979, however, when the author arranged for Durán to see the longer TV interview of Oswald made in New Orleans, she said she "was not sure if it was Oswald or not . . . the man on the film is not like the man I saw here in Mexico City. . . . The man on this film speaks strongly and carries himself with confidence. The man who came to my office in Mexico City was small and weak and spoke in a trembling voice."

In notes she made on the incident, Durán wrote that the visa applicant had been at most about 5'6" tall. "Short . . . about my size," she told Assassinations Committee staff. Durán is a little woman, only 5'3½". Again, the authentic Oswald's height was 5'9 ½".

In her very first interview, responding to questioning the day after the assassination, Durán described the Oswald at the Embassy as having been *"rubio, bajo"*—which translates as "blond [or "fair-haired"], short."[9] Azcue, for his part, told the Assassinations Committee that he remembered the visitor as having been "dark blond." Oswald, according to an FBI document dated August 1963, had "light brown" hair.

One might put these anomolies down to faulty memory—and dismiss the discrepancy over the visa applicant's height—were it not for the spontaneous recollection of another Mexico City witness.

Oscar Contreras was a law student at Mexico City's National University in 1963. One evening at the time of the Oswald incidents in Mexico, he told the author, he and three friends were sitting in a university cafeteria talking. They all held left-ist views, and he belonged to a group that supported the Castro revolution—as did many Mexicans—and had contacts in the Cuban Embassy. As they chatted, a man at a nearby table came over and introduced himself, spelling out his entire name—"Lee Harvey Oswald."

Contreras and his friends laughed, for "Harvey" and "Oswald" were familiar to them as the names of characters in a popular cartoon about rabbits. Indeed, Contreras said, that was why the name stuck in his mind.

Like Consul Azcue, Contreras said the "Oswald" he met that evening looked older than thirty. Like Sylvia Durán, he recalled that Oswald was short—he, too, thought at most 5'6". Contreras, who was himself 5'9", clearly recalled having looked *down* at the man he still remembered as "Oswald the Rabbit."

With minor variations, Contreras' "Oswald" offered the students a familiar account of his background.[10] He had had to leave Texas, he said, because the FBI was bothering him. He declared that life in the United States was not for him. He wanted to go to Cuba, but for some reason the people at the Cuban Consulate were so far blocking his visa application. Could the students help—through their friends in the Embassy? Contreras and his friends said they would try.

When they talked to their Cuban contacts—they included Consul Azcue and a Cuban intelligence officer—they were warned to break off contact with this "Oswald." The Cubans said they suspected that his purpose was to infiltrate left-wing groups. When Oswald next came to see them, Contreras and his student friends told him that the Cubans did not trust him and were not going to give him a visa. "Oswald," who ended up spending the night at the students' apartment, was still begging for help in getting to Cuba when he left the following morning.

The next time Contreras heard the name Oswald, he said, was after the assassination. He had no love for the United States and did not report his encounter with "Oswald" to American authorities. Only four years later, having made the acquaintance of the then U.S. Consul, did he mention it in conversation. The Assassinations Committee found records showing that the lead had been considered "the first significant development in the investigation of the Kennedy assassination after 1965."

Having interviewed Contreras twice, the author thought him a credible witness. He had gone on to become a successful journalist—eventually the editor of *El Mundo*, the newspaper serving the town of Tampico.[11]

How, though, would the Oswald whom Contreras met have found his way into the student milieu? In 1994, in Mexico City, the author interviewed an attorney named Homobono Alcaraz. He had featured in FBI reports as having said that, while studying law—like Contreras—he, too, had met and talked with Oswald. The encounter, Alcaraz told the author, had occurred at Sanborn's restaurant, in the company of two or three other American students—all of them, like Alcaraz himself, Quakers.[12]

The students' talk had centered on the difficulties involved in getting to Cuba. Oswald, Alcaraz recalled, eventually left with one of the Americans—whom Alcaraz remembered as having been named Steve "Kennan, or Keenan" (Alcaraz had trouble pronouncing or spelling the name) from Philadelphia. They went off together on his motorbike, Oswald riding pillion, headed for the Cuban Consulate. Recent research established that a student from Philadelphia named Steve Kenin did visit and live for some time in Mexico, did frequent a Quaker guest house, and did ride a motorbike—and did travel to Cuba.[13]

The physical description Oscar Contreras supplied, like the anomalies arising from much of the Cuban Consulate scenario, has contributed to suspicion that the Oswald who visited the Consulate was an impostor. Pause, though, to consider the evidence official investigations accepted—that it *was* the real Oswald who pestered the Cuban officials. That evidence is persuasive if not conclusive.

The signature on the visa application form, graphologists told the Assassinations Committee, was Oswald's. Consular assistant Sylvia Durán had, as noted, required passport-size photos for the visa, recommended a nearby photographic service, and said her visitor later returned with the necessary photos. The picture affixed to the surviving application form certainly appears to be that of Oswald.

Some ifs and buts remain. Absent cast-iron evidence, graphologists' views are not legally considered reliable. There is doubt, too, about the visa photos' provenance. Investigation following the assassination indicated that the pictures had not been taken at any local Mexico City establishment. As for Sylvia Durán, she could not remember for sure when precisely she handed the visa application forms to her visitor and at what stage the applicant signed. Sometimes, she said, she would allow the signed forms to leave the building. Her boss, Azcue, for his part, told the Assassinations Committee that he could "almost assure" them that the clothing worn in the visa photo was different from that worn by the man he met.

Following the imposture notion, one might assume that an operative impersonating an individual would have had access to authentic photographs and familiarity with the signature of his subject.

There is more, though, information that—for this author— seems to clinch the matter so far as the Oswald at the Cuban Consulate is concerned. After the assassination, the name and phone number of consular assistant Sylvia Durán were found scrawled in Oswald's address book. There is the fact, too, that—though his wife, Marina, initially denied all knowledge of a Mexico trip and visits to the embassies—she eventually acknowledged that her husband told her about it.[14]

The House Assassinations Committee Report stated that the Committee thought "the weight of the evidence" indicated that Oswald visited both the Cuban Consulate and the Soviet Embassy.[15] Its 410-page study of the complex Mexico episode said, nevertheless, that the evidence pointing to impersonation of Oswald was "of such a nature that the possibility cannot be dismissed." The Committee's Final Report noted, too, that it focused on the possibility that an impostor visited the Soviet Embassy or Cuban Consulate "during one or more of the contacts in which Oswald was identified by the CIA."

If an Oswald impostor did operate in Mexico City, could the CIA have been involved? The Agency did impersonate people there, and within months of the Oswald visit. A real-life scenario, with striking similarities to the game suspected to have been played when Oswald was there has surfaced, in a CIA document.

Just two months before the Oswald appearances, a U.S. citizen from Texas named Eldon Hensen twice made phone contact with the Cuban Embassy. He could not himself come to the Embassy, he told an aide, because "an American spy might see him"—but gave the name of his hotel. Hours later, he received a call from a man who identified himself as a member of the Embassy staff. They duly met and talked, and Hensen offered to work on behalf of the Cuban government on his return to the United States.

The Cuban "aide" had, in fact, been in the pay of the CIA. "At station request," read a subsequent Agency cable to HQ, "[name withheld] posing as CUBEMB officer made contact . . . lured Subj[ect] to hotel restaurant . . . [second name redacted] witnessed meeting from nearby table . . . [withheld word, probably the FBI] informed . . . will handle stateside investigation."

By using its audio surveillance of the Cuban mission, the Agency had entrapped would-be pro-Castro activist Hensen. "A standard operation there," former Assassinations Records Review Board Executive Director Jeremy Gunn said in 2003, "was to impersonate Americans in telephone contact with the [Soviet] Embassy." There is no good reason to suppose the CIA dealt otherwise with the Cuban mission.

Assassinations Committee investigators strove for months to get the CIA to cooperate in its search for the truth about Mexico City—and emerged certain that the Agency was hiding something. What follows draws on documents that they, and later the Assassinations Records Review Board, did succeed in extracting. It provides a glimpse, but only a glimpse, of what really occurred.

On October 8, 1963, a week after the supposed Oswald visits to the embassies, CIA Mexico City Chief of Station Winston Scott sent a name trace request to headquarters in Langley on an:

American male who spoke broken Russian said his name Lee OSWALD (phonetic), stated he at SOVEMB on 28 Sept . . . Have photos male appears be American entering Sovemb 1216 hours, leaving 1222 on 1 Oct. Apparent age 35, athletic build circa 6 feet, receding hairline, balding top . . ."

Scott was sending in his query on the basis of surveillance photographs of the individual in question, one of which is reproduced in this book (see Photo 36). CIA headquarters knew Oswald did not answer the description sent in by Scott, as it made clear in a response to the Mexico station. "Oswald," a staffer wrote, "is five feet ten inches, one hundred sixty-five pounds, light brown wavy hair. . . ."

The same day, October 10, however, a teletype went out from

CIA headquarters to the FBI, the State Department, and the U.S. Navy—suggesting the older man might be one and the same as Oswald. Having noted the basics about the thirty-five-year-old, balding six-footer who had visited the Soviet Embassy, the headquarters message went on to state:

IT IS BELIEVED THAT OSWALD MAY BE IDENTICAL TO LEE HENRY [sic] OSWALD, BORN ON 18 OCTOBER 1939 IN NEW ORLEANS, LOUISIANA. A FORMER U.S. MARINE WHO DEFECTED TO THE SOVIET UNION IN OCTOBER 1959 AND LATER MADE ARRANGEMENTS THROUGH THE UNITED STATES EMBASSY IN MOS-COW TO RETURN TO THE UNITED STATES WITH HIS RUSSIAN-BORN WIFE, MARINA NIKOLAEVNA PUSA-KOVA [sic], AND THEIR CHILD . . .

These documents alone were to lead to prolonged struggles between the CIA and investigators, congressional committees and private researchers alike. Who was the American at the Soviet Embassy who "identified himself as Lee Oswald" but looked totally unlike him—ten years older, taller, and heavier-built? Could that be confirmation that someone had impersonated Oswald?

Agency spokesmen were at pains to explain that there really was no mystery at all. According to the CIA, the raw data on the "Oswald" visit to the Soviet mission had initially been associated with a picture of another "person known to frequent the Soviet Embassy," who had been there three days after the Oswald visit. Someone at the CIA's Mexico City station had mistakenly "guessed" that the heavily built man of thirty-five and Oswald were one and the same.

On receiving the misleading report, headquarters in Washington had then supposedly tried to sort out the discrepancy between the photos of the thirty-five-year-old and the contradictory file details of the real Oswald collected during his time in Russia. The task was made more difficult, the CIA would later claim, by the supposed fact that the Agency at that point had no photograph of the real Oswald. "CIA did not have a known photograph of Oswald in its files before the assassination of President Kennedy either in Washington or abroad," CIA officer Raymond Rocca, who as head of Research and Analysis was a senior colleague of Counterintelligence chief James Angleton— was to write in a 1967 memorandum. More than a decade after the assassination, then CIA Director William Colby would still be saying of the man who was not Oswald: "We don't to this day know who he is."

Some documents, however, contradict these claims. Right after the assassination, when Mexico station chief Winston Scott sent photos of the man who was not Oswald to headquarters, he noted that they were "photographs of a certain person who is known to you." Months later, the CIA would tell the Warren Commission it "could be embarrassing to the individual involved, who as far as this Agency is aware had no connection with Lee Harvey Oswald or the assassination."[16]

The CIA's claim that it had no photograph of the real Oswald on record, moreover, does not stand up. The Agency's own files indicate that it did have pictures of the real Oswald at the time of the Mexico affair. Less than four months after the assassination, when the CIA sent the Warren Commission what it called "an exact reproduction of the Agency's official dossier [on Oswald] . . . exact copies of all material in this file up to early October 1963"—the time of the Mexico episode. Included in the dossier were clippings from the *Washington Post* and *Washington Evening Star* dated 1959, reporting the authentic Oswald's defection to the Soviet Union—and featuring news agency photographs of Oswald.[17]

The CIA indulged in shadow-boxing with the Warren Commission after the assassination. Faced with a request for three Agency cables that dealt with the matter of the photos of the man who was not Oswald, it played for time. In an internal memorandum, Counterintelligence chief Angleton's colleague Rocca expressed his boss' desire to "wait out" the Commission.[18] Wesley Liebeler, one of the few Commission attorneys who had direct contact with CIA personnel, would recall that the Agency had been so secretive about the photographs as to be virtually useless.

The photograph puzzle prompted yet another question. Whether or not the photographs of heavily built man at the Soviet Embassy had anything to do with the case, they were evidence—as reported earlier in these pages—that CIA cameras did indeed photograph people visiting Communist embassies. That being so, should not the Agency have pictures of whoever *did* go to the Soviet and Cuban Embassies—on several occasions—using the name Oswald? Photographs of him there, after all, would clear up the matter once and for all. Where are they?

The CIA has always denied having obtained any such photographs, and offered a variety of explanations. The camera at the Soviet Embassy, according to an internal CIA document, did not operate on weekends. That would explain why there were no pictures of Oswald on the Saturday he is said to have visited the Soviets. The cameras at the Cuban mission were also apparently not used at the weekend. Yet there were a total of four "Oswald" visits, combining those to the Cuban and

Soviet missions, on Friday, September 27—a weekday. Why, then, would there be no photographs from any of those total of eight entrances and exits?

A senior CIA officer who served in Mexico accounted for the absence of photos at the Cuban Consulate by claiming that the camera at that site happened to break down during the Oswald visit to Mexico City. Documents now available, however, show that not one but two cameras covered the entrances to the Cuban mission on September 27. One of those cameras was activated for the first time that very morning, and—it appears—worked that day.

What then of the photo surveillance at the Soviet Embassy? Freedom of Information suits eventually extracted the information that no less than twelve photographs were taken of the man who was not Oswald. They show the mystery man in various poses and wearing different clothes, and one of them was taken on October 1—one of the days an "Oswald" supposedly went to the Soviet Embassy. Why do we have no CIA pictures of Oswald there?

The Assassinations Committee investigators' report noted that an "Oswald" made at least five visits to the Communist embassies, perhaps as many as six. It was hard to believe that CIA cameras failed to pick him up even once. In a draft manuscript he left behind when he died, former Chief of Station Scott wrote that there had been such photos. Several other former Agency officers, moreover, said CIA cameras got pictures of Oswald, or of someone identified as Oswald, on visits to the two missions.

The Committee speculated that "photographs of Oswald might have been taken and subsequently lost or destroyed . . ." It did not question how the CIA could have lost pictures of Oswald—of all people. And why would the Agency *destroy* such photographs? In its 1998 report to President Clinton, the Records Review Board probably got close to the truth when it wrote carefully that the "CIA reports that it did not *locate* [author's emphasis] photographic evidence of Oswald's visits." If the CIA did have photographs of the real Oswald entering the embassies, and entering alone, one can be sure it would have been delighted to produce them long ago.

The CIA's account of its other surveillance system in Mexico City, the tapping and bugging of Communist embassies, is also feeble. If the embassies were bugged and their telephones tapped, and if that is how some of the intelligence on Oswald was gathered, where are the sound tapes?

Asked about the recordings in 1975 on CBS' *Sixty Minutes* program, then CIA Director William Colby responded vaguely that he thought there had been Oswald voice recordings from the embassy contacts. There had indeed.

The file shows that the Agency tapped a phone call—supposedly from the Cuban Consulate to the Soviet Embassy—by a man the CIA indicated was Oswald, purportedly on Saturday, September 28. According to the CIA record, there were also two tapped Oswald conversations with the Soviet Embassy on Tuesday, October 1. Having listened to both calls, the transcriber said they involved the same caller.

According to information the CIA supplied to the Warren Commission about those calls, "The American spoke *in very poor Russian . . .* [author emphasis]." The speaker's ability in Russian is elsewhere described as "terrible, hardly recognizable." That does not sound like the real Oswald, who had achieved a good standard of spoken Russian while in the Soviet Union and on his return to Texas impressed the Russian community with his fluency in colloquial Russian. Sylvia Durán, moreover, insisted that the Oswald who visited her took no part in the call she made to the Soviet Embassy to discuss the visa request. He did not use the telephone while in her office, nor did he say anything in Russian.

The CIA stance on the Mexico City episode—that until Oswald's name surfaced after the assassination his embassy visits were simply routinely logged, not at the time assigned any importance—is not borne out by the account of the Mexico City transcriber and translator who worked on the taped material. Located years later by a *Washington Post* reporter, they said the Oswald tapes triggered a departure from routine. "Usually," the translator said, "they picked up the transcripts the next day. This they wanted right away." Former Chief of Station Scott, moreover, wrote in his draft memoir that Oswald had been "a person of great interest to us during this September 27 to 2 October period."

The CIA told the Assassination Records Review Board it "destroyed tape[s] containing Oswald's voice and other related calls as a matter of routine procedure." The Agency's position was, as it had long been, that tapes of no particular intelligence value were wiped after two weeks and recycled.[19] In a 2005 interview, however, former Mexico case officer Anne Goodpasture—referring to the recording of an October 1 Oswald exchange—said it had been seen as significant. While the original tape had been erased for reuse, it had first been copied on to a separate tape— the usual practice with the most interesting tapes.[20]

The claim that the Oswald tapes were all erased is untenable. Compelling evidence indicates that they survived until long after the assassination—and that someone did imperson-ate Oswald.

Within twenty-four hours of the assassination, FBI Director Hoover had a preliminary broad analysis of the case. It was five pages long and unremarkable except for one paragraph. It read:

> The Central Intelligence Agency advised that on October 1, 1963, an extremely sensitive source had reported that an individual identifying himself as Lee Oswald contacted the Soviet Embassy in Mexico City inquiring as to any messages. Special agents of this Bureau, who have conversed with Oswald in Dallas, Texas, have observed photographs of the individual referred to above and *have listened to a recording of his voice. These Special Agents are of the opinion that the above-referred-to individual was not Lee Harvey Oswald* [author's emphasis].

On the morning of the same day, November 23, senior Hoover aide Alan Belmont reported that he learned as much from the Dallas Special Agent in Charge, Gordon Shanklin, who had told him Dallas agents thought "neither the tape nor the photograph pertained to Oswald."

The message seemed crystal-clear. The CIA had sent to Dallas both a picture and a sound recording of the man its surveillance had picked up using the name "Lee Oswald"—and neither pic-ture nor tape matched the Oswald under arrest.

The same morning, Director Hoover telephoned the new President, Lyndon Johnson, to brief him on what appeared to be the facts about the assassination. The transcript includes the following exchange:

Johnson: Have you established any more about the [Oswald] visit to the Soviet Embassy in Mexico in September?

Hoover: No, that's one angle that's very confusing for this reason. We have up here the tape and the photograph of the man who was at the Soviet Embassy, using Oswald's name. That picture and the tape do not correspond to this man's voice, nor to his appearance. In other words, it appears there was a second person who was at the Soviet Embassy down there.[21]

Years later, when Assassinations Committee staff queried the Hoover memo and phone conversation with Johnson, the responses of the CIA and FBI suggested the reference to an "Oswald" recording had merely been a mistake—reflecting muddle in the rush of events after the assassination.[22] The change of story by the FBI, however, along with anomalies in the documentary record, feeds into suspicion that "Oswald" tapes were part of a package of material flown from Mexico City to Dallas on the night of the assassination, and that they were reviewed there. There was such a flight, and it did carry material from the CIA in Mexico.[23]

While a transcript of the Hoover conversation with Johnson has survived, the recording—made on an IBM machine—has not. There is now only a hissing noise on the relevant fourteen minutes of the recording. A report by the company that tried to recover the audio on behalf of the Johnson Library and National Archives, states that "most likely [the recording] was intentionally erased."

FBI Director J. Edgar Hoover was known for his loathing of the CIA—and for the irate notations he habitually scrawled on reports and memoranda. Weeks after the assassination, at the bottom of a memo relating to another CIA matter, he wrote: "I can't forget . . . the false story re Oswald's trip to Mexico." It was, he said, an example of the Agency's "double-dealing."

This author interviewed three witnesses who flatly contradicted the CIA's claim that no Oswald tape was retained until the assassination. Former Warren Commission attorneys William Coleman and David Slawson said they listened to "Oswald tapes" during a visit to the CIA station in Mexico as late as April 1964—months after the President was killed. (A third Warren lawyer, David Belin, said during a television interview: "The Warren Commission had access to the tape.")

Coleman, a senior counsel then, later to become a member of President Reagan's cabinet, said he had "enough curiosity that I listened to *all* that I could make any words out of at all. And at odd times I asked for the transcript—not in lieu of the oral version, only to back it up. Having been a trial lawyer, I knew that the worst thing in the world would be to say that I read a transcript only . . . then find later that there was a difference."

Coleman said he heard the recording in a "secure" room. He noted that it was scratchy, as surveillance tapes often are, and that—with no reason at the time to think an impostor might have been at work—he and his colleague made no effort to compare the voice with other recordings to establish that it was identical to the known voice of alleged assassin Oswald. Slawson, for his part, recalled the name of the officer whom CIA station chief Winston Scott had assigned to play the recording for him and his colleague.

The author tracked down that officer, by then retired, and—though only on learning that Coleman and Slawson had acknowledged having heard the recorded material, and on the strict condition that I publish neither his name nor his rank—the officer confirmed that the recording had survived the assassination, and that Scott had assigned him to play it for the visitors from the Warren Commission.[24]

There is something else, something seen as revelatory by the researchers who have done the most extensive analysis of relevant Agency files.[25] It is a CIA response to Station Chief Scott in Mexico, responding to his name trace request of October 8 describing the visit to the Soviet Embassy by the man who was not Oswald. Over three pages, the response summarized Oswald's history of defection to Russia, marriage to a Soviet citizen, and apparent disillusion with life there:

> "Latest HQDS info was [State Department] report dated May 1962 stating [it] had determined Oswald is still U.S. citizen and both he and his Soviet wife have exit permits and Dept [of] State had given approval for travel with their infant child to USA."

That, however, was not the most recent information CIA headquarters had received on Oswald. The files show that the Agency knew all about his return to the States, that he had since been interviewed by the FBI, about his life in Dallas; correspondence he had had with the Soviet Embassy in Washington, DC, and with communist organizations; his move to New Orleans; his Fair Play for Cuba activity; and his purportedly angry encounter with the DRE's anti-Castro exiles, and the subsequent arrest. The FBI had copied its most recent FBI report on Oswald's progress to the CIA less than a week before the incorrect transmission that purported to brief the CIA station chief in Mexico—yet withheld the latest information from him.

The massive omission was hardly inadvertent. The draft of the response to Mexico had been reviewed by three different officers in CIA Counterintelligence, seen and authenticated by the chief of Covert Operations for the Western Hemisphere— which included Mexico—and finally transmitted under the name of Tom Karamessines, assistant to then Deputy Director for Plans Richard Helms. Jane Roman, a senior aide to Counterintelligence chief Angleton, helped prepare and signed off on the inaccurate message. Interviewed in 1995, in retirement, she had extraordinary things to say.

"I'm signing off," Roman acknowledged, "on something that I know isn't true." The message, she said on studying it, was "indicative of a keen interest in Oswald held very closely on the need-to-know basis. . . . There has to be a point for withholding information . . ." Those with final authority over the content of the message, Roman speculated, may have thought that "somehow . . . they could make some use of Oswald. I would think that there was definitely some operational reason to withhold it, if it was not sheer administrative error, when you see all the people who signed off on it."

If, as Roman explained, she had not had ultimate responsibility for what the message did or did not contain, who had? "The only interpretation I could put on this," she said—noting the language used in the message and the identity of its signatories—

"would be that [the] SAS group would have held the information on Oswald under their tight control."

The SAS, or Special Affairs Staff, oversaw all anti-Castro operations. "The Cuba task force," Roman surmised, would have "got word how to handle this. . . . Well, I mean they hold it within themselves. . . . And I wasn't in on any particular goings-on or hanky-panky as far the Cuban situation."

The CIA's chief of Cuban operations in 1963—a man in charge of a great deal of hanky-panky—was David Phillips, a rising star who was to go on to become chief of the Western Hemisphere Division. He traveled widely in 1963, but was based in Mexico City.

As early as 1961, documents show, Phillips had supervised the CIA's propaganda efforts to counter the Fair Play for Cuba Committee. At that point, his fellow officer Howard Hunt was to testify, he "ran" the DRE—the anti-Castro group whose members were two years later to engage in a supposed clash with Oswald in New Orleans. An agent reporting to Phillips in 1961, documents show, spied on a young man who was "actively engaged in the organization of a local chapter of the Fair Play for Cuba Committee"—a mirror image of the activity in which Oswald would seemingly engage in New Orleans.

In Mexico City, at the time of the Oswald episode in 1963, Phillips headed the unit responsible for surveilling the Cuban Consulate. He would later go public in saying that Oswald's visits had not been caught on camera. He and his team, he wrote, "spent several days studying literally hundreds of photographs available to the CIA before and during Oswald's trip to Mexico City. He did not appear in any of them." As reported earlier, this Phillips claim conflicts with what is known of the camera surveillance. Assassinations Committee investigators did not believe it.

Phillips it was, too, who told the Assassinations Committee that recordings made during the Oswald visit had been "routinely destroyed"—wiped—a week or two later and recycled. "There's no question," he told another interviewer, "that's what occurred to Oswald's conversations. They don't exist anymore." Oswald, Phillips wrote, had been "just another blip." That, of course, is contrary to the statements of Station Chief Scott in his draft manuscript—"we kept a special watch on [Oswald] . . . he was of great interest to us."

Phillips is known to have lied under oath about other matters. In 1975, in sworn testimony to a Senate committee, he would assert that the overthrow and death of Chile's President Allende two years earlier had been the result of a home-grown coup, not because those involved were supported, encouraged, or even winked at by the CIA. In fact, the Agency long strove to engineer the coup. In 1999, a decade after Phillips' death, the National Security Archive—an independent organization— obtained CIA records indicating that he had headed the Task Force involved in a plot to kidnap a Chilean general—even supplied machine guns for the operation. The general was killed by other plotters with whom the CIA had also been cooperating. Phillips' statements in connection with the Kennedy assassination are highly controversial, and he will feature in these pages again.

The name of the overall head of CIA Counterintelligence, James Angleton, figures significantly in the mysteries of Mexico City—which was part of his fiefdom. Intent on bringing additional pressure on the Cubans and Soviets in Mexico

City, he had pushed for the establishment of a special, independent undercover unit, clashing in the process with Station Chief Winston Scott. It was Angleton who pushed, after the assassination, to "wait out" the Warren Commission on its query on the matter of the photographs of the man who was not Oswald.

When Scott died suddenly in 1971, retired but still living in Mexico, Angleton flew down from Washington, DC, the moment he heard the news. The day after the funeral, he turned up at the widow's door accompanied by John Horton, the station chief of the day. Angleton wanted access to the dead man's study, a holy of holies to which Scott had admitted no one, access to his papers and to "any classified material he kept." Among the material found there, Horton was to recall, was a stack of reel-to-reel tapes labeled "Oswald."[26]

The next day, after Angleton had left, a truck removed three large boxes and four suitcases containing the tapes, Scott's draft memoir containing his account of the Oswald episode, and much else. All were shipped to Washington. A former CIA headquarters officer, Paul Hartmann, who for twelve years maintained the HQ file on Oswald, was to recall having received "a package of tapes concerning the Oswald case. . . ."

The story of the Mexico City tapes had a melancholy apparent ending in the 1980s, when Michael Scott, son of the deceased station chief, sent the CIA a Freedom of Information request for some of the material that had been taken from the family home. Months later, the record shows, the items seized by Angleton became the subject of a CIA destruction order. According to the order, they consisted of "operational research [including] activities of a sensitive nature or those which were transitory targets of opportunity."

It is reasonable to speculate that the eventual fate of the remaining "Oswald" tapes was their willful destruction.

If there was imposture in Mexico City, the CIA operatives involved must have had a motive for the deception. If there has been an Agency cover-up of events—one that includes the withholding and in the end the destruction of "Oswald" recordings—there has to have been a reason. Some possible explanations:

The Texan Eldon Hensen, who like Oswald offered his services in the Cuban cause, was apparently manipulated by a CIA impostor posing as a Cuban Embassy aide, both to thwart his activity and, perhaps, gauge the Cuban response to similar approaches. Was imposture also used in Oswald's case, to counter his plans and monitor Cuban and Soviet responses?

The FBI and the CIA, the files clearly show, were both aggressively involved in countering the Fair Play for Cuba Committee at home and abroad. The object was to penetrate the Committee's operations and damage it with black propaganda. The evidence of New Orleans may suggest that, wittingly or unwittingly, Oswald was used to exactly those ends before leaving for Mexico. Was that also the CIA's purpose in Mexico City? If so, the concept can be seen as a legitimate operational sideshow that was harmless enough—until Oswald was named as President Kennedy's alleged assassin. When catastrophe occurred, was there a rush to cover up the "harmless" operation?

The Agency's greater purpose, of course, was to overthrow the Castro regime by almost any means short of overt military invasion. Activity to that end ranged from black propaganda to the assassination of Fidel Castro himself—and Castro knew it.

Some of the information to be covered in these pages will suggest that there were those who sought to manipulate Oswald's visit to Mexico for a far more sinister purpose. And that renegade anti-Castro forces within the CIA or used by it sought to assassinate President Kennedy and by manipulation of Oswald, and through true or false facts that could be pinned on him, lay the blame on Castro. That done, they would have surmised, the United States would be almost bound to retaliate by invading and toppling the Cuban Communist regime.

CHAPTER 20

Facts and Appearances

"Truth: An ingenious compound of desirability of appearance."

—Ambrose Bierce, *The Devil's Dictionary*

The real Lee Harvey Oswald made a mundane return to the United States. The trip home to infamy was another bone-shaking bus journey, not to New Orleans but to Dallas, Texas, and a night at the YMCA. He made a weekend visit to his wife, Marina, now awaiting the birth of a second child at the home of her friend Ruth Paine on the outskirts of the city—a contact that was to have a pivotal effect on Oswald's destiny.

Ten days after his arrival in Dallas, Paine told a neighbor, Linnie Mae Randle, that Oswald was having trouble finding a job. There might be an opening, Randle thought, at her brother's place of work. Oswald followed up and two days later started the last job of his life, as an order-filler at a warehouse that handled the distribution of educational books—the Texas School Book Depository.[1]

Superficially, the last forty days of Oswald's life were unremarkable. After five days renting from a first landlady with whom he did not get on, he took a room at 1026 North Beckley—registering under the name "O. H. Lee." To the owners of the house and to fellow tenants, Oswald seemed quiet, lonely. He spent most evenings reading or watching television, rarely made conversation. He visited Marina almost every weekend.

The women made an occasion of Oswald's twenty-fourth birthday, which fell on October 18. Ruth brought wine, decorated the table, and baked a cake. The cake was carried in aglitter with candles, and everyone sang "Happy Birthday, Lee." Oswald was visibly moved, and his eyes filled with tears. He rejoiced when Marina gave birth two days later to their second child, another daughter. In some ways, it seemed, the rickety marriage was recovering a little. Oswald seemed interested in reestablishing a domestic life, and talked of their setting up house together again.

At work at the Book Depository, Oswald's supervisor thought he "did a good day's work" and deemed him an above-average employee. According to his wife, Oswald said he was saving money. He may have anticipated an early end to his employment. Around November 1, three weeks before the assassination, Oswald wrote in a letter to the Internal Revenue Service that he had "worked only six months in the fiscal year of 1963." Days later, he supposedly told Marina that "there was another job open, more interesting work . . . related to photography." There is no knowing what he meant, in the letter to the taxman or in the alleged remark to his wife.[2]

During the final two weeks of the saga, a new, unwelcome development occurred. There were visits that were reported to Oswald by Marina and her hostess, Ruth Paine, by a Dallas FBI agent named James Hosty. Seven months earlier, when routine reports had picked up Oswald's subscription to the *The Worker*,

NOT IN YOUR LIFETIME

the American Communist Party newspaper, the record indicates, Hosty had suggested the Oswald case be reopened. Now, on November 1, having learned from the CIA that somebody using the name Lee Oswald had visited the Soviet Embassy in Mexico City, and on learning from New Orleans that the Oswald family had departed—leaving Ruth Paine's address for forwarding purposes—Hosty turned up on Ruth Paine's doorstep. By his account, and according to Ruth and Marina, he said merely that he would like to talk to Oswald and asked how to contact him. The women said Oswald worked at the Book Depository. When Hosty called by again, asking for the address of Oswald's rented room, the women said they did not have the telephone number. Their accounts suggest that, though they did know it, they withheld it because Oswald had said the FBI was out to harass him.

News of Hosty's visits plunged Oswald into a black mood, according to Marina. The day after the second one, he apparently appeared at the FBI office in Dallas asking to see Hosty. Told the agent was out to lunch, according to a receptionist, he produced an envelope, said "Get this to him," and departed. After the assassination, however, the FBI would conceal not only the contents of the envelope, but also its very existence. What the note contained remains uncertain even today.

The note's existence remained unknown until 1975, when a journalist learned of it from an FBI contact. The sorry story was eventually pieced together by the House Committee on the Judiciary, the Senate Intelligence Committee, and then the Assassinations Committee. Former FBI staff, including Agent Hosty, admitted that there had not only been a note but that it had been destroyed within hours of Oswald's death. The receptionist who had taken delivery of it, Nannie Fenner, made a dramatic claim. She said she had gotten a look at the note and that it read roughly:

Let this be a warning. I will blow up the FBI and the Dallas Police Department if you don't stop bothering my wife.

Lee Harvey Oswald

Agent Hosty said Mrs. Fenner was wrong, that she was unreliable. Besides, he said, the note had been folded in such a way as to conceal the contents. According to him, it had read more or less as follows:

If you have anything you want to learn about me, come talk to me directly. If you don't cease bothering my wife, I will take appropriate action and report this to the proper authorities.

There was nothing especially out of the ordinary about that, Hosty said, and the note remained in his work tray until after the President's assassination. If the note was so innocuous, though, the rest of the story makes little sense. Within hours of the assassination, according to Hosty, he was called into the office of Special Agent in Charge Gordon Shanklin. Shanklin, "agitated and upset," got Hosty to explain the recent contacts with Ruth Paine and Oswald's wife and how the note had reached him. Then, after Oswald in turn had been murdered, he summoned Hosty again.

According to the agent, his superior took the note from a desk drawer saying, "Oswald's dead now. There can be no trial. Here—get rid of this." Then, as Hosty tore the note up in front of him, Shanklin cried: "No! Get it out of here. I don't even want it in this office. Get rid of it." Hosty then took the note to the lavatory and—his words—"flushed it down the drain."

Days later, Shanklin asked for an assurance that he had done as ordered.

Shanklin, for his part, flatly denied having known anything about the note. Former Assistant Director William Sullivan, however, said Shanklin had often mentioned an "internal problem" over a message from Oswald. A Dallas supervisor, Agent Howe, said he had taken the note to Shanklin after finding it in Hosty's work tray after the assassination. Howe had the impression that Shanklin "knew what I had and—for what reason I don't know—he didn't want to discuss it with me."

Shanklin's is the most dubious of the unsatisfactory FBI statements about the note. (He it was, the reader will recall, who initially said tapes of "Oswald" in Mexico City had arrived in Dallas and been heard to contain a voice that was not the real Oswald's—only to retract the report hours later.) The House Assassinations Committee said it "regarded the incident of the note as a serious impeachment of [both] Shanklin's and Hosty's credibility." During his testimony to the Judiciary Committee, Shanklin was warned that he might be open to prosecution for perjury.[3]

A second piece of documentary evidence escaped yet another call for destruction by Agent-in-Charge Shanklin. On November 9, while visiting the Paine household, Oswald apparently wrote a letter to the Soviet Embassy in Washington, DC. It referred to having visited the Soviet Embassy in Mexico City, and suggested that he and his wife still wanted to return to the Soviet Union. Oswald had had to curtail his trip to Mexico City, the letter said, because renewal of his visa would have involved using his "real name." The FBI was no longer interested in Oswald's Fair Play for Cuba Committee activities, it went on, but Agent Hosty had warned against him starting them again in Texas.[4]

There is also a puzzling background to this document. We know of its existence from two sources—from a routine intercept of mail addressed to the Soviet Embassy and from Ruth Paine, who after the assassination passed Agent Hosty a copy of a draft she said she found. Oddities include the fact that Oswald had supposedly left the draft lying on Mrs. Paine's desk, as though he wanted her to find it. As for the letter's contents, there is the clear implication that Oswald used a false name in his travel to Mexico City (actually, the name on his Mexican tourist card —"Lee, Harvey Oswald"—reads more like a clerical error than a pseudonym). As for the suggestion that he wished to return to Russia, everything we know of Oswald's actual attitude suggests he had no intention of doing so.

The comments in the letter to the Soviets about the Dallas FBI, meanwhile, bear no relation to the known facts. According to the record, Oswald and Hosty had not met, and Hosty had not warned him against doing anything. When Hosty received the letter from Mrs. Paine and showed it to his boss, Gordon Shanklin, Shanklin reacted just as he had in the case of the note Oswald left at the FBI. He "became highly upset and highly incensed," according to Hosty, and ordered the letter destroyed.[5]

Why the rush to cover up? A plausible explanation is that Oswald may have been embroiled in U.S. intelligence activity, as he had perhaps been in New Orleans and in Mexico City. Some part of the intelligence apparatus may have been informed of—had perhaps even directed—what was going on. Far in the future, Hosty himself would strongly suggest that the order to destroy the Oswald note received at the Dallas office originated at FBI headquarters, perhaps at the top. He hinted darkly, too, at revelations to come.

"I am the one," Agent Hosty said of the House Assassinations Committee, "they are afraid is going to drop bombs—if they are going to try to contain this like the Senate Intelligence Committee and the Warren Commission, they don't want me there."

As the weeks leading up to the assassination unrolled, real-life oddities continued. On November 1, the day of Hosty's first visit to the Paine household, Oswald reverted to an old practice and rented a post-office box in downtown Dallas. The rental form authorized two nonprofit organizations to receive mail at the box—the Fair Play for Cuba Committee, and the American Civil Liberties Union (ACLU). This last was a new departure for Oswald. Unlike the FPCC, the ACLU existed not for a political purpose but to champion civil liberties—the rights of the individual, the right to fair trial, and freedom of speech.

When a few days later Oswald became a member of the ACLU, he asked how he could get in touch with "ACLU groups in my area." Neither the new membership nor the inquiry made any sense. Oswald had been to a local ACLU meeting ten days earlier in the company of Ruth Paine's husband, Michael—the couple were members of the organization. He had himself spoken briefly at the meeting and chatted with other attendees afterward. So Oswald had no innocent need to write to the other end of the country for information on ACLU activities in Dallas. As for joining the ACLU, he had told Paine he would never do so—because it was too apolitical.

A letter Oswald wrote to the U.S. Communist Party on the day he opened his post-office box, moreover, showed that he knew perfectly well where and when Dallas area ACLU meetings were held. He asked, too, for advice on how to heighten "progressive tendencies" in the local branch. Was Oswald launching off on some dark scheme involving the ACLU, similar to his seemingly staged activities in New Orleans? Whatever the purpose, a further clue throws a glimmer of light on Oswald's last days, linking him—once again—to New Orleans.

Before leaving for Dallas via Mexico, Oswald had himself arranged for the New Orleans post office to forward mail to Ruth Paine's house. In the second week of October, however, some other person in New Orleans—someone whose handwriting was not Oswald's—filed a second change-of-address card duplicating Oswald's original request. A Warren Commission lawyer, alerted to the anomaly, saw the problem at once. "Let me come bluntly to the point," he said, "Oswald wasn't in New Orleans on October 11. He was in Dallas." Someone else, identity unknown, was apparently taking the trouble to look after Oswald's business in Louisiana. The New Orleans connection had not ceased with his departure.[6]

The notion that one or more unidentified people were in touch with Oswald in the last weeks before the assassination does not stand alone—contrary to the impression given by the Warren Commission. On calls Oswald made and received at both Dallas boarding houses he used, witnesses recalled, he spoke in a "foreign language." The party on the other end of the line, one might think, was usually his Russian wife, Marina—who did speak with him on the phone. People at both boardinghouses, however, would say that they thought a male caller had telephoned, and that Oswald also spoke in a foreign tongue on those calls.[7]

There were other calls that were neither traced nor explained. The manager of an Enco service station, across the street from the second rooming house, recalled Oswald asking for "change with which to make long distance calls . . . from a coin tele-phone booth located at the side of his station." He made at least two such calls, some six weeks before the assassination. Efforts to trace calls made from the booth failed to reveal whom Oswald had phoned.

A further credible report about a phone call reached the FBI within days of the assassination—one that has received little if any notice. A Louisiana operator drew her supervisor's atten-tion to a call she had handled just a day—perhaps two—before President Kennedy was killed. It had been, she said, a "prepaid, long distance, person-to-person call to Lee Harvey Oswald at the Texas School Book Depository." The caller had been "an adult female," believed to have been phoning from Slidell, Louisiana. Slidell is thirty-one miles from New Orleans, scene of Oswald's Cuba-related doings that summer, and just ten miles from a camp where anti-Castro exiles had been training. Carlos Bringuier of the DRE, with whom Oswald had his suspect street encounter in New Orleans, had been involved with the exiles in question. The identity of the person who called Oswald from that location just before the assassination, and the reason for the call, remains unknown.[8]

After any crime that makes news, anywhere in the world, police reports flood in from people who claim to have seen or have information on the chief suspect. Some turn out to be genuine cases of mistaken identity, others mischievous. The Kennedy assassination sparked hundreds of Oswald sightings, most of which were eventually discounted. Some were of potential sig-nificance, either because of the apparent integrity of the witness reporting or because the detail provided appeared credible. Most of those sightings, though, were also eventually discarded, like jigsaw pieces that get into the wrong box.[9]

In light of all the information now available, however, a recurring feature of such "Oswald" reports deserves attention. Several of them stated that a man accompanying "Oswald" had looked Hispanic—perhaps Cuban. In some of the reports, the reference was specific.

A former New Orleans immigration inspector, testifying years later to the Senate Intelligence Committee, said he was "absolutely certain that he interviewed Lee Harvey Oswald in a New Orleans jail cell" before April 1, 1963—before the authentic Oswald even arrived in New Orleans that year. The inspector was sure of the time frame and sure, too, that the man had been "claiming to be a Cuban alien." Having established that this was a false claim, he pursued the matter no further.[10]

In the second week of October in Dallas, just weeks before the President was killed, according to a Dallas citizen, a man described as "identical" to Oswald was present at a local meeting of the DRE, the anti-Castro group that crops up so frequently in this story. Also attending, apparently, was the extreme right-wing General Walker, whom the real Oswald had allegedly tried to kill several months earlier.

A mere five days before the assassination a citizen of Abilene, two hundred miles west of Dallas, picked up a note left for one of his neighbors, Pedro González. It was, the citizen was to recall, an urgent request to call one of two Dallas telephone numbers, and the signature read "Lee Oswald." González appeared nervous when handed the note, and minutes later was seen using a public telephone. Previously, the citizen said, he had seen a man resembling Oswald at González's apartment, accompanied by a second, older American from New Orleans. González, who headed a local anti-Castro group called the Cuban Liberation Committee, was known to be a friend of Antonio de Varona, leader of the CIA-backed Cuban Revolutionary Council.[11]

De Varona had, within days of the Abilene incident, stayed at the home of a close relative of a woman whose Oswald sighting troubled official investigators and remains a focus of research to this day. The sighting is troubling because—if it occurred as reported—it linked Oswald indisputably to the anti-Castro movement, to CIA operatives, and to New Orleans.[12]

The Odio Incident

It had been evening in Dallas, in late fall, when someone rang the doorbell at Apartment A, Crestwood Apartments. Inside, Silvia and Annie Odio were not expecting visitors. Annie went to the door first, peered out without releasing the night chain, then called to her elder sister. Silvia, glancing through the crack, saw that there were three men standing there—two Hispanics and an American. Though they were strangers, the way they introduced themselves—showing knowledge of her family and an associate—led her not to turn them away. The conversation that followed marked the start of a tantalizing puzzle. The Odio incident has been called "the proof of the plot."

Silvia and Annie Odio came from a wealthy upper-class family that had long been prominent in revolutionary politics in Cuba. Their father, Amador, supported Fidel Castro in the underground fight to overthrow the Batista dictatorship, hoping that the outcome would be democratic government in his country. When Castro delivered communism, however, Amador had begun working against the new regime. Arrest followed, for harboring on his estate a man wanted for involvement in a plot to kill Castro. By 1963, Odio and his wife were political prisoners, their family scattered in exile. Silvia, twenty-six years old, and Annie, seventeen, had joined the growing exile community in Dallas.

There, following in her father's footsteps, Silvia had become politically active and joined the group Junta Revolucionaria (JURE). Though its members opposed Castro and communism, many in exile politics considered the group dangerously leftist. The men who came to the Odio sisters' apartment in fall 1963 said they were members of JURE, which was why she agreed to talk to them.

Although Odio was to tell her story repeatedly to the authorities, she gave no press interviews until 1978, when she spoke with the author. Then, and on numerous occasions later, she relived a frightening experience. The author also interviewed her sister.

It had swiftly become clear during the conversation at the Odio apartment that one of the two Hispanics was the group's leader. He was tall, looked about forty, and said his "war name" was Leopoldo. The second Hispanic, who was shorter and wore glasses, was addressed as "Angelo" or "Angel." Like Leopoldo, he had an olive complexion and could have been either Cuban or Mexican. The third, much younger, man was American. He stood quietly by, saying little or nothing, as Leopoldo explained why they had come.

They had traveled from New Orleans, he said, and the three men did look weary and unshaven, as if after a long trip. As well as being JURE members, Leopoldo asserted, they were working with the blessing of the Cuban Revolutionary Council, the government in exile. The men, who knew the underground name of Silvia's father, mentioned details about events in Cuba that only an insider was likely to know. They were evidently familiar with recent plots to assassinate Castro. Leopoldo and his comrades were trying to raise funds for anti-Castro operations, he said, and wanted Silvia's help—specifically, in translating fund-raising letters to U.S. businessmen into English.

Impressed though she was by the visitors' knowledge, Silvia Odio felt uneasy, leery of dealing with people she did not really know. She told the visitors she wanted no part in a campaign of violence, and the discussion ended inconclusively. The men left in their red car, supposedly to begin another long journey.

All the time the men had been at the apartment, the young American had said hardly a word. He had merely stood watching and listening, in Odio's words, "sort of looking at me to see what my reaction was, like somebody who is evaluating the situation." Eight weeks later, Silvia—and her sister Annie—were to react with fear and bewilderment when they saw pictures of the man arrested for shooting President Kennedy. The American in the group that came to their door, Silvia would say she recalled with a jolt, had been introduced as "Oswald"—"Leon Oswald." She had a further, sinister, reason to remember him.

Leopoldo, who had introduced "Oswald" when the men came to the door, had telephoned Silvia less than forty-eight hours later. He again brought up the request for assistance, but also seemed keen to discuss something else. "What," he asked, "did you think of the American?" Remembering how quiet the American had been, Silvia said she had not really formed an opinion. Leopoldo then made a number of remarks that Silvia found chilling at the time and more so, obviously, later.

He said of Oswald: "Well, you know, he's a marine, an ex-marine, and an expert marksman. He would be a tremendous asset to anyone, except that you never know how to take him." As she listened, Silvia Odio wondered what she was expected to say. Then Leopoldo went on: "He's kind of loco, kind of nuts. He could go either way. He could do anything—like getting underground in Cuba, like killing Castro." Then: "The American says we Cubans don't have any guts. He says we should have shot President Kennedy after the Bay of Pigs. He says we should do something like that."

That was all. Leopoldo appeared to have little else to say, and the conversation ended. Silvia Odio never heard from him again. She had felt even during the phone call, she told the author, that there was something wrong, something sinister and deliberate about it. "Immediately," she said, "I suspected there was some sort of scheme or plot."

Silvia was at work when, just weeks later, news broke that the President had been shot in the city in which she and her sister lived. Her head filled with frightening thoughts. When broadcasts confirmed that President Kennedy was dead, her boss decided all the staff could go home. Silvia, who was prone to fainting fits, passed out on her way to the parking lot and was taken to a hospital.[13]

Across the city, her sister Annie had watched the President drive past, waving to spectators, before the shooting. That afternoon, when she saw Oswald's picture on the television, her first thought was, "My God, I know this guy and I don't know from where. . . . Where have I seen this guy?" Soon, on being told her sister had been taken ill, Annie visited Silvia in the hospital—and at once said that she knew she had seen Oswald somewhere before but at first could not quite place him. Silvia, who had begun to cry, reminded her of the three men who had visited their apartment. She told Annie, too, about the disturbing call from Leopoldo.

There was a television in the hospital room, and now Silvia, too, saw pictures of Oswald. "Annie and I looked at one another and sort of gasped," she told the author, "She said, 'Do you recognize him?' She said, 'It is the same guy, isn't it?' I said, 'Yes, but do not say anything.' "

The sisters were frightened, worried that their encounter with "Oswald" and his two companions had somehow placed them in danger. With their parents far away in Cuba in Castro's prisons, they felt very much alone. Silvia suffered from a physical condition that frequently caused blackouts when she was under stress—as when she learned of the assassination. Annie was a scared girl of seventeen. They decided to say nothing to the authorities of their disquieting experience, which only became known purely by chance, when another Odio sister mentioned it to an American friend.

A series of casual conversations finally brought the incident to the attention of the FBI, which at first expressed little interest. The matter was not pursued with vigor until the following summer, when the Warren Commission's work was well advanced. When there was a serious follow-up, it emerged that there was every reason to believe the sisters' account—not least when it emerged that she had discussed it with another witness *before* the assassination. Evidence was available, too, that she had reported the incident—again before the assassination—in a letter to her father in Cuba. Coupled with the fact that not only Silvia but Annie recalled the visit and said the mysterious American had resembled Oswald, the information was impossible to ignore.

"Mrs. Odio has been checked out thoroughly . . ." Warren Commission attorney David Slawson was to write. "The evidence is unanimously favorable, both as to her character and reliability and as to her intelligence." His colleague Wesley Liebeler wrote—as to whether Oswald was at Odio's home—"Odio may well be right. The Commission will look bad if it turns out that

she is." To Slawson, Odio was "the most significant witness linking Oswald to anti-Castro Cubans."

There was a problem, though, one that the Warren Commission never resolved. While the actual date of Odio's encounter
was never pinned down, investigation focused on the period September 24 and 29—in particular the middle of that time frame.
This was a period when the authentic Oswald was ending his
stay in New Orleans and setting off for Mexico City. He could
not have been at Odio's apartment, by any account of his movements, unless he had been flitting around the country not by
bus—the way he reached Mexico City—but by some other very
speedy form of transport. There was no evidence that Oswald
had traveled by commercial airline.

Nevertheless, the Odio evidence remained troubling. In the
dying days of the Commission, Chief Counsel Lee Rankin wrote
to FBI Director Hoover, "It is a matter of some importance to
the Commission that Mrs. Odio's allegations either be proved
or disproved." On September 21, 1964, as the Warren Report
was being finalized, Hoover reported that his agents had traced a
man named Loran Hall, a "participant in numerous anti-Castro
activities," who said he had been in Dallas at the relevant time
and had visited Silvia Odio along with two associates—Lawrence Howard and William Seymour. Hall said one of his friends
looked like Oswald, and Hoover seemed satisfied that it was this
resemblance that had led to all the fuss. On that basis, a last-
minute passage was inserted in the Warren Report, implying that
Odio's account had been a matter of mistaken identity.

The FBI, however, had for a while withheld a crucial fact from
the Commission. Faced with denials by his companions that they
had been at the Odio sisters' apartment, Hall had recanted his
story. Then, when the FBI belatedly came clean—after the War-

ren Report had gone to press—the Commission, in turn, failed to include a correction in the volumes of evidence that accompanied the Report.

Analysis done in recent times, though, suggests a solution to the knotty question of when the Odios' Oswald encounter occurred, and how it may have fit into Oswald's known movements. In her first conversation with the FBI, Silvia Odio had herself dated the visit to the apartment as having occurred in "late September or early October." In his 2008 book on the assassination, the historian David Kaiser suggested the date of the visit may well have been as late as October 3—a day Oswald had been not en route *to* Mexico City but arriving back in Dallas.

If Professor Kaiser is right, the possible implications of the anti-Castro trio's visit to Silvia Odio—and the pointed statement to her that "Leon Oswald" believed that President Kennedy should be killed—becomes additionally ominous. For the local press had reported only days earlier that a presidential visit to Texas—including Dallas—was planned for the third week of November.

Kaiser may indeed be right in thinking that the Odio incident occurred on October 3. Hotel records showed that Loran Hall and two male companions were in Dallas that day. Hall, whose "explanation" of the Odio matter—shortlived though it was—served to relegate the matter to the Warren Commission's trivia pile, deserves a closer look. He turned up again in 1967, when the New Orleans aspects of the assassination case were aired publicly, and again muddied the waters with information that led in useless directions. In 1977, he gave evidence to the Assassinations Committee only with great reluctance. When he eventually did so, on a basis that ensured that he could not be prosecuted as a result of anything arising from his testimony, he maintained that he had never claimed to have visited Silvia Odio. In its final Report, the Committee characterized his original tale as an "admitted fabrication."

Hall, alias "Lorenzo Pascillo," was a thirty-three-year-old former U.S. Army sergeant who reportedly had training in counterintelligence. He was also said to have trained Cuban exiles at a camp on Lake Pontchartrain outside New Orleans— the same camp to which Oswald had allegedly been taken at one point. Hall had gone to Havana in 1959, before the fall of the Batista dictatorship, to work in the casino of the Capri Hotel, which was controlled by Santo Trafficante, one of the Mafia leaders who has been named in connection with killing President Kennedy. After the fall of the regime, by Hall's own account, he and Trafficante shared a Quonset hut in a Castro detention camp.

Notes of Hall's interviews with congressional investigators indicate that the CIA made contact with him the day after his release and repatriation. A CIA document says the interest in Hall was solely "for debriefing." His son, however, said in court testimony that his father was for many years a CIA operative.

The Odio encounter remains today an incident that cannot be ignored yet resists explanation. The House Assassinations Committee's firm conclusion, however, was that it believed the Odio sisters and accepted that they had indeed met a man who had been introduced as Leon Oswald and looked like Oswald. It was, as a Committee report noted in fine understatement, "a situation that indicates possible conspiratorial involvement."

What sort of involvement? If Oswald was a genuine pro-Castro leftist, as the Committee thought, what was he doing at

Odio's home in the company of anti-Castro activists? The Committee speculated—though without conviction—that Oswald, as part of a leftist assassination plot, perhaps associated with the exiles in order to implicate the anti-Castro side in the President's murder. The other, contrary, interpretation, espoused by many researchers, is that anti-Castro operatives deliberately used Oswald, or the name of the real Oswald, to set him up as a fall guy for the assassination.[14]

Absent any certainty—except that the Odios' account is credible, an unresolved part of the assassination story—we are left with the comments of two of the main protagonists.

"As it stands right now," Loran Hall said in a taped 1977 interview, "there's only two of us left alive—that's me and Santo Trafficante. And as far as I'm concerned we're both going to stay alive—because I ain't going to say shit."

Silvia Odio ended her interview with the author with a poignant thought. Asked what haunted her most about her experience all those years ago, she replied, "It is the thought that perhaps, somehow, I could have prevented the assassination."

CHAPTER 21

Countdown

"The Kennedys were playing with fire."
—former Secretary of State Dean Rusk, on the
brothers' duplicity over Cuba, 1994

In the fall of 1963, at the very time Odio was introduced to
Oswald in Dallas, President Kennedy made moves in secret
that, if discovered—as they likely were—offered those violently
opposed to Castro greater cause than ever to take drastic action.
On September 19, U.S. Ambassador to the United Nations
Adlai Stevenson phoned the President with news of a remarkable
development. Tentatively, through an obscure African diplomat
and others, Fidel Castro let it be known that he was interested
in reaching some sort of accommodation with the United States.

The Cuban leader's message, very different from his public rant-
ings, had been passed on—over coffee at U.N. headquarters—to
William Attwood, Special Adviser to the American delegation.
Attwood had previously met and talked with Castro and was well
regarded by Kennedy. The sense of the message, passed on by
Guinea's ambassador to Cuba, was that Castro was uneasy about
the degree to which Cuba had become tied to the Soviet Union,
was at odds with his own hardliners, and wanted to redress the

balance by finding an accommodation with the United States. It sounded as though he wanted talks about talks.

This had the potential for breakthrough as momentous as, say, the first tentative contacts between Egypt and Israel in the 1970s. Kennedy responded rapidly, giving the go-ahead for contact between Attwood and Cuba's delegate at the United Nations, Carlos Lechuga—on two conditions.[1] First, it should not appear that the United States had solicited the discussions and, second, any contacts were to be secret.

"Secret" meant that only those with need to know should be told. Kennedy was already in conflict with those in his own cabinet who opposed talk of withdrawal from Vietnam, and with those who looked sourly on his policy of global disengagement. Going soft on Cuba, moreover, would enrage those at the CIA who had for years been passionately involved in the fight to topple Castro. "Unfortunately," Ambassador to the United Nations Adlai Stevenson told Attwood, "the CIA is still in charge of Cuba." To some at the State Department, too, the very idea of accommodation was heresy. The President wanted to find out more about the Castro approach, but he wanted it done quietly and at arm's length.

Attwood already had a willing go-between for the coming contacts with Havana. This was Lisa Howard, an ABC News reporter who had interviewed Castro in Havana—and, moreover, had a sexual dalliance with him. She had told the President about the trip—including the bedroom encounter—on her return. "She mentioned that Castro hadn't taken his boots off," recalled the author Gore Vidal, who knew both Kennedy and Howard, "Jack liked details like that." Much more seriously, the reporter had gained the impression that Castro was ready to talk, and had come back and reported as much—

eventually in print. Now, Attwood recruited Howard to help with his mission, promising an exclusive story should anything come of the contacts.

On September 23, the reporter engineered a cocktail party at her Manhattan apartment, to which Attwood and Lechuga were invited. At a discreet distance from other guests, the American and the Cuban talked cautiously for about half an hour. Lechuga indicated that progress might be possible, that Castro might want to meet with Attwood.

The following morning saw Attwood on an early shuttle to Washington, DC, and a meeting with Robert Kennedy, who agreed that contacts could be worthwhile. Then he and Lechuga met again. Through the month of October, as the days ticked by toward tragedy in Dallas, the secret diplomacy continued. Hoping to move things along, Attwood got the President to discuss Cuba with Jean Daniel, an eminent French journalist who was due soon to fly to Cuba to see Castro.

At their meeting, President Kennedy surprised Daniel by expressing vigorous approval for the basic principles of the Cuban revolution. The United States, he said, had been to blame for many of the evils of the old Batista regime. While warning that he would not tolerate Cuban subversion in Latin America, the President said he now "understood the Cubans." He asked Daniel to come to see him again on his return, following the upcoming visit to Cuba, to brief him on his exchanges with Castro. Daniel was being used, he realized, as an "unofficial envoy."

Meanwhile, Attwood's secret diplomacy seemed to be getting somewhere. Castro's trusted aide and personal physician, Rene Vallejo, suggested through Lisa Howard that Attwood fly to a one-on-one meeting with Castro at Varadero, on Cuba's north coast.

On November 5, a recently released White House tape shows, Kennedy and National Security Adviser McGeorge Bundy discussed how to move the matter forward. The President suggested getting Attwood "off the payroll," so that—if leaked—any contact with Castro could appear unofficial, "deniable." The President was interested, Attwood noted in his diary, in the possibility of "taking Castro "out of the Soviet fold . . . perhaps wiping out the Bay of Pigs and getting back to normal."

The administration was playing a dangerous double game. A previous chapter of this book reviewed the likelihood that the Kennedy brothers had been aware of plans to kill Castro earlier in the presidency.[2] Through the fall of 1963, in the very weeks Kennedy was authorizing a dialogue with Castro, CIA officers again met with Castro's aide Rolando Cubela, whom the Agency believed—mistakenly—to be a traitor set on the regime's overthrow.

Several times in early September, Cubela and his CIA case officer Nestor Sanchez—who answered to the head of Cuba operations, Desmond FitzGerald—met at a safe house in Brazil. In early October they met again in France, at a house outside Paris. On October 11, Sanchez reported that Cubela wanted Robert Kennedy's personal assurance that the United States would support "any activity" he might undertake against Castro. On October 29, FitzGerald himself flew to Paris and, representing himself as Robert Kennedy's personal emissary, told Cubela that Washington would back any anti-Communist group that would "neutralize" the Cuban leadership. He and Cubela also discussed what weapon might be used to kill Castro, and Fitzgerald later approved weapons being provided.[3]

ANTHONY SUMMERS

There is no compelling reason to think that these CIA officers acted, as Kennedy loyalists have maintained, without authority.[4] Documents and interviews made public since 2005 seem to indicate that there was also another plan in the works, one that envisaged a coup utilizing a second supposed traitor in Castro's government apparatus. The game plans, both for the Cubela operation and for the second alleged plot, envisaged Castro being killed.[5]

Could there really have been duplicity on such a breathtaking scale? Did the Kennedys open a peace parley with Castro while simultaneously pressing ahead with murderous schemes to get rid of him? In a 1994 interview, former Kennedy Secretary of State Dean Rusk told the author that he had learned of the coup planning—after the assassination—from the committee in the National Security Council that was working on it." That is, from the Special Group, effectively directed by Robert Kennedy. "There's no particular contradiction there," Rusk said. "It was just an either/or situation. That went on frequently." The Kennedy brothers, he said, had been "playing with fire."

If Castro discovered he was being two-timed—and that seems overwhelmingly likely, given that Cubela seems to have remained loyal—how would he respond? And what if one of the more virulent anti-Castro exile factions (and perhaps some of their CIA backers) learned of—and believed to be real and ongoing—the peace feelers between Kennedy and Castro? How would *they* react? When briefed by Attwood on the status of the dialogue with the Cubans, Robert Kennedy had voiced concern about security. It was, he feared, "bound to leak."

The risk was surely greater than the Kennedys knew, and increasing with every week that passed. The CIA had known for months about Lisa Howard and her information on Castro's

368

comments about a possible rapprochement—she had talked with Agency officials following her return from Cuba. Yet it was Howard whom Attwood used when in late October, wishing to maintain momentum, he sought to get a message through to Castro. From her New York City apartment, Howard made a string of calls to Castro's aide Vallejo in Cuba. Then Attwood himself tried calling from Howard's phone. Getting through meant hours of loose talk on vulnerable open lines.

This was a naïve way of going about a mission that was supposed to be secret. The CIA had long since succeeded in placing agents hostile to Cuba inside the Cuban mission to the United Nations headed by Carlos Lechuga, who of course knew about Attwood's work. Making overseas calls in those days, moreover, involved going through an operator—an insecure procedure. The National Security Agency intercepted calls to Havana, and other U.S. intelligence agencies reaped the informational harvest.[6]

"I think the CIA must have known about this initiative," Arthur Schlesinger, former Kennedy Special Assistant and the presidency's preeminent chronicler, told the author. "They must certainly have realized that Bill Attwood and the Cuban representative to the U.N. were doing more than exchanging daiquiri recipes. . . . They had all the wires tapped at the Cuban delegation to the United Nations." On at least one of Lisa Howard's calls to Havana, Attwood was to recall, she said the President was personally committed to the ongoing contacts.

"If the CIA did find out what we were doing," Attwood said he realized later, that could have "trickled down to the lower echelon of activists, and Cuban exiles, and the more gung-ho CIA people who had been involved since the Bay of Pigs. If word of a possible normalization of relations with Cuba leaked to these people, I can understand why they would have reacted so violently. This was the end of their dreams of returning to Cuba, and they might have been impelled to take violent action. Such as assassinating the President."

Arthur Schlesinger agreed. "Undoubtedly, if word leaked of President Kennedy's efforts," he said, "that might have been exactly the kind of thing to trigger some explosion of fanatical violence. It seems to me a possibility not to be excluded."

Far away from New York City and Washington, DC, the prelude to tragedy had been unfolding. As Attwood made his not-so-secret contacts with Cuba, Lee Oswald—and at some stage apparently an Oswald imposter—had badgered Cuban and Soviet diplomats in Mexico City to grant him visas. There, too, CIA recording devices recorded the action. At about the same time in Dallas—perhaps on October 3—Silvia Odio had been visited by two anti-Castro operatives accompanied by the quiet American they called "Leon Oswald." The "Oswald" who—the operatives' leader would tell her in that odd phone call, just days after the first public reporting of a coming presidential visit to Dallas—apparently said the exiles "should have shot President Kennedy after the Bay of Pigs."

On October 1, at a house in the Dallas suburb of Farmers Branch, the local John Birch Society hosted three venomously anti-Kennedy exiles. A member of the audience taped what was said and later provided the recording to a senior Dallas police officer, who years later provided a copy to the author. On the tape, a Bay of Pigs veteran named Nestor Castellanos can be heard reviling the President: "Get him out! Get him out! The quicker, the sooner, the better. He's *doing*

all kinds of deals [author's emphasis]. . . . Mr. Kennedy is kiss-
ing Mr. Khrushchev. I wouldn't be surprised if he had kissed
Castro, too."

After referring to plans for an anti-Kennedy demonstration,
Castellanos tells his audience, "We are waiting for Kennedy the
twenty-second [November], buddy. We are going to see him, in
one way or the other. We're going to give him the works when he
gets in Dallas." While no evidence links this speaker to the coming assassination, his speech reflects the passionate antipathy to
the President among anti-Castro activists.

Before Dallas, the President was to visit Chicago—on
November 2—and Miami—on November 18. In Chicago,
three days before Kennedy arrived, the Secret Service learned
of a potential threat to his life. Police arrested a former marine
with a history of mental illness named Thomas Vallee, who was
found to be in possession of an M-1 rifle and three thousand
rounds of ammunition. Vallee, a member of the John Birch
Society, was an outspoken opponent of the Kennedy administration. According to a former Secret Service agent there
was also another threat in Chicago, involving a four-man team
armed with high-power rifles. One member of the team, the
agent said, was a Hispanic.[7]

The visit to Chicago was canceled at the last minute, when
crowds were already massing to greet the President. It is not
clear whether the reason for the cancellation was a crisis following the assassination of President Diem in Vietnam, or
because the President was feeling unwell—or in light of a murder threat.

On November 6 in Dallas, Oswald left his note at the office of
the FBI, the note Bureau officials would destroy after the assassination.[8] On November 9, in Miami, the head of police intelligence

sat listening to a fuzzy tape-recording of a conversation between a known right-wing extremist, Joseph Milteer, and a trusted police informant. The transcript, made later that day, ran as follows:

Informant:	I think Kennedy is coming here on the eighteenth, or something like that to make some kind of speech. . . .
Milteer:	You can bet your bottom dollar he is going to have a lot to say about the Cubans. There are so many of them here.
Informant:	Yeah. Well, he will have about a thousand bodyguards, don't worry about that.
Milteer:	The more bodyguards he has, the easier it is to get him.
Informant:	Well, how in the hell do you figure would be the best way to get him?
Milteer:	From an office building with a high-powered rifle He knows he's a marked man. . . .
Informant:	They are really going to try to kill him?
Milteer:	Oh yeah, it is in the working.
Informant:	Boy, if that Kennedy gets shot, we have got to know where we are at. Because you know that will be a real shake if they do that.
Milteer:	They wouldn't leave any stone unturned there, no way. They will pick somebody up within hours afterwards, if anything like that would happen. Just to throw the public off.

Captain Charles Sapp, head of Miami's Police Intelligence Bureau, and his team of a dozen detectives had worked closely with the Secret Service during a previous presidential visit to

Miami. Now, with the President due on November 18—four days before the shots that would kill him in Dallas—Sapp had new cause to worry.

Milteer, the extremist on the tape, was a wealthy agitator and member of a galaxy of ultra-right-wing groups including the National States Rights Party, which had close links to anti-Castro extremists. Sapp passed on the remark that the President's assassination was "in the working" to other agencies. The Secret Service did check on Milteer's whereabouts, and there was an assassination alert on November 18, when Kennedy arrived in Tampa, his first stop in Florida.

The second stop was in Miami, where the President addressed the Inter-American Press Association about Cuba, a speech that—Arthur Schlesinger was to write—had been carefully crafted for listeners across the straits in Havana, Cuba.

It was freighted with significance.

"It is important to restate what divides Cuba from my country . . ." Kennedy told his listeners. "It is the fact that a small band of conspirators has stripped the Cuban people of their freedom and handed over the independence and sovereignty of the Cuban nation to forces beyond the hemisphere. They have made Cuba a victim of foreign imperialism . . . a weapon in an effort dictated by external powers to subvert the other American republics. This, and this alone, divides us. As long as this is true, nothing is possible. Without it, everything is possible. . . . Once Cuban sovereignty has been restored we will extend the hand of friendship and assistance."

This has become known as the "signal" speech. The headline over the UPI report of the speech in the following day's newspapers was "Kennedy Virtually Invites Cuban Coup." The report said the President had "all but invited the Cuban people to overthrow Fidel Castro's Communist regime and promised prompt U.S. aid if they do. . . . The President said it would be a happy day if the Castro government is ousted."

According to a 1976 Senate Intelligence Committee report, the CIA's Desmond FitzGerald, had helped write the speech. Word was passed to Castro aide Rolando Cubela, with whom FitzGerald had met so recently to discuss the murder of the Cuban leader, that the reference to a "small band of conspirators" was to the Cuban government—a reference designed to reassure him that the President personally supported a coup.[9]

Whomever in Havana the "signal" message was precisely intended for—and it seems to this author that it sent encouragement to any and all of Castro's enemies—it conflicted directly with the ongoing peace feelers entrusted to William Attwood. Even as the President flew home from Florida, Attwood was on his way to another tussle with the telephone in reporter Lisa Howard's apartment.[10] As they strove to nail down an acceptable formula for talks, he and Castro's aide Vallejo had continued to be thwarted by telephone delays and broken connections. Now at last, in the early morning hours of November 19, they did have a proper conversation.

Though Attwood did not know it at the time, he was effectively speaking to Castro himself—the Cuban leader was seated at Vallejo's side throughout the conversation. Castro still hoped a U.S. representative would come to Cuba. There was no way he could himself come to the United States, yet this was a matter only he could deal with. The Cuban side, for their part, would submit an agenda for the proposed talks. Castro gave an assurance, meanwhile, that Che Guevara, his close comrade and a hardliner who favored maintaining the relationship with the Soviets, would not be involved.

Later on November 19, at an initial meeting with Castro in Havana, the French journalist Jean Daniel briefed the Cuban leader on his recent talk with President Kennedy. For now, Castro responded, he could not discuss the future of Cuba's links with Moscow. Nevertheless, he said, he saw new hope for a breakthrough in relations with the United States—under Kennedy as President.

"He still has the possibility," Castro said, "of becoming, in the eyes of history, the greatest president of the United States, the leader who may at last understand that there can be coexistence between capitalists and socialists, even in the Americas. . . . I know, for example, that for Khrushchev, Kennedy is a man you can talk with. . . . Personally, I consider him responsible for everything, but I will say this: He has come to understand many things over the past few months; and then, too, in the last analysis, I'm convinced that anyone else would be worse."

When Daniel saw the President again, Castro added, he could "tell him that I'm willing to declare [leading Republican contender of the day Barry] Goldwater my friend if that will guarantee Kennedy's reelection! . . . Since you are going to see Kennedy again, be an emissary of peace."

In the United States, meanwhile, William Attwood had called the White House to report on his latest stint on the phone to Cuba. Adviser McGeorge Bundy had again briefed the President. As had been mooted earlier, Attwood was to "see what could be done to effect a normalization of relationship." The President would decide "what to say to Castro" and brief Attwood as soon as Havana came up with an agenda. Kennedy would not be leaving Washington, Bundy said, except for a brief visit to Texas . . .

Dallas.

On November 21, according to an informant reporting to the Secret Service, a Cuban exile named Homer Echevarría fulminated against the President while negotiating a covert arms deal. The money for the guns would be ready shortly, he said, "as soon as we take care of Kennedy." Later investigation would establish that Echevarría's associate in the arms deal had been the military head of the DRE—that group again—and financing was coming from "hoodlum elements"—the Mafia.

On the morning of November 22, CIA's Cuba chief Desmond FitzGerald held a meeting to discuss plans—said to have been in their final stages—for Castro's removal. The meeting was "the most important I ever had on the problem of Cuba," recalled Enrique Ruiz-Williams, a Bay of Pigs veteran and member of the inner coterie of the administration's anti-Castro deliberations.

Were coup plans indeed in their final stages? "If Jack Kennedy had lived," FitzGerald would tell colleagues four months after the assassination, "I can assure you we would have gotten rid of Castro by last Christmas."

On November 22, at a further meeting in Paris—with FitzGerald's knowledge and approval—CIA case officer Nestor Sanchez handed Cubela—the presumed traitor—an alternative assassination device with which to kill Castro, a Paper Mate pen modified to serve as a poison syringe. Just two days earlier, barely twenty-four hours after John F. Kennedy had approved pressing on with peace feelers toward Castro, CIA technicians had worked through the night preparing the weapon. As Sanchez and Cubela ended their meeting, news came through that the President had been shot dead in Dallas.[11]

Desmond FitzGerald died four years later, never having told official investigators of his role in the plots to kill Castro. According to his family, he would never afterward speak of the President's assassination.

Lisa Howard, the CBS journalist who had acted as go-between to Castro officials during the Attwood peace initiative, died two years after the assassination.[12] "Lisa had seen herself as a Joan of Arc," her friend Gore Vidal recalled, "rushing between the two sides to help bring peace. Castro had told her of the efforts by the CIA against him, and it upset her to think that the Kennedys had been talking peace when they were also out to do him in. I think all this is why Bobby never really wanted Jack's assassination investigated. Because the more they dug up, the more quickly they would ask whether Castro had done it to forestall the Kennedys. And the Kennedys would come to be regarded as American Borgias."

Two hours after hearing that his brother was dead, Robert Kennedy placed a call to the Ebbitt Hotel on H Street NW, in Washington, DC, a nondescript establishment the CIA used to lodge Cuban exiles. His call was to the room of Enrique Ruiz-Williams, just back from the meeting to discuss plans for Castro's violent overthrow and now in conversation with the author Haynes Johnson, who was working on a book about the Bay of Pigs. Kennedy spoke with them both, and said something remarkable. "Kennedy was utterly in control of his emotions when he came on the line," Johnson was to write, "and was studiedly brisk as he said, 'One of your guys did it.' "[13] The public face of alleged assassin Oswald, of course, was the very opposite of an anti-Castro activist.

Robert Kennedy flailed around in his immediate first suspicions. "At the time," he was to tell his aide Walter Sheridan, "I asked [CIA director] McCone . . . if they had killed my brother, and I asked him in a way that he couldn't lie to me, and they hadn't." McCone was a Kennedy appointee, though, and some of those handling the dark side of anti-Castro operations may not have kept him fully informed. The President's brother came to realize that.

On December 9, 1963, Arthur Schlesinger discussed the assassination with Robert Kennedy. "I asked him, perhaps tactlessly, about Oswald. He said that there could be no serious doubt that he was guilty, but there was still argument whether he did it by himself or as a part of a larger plot, whether organized by Castro or by gangsters. He said that the FBI thought he had done it by himself, but that McCone thought there were two people involved in the shooting."

In spite of his doubts, Robert played no role in the ensuing investigation, although as Attorney General he was the nation's senior law officer. "There was no way of getting to the bottom of the assassination," wrote Harris Wofford, a former special assistant in the Kennedy White House, "without uncovering the very stories he hoped would be hidden forever. So he closed his eyes and ears to the cover-up that he knew (or soon discovered) [former CIA Director] Allen Dulles was perpetrating on the Warren Commission, and took no steps to inform the Commission of the Cuban and Mafia connections that would have provided the main clues to any conspiracy."

Further inquiries were undesirable, the President's brother told William Attwood, for "reasons of national security."

CHAPTER 22

Casting the First Stone

"Time's glory is to calm contending kings,
To unmask falsehood, and bring truth to light."
—William Shakespeare, *The Rape of Lucrece*

Four days after John F. Kennedy's funeral, President Lyndon B. Johnson summoned Chief Justice Warren to the White House to press him to chair the commission of inquiry into the assassination. When Warren proved reluctant—he did not think a member of the Supreme Court should serve on a presidential commission—Johnson appealed to his sense of duty to the nation. "The gravity of the situation was such," Warren recalled Johnson telling him, "that it might lead us into war . . . it might be a nuclear war." According to Johnson himself, he showed the Chief Justice a report he had received about "a little incident in Mexico City." War could come, he said, "if the public became aroused against Castro and Khrushchev"—a war that, the Defense Secretary had told him, "might cost the loss of forty million people."

Only a year after the Cuban Missile Crisis, when the world had come closer to nuclear war than at any time before or since, the new President apparently felt he was staring into the abyss.

The Soviet Union ordered a nuclear alert, fearing it would be blamed for the assassination. Drawing on his privileged access to closely held information, former Assassinations Committee Chief Counsel Robert Blakey told the author, "The Russians were on alert, and it looked like the beginning, or the possible beginning, of nuclear war. My distinct understanding," he wrote in February 2013, "was that the military in the Soviet Union and the United States were on full alert. SAC [Strategic Air Command] bombers were in the air in force."

Cuba was a potential target. Citing contemporary sources, Oswald's FBI case agent James Hosty wrote decades later that "fully armed [U.S.] warplanes were sent screaming toward Cuba. Just before they entered Cuban airspace, they were hastily called back. With the launching of warplanes, the entire U.S. military went on alert."

The best information available, a contemporary memo to the executive secretary of the National Security Council, indicates that U.S. Southern Command went to DEFCON 4, while the Pacific Command went to DEFCON 3, a higher alert status.

The crisis, former Chief Counsel Blakey told the author, ended only when President Johnson personally assured the Soviets that the United States had no evidence of Soviet involvement and planned no reprisals.

If public statements meant anything, Cuba's position was clear within hours. "Despite the antagonisms existing between the government of the United States and the Cuban revolution," said Havana's U.N. ambassador Carlos Lechuga—one of the key players in the recent efforts to arrange a dialogue between Washington, DC, and Havana, Cuba. "We have received with profound displeasure the news of the tragic death of President Kennedy."

In Cuba, the French journalist Jean Daniel had been with Castro at the moment he took a call from Cuban President Osvaldo Dorticós, informing him of the shooting.[1] Castro, Daniel later recalled, sat back in his chair and repeated three times, "*Es una mala noticia*. . . .This is bad news." Then he fell silent. Castro said he thought the deed "could equally well have been the work of a madman or a terrorist."

A second call said Kennedy might still be alive, that there might be hope of saving him. If he were saved, the Cuban leader said, he would effectively be "already re-elected [for a second term]." He said it, Daniel noted, with an air of satisfaction. News that the President had died came as those present listened to NBC radio broadcasting from Miami. Castro rose to his feet. "Everything is changed," he said, " Everything is going to change. . . . The Cold War, relations with Russia, Latin America, Cuba, the Negro question . . . all will have to be rethought. I'll tell you one thing: At least Kennedy was an enemy to whom we had become accustomed. This is a serious matter, an extremely serious matter."

A fifteen-minute break in broadcasting followed, broken only by the tones of the American national anthem on the radio. "Strange indeed was the impression," Daniel wrote, "on hearing this anthem ring out in the house of Fidel Castro, in the midst of a circle of worried faces. . . . 'Now,' Fidel said, 'they will have to find the assassin quickly, otherwise you wait and see, I know them, they will try to put the blame on us for this thing. . . .' "

Castro and Daniel were on the road in a car, still listening to the radio, when a commentator suggested that the alleged assassin was "a spy married to a Russian." It would be his turn next, Castro said, and so in a sense it was. Word came that Oswald had been a member of the Fair Play for Cuba Committee and a

Castro admirer. "If they had had proof," Castro said, "they would have said he was an agent, a hired killer. In saying simply that he is an admirer, this is just to try and make an association in people's minds between the name of Castro and the emotion awakened by the assassination. This is a publicity method, a propaganda device. It's terrible." As the radio began calling Oswald a "pro-Castro Marxist," Castro canceled his planned schedule and—Daniel believed—ordered a state of alert.

Castro had been right about the reflex reaction of many in the United States. Newspaper editorials were to speak darkly of "The Enemy Without," and a Gallup Poll revealed that a large number of Americans thought Russia, Cuba, or "the Communists" were involved. In Dallas on the night of the assassination, Assistant District Attorney William Alexander spoke of charging Oswald with having murdered the President "as part of an international Communist conspiracy."

President Johnson, already back in Washington, DC, saw to it that there would be no such charge. Henry Wade, the District Attorney himself, would recall receiving not one but three calls from an aide to the new President. "Washington's word to me," he said, "was that it would hurt foreign relations if I alleged a conspiracy. . . . I went down to the police department . . . to make sure the Dallas police didn't involve any foreign country in the assassination."

At the very start of his presidency, Johnson had acted to prevent what he thought could potentially be global catastrophe. It was a measure that will surely endure as an act of sanity and statesmanship. Nevertheless, the new President himself would come to suspect there had been a conspiracy, and that Castro had been involved. He was to share variations on that theme with at least five people, none of whom would feel free to speak publicly until after his death.

"I'll tell you something that will rock you," he told ABC TV's Howard K. Smith in 1968, just before the end of his own presidency, "Kennedy was trying to get to Castro, but Castro got to him first. . . . It will all come out someday." Out of office, during an interview with CBS's Walter Cronkite, he said he had never been "completely relieved of the fact that there might have been international connections. . . . I don't think we ought to discuss the suspicions, because there's not any hard evidence that Oswald was directed by a foreign government. . . . He was quite a mysterious fellow, and he did have connections that bore examination."[2]

In 1971, over coffee with Leo Janos, one of his former speechwriters, he said he had "never believed Oswald acted alone, although I can accept that he pulled the trigger." He explained that the United States "had been operating a damned Murder Inc. in the Caribbean," and speculated that the assassination had been retaliation for the CIA's efforts. Finally, not long before his own death in 1973, he told Hearst columnist Marianne Means that he thought Oswald had shot his predecessor "because he was under either the influence or the orders of Castro."[3]

Kennedy's successor had spoken off the record, surely guessing that one or all of his listeners would publish his remarks once he was gone. So they did, and it was tantalizing stuff. Contrary to what Johnson had told ABC's Smith, however, evidence that Castro had a hand in the assassination has not "all come out."

What really triggered Johnson's suspicion, encouraging the notion of a Castro hit, was an account he heard in 1967 from the columnist Drew Pearson—as had others, including Earl Warren. Pearson and his colleague Jack Anderson, for their part, had received their information from a prominent Washington attorney named Edward Morgan. Morgan, in turn, was retailing a story offered by his client—none other than John Roselli, the Mafia gangster who had helped the CIA in the early plots to kill Castro.

Top mobsters do not push to get stories into the press out of a sense of public duty. Roselli's motive? The House Assassinations Committee, noting that his story of Cuba-related skullduggery coincided with the mobster's efforts to avoid prosecution and deportation back to Italy, thought it possible that Roselli "manipulated public perception of the plots . . . to get the CIA to intervene in his legal problems, as the price for his agreeing to make no further disclosures."

The story Roselli peddled had three main elements: that mobsters had at one point been recruited to assist the CIA in attempting to assassinate Castro, that Robert Kennedy may have approved efforts to kill the Cuban leader, and that Castro riposted by sending assassins to the United States to kill President Kennedy. The first two elements, as described in these pages, were factual. The third element, however, had no substance to it. The best Roselli came up with to support his allegation of Castro involvement was that he and associates had received "feedback furnished by [unidentified] sources close to Castro." This was a slender reed on which to hang the allegation that preoccupied Johnson to the end of his life.[4] On the basis of barely any solid information, however, the insinuation that Castro had a hand in the Kennedy assassination proved durable.

There was something that appeared to nourish the suspicion that Castro retaliated against President Kennedy, a statement the Cuban leader himself had reportedly made two months before the assassination.

On the night of September 7, 1963, while attending a reception at the Brazilian Embassy in Havana, Castro had settled down in a chair and uttered a stream of vituperation against John F. Kennedy. He had called the President "a cretin . . . the Batista of his times . . . the most opportunistic American President of all time." He had denounced recent exile raids and said—according to the report filed by Daniel Harker of Associated Press—"We are prepared to fight them and answer in kind. United States leaders should think that if they are aiding terrorist plans to eliminate Cuban leaders, they themselves *will not be safe* [author's emphasis]."[5]

Had the Cuban leader very loudly issued a public warning— one he wanted to be heard in Washington—that he was aware of American plans to kill him or senior colleagues, and would respond in kind? The Cuban leader was to deny it repeatedly, most formally in 1978 to House Assassinations Committee members and staff who visited Havana.

"I said," he asserted, referring to the much-quoted comment, "something like those plots start to set a very bad precedent . . . that could become a boomerang against the authors of those actions . . . but I did not mean to threaten. . . . [It was] rather, like warning that we knew . . . I didn't say it as a threat. . . . For three years, we had known there were plots against us . . . the conversation came about very casually, you know."

The idea that Cuba could have been involved in President Kennedy's death, Castro said, was "insane . . . I never heard anyone suggest or even speculate about a measure of that sort, because who could think of the idea of organizing the death of the President of the United States? That would have been the most perfect pretext for the United States to invade our country, which is what I have been trying to prevent all these years. . . . What could we gain from a war with the United States? The United States would lose nothing. The destruction would have been here."

Cuba's Marxist policy, Castro told other interviewers, left "no room for liquidation of leaders of any social system through terrorist acts." During the bitter struggle to overthrow Batista, Castro's forces did not try to kill the hated dictator. In the fall of 1963, in light of the secret dialogue about accommodation, would it have made sense for Castro to plot Kennedy's death? Had he been so duplicitous, he told the Committee, U.S. retaliation would almost certainly have swept away the revolution and Castro with it. Castro was aware too, that, even had Cuba's role not been discovered, there was the possibility that a successor to Kennedy would prove as tough or even tougher toward Cuba.

There is another reason to doubt that Castro's reported remark at the Brazilian Embassy was a real threat to President Kennedy's life, a reason he did not articulate himself. Had he really intended harm to the President, would Castro have announced it to the press two months in advance?

The Assassinations Committee considered the fact that news of Castro's "threat" remark had been published in New Orleans just a few weeks before Oswald's trip to Mexico City. If Oswald read the story, might he have convinced himself that killing the President would make him a sort of revolutionary hero?

That idea hardly squared with the consistent evidence that Oswald thought well of President Kennedy. In custody after the assassination, asked whether he thought Cuba would be better off with the President dead, Oswald replied that, "since the President was killed someone would take his place, perhaps Vice

President Johnson, and . . . his views would probably be largely the same as those of President Kennedy."

Oswald's statements before the assassination carry more weight, but leave the same impression. Asked in the radio debate in New Orleans whether he agreed with Castro's remarks that President Kennedy was a "ruffian and a thief," Oswald said he did not agree with that wording. He thought, however, that the CIA and the State Department had made "monumental mistakes" over Cuba.

Lieutenant Martello, the police intelligence officer who spoke with Oswald after the street fracas in New Orleans, recalled that Oswald "in no way demonstrated any animosity or ill-feeling toward President Kennedy. . . . He showed in his manner of speaking that he liked the President." No one ever would make a credible allegation that the alleged assassin had anything but good to say about John F. Kennedy.

The House Assassinations Committee found "persuasive reasons to conclude that the Cuban government was not involved in the Kennedy assassination." Were the multiple stories that seemed to link Oswald to Castro's Cuba merely opportunistic efforts, after the fact, to turn the assassination to propaganda advantage? Or is it possible that some of them were part of a conspiracy designed to do away with President Kennedy and— by linking Oswald to Havana—provoke U.S. retaliation against Cuba, even at the risk of causing a nuclear conflict?

The evidence suggests that painting a track of guilt that led to Havana was deliberate, even perhaps preconceived.

At noon on November 25, the day after the real Oswald had been silenced forever, a young Nicaraguan named Gilberto Alvarado walked into the American Embassy in Mexico City.[6]

What he had to say was so important, he said, that he had to see the Ambassador himself. During a visit to the Cuban Consulate in mid-September, he claimed, he had seen Oswald on a patio talking with a thin black man. They had then been joined by a tall Cuban who passed money to the black man. Then, Alvarado asserted, he heard the black man tell Oswald in English, "I want to kill the man." Oswald replied, "You're not man enough—I can do it." To which the black man responded in Spanish, "I can't go with you. I have a lot to do." Oswald replied, "The people are waiting for me back there." The black man then handed Oswald $6,500 in large-denomination notes, adding by way of apology, "This isn't much." And the supposed meeting ended.

Alvarado claimed he had tried to warn the Embassy about all this before the assassination, but had been rebuffed as a time waster. Now, his account set the wires humming between Mexico City and Washington. It seemed there could be something to it—CIA staff knew from surveillance coverage that an "Oswald" had visited the Cuban Consulate. Ambassador Thomas Mann, who had expressed suspicion of Cuba within hours of the assassination, urged his staff to give Alvarado's tale serious attention.

Alvarado's claim was flashed to Washington for the attention of the FBI and the State Department—and the White House, where it became one of the first pieces of "evidence" to sow the idea of a Castro conspiracy in the new President's mind. Twenty-four hours later, the CIA reported information "from a sensitive and reliable source" that tended to confirm Alvarado's story.

"In reading Oswald's rather complete dossier," Ambassador Mann explained in a later message, "I did not get an impression of a man who would kill a person he had never met for a cause, without offers from the apparatus to which he apparently belonged, when there was nothing in it for him. I therefore had a feeling—subjective and unproven to be sure—that either in Mexico or the United States someone had given him an assignment and money. . . . Castro is the kind of person who would avenge himself in this way." The Ambassador reminded Washington of the AP story of September that had quoted Castro as saying U.S. leaders would "not be safe."

On November 27, the Embassy's legal attaché relayed a press statement put out by a "former Cuban diplomat"—a prominent exile—that stretched what AP's "threat" story had actually said. In the diplomat's version, Castro had said, "Let Kennedy and his brother Robert take care of themselves, since they, too, can be the victims of an attempt which will cause their death."

Washington reacted very cautiously. An FBI supervisor, Laurence Keenan, was sent to Mexico with orders to damp down any suggestion of conspiracy. He stressed to Ambassador Mann that the FBI position was—as it was to remain—that Oswald and Oswald alone had killed the President. The State Department, for its part, sent Mann a telegram he never forgot. Years later, when interviewed by the author, he was still irritated by what he recalled as "an instruction from Washington to cease investigation." Even as the Ambassador fumed, however, it was becoming apparent that there was something rum about Alvarado's story.

Questioned by Mexican officials, the young Nicaraguan admitted that his story had been a fabrication. He had never seen Oswald, had not seen money change hands, had not tried to alert the American Embassy before the assassination. Then, however, when U.S. officials continued to show interest, he reverted to the original story and claimed that the Mexicans had pressured him into the retraction. A polygraph test, however, indicated that he might be lying. Alvarado then acknowledged that he "must be mistaken," was uncertain when the incident had occurred, and said he had merely seen "someone who looked like Oswald." Officials in Washington, DC, decided once and for all that there was nothing to the story.

In Mexico City, Ambassador Mann still felt Alvarado should have been flown to the United States for further questioning. In that he was right. Having apparently lied made Alvarado no less relevant to the investigation. For the nature of his story, and his background, suggested that the attempt to tie Castro to the assassination had been no spur-of-the-moment impulse.

Consider Alvarado's claim that he heard Oswald tell his companion, "You're not man enough [to kill the man]. I can do it." That echoed almost exactly what Silvia Odio in Dallas had been told by her mysterious anti-Castro visitor "Leopoldo." Alvarado, too, quoted Oswald as having said that Cuban exiles "don't have any guts . . . should have shot President Kennedy after the Bay of Pigs." The two accounts could be from the same bad film script—but by what scriptwriter?

Alvarado said he was a Nicaraguan intelligence agent, that he had been at the Cuban Embassy on a mission to try to get into Cuba. The Nicaraguans denied it, claiming to the contrary that he was a known Communist—an implausible suggestion to make about an individual who had tried to implicate Communist Cuba in the assassination. The Americans believed Alvarado was indeed a Nicaraguan agent. A CIA document notes that he had been a "regular informant of the Nicaraguan secret service, an officer of which has provided this agency with [Alvarado's] reports for over a year."

Then Nicaraguan dictator Luis Somoza was an avid supporter of the anti-Castro exiles, as was natural for Central America's version of the former Cuban dictator Batista. His country had served as a principal assembly point for the Bay of Pigs invasion, and remained open house for the CIA and its Cuban protégés. Nicaragua hosted anti-Castro leader Manuel Artime, who commanded two bases in the country and had a role in the CIA plot to kill Castro using Rolando Cubela. Artime's associate and friend was Howard Hunt, the Agency propaganda specialist who said he had been one of the first to recommend that Castro be killed.[7]

In spite of the holes in Alvarado's claim about Oswald, his allegation was brought to President Johnson's attention on at least three occasions and for some time remained a live issue.[8] Even as that allegation lost its head of steam, moreover, others proliferated.[9]

On December 2, a new Mexico City witness came up with a variation on Alvarado's theme. Pedro Gutiérrez, a credit investigator, sent a letter to President Johnson saying that that he, too, had seen Oswald being handed money—by his account—outside the Cuban Embassy. Gutiérrez's story, which caused further extensive investigation, led nowhere. He turned out to be a zealous anti-Communist with a background of agitation.

Within a day of Gutiérrez's allegation, a "sensitive source" told the CIA about a Cubana Airlines flight that had supposedly been delayed for hours at the Mexico City airport on the night of the assassination—waiting for a mysterious passenger. When he at last arrived, by private aircraft, he had allegedly traveled on to Havana concealed from fellow passengers in the pilot's cabin. Checks revealed that, in fact, the Cuban aircraft had left for Havana before the second plane arrived. Another claim that led nowhere.[10]

Some allegations had the ring of calculated black propaganda. A prominent exile writer, Salvador Díaz-Versón, claimed that while in Mexico City, Oswald had met at restaurant with the Cuban Ambassador and Sylvia Durán, the secretary who dealt with his visa application. His source for this, Díaz said, was a fellow exile journalist living in Mexico, Eduardo Borrell Navarro. Interviewed for the author, Borrell said he, in turn, had gotten his information from anti-Castro Cubans—they had been surveilling their pro-Castro counterparts before the assassination. Borrell spoke of his own long and close relationship with officials at the U.S. Embassy, and said his sources were close to U.S. intelligence.

Along with all these claims, there was a matter that an Assassinations Committee report characterized as an allegation that "although related to certain facts, cannot be substantiated." Late on the night of the assassination, according to former U.S. diplomat Clare Booth Luce, the wife of wealthy publisher and editor-in-chief of *Time* and *Life* magazines, Henry Luce, she had received a call from a Cuban exile she knew well. Like some other wealthy Americans, Mrs. Luce supported the anti-Castro movement by funding one of the motorboats the exiles used for raids on Castro's Cuba. The man phoning was one of her protégés, and he had called from New Orleans.

The purpose of the call was to tell Mrs. Luce that her exile protégé and two comrades had met Oswald during the summer, that he had tried to infiltrate their group, and had offered his services to help kill Castro. The exiles had unmasked him as a member of the Fair Play for Cuba Committee, however, taken pictures of his street actions and taped him talking about Cuba within his "communist cell." According to Mrs. Luce's caller, Oswald had made "several" trips to Mexico City and had returned with funds.

With that, Mrs. Luce said, the voice from New Orleans launched into a familiar litany. Oswald had boasted he was "a crack marksman and could shoot anybody—including the President or the Secretary of the Navy."[11] There was "a Cuban Communist assassination team at large and Oswald was their hired gun."

The Committee found that Mrs. Luce's protégés in 1963 had been in the DRE, the exile group represented in New Orleans by Carlos Bringuier, who had taken part in the street fracas with Oswald over his Fair Play for Cuba leafleting.[12] Here again, then, in a call to the wife of a man at the top of *Time*—that mighty media outlet—was the scenario of a Communist Oswald who supposedly bragged about his marksmanship and spoke of killing the President. Shades of the Silvia Odio incident, and the Mexico City allegations.

The most revealing detail of the Luce episode, however, was the reference by her caller to Oswald's travel to Mexico City. Mrs. Luce was sure she had received the call late on the night of the assassination—she recalled the phone ringing while she and her husband were watching the television coverage. Oswald's visit to Mexico City, however, did not become known to the public until forty-eight hours *later*. On the night of November 22, the record indicates, Oswald's visit to Mexico City was known only to Oswald himself, perhaps to his wife, Marina—and to U.S. intelligence.

If the call to Mrs. Luce was another fable designed to incriminate Castro's Cuba, ready-made to generate massive publicity,[13] it suggests collaboration between the exiles and an element of American intelligence.[14] Tracking back, the indications are that an effort to link Oswald firmly to Castro's Cubans had begun as early as September, in Mexico City.

*　　*　　*

Oscar Contreras, the then law student who said he was button-holed in the university cafeteria by an Oswald other than the authentic Oswald, offered food for thought.[15] Perhaps he was being over-suspicious, Contreras told the author, but he had never been able to understand how—of all the thousands of students in Mexico City—the man who called himself Oswald picked on three who really did have contacts in the Cuban Embassy. Nothing about the evening, or the moment, had had anything to do with Cuba.

Contreras recalled, too, how emphatically Cuban officials at the Consulate later warned them off seeing any more of Oswald. They did so, they said, because they thought even then that the young American might well be "some sort of provocateur, sent by the United States to go to Cuba with evil intent." The Cuban Consul's colleague, Alfredo Mirabal, recalled that his impression "from the very first moment was that it was in fact a provocation." Disquieting leads suggest that the Cubans' suspicion, voiced weeks before the assassination, was not mere paranoia.

According to Ernesto Rodríguez, who claimed to have been a CIA contract agent in Mexico City in 1963, Oswald had given both the Soviets and the Cubans information about a current CIA plan to assassinate Fidel Castro—had even talked about it on the telephone.[16] He offered to share more information, Rodríguez said, were he granted a Cuban entry visa. The story fed into the theory that Castro may have responded to Oswald's information by striking first—in Dallas.

Another account, if true, indicates flatly that a U.S. intelligence officer attempted to concoct information about Oswald in Mexico City. Exile leader Antonio Veciana, who said he saw Oswald in the company of his American contact, "Bishop," just weeks before the Mexico episode,[17] added that—after the assassination—Bishop gave him a new task. "He asked me to get in touch with a cousin of mine who worked in the Cuban Embassy in Mexico City, Guillermo Ruiz. Bishop asked me to see if Ruiz would, for money, make statements stating that Lee Harvey Oswald had been at the Embassy a few weeks before the assassination. I asked him whether it was true that Oswald had been there, and Bishop replied that it did not matter whether he had or not. What was important was that my cousin, a member of the Cuban diplomatic service, should confirm that he had been."

Veciana did have a cousin by marriage named Ruiz, who worked—fronting as a diplomat—for Castro's intelligence service. According to Veciana, however, he was unable to contact Ruiz as quickly as Bishop had wished. Before he could do it, Bishop told him to "forget the whole thing and not to comment or ask any questions about Lee Harvey Oswald."[18]

Veciana may well have told the truth. A former associate who worked with Veciana when he was chief of sabotage for the People's Revolutionary Movement in Havana said, "Veciana was the straightest, absolutely trustworthy, most honest person I ever met. I would trust him implicitly."[19] The Assassinations Committee investigator's report on him stated that "Generally, Veciana's reputation for honesty and integrity was excellent. He appeared credible to this author in the course of many contacts, and important information he provided checked out."

"Bishop," Veciana said, "did work for an intelligence agency of this country, and I am convinced that it was the CIA. . . . The impression I have is that the Mexico City episode was a device. By using it, Maurice Bishop wanted to lay the blame for

President Kennedy's death fairly and squarely on Castro and the Cuban government."

If that was the ploy, it came close to succeeding. Even today, some still think Castro was behind the Kennedy assassination.[20]

In the late 1970s, the author interviewed the son of the late Mario García Kohly Sr., a prominent activist and for a time self-styled president-in-exile of Cuba. An extreme rightist bitterly opposed to President Kennedy's policy, he had, by 1963, long since broken with the mainstream exile movement. On hearing the news that Kennedy had been killed, Mario Kohly Jr. said, he called his father—after opening a celebratory bottle of champagne.

"My father," he told the author, "seemed elated and quite relieved. He seemed more pleased, I would say, than surprised. I am sure he had knowledge of what really happened in Dealey Plaza." The younger Kohly would not say who he believed killed Kennedy. "Let's just say," he responded," it is very possible the assassination was done by the anti-Castro movement in the hopes of making it look like Castro had done it. If they could blame the assassination of President Kennedy on Fidel Castro and arouse enough indignation among the American people, this would have helped the movement to get the support we needed to regain our country. In other words, they either would have supported a new invasion against Castro or might have invaded Cuba themselves."

It never happened, of course. As the months went by, it became apparent that Washington had put aside plans for intervention in Cuba. Even as the exiles' military plans were consigned to the political trash can, so too was talk of reaching an accommodation with Fidel Castro. Three days after the assassination, when U.S. diplomat William Attwood received formal confirmation that Havana wished to proceed with talks, President Johnson was briefed on the contacts of recent weeks. The new President, preoccupied as he was with the accelerating U.S. involvement in Vietnam, evinced no interest. Word came back," Attwood recalled, "that this was to be put on ice for the time being, and 'the time being' has been ever since."

The Kennedy era was over, its promise vanishing into mythology as surely as the flame on the President's grave flickered in the wind. With Lee Oswald dead, the Warren Commission made little of the inconsistencies of the case—the Silvia Odio incident, the suspect scenario in Mexico City, and the indications that there may have been more than one gunman. Late in the inquiry, faced with the imponderables of the Odio evidence, Chief Counsel Rankin spoke volumes when he said wearily, "At this stage, we are supposed to be closing doors, not opening them."

Behind one of the doors stood the surviving principal in the case, Jack Ruby. That door, too, was better left closed.

CHAPTER 23

The Good Ole Boy

*"The pattern of contacts did show that individuals
who had the motive to kill the President also had
knowledge of a man who could be used to get access
to Oswald in the custody of the Dallas police."*

—House Select Committee on Assassinations
Report, 1979

Seven months after the assassination, in a nondescript room
at Dallas County Jail, the Chief Justice of the United States
presided over a vital interrogation. Earl Warren, accompanied
by then Congressman Gerald Ford and a pack of lawyers, was
going through the motions of questioning Jack Ruby.[1] The man
who had silenced Lee Oswald sat shifting uneasily, chewing his
lower lip, sometimes drying up altogether. If he was afraid the
Warren Commission would prove hard to handle, Ruby worried
unnecessarily. The interrogators listened with equanimity to the
well-rehearsed story of why he murdered the accused assassin.

Ruby testified:

No one . . . requested me to do anything. I never spoke to
anyone about attempting to do anything. . . . No underworld

person made any effort to contact me. It all happened that Sunday morning. . . . The last thing I read was that Mrs. Kennedy may have to come back to Dallas for a trial for Lee Harvey Oswald and I don't know what bug got hold of me. . . . Suddenly, the feeling, the emotional feeling came within me, that someone owed this debt to our beloved President to save her the ordeal of coming back. I had the gun in my right hip pocket, and impulsively, if that is the correct word here, I saw him [Oswald] and that is all I can say. . . . I think I used the words, "You killed my President, you rat."

Ruby presented himself as the misguided exponent of his own brand of sentimental patriotism, and the Warren Commission saw no need to probe further.

A month earlier, the two lawyers charged with the Ruby investigation, Leon Hubert and Burt Griffin, had fired off a long memorandum to Chief Counsel Lee Rankin. It laid out, in precise detail, areas they felt had been inadequately investigated, emphasizing that the Commission had yet to disprove that "Ruby killed Oswald at the suggestion of others." Their recommendations were followed up only in a halfhearted sort of way, for—as Griffin put it—"They were in a different ball game than we were. . . . They really thought that ours was crazy and that we were incompetent." Hubert resigned, on the understanding that he would still be present at the forthcoming interview with Ruby. The promise was not kept. Warren, Ford, and Lee Rankin departed for Dallas without informing Hubert. The Commission's specialists on Ruby, the two men most qualified for the job, were excluded from questioning the man who perhaps held the key to unsolved areas of the assassination.

The Commissioners who did talk to Ruby found it a tedious chore. Ruby rambled on for hours, often irrelevantly, about his activities before the murder. He prattled about his Jewish origins and how Jews would be killed in vast numbers because of what he had done. He seemed frightened, so much so that Chief Justice Warren apparently dismissed him as a psychiatric case. That was insufficient justification for what happened before the interview ended.

Ruby had been doodling on a notepad. Then he cried: "Gentlemen, unless you get me to Washington, you can't get a fair shake out of me. . . . I am not a crackpot, I have all my senses—I don't want to avoid any crime I am guilty of." Eight times in all, Oswald's murderer begged the Chief Justice to arrange his transfer to the capital for further questioning and lie-detector tests. Warren told him it could not be done. In the Warren Report, published a few months later, Ruby was characterized as merely "moody and unstable," one lone nut who had killed another. His background and activities, the Report said, "yielded no evidence that Ruby conspired with anyone in planning or executing the killing of Lee Harvey Oswald."

Fifteen years later, the House Assassinations Committee replaced the Commission's certainty with a cobweb of suspicion. Along with its finding that the assassination evidence pointed to conspiracy, the Committee portrayed a Ruby who had, for years, been involved with some of the people most motivated to kill the President. They found that vital matters had been glossed over in the original inquiry and that Ruby probably received "assistance" in gaining access to the police station basement where he shot Oswald.

The most startling revelations about Oswald's killer concerned his involvement with organized crime and with Cuba.

The Warren inquiry had declared there was "no significant link between Ruby and organized crime," dismissing what it called "rumors linking Ruby with pro- or anti-Castro activities." Given the material the Warren staff possessed even then, it is hard to believe the Report's authors expected to be taken seriously. Ruby's life story is the dossier of a sort of gangsters' groupie.

It began in Chicago. Jacob Rubenstein—Ruby's name at birth—came into the world in 1911, the fifth of eight children born to Polish immigrant parents, a drunkard father and a slightly crazed mother. All eight offspring ended up in foster homes. Jacob never made it past the eighth grade. By the age of sixteen he was known as Sparky to his pals, a tough, street-smart kid roaming Chicago's West Side who earned the occasional dollar by running errands—for a boss whose name is synonymous with violent crime, Al Capone.

The record of Jacob's early life is one of an apprenticeship in petty crime—ticket scalper, racetrack tip-sheet vendor, dealer in contraband music sheets, and nightclub bouncer. He had some minor brushes with the law and earned a reputation for senseless violence. In 1937, he took a real job of sorts—as what he later liked to call "organizer" for a local branch of the Scrap Iron and Junk Handlers Union. The union leadership had been commandeered by stooges for Chicago's leading racketeers, and Ruby was a bagman for the new president, John Martin. He once pulled a gun while trying to recruit members in a scrap-paper plant. When Martin shot down his predecessor, Ruby was pulled in for questioning.

Years later, the Warren Commission would accept his claim to have "left the union when I found out the notorious organization had moved in there." In fact, Ruby stayed on for some time. The Warren Commission ignored, too, an FBI interview with a Chicago crime figure who said Ruby had been "accepted and to a certain extent his business operations controlled by the syndicate." After a wartime spell in the U.S. Air Force, Ruby left Chicago for Dallas and the nightclub business.

By his own account, reportedly, the move was at the direction of his Mob associates. A Dallas businessman who knew Ruby well, Giles Miller, told the author Ruby would "discuss how he was sent down here by 'them'—he always referred to 'them'— meaning the syndicate. He always complained that if he had to be exiled, why couldn't he have been exiled to California or to Florida? Why to this hellhole Dallas?" According to Luis Kutner, a former attorney on the Kefauver Committee—the 1950 Senate probe into organized crime—the staff learned that Ruby was "a syndicate lieutenant who had been sent to Dallas to serve as a liaison for Chicago mobsters."

A Mob emissary, Paul Jones, tried in 1946 to bribe the Dallas District Attorney and Sheriff to let the syndicate operate in the city.[2] Decades later, when Ruby shot Oswald, former Sheriff Steve Guthrie came forward to say Ruby had been the man named by Jones to run the proposed operation—a gambling joint fronting as a restaurant and nightclub. The Chicago contacts who introduced Jones to Ruby, Paul "Needle Nose" Labriola and Jimmy Weinberg, were close to the man who at the time ran organized crime in Chicago, Sam Giancana. Giancana, as noted earlier, would in the distant future play a prominent role in the CIA-Mafia plots to kill Fidel Castro.

In Dallas, Ruby made a sort of career for himself as the proprietor of shady nightspots known for after-hours drinking and violent brawling. He beat up those who crossed him, but escaped serious trouble by being careful to dispense favors to policemen. Underworld sources said Ruby was "the payoff man for the Dallas Police Department," a man who "had the fix with the county authorities." Further afield, Ruby apparently played more dangerous games.

In 1956, he was named by an FBI informant as the man who "gave the okay to operate" in part of a major drug-smuggling scheme. Enter, soon after, Ruby the gunrunner to Cuba. His Cuba connection would appear to link him to Santo Trafficante, the Mafia chieftain who was reportedly later to prophesy that President Kennedy "was going to be hit." Ruby's apparent connections led to the core of the most enduring suspicions as to who really killed Kennedy.

So far as could later be established, Ruby's interest in Cuba began six years before the assassination. According to James Beard, a former associate, he stored guns and ammunition at a house on Texas's southern coast, prior to ferrying the weaponry into Cuba. Beard said he saw "many boxes of new guns, including automatic rifles and handguns" loaded aboard a military-surplus vessel, and that "each time the boat left with guns and ammunition, Jack Ruby was on it." The shipments were destined for Fidel Castro's revolutionaries, then still fighting to topple Batista. In the years before the revolution, Castro was supplied and supported from the United States, not least by the leaders of organized crime—currying favor against the possibility that Castro were to prove victorious.

According to Texas gunrunner Robert McKeown, whom the author interviewed, Ruby continued to ship in military supplies after Castro did seize power.[3] By the spring of 1959, moreover, he was pursuing another project. He "wanted to talk about getting some people out of Cuba" on behalf of "a man in Las Vegas." After the assassination, when it emerged that Ruby had been in Havana in 1959, he said he had merely taken an eight-day vacation in Cuba at the invitation of a man named McWillie.

Lewis McWillie, one of Ruby's closest friends, had—in the words of a contemporary FBI report—"consolidated his syndicate connections through his associations in Havana, Cuba, with Santo Trafficante. . . ." He was in Cuba managing the Tropicana nightclub, in which Trafficante had a major interest. He had organized and paid for a weeklong trip to Havana for Ruby, McWillie was to say, in hopes that Ruby would get friends in the press to promote the club. Other information, however, suggests there was more than one visit—and activity that fit not at all with the story of a freeloading vacation in the Caribbean.[4]

Cuban immigration files were to show that Ruby arrived in Havana on August 8, 1959, flying in from New Orleans. Far from staying in Havana for just a few days, he was still there a full month later. Three witnesses, two attorneys and an architect, recalled having encountered Ruby at the Tropicana Casino in the first week of September, over Labor Day weekend. On September 8, Ruby mailed a postcard from Havana to a female friend in Dallas, mentioning in passing that "Mac"—presumably McWillie—"says hello." An exit card showed that he flew out of Havana three days later. His travels, however, were not over.

Within twenty-four hours of leaving Havana, documents showed, Ruby entered Cuba again—this time from Miami—stayed for a night, then left for New Orleans. So Ruby made at least two trips, the first lasting more than a month, followed by a forty-eight hour shuttle that can hardly have been part of the pleasure trip Ruby and McWillie claimed. There were almost certainly other visits.

Elaine Mynier, a mutual friend of Ruby and McWillie who worked at the Dallas airport, said she "frequently" saw Ruby and

McWillie coming and going. A Delta Airlines agent at New Orleans spoke of Ruby's "numerous flights." On August 10, two days after his first arrival in Havana, a police report had Ruby in Dallas being interviewed about traffic violations. Bank records for the following week placed him in Dallas accessing his safe-deposit box. On August 31, too, he was apparently in Dallas, and he was there again four days later. The Assassinations Committee would conclude that Ruby made at least three trips to Cuba, perhaps more, and "most likely was serving as a courier for gambling interests."[5]

While in Cuba, information strongly suggests, Ruby met not only with Lewis McWillie, but also with Santo Trafficante. In the summer of 1959, as one of the most prominent targets of Castro's gradual clampdown on Mafia gambling and narcotics operations, Trafficante was confined at the Trescornia detention camp on the outskirts of Havana. A former detainee named John Wilson, who was held in the camp at the same time, was to contact U.S. authorities in 1963 when news broke that Jack Ruby had killed alleged assassin Lee Oswald.[6] At Trescornia, he reported, he had known "an American gangster called Santos [sic]," and that "Santos" had been "visited several times by an American gangster-type named Ruby" who "would come to prison with [a] person bringing food."[7]

Years later, in an appearance before the Assassinations Committee, Trafficante would say carefully, "I never remember meeting Jack Ruby . . . I don't remember him visiting me, either. . . . I never had no contact with him. I don't see why he was going to come and visit me." The Committee concluded that there was "considerable evidence" that Ruby did visit Trafficante at the camp. It linked him, too, to Trafficante associates in Dallas. One, an old Cuba hand named Russell Matthews, was described by one of his own attorneys as "probably the closest thing to the Mafia we've ever seen in Dallas." There was also James Dolan, described as one of Dallas' "most notorious hoodlums," a man who committed acts of violence on Trafficante's behalf, and who was also linked to the Marcello network in New Orleans. The telephone number of a Trafficante associate named Jack Todd was found in Ruby's car after he shot Oswald.

Once they realized their day in Cuba was over, of course, crime bosses had begun backing the anti-Castro cause. Some, notably Trafficante, would agree to help CIA plans to murder Castro. Ruby, however, may at some stage not have played the Cuban game according to the Mob's new rules. One of Ruby's lawyers was to note that Ruby was fearful because "he had tried to arrange some sort of a deal with Cuba after Fidel Castro overthrew the Batista regime." A psychiatrist who visited Ruby reported that there was, "considerable guilt about the fact that he sent guns to Cuba; he feels he helped the enemy and incriminated himself." Ruby told the psychiatrist, "They got what they wanted on me.". He did not say who "they" were.

Ruby's first lawyer after he killed Oswald, Tom Howard, told the press that his client's mind had simply gone blank at the moment of shooting Oswald. It was, the lawyer said, a case of "temporary insanity." Insanity or conspiracy? Ruby's behavior before the Oswald shooting provides some clues.

For a man judged by the Warren Commission to have "no significant link" with organized crime, 1963 caught Jack Ruby in a hail of coincidences. The Assassinations Committee, which used a computer to analyze the phone records of Ruby and other key individuals for the days and weeks before the assassination, found that men with the motive to kill the President had knowledge of Ruby's "possible availability."

In early October, just after the public announcement of the President's forthcoming Dallas visit, a call went from Ruby's telephone at his Carousel Club to a Louisiana number listed under the name of the ex-wife of Russell Matthews, the Trafficante associate from the Cuba days.

Late in October, Ruby called Irwin Weiner, a Chicago bondsman who headed the insurance company that underwrote the pension fund of Jimmy Hoffa's Teamsters Union. He would later be charged with helping to defraud the Teamsters' pension fund of $1.5 million—and found not guilty after the government's chief witness had been shot dead by masked men. Weiner also knew Sam Giancana and Santo Trafficante. Two weeks before the assassination, Ruby had a conversation with Robert "Barney" Baker, whom Robert Kennedy had called Hoffa's "roving ambassador of violence." The next day, Ruby called another Hoffa lieutenant, Murray "Dusty" Miller, then phoned Baker again.[8]

Ruby, and some of those who had been in contact with him, would claim such calls had related to an effort by Ruby to solve problems he was having with the American Guild of Variety Artists, the entertainers' union. Weiner, however, refused to discuss the nature of his Ruby call when questioned, and years later told a reporter their exchange had had nothing to do with labor troubles.[9] Barney Baker, Hoffa's henchman, claimed he and Ruby indeed discussed union problems. Why, though, would Jimmy Hoffa's strong-arm man take time out to help with Ruby's petty worries? The Ruby-Baker calls came at a time when Hoffa was under increasing attack from the Kennedy Justice Department. He had spoken of wanting both Kennedy brothers dead, as reported earlier, and he was close to Trafficante.

Assassinations Committee staff also probed a one-minute call Ruby made three weeks before the assassination to a New Orleans number, CH 2-5431, which turned out to be the office number of Nofio Pecora, a lieutenant of Mafia boss Carlos Marcello. Marcello himself, a man who used the telephone only with extreme caution, had placed a call to CH 2-5431 in midsummer 1963.

Oswald's uncle Charles Murret was an associate of Pecora. Oswald had been bailed, following the New Orleans street fracas over his Fair Play for Cuba Committee activity, thanks to the intervention of Emile Bruneau, another Pecora associate— eleven months after Marcello had reportedly talked of having the President murdered and "setting up a nut to take the blame." Pecora "declined to respond" when asked by the Assassinations Committee about the Ruby call. He later said he "did not recall" speaking with Ruby, did not know him, and suggested he might have taken a message for somebody else on his property. The Committee was "dissatisfied" with these responses.[10]

Early investigators knew nothing about another factor the Committee uncovered. Jack Ruby was in dire financial straits in 1963, had borrowed more than a thousand dollars from the bank, was being pursued for rent arrears on his club premises, and the Internal Revenue Service was after him for nearly $21,000 in unpaid taxes—a figure that by midsummer rose to almost twice that figure. Yet suddenly, in the very last days before the assassination, Ruby began behaving as though he expected his finances to take a dramatic change for the better.

Ruby had long lived out of his hip pocket or left money littered around his apartment. On November 15, however, he began using a safe and discussed embedding it in concrete in his office. On November 19, three days before the assassination,

Ruby told his tax lawyer that he had a "connection" who could supply him with money to settle his debts to the IRS. That day, according to Ruby's bank record, there had been a mere $246 in his Carousel Club account. Three hours after the President's assassination, however, Ruby would go to his bank carrying the then huge cash sum of $7,000—some $53,000 at today's rates— in large bills stuffed in his pockets. He deposited none of the money, and about half of it had vanished by the time he was arrested two days later.[11]

The Assassinations Committee was to conclude that those with the motive to assassinate the President had in Jack Ruby "knowledge of a man who had exhibited a violent nature and who was in serious financial trouble." Did the Mob take up its option?

The Weekend of the Killings

Shortly before 10 p.m. on November 21, Ruby went to dinner at the Egyptian Restaurant in Dallas with a longtime crony named Ralph Paul. The Egyptian was owned by one Joseph Campisi, whose description in official records ranged from being a "negative" member of organized crime to "suspected" and "definite." Campisi knew associates of Santo Trafficante Jr. and had a longstanding relationship with Joseph Civello, who reportedly ran Dallas operations for Carlos Marcello. He would tell the FBI after the assassination that he knew nothing about Ruby's background—yet later visit him in jail.

On the morning of the assassination Ruby dallied for hours in the offices of the *Dallas Morning News*. He ate breakfast there, and was noticed by a number of employees during the morning. He was in the advertising department—discussing publicity for his clubs—until 12:25 p.m., and he was there minutes after 12:30, when the shots rang out just blocks away in Dealey Plaza. His presence at the *Morning News* gave Ruby a viable alibi and more. Even before news that the President had been shot flashed through the newspaper's offices, he was seated at a desk—a copy of the morning paper in hand—holding forth angrily about the now infamous black-bordered advertisement that "welcomed" President Kennedy to Dallas. When news of the shooting did come in, and people gathered round a television, Ruby appeared "obviously shaken . . . sat for a while with a dazed expression in his eyes."

Dallas Morning News journalist Hugh Aynesworth, whose view was that Ruby had "feigned surprise" at news of the assassination, made a good point. Given that Ruby knew the President was in town, and given that the *Dallas Morning News* offices were a two-minute walk from Dealey Plaza, why had Ruby—if devoted to the President as he claimed—not bothered to go see him pass by?

Ruby soon began a telephone marathon. He called his club, saying he might decide to close up. He made a show of a call to his sister, handing the phone to a newspaper employee so that he could hear the sister cry out, "My God, what do they want?" As he left the newspaper building, Ruby would claim afterward, he was in tears. Twenty minutes later he was in the throng at Parkland Hospital, where reporters were awaiting news of the President's condition. He tugged the sleeve of White House correspondent Seth Kantor, who had known him when he worked in Dallas, said what a terrible thing the shooting was, and asked whether he ought to close his clubs. Kantor said he thought he should and hurried on.[12]

Ruby did order the closure of his clubs, then launched into

a spate of calls to relatives, friends, and businesspeople. One remembered him sounding very "broken up." His sister recalled him saying, "I never felt so bad in my life, even when Ma or Pa died." Was this a genuine reaction, or a show intended to build up the image of the Ruby, who would claim he shot Oswald on an impulse?

That evening, over a period of almost five hours, Ruby was seen repeatedly at the police station where Oswald was being held. At about 7:00 p.m., according to a reporter who knew him, he emerged from an elevator on the floor where Oswald was being questioned, walking between two journalists, hunched over and writing something on a piece of paper. Then he was seen hanging around outside the Homicide office where Oswald was being interrogated. According to the reporter, Ruby "walked up to the door of Captain Fritz's office and put his hand on the knob and started to open it." Officers on the door blocked his way at the last moment.

Ruby then left the police station, and showed up at a synagogue at a special service in memory of the President. The rabbi, who spoke with him, noted that he said nothing about the assassination. Then Ruby was off to the police station again, carrying a supply of corned-beef sandwiches for policemen he knew. He was still there after midnight when Oswald was led briefly into the mob of pushing, shouting reporters. Minutes later, when the District Attorney told the press that Oswald belonged to the Free Cuba Committee, Ruby piped up and corrected him. The D.A., he said, meant not Free Cuba—an anti-Castro group—but, as had by now been made public, the Fair Play for Cuba Committee, the pro-Castro group.

Ruby may have hoped to kill Oswald that first night at the police station. As he mingled with journalists and policemen, he was later to admit, he had his .38-caliber revolver with him.[13] The hubbub at the station eventually eased off, but Ruby kept going. First he dropped into a nearby radio station. Then, in the wee hours, he spent an hour or so talking in a car with an off-duty policeman. This was Patrolman Harry Olsen, who had with him one of the women who worked in Ruby's club. As they talked, the couple was to recall, Ruby cursed Oswald. He, for his part, would belatedly claim that Olsen told him "they should cut this guy [Oswald] inch by inch into ribbons."[14]

Still not done, Ruby went to the other Dallas paper, the *Times-Herald*, and told more people how upset he was about the assassination. He went home at last at 4:30 a.m., but not to sleep. Ruby rousted his roommate, George Senator, and an employee out of bed and dragged them off by car on a bizarre dawn expedition. To the puzzlement of his companions, he had them photograph a large signboard that bore a poster attacking the Chief Justice of the United States. Senator and the employee could not make out whether Ruby thought the poster was the work of Communists, the John Birch Society, or a combination of both. Then at last, having added irrationality to the sustained show of grief, Ruby went home to bed.

The next day, Saturday, at noon, senior officers began to discuss when to move Oswald from the police station to the county jail. There was talk of doing it that afternoon. In two calls to a local newsman, Ruby asked for information on the move. At 4:00 p.m., the time first considered for the transfer, he was back at the police station again. Police Chief Curry, however, advised the press to return next morning at 10:00 a.m.

That night, with the murder of Oswald less than twenty-four hours away, Ruby made more calls. At 10:44 p.m., a call went from Ruby's sister's apartment to Ralph Paul, the associate with whom he had dined two nights previously. One of his employees, who was to say she remembered Ruby having called, overheard Paul say something about a gun and exclaim, "Are you crazy?"[15]

Starting around 11:00 p.m., at his club, Ruby made multiple calls to Galveston, in the southeast of the state, trying to reach Breck Wall, a friend who was on his way there from Dallas. When he found Wall had yet to arrive, Ruby phoned Paul repeatedly at home until—at 11:44—he finally got through. The business that had been so pressing took only two minutes to conclude. Then, pausing just long enough to get the dial tone back again, Ruby made yet another brief call to Paul's home number.

When FBI agents questioned him soon after Oswald's murder, Paul did not mention these late-night calls. Later, he said Ruby had called merely to say other clubs in town were doing poor business. Wall, whom Ruby had striven so hard to reach long-distance, said the call had been merely about union business—the same explanation offered for Ruby's conversations a week or so earlier with Hoffa's aide Barney Baker.

On the morning of Sunday, November 24, Ruby and his roommate, George Senator, were to claim, Ruby stayed in his apartment till nearly 11:00 a.m.[16] Other evidence suggested Ruby was out and about early that morning near the police station. Three television technicians said they saw him near their outside broadcast van. At 9:30 a.m., according to a church minister, Ruby and he traveled together in the station elevator—Ruby, he said, got out at the floor on which Oswald was being held.

Ruby was at home about an hour later, however, when one of his strippers called to ask for money. He sounded abrupt and pressed for time, but promised to wire her some cash. The money for the stripper is central to understanding the final events that led to Oswald's murder. For Oswald, at that point, had just one hour to live.

Ruby left his apartment shortly before 11:00 a.m., his pockets stuffed with more than two thousand dollars in cash—and his gun. Having parked his car downtown, he walked to Western Union—along the street from the police station—to send, as promised, twenty-five dollars to the stripper who had called earlier. The time stamp on the transaction read 11:17 a.m. The timing was important—it contributed to the argument that Ruby's actions just minutes later would be a crime of passion, not a planned execution.

Rapidly, Ruby made his way into the heavily guarded police station basement, penetrating an area that was supposedly accessible only to policemen and reporters. Two minutes later, handcuffed to a detective, the prisoner was brought down to the basement by elevator. A lawyer named Tom Howard peered into the basement jail office, said, "That's all I wanted to see," and walked away. Seconds later, Oswald was led out of the office into the glare of television lights, on his way to the car waiting to convey him to the county jail. He never reached it.

One of the police officers, Detective Billy Combest, saw Ruby stride swiftly forward. "He was bootlegging the pistol like a quarterback with a football. . . . I knew what he was going to do . . . but I couldn't get at him." Ruby fired one destructive bullet into Oswald's abdomen. It ruptured two main veins carrying blood to the heart and tore through the spleen, the pancreas, the liver, and the right kidney. Oswald never spoke another word, and died soon after at Parkland Hospital.

One of the first officers to talk to Ruby under arrest quoted him as saying, "Well, I intended to shoot him three times." The man who was to be his first attorney was Tom Howard, the man who had looked through the jail-office window seconds before Oswald was shot. Howard, a maverick local lawyer with a police record of his own, had six minutes with Ruby that afternoon. It was he whom Jack Ruby would identify, months later, as having originated the claim that he shot Oswald to save the President's widow the trauma of returning to Dallas to testify in court. "It was not my idea," he was to write in a note to another of his attorneys, "to say I shot Oswald to keep Jackie Kennedy from coming back here to testify. I did it because Tom Howard told me to [say so]."

The world would never know what Ruby's motive really was. Nor would it ever be known for sure how—with split-second timing—he managed to get into position to do it. A police report would state that he got into the basement because of a "series of unfortunate coincidences which caused a momentary breakdown in the security measures." The Warren Commission decided he was just plain lucky, that he got in by slipping past a policeman guarding the car ramp that gave entry to the building from Main Street. It suggested that the officer in question, Roy Vaughn, had been distracted by a police car leaving the basement.

This ignored Vaughn's own testimony and that of several others. Vaughn knew Ruby, and said no one could have got past him unobserved. All three of the senior police officers in the car, two of whom also knew Ruby, were sure no one had been on the ramp as they drove out. Another officer, Sergeant Don Flusche, said he was sure "beyond any doubt in his mind that Jack Ruby, whom he had known for many years, did not walk down Main Street anywhere near the ramp." Corroboration came from a cabdriver who had been watching the ramp closely—he had been hired to pick up an enterprising journalist who planned to follow the Oswald transfer car. Another reporter, who stationed himself in the middle of the ramp inside the basement, was sure no one walked past him in the five minutes before Oswald was killed.

According to the notes of the Secret Service agent who first questioned Ruby, Forrest Sorrels, Ruby at that point said nothing about how he had gotten into the basement. FBI agent Ray Hall, who interrogated him later, noted that he "did not wish to say how he got into the basement or at what time he entered." Ruby was to hold to that position for twelve days. Only a month later was he to say he had entered via the Main Street ramp.

Several policemen present at the initial interrogations wrote reports consistent with Sorrels' and Hall's accounts, indicating that Ruby had refused to respond to questions about that. Sergeant Patrick Dean, however, who had been in charge of basement security at the time, claimed in a second report—written the following day—that Ruby had "stated to me *in the presence of Mr. Sorrels* [author's emphasis] that he had entered the basement through the ramp entering on Main Street." Three other officers, who had also been present during Sorrels' or Hall's questioning, backed up Dean's version.[17]

The Secret Service's Sorrels, who had taken careful notes, was astonished by the claim he had missed such an important point, and Warren Commission counsel Burt Griffin did not believe he had. Griffin called one of the officers a "damned liar" to his face. So sure was he that Dean had lied that he broke off in the middle of taking the sergeant's testimony, sent the stenographer out of the room, told Dean he did not believe him, and asked him to reconsider. Dean reacted with righteous indignation, and the story leaked to the press. Griffin was recalled to Washington, DC, and the Warren Commission chose to use Dean's account.

This in spite of the fact that Dean failed a lie detector test—even though he was allowed to write the questions himself. "I was nervous and hypertensive," he said, "so I flunked it. Or rather it was inconclusive." The written record of the test was nowhere to be found when the Assassinations Committee looked for it in the 1970s. "You have to suspect the possibility," a former Warren Commission attorney was to say, "that Dean, at a minimum, had seen Ruby enter the basement and had failed to do his duty." This begged a further question. If police officers lied, did they do so merely to cover up bungled security? Or did they cover up a more sinister truth, that one or more policemen actively conspired with Ruby in the murder of Oswald?

A Dallas police inquiry concluded that Ruby knew up to fifty officers personally. Sergeant Dean had known him since the early 1950s, and admitted that Ruby gave him and other favored officers bottles of whiskey for Christmas. Did Ruby's generosity to the police pay off when he needed to get at Oswald? A report of an interview with Ruby states that he "became very emotional . . . almost to the point of hysteria in his efforts to protect any police officer from being implicated in his entrance into the basement of City Hall."

The controversy over precisely how and why Ruby got into the basement aside, there remains the matter of his timing? Was it just luck that he arrived at precisely the right moment, or was he tipped off? If Ruby had stalked Oswald for thirty-six hours, as the evidence indicates, why had he not shown up at 10:00 a.m. on the Sunday morning—the time Chief Curry had publicly suggested Oswald's transfer was likely to take place? How did Ruby, who was at home in the early part of the morning, know that the transfer had been delayed?

It was at 9:00 a.m. on Sunday that senior officers had begun issuing the detailed orders for Oswald's actual transfer. Though the projected 10:00 a.m. move was deferred, it was agreed that Oswald would be moved within hours. For the first time, too, it was decided that Oswald would be taken out through the basement. Of the officers who learned that key information, three names came under most scrutiny.

Television videotape of the moment before Oswald was shot showed Ruby seemingly sheltering behind the ample form of Officer William "Blackie" Harrison. Harrison denied having had any contact with Ruby that morning. When he took a lie detector test, having prepared by taking tranquilizers, the results were reportedly "not conclusive."[18]

Officer Harrison, who had known Ruby for eleven years, was twice away from his colleagues in the hours before Oswald was shot. He and Detective L. D. Miller had been at a diner on a coffee break when summoned back to take part in the basement security operation. Miller, for his part, at first refused to give a sworn deposition. Then, when he did testify, he acknowledged that Harrison had received a telephone call from "an unknown person" while at the diner. Harrison claimed the call had been the one ordering them back to headquarters. At the station, when members of Harrison's unit trooped down to the basement at 11:10 a.m., they encountered Harrison on his way up from the sub-basement. He had been down there, he said, getting cigars. It may be relevant that there were four telephones on the way to the machine that dispensed cigars.

Another officer detailed to the basement operation, Lieutenant George Butler, had known Ruby since the 1940s.[19] Butler had been calm and controlled in the thirty-six hours following the assassination, according to a reporter. Before Oswald's transfer, however, his poise "appeared to have deserted him completely . . . so nervous that . . . I noticed his lips trembling."

Finally there was Sergeant Dean, with his dubious claim about what Ruby had said of his means of entry. Dean had reportedly been on good terms with Joe Civello, the Dallas Mafia figure who—insiders accepted—represented Mob boss Carlos Marcello in Texas. Civello had invited Sergeant Dean to dinner as far back as 1957. It was a disturbing association to find in the background of the policeman who was in charge of security in the police station basement at the time Oswald was killed.[20]

Delinquent though it was in following up Ruby's links to organized crime and to Cuba-related activity, the Warren Commission did ask the CIA for any available information on ties between Ruby and a number of individuals and groups. Many weeks later, the CIA responded that "an examination of Central Intelligence Agency files has produced no information on Jack Ruby or his activities."

Neither the CIA nor the FBI told the official inquiry what both agencies knew of the report that Ruby had once visited Mafia boss Santo Trafficante in Cuba. John Roselli, senior mobster and key contact man in the CIA-Mafia plots to kill Castro, discussed Ruby before he himself was murdered. Allowing for the self-interest implicit in his main allegations, which implicate Castro in the Kennedy assassination, Roselli's comments on Oswald's killer—to the columnist Jack Anderson—remain interesting. "When Oswald was picked up," Anderson quoted Roselli as saying, "the underworld conspirators feared he would crack and disclose information that might lead to them. This almost certainly would have brought a massive U.S. crackdown on the Mafia. So Jack Ruby was ordered to eliminate Oswald."

Ruby succumbed to cancer in 1967, still in prison, after the death sentence imposed on him for Oswald's murder had been overturned on appeal. He left hints behind him, whether true or false, whether sane or the product of a disturbed mind. He had told the Warren Commission members who questioned him that he had been "used for a purpose." He told a psychiatrist that he had been "framed into killing Oswald" that the assassination had been "an act of overthrowing the government," and that he knew "who had President Kennedy killed."

While searching through old videotapes in Dallas, the author found a fragment of a rare television interview with Ruby, one that had not at the time been shown on national television. Slumped in a chair during a recess in his interminable series of court appearances, Ruby had come out with: "The only thing I can say is—everything pertaining to what's happened has never come to the surface. The world will never know the true facts of what occurred—my motive. In other words, I am the only person in the background to know the truth pertaining to everything relating to my circumstances."

Others, long gone now as Ruby is gone, did not answer history's many questions. The statements of key figures associated with the case, however, suggested they had guilty knowledge.

CHAPTER 24

Hints and Deceptions

"Three may keep a secret, if two of them are dead."

—Benjamin Franklin

Santo Trafficante, the Florida mafia boss, was forced by subpoena
to testify on oath before the Assassinations Committee in 1977.
The questions put to him included the following:

* Did you ever discuss with any individual plans to assassinate
  President Kennedy?
* Prior to November 22, 1963, did you know Jack Ruby?
* While you were in prison in Cuba, were you visited by Jack
  Ruby?

In response to all four questions, Trafficante responded, "I
respectfully refuse to answer pursuant to my constitutional
rights under the First, Fourth, Fifth, and Fourteenth Amend-
ments." "Pleading the Fifth" invokes the constitutional
principle that no one can be forced to give evidence that may
be self-incriminating.

Trafficante testified again, in secret, having been granted immunity from prosecution arising from what he might say. Then, in late 1978, he appeared at a public hearing to deny having said—in advance of the assassination, as alleged—that President Kennedy was "going to be hit." Asked whether he had been aware of threats to the President made by his Louisiana counterpart Carlos Marcello, he replied, "No, sir; no, no chance, no way."

There was also, however, a comment Trafficante made in 1975 on an audiotape recorded during an FBI surveillance operation. "Now only two people are alive," an FBI microphone had picked up Trafficante saying—in conversation with Marcello— "who know who killed Kennedy."

What he meant remains unknown and unknowable.[1] Trafficante died in 1987, following heart surgery. Teamsters leader Jimmy Hoffa, who had been his friend and who allegedly wanted both Kennedys dead, had vanished twelve years earlier—probably murdered by criminal associates.

Sam Giancana, the Chicago Mob boss who conspired with Trafficante and the CIA to kill Cuba's Fidel Castro, was also long dead. He had been found in 1975, lying face-up in a puddle of blood, just when the Senate Intelligence Committee was preparing to question him about the Castro plots. He had been shot once in the back of the head and six times—in a neatly stitched circle—around the mouth. It was the Mob's way, sources said, of warning others not to talk. It was suspected that Trafficante had ordered the hit.

John Roselli had been killed soon after Giancana and Hoffa. What was left of him was found crammed into an oil drum, floating in Miami's Dumfoundling Bay. He had testified to the Senate Intelligence Committee and was due to appear again. Trafficante was again a suspect. Before Roselli died, it was reported, he had suggested that his former associates in the Castro assassination plots had gone on to kill President Kennedy. Within weeks of his death, the House of Representatives voted by a huge majority to reopen the Kennedy case—a decision that led to the formation of the House Assassinations Committee.

The Committee finding, in 1979, was that "extensive investigation led it to conclude that the most likely family bosses of organized crime to have participated in [planning the President's assassination] were Carlos Marcello and Santo Trafficante." While both had had "the motive, means, and opportunity to plan and execute a conspiracy," though, the Committee was unable to pin anything on them.

Carlos Marcello, the boss of the Mafia in the southeastern United States, had like Trafficante appeared before the Assassinations Committee. His principal business in life, he had earlier had the audacity to tell another committee, was as a tomato salesman earning about $1,600 a month. His answers related to the President's assassination were no more illuminating.

Asked whether he ever made a physical threat against the President, Marcello replied, "Positively not, never said anything like that." Trafficante, he said, had never talked with him about assassinating Kennedy. Their contacts had been "strictly social." He did not know of any discussion with U.S. officials about killing Fidel Castro, had not been to Cuba before or after 1960, never had any interests there. He "never knew" either the alleged assassin, Lee Oswald, or Jack Ruby. He professed ignorance of Cuban exile activities near New Orleans—though he acknowledged having known Guy Banister. He had also known David Ferrie, he said, but not in the context of the assassination.

More, just a little more, emerged from FBI surveillance obtained during a bribery probe in 1979, when microphones planted in Marcello's home and office again picked up snatches of relevant conversation. It was the year the Assassinations Committee was winding up its work, and—on several occasions—mikes picked up the mobster repeating, as though he wanted to be overheard, the sort of "No, I never" denials he had made when testifying. Once, however, when a visitor asked his reaction to the Committee's suspicions as to his role in the assassination, the mobster told the man to shut up. Then there was the sound of a chair being pushed back, of the two men walking out of the room. In the last words picked up, Marcello could be heard telling his companion that this was a subject better discussed outside. Going "outside" to discuss sensitive matters, the record shows, was something Marcello did on more than one occasion.[2]

An informant the FBI used in that surveillance operation, a man named Joseph Hauser, later claimed he got Marcello to discuss the assassination. According to Hauser, the mobster admitted both that he had known Oswald's uncle Charles Murret, and that Oswald himself had at one point worked as a runner for the betting operation run for Marcello by Sam Saia. Even more provocative was something that—according to Hauser—Marcello's brother Joseph said. Edward Kennedy was about to run for the White House, and Hauser raised the subject of the "rough time" the elder Kennedys had given Marcello back in the 1960s. "Don't worry," Joseph supposedly replied, "We took care of them, didn't we?"

Oswald's uncle Charles had indeed been involved in gambling activity, and he was an associate of Sam Saia. Saia was a powerful figure in bookmaking, and he was reputedly close to Carlos Marcello. What Marcello is said to have confided is thus plausible—but it is not evidence. Of the surveillance tapes thus far released, none show that Marcello made these admissions, or that his brother's remark about having "taken care" of the Kennedys was made. One wonders, too, whether, if it was made, it was meant seriously.

There is more, similar, material, in this case reflected in FBI records. It dates to the mid-1980s, when the Mob boss had at last been jailed—on charges of racketeering, wire fraud, and conspiracy to bribe a federal judge. It was then that a fellow prison inmate named Jack Van Laningham, who was being used by the FBI in another surveillance operation against Marcello, made a new allegation that the Mob boss had admitted involvement in the Kennedy assassination. The FBI file contains a report on what, according to Van Laningham, Marcello told him and another inmate while they were sitting "outside in the patio" of the prison yard. As originally circulated, with Van Laningham's name withheld, it reads as follows (see facsimile on next page):[3]

A confidential source who has provided reliable information in the past furnished the following:

On December 15, 1985, he was in the company of CARLOS MARCELLO and another inmate at the FEDERAL CORRECTIONAL INSTITUTE (FCI), Texarkana, Texas, in the court yard engaged in conversation. CARLOS MARCELLO discussed his intense dislike of former President JOHN KENNEDY as he often did. Unlike other such tirades against KENNEDY, however, on this occasion CARLOS MARCELLO said, referring to President KENNEDY, *op cit.*

"Yeah, I had the son of a bitch killed. I'm glad I did. I'm sorry I couldn't have done it myself.

1

FEDERAL BUREAU OF INVESTIGATION

Date of transcription___3/7/86___

A confidential source who has provided reliable information in the past furnished the following:

On December 15, 1985, he was in the company of CARLOS MARCELLO and another inmate at the FEDERAL CORRECTIONAL INSTITUTE (FCI), Texarkana, Texas, in the court yard engaged in conversation. CARLOS MARCELLO discussed his intense dislike of former President JOHN KENNEDY as he often did. Unlike other such tirades against KENNEDY, however, on this occasion CARLOS MARCELLO said, referring to President KENNEDY, "Yeah, I had the son of a bitch killed. I'm glad I did. I'm sorry I couldn't have done it myself."

Investigation on___3/4/86___ at___Seagoville, Texas___ File DL 183A-1035-Sub L

SAs RAYMOND A. HULT and
by___THOMAS K. KIMMEL, JR.___TKK/dli Date dictated___3/6/86___

This document contains neither recommendations nor conclusions of the FBI. It is the property of the FBI and is loaned to your agency; it and its contents are not to be distributed outside your agency.

Later, in a letter to an FBI agent, Van Laningham quoted Marcello as saying he had known Santo Trafficante, who had been his partner in the gambling rackets in Cuba. He had "hated" the President and his brother the Attorney General. He had been "introduced to Oswald," the Mob boss supposedly told Van Laningham, "by a man named Ferris, who was Marcello's pilot"—a reference presumably to David Ferrie—and had thought Oswald "crazy." He had backed Ruby in business in Dallas, and Ruby had come to Louisiana to "report" to him.

This was truly damning information, if Marcello really did admit that he ordered the President killed. But does Van Laningham's allegation have a basis in truth?

The former Senior Supervisory Resident Agent at the FBI office near the prison, Thomas Kimmel, Jr., was interviewed for this book in 2013. He confirmed that Van Laningham had indeed been used in an operation targeting Marcello in prison, and that he did make the allegation quoting Marcello on the assassination. As the relevant memo shows, he duly passed the information on to FBI headquarters.

Van Laningham, who was also interviewed for this book, claimed the FBI "did not want me to go into the Kennedy thing whatsoever. . . . The FBI doesn't want anybody to know that." According to the former inmate, similar statements the Mob boss made on other occasions to involvement in the assassination had been recorded by the FBI bug with which Van Laningham had been provided. According to former agent Kimmel however, "There was nothing remotely resembling that" on the tapes. Ron Sievert, the prosecuting attorney who supervised the Marcello surveillance operation, said in a 2013 interview for this book that there was "absolutely nothing to corroborate " the claim by Van Laningham.

Former Agent Kimmel said he reported the purported Marcello admission to superiors because it was his duty to do so. He did not, though, recall receiving any significant reaction. His own view, looking back in 2013, was as follows. "I don't doubt that Carlos made the statement. I don't think Van Laningham is fabricating that. . . . We got to the point where we thought Carlos would say almost anything. And even if he said something on the tape it would not be credible. Carlos was old. Carlos was on the outs. . . . I thought there were indications of senility on Carlos' part, and thought a jury or a judge would agree. . . .no matter what Carlos said." Supervisory attorney Sievert agreed that "there was also the mental capcity issue."

By 1989, three years after the episode Van Laningham reported, Marcello had suffered a series of strokes and was in a state of what an attending doctor described as "senility." That year, employees at a prison medical center reported having heard Marcello say—in the early hours of the morning, while in bed—"That Kennedy, that smiling motherfucker, we'll fix him in Dallas." The old man rambled on to that effect, apparently under the delusion that the jail employees were his bodyguards and that the assassination had not yet occurred.

This time the FBI did eventually follow up by questioning Marcello—both about that comment and the "I had the son of a bitch killed" remark Van Laningham had reported several years earlier. Marcello denied having said anything of the kind. He was released from prison soon afterwards and died in 1993 at the age of 83.[4]

The indications that there was a conspiracy to kill the President, however, do not end with the information allegedly sourced directly to Marcello and Trafficante.

There is, first, the account of a minor public figure named John Martino, an associate of Trafficante. In private, according to his wife, he said in advance that the assassination was going to occur. In an interview with the author, his widow Florence vividly recalled what her husband said and did on November 22, 1963.

"John insisted he wanted to paint the breakfast room that day," Mrs. Martino said, "We were supposed to go out to the Americana [in Miami Beach] for lunch. . . . But it was on the radio about [the visit to] Dallas. . . . And he said, 'Flo, they're going to kill him. They're going to kill him when he gets to Texas.' " She asked her husband what he meant, but he would not elaborate. Then, at lunchtime, the Martinos' seventeen-year-old son, Edward, saw breaking news of the assassination on television.

"When I called them in," Edward told the author in 1994, "my father went white as sheet. But it wasn't like 'Gee whiz!'—it was more like confirmation." "Then," according to Mrs. Martino, "John was on the phone. . . . He got I don't know how many calls from Texas. I don't know who called him, but he was on the phone, on the phone, on the phone."

New Jersey-born John Martino, who was fifty-two in 1963, had worked in the slot-machine rackets and was knowledgeable about electronics. Before the Cuban revolution, he had run surveillance at a Havana casino owned by Santo Trafficante Jr. Then, on returning to Cuba after the Castro takeover, he was thrown into jail—by his own account for trying to liberate cash that Trafficante had been obliged to leave behind. On his release, in 1962, he had thrown himself into both the propaganda war against Castro and into clandestine efforts to topple the Cuban leader.[5]

An early FBI report characterized Martino as Trafficante's

"close friend," and the mobster was seen at his home in the mid-1960s. He was said to have worked with mobster John Roselli, and to have taken part in one of the plots to kill Castro. CIA documents, and the author's interviews with his family, indicate that Martino also had contacts with the CIA and the FBI. William "Rip" Robertson, a CIA agent who had defied presidential orders by going ashore at the Bay of Pigs in 1961, was a familiar face at his home. In the spring of 1963, Martino personally took part in an operation to insert fighters into Cuba that included Cuban exiles, CIA operatives—and even, for propaganda purposes, journalists from *Life* magazine.[6]

After November 22, Martino was at the forefront of efforts to suggest that Cuba was behind the assassination. He was a prime source, perhaps the originator, of the story that Oswald had been involved in pro-Castro activity not only in New Orleans but in Florida. He claimed that Oswald, rather than merely visiting Mexico City, had flown secretly to Cuba—and been paid by Castro to shoot Kennedy. Pressed to reveal his source, Martino named him as Oscar Ortiz, a member of an anti-Castro group "too sensitive to name." The FBI could locate no "Ortiz," and there the matter ended.

What Martino said in private to those he knew well was the exact opposite of his time-wasting exercise in pointing the blame at Castro for the murder of the President. In a exchange after the assassination, he made a brief comment to John Cummings, a young reporter he had come to trust following his release from jail in Cuba. He said, Cummings told the author, that "there had been two guns, two people involved" in Dallas. . . . "When I asked if anti-Castro Cubans were involved, he said, 'That's right.' But very often with Martino, you knew there wasn't any point in asking more."

Martino brought the subject up again only many years later, in 1975, when he was suffering from heart disease. "I called him in the spring," Cummings said, "and he told me he was ailing, and I went to see him. And he came out with a mea culpa about JFK. He told me he'd been part of the assassination of Kennedy. He wasn't in Dallas pulling a trigger, but he was involved. He implied that his role was delivering money, facilitating things. . . . He asked me not to write it while he was alive."

Cummings kept his word, not least perhaps because, the last time he saw Martino alive, Trafficante's former associate came up with what amounted to a diversion—an assertion that he had in 1963 himself met Oswald in the company of an FBI agent named "Connors." Former agent James O'Connor, the record shows, had been one of those to whom—soon after the assassination—Martino had spun his "Oswald-the-Castro-agent" line.[7]

Also months before he died, however, he told a close business associate named Fred Claasen that he had personal knowledge of a plot behind the President's assassination. As reported in the chapter of this book that deals with the shooting of Officer Tippit, Martino said: "The anti-Castro people put Oswald together. Oswald didn't know who he was working for—he was just ignorant of who was really putting him together. Oswald was to meet his contact at the Texas Theater [the movie house where Oswald was arrested]. They were to meet Oswald in the theater and get him out of the country, then eliminate him. Oswald made a mistake. . . . There was no way we could get to him. They had Ruby kill him."[8]

A further, and final, detail came to the author from Martino's widow, Florence. Right after the assassination, she recalled, her husband told her, "When [the police] went to the theater and got Oswald, they blew it. . . . There was a

Cuban in there. They let him come out." He said, "They let
the guy go, the other trigger."[9]

Coming, as the allegation did, from a man who had been
close to Mafia boss Trafficante and deeply involved with the
anti-Castro movement, was this make-believe? Or did it, perhaps, reflect what really happened?

An anti-Castro Cuban, a man with a known record as an
assassin—and a connection to Mob boss Santo Trafficante—
reportedly did claim to have fired at the President on November
22. Fresh information, published here for the first time, surfaced
in 2007 in an unexpected call to former House Assassinations
Committee Chief Counsel Robert Blakey. Eighty-one-year-
old Reinaldo Martínez Gomez, himself a Cuban exile living in
Miami, said he had information he wished to share before he
died. Professor Blakey, together with this author, listened to the
essence of Martínez's account, then flew to Florida to question
him in detail and tape an interview.

Martínez wanted to talk about a man who had been his best
friend when they were both students in Cuba, Herminio Díaz
García. They had been "inseparable," going fishing, attending
cockfights—a national pastime in that country—and practicing
shooting. Díaz was fascinated by guns, and became quite a marksman. The two friends' paths in life diverged. Martínez went to
work in a hardware store and wound up running it. Díaz was "very
quiet, introverted—and exceptionally brave," but showed little
interest in a conventional career. The one thing he was professional about, his friend told us, was "in the use of firearms. He
was passionate about shooting, whether with rifle or pistol. This
was his obsession—he always had one [a weapon] with him."

It is a matter of record that in the late 1940s, in Mexico, Díaz murdered a former Cuban police chief. Several years later, he attempted to assassinate the President of Costa Rica. In the late 1950s, according to Martínez, he plotted to kill the Cuban dictator Fulgencio Batista.[10] Over a period, his friend thought, Díaz probably murdered twenty people.

Martínez told the author, and a CIA document suggests, that Díaz returned to Cuba at the time of the 1959 revolution. He may have joined Castro's forces for a while. What seems to have motivated him, though, was less political fervor than a desire to be behind a gun and—in Martínez's opinion—money. Martínez's recollections, and the U.S. government record, show that Díaz at once point headed security at Havana's Riviera Hotel and casino. In other words, he too worked for Santo Trafficante.

Several times in 1959, Díaz—who at the time had no car—asked Martínez to drive him to the detention camp where the Mob boss was being held. "I went there with Herminio five or six times," Martínez recalled, "and there was a waiting room where I sat while he went in to see Trafficante. On one of the visits, I noticed a particular man—he caught my attention because in Cuba in July or August it is really hot, and this man was dressed in a double-breasted woolen suit and felt hat. [When] I asked Herminio, 'Chico, is he mad?', he told me it was Jack Ruby, a friend of Santo, who had come to see him." As Ruby had indeed visited, as described in the preceding chapter of this book. "The image of that man dressed that way in a climate as hot as it gets in Cuba stayed with me, and came back to me again when I saw Ruby kill Lee Harvey Oswald in Dallas. . . . It looked like he still hadn't taken off the suit."

Trafficante was released from the camp soon afterward. His

reward was to be given a new job as head of security at the casino. Soon enough, however, the rush of events separated Martínez and Díaz. Díaz's job ended when Castro shut down gambling altogether, and he eventually left on a merchant ship. Martínez, who was to be in and out of Castro's prisons—he said on currency offenses—never saw his friend alive again.

Martínez was in jail several years later, in early June 1966, when officials rousted him out late one night to show him a mugshot of Díaz and ask him to identify it. When Martínez replied that the picture was of his friend Díaz, they retorted: "He *was* your friend"—then showed him a photo of Díaz's bloodied corpse on a stretcher. Díaz had been killed, documents and press coverage confirm (see facsimile below) during a failed raid in which he and a comrade had intended to kill Castro. Martínez's name had been found on a list in Díaz's pocket.

That would have been the end of it, Martínez said, were it not that—several months later—the man who had led the raid in which Díaz died, Tony Cuesta, wound up in the same prison as Martínez. Cuesta was recovering from terrible injuries he had suffered before being captured—the loss of an arm, virtually total sight loss, and hearing problems. It was to Martínez, who was assigned to work in the infirmary, that he came for minor treatment. The two men discovered that they had something in common, a long acquaintance with the dead man they had both known as "Herminito."

One day, Martínez said, Cuesta told him something he would never forget. He spoke of the night of the failed exile raid, of how he and Díaz had sat talking in the boat waiting for the tide to be right for a landing. Then, as Martínez recalled it in his interview with Blakey and the author: *"Que Herminio le había confesado a él, a Tony Cuesta, que Herminio había tenido participación en la muerte del Presidente de Los Estados Unidos."* (Herminio had confessed to him, to Tony Cuesta, that Herminio had taken part in the death of the President of the United States.)

Cuesta did not elaborate and—according to Martínez—he did not press him. "I had learned to be very reserved in prison. Aside from the fact that I was with Tony Cuesta, there [in prison] you couldn't converse with your own shadow. I didn't pressure him to tell me more. . . . We spoke of other things. . . . I think in that moment he had not been lying to me. . . . I don't believe he had any reason to lie to me. Because, given the state he was in [with his wounds], I don't think a man makes things up."

Had Martínez believed Díaz took part in the President's assassination? "I did not believe it and neither did I disbelieve it. Because I had no evidence—to know whether it was true."

Martínez and his family left Cuba for Florida some thirteen years later, in the Mariel boatlift of 1980. In Miami, when he went to see Remigio "Cucú" Arce, an old friend from Cuba back in the 1940s, he got what appeared to be confirmation of what he had heard from Cuesta. In his cups one day, Arce, who had known Herminio Díaz García well—it was he who had introduced Martínez to Díaz in the first place—confided: "Listen, the one who killed the President was our little friend." Which little friend? "Herminio."

Troubled, Martínez told the author, he had gone to the FBI to report what he had been told. The agent with whom he spoke did not seem interested.

Martínez has died since being interviewed, and there is no way now to assess the credibility of his account. The principal source he cited, the prominent exile activist Tony Cuesta, died in 1992. Remigio Arce is dead, too.

The strength of Martínez's account lies in the fact that his friend Herminio Díaz García did have a known track record as an assassin. The record shows, moreover, that he was an associate of Santo Trafficante and was involved in the struggle against Castro. There is a possible weakness to his account, however. Long before Martínez linked Díaz to President Kennedy's assassination, researchers had heard it from a Castro official. In the 1990s, former Cuban intelligence chief Fabián Escalante informed researchers that Cuesta had told him of Díaz's supposed role in the assassination shortly before his release from prison in 1978.[11] Martínez, moreover, discussed Cuesta's claim with Escalante— he told the author—when he revisited Cuba in 2005.

Those who believe Castro had a hand in the Kennedy assassination will see Martínez's account as merely a further piece of Cuban propaganda, disinformation designed to deflect suspicion away from Havana. When the author put this to Martínez, he just shrugged. He was telling the story now, he said, because he was nearing the end of his life and because: "*Es la verdad—mi verdad*. It is the truth—my truth."

Truth was always a commodity in short supply where exile groups and their CIA backers were concerned. At the center of the fog of unknowns, now as then, are the roles of the CIA and the DRE, the militant exile group that had that strangely stagey clash with Oswald in New Orleans.

The DRE, in the words of an Agency memorandum, had been "conceived, created, and funded by the CIA." By 1963, it funded the DRE to the tune of $51,000 a month—or $385,000 at today's rates—regularly delivered to the group's leaders in a brown paper bag. A problem had arisen, however. Not satisfied with a psychological warfare role, the group's leaders insisted on taking the paramilitary fight against Castro—even when doing so conflicted with Kennedy administration policy. A new CIA case officer, appointed in the months before the President's assassination, had the task of trying to steer the DRE away from military activity and towards political action and intelligence collection.

This fit well with the way the exiles of the DRE handled Lee Oswald in New Orleans. There was the street confrontation, a visit to Oswald's apartment by a DRE man posing as a fellow supporter of Castro, and a call for congressional investigation of Oswald.[12] Then, within hours of Oswald's arrest after the assassination, there was a DRE information blitz to hammer home the message that the killer was a leftist supporter of Fidel Castro.

The CIA did not inform the Warren Commission that it had created and subsidized the DRE, even though the group's connection to Oswald was potentially of great significance.[13] The Agency's behavior toward the House Assassinations Committee in the matter, meanwhile, amounted to downright obstruction.

The Committee pursued its numerous requests to the CIA under a working arrangement negotiated by Chief Counsel Robert Blakey, an arrangement that—in theory—offered better access to Agency material than that enjoyed by any previous congressional probe. As things turned out, however, Committee staff found themselves frustrated by procrastination and an "inability to find" what was requested. Two investigators became so desperate to get responses to their requests, they told the author, that they would arrive at CIA headquarters before the liaison office opened and leave only when it closed.

Only years later did anyone discover just whom the CIA had called back from retirement to supervise liaison with the Committee. He was George Joannides, the very former case officer who had been assigned to the DRE in 1963. Joannides had been in almost constant touch with the DRE in the months before the assassination, and immediately afterward had handled its leaders' request for clearance to generate publicity about Oswald's pro-Castro activity. On the day in 1964 that the Warren Commission wrote to the DRE's Carlos Bringuier to come to Washington, DC, a travel form shows, Joannides flew to New Orleans. In the late 1970s, as liaison to the Assassinations Committee, however, he concealed this background. Joannides even claimed, according to one investigator, that "he could not find any records indicating the name of the DRE's control officer."[14]

This gross deception was exposed only in 1998, to the outrage of those who had been duped.[15] Had he known the truth during the Committee's tenure, former Chief Counsel Blakey said, he would have demanded that Joannides be removed as liaison officer and be questioned on oath as a material witness. That was the mildest of Blakey's comments. He called the ruse that had been perpetrated on the Committee "criminal . . . a willful obstruction of justice. . . . Anyone who corruptly endeavors to influence, obstruct, or impede the power of inquiry [by Congress] is guilty of a felony."

"The Agency set me up . . ." the former Chief Counsel said, "I no longer believe anything the Agency told the Committee." Professor Anna Nelson, who had been a member of the Assassination Records Review Board, felt that the CIA had "destroyed the integrity of the probe made by Congress" and suggested a congressional probe of "the CIA's alleged corruption of its inquiry into the Kennedy assassination." Judge John Tunheim, the Records Review Board's former chairman, said the episode showed that "the CIA wasn't interested in the truth about the assassination."

Washington reporter Jefferson Morley, who was first to reveal Joannides' duplicity, has fought a long court battle to obtain further relevant records on the officer's activity. A decade on, as these pages went to press, the fight had gone all the way up to the federal Court of Appeals. The CIA claimed it could locate no monthly reports by Joannides for the period, even though—for the officers who preceded and succeeded him—the filing of regular reports was routine. The Agency refused to release 295 documents from Joannides' administrative file—on "national security" grounds.

In 1981, after his work as liaison for the Assassinations Committee, Joannides received one of the CIA's highest awards, the Career Intelligence Medal. Yet even the memo approving the award has been withheld—again citing "national security."

A National Archives request to review the withheld Joannides material has also been turned down. And this when the documents withheld concern a man who has been dead for more than twenty years and—if the records do relate in any way to the Kennedy assassination—to a murder half a century old.

Just as CIA material on Joannides remains unavailable, so, too, do 605 pages on David Phillips, who was the Agency's chief of Cuban operations in November 1963. As reported in previous pages, Phillips supervised early efforts to counter the pro-Castro Fair Play for Cuba Committee, headed the unit responsible for surveillance during the Oswald visit to Mexico City in 1963, and is also believed to have promoted the fortunes of the DRE exile group from the outset. He aroused the suspicions of Assassinations Committee staff for another reason.

The Committee gave serious consideration to the possibility that David Phillips was the man behind the pseudonym "Maurice Bishop," the officer alleged by Alpha 66 leader Antonio Veciana to have met with Oswald before the assassination and—after it—to have ordered the fabrication of a phony link between Oswald and a Cuban diplomat in Mexico.*

Investigators asked Ross Crozier, a former CIA officer who had served at the Agency's Florida headquarters, to respond to three names: "Bishop," "Knight", and the true name of an officer who had once worked out of Havana. Crozier at once stated correctly that the latter was the true name of a man he had met. The name Knight, he recalled, had sometimes been used by Howard Hunt. "Bishop," he said, had been a name David Phillips used. He coupled the name "Bishop," moreover, to the first name "Maurice"—a name the Committee investigators had not mentioned.[16]

Phillips, however, flatly denied the suggestion that he might have been Veciana's case officer. Veciana, for his part, would say of Phillips only, "It's not him. . . . But he knows." Committee investigators were faced with a nomenclature puzzle they never resolved—and eventually ran out of time.[17] This author, however, traced a person whose statements corroborated Veciana's claim that his clandestine contact used the name Bishop.

---

* See "Bishop" references in Chapter 18. The Assassinations Committee Report referred only to a "retired officer" having been considered as "Bishop," but the officer is repeatedly identified as Phillips in the related Appendix.

The new witness was a Cuban exile—a woman who requested anonymity—who had earlier, before they both left Cuba, worked as Veciana's secretary in Havana. In exile, when he became a leading activist, she had agreed to act as a sort of human answering machine and take messages for him. During the interview, the author ran through a large number of names of people who might have called—all of them entirely imaginary except the name "Bishop." She promptly responded that, of all the names mentioned, the one name she remembered was Bishop. That name, she said, was linked in her mind to that of a American woman called Prewett.

"Prewett," it emerged, turned out to be Virginia Prewett, a Washington journalist who long specialized in Latin American affairs. In her articles in 1963, the files showed, she praised the raids on Cuba by Veciana's group Alpha 66 and lambasted the Kennedy administration for clamping down on exile activity. In an interview with the author, she admitted having had contact with Alpha 66. Asked about Veciana, she said initially, "Where is he now?"—then backed off and claimed she had never met him. Asked about Bishop and the CIA, Prewett said at first, "Well, you have to move around people like that,"—then that she had not known him. Asked about David Phillips, she said she had never met Phillips. Phillips himself, asked about Prewett, said they had met on more than one occasion and that he had known her quite well.

The Assassinations Committee, in 1979, declared itself not satisfied with either Phillips' or Veciana's answers on the matter of Maurice Bishop. The Committee "suspected Veciana was lying when he denied that the retired officer [Phillips] was Bishop." It said of Phillips that he "aroused the Committee's suspicion when he told the Committee he did not recognize Veciana as the founder of Alpha 66, especially since the officer had once been deeply involved in Agency anti-Castro operations."

The investigator whose special focus had been investigating Phillips, Gaeton Fonzi, wrote later that Phillips had "committed perjury before the Committee. It could have been proven, [and] he would have been convicted." Former Chief Counsel Robert Blakey restricted himself to saying drily that the Committee had been "less than satisfied" with Phillips' candor.

A graduate of the Johns Hopkins School of Advanced International Studies, Glenn Carle, has recalled how Phillips helped him get into the CIA in the early 1980s—a favor that launched him on a long career as a Clandestine Services officer. In conversation with Phillips, he recalled in 2013, he asked him about the allegation that he had been "Bishop." The response he received is startling, given Phillips's history of flat-out denial.

"He did not say, 'Yes, I am Maurice Bishop,' Carle remembered, "It was clear to me, however, that he was the man who had used the Bishop alias. . . . Phillips' reaction was to acknowledge that he was the man in question. . . . He tacitly accepted its accuracy; but he did not explicitly confirm to me that he had done what he was accused of doing: meeting with Oswald. He avoided discussing this point."[18]

Asked by his brother David whether he had been in Dallas on November 22, 1963, Phillips reportedly replied, "yes." He vouchsafed no more than that, and died soon afterward, in 1998.

Phillips attracted controversy even from the grave. He left behind the draft of a novel featuring a character who had been a CIA officer based in Mexico City, as he himself had been in real life. "I was one of those officers who handled Lee Harvey Oswald," Phillips the author had his fictional character write in a letter. "We gave him the mission of killing Fidel Castro in

Cuba. . . . I don't know *why* he killed Kennedy. But I do know he used precisely the plan we had devised against Castro. Thus the CIA did not anticipate the President's assassination, but it was responsible for it. I share that guilt."

Shortly before his death, Phillips had talked on several occasions with a former Assassinations Committee staffer named Kevin Walsh. "My private opinion," he told Walsh in all apparent seriousness, "is that JFK was done in by a conspiracy, likely including rogue American intelligence people."

This very senior former CIA officer—Phillips had eventually risen to be chief of the Western Hemisphere Division—knew well that this extraordinary remark would be quoted. Was it mischievous, a thumbing of the nose at those he saw as having tormented him? Or did he know something the public did not, something that—even if he personally was innocent in the assassination—he felt bound to conceal? What is not in doubt was that Phillips, and others from the Agency before him, had ducked and weaved and dissembled in the face of official investigation.

The CIA-Mafia Cuba plots, the Assassinations Committee declared in 1979, "had all the elements necessary for a successful assassination conspiracy—people, motive, and means—and the evidence indicated that the participants might well have considered using the resources at their disposal to increase their power and alleviate their problems by assassinating the President. Nevertheless, the Committee was ultimately frustrated in its attempt to determine details of those activities that might have led to the assassination. . . ."

Former Warren Commission counsel Burt Griffin, a judge in later life, blamed the federal intelligence agencies for the failings of both the official investigations. "I feel betrayed," he said, "I feel that the CIA lied to us, that we had an agency of government here which we were depending upon, and that we expected to be truthful with us, and to cooperate with us. And they didn't do it. The CIA concealed from us the fact that they were involved in efforts to assassinate Castro, which could have been of extreme importance to us. Especially the fact that they were involved in working with the Mafia."

Griffin felt the same about the FBI, because it had not pursued the leads that pointed to possible conspiracy. "What is most disturbing to me," he said, "is that these two agencies of government, that were supposed to be loyal and faithful to us, deliberately misled us."

"Consider the possible reality," he had suggested to the House Assassinations Committee, "that under the American system of civil liberties and the requirement of proof beyond a reasonable doubt, it is virtually impossible to prosecute or uncover a well-conceived and well-executed conspiracy."

In 1979, Committee Chief Counsel Robert Blakey believed a prosecution was possible in the case of President Kennedy's assassination. There were at that time, he said, still "living people who could have been involved" in the President's assassination. "These people," he went on, "should be vigorously investigated by all constitutional means. . . . There are things that can be done, in a criminal justice context, to move this towards trial." Blakey thought he could "come close" to securing convictions.

To all intents and purposes, however, the U.S. Justice Department sat on its hands—a lapse the former chief counsel termed "diabolical." As the new century began, though, Blakey became resigned to the fact that it was too late for prosecutions. The mysteries surrounding the murder of the 35th president of the

United States, he now conceded, would never be solved, for John F. Kennedy's death no longer seemed to matter. As a generational milestone of national trauma, November 22, 1963 had been replaced by September 11, 2001.

"Everybody will know who I am now," Lee Oswald had remarked while being interrogated. Fifty years on, however, Oswald remains ill defined, a figure in the fog of incomplete investigation and the absence of real official will to discover the full truth.

None of the key characters in the tragedy now remains alive. Oswald is in his reinforced grave at Fort Worth's Rose Hill Cemetery, Jack Ruby in a Jewish cemetery in Chicago, Carlos Marcello in his tomb near New Orleans, Santo Trafficante in a mausoleum at La Unione Italiana Cemetery outside Tampa. The men whose job it was to "keep the secrets" of their epoch—Richard Helms, James Angleton, David Phillips, George Joannides—all are gone.

The murder victim, John F. Kennedy, slumbers on in his place of honor at Arlington National Cemetery in Virginia, beneath a flickering flame.

Image Gallery

2. The killing ground. Dealey Plaza, from the Book Depository window where a gunman allegedly lay in wait.

3. Seconds before the shooting started. At about this moment, the Governor's wife remarked to the President, "Mr. Kennedy, you can't say Dallas doesn't love you."

4. Was there one person, or two, behind the sixth-floor windows? (see inset)

5. The ambush. Beyond the stricken President is the area of the grassy knoll where House Assassinations Committee acoustics experts placed a second gunman – a finding now challenged. Some suspected that one of the objects in this damaged Polaroid photograph (see box) may be a man's head.

6. Did a second gunman fire at the President from this vantage point to his right front? The witness pointing, railroad supervisor Sam Holland, said he saw smoke by the picket fence.

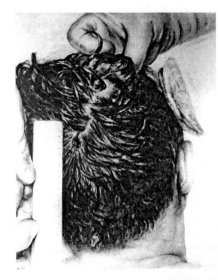

7. A botched autopsy. One of the medical drawings published by the House Assassinations Committee. The medical panel, working from an original photograph, concluded that the early doctors made a four-inch error in placing an entrance wound in the President's head. (medical illustration drawn from photograph)

8. Best evidence. Some of the autopsy photographs have been seen by the public, some not. Confusion continues. No damage to the rear of the President's head is seen in this photograph. Yet Dallas doctors described a massive wound. The explanation may be that the scalp is being pulled down for the photograph, thus covering a gaping hole.

9. Lee Oswald, aged 20, at the time of his defection to the Soviet Union.

10. Surveillance by chance? Oswald (arrowed) photographed in 1961 in the Soviet city of Minsk. The photo, taken by American tourists, reached CIA files.

11. Giving up on communism? Oswald and his Soviet wife Marina leave Minsk by train in 1962. While en route – in Holland or when he reached the United States – was the defector questioned by U.S. intelligence?

12. The friend with links to American intelligence. George de Mohrenschildt, who became Oswald's mentor in Dallas, has been linked to the CIA and to U.S. Army Intelligence. Just as the House Assassinations Committee was planning to question him, he killed himself.

13. 14. 15. The rifle found at the scene. Ordered in the name of "Hidell," it led straight to Oswald. Was Oswald's finger on the trigger on the day of the assassination? Did the almost intact bullet (left) cause both the President's first wound and the Governor's multiple injuries?

16. 17. Most accept that this photograph shows Oswald holding the rifle later retrieved at the scene of the assassination. One copy, which showed up years later, bore the words, in Russian: "Hunter of fascists, ha-ha-ha!!!" (below) Though the dedication appears to be Oswald's, the handwriting does not resemble that of the alleged assassin.

18. 19. A spontaneous incident, or was it staged? Cuban exiles appeared to clash with Oswald as he handed out pro-Castro leaflets in New Orleans. It may, though, have been a phony incident, part of a U.S. intelligence operation against the Fair Play for Cuba Committee.

20. Fidel Castro. Some still suspect he was behind the President's assassination. Others think there was an effort to fabricate information linking him to the crime.

21. Santo Trafficante, said to have forecast that the President was "going to be hit." Oswald's killer, Ruby, knew several Trafficante associates and may himself have visited the Mob boss.

22. John Roselli, a close Trafficante associate, was used by the CIA in its plots to kill Fidel Castro. He was murdered before Senate Committee questioning resumed. Did Trafficante order the hit?

23. (above)Teamsters leader Jimmy Hoffa, who was close to Mafia boss Carlos Marcello, long feuded with Robert Kennedy and reportedly favored killing both brothers.

24. (right) New Orleans mob chieftain Carlos Marcello, quoted as having spoken before the assassination of "setting up a nut to take the blame" and – long afterwards – as boasting that he had "had the son of a bitch" – the President – "killed."

25. Allen Dulles, former CIA Director, served on the Warren Commission. He did not tell his colleagues about the CIA's plots to kill Castro – and privately advised CIA officers on how to respond to questions as to Oswald's possible links to the CIA.

26. James Angleton, CIA Counterintelligence chief, urged "waiting out" the Commission on a key matter, and later ordered the seizure of key documents – which were then suppressed

27. Richard Helms, a senior CIA official in 1963, later shrugged off the failure to acknowledge the Castro assassination plots with: "It's an untidy world."

28. William Sullivan, an FBI Assistant Director, spoke of an "internal problem" over a note Oswald had left at the Dallas FBI office – the note had been ordered destroyed.

29. 30. 31. 32. 33. A crossroads for conspirators? The building at 544 Camp Street, in New Orleans, housed Guy Banister (top right) and was frequented by David Ferrie (below) both anti-Castro activists. How come, then, that the 544 address was stamped on a *pro*-Castro document Oswald handed to the FBI? Banister's employee Delphine Roberts (below) said Oswald used the office with Banister's connivance.

34. Proof that Ferrie knew Oswald? This photo, not discovered until 1993, appears to show Oswald (circled, far right) and Ferrie (circled, far left) eight years before the assassination, in a Civil Air Patrol group.

35. 36. 37. Mystery in Mexico. Agents filmed and bugged the Cuban and Soviet missions in Mexico City for the CIA – and were watched and photographed in turn by Castro's intelligence service. A CIA message implied that the stocky man (top right) had used Oswald's name at the Soviet consulate. CIA station chief Winston Scott (right) wrote that his cameras got photos of the real Oswald, but none ever surfaced.

38. 39. Did the man who was CIA's chief of Cuba operations in 1963, David Phillips, operate as "Maurice Bishop," the name allegedly used by an officer said to have met with Oswald before the assassination and – afterwards – to have sought to fabricate evidence linking Oswald to Cuban diplomats in Mexico City?

40. 41. Testimony that could not be ignored. Silvia Odio in Dallas. She and her sister later recalled a visit by anti-Castro activists, one of whom – they believed – had been 'Oswald'. The activists' leader later spoke of the Oswald figure with Odio in a way that seemed designed to incriminate him. Loran Hall (right), who became part of this scenario, was an associate of Mob boss Santo Trafficante.

42. 43. Carlos Bringuier (left), who clashed with Oswald in New Orleans, was one of a group of anti-Castro activists handled by CIA case officer George Joannides (right). Joannides later hid this connection from the House Assassinations Committee.

44. The end of the interrogation, the moment Jack Ruby shot Oswald dead.

45. 46. Trafficante associate John Martino (left) said "The anti-Castro people put Oswald together...They had Ruby kill him." The author was told in 2007 that Herminio Diaz, who had worked for Trafficante and was a known assassin, (far left in photo below) admitted having "taken part in the death of the President of the United States."

Illustration Credits

1. John Fitzgerald Kennedy by Aaron Shikler, The White House Historical Association (White House Collection). 2. R. W. 'Rusty' Livingston Collection/The Sixth Floor Museum at Dealey Plaza. 3 & 4. Jack Weaver. 5. Corbis. 6. Courtesy of Jeff Wallace. 7 & 8. Courtesy of US Government Printing Office/Assassinations Committee files. 9 – 11. Warren Commission Exhibit. 12. Courtesy of Jeanne de Mohrenschildt. 13–19 Warren Commission Exhibits. 20. Bettmann/Corbis. 22. Clark Co. Sheriff's Office, Las Vegas mugshot. 23 & 24. Bettmann/Corbis. 25–27. CIA. 28. FBI. 33. Ronan O'Rahilly 34. John Ciravolo. 35. Courtesy of Cuban Government. 36. CIA. 37. Courtesy of Michael Scott. 38. House Assassinations Committee. 40. Courtesy of Silvia Odio. 41 & 42. House Assassinations Committee 43. CIA. 44. National Archives. 45. Courtesy of Mrs Martino. 46. *Granma*, Cuba. 47. Niall McDiarmid/Alamy.

Acknowledgments

The mainstream media has long tended to treat serious Kennedy assassination researchers as though they are mere cranks or sensation-seekers. Cranks do, of course, fool around on the fringes of all controversial events, not least in the age of the Internet, and they obscure credible work. In the Kennedy case, there has also been the scholarship and persistence of a number of committed citizens, whose work filled the gap left by official investigation and neglectful journalism. It was largely their work that led to fresh investigation by congressional committees—including the House Assassinations Committee, which concluded in 1979 that the President's death was probably the result of a conspiracy. A further reward, in 1992, was the passing of the John F. Kennedy Assassination Records Act, which secured the release of millions of pages of previous withheld documents. A handful of citizens can still budge a resistant establishment.

Many independent researchers, and some of those who headed or staffed the congressional probes, have been of great assistance to me. Two, in particular, gave me access to their unique fund of knowledge and research material—and guided me away from red herrings. They were the late Mary Ferrell, in Texas, and—to this day—Paul Hoch in California. Mrs. Ferrell was known to reporters and researchers around the world for her tireless and meticulous research. Over almost the entire period since the assassination, Paul Hoch has deservedly earned a reputation for fine scholarship and innovative insight. I am indebted to them both for their friendship and guidance. Paul, for his sins, has read and annotated the drafts of all editions of this book.

A mere handful of professional reporters have ever worked on the case with lasting diligence. One is Jefferson Morley, formerly of the *Washington Post*, who has been generous with collegiate help on this latest lap. During an earlier phase, there was Earl Golz, formerly of the *Dallas Morning News*, who worked the story remorselessly—often in the face of editorial reluctance—and the late Seth Kantor of the *Atlanta Constitution*, whose 1978 book on Jack Ruby remains an essential resource. During the current work, author Gus Russo has helped lasso some FBI material.

Thanks for help during work on this edition are due to Rex Bradford, a research dynamo, and Bill Kelly, who runs the blog JFKCounterCoup. The late Sylvia Meagher, whose book *Accessories after the Fact* helped convince Congress that the case should be reopened, gave generously of her time in the 1970s. Others who helped selflessly have been Dan Alcorn; Mark Allen; Professor Peter Dale Scott; Robert Dorff; the late Bernard Fensterwald and James Lesar of the Assassination Archives and Research Center in Washington, DC; Jones Harris; the late Larry Harris, who focused above all on the Tippit case; Harry Irwin; Tom Johnson; the late Penn Jones; David Lifton; Gary Mack; Dick Russell; Gary Shaw; the late Kevin Walsh; Alan Weberman; the late Harold Weisberg and Jack White; and Mark Zaid.

I am indebted to the late Dr. Vincent Guinn, the metals analyst whose work on the ballistics evidence was central to the House study. Dr. Cyril Wecht, the combative forensic pathologist from Pennsylvania, corresponded over many months—though I have not necessarily agreed with his theories! Former British

Detective-Superintendent Malcolm Thompson helped with photographic expertise. In the intelligence area, I thank John Marks of the Center for National Security Studies; the late Ray Cline of the Center for Strategic and International Studies, who gave good advice; Marion Johnson of the National Archives, who was endlessly patient during the writing of the first edition of this book; and Amy De Long, who gave assistance in 2013. The late Dave Powers, Curator at the John F. Kennedy Library, was helpful. The work done by former Army intelligence analyst John Newman, who contributed a postscript to the previous edition of this book, has continued to be helpful.

David Kaiser, former professor of history at the Naval War College, whose 2008 book contains some of the best recent scholarship on the assassination, courteously responded to me. David Barrett, professor of political science at Villanova University, generously shared a key document.

Senator Richard Schweiker of the Intelligence Committee, and the late Judge Richardson Preyer, chair of the House Assassinations Committee, gave patient help and advice. So, more recently, has the former chief counsel of the House Assassinations Committee, G. Robert Blakey—professor emeritus of law at the University of Notre Dame—with whom I shared a stimulating research expedition in 2007. A number of dedicated congressional staff who spoke with me must remain anonymous. It is an honor, however, to mention Gaeton Fonzi, a man of courage and integrity with whom I had the privilege of working after his work for the House Assassinations Committee was done. His colleagues' nickname for him was "Ahab"—and he never let up until the illness that led to his too-early death in 2012.

In Cuba, officials were cooperative and generous with facilities. I was neither credulous nor cynical about what they told me—an attitude I learned, in this case, also to take with U.S. officialdom.

My work on the case began in 1979 when—with the able Michael Cockerell—I made a television documentary that was shown on the BBC and around the United States. Independent filmmaker Ronan O'Rahilly provided further research opportunities and encouragement. Neither of those film operations could have been achieved without the skill and comradeship of my friends from long-ago days of danger in Vietnam and the Middle East, cameraman Raymond Grosjean and his sound engineer, the late Georges Méaume. In 1993, the producers of the *Frontline* program gave me the opportunity to follow Oswald's trails in Russia and Mexico. Personal thanks, for his part in that project, to my old BBC colleague Bill Cran.

Gratitude, too, to *Vanity Fair* magazine, which commissioned me to write a major 1994 article on the case. Editor Graydon Carter, and his colleagues Wayne Lawson and Robert Walsh, steered the piece to press with an attention to accuracy that remains so lacking in the handling of this story by most of the media.

Since 2006, in connection with developing new information, I thank Charles Cardiff, Libia Winslow, and Siobhán Murray— for translation from Spanish—Emer Reynolds of Crossing the Line Films in Dublin, and Gordon Winslow in Miami. Professor Sanjeev Chatterjee of the University of Miami School of Communication generously provided a film crew. I thank, too, Sra. Marta Martínez for her hospitality and—later, after her husband's death—her courteous help.

Friends who helped and encouraged over the years included Fenella Dubes; Mariko Fukuda; Esme and Larry Gottlieb; Willie and Bríd Henry; and, sadly gone now, Jane Bradbeer, Vicky

Mason, and James Villiers-Stuart. Susan Hart, who typed the original manuscript, was an unfailing source of help. Cynthia Rowan urged me on and applied an eagle eye to the first draft. For this edition, the trusty Sinéad Sweeney produced essential transcripts at short notice. Publishers Simon Thorogood at Headline in the UK, and Jane Friedman at Open Road Media in New York, have been ever supportive. Stephanie Gorton and Pete Beatty at Open Road steered this edition to completion. Lauren Chomiuk and Joan Giurdanella were super-thorough copyeditors, and James Edgar designed the UK cover.

My gratitude, as always, to the literary agent who keeps bread on our table in these tough times for the publishing industry, Curtis Brown chairman Jonathan Lloyd. The serenity of his assistant, Lucia Rae, keeps everyone sane.

I thank those loyal Americans, especially those in intelligence, who agreed to talk—albeit on occasion off the record. In a true democracy, loyalty is due ultimately not to bureaucracies and formal oaths of secrecy, but to personal conscience and the public interest.

I could not have done worthwhile work on this case, at any point in the past twenty years, without the professional skills and the love of the most indispensable colleague of all, my wife and professional partner, Robbyn. For this edition in particular, her hard work and wisdom has been vital.

Sources and Notes

Abbreviations

If not described in full, source books are referred to here under the authors' names and the notation Full details of these can be found in the bibliography.

Information deriving from research done by the author and Robbyn Swan for their December 1994 *Vanity Fair* article, "The Ghosts of November," will be referred to by the abbreviation VF.

Citations referring to official reports will be abbreviated as follows:

Warren Commission Report, Report, p. –.

Material in the twenty-six volumes that accompany the Warren Commission Report are referred to by volume and page, e.g., XXII.25.

Warren Commission Exhibits are referred to as, e.g., CE 2021.

Warren Commission Documents are referred to by document number, e.g., CD 16.

The *Report of the House Select Committee on Assassinations* (1979) is referred to as, e.g., HSCA Report, p.–.

The twelve Kennedy volumes of *Hearings and Appendices* of the House Select Committee on Assassinations are referred to by volume and page number, e.g., HSCA V.250.

References to documents held by the National Archives and Records Administration are cited as NARA and their record number, e.g., NARA 124-10193-10468.

The *Interim Report* (1975) of the *Select Committee to Study Governmental Operations with Respect to Intelligence Activities, United States Senate—Alleged Assassination Plots Involving Foreign Leaders* is referred to as Sen. Int. Cttee., *Assassination Plots*.

The Final Report of the above Select Committee (1976), entitled *The Investigation of the Assassination of President John F. Kennedy: Performance of the Intelligence Agencies*, is referred to as Sen. Int. Cttee., *Performance of Intelligence Agencies*.

Assassinations Records Review Board citations are referred to as AARB.

All the above are published by the U.S. Government Printing Office and listed in the bibliography to this book. Most are available online at MaryFerrell.org.

Preface

XII   From the start: Prof. Sheldon Appleton, "The Mystery of the Kennedy Assassination: What the American Public Believes," *The Public Perspective*, November/December 1998.
2013 poll: Conservative Intelligence Briefing, January 25, 2013.
2009 poll: CBS News, February 11, 2009.
"probably" HSCA Report, p. 1.
Warren: *New York Times*, February 4 & 5, 1964; *Washington Post*, February 4, 1964; *Los Angeles Times*, February 5, 1964; *Dallas Morning News*, February 5, 1964.

XIII   *Note 1*: Until the collapse of the Soviet Union, certainly, intelligence information involving the Soviets was highly sensitive. Most of the information about the KGB defector

Yuri Nosenko, and his claim to have knowledge of how the KGB had handled Oswald in the Soviet Union, was long top secret (see Chapters 8 and 10). CIA operations in or against Castro's Cuba—especially where they involve living people—may yet be sensitive. The Mexican authorities' part in CIA surveillance operations in Mexico City (see Chapter 19) may still be seen as politically sensitive within Mexico.

Army Intelligence files: See Chapters 5 & 16.

Secret Service destroyed: ARRB Report, p. 149 & see p. 64–

Naval Intelligence files: *ibid.*, p. 157, "The Railroading of LCDR Terri Pike," by William Kelly, www.jfkcountercoup.blogspot. com, corr. William Kelly, transcript int. CDR (USNR) Robert. D. Steele, February 1, 2013, HSCA XI.541

Archives Stated: Gary M. Stern, General Counsel to Jim Lesar, Assassination Archives & Research Center, June 12, 2012.

Blakey: ("bureaucratic jargon") *Salon*, June 14,2012; ("playing") Robert Blakey to Paul Hoch *et al.*, February 11, 2013.

XIV "unless the President": Stern to Lesar, *supra.*

1. Ambush

5 Poem: *Poems* by Alan Seeger (Charles Scribner & Sons, 1916).

Kennedy and danger in Dallas: Manchester, *op. cit.*, pp. 13, 15, 45.

6 Leading lights: Major General Edwin Walker, Mayor Earle Cabell, H. L. Hunt.

Kennedy talk/speeches: Manchester, *op. cit.*, pp. 86, 96.

Advertisement: *Dallas Morning News*, November 22, 1963; XVIII.835; inserted by John Birch Society members and rightists.

Kennedy comment: Manchester, *op. cit.*, p. 137; and Bishop, *op. cit.*, p. 25; VII.455—testimony of Kenneth O'Donnell.

7 Miami scare: CD 1347/20 and author's interview with Miami Police Intelligence Captain Charles Sapp, 1978; but see HSCA Report, p. 635n44.

Spectator comment: Manchester, *op. cit.*, p. 154.

Nellie Connally comment: IV.147, IV.131.

9   Officer's remark: Bishop, *op. cit.*, p. 147.

Time: (calculated for HSCA) HSCA II.40; HSCA Report, p. 48 (Agent Youngblood noticed the clock on the Book Depository).

President's cry: II.73, 74.

Note 1: It has been suggested that Secret Service Agent Kellerman imagined he heard the President speak, because of the possibility his throat wound made speech unfeasible. Doctors differ on this point, but it seems speech may briefly have been possible (HSCA VII.278, 295, 305).

Events in car: (Mrs. Kennedy's cry) V.179–; ("You know when he was shot") Theodore White's unpublished notes on his interview with Mrs. Kennedy, November 29, 1963; JFK Library—for this citation, the author is indebted to David Talbot and his book, *Brothers*, New York: Simon & Schuster, 2007, p. 247–; (Mrs. Connally) IV.148; (Gov. Connally) IV.133; ("buckshot") HSCA I.54.

10   Doctor breaks news: Manchester, *op. cit.*, p. 215.

I. DALLAS: The Open-and-Shut Case

2. The Evidence Before You

13   Cartridges found: III.283 (Mooney).

Gun found: III.293 (Boone) and VII.107 (Weitzman); (described) III.392 (Frazier) IV.260 (Day).

14   *Note 1*: There has been controversy over the identification of the rifle, because it was initially described as a Mauser. Although one of these descriptions came from one of the officers who found the weapon (who was familiar with guns), the author believes this was simply a mistake. The author does not subscribe to the theory that the rifle was subsequently switched for the one supposedly owned by Lee Harvey Oswald, as some claim. HSCA experts

agree confusion is the probable explanation (HSCA VII.372). But see Dick Russell, *op. cit.*, for suggestion the Carcano was found on the *fourth* floor. (Russell, *op. cit.*, p. 568)

Bullet fragments (listed): HSCA VII.365.

Intact bullet (found): Report, p. 79.

Note 2: The bullet was found by Darrell Tomlinson, the hospital's chief engineer, when he moved the stretcher. Tomlinson was not at all convinced that the stretcher was the one that had been used for Governor Connally. The Warren Commission, however, decided it was that stretcher. The uncertainty has fueled suspicions that the bullet was perhaps planted as part of a plan to inculpate Lee Oswald. To this author, that posits too complex a plot and is improbable. (Report, p. 79, and VI.126–.)

Cartridges, bullets, and fragments linked to rifle: Report, p. 84–; HSCA VII.367–.

Note 3: Admiral Osborne, who attended the Kennedy autopsy, said he saw and even handled an intact bullet during the procedure. He thought it turned up in the body's wrappings, though he was open to the possibility that it arrived independently— which may mean he merely saw the famous "single bullet" later, after its separate transfer from Dallas. However, the possibility remains that he did see a second mystery bullet, and full questioning of the other doctors should have been able to resolve this (Lifton, *op. cit.*, Chapter 29, & HSCA VII.15). Speculation has also arisen because FBI agents signed a receipt for a "missile" received from the autopsy doctors (Lifton, *op. cit.*, & HSCA VII.12).

15   Argument over body: McKinley, *op. cit.*, p. 120.

"at gunpoint": int. Dr. Robert Shaw, 1978.

Helpern: Marshall Houts, *op. cit.* p. 52.

Not shaved/not sectioned: VF, December 1994, HSCA interviews released 1995; and HSCA VII.17, 25.

16   Baden: HSCA I.298; and cf. HSCA VII.177.

Handicapped: HSCA VII.13; and VF, December 1994; HSCA VII.13–; and cf. State of Louisiana v. Clay Shaw—Finck testimony, February 24, 1967; and (on clothing) HSCA VII.192.

Kennedy disease: *New York Times*, October 6, 1992, report on *Journal of the American Medical Association* article just published.

Autopsy summary: Report, p. 86, HSCA VII.6–, 87–.

17   Probed: CD7.4; HSCA VII.12–.

Series of reexaminations: HSCA VII.3–, 89.

Small wound: HSCA VII.85; and *cf.* HSCA VII.175–.

Serious mistake: HSCA VII.104; and *cf.* HSCA VII.176.

18   *Note 4*: Some photographs were apparently "liberated" by a person working for the House Assassinations Committee, and others were reportedly produced by a former Secret Service photographer, James Fox. In August 1979, a freelance journalist, Harrison Livingstone, revealed that he had copies of five Kennedy autopsy photographs. They were eventually published in his book *High Treason*, written with Robert Groden. (See *New York Times*, August 19, 1979, and Bibliography.)

Head wound: See Thompson, Josiah, *op. cit.*, and Lifton, David, *op. cit.*, for early and late studies of entire autopsy area; VF, December 1994.

Hill: Livingstone/Groden, *op. cit.*, p. 388. Jacqueline Kennedy: Lifton, *op. cit.*, p. 312 and *Nova* (PBS-TV program), November 15, 1988.

McClelland: VI.33, (drawing) Thompson, *op. cit.*, p. 140;

19   Parkland descriptions: Lifton and Livingstone/Groden, *op cit.* Clark: Lifton, p. 318.

20   Custer (and colleague Edward Reed): Lifton, *op. cit.*, p. 773.

Secret Service: VF, December 1994, and HSCA interviews released 1995.

drawings: *ibid.*; Bashour: Livingstone/Groden, p. 39.

22   McClelland: int. May 1989.

Note 5: Dr. McClelland's statement is supported by the autopsy surgeons' report of January 26, 1967, reprinted in Harold Weisberg, *op. cit.*, *Post-Mortem*, pp. 577–579.

Vanished photos: (Humes) HSCA VII.253; (Finck) HSCA interview released 1994, p. 90; (Director of Photography)

John Stringer, HSCA Agency File No. 002070.

23 Photos forgery: *VF*, December 1994; HSCA VII.37; *Boston Globe*, June 21,1981; Lifton, *op cit.*

Note 6: The Assassinations Committee's study of the autopsy materials led to scandal, when a safe containing the pictures and X-rays was opened. A folder had been removed, and one photograph of the dead President ripped out of its cover. A fingerprint check located the culprit, a CIA employee named Regis Blahut assigned to protecting secret CIA documents temporarily in the custody of the Committee. He was fired, and the CIA told the Committee that Blahut had acted out of "mere curiosity." The picture in which Blahut was apparently especially interested featured the late President's head, and thus was one of those that was at the center of controversy about the source of the shot or shots that caused the fatal head wound. (*Washington Post*, June 18, 19, 28, 1979; *Clandestine America*, III.2, p. 4; statement by Rep. Louis Stokes to House of Representatives, June 28, 1979.)

Missing brain: HSCA VII.25, Assassinations Record Review Board, contact report, April 1, 1997, posted on http://jfkcountercoup2.blogspot.ie.

24 McClelland on X-rays: *Inside Edition* (TV program), July 1989.

Custer: *VF*, December 1994.

Mantik: *ibid.*, & int., 1995.

Note 7: The authenticity of the autopsy photographs and X-rays was questioned as early as 1981, in the book *Best Evidence*, by David Lifton (see Bibliography). His thesis, that the President's body was tampered with surgically between Dallas and the Bethesda autopsy, is dealt with at length in the Aftermath chapter of the previous (Paragon) edition of this book, published at the time under the title *Conspiracy*. The theory seems preposterous, yet it is hard to dismiss the testimony of many of the witnesses Lifton interviewed. He certainly raised troubling questions about the movement of the President's body.

Zapruder film: http://www.youtube.com/watch?v=kq1PbgeBoQ4

& available for viewing at National Archives.

26   Dictabelt: author's research in Dallas, 1978; HSCA II.16, 107.
Acoustics: HSCA II.17–, V.645; author's ints.
with Barger, November 1978; HSCA V.645, *op cit.*
HSCA VIII, V.652, V.671–, V.592, V.679, HSCA Report, p. 65, and V.674.

27   HSCA acoustics finding: HSCA Report, p. 1; "beyond reasonable doubt": HSCA V.583.

28   Academy of Sciences: Ramsey Report, 1982.

29   Responsible researchers: e.g., "The acoustic evidence in the Kennedy assassination," paper by Michael O'Dell, http:// mcadams.posc.mu.edu/odell/; author's corr. O'Dell & Paul Hoch, 2012.
2010 book: Donald Thomas, *Hear No Evil*, Ipswich, MA: Mary Ferrell Foundation, 2010.
Further studies: 2013 papers by Michael O'Dell, further analyzing HSCA's original tests, shared with the author.
Blakey: int., May 3,1989, & *re* witness testimony, Blakey email to Kaiser *et al.*, October 12, 2012.

3. How Many Shots? Where From?

31   Huxley: *Collected Essays*, vol. 8.
Survey of people on number of shots: HSCA VIII.142.

32   Acoustics specialists: "Firearms Investigation, Identification and Evidence," Hatcher, Jury and Weller, 1957, p. 420, Secret Service memo March 7, 1964 (S.S. Files 221–229).
Rear right outriders: James Chaney and D. L. Jackson.
Five in the car: Mrs. Kennedy (V.180); Connallys (IV.132, 145); Agent Kellerman (II.74; XVIII.724; II.61) (he believed there were more than three shots); Agent Greer (II.130).
Rear left outriders: B. J. Martin (VI.292); B. W. Hargis (VI.294); and *New York Daily News*, November 24, 1963.

33   Moorman: XIX.487; XXII.838; XXIV.217.
Brehm: XII.837.

Newman: XIX.488; XXII.842; XXIV.2; IV.218.

Orr: conversation with Dallas researcher, November 22, 1963, and subsequently. Orr was never interviewed by any official body.

Acoustics: testimonies of Barger (HSCA II) and Weiss/Aschkenasy (HSCA V).

34 Blakey summary: HSCA V.690.

Time frame: HSCA V.724.

Two shots sounded like one: Report, p. 87.

Origin of third shot: HSCA VIII.5.

35 Origin of knoll shot: HSCA VIII.10.

Ford: Article in *Life* magazine, October 2, 1964.

Survey *re* direction of shots: HSCA Report, pp. 87, 90.

Note 1: The first useful survey on shots was *Fifty-One Witnesses: The Grassy Knoll* by Harold Feldman (San Francisco: Idlewild Publishing, 1965). The author took this, the most perspicacious early work, into account. It agrees, in basic conclusions, with the HSCA findings.

Mrs. Kennedy: V.180.

Governor Connally: IV.132–.

36 Mrs. Connally: IV.149.

Greer: II.129.

Kellerman: XVIII.724 and II.61.

Left outriders: VI.293 (Hargis) and VI.289 (Martin).

Chaney: unidentified film interview in police station and taped interview for KLIF, Dallas, on record *The Fateful Hours*, Capitol Records.

O'Donnell: VF, December 1994, drawing on O'Neill's biography; and ints. O'Neill and Dave Powers.

Moorman: XIX.497; XXII.838; XXIV.217.

Orr: conversation with Dallas researcher, November 22, 1963, and subsequently.

Brehm: XXII.837.

Newman: XIX.490; XXII.842; XXIV.219.

37 Book Depository witnesses: manager, William Shelley (VI.328);

superintendent, Truly (III.227); TSBD vice president, O. V. Campbell (XXII.638); vice president publishing company, S. F. Wilson (XXII.685).

Sorrels: XXI.548; (later testimony) VII.347.

Landis: XVIII.758.

Decker: verbatim from police radio traffic recording of November 22, 1963 (as published in JFK Assassination File by Jesse Curry, 1969). (See bibliography.)

38   Arnold: interviewed by Earl Golz for *Dallas Morning News*, August 27, 1978 (seen by Yarborough) *Dallas Morning News*, December 31,1978); never interviewed by HSCA, interview of Arnold by Golz, May 23,1979.

40   Railway supervisor: S. M. Holland testimony VI.239–.

Woodward and friends: *Dallas Morning News*, November 23,1963. (Woodward's position indicated in XXIV.520.)

Chism and wife: XXIV.204, 205.

41   Millican: XIX.486.

Jean Newman: XXIV.218. Not to be confused with Gayle Newman, mentioned earlier.

Zapruder: CD 87; HSCA Report, p. 89.

Holland: (police statement): XXIV.212; (testimony) VI.239; interview of Holland by Mark Lane (on film) taken from transcript of *Rush to Judgment*, transmitted on BBC-TV, January 29, 1967.

42   Eight other witnesses: (Frank Reilly) VI.230; (Nolan H. Polton) XXII.834; (James Simmons) XXII.833; (Clemon Johnson) XXII.836; (Andrew Miller) VI.225, XIX.485; (Richard Dodd XXII.835; (Walter Winborn) XXII.833; (Thomas Murphy) XXII.835. (See also HSCA XII.23.)

Bowers: VI.284, testimony of Bowers; and filmed interview by Mark Lane, March 31, 1966; Lane, *op. cit.*, p. 23–.

Gunpowder (Mrs. Cabell) VII.486–, (Yarborough) Feldman, *op. cit.*, unpaginated; (Roberts) Feldman, *op. cit.*, unpaginated; (Brown) VI.233–; (Baker) VII.510–.

43   Smith: VII.535; *Texas Observer*, November 13, 1963; ints. by author, August 1978; XXII.600.

Moorman photograph: HSCA VI.125–; Zapruder on CBS (Rather error): tape of KRLD, Dallas CBS affiliate-reel 65A.7 (inventory of tapes of Dallas radio stations, National Archives).

44 Frames reversed (original error): XVIII.70–; "printing error": Hoover letter to Ray Marcus, December 14, 1965.

Hargis: VI.293–295; Curry, *op. cit.*, p. 30.

Martin: VI.289.

45 Harper: CD 1269, p. 5; HSCA VII.24.

"covered with brain tissue": HSCA Report, p. 40.

HSCA conclusion: HSCA Report, p. 1; HSCA V.690–.

Neuromuscular reaction: HSCA 1.415.

Medical panel supported reaction thesis: HSCA VII.174, 178.

Entrance wound: HSCA VII.176, 107; and HSCA I.250 (brain should have been sectioned); HSCA VII.134; (bullet path) HSCA VII.135.

46 Guinn tests: HSCA I.507; (testimony) HSCA I.491; int. Dr. Guinn, November 1978; *Analytical Chemistry*, Vol. 51, p. 484A, April 1979.

Note 2: Dr. Guinn was unable to test one fragment found in the car, part of the copper jacket rather than lead (HSCA I.515). In their analysis, the firearms panel concluded that this was the base of a 6.5-mm bullet and believed it had been fired through the rifle found at the Depository (HSCA VII.369). This, probably, was the fragment referred to by Congressman Dodd in public session as "not easily identifiable as a result of neutron activation tests" (HSCA V.696).

One of the fragments recovered from the floor of the limousine has vanished since 1963 (HSCA VII.366n). In addition, Guinn reported finding one fragment container empty, a can that had apparently contained particles from the car's damaged windshield. Nor were any samples left from a curb that had reportedly been struck by a bullet. Guinn assumed these had simply been "used up" in earlier FBI tests (HSCA I.196 and letter to author, August 10, 1979). This, at any rate, is the way the HSCA decided to account for the difference in weight and count of fragment material originally listed by the FBI and that handed to Guinn (HSCA Report, p. 599n33). Clearly, the fragments were, at one stage, at least poorly cataloged and monitored. Some will suspect a more sinister explanation. See also *Note 6* on problems with possible missing fragments in connection with Governor Connolly's wrist and the magic bullet (later in this chapter).

Ballistics link fragments to gun: HSCA VII.369.

47   Warren investigators & "magic bullet theory": Report, p. 105.

Note 3: Norman Redlich, Warren Commission lawyer, said on March 23, 1965, "To say that they were hit by separate bullets is synonymous with saying that there were two assassins." (See *Inquest* by E. J. Epstein, p. 55.)

48   Helpern: Marshall Houts, *op. cit.*, pp. 9, 59.

Note 4: Helpern was quoting the Warren Commission description of the bullet. The HSCA firearms panel found it to weigh 157.7 grains, however (HSCA VII.368, 372).

Shaw: int, 1978; and HSCA I.268, 302.

49   McCloy: *VF*, December 1994.

Boggs: June 11, 1965, interviewed by E. J. Epstein for *Inquest* (p. 148).

Cooper: interview for BBC, produced by author, 1978.

Russell: interviewed by Alfred Goldberg, May 5, 1965, reported in *Inquest* by E. J. Epstein, p. 148; and interviewed in 1970 for *Whitewash IV* by Harold Weisberg, p. 212; see also *New York Times*, November 22, 1966, VF, December 1994.

HSCA on "magic bullet": HSCA Report, p. 47.

Forensic panel on "magic bullet": HSCA VII.179.

Ballistics experts: (tests on bullets) HSCA I.411; (bullet fired in rifle) HSCA VII.368.

Guinn test: HSCA I.533.

50   HSCA sequence: HSCA Report, pp. 1, 46– & HSCA V.690.

Journal of the American College of Surgeons article: May 1994.

Note 5: Case Closed, a 1993 book by lawyer Gerald Posner (see

Bibliography), argued that computer enhancement "settles the question" of the timing of the shots, and that test-firing "provided the final physical evidence necessary to prove the single-bullet theory." Posner failed to tell readers in the first edition of his book that the computer work had been done for the prosecution side in a mock trial of Oswald conducted by the American Bar Association. (Gerald Posner, *op. cit.*, pp. 317, 402; *Case Open*, by Harold Weisberg, *op. cit.*, pp. 57–79; and int. Dr. Angela Meyer of FAA, 1994).

51 Op. room supervisor/policeman: Audrey Bell, conv. with author, 1978; and Patrolman Charles Harbison, in *Dallas Morning News*, April 3, 1977; int. by Earl Golz, September 1977; and *cf.* Dallas Police property list, released by Dallas Municipal Archives and Records Center, 1992; HSCA VII.156 and Fig. 17, HSCA VII.392; Report, p. 95.

Note 6: As to doubt whether relevant bullet was found on Connolly's stretcher, see *Note 3* to Chapter 2. In 1978, HSCA wound ballistics expert Sturdivan did say he felt more was missing from the magic bullet than is accounted for by the surviving fragments and surmised that some had been lost. (HSCA 1.412) Some fragments have indeed vanished since 1963 (see *Note 2* on Guinn tests). Their loss, without proper accounting, fueled suspicion by some researchers that they were maliciously removed.

Finck: VF, December 1994.

Connally death/fragment: *ibid.*, *New York Times*, UPI, June 19, 1993.

52 Jenkins: David Lifton, *op. cit.*, p. 613; and *cf.*

Jenkins HSCA int., memo 002193, released 1995.

Throat merely probed: HSCA int. Dr. Thornton

Boswell, memo 002071, released 1995; (not sectioned) affidavit of FBI Agent James Sibert, October 24, 1978, released with HSCA Agency File no. 002191, in 1995.

53 McClelland: int., May 4, 1979; Livingstone & Groden, *op. cit.*, p. 394.

Robinson: HSCA int., Agency File no. 000661, released 1995.

Crenshaw: VF, December 1994; and Charles Crenshaw *et al.*, *op cit.*

Burkley: HSCA int. Burkley (undated), 1977, in AARB MD 19, www.maryferrell.org, & AARB Report, p. 131, *re* reported Burkley belief that there had been a conspiracy to kill the president. Baden: HSCA Report, pp. 80, 604n106.

54   Mantik, Riley: *VF*, December 1994; and int.

Mantik, 1995.

Note 7: More fully, the 2006 study's findings were that "a conclusion of material evidence for only two bullets in the questioned JFK assassination specimens has no forensic basis. . . . Although collateral information from the overall investigation might very well narrow the choices, as stand-alone primary evidence, the recovered bullet fragments could be reflective of anywhere between two and five different rounds fired in Dealey Plaza that day."

The study continues with the somewhat opaque observation that: "Only the near-complete mass of CE-399, the stretcher bullet, precludes the conclusion of one to five rounds. Moreover, the fragments need not necessarily have originated from MC [Mannlicher-Carcano] ammunition." (*Journal of Forensic Sciences*, July, 2006, Vol. 51, No. 4)

4. Other Gunmen?

56   Curry: Curry, *op. cit.*, p. 61.

Secret Service man with gun: picture in *The Torch Is Passed* (AP 1964) p. 17; and HSCA Report, p. 606n55.

Willis: HSCA XII.7; (photographs) HSCA VI.121.

Price: XIX.492; interview of Price by Mark Lane, March 27, 1966; HSCA XII.12.

57   Bowers: VI.284; filmed interview by Mark Lane, March 31, 1966; HSCA XII.12–.

Smith: VII.535; *Texas Observer*, December 13, 1963; ints. with author, August 1978 and subsequently.

Note 1: The Assassinations Committee was unable to resolve the problem created by Officer Smith's sighting of a man who showed Secret Service credentials. It considered the possibility that he had mistaken an Army Intelligence agent for a Secret Service man, given that some evidence shows that Army Intelligence officers were in the Dealey Plaza area. The Department of Defense, however, said the record contained nothing about such agents being active in Dallas on November 22. The Committee thought it possible that Dallas Police plainclothes detectives might have been taken for Secret Service agents. British researcher Chris Mills has since argued that the mystery man may have been a real Secret Service agent, Thomas "Lem" Johns. A former NBC cameraman, David Wiegman, has recalled seeing Johns on the knoll. But questions remain, not least over the unkempt appearance of the man Officer Smith encountered. That hardly fits the image of a Secret Service man on duty in the public eye. (HSCA Report, p. 183–; and "The Man Who Wasn't There," an article by Chris Mills, *Dallas '63*, www.manuscriptsservice.com/DPQ/mills-1htm

58 Arnold: *Dallas Morning News*, August 17, 1978; int. by Earl Golz, May 23, 1979.

Summers: int. by Gary Mack for "Sixth Floor Museum," 2002, *Nova*, PBS, 1988.

Curry: int. by author, December 1977.

Tilson: int. by Earl Golz of *Dallas Morning News* & *Dallas Morning News*, August 20,1978.

59 Other reports of cars: HSCA XII.13–.

Rowland: II.175; (and FBI) II.183.

60 Henderson: XXIV.524 (to FBI); interviewed by author, 1978, and by Earl Golz, in *Dallas Morning News*, December 19,1978. (In Henderson's FBI statement, which is reported speech, it is not clear if she is discussing the specific sixth-floor window.)

Walther: XXIV.522 (to FBI); also, int. by author, 1978; and by Earl Golz of *Dallas Morning News*, 1978; recorded int. by Larry

Schiller for Capitol Records, *The Controversy*, 1967.

61 Powell: traced and interviewed by Earl Golz for *Dallas Morning News*, December 19, 1978.

62 Questioning at jail: Bugliosi, *op. cit.*, p. 836.

Clerks: VI.194 (R. Fischer); and VI.203 (Edwards); and XXIV.207–.

Brennan: III.145; XI.206–.

Euins: II.209; VI.170; VII.349.

63 Worrell: Report, p. 253; II.190.

Mayor's wife and photographers: VII.485– (Mrs. Cabell); 11.155 (R. Jackson); and VI.160 (M. Couch).

Radio calls: XXIII.916—transcript of police radio Channel 1; and Curry, *op. cit.*, p. 43–.

Three employees: Report, p. 70–.

Warren did not establish: Report, p. 144.

64 Citizen call on radio: XVII.408, transcript of police radio Channel 1; (time) Report, p. 165.

Suspect description: XXIII.859–, transcript of police radio Channel 1.

Brewer: VII.4.

65 Ticket seller: VII.10– (J. Postal).

McDonald: interview with author, 1978; III.299.

Oswald cry: III.300 (McDonald).

5. Did Oswald Do It?

66 Oswald excuse for leaving scene: Report, p. 600.

Fritz: Report, 599 (p. 13, Fritz report).

Interrogation sessions: Report, Appendix XI, which contains reports of Captain Fritz, FBI Agents Hosty, Bookhout, Clements, Secret Service Inspector Thomas Kelley, and U.S. Postal Inspector H. D. Holmes.

Note 1: The Warren Report stated that Fritz kept no notes of the interrogation and that no stenographic or tape recordings were made. Fritz had in fact made scrawled notes, and these were released by the Assassination Records Review Board in 1997. They do not significantly change the existing knowledge of what Oswald said when interrogated. (No notes: Report, p. 180; released: AARB press release, November 20, 1997, www.maryferrel.org.)

67 Oswald statements to press: all are taken by the author from contemporary radio and TV tapes.

68 Cartridges found: III.283 (Mooney).

Gun found: III.293 (Boone); VII.107 (Weitzman).

Rifle described: III.392 (Frazier); IV.260 (Day).

Palm print: IVH.258 (Day).

Klein's: VII.364 (Waldman); VII.370 (Scibor).

69 Oswald's writing: VII.420 (Cadigan); IV.373 (Cole).

Hidell card: VII.58 (Hill).

Fibers: IV.83– (Stombaugh).

Marina on rifle: I.26, 52 (Marina Oswald).

Police search: VII.229 (Rose); VII.548 (Walthers); IV.286.

Liebeler: *VF*, December 1994.

70 Frazier: II.222 (Buell Frazier).

Frazier sister: II:248 (Linnie Randle).

Bag found: IV.266 (Day).

Prints on bag: Report, Appendix X.565–; IV.3 (Latona).

Fibers on bag: IV.77 (Stombaugh).

Photographs found: VII.231– (Officers Adamcik, Moore, Stovall, Rose).

Marina on photographs: I.15, 117; V.405.

71 Imperial Reflex: IV.284 (Shaneyfelt).

Marks on "magic bullet": III.429 (Frazier); III.498 (Nicol); HSCA VII.368.

Tippit ballistics: dealt with extensively in Chapter 6.

Oswald charged on Tippit count: Report, p. 198.

Alexander decision: int. with author, 1978.

Curry account: Curry, *op. cit.*, p. 79.

Note 2: There may be some doubt as to whether Oswald was actually arraigned for the President's murder. An FBI report of November

25, 1963, states categorically, "No arraignment on the murder charge in connection with the death of President Kennedy was held, inasmuch as such arraignment was not necessary in view of the previous charges filed against Oswald and for which he was arraigned." (CD5.400) Homicide Captain Fritz, Police Chief Curry, and Judge Johnston (IV.221; IV.155; XV.507–), however, said Oswald was charged. The time given was 1:35 a.m. Yet Officer J. B. Hicks, who was on duty in the relevant office until after 2:00 a.m., was certain Oswald was not arraigned at 1:35. Another FBI report, classified until 1975, indicates that Oswald was never arraigned on the presidential charge (CD 1084A.11). The author's interview with Assistant District Attorney Bill Alexander suggests the charitable explanation—that officials confused the arraignment on the presidential charge with the earlier one involving Officer Tippit.

72   Oswald's comments on rifle (and on all points unless indicated): Report, Appendix XI.

Note 3: Nobody at the Dallas post office concerned was ever formally asked whether they recalled handing a hefty package to somebody claiming to be the holder of Box 2915 a few months previously. The way such a package was delivered to a box holder was by leaving an advice note asking him to call at the counter. No postal worker recalled having given Oswald any such package. (Meagher, *op. cit.*, p. 50.)

73   Warren Report on Hidell: Report, p. 313, 644–, 292.
Heindel: VIII.318.

74   "Hidell" card in wallet: VII.58 (Hill); and see discussion in Meagher, *op. cit.*, p. 185.
Oswald identifies himself as Hidell: VII.228, but see also VII.187–.
Public discussion of Hidell: Meagher, *op. cit.*, p. 188.

Note 4: Some have inferred that the Hidell identity card was fabricated by the authorities to link Oswald with the mail order for the rifle. This is impossible to square with Oswald's handwriting on the order form, without assuming a plot to frame Oswald involving law enforcement officials across the United States. The author rejects that notion, not because it is inherently implausible that a man would be framed by the authorities, but because the deception involved would have involved too many people and been too vulnerable to exposure.

"Hidell" and military intelligence: Paul Hoch memo on "Army Intelligence, A. J. Hidell, and the FBI," October 8, 1977; FBI document 105-82555 (unrecorded) (original in 62-109060-811); *Dallas Morning News*, March 19,1978; HSCA Report, p. 221.

75   Both names in Oswald wallet: VII.228.

76   *Note 5*: FBI records show that Lieutenant Colonel Jones told the FBI that Hidell was an associate of Oswald, not a name used as an alias. The signature "A. J. Hidell" appears as "Chapter President" on a Fair Play for Cuba Committee card Oswald showed the police in New Orleans after his arrest following a demonstration over Cuba. Handwriting experts were of the opinion this was signed by Marina Oswald (HSCA VIII.238). The point here is that Oswald was using Hidell—whether he existed or not—as somebody *other than* himself. The same is suggested by the discovery in Oswald's effects of an index card for Hidell, along with cards for real people (Meagher, *op. cit.*, p. 197). Oswald was not carrying a Hidell ID when questioned in New Orleans (X.52–). See full discussion of this episode in this book, Chapter 17, "Blind Man's Bluff in New Orleans."

Shanklin affair: HSCA Report, p. 195–; (interviewed by HSCA) HSCA Report, p. 627.

77   Oswald's intelligence: (school record) Texas Attorney General's Report, VIII.2965.30d (the record also says Oswald's IQ was "in the upper range of bright, normal intelligence"; (intelligence noted in Marines) VIII.290, 297, 300.

Oswald offers garage information: Report, p. 603.

78   *Note 6*: Captain Fritz suggested (Report, p. 607) that the police had the backyard pictures by 12:35 p.m. on November 23. In light of the version of events offered by the policeman who

found the pictures, that appears not to have been accurate. (VII.193, 231; HSCA VI.139).

79 Persuasive evidence on pictures; (experts) Warren Report, p. 125 and HSCA VI.161; (Marina) I.117, 16.

Letter signed "L. H.": see Albert Newman, *op. cit.*, p. 154–, et. seq.

Taking of photographs: (Marina) I.117, 16, and HSCA II.241; (Marguerite) I.148; (White) HSCA II.321; HSCA VI.141; (fellow officer) HSCA VI.153.

80 Police reenactment: Warren Commission Exhibit (photographs only at LBJ Library, Austin, Texas).

Marina: (on burning picture) McMillan, *op. cit.*, p. 441; (on Oswald and rifle) II.415.

Note 7: The Warren Commission based much of its case against Oswald on Marina's testimony—though the very fact that she was Oswald's wife would have disqualified her testimony had her husband come to trial.

Marina "lying": Warren Commission memorandum, Redlich-Rankin, February 28, 1964.

81 HSCA on Marina: HSCA Report, p. 55.

Marina lapses of memory: HSCA XII.332.

Oswald colleague: X.201, Dennis Ofstein testimony.

82 *Note 8*: Oswald may have signed one copy of the rifle photograph and given it to his Dallas associate George de Mohrenschildt. This possibility is dealt with in Chapter 12, "Oswald and the Baron."

83 Fibers: (FBI) Report, p. 124; (Oswald on shirt change) Report, pp. 605, 613, 622, 626.

Independent analysis: *Frontline*, PBS, November 16, 1993; VF, December 1994.

Day: IV.261 (Day).

84 *Note 9*: Lieutenant Day did not release the palm print to the FBI until November 26, 1963.

Location of print: IV.260 (Day).

Print old: int. of Day by Robbyn Swan, 1994.

Rods: Howard Roffman, *op. cit.*, pp. 56, 146, 158–160, 174, *et al.*; Ray and Mary La Fontaine, *op. cit.*, p. 371.

85   Shorter package: II.239 (Buell Frazier); II.248 (L. Randle);
     IX.475 (Krystinik).

     Oiled gun: XXVI.455.

     Inquiry conclusions: (Warren) Report, p. 137– & see HSCA
     Report, p. 57.

86   No ammunition: VII.226; XXVI.63.

     Note 10: John T. Masen, of Masen's Gunshop (CE 2694 and
     CD 897.83–), told the FBI he acquired and sold ten boxes
     of Mannlicher-Carcano ammunition in 1963. Masen had
     been investigated for violation of the Firearms Act before the
     assassination (CD 853A.2) and admitted an association with a
     prominent member of Alpha 66, Manuel Rodriguez. (See Index
     for other references to Alpha 66. At least one of its senior mem-
     bers has a major role in the mystery.)

87   Dodd theory: HSCA Report, p. 484– (*Option one*).

88   Oswald's shooting record: XI.302.

     Former marine on Oswald's shooting expertise: VIII.235 (Nelson
     Delgado).

89   Oswald statements on whereabouts: Report, pp. 600, 613.

     Prints on cartons: (Oswald's) IV.31—Latona; (unidentified
     print) Report, pp. 249, 566.

     Note 11: Astonishingly, not all the employees of the Book
     Depository were fingerprinted. After the workers known to
     have handled cartons had been checked and ruled out, the
     Depository superintendent "requested that other employees
     not be fingerprinted." (XXIV.7) Obligingly, the authorities
     went along with his request.

     Chemical test: IV.275 (Day); CD 5.145, 152.

     Note 12: Nitrate deposits were found on Oswald's hands, which
     was consistent with his having fired a handgun, like the one
     he allegedly used to shoot policeman Tippit. Similar depos-
     its could also, however, have resulted from handling printed
     matter (as Oswald did in his job) or from urine splashes. The
     nitrate test has long since been considered outmoded and
     unreliable.

Givens: Report, p. 143; (narcotics) Roffman, *op. cit.*, p. 177; XXIII.873; VI.355; (FBI questioning, November 22) VI.355.

90 Oswald at 11:45 a.m.: III.168 (Williams); VI.337 (Lovelady).

Chicken bones/lunch: III.169– (Williams); III.288 (Mooney); VII.46 (Hill); VII.121 (Boyd); VII.105 (Johnson); VII.146 (Studebaker); VI.330 (Shelley); VI.307 (Brewer); IV.266 (Day).

91 Jarman: III.200– (Jarman).

Norman: III.189 (Norman).

Shelley: VII.390 (Shelley).

Piper: VI.383 (Piper).

Note 13: It appears that Jarman years later said that—like Givens—he observed Oswald on the first floor as early as noon. He did not say this in his more contemporary Warren Commission testimony. With Piper, Shelley (and Givens), this would make four witnesses who saw Oswald downstairs at noon. In his 2007 book, Vincent Bugliosi questioned whether it was noteworthy that Oswald had described seeing Jarman and Norman, but his argument appears to hinge to a degree on whether Oswald actually had lunch *with* the two men—something Oswald did not claim to have done. (HSCA Report, p. 57, referring to an HSCA interview; III.201; Vincent Bugliosi, *Reclaiming History, The Assassination of President John F. Kennedy*, New York: Norton, 2007, p. 830).

92 "Going up to eat": XIX.499 (Piper).

Carolyn Arnold: conversations with author, November 1978; also with Earl Golz of *Dallas Morning News*, November 26, 1978; FBI report V.41.

Note 14: Carolyn Arnold later remarried.

Note 15: Mrs. Arnold's 1978 comments seem important, if true. The author received a letter from Associate Professor James Chalmers, of the Department of Political Science at Wayne State University in Detroit, expressing doubt on Mrs. Arnold's 1978 version of events. He suspected that the passing of time led her to enlarge on what she really saw, and that the original

FBI report cited here is the accurate version. There is, too, the statement of Pauline Sanders, a Depository clerk who said she left the second-floor lunchroom at about 12:20 p.m.—and did not see Oswald that day at all.

Chalmers, for his part, pointed out that Mrs. Arnold herself signed a 1964 affidavit stating that, having left the Depository at "about 12:25," she "did not see Lee Harvey Oswald at the time President Kennedy was shot." Chalmers also pointed out that Oswald, as reported by agents who were present during his interrogations, spoke variously of having lunched on either the first or second floor. But Mrs. Arnold's 1964 affidavit should not necessarily lead us to doubt her 1978 account. When Kennedy was shot, Arnold was outside the Depository. The 1964 affidavit does not cover what she may have seen before leaving the building. The author found Mrs. Arnold credible when he spoke with her in 1978. On contacting her again in 1993, it emerged that she had been much harassed as a result of publicity following publication of the original edition of this book. Nevertheless, speaking through her husband, she confirmed that her version of events remained the same as in 1978. (Letter to author from Associate Professor James Chalmers, April 20, 1993; int. Mr. Arnold, 1993; and see Sanders & 1964 affidavit, CE 1381.)

93 Haste by FBI: *The Secret Life of J. Edgar Hoover* by Anthony Summers; New York: Pocket Books, 1994; pp. 367, 519.

Rowland: II.169, 183(Arnold Rowland); VI.181, 185 (Barbara Rowland).

94 Motorcade approaching at 12:15 p.m.: XVII.460; XXI.390, 911.

Mrs. Arnold's leaving time: XXII.635 (Baker); XXII.656 (Johnson); XXII.671 (Rachey); XXII.645 (Dragoo); Brennan: III.142 (Brennan).

Brennan at lineup: Report, p. 145 (see also for both Brennan comments to FBI).

Brennan and "Communists": III.148 (Brennan).

Eyesight: III.147, 157 (Brennan).

Brennan and "no recoil": III.154 (Brennan).

95   Brennan and "smoke in knoll area": III.211.

Report on Brennan: Report, p. 146.

Oswald's brown shirt: XXIII.417; XXVI.445; II.250; III.257; CD 1405; *Life* magazine, October 2, 1964, p. 8; (pictured in color) Model and Groden, *op. cit.*, p. 137.

Oswald's "reddish" shirt: Report, pp. 605, 613, 622, 626.

Policeman on shirts: III.263; III.257 (Baker).

Note 16: An analysis of a film made by a citizen named Charles Bronson (reported in *Dallas Morning News*, November 27,1978) suggested that (at 12:24 p.m.) one of the moving figures on the sixth floor wore "purplish red" upper clothing. Oswald claimed during his questioning that he had changed his shirt at his roominghouse after leaving the Depository and before his arrest. He said, according to reports of his interrogation, that the shirt he discarded was "reddish-colored" or "red." No such shirt was ever traced. So far as is known, he owned only brown, light brown, and blue shirts (XVI.515). What's more, he was remembered as wearing a tan shirt by a neighbor who saw him leave for work on the day of the assassination (II.250). Yet Officer Baker's testimony (III.263, 257) does seem to corroborate Oswald's statement that he had changed into a darker shirt. It is not really clear what color shirt Oswald wore to work that day. While the matter remains unresolved, it was evidently not white or light-colored—and that is the color clothing reported by most of those observing a window gunman. (The shirt Oswald was wearing when arrested is preserved at the National Archives.)

Rowland on shirt: II.171.

Brennan: III.145.

96   Clerks: VI.194 (Fischer); VI.203 (Edwards); also XXIV.207, 208.

Mrs. Walther: interview with Earl Golz, November 1978 (in line with early statement, XXIV.522).

Baker: III.244– (Baker).

97   *Note 17*: Baker himself initially wrote in his statement

(XXVI.3076) that he "saw a man standing in the lunch-room *drinking a Coke* [author's emphasis]." He subsequently crossed out "drinking a Coke." One of the details announced by Police Chief Curry was that Oswald was seen by Baker and the building superintendent, Roy Truly, carrying a Coke (Leo Sauvage in *Commentary*, *op. cit.*, p. 56). If that were not so, it is hard to see how such a precise detail arose in the first place. Yet Baker and Truly ended up saying Oswald had nothing in his hand when they met him (Report, p. 151). The question is important to the issue of whether Oswald could have got down from the sixth floor to encounter Baker and Truly when he did. Even without a pause to obtain a Coke, it would have been a close shave. If Oswald purchased and started drinking a Coke by the time of the encounter with the policeman, then the known time frame is stretched to bursting point—some would say beyond. (Oswald himself, incidentally, told the chief of Homicide he was "drinking a Coca-Cola when the officer came in.") (Report, p. 600.) In this author's opinion, the balance of the evidence suggests he was.

A relatively new book, which the author received only as this edition went to press, is relevant to the timing of Oswald's descent to the lunchroom. In *The Girl on the Stairs*, author Barry Ernest examined the account of a Book Deposi-tory witness named Victoria Adams. Adams claimed she and a colleague hurried down the stairs from the fourth floor without seeing or hearing Oswald making the same descent. The crucial factor, the *exact* time they actually went down the stairs, however, remains unclear. Citing the evidence of other testimony and contemporary film footage, Gary Mack, today the curator of the Sixth Floor Museum in Dal-las, believes Adams descended the stairs *before* Oswald—and that this explains why the women did not see him. (Barry Ernest, *The Girl on the Stairs*, Gretna, LA: Pelican, 2013, Mack corr., 2013)

Reconstructions: For extensive discussion, see Roffman, *op. cit.*, p. 201–; Meagher, *op. cit.*, p. 70–; (Assassinations Committee, 1979) HSCA Report, p. 601n123.

President late: Report, p. 3; XXII.613– (and see especially 616); Report, p. 643.

98 Oswald asked workmate: III.201 (Jarman).

Curry: *VF*, December 1994.

99 *Note 18*: The two newsmen who recalled being directed to a phone were Robert MacNeil, then a reporter for NBC, and Pierce Allman, then program director for WFAA TV. Both men remembered the encounter but did not recall the individual who pointed out the phone well enough to say he had been Oswald. (crew-cut man: Report, p. 629; MacNeil: "Covering the Kennedy Assassination," MSNBC; Allman: Wardlaw to Gannaway, February 18, 1964, Dallas PD, Criminal Intelligence files, Box 13, www.jfk.ci.dallas.tx.us, CD 354.)

Supervisor: III.279 (Mrs. Reid).

Foreman: XXIV.226 (Shelley).

Bus ticket: IV.211 (Fritz); VII.173 (Sims).

Taxi driver: II.260 (Whaley).

6. The Other Murder

101 Alexander quoted: int. 1977.

Roberts: VI.438; VII.439.

102 Check on cars: XXV.909; XXIV.460.

Oswald name crops up: Report, p. 9 (in Hill 1:51 p.m. radio report); XXI.40, 397; (Beckley address discovered after 2:00 p.m.) Report, p. 601.

103 Order to Tippit at 12:45: IV.179 (Curry); XXIII.844.

Tippit call at 12:54: IV.179, 184 (Curry); VII.75 (Putnam); XXIII.849–.

Call to Tippit at 1:00 p.m.: XVII.406 (precise time pinpointed by private study of police tapes).

Tippit call at 1:08 p.m.: XVII.407.

Citizen's call at 1:16 p.m.: XVII.408.

Report scenario: Report, pp. 6, 7, 165.

104 Markham according to Report: Report, pp. 167, 168.

Markham statements: III.305–, 321–342; VII.409–.

Death instantaneous: Report, p. 165; (Benavides testimony) VI.446–.

Crowd: III.336, 354; VI.448–.

105 Ammonia: IV.212 (Fritz).

Note 1: Attention has been drawn to the fact that one witness in the Tippit case, Warren Reynolds, was shot in the head two days after telling the FBI he could not identify Oswald. There was no apparent cause for the shooting. Reynolds recovered and later agreed he thought the fleeing gunman had been Oswald after all. Within a week or two of the Reynolds shoot-ing, a key witness in that affair was found dead in a police cell, having apparently hanged herself. She had herself earlier mentioned an association with Jack Ruby and his club. The brother of a Tippit witness was shot dead, and many assumed it was a matter of mistaken identity. While these incidents arouse speculation, there is nothing evidentiary to link them to the Tippit or Kennedy killings. However, it is clear they were inadequately investigated. (Injured witness: XXV.731; XI.437; XI.435; dead brother, (Eddy Benavides): Meagher, op. cit., p. 299).

Ball: debate in Beverly Hills, California, December 4, 1964. Lane, op. cit., p. 161.

Clemons: interview filmed by Mark Lane, March 3, 1966; interview report by George and Patricia Nash, New Leader, November 12, 1964; notes of int. by Earl Golz and Tom John-son, 1965.

106 Wright: Nash interview—New Leader, November 12, 1964.

Note 2: Myers's book is With Malice: Lee Harvey Oswald and the Mur-der of Officer J. D. Tippit, Milford, MI: Oak Cliff Press, 1998.

Best evidence/forensic: See Myers, op. cit., p. 250– & previous edition of this book (New York: Marlowe, 1998), p. 69–.

107 Travel possible in time frame?: *ibid.*, p. 72–.

108 Alexander: ints. by author, December 1977 & August 1978.

Note 3: Alexander pointed out that the alleged assassin was close to U.S. Highway 67—R. L. Thornton Freeway—when he supposedly clashed with the policeman, and may have been returning from it. Highway 67 is the route to Red Bird Airport, then a field for small aircraft on the outskirts of Dallas. Alexander speculated (interview with this author, 1978) that Oswald may have expected to be picked up and taken to the airport, but that something went wrong at the rendezvous, and the getaway failed.

109 Record shop: Hurt, *op. cit.*, p. 163–, but see Bugliosi, *op. cit.*, p. 583–.

Mechanic: HSCA XII.37, 39, 40.

Note 4: The author is indebted to researcher William Kelly for his summary of this episode. Kelly points out that the owner of the car in question, aside from being a friend of Tippit, worked for Collins Radio in nearby Richardson, Texas. That same month, Collins Radio had received publicity in connection with its lease of a ship, the *Rex*, involved in a CIA operation to land commandos in Cuba. Alleged assassin Oswald had been introduced to a Collins executive, retired Admiral Chester Bruton, by George de Mohrenschildt. (Research supplied to the author by William Kelly; and see De Mohrenschildt references in this book.)

HSCA on Tippit: HSCA Report, p. 59–.

110 *Note 5*: The Mafia associate was John Martino—see index under "Martino"—his claims are covered in Chapter 24. Additionally, a Dallas police source was years later to report a allegation he said had been made to him by Max A. Long, a sometime boxer and "motel-bar operator" with a criminal arrest record. When Oswald killed Tippit—outside 404 East 10th Street—Long said, he had been on his way to a "safe house" at 324 East 10th. Long said he knew Jack Ruby and other figures who have been linked to the assassination.

He has been linked, under variants of his name, to two addresses on 10th Street—the homes at 324 and 317. The report was turned over to the FBI, but it is not clear that it ever received serious attention. Long died in 1980. (Myers, p. 360, citing FBI 62-109060-9866, August 24, 1977)

7. A Sphinx for Texas

111 LeCarre: quoted in Arthur Schlesinger article, *Cigar Aficionado*, November/December, 1998.

Curry: int. 12/77.

Alexander: int. 12/77.

112 Oswald motive: Report, pp. 421, 423; HSCA Report p. 61–.

Robert: *VF*, December 1994.

113 Oswald on JFK: Report, p. 627, report of Secret Service Inspector Kelley;(Marina) HSCA II.252, 217, 209; McMillan, *op. cit.*, pp. 194, 350; HSCA XII.361, 413; (Martello) X.60; (eve of murder) HSCA XII.413, 331; *VF*, December 1994.

114 *Note 1*: An exception—the only exception so far as the author knows—was Volkmar Schmidt, an oil industry geologist who met Oswald at a social occasion in Dallas early 1963. Thirty years later, he said in an interview that Oswald had been: "extremely critical of President Kennedy, and he was just obsessed with what America did to support this invasion [of Castro's Cuba] at the Bay of Pigs, obsessed with his anger towards Kennedy." In an FBI interview within a week of the assassination, however, Schmidt had recalled nothing like this. On the contrary, he had asserted that—in a conversation on politics that lasted several hours and during which Oswald appeared "very frank"—Oswald "did not speak of President Kennedy or his policies." Against that background, no credence can be given to Schmidt's later claim. (Epstein, *Legend*, p. 483–, Gus Russo, *Live by the Sword*, Baltimore, MD: Bancroft, 1998, p. 120, citing int. for *Frontline* program; (int. by FBI) int. Volkmar Schmidt,

November 29, 1963, FBI 105-82555, Oswald HQ file, Section 22) Oswald to president of Bar Association: VII.329 (Nichols).

Abt: report of Inspector Kelley, Report, p. 627; www.spartacus.schoolnet.co.uk/USAabtJ.htm

115 Robert Oswald: I.468; (diary) XVI.901.

Johnson: CBS News, "The American Assassins," Part II, November 26, 1975.

116 Warren: *New York Times*, February 5, 1964, p. 19.

FBI spokesman: int Inspector Hoynden, December 1977.

117 HSCA stymied: author's ints. with HSCA sources, 1978–1979; HSCA Report, p. 490 (end of dissent by Congressman Dodd).

Johnson: Warren Commission memorandum by lawyer Melvin Eisenberg, February 17, 1964.

Marina Oswald mysteries: see Chapter 10, "Mischief from Moscow."

Russell: Warren Commission Executive Session transcript for January 21, 1964.

118 Meller: CD 950, interview of Meller by Dallas police officers Hellingshausen and Parks, February 17, 1964.

Moore: ints. (widow) Jeanne de Mohrenschildt, 1978 (she corroborated her husband's version of Moore's remarks); and George de Mohrenschildt interview with Edward Epstein, March 29, 1977, *Legend, op. cit.*, p. 186.

Kantor and Hendrix: Kantor, *op. cit.*, p. 198–; *El Paso Herald-Post*, September 24, 1963; (Homestead) "Bayo-Pawley Affair," *Soldier of Fortune*, Spring 1976; and see Hendrix references, Thomas Powers, *op cit.*

119 Army Intelligence: memo attached to FBI document 105-82555 (unrecorded; original in 62-109060-811); *Dallas Morning News*, March 19, 1978, quoting FBI documents; HSCA Report, p. 221.

120 Preyer: int., 1978.

HSCA on (lack of) agency involvement: HSCA Report, p. 2.

Note 2: The "serious allegation" referred to is the charge by a former anti-Castro exile leader that he saw his American Intelligence case officer—a who used the cover name "Maurice Bishop"—with Oswald shortly before the assassination. The same officer allegedly attempted to build up a false story that Oswald had been in touch with the Cuban Embassy in Mexico City. The episode will be dealt with later in the book. (See also Index references to "Bishop.")

Chief counsel's comment that the allegation remained "undiscredited": HSCA IV.476.

Warren Report on agencies and Oswald: Report, p. 327.

Dulles: Warren Commission Executive Session, January 27, 1964.

121 Newsman's question: contemporary news film.

Combest: int., August 1978.

122 *Note 3*: In the 1978 interview. Combest also said that Oswald accompanied his headshaking with "a definite clenched-fist salute." This cannot be taken as good evidence of a political gesture, given Oswald's condition at that moment. It may indeed have been an expression of pain. Combest said nothing about the "salute" in his statements on Warren Commission testimony (XII.185 and XIX.350).

Artificial respiration: Manchester, *op. cit.*, p. 604.

Oswald prints taken: XVII.308; *Fort Worth Press*, November 25, 1963.

II. OSWALD: Maverick or Puppet?

8. Red Faces

125 Oswald quote: XVI.817; letter to Robert Oswald, November 26, 1959 (from Moscow).

"Communist conspiracy": William Alexander, an Assistant District Attorney, quoted by Manchester, *op. cit.*, p. 326.

Colby recalled: Colby memo, September 6, 1975, no. 1188-1000, JFK files, Box 60, Folder F1, NARA.

126 Nosenko: Epstein, *Legend, op. cit.*, p. 11.

Schweiker: int. 1978.

Epstein book: Epstein, *Legend, op. cit.*

127 Angleton: quoted by Seymour Hersh in *New York Times Magazine*, June 25, 1978, from Angleton testimony to Senate Intelligence Committee, 1975 (Book III, 1976).

Young Oswald & Communism: (statements of mother) interview of Marguerite Oswald in *New York Times*, December 10, 1963; XIX.319; (high school friend) VIII.18—William Wulf; (second friend) HSCA IX.109; (writing to Socialist Party) XXV.140.

Note 1: The Oswald letter to the Socialist Party, which included the statement "I am a Marxist and have been studying Socialist principles for well over fifteen months," appeared in an unusual way. An FBI report of December 18, 1963, less than a month after the assassination, states that it had turned up that day "during routine processing of inactive files of the Socialist Party of America," stored in the library at Duke University, North Carolina. Although there is no concrete reason to doubt the letter's authenticity, it is odd that this document was discovered among hundreds of other papers, quite by chance, so soon after the assassination. It became the documentary proof that Oswald was a budding left-winger even before his enlistment in the Marine Corps (XXV.140). For further discussion of the origins of Oswald's ostensible Socialism, see Chapter 17, "Blind Man's Bluff in New Orleans."

128 Interest in Marines: Report, p. 384.

"Confidential": XIX.665.

Atsugi period dealt with in Warren Report, Appendix XIII.

129 Officer's comment: Captain Gajewski, Epstein, *op cit.*

Legend, op. cit., p. 68.

Oswald as crew chief: VIII.291, Lieutenant J. E. Donovan testimony.

Oswald intelligence: Gator Daniels, int. cited in Epstein, *Legend, op. cit.*, p. 70.

130 U-2: primary sources are Gary Powers, *Operation Overflight*; Harry Rositzke, *CIA's Secret Operations*; Fletcher Prouty, *The Secret Team*; eds. Gary Powers & Harold Berman, *The Trial of the U-2*, Chicago: World Publications, 1960; David Wise & Thomas Ross, *The Espionage Establishment*. Edward Epstein in *Legend* provides the best detail of the U-2 operation at Atsugi, and Oswald's familiarity with it.

Note 2: In a 2008 book on Oswald and activity at Atsugi, former Marine Corps intelligence officer Jack Swike—who served at Atsugi during approximately the same period as Oswald—asserted that the base indeed housed a nuclear facility. (www.themissingchapter.com/leeharveyoswald1.html, referring to Jack Swike, *The Missing Chapter: Lee Harvey Oswald in the Far East*, www.createspace.com, 2008).

131 Donovan talk with Oswald: as reported in Epstein, *Legend*, *op. cit.*, p. 280–282. The conversation took place not at Atsugi but at the Cubi Point base in the Philippines.

Picture-taking: Epstein, *Legend*, *op. cit.*, p. 69.

Affair with hostess and subsequent liaisons: Epstein, *Legend*, *op. cit.*, p. 71–.

Note 3: Among other possibilities, Oswald may have had additional money from black market activity. A former marine who served with him is cited to that effect in the 2008 book cited in *Note 2*, *supra*.; www.themissingchapter.com/leeharveyoswald1.html.

132 Self-inflicted shooting and quarrel incidents: Report, p. 683–.

Taiwan: Report, p. 684; shots in wood: Epstein, *Legend*, *op. cit.*, p. 81.

Note 4: In his book *Missing Chapter*, mentioned in an earlier note to this chapter, former Atsugi officer Jack Swike asserted—contrary to the Warren Report account—that Oswald did not go to Taiwan. (www.themissingchapter.com/leeharveyoswald1.html)

Eurasian: Epstein, *Legend*, *op. cit.*, p. 83 & see Report, p. 684

133 Santa Ana and Donovan: VIII.290, 297, 300.

Russian enthusiasm in California: Report, p. 685 & and related documents.

Name on jacket: VIII.316.

Thornley: James/Wardlaw, *op. cit.*, p. 5; (on Marxism) Report, p. 685.

134 Delgado: VIII.241.

Senior Angleton aide: Rocca memorandum to Rockefeller Commission on CIA activities within the United States, May 30, 1975; *op. cit.*

Note 5: The Angleton aide was Raymond Rocca, a longtime senior colleague who—Angleton's biographer wrote—"led the effort to reconstruct the past." (Tom Mangold, *Cold Warrior*, London: Simon & Schuster, 1991, p. 38).

135 Oswald in spring 1959: Report, p. 688.

Mother's injury: Robert Oswald, *op. cit.*, p. 93; XVI.337.

HSCA on Marines record and discharge: HSCA Report, p. 219–.

Oswald brother: Robert Oswald, *op. cit.*, p. 95.

136 Oswald U.S.A.-Soviet Union trip: Report, p. 690. The Warren Report was in error on details of this journey, discrepancies that left the Assassinations Committee at a loss in 1979. This is covered in the next chapter.

"De Luxe": int. Rimma Shirokova, Moscow, 1993.

Easy access and Soviets: HSCA Report, pp. 212, and 212–221.

Note 6: The possibility of a Stockholm visit was first raised in a report three days after the assassination (November 25, 1963) in *Dagens Nyheters*, the leading Swedish newspaper. It reported as fact that Oswald "passed through Sweden . . . on his way to the Soviet Union." The article stated that "after an unsuccessful attempt to get a Russian visa in Helsinki, he went to Stockholm, where he rented a hotel room. Two days later, he was able to continue his journey to Moscow. That indicates the Russian Embassy gave him a visa." Jones Harris, an independent researcher, reported confirmation, from a CIA source, that Swedish intelligence confirmed the detour to Stockholm. There was nothing about it in the Warren Report, or in the HSCA Report in 1979.

CIA/State studies : XXVI.156, 165, 158; HSCA IV.241.

Moscow arrival: HSCA Report, p. 212.

Oswald at American Embassy: Report, p. 260.

Allegiance letter: Report, p. 261.

137 Oswald on giving Soviets information: Report, p. 748; XVIII.908.

McVickar reaction: XVIII.153–.

Associated with Communists: IX.242—testimony of George de Mohrenschildt.

Note 7: De Mohrenschildt, the Russian emigré who was to befriend Oswald in Texas after his return from the Soviet Union, said: "He [Oswald] told me that he had some contacts with the Communists in Japan, and they—that got him interested to go and see what goes on in the Soviet Union." Statements by de Mohrenschildt, however, must be read in the light of the evidence about de Mohrenschildt's background (see Chapter 11).

9. Cracks in the Canvas

138 Russell quote: conversation with researcher Harold Weisberg, 1970.

Delgado: VIII.242.

Block: int. by Epstein for *Legend*, p. 86.

139 Thornley: affidavit January 8, 1976.

140 Russian language: Report, p. 685; VIII.307; XIX.662 (took Russian test February 25, 1959).

Powers: VIII.275, 283; Epstein, *Legend, op. cit.*, p. 83.

Quinn episode: VIII.321—Roussell testimony; Quinn XXIV.430; VIII.293—Donovan testimony; int. of Quinn by Epstein, *Legend, op. cit.*, p. 87.

141 Executive session: transcript of Warren proceedings, January 27, 1964.

Self-inflicted wound: ints. former marines by Epstein, *Legend, op. cit.*, p. 283.

142 Taiwan to Atsugi: HSCA Report, p. 220 (citing Department of

Defense letter, 6/22/78); Folsom DE I.3; see also "From Dallas
to Watergate" by Peter Dale Scott, *Ramparts*, November 1973;
(Rhodes) quoted by Epstein in *Legend, op. cit.*, p. 81.

Medical record: IX.603; VIII.313–; XIX.601.

Doctor/"line of duty": int. Dr. Paul Deranian, 1979.

143   "Secret" clearance?: VIII.298 (Donovan); VIII.232 (Delgado);
      HSCA Report, p. 219 (HSCA); XI.84 (Thornley).

144   Marine report on clearance: XXIII.796 (Director of Personnel's
      report).

Oswald bank account: XXII.180.

Note 1: Doubt also surrounds how Oswald managed to cover the
considerable expenses he was to incur at times in the years to
come.

Report on Moscow trip: Report, p. 690.

Date stamps: XVIII.162.

145   Direct flight: XXVI.32.

Note 2: The UK/Finland travel anomaly over the years led to
speculation that Oswald traveled from London to Helsinki by
military aircraft. That seems unlikely, not least because military involvement would have made nonsense of the cover of an
otherwise civilian trip. The House Assassinations Committee,
after intensive research, declared itself "unable to determine
the circumstances regarding Oswald's trip from London to Helsinki." Though the anomaly has never been resolved by official
investigation, one independent researcher has surmised that
Oswald could have reached Helsinki by commercial airplane—
in the time available—by a zigzag route. ("unable": HSCA
Report, p. 211; researcher: "The Man Who Wasn't There," by
Chris Mills, article in *Dallas '63*, British journal)

Torni/Kurki: Report, p. 690.

Note 3: After the assassination, Oswald's mother, Marguerite,
would declare her belief that her son had been "an intelligence
agent of the U.S. government." Though Mrs. Oswald frequently overdramatized, her claim that Oswald was involved
with American intelligence does not stand entirely alone.

In 1978, a former CIA finance officer who had once served in Tokyo, James Wilcott, would testify to the Assassinations Committee that he had been told by a CIA colleague that Oswald had been "recruited from the military for the express purpose of becoming a double-agent assignment [sic] to the USSR." Wilcott alleged that the colleague told him the cryptonym," or code designation, assigned to Oswald. The CIA, Wilcott asserted, had had some kind of special "handle" on Oswald, perhaps because it was known that he had "murdered someone or committed some serious crime." Though the Assassinations Committee staff found Wilcott's story inconsistent, and though his evident antipathy toward the CIA harmed his credibility, the gist of his claim about an Oswald link to a murder or crime perhaps cannot be entirely ruled out. A Marines guard, Martin Shrand, did die in suspicious circumstances—shot dead with his own weapon—on the same base as Oswald in the Philippines. Though the death was eventually ruled to have been accidental, one marine—D. P. Camerata—was to refer to having heard "a rumor to the effect that Oswald had been in some way responsible for the death." On the other hand, former Marines officer Jack Swike—who has been cited in the notes to the previous chapter—wrote in his 2008 book that Oswald was not in the vicinity when Schrand was shot. (Marguerite Oswald: XXVI.40; and *A Citizen's Dissent* by Mark Lane, p. 9 [see Bibliography]; Wilcott: *New York Times*, March 27, 1978; *Clandestine America*, II.3; HSCA Report, p. 198–; Schrand: Report p. 664; VIII.316; VJ.II.281; XXV.864; Epstein, *Legend, op. cit.*, p. 75; "rumor": VIII.316, statement of D. P. Camerata, & see also HSCA XI.542; Swike: www://themissingchapter.com/leeharveyoswald1.html.)

McCone/Helms: V.120.

Assurances to HSCA: HSCA Report, p. 198.

146   Helms and Castro plots: *Sen. Int. Cttee. Assassination Plots:*, pp. 101, 103.

Senator Morgan exchange: Sen. Int. Cttee., *Performance of Intelligence Agencies*, p. 70.

"Untidy world": HSCA IV.172.

Helms conviction: *New York Times*, November 25, 1977.

147 "honorable men": Richard Helms, "Global Intelligence and the Democratic Society," speech to American Society of Newspaper Editors, April 14, 1971, cited in "Richard Helms: The Intelligence Professional Personified, by David Robarge of CIA history staff, www.cia.gov/library/center-for-the-study-of-intelligence/csi-publication/csi-st.

Angleton: FBI memorandum, Sullivan to Belmont, May 13, 1964.

Angleton/Dulles: Sen. Int. Cttee., *Performance of Intelligence Agencies*, p. 69.

Dulles coaching officers: Murphy to DDP, CIA document 657–831, April 13, 1964, www.maryferrell.org.

148 "201" file: CIA Information Coordinator letter to the author, February 15, 1979, and to James Tague, August 18 1977; int. John Newman, 1995.

"201" defined: HSCA Report, p. 200, and independent sources.

"201" opening: CIA document 1187-136, Chief Counterintelligence Staff to Executive Assistant to Deputy Director of Plans (later styled Operations), September 18, 1975 (somewhat mangled, it seems, in HSCA Report, p. 200–); int. John Newman, 1995.

149 Snyder: (according to CIA and Snyder) HSCA Report p. 214–; see also CIA document 609-786 (p. 2), which says Snyder joined CIA in 1949 and "apparently resigned" in 1950; *Who's Who in the CIA*, published by Julius Mader, Berlin; 1968 (leftist publication); and see John Newman, *op. cit.*, References.

Hallett: int. by Robbyn Swan, 1994.

"Would not always": HSCA Report, p. 197.

Harvey notes: released to the Assassinations Committee, 1978; see HSCA Report, p. 204.

150 *Note 4*: The extract is from Harvey's files on "ZR/RIFLE," a CIA draft plan for "a capability to perform assassinations." Though the files included proof of CIA links with professional assassins, there is no evidence that the material has any relevance to the Kennedy assassination. (Harvey notes released to the Assassinations Committee, 1978 & HSCA Report, p. 204).

Dulles/Boggs exchange: Warren Commission Executive Session, January 27, 1964.

HSCA & Military intelligence possibility: HSCA Report, p. 224.

151   Navy reaction: VIII.298, testimony of Lieutenant Donovan.

Note 5: The Assassinations Committee received information suggesting that the Marine Corps took a hitherto unknown interest in Oswald after the President's death. The Committee was informed by former Marines navigator Larry Huff that—in December 1963 and early 1964—he took part in transport operations involving a team of military CID investigators. Huff, who retained personal logs for the period, said the group of about a dozen investigators were flown to Japan, en route to the Atsugi base where Oswald had once served. Huff said he learned from his passengers that the purpose was to investigate Oswald's activities at Atsugi. When he picked the group up to take them back to base later, they told him something of their investigation and gave him sight of their report, which was, Huff said, marked "Secret—For Marine Corps Eyes Only." It contained a psychological evaluation of Oswald that concluded the alleged killer "was incapable of committing the assassination alone." Huff also believed that a similar military team had been dispatched to Dallas. The Committee could find no trace of the supposed report. Late in its research, however, the Committee obtained confirmation from another crew member that the flights to and from Japan had taken place. The Committee left the matter unresolved. (HSCA XI.541).

"Damage assessment" and defections/Fox:
Epstein, *Legend, op. cit.,* pp. 102, 366.

Rash of defectors: HSCA XII.437–; and correspondence between Hugh Cumming, *op cit.*

Director of Intelligence at State Department, and Richard Bissell (CIA Deputy Director for Plans), October–November 1960, and attachments.

Note 6: The Rand employee was Robert Webster, a plastics expert who defected after working at an American exhibition in Moscow. He had been employed by the Rand Development Corporation, an entity purportedly separate from the better known CIA-funded Rand Corporation.

There are parallels between the Soviet odysseys of Webster and Oswald. Webster told U.S. officials of his intention to defect less than two weeks before Oswald did the same. Webster, also a former U.S. Navy man, had a relationship with a Soviet woman thought to have been linked to the KGB. The Soviet wife Oswald married was also suspected of having intelligence connections. Webster left the USSR, apparently disillusioned, a fortnight before Oswald.

There are CIA and FBI files, meanwhile, on another American, Marvin Kantor, who was in Russia at the same time as Oswald. Kantor spent time in 1958 and 1959 in Minsk, where Oswald also lived while in the Soviet Union. One of Kantor's friends there, he said later, had been a young man named Igor (LNU), son of a Soviet army general. When Oswald was in Minsk, he, too, had a friend—Pavel Golovachev—whose father was a Soviet army general. Years later, reportedly, it emerged that he had been a KGB informant. (Webster: see sources for "defectors," above; Rand: Canfield & Weberman, *op. cit.*, p. 24–; author's consultation Peter Dale Scott and Scott's unpublished ms., "The Dallas Conspiracy," 11.11, CD 5.259, McMillan, *op. cit.*, p. 107; Kantor: Memo to Director, March 2, 1965, CIA Segregated collection, Reel 44, Folder J, CIA document 1004-400. Golovachev is mentioned in Oswald's "Historic Diary").

152 Otepka: Otepka interview, 1971, reported in Fensterwald/Ewing, *op. cit.*, p. 230.

10. Mischief from Moscow

153 "A Communist": Lenin, Collected Works, Vol. XVII.

Oswald reading disability (expert opinion): XXVI.812–.

"Historic Diary" excerpt: XVI.94; XXIV.333.

154 *Note 1*: The Warren Commission concluded that Oswald wrote the "Diary" but did not start writing until he arrived in Minsk (Report, p. 691). E. J. Epstein (*Legend*), citing handwriting analysis and other factors, concluded that the "Diary," was put together after the dates described. HSCA experts' conclusions, XII.236. Marina Oswald said in 1978 (XII.391) that Oswald would write several days in a row or sometimes skip for a week or so.

indicating deception: XII.452.

Note 2: As this edition went to press, the author learned of— but was unable to give full attention to—a lengthy study of Oswald's Soviet period by Canadian author Peter Vronsky. It is evidently the result of much research and original interviewing. (Vronsky, "Lee Harvey Oswald in Russia" website).

Hospital records: XVIII.450.

Shirokova: int., Moscow, 1993.

Note 3: In the "Historic Diary," Oswald wrote of an "elderly American" at the hospital who was distrustful of Oswald for being evasive about why he was in Moscow. Though the FBI was able to check this reference—because in those days so very few Americans passed through Moscow—the only older American who had then been at the hospital was certain he had not encountered Oswald, or any other American. ("Elderly American": "Historic Diary" entry for October 26, 1959; CIA document 1168-432-5 and related documents. As to the Soviet hospital record as released, the Assassinations Committee noted that the signatures of Soviet officials on documents concerning Oswald were all illegible. One of the hospital documents related to Oswald's "suicide attempt" is dated April 25, 1953 (HSCA XII.451–, 494).

Psychiatrist recalled: int. Dr. Lydia Ivanova Mikhailina, Moscow, 1993 & her later considered commentary on file.

155 Intourist guides: Report, p. 260.

Other defector: Epstein, *Legend, op. cit.*, p. 295.

Note 4: Oswald was interviewed in his hotel room on November 16, 1959, by an American reporter (Report, p. 696), and at the end of November, the U.S. Embassy informed the State Department (Report, p. 750) that he had left the hotel "within the last few days." According to the Soviet record, as presented to the Warren Commission (XVIII.404), Oswald was in Moscow until January 4. Oswald may have been taken somewhere else before being moved to Minsk. In his own notes about his stay in Russia, he says he started work in Minsk in June 1960. This would dovetail with a report by a Soviet citizen who walked into the British Embassy in Moscow after the assassination. The citizen (whose name the author withholds) told British and U.S. diplomats that in April–May 1960 he saw Oswald, under KGB control, in the city of Gorky. He also alleged that he knew Marina Oswald to be attached to the KGB. Other, wilder claims by this individual threw doubt on his credibility. But there might be some truth to the Gorky aspect of the story. It has been reported that there was a KGB spy school in Gorky, notably by George Carpozi, the author of *Red Spies in Washington* (New York: Simon and Schuster, 1968, p. 12), who stated: "Most prospective intelligence agents are sent to the notorious Marx-Engels Institute in Gorky." (For Soviet citizen's report, see XXVI.735–; CD 1378; CD 1443; for Oswald's time of starting work in Minsk, see XVI.287.)

"after a certain time": XVI.121.

156 Minsk/ "living big": "Historic Diary," XVI.99 & photographs of life in Russia recovered after assassination.

Marina sketch: I.84; XXII.740.

Meetings at dances: XVI.102; "Historic Diary" entries, March 1961.

Subsequent courtship and marriage: Report, p. 703; (proposal)
XXII.750; XVIII.604; HSCA XII.354.

157 Warren Commission doubt: transcript of proceedings of Executive Session of Warren Commission, January 27, 1964.

Marina on husband's innocence: *Life* magazine, November 29, 1963.

"fateful rifle": I.119—testimony of Marina Oswald.

not sure husband's gun: I.119 and V.611—testimony of Marina Oswald.

Walker allegation: 1.16—testimony of Marina Oswald.

Nixon allegation: V.387—testimony of Marina Oswald; see also Newman, *op. cit.*, p. 349; Report, p. 189.

"he is not guilty": Ernst Titovets, *Oswald Russian Episode*, Minsk: MonLitera, 2010, pp. 417, 451n83.

Russell: proceedings of Executive Session of Warren Commission, January 27, 1964.

158 Redlich: HSCA XI.126 (reproduction of Warren Commission memo from Redlich to Chief Counsel Rankin, February 28, 1964).

Introduction: XVI.102 (entry for March 17, 1961); (biography) McMillan, *op. cit.*, p. 59; I.90–; XXII.745, 750, 267; XXIII. 402; HSCA XII.324, 351; HSCA II.208; and Warren I.88.

Titovets remembered: Titovets, *op. cit.*, 219–.

159 Uncle: XXII.745 and I.90; (rank) HSCA XII.323. The uncle was Ilya Prusakov.

Leaving first job: Report, p. 703; CIA doubts—Epstein, *Legend, op. cit.*, p. 304.

Marina at "Rest Home": XXII.745.

Name and address: CIA document 624-823 (Appendix C).

Note 5: The other American defector was Robert Webster, who had interesting parallels to Oswald. See Chapter 9, *Note 6.* Research in 1993, when Russian became open to journalists, located the man who had lived at the Leningrad address in Marina's address book. He said he did not remember Webster, but his brother—who still lived there—did recall the American. (Robbyn Swan ints., Russia, 1993).

"Prostitution": Titovets, p. 244–, 438n7 & see Norman Mailer, *Oswald's Tale*, London: Little, Brown, 1995, p. 156, author's conv. Mailer.

160   "Bugged": Titovets, p. 191–.

Russian press: *ibid.*, p. 195, citing *Izvestia*, August 8, 1992.

Nosenko: WC documents 434 & 451, released in 1975, from related Commission memoranda and from HSCA Report, pp. 101–, HSCA II.436, 453, 499, 517, 525, III.624, HSCA XII.475, 585–. See also full-length study by Edward Epstein in *Legend, op. cit*; article by Jack Nelson in the *Los Angeles Times*, March 28,1976; and John Barron, *op. cit.*, p. 452. The author also drew on his own conversations with James Angleton in 1976 and 1978, & lengthier reporting on Nosenko in the previous edition of this book (Marlowe, 1998). Additional background from Nosenko presentation of HSCA Chief Counsel Blakey, HSCA 11.436 (and attached documents); and HSCA XII.475–.

161   *Note 6:* The other Soviet defector was Major Anatoli Golitsin. (see Nosenko sourcing above).

Note 7: Defector Nosenko was closely confined and interrogated for years. He was over a period kept in a small windowless cell, deprived of sound and reading material. In one week in 1966, he had to submit to lie detector tests for 28½ hours. At last, in 1968, he was given a new name and paid some compensation.

"staggering": Richard Helms with William Hood, *A Look Over My Shoulder.* New York: Random House, 2003, p. 241.

Rositzke: XVIII.128.

Miler: int.by Edward Epstein, *Legend, op. cit.*, pp. 30, 278; (deputy chief) HSCA XII.624.

162   "odd": Helms, *op. cit.*, p. 241

"Absolutely unthinkable": John Hart (CIA-appointed witness to HSCA), HSCA II.487.

U-2: see sourcing *re* U-2 in Chapter 8, *supra.*

Note 8: Since the collapse of the Soviet Union, Sverdlovsk has reverted to its pre-revolutionary name, Ekaterinburg.

Powers had no doubt: *The Times* (London), April 20, 1971.

Note 9: The former deputy chief of the CIA's Soviet Bloc Division told the Assassinations Committee (HSCA XII.626) that it had not been proven Oswald knew much about the U-2. It has not been proven, yet this same witness agreed that Oswald worked with radar 500 yards from the U-2 runway, and his radar unit tracked the aircraft. Thus, said the witness, "certain things as to speed and altitude might have come to Oswald's attention." Those were exactly the details the Soviets were interested in at the time.

Theories about Oswald and the shootdown of the U-2 have proliferated over the past half century: that the plane was not—as long believed—at its high operating altitude when shot down, which might make information from Oswald irrelevant; that Oswald was manipulated into defecting because CIA Counterintelligence, suspecting the existence of a mole within the Agency, wished to gauge Soviet knowledge of the program; and, in the London *Times* in 2010, the suggestion that—whatever the circumstances of the U-2 shootdown—U.S. interpretation of the event was fogged by the accidental downing of a Soviet interceptor airplane. A recent article, which speculates that Oswald's 1959 defection was orchestrated by U.S. intelligence, cites information suggesting that the CIA knew the U-2 was vulnerable to shootdown and was planning to replace it. (See New York, Marlowe, edition of this book, 1998, p. 137–, *The Times* (London), May 1, 2010, Mark Prior,"Oswald and the U-2 Program, www.ctka.net/2012/LHO_U2_Mark_Prior. html.) Oswald's letter home: XVI.871—Oswald to brother Robert, February 1962.

163 May Day party: XVI.100—"Historic Diary."

Oswald reference to Moscow visit: X.203—Ofstein testimony; and CD 205.473.

Note 10: The later acquaintance was Dennis Ofstein, a later fellow employee in Dallas.

Soviets behind assassination?: (Warren) Report, pp. 21, 655–; (HSCA finding) HSCA Report, p. 108.

Semichastny: "Who Was Lee Harvey Oswald," transcript, Frontline, November 16, 1993, www.pbs.org, & author's int. 1993.

11. An "Intelligence Matter"

165   Eisenhower: quoted by Wise and Ross, *op. cit.*, 287.

Note 1: Oswald referred in his letter to an earlier one, along the same lines, that he said he had sent in December. The Embassy, in the shape of Consul Snyder, replied saying the earlier letter had never arrived.(Report, p. 701, HSCA XII.455).

166   Oswald "learned": XVIII.380; XVI.705, XVIII.137, 158.

Passport returned: V.284; XVIII.160–.

Lookout card: Report, pp. 722, 750.

Note 2: More astonishing, Oswald was to be issued a passport within twenty-four hours as late as 1963, when he applied for a new passport for yet more travel to Communist countries. (Report, p. 774.)

Strict control by FBI and State: Meagher, *op. cit.*, p. 335.

167   Johnson: ("thin line") John Newman, *op. cit.*, pp. 72, 78; (NANA/ continuing interest) *ibid.*, p. 61–, 538–, VF, December 1994, HSCA Report, p. 214, CIA documents April 5, 9 & 12, 1957; May 5, 1958; February 8, 1961; October 25, 1962; December 2, 1965; ("he hoped") XI.463, John Newman, *op. cit.*, p. 73–; ("I think") CIA Contact Report, December 11, 1962, www.maryferrell.org; ("Witting Collaborator") CIA documents, January 1975—released 1993; interviews by Robbyn Swan, 1994; ("official business") memo, Rosen to Belmont, November 23, 1963, FBI no. 105-82555.

Note 3: Interviewed on behalf of this author in 1994, Johnson—by then long since known by her married name, Priscilla Johnson McMillan—said: "My bottom line is that I never worked for the CIA. . . . I don't know what was in the mind of the person who put me down as a Witting Collaborator . . . [In Moscow] I had no way of knowing who in the American Embassy, say, worked for the CIA and who didn't." McMillan never knowingly discussed Oswald with the CIA, she maintained. (int. Robbyn Swan, 1994) In 1963, soon after the assassination, McMillan had early access to Marina Oswald and—after years of delay—published *Marina and Lee*, a book that portrayed Oswald as the lone assassin. (See Bibliography.)

Navy message: XVIII.116, 367; John Newman, *op. cit.* p. 446.

Minsk photographs: Report, p. 267–, XX.474 (Kramer Exhibits 1 & 2); XX.474; XI.212; II.212–; CIA document 614-261, March 20, 1964; CIA 948-927T; CD 859; CD 1022; CD 871; HSCA Report, pp. 198, 206, 630, HSCA XII.639; int. Rita Naman, June 1979; CD 859a, Dallas to Seattle, April 13, 1964, FBI 105-82555, www.maryferrell.org.

168 *Note 4*: According to the Oswald "Historic Diary," the defector returned to Minsk—following a visit to the U.S. Embassy in Moscow—on July 14, 1961, three weeks *before* the date of the tourists' first encounter with him in Moscow, which Naman said occurred on August 1. That day, according to Oswald's written account, he was in Minsk. Naman, however, was sure of her dates. This is an anomaly that, while it may be further evidence that the Oswald "Historic Diary" is bogus, does nothing to detract from the impression that Oswald's encounters with the tourists were not chance but planned ("Historic Diary": HSCA VIII.290).

169 *Note 5*: An hour before the meeting with Oswald in Minsk, Naman said, she was intensively questioned by an official in plain clothes who demanded to know the true purpose of the women's visit to Russia. While in Moscow, the women had given a copy of *Newsweek* to a man who told them he was a student—and the official accused Naman of speading anti-Soviet propaganda. Later, on crossing the Soviet border into Poland, the same official questioned the trio again. The women's car, Naman said, was "virtually taken apart" in a thorough search, and the women figured the searchers were looking for documents. This Soviet interest in the women may not be relevant to the Oswald story.

Note 6: This was a time when the CIA was running what it called its American Visitors Program, which enlisted the "cooperation, for limited purposes, of carefully selected persons traveling in the Soviet Union." In large part, the aim was to get information and photographs of Soviet places and installations. It seems possible, though, that the program was also used to make contact with human targets like defector Oswald.

Other vestigial evidence may indicate that someone in the United States, identity unknown, was in touch with Oswald while he was in the Soviet Union. One of his Minsk girlfriends, Ella German, recalled him having said in 1960 that he had been getting letters from "a cousin," who had sent him books. There was a cousin, Marilyn Murret, who was to be quoted in a 1964 newspaper as saying she knew in advance about Oswald's trip to Europe. Murret would tell the Assassinations Committee that, contrary to rumors to the contrary, she had never had links to the CIA nor, to her knowledge, ever worked for a government agency.

Ernst Titovets, the Minsk acquaintance cited in Chapter 11, kept two books Oswald had given him—as a farewell gift before leaving for home in 1962—which he said had been mailed to him by someone in the United States. The books were *The Power of Positive Thinking*, by Norman Vincent Peale, and *As A Man Thinketh*, by James Allen. Both had been inscribed on the flyleaf in longhand, but Oswald snipped out the inscriptions with a razor blade before giving the books to Titovets. (Visitors Program: HSCA Report, p. 198, Rositzke, *op. cit.*, p. 58; Murret: HSCA records on Marilyn Murret, released 1994, including January 16, 1978, report of Robert Buras, and transcript of the November 6, 1978, Murret depo-

sition for HSCA; also FBI documents, including letter from
Director to J. Lee Rankin of May 19,1964, Justice Department summary of May 7 and 22, 1964; Department of the Air
Force report of contact with John Pic, dated [month unclear]
16, 1962; Warren Commission testimony of Murret, May 6,
1964; and syndicated column of Paul Scott, as published in
the *Knoxville* [Tennessee] *Journal*, April 11, 1977; books: ints.
Ernst Titovetz, 1993–1994; and see Newman, *op. cit.*, p. 193–,
Titovets, op.cit., pp. 163, 322, XVI.155).

Colby: int. for CBS News, *The American Assassins*, November 26,
1975.

170 Davison expelled: HSCA Report, p. 215–; David Wise, *Molehunt*, New York: Random House, 1992, pp. 60, 120n; *The
Penkovskiy Papers*, New York: Avon Books, 1966, p. 381.

Davison in address book/Davison comments: CIA 1281-1024;
CD 87; CD 235; CD 409; CD 1115; CD 11; XIII.103; Wise &
Ross, *op. cit.*, p. 268 (see Bibliography), CIA report, file no.
61-01-04, HSCA, Record no.180-10147-10166.

Note 7: Penkovsky, who had spied for the CIA and Britain's MI6,
was executed by the Soviets in 1963. The address Dr. Davison
gave the Oswalds was in Atlanta, Georgia, where his mother
Natasha lived. Davison told the Assassinations Committee
his mother would welcome the Oswalds should they travel via
Atlanta on their way to Texas. Though at the time they met
Davison, there were apparently no plans for the Oswalds to
travel through Atlanta, their flight was in fact to make a stopover there en route to Texas. It appears to have been a brief
stop, however, allowing no time to leave the airport to visit
anyone. The author knows of no other information linking
the Oswalds to Atlanta. Oddly, though, George de Mohrenschildt, Oswald's later mentor in Dallas, was to write after
the assassination that the Warren Commission skimped full
investigation of "Lee's activities in *Atlanta* [author's empha-
sis], New Orleans, and Mexico City."

Another scrawled note in Oswald's address book, also presumably written in Moscow, reads: "K-42000, 384, 1-2 DINNER, Jelisavcic." Jelisavcic, research indicates, was Mikhailo Jelisavcic, the manager of American Express in Moscow. "K-42000" was his telephone number and "384" the number of the room at the Hotel Metropol that was his office. Oswald, of course, had reason to visit American Express—in connection with the imminent journey back to the West. Though American Express had reportedly been used as cover by U.S. intelligence in earlier years, and though documents suggest Jelisavcic was on good terms with U.S. Embassy officials, and though the FBI would years later probe the "possible compromise of Jelisavcic by Soviet intelligence," there is no basis for the notion that he worked for either U.S. or Soviet intelligence—as some have claimed. Oswald's scrawled "1-2 DINNER" may merely refer to the hour at which Jelisavcic would be absent from his office. Oswald's notebook also reflects contact with the Rotterdam American Express office during his forthcoming travel through Holland. (Atlanta route: XVI.616; XVIII.16; Davison's mother: XVI.37; XVI.50; brief stop?: I.330; *Tilley v. Delta Airlines*, February 1, 1966, http://sc.findacase.com (re. schedule of Delta flight); skimped: HSCA XII.250; Jelisavcic: CD 1115; Memorandum *re* addresses in Oswald address book, FBI file 62-117290 HSCA HQ Bulky file 456x6; SAC New York to Director, December 17, 1968, FBI Airtel, John Armstrong papers, Box 16, Book 2, Tab 20, Baylor University Archives; CIA Appendix C to Chron. of Oswald in USSR, Mary 26, 1964, p. 55; CD 680; Director to SAC New York, January 8, 1965, FBI 105-82555, Oswald HQ file, Section 224; American Express intelligence: AP, July 29, 2010, "The CIA's Temporarily Unavailable Records," National Security Archive, June 6, 2012)

171 Train journey: XVI.137, 144.

Helmstedt: XVIII.168; XVI.144, 147; research contributed by Sidney A. Martin; http://oswaldinholland.weblog.nl; Perry Vermeulen, *Lee Harvey Oswald, via Rotterdam naar Dallas*, Holland: Tirion Sport, 2008.

172 Accomodation: XVIII.615; I.101 (testimonies, U.S. Embassy

staff); Marina—HSCA 11.289, 310; HSCA XII.369 (Marina alternately spoken of Amsterdam and Rotterdam).

Executive session: transcript of proceedings of Warren Commission, January 27, 1964.

Holland research: author's 1993, drawing on CE 18, pp. 51, 42, 47; Vermeulen, *op. cit.*, http://oswaldinholland.weblog.nl.

173 *Maasdam* crossing: 1.101, (testimony, Marina Oswald); Report, p. 712; http://oswaldinholland.weblog.nl.

Note 8: The Oswalds were listed on the *Maasdam's* passenger list, though the Commission found no one who recalled having seen them on board. Oddly, Marina is on record as having said they "arrived in New York *by air* [author's emphasis] . . . stayed in some hotel in New York City for one day and then went by train to Texas [author's emphasis]." Though Marina spoke in the presence of two qualified translators, the anomaly—the author guesses—was probably the result of an error in translation. (ship's manifest, obtained by author, 1993; "*by air*": XXIII.407–Secret Service report of Marina Interviews, November 26–28, 1963)

174 Raikin: Report, p. 173.

American Friends: "From Dallas to Watergate" by Peter Dale Scott, *Ramparts*, November 1973.

Oswald & anti-Castro exiles: The reference is to 544 Camp Street, New Orleans. See Chapter 17, "Blind Man's Bluff in New Orleans."

Form Oswald signed: XIX.680.

175 ONI no action: John Newman, *op. cit.*, p. 264.

Not placed on list: XVII.801.

FBI security case: Report, p. 434.

FBI asked Oswald: Report, p. 434.

Declined polygraph: Dallas FBI office memorandum to HQ, July 10, 1962, Sen. Int. Cttee., *Performance of Intelligence Agencies*, p. 88.

case closed: Report, p. 435.

Note 9: There would be further contacts between Oswald and the FBI in the period leading up to the assassination, and the nature of his relationship with the Bureau—to be covered later in these pages—is clouded.

Fox: Epstein, *Legend*, *op. cit.*, p. 312.

176   *Note 10*: Webster has appeared earlier in these pages, in Chapter 9: *Note 6* and Chapter 10: *Note 5*. Other returning defectors questioned were Libero Ricciardelli, a World War II Air Force hero who returned from Russia with his family in 1963, and Bruce Davis, a soldier who had deserted from the U.S. Army in Germany. The Assassinations Committee Report found, however, that the CIA did not automatically contact returning defectors. Indeed, an Assassinations Committee study found that of twenty-two returnee defectors who returned in the relevant timeframe (out of an original list of 380) only four were interviewed by the CIA. (Ricciardelli/Davis: HSCA, XII.437, John Newman, *op. cit.*, p. 184; not automatically: HSCA Report, p. 209).

"Laying on interviews":Casasin to Haltigan, November 25, 1963, CIA, HSCA Record no. 104-10059-10181.

"REDWOOD"/ "KUJUMP": Research Aid: Cryptonyms and terms in Declassified CIA Files, www.nara.gov.

Note 11: Having previously been released with redactions, Casasin's memo was in released virtually in full in 1996. "Thomas Casasin" is a pseudonym, not a real name. The sense makes clear that the timeframe of the discussion by CIA officers was mid-1962—the Assassinations Committee accepted that a reference in the memo to "1960" was incorrect. Committee interviews located no other CIA employee who recalled the discussion, and found no evidence of Agency contact with Oswald. (redactions: HSCA IV.210; not real name: Memo for the Record, June 29, 1978, HSCA Record no. 104-10066-10201; not "1960"/no other: HSCA Report, p. 208)

177   Deneselya: HSCA Report, p. 208, Henry Hurt, *Reasonable Doubt*, New York: Holt, Rinehart & Winston, 1985, p. 247–, Russo, *op. cit.*, p. 122–, Ewing to Gabrielson, June 5, 1980, JFK Box no. 59, Folder F15, www.maryferrell.org, citing UPI March 31, 1980 &

see "Who Was Lee Harvey Oswald," by Joan Mellen, www.mary-
ferrell.org.

Psychiatrist: CBS Evening News, June 30, 1975, Epstein, *Legend*,
op. cit., p. 312n14, HSCA XII.451.

Note 12: Deneselya reportedly first told his story to Senator
Richard Schweiker of the Senate Intelligence Committee,
and certainly did tell it to the Assassinations Committee. He
talked with PBS's *Frontline* program in 1993, and has spoken
with other researchers. The Assassinations Committee looked
for but failed to locate the contact report to which he referred.

There are numerous CIA reports on an American named
Marvin Kantor, who had made two visits to Minsk, and had—
like Oswald—once served in the Marine Corps. Details about
Kantor, however, do not fit the man referred to by either Deneselya or by the unnamed psychiatrist. Unlike Oswald, Kantor
was not a defector—he had a relative in Minsk—and had
not worked at the Minsk plant. He returned to the United
States with a Danish wife, not a Soviet bride, and came back
not in 1962 but in 1961. There remains the possibility that
the unnamed psychiatrist's subject, as he himself wondered,
might have been not Oswald but returned defector Robert
Webster. Webster had lived with a woman in the USSR,
but he had not married her and did not bring her with him
to the United States. (Deneselya: as sourced above; Kantor:
Kantor entry, Mary Ferrell database, www.maryferrell.org;
DDP, CIA to Director, FBI September 1, 1961, NARA 104-
10173-10084, August 23, 1963, NARA 104-10173-10085, &
undated, NARA 104-10173-10990; DDP, CIA to Director,
Civil Service, May 6, 1964, NARA 104-10173-10087; Metz
to Director, FBI, March 2, 1965, NARA 104-10059-10182;
see references to Webster *supra*.)

"Andy Anderson": ("signed off"/ officers) Russo, *op. cit.*, p. 122,
citing work with "Who Was Lee Harvey Oswald," *Frontline*,
November 16, 1993; (consultant) John Newman, int. for
Frontline; ("Anderson" document) MFR *re* Oswald/Alvarado,

December 3, 1963, NARA 104-10408-10347.

Note 13: For a detailed summary of the Anderson entry and its discovery by Newman, see Gus Russo, *op. cit.*, p. 122–.

178 former deputy chief: *ibid.*; and *VF*, December 1994.

"big billboard": int. John Newman., *VF*, December 1994.

Moore: int. Jeanne de Mohrenschildt, & see de Mohrenschildt sources in Chapter 12.

12. Oswald and the Baron

179 Jeanne de Mohrenschildt quote: Bill O'Reilly int. 1977 for WFAA TV, cited at www.reopenkennedycase.net.

Gregory call: II.337, testimony of Peter Gregory.

de Mohrenschildt: Report, p. 282–; (de Mohrenschildt background) IX.166, 285–testimony of de Mohrenschildt; FBI file on de Mohrenschildt; HSCA XII.49–; HSCA Report, p. 217–; author's interviews with Jeanne de Mohrenschildt, 1978–1979. Except where indicated, material on De Mohrenschildt is taken from these sources.

Note 1: George de Mohrenschildt's father, Sergei von Mohrenschildt, had been a Marshal of Nobility in the province of Minsk, where decades later Oswald had spent most of his time in Russia. George had grown up on a family estate in Poland, trained at the elite Polish cavalry academy, then studied at a university in Belgium. He had come to the United States in 1938.

180 OSS: CIA document 18-522—Helms memo to Warren Commission; (application) CD 531.3; CD 777A.3; CD 533.57.

Cogswell: *New York Daily News*, April 12, 1977; see, however, HSCA XII.60, noting that Cogswell generated information on De Mohrenschildt for HSCA.

CIA file shows: CIA document 18-522.

Offer to State Department: Report, p. 283.

181 Something for State Department?: testimony of Mrs. Igor Voshinin, HSCA VIII.425.

Note 2: De Mohrenschildt told the Warren Commission he had never been an agent of any government, or been in the pay of any government, except the American government, the ICA (International Cooperation Administration, a forerunner of AID, the Agency for International Development). In an unpublished memoir, obtained later by the Assassinations Committee, he wrote: "I never, never worked for CIA." (IX.212 & XII.314)

Orlov interview: Epstein, *Legend, op. cit.*, p. 314.

Bouhe: testimony, VIII.355.

De Mohrenschildt on Moore to Warren: IX.235–.

Note 3: In a muddled answer, de Mohrenschildt said in his testimony that the others with whom he might have spoken about Oswald were George Bouhe, the doyen of the Russian community in Dallas, and/or Max Clark, an attorney who had previously been head of security for the Convair Aircraft Corporation (IX.235–, & see FBI agent James Wood's report, March 22, 1964, Everett Glover statement to FBI, February 28, 1964, CD 555 & HSCA XII.54.

182 Moore employed: HSCA Report, p. 217–; HSCA XII.54.

Jeanne on Moore: ints. 1978/1979.

Note 4: George de Mohrenschildt himself referred to the meeting with Moore in an unfinished manuscript he left behind at his death. "A short time after meeting Lee Harvey Oswald, before we became friends," he wrote, "I was a little worried about his opinions and his background. And so I went to see Mr. J. Walton Moore, to his office . . . and asked him pointblank: 'I met this young ex-marine, Lee Harvey Oswald. Is it safe to associate with him?'" And Mr. Moore's answer was: "He is OK. He is just a harmless lunatic."

On the day he died, in 1977, de Mohrenschildt claimed in an interview: "I would never have contacted Oswald in a million years, if Moore had not sanctioned it." The interview, with author Edward Epstein, was never completed—nor did the Assassinations Committee ever hear his account. Hours after speaking with Epstein, and on hearing that a House Asassinations Committee investigator wished to speak with him, de Mohrenschildt was found shot dead—an apparent suicide. The ensuing investigation established that de Mohrenschildt had suffered from depression, had spent three months in a mental institution the previous year, and had made previous suicide attempts. What he wrote in his unfinished manuscript—if relevant passages were written in the months before his death—and what he told Epstein, are obviously of dubious value. That is why later statements attributed to George de Mohrenchildt material have been relegated to this note.

Jeanne de Mohrenschildt, however, was entirely rational in lengthy conversations with the author, and appeared to have good recall. The one conflict between her account of the initial conversation with Moore and her late husband's was that she said the exchange with Moore occurred not at Moore's office but over dinner at the de Mohrenschildt's home.

Research in 2012 indicated that a large number of documents on de Mohrenschildt are still withheld. (Manuscript: obtained by author from attorney Patrick Russell, & see HSCA XII.69–; "I would never": Edward Epstein, *The Assassination Chronicles*, New York: Carroll & Graf, 1992, p. 559; HSCA investigator: Gaeton Fonzi, *The Last Investigation*, New York: Thunder's Mouth, 1993, p. 192; shot dead: Death Investigation, Palm Beach, Florida, Sheriff's Office, March 29, 1977; Jeanne: ints. by author 1978–1979; documents withheld: NARA withholding list shared with William Kelly.

"No commenting": Epstein, *Legend*, *op. cit.*, p. 315n15.

Moore fobbed off: "Three Witnesses," Dick Russell article, *New Times*, June 24, 1977.

183 "Periodic": HSCA XII.54–.

Oswald "delightful": from "Three Witnesses," article by Dick Russell, *New Times*, June 24, 1979.

184 "Whatever": IX.96, Gary Taylor testimony; author's interview, 1978.

Note 5: It may be significant that Oswald, for all his apparent poverty, had just finished repaying the $200 his brother had lent him to help with the travel from New York. ($200 repaid to brother: Report, pp. 741–).

185 YMCA and post-office box: Report, pp. 719–720. Jaggars-Chiles-Stovall: Report, p. 719 and related sources.

Ofstein: X.202, Dennis Ofstein testimony.

186 *Note 6*: There is controversy as to whether there was in fact a Minox, and some claim that an evidence photograph shows only an *empty* Minox camera case and a Minox light meter. Months after the assassination, the FBI would claim there was no Minox camera. The police, however, declined to change the manifest. Assistant District Attorney Bill Alexander, who himself owned a Minox, said there was a camera and that he personally worked its mechanism. Warren De Brueys, the FBI agent who took Oswald's possessions to Washington, DC, said in retirement that he did not remember a Minox. He added, however, that there were "limitations as to what I can say. . . . I have signed the secrecy agreement before leaving the Bureau." An Assassinations Committee lawyer said a Minox camera had indeed been seized. (Minox: HSCA XII.390 and 373, *Dallas Morning News*, Earl Golz article, August 7, 1978, (controversy) "Missing Minox or Major Mistakes?" http:// jfkassassination.net; (Alexander) int. 1978).

"Micro dots": XVI.53.

Note 7: Oswald may have used equipment available at Jaggars-Chiles-Stovall to forge the "Hidell" draft card he carried. An FBI expert has said that the forgery involved a very accurate camera "such as are found in photographic laboratory and printing plants." (IV.388).

187 New Year greeting and reading material: Report, p. 722; (*Time*) CD 1231; XXII.270.

Suggestion Marina return to USSR: I.35, Marina Oswald testimony.

Wrote to Soviet Embassy: I.35; XVI.10.

Buying guns: Report, pp. 119, 174, 723, and Chapter 5, *supra*.

188 Reports on Walker shooting: Report, p. 20 and HSCA Report, p. 61.

189 Oswald's conversations on Walker: IX.256.

De Mohrenschildt testimony & HSCA XII.201; FBI int. with Volkmar Schmidt, NARA (unrecorded), Epstein, *Legend, op. cit.*, p. 205.

Photographs: Report, p. 185.

190 Marina on Oswald and rifle: Report, p. 723–, XXII.763, 785; XXIII.393, 402; XXII.778; I.14; XXII.197, 785; V.397–399; HSCA II229, 231 & see IX.249, 316.

Photograph with guns and newspapers: Report, pp. 125–128.

Oswald stopped working: Report, p. 724; CD 7.128; CD 6; CD8; XXIII.696; XIII.529; XXII.278.

Walker incident: Report, pp. 183–187.

191 Walker ballistics: Report, p. 186; HSCA VII.370, I.472, HSCA I.502; (police report) HSCA Report, p. 98n4; XXIV.39. (press reports) *Dallas Morning News*, April 11 & 12, 1963, *New York Times*, April 12, 1963.

Note 8: Major General Walker added his own note of confusion on the question of the bullet. After seeing the exhibit shown in the Assassinations Committee hearings, the General said it was not the bullet he recovered in his house in 1963. He said the original projectile was so battered it was hardly recognizable as a bullet at all—far less so than the bullet shown in the Committee hearings. While the General was an irascible eccentric on political matters, he was an experienced soldier and he was talking about the bullet that nearly killed him. No check was apparently made of the chain of possession of the bullet. (ints. Walker, 1978; and see photograph of bullet, HSCA VII.390.)

192 "Something truly remarkable": Report, p. 724;

De Mohrenschildt version: Report, p. 282;

Marina version: XXII.777; HSCA II.234, & see analysis of "gun in closet" incident, Meagher, *op. cit.*, p. 127.

Previous year: HSCA XII.52.

1967 photograph find: ints. Jeanne de Mohrenschildt; George de Mohrenschildt letter April 17, 1967, cited at McMillan, *op. cit.*, p. 489n9; back of photograph is shown HSCA VI.151; (Oswald's handwriting) HSCA II.396; (translation) HSCA II.388; (rewritten in pencil) HSCA II.386, 388 & see HSCA II.295–, 243, 306, 315, HSCA XII.336.

Note 9: There is an example of such fallibility in the work of the HSCA's handwriting panel. It concluded that two Oswald signatures differed in many details from other Oswald signatures (HSCA VIII.235). The two signatures in question are on receipts for wages at Oswald's Dallas place of work—surely most likely to have indeed been signed by Oswald.

Another point on the same lines arises from a further inscription on the back of the photograph, presumably written since 1967. It reads "copyright G. de M." The HSCA experts did not think it had been written by de Mohrenschildt (HSCA II.385). De Mohrenschildt's lawyer, however, has said that de Mohrenschildt told him—as indeed seems most probable—that he did write the notation (letter of Patrick Russell to author, June 18, 1979). Handwriting evidence should always be weighed in the light of other available evidence.

194 Oswald finances/repayments: Report, Appendix XIV; XVII.646; XVIII.277, 316; XIX.252; XXII.86, 122; XXI.163; V.316; HSCA XII.338.

Oswald earnings in seven-week period: XXII.227, XXII.380.

Note 10: The State Department mailed Oswald a receipt showing that his debt was cleared on March 9.

Money order for rifle: Report, p. 119.

Note 11: While the postal money order was purchased early in the morning—and the post office did not open until 8:00 a.m. (VII.295). Oswald's work time sheet shows that he had clocked in by 8:00 a.m. that day (XXII.605). How he managed to get to the post office has been debated, along with the possibility that someone else sent off the order on his behalf. It was suggested (McMillan, *op. cit.*, p.485n8), that Oswald actually went to work only after visiting the post office, and filled in a false time on his time sheet to make it appear he had started work promptly at 8:00 a.m. A check of Oswald's time sheets (XXIII.538), however, revealed an instruction to employees that "time shown heron must agree with *clock register*." If Oswald had to abide by a mechanical clocking device, it would perhaps have been difficult to falsify his arrival time at work.

Coleman: HSCA Report, p. 98n4; see also XXVI.437, 753.

195 Oswald's driving capability: Report, p. 321.

Surrey: V.446; HSCA Report, p. 98n4.

Claunch: interview with Gary Shaw, independent researcher.

Note 12: The author drew on the Assassinations Committee summary of Walter Coleman's evidence, because it was the most up-to-date account. However, there are minor discrepancies between this and relevant documents in the Warren Commission volumes. In those reports, the Ford was "white or beige" and older. One of the Warren versions refers to the Ford leaving at speed, while the other does not (XXVI.437–; XVI.753; HSCA Report, pp. 61n5, 98n4).

HSCA on Walker shooting: HSCA Report, pp. 61n5, 98n.

196 November 22 police call *re* Chevrolet: XXIII.888.

Walker & Cuba: int., 1979.

Walker arouses exiles: XXVI.738, statement of Mrs. Connell.

197 Surrey and leaflet: Report, p. 298; XVIII.646.

Seven Days in May and JFK: The Celluloid Muse by Higham and Greenberg, p. 92; Schelsinger, *The Imperial Presidency*, pp. 198, 417, Fletcher Knebel and Charles W. Bailey, *Seven Days in May*, New York: Harper and Row, 1962.

De Mohrenschildt in Haiti: HSCA XII.55–(including CIA document 431-154B); (Kail) HSCA XII.57 and HSCA X.42; (plot) Herbert Atkin, quoted in "Three Witnesses," Dick Russell article, *New Times*, June 24, 1977.

Postcard: int., Jeanne de Mohrenschildt, 1978.

Anikeeff: Newman, *op. cit.*, p. 278–; and int. Newman, 1995.
Rocca: Rocca to OGC, 7D01, September 28, 1964, JFK 104-
10105-10196, www.maryferrell.org.

III. CONSPIRACIES: Cuba and the Mob

13. The Company and the Crooks

201 Assassinations Committee staff report: HSCA X.3.

202 Hunt forms CRC: Hunt, *op. cit.*, pp. 40–50, 182–189.

Hunt recommendation: *ibid.*, p. 38.

Nixon: "Cuba, Castro and John F. Kennedy" by R. M. Nixon, *Reader's Digest*, November 1964.

203 Nixon tape: Nixon to H. R. Haldeman, July 23, 1972.

204 Hunt: Hunt quotes are from author's int. Hunt, 1978, unless otherwise indicated.

Dulles encouraged: Schlesinger, *Robert F. Kennedy*, p. 452.

CIA intelligence reports on uprising: int. Hunt , 1978.

"Treason": RFK int. for JFK Oral History program, March 1, 1964.

"Splinter CIA": e.g. *New Times*, April 25, 1966.

205 Harvey: Sen. Int. Cttee. *Assassination Plots*, p. 66.

Pepe San Román: int. for "The CIA's Secret Army," CBS, June 10, 1977; HSCA X.9; Haynes Johnson, *op. cit.*, p. 17.

206 Kohly: int., 1978.

"No long-term": Cuba Study Group, Recommendation 6, June 13, 1961, Schlesinger Papers.

RFK enthusiasm: *Sen. Int. Cttee. Assassination Plots*, p. 141.

207 JM/WAVE: HSCA X.ll; (statistics: Thomas Powers, *op. cit.*, pp. 136, 139nl6).

Kennedys and captured exiles: Schlesinger, *Robert F. Kennedy*, Chapter 21.

Miami speech: *JFK Public Papers* (1962), pp. 911–912.

208 U.S. assurances: Schlesinger, *Robert F. Kennedy*, p. 257.

JFK on Republicans: Arthur Schlesinger journal, October 30, 1962.

209 *Note 1:* In his book *We Now Know: Rethinking Cold War History* (New York: Oxford University Press, 1997), Professor John Gaddis concluded that the missiles were removed. The view that they may not have been remains dubious speculation.

Clamp down: Sen. Int. Cttee., *Performance of Intelligence Agencies*, p. 11–; raid March 17–18, 1963 and State Department reaction: *Dallas Times-Herald*, March 19, 1963; JFK acted: *Dallas Times-Herald*, March 22, 1963; March 26 raid: Albert Newman, *op. cit.*, p. 326; "Cuba protests": *Dallas Times-Herald*, March 28, 29, 30, 1963; U.S. action: *Dallas Times-Herald*, March 31, 1963; boat seizures: *Dallas Times-Herald*, April 1, 1963.

Soviets began: *Dallas Times-Herald*, March 22, 1963; JFK press conference, *JFK Public Papers* (1963) April 3, 1963.

210 Nixon speeches: to American Society of Newspaper Editors, April 20, 1963; *Dallas Morning News*, April 21, 1963; HSCA X.13.

Cuban Revolutionary Council funds cut: Schlesinger, *Robert F. Kennedy*, p. 540; Albert Newman, *op. cit.*, p. 333; HSCA X.13.

Sapp memo: to Assistant Chief of Police Anderson, April 4, 1963; int. Sapp, 1978.

Handbill: Manchester, *op. cit.*, p. 53.

211 Fontainebleau meeting/CIA-Mafia collaboration: int. Joe Shimon, 1978; also *Sen. Int. Cttee. Assassination Plots*, 1975; HSCA X.151–; HSCA IV.126; HSCA Report, p. 114–. References hereafter to CIA-Mafia plots are from those sources unless otherwise indicated.

212 ONI and OSS & Mafia: Thomas Sciacca, *Luciano*, New York: Pinnacle Books, 1975; , Richard H. Smith, *OSS: The Secret History of America's First Central Intelligence Agency*, Berkeley, CA: University of California Press, 1972; ed. Anthony Cave Brown, *The Secret War Report of the OSS*, New York: Berkeley Publishing Corp., 1976.

213 Lansky, Trafficante, and Cuba: "The Hughes-Nixon-Lansky Connection," *Rolling Stone*, May 20, 1976; Ed Reid, *op cit.*

215 Initial Mob plotting: HSCA X.175–, 194n213.
Dulles: HSCA XI.66.
Maheu background: *Sen. Int. Cttee. Assassination Plots*, p. 74n4.
Giancana and Cuba: Hougan, *op. cit.*, pp. 335, 337.

216 Trafficante background: Reid, *op. cit*; *Sen. Int. Cttee. Assassination Plots*; Hearings of McClellan Committee, 1959, pp. 124–132; Alfred McCoy, *Politics of Heroin in Southeast Asia*, New York: Harper Colophon Books, 1972, pp. 27, 55; Hank Messick, *Lansky*, New York: Berkley Medallion Books, 1971, pp. 195, 215; HSCA V. 419–.
Trafficante as "Pecora": HSCA V.257.
De Varona: Dan Moldea, *The Hoffa Wars*, New York: Paddington Press, 1978, p. 133.

217 HSCA speculation: HSCA Report, p. 114.
Szulc: "Cuba on Our Mind," *Esquire*, February 1974.
Smathers: "Were Trujillo, Diem, CIA Targets Too?" by Jack Anderson, UFS syndicated article, *Miami Herald*, January 19, 1971; conv. 1978; and int. by D. M. Wilson for JFK Oral History Program, March 31, 1964.
RFK, Giancana, and plots: *Sen. Int. Cttee. Assassination Plots*, p. 129–; HSCA X.187.

218 RFK "stops" plot: *New York Times*, March 10, 1975; also int. of Frank Mankiewicz, October 29, 1969 for RFK Oral History Program.
CIA officials' refrained: e.g. in Thomas Powers, *op. cit.*, Chapter 9.
Helms recalled: Helms with Hood, *op. cit.*, p. 188.

219 Bissell: *VF*, December 1994 (drawing on interviews of Bissell by Jan Weininger). For another reading of Bissell on this subject, see Evan Thomas, *The Very Best Men, Four Who Dared: The Early Years of the CIA*, New York: Simon & Schuster, 1995.
Harvey told I. G.: *ibid.*, pp. 132, 137.
Former officer: int. Jan Weininger, citing her int. of case officer, 1994.

Smathers: int. by Robbyn Swan, 1994.

Note 2: Judith Campbell is frequently named as Judith "Exner," her later married name. Judith Campbell was her name during the Kennedy administration.

Campbell: *Sen. Int. Cttee. Assassination Plots*, p. 129; Judith Campbell as told to Ovid Demaris, *My Story*, New York: Grove, 1977; "Jack, Judy, Sam and Johnny," *New Times*, January 23, 1976; *New York Post*, December 22, 1975; author's articles, *New York Daily News*, October 6, 7, 8, 1991; ints. Exner, 1990–1992; int. Evelyn Lincoln, 1991.

220 Halpern: Evan Thomas, *op. cit.*, p. 403, *American Heritage* magazine, November 1995, p. 60, and int. Mark Allen, 1995.

Giancana on wiretap: Robert Blakey & Richard Billings, *The Plot to Kill the President*, New York: Times Books, 1981, p. 383.

14. The Mob Loses Patience

221 Trafficante quote: int. José Alemán,1978; originally quoted in the *Washington Post*, May 16, 1976 (explained later in this chapter).

RFK on organizer: Schlesinger, *Robert F. Kennedy, op. cit.*, p. 8.

222 "shooting fish": *ibid.* p. 62.

223 Hoffa on RFK: ("bastard") James R. Hoffa, as told to Oscar Fraley, *Hoffa: The Real Story*, New York: Stein and Day, 1975, pp. 107–115; ("monster") Ralph and Estelle James, *Hoffa and the Teamsters*, New York: Van Nostrand, 1965); ("brat") BBC int. of Hoffa, 1975.

Hoffa to Teamsters on RFK: *International Teamster*, February 1959.

JFK replied: "The Mafia, the CIA, and the Kennedy Assassination," *Washingtonian*, November 1975.

RFK on gangsters: Schlesinger, *Robert F. Kennedy, op. cit.*, p. 240.

224 RFK on Hoffa associates/syndicate: Schlesinger, *Robert F. Kennedy, op. cit.*, p. 75.

RFK on Baker: Schlesinger, *Robert F. Kennedy, op. cit.*, p. 60.

RFK on "private government": Robert Kennedy to Sen. Govt. Operations Cttee., September 25, 1963.

Hoffa prime target: Walter Sheridan, *The Fall and Rise of Jimmy Hoffa*, New York: Saturday Review Press, 1972, p. 193.

225 Hoffa's "seamy" information on Kennedys: cited Jim Hougan, *op. cit.*, p. 119.

Note 1: The author's book *Goddess: The Secret Lives of Marilyn Monroe* (New York: Open Road Integrated Media, 2013, and London: Orion, 2012) is a full-scale biography that includes the star's relationships with the Kennedy brothers.

"Fuck Hoover!" int. William Roemer, 1988; William Roemer, *Man Against the Mob*, New York: Donald Fine, 1989, pp. 118, 214; int. Neil Welch, 1988.

Giancana & RFK: McClellan Committee hearing June 9, 1959, 86th Cong., 1 Sess., 18672–.

226 Giancana crime career: *New Times*, January 23, 1976; and Robert Blakey to author, 1979.

Kennedy prosecution record: Department of Justice figures, HSCA V.435; *Congressional Record*, March 11, 1969, S2642; research of Katherine Kinsella for author, 1978; HSCA V.434–.

Salerno: quoted in *JILE*, Indiana Police Association journal, Spring 1979.

Weisburg/Bruno wiretap: HSCA V.443, 458.

227 Fithian: *JILE*, Indiana Police Association journal, Spring 1979.

HSCA assessment: HSCA Report, p. 161.

228 Partin episode: ints. Judge Hawk Daniels, 1978; int. Edward Partin, 1978; "An Insider's Chilling Story of Hoffa's Savage Kingdom," *Life* magazine, May 15, 1964; HSCA Report, p. 176–.

229 JFK told Bradlee: Benjamin Bradlee, *Conversations with Kennedy*, New York: W. W. Norton, 1976, p. 125–.

Trafficante & Kennedys: McClellan Committee Hearings, 1959 (p. 12432).

Alemán episode: int. José Alemán, 1978; originally reported by George Crile in the *Washington Post*, May 16, 1976. Alemán testimony, HSCA V.301 (incorporating staff reports); HSCA

Chief Counsel, HSCA V.345; HSCA Report, p. 172–; Moldea, *op. cit.*, p. 427n46.

Note 2: The date of the alleged Alemán-Trafficante conversation is unclear. It was first reported (*Washington Post*, May 16, 1976) as September 1962. Alemán himself was unsure because he had at least three meetings with Trafficante during that general period. In his testimony to the Assassinations Committee he spoke of June–July 1963 (HSCA V.303).

230 Hoffa millionaire: *Playboy*, December 1975.

231 Note 3: The Bureau denied this allegation by Alemán.

Marcello: (Ed Reid quoting Aaron Kohn) Reid, *op. cit.*, p. 156; (syndicate income) HSCA IX.65; (elusive) *ibid.*, p. 154; (Cuban involvement) Jim Hougan, *op. cit.*, p. 335 (quoting FBI); (link to Hoffa)int. Judge Daniels, 1978; (Marcello, Hoffa and Nixon contribution) Moldea, *op. cit.*, p. 108; (bribe in Hoffa case) Reid, *op. cit.*, pp. 159–60; (birth and deportation)Reid, *op. cit.*, p. 151–; (influence) HSCA IX.52, 88n52; and Aaron Kohn, quoted by Fensterwald/Ewing, *op. cit.*, p. 307.

233 Note 4: One report said Marcello was picked up by two CIA agents posing as Justice Department officers (Hougan, *op. cit.*, p. 113). The Assassinations Committee staff report, however, specified that they were Immigration Service officers (HSCA IX.71).

234 Marcello "threat": ints. Edward Becker, 1978, 1992; originally revealed by Ed Reid, *op. cit.*, p. 161–; Becker int. by Earl Golz, *Dallas Morning News*, December 1978; HSCA Report, p. 171–; HSCA IX.75; int. Julian Blodgett, 1992; and see Anthony Summers, *Official and Confidential: The Secret Life of J. Edgar Hoover*, New York: Putnam, 1993, p. 327–.

235 Note 5: Ed Reid, who first reported the alleged Marcello threat in his book *The Grim Reapers* (see Bibliography), was the winner of many journalism awards, including a Pulitzer Prize in 1951. He became an acknowledged specialist on organized-crime operations for that period.

Note 6: Neither Roppolo nor Liverde (which should perhaps be rendered "Livaudais"), the other associate who allegedly attended the meeting, was interviewed by the Assassinations Committee. They should have been. ("Liverde," Becker has said, may have been a member of the Liberto family, one of whose members was suspected of conspiring with Marcello to murder Dr. Martin Luther King Jr.).

236 *Note* 7: Apparent corroboration of the Hoffa/Trafficante/Marcello involvement in President Kennedy's death appeared in 1994, in *Mob Lawyer* by Frank Ragano, the longtime attorney for all three. Ragano wrote that Hoffa had sent him to see Marcello and Trafficante in July 1963, to ask them to have the President killed. After the assassination, Ragano claimed, Hoffa exclaimed, "I told you they could do it," while Marcello said, "Tell [Jimmy] he owes me big." Ragano also claimed that, days before his death in 1987, Trafficante effectively confessed to the crime—saying: "Goddamn Bobby. Carlos [Marcello] fucked up. We shouldn't have killed John. We should have killed Bobby." While some have expressed belief in Ragano's account, this author finds the Trafficante "confession" story dubious. The author looked into whether Trafficante was where Ragano said he was on the day Ragano said he met with him, and decided it was unlikely, if not impossible. Exposing Ragano as a liar, however, would not dispose of the "Mob dunnit" theory—nor of the notion that Trafficante and Marcello played some part in Kennedy's murder. For more detail on the author's probe of the Ragano story, see VF, December 1994.

Blakey on Mob guilt: *Newsweek*, July 30, 1979.

15. Six Options for History

238 Johnson predicts visit: *Dallas Times-Herald*, April 24, 1963 (reporting Johnson speech previous evening).

April 24 departure: II.459, Ruth Paine testimony.

Murrets and Oswald call: VIII.135, 164.

Uncle's Mafia link: HSCA Report, p. 170; HSCA IX.95.

239 HSCA on Soviets: HSCA Report, p. 103.

Oswald lone gunman: Report, p. 423.

240 *Note 1*: The thesis postulating Soviet involvement in the assassination was expounded—fatuously—by the British writer Michael Eddowes in his book *The Oswald File* (see Bibliography). Eddowes suggested that the real Oswald never returned to the United States. Eddowes based his theory mostly on discrepancies in the heights recorded for Oswald on official documents, which seem to show that the Oswald who returned from Russia was considerably shorter than the Oswald who served in the Marine Corps. Eddowes suggested that the fake Oswald killed President Kennedy on orders from Soviet leader Khrushchev. The monstrous political implications aside, this theory founders on the fact that the fingerprints of Marine Oswald are identical with those of the Oswald who died in Dallas. To accept Eddowes' theory one would also have to believe that Oswald's mother was fooled by the fake Oswald on his arrival from Russia. Nevertheless, Eddowes succeeded in persuading Texas courts to order the exhumation of Oswald's body for tests to determine whether the corpse was really his. On exhumation, according to the authorities, the body was declared to be what it was buried as in 1963—that of the authentic Oswald.

Johnson swung: see Anthony Summers, *Official and Confidential: The Secret Life of J. Edgar Hoover*, New York: Putnam, 1993, p. 330 and sources.

Note 2: Long after the Warren inquiry, when the existence of the CIA plots to kill Castro was revealed, some former Commission members were outraged, saying the CIA had kept them in the dark. According to Earl Warren's son, however, the Chief Justice did learn about the plots. (VF, December 1994; ints. Warren's son Earl Warren Jr., and his grandson, Jeff Warren, 1994; outrage of some Commission members: e.g., author's ints. Burt Griffin, for BBC, January 1977.)

Coleman: int. 1994.

Warren & HSCA on Cuban role: Report, p. 21, HSCA Report, p. 129.

241 *Note 3:* The author first referred to was Gus Russo, who in 1998 wrote *Live by the Sword: The Secret War Against Castro and the Death of JFK* (Baltimore, MD, 1998). The passage cited is at p. 459. The former CIA analyst, Brian Latell, wrote *Castro's Secrets: The CIA and Cuba's Intelligence Machine* (New York, Palgrave Macmillan, 2012). The author's thesis is summarized at p. 247.

Note 4: See Chapter 22, "Casting the First Stone."

HSCA on top mobsters: Report, p. 1.

242 *Note 5:* Robert Blakey, a former special prosecutor in the Kennedy Justice Department, spent the greater part of his career as professor of law at Notre Dame University, and director of the university's Institute on Organized Crime. The quotation is taken from p. xiv of his book *The Plot to Kill the President* (New York, Times Books, 1981) coauthored with Richard Billings, who had been editorial director of the House Committee.

Note 6: The book is *The Road to Dallas: The Assassination of John F. Kennedy*, by David Kaiser (Cambridge, MA, Belknap, 2008). Kaiser's view, in essence, is that the assassination was the result of "a conspiracy of mobsters and misfits." (See his book, pp. 8, 414.)

Marcello acknowledged: Lamar Waldron with Thom Hartmann, *Ultimate Sacrifice: John and Robert Kennedy, the Plan for a Coup in Cuba and the Murder of JFK*, New York: Carroll & Graf, 2005, pp. 12, 818.

Edwards: Fensterwald, *op. cit.*, p. 148.

243 Hart: *Denver Post*, May 2, 1976.

244 Fonzi: see Bibliography.

Note 7: The late Gaeton Fonzi's 1993 book was *The Last Investigation* (New York: Thunder's Mouth Press). The references cited are on pp. 404, 409.

Note 8: The former analyst, who is also a trained historian, is John Newman, whose 1995 book was *Oswald and the CIA* (New York: Carroll & Graf). He contributed a postscript to the previous edition of this book.

245 *Note 9*: The former *Washington Post* journalist, Jefferson Morley, is the author *Our Man in Mexico: Winston Scott and the Hidden History of the CIA*, Kansas, MO: Univ. Press of Kansas, 2008. For the references used, see that book, p. 238, and Morley's article "What Can We Do About JFK's Murder?" (*The Atlantic*, December 21, 2012)

Road map: Robert Blakey, in introduction to *The Final Assassinations Report* (see *Report of the Select Committee* in Bibliography).

16. Viva Fidel?

246 Liebeler: Hearings, XI.414.

Delgado: VIII.241.

Oswald spring letter: XX.511, Oswald undated letter date is best fixed between March 23 and April 2, see Albert Newman, *op. cit.*, p. 328; also XXII.796; reports of policemen Harkness and Finigan, who observed "unidentified white male" with pro-Castro placard.

247 FBI reading FPCC mail: XVII.773, report by FBI agent Hosty, referring to information supplied by informant on April 21, 1963.

1962 envelope: FBI exhibit 413 in National Archives, envelope from FPCC to Oswald, postmarked "1962," found among Oswald's effects after the assassination. The address on the envelope narrows the date down to the period August 4 and October 8, 1962.

Late May letter to FPCC: XX.512.

FPCC reply: XX.514—letter is dated May 29.

248 Printing: (Jones) Report, pp. 407, 728; XX.771; XXII.797; XXV.587, 773; (Mailer's) XXII.800; XXV.770–.

Note 1: When interviewed by the FBI after the assassination, however, neither Jones employee questioned thought that the man who ordered the leaflets—using the name "Osborne"—looked like the FBI photograph of Oswald. An employee at a company that printed other material, however—and who said his customer used the name "Osborne"—did identify Oswald from a photo. (Kaiser, *op. cit.*, p. 212, citing FBI documents).

"Hidell": Report, pp. 578, 615; (Marina signs) Report, p. 578; (handwriting experts) HSCA VIII.238; see also Chapter 5, *supra.*

Note 2: Only one person has acknowledged familiarity with Oswald's use of the name Hidell in advance of the assassination. That is Oswald's wife, Marina, who eventually said Oswald persuaded her to sign the name in the space for "President" on his New Orleans Fair Play for Cuba Committee card. Handwriting analysis indicated she did indeed do this.

Worker letter: XX.257.

Port demonstration: XXII.806 (report of Patrolman Girod Ray).

249 Library visits: New Orleans FBI report dated November 27, 1963, FBI 105-82555, Section 12, www.maryferrell.org.

Seminary visit: XXV.926–; (with Murret) HSCA IX.95.

Corr. Soviet Embassy: I.35; XVI.10–20; XVIII.506.

250 Bringuier visit: XIX.240; XXV.773; (next day) X.37; XXVI.768.

Oswald-Bringuier incident: XI.358; XXV.90, 773; XXVI.348, 578, 768; CD 6.223. int. Bringuier, 1978; Bringuier, *op. cit.*, p. 25–.

251 Martello/Austin: James/Wardlaw, *op. cit.*, p. 12.

Oswald/editor: XXI.626.

Long John Nebel call: "If Ruby had Missed, They Would have Listened," Bob Consadine column, *New York Journal American*, February 28, 1964[?] in FBI 105-82555-A.

August 16 incident: X.41, 61, 68; XVI.342; XXV.771; CD 206.216–; CD 114.629; CD 75.69–.

Radio interview: X.49; XI.160–.

252 Debate: X.42; XI.171; XVII.763.

Warren Commission rationale: Report, p. 412.

253 August 1 letter: Oswald to Lee, August 1, 1963, FBI 105-38431, www.maryferrell.org.

254 Bringuier call to supporters: XIX.175.

255 CIA , FBI & Army Intelligence clandestine ops.: Sen. Int. Cttee., *Performance of Intelligence Agencies*, p. 66; HSCA Report p. 224; int. John Marks, author of *CIA and the Cult of Intelligence* (see Bibliography), quoted in Anson, *op. cit.*, p. 284.

"We did everything": int. Joseph Burkholder Smith, 1994.

"We have in the past": article in Dallas newspaper (uncited), filed by FBI, August 5, 1963, obtained from researcher Paul Hoch.

257 John Glenn: Hearings, House Committee on Un-American Activities, November 18, 1963.

258 "the undersigned": NARA 104-10308-10163, dated July 10, 1963.

259 DRE and Bringuier: HSCA X.81n; (CIA memo) CI/R&A (Counter Intelligence Research and Analysis), "Garrison and the Kennedy Assassination," June 1, 1967, and Enc. 6 to CIA CI/R&A memo for the record, April 3, 1967; and see John Newman, *op. cit.*, Bringuier refs.; (Borja) HSCA X.85; CIA memo addressed to Deputy Director for Support, May 1, 1967; and CIA document C5A, February 11, 1963.

Hunt on Phillips: HSCA testimony of E. Howard Hunt, Pt. II, November 3, 1978, p. 29, released under JFK Records Act.

260 *Note 3*: Though this author as yet sees no cause to doubt Stuckey did get the Oswald briefing from the FBI, the historian David Kaiser did express doubt in his 2012 book *The Road to Dallas*. (McMillan, *op. cit.*, p. 352—citing letters from Stuckey, especially that of January 4, 1976, obtained by author from a confidential source; Hearings XI.162, Kaiser, *op. cit.*, p. 225.)

Quiroga: CIA memorandum, c. May 1967, *re*

"CIA involvement with Cubans and Cuban Groups Now or Potentially Involved in the Garrison Investigation"; see also Newman, *op. cit.*, p. 600, source 87, and Quiroga index refs.

Butler/INCA: XXII.826; John Newman, *op. cit.*, p. 342–; (and CIA memos) May 3 & July 20, 1965, August 1, 1966 & July 28, 1970, file A-135263, released to National Archives, 1995; (production manager) Weisberg, *op. cit.*, p. 51.

261 Warren Report on exposé: Report, p. 729.

FBI record re. Stuckey: John Newman, *op. cit.*, p. 343.

Oswald initiative: Quigley report of August 27, 1963, FBI 62-109060, JFK HQ file, Section 173.

Quigley meeting: XXVI.95–; X.53; XVII.758.

Quigley 1961: IV.432–, testimony of Quigley.

262 FBI & Oswald security case: Sen. Int. Cttee., *op cit.*

Performance of Intelligence Agencies, p. 89–.

Note 4: The case was only reopened several months later, when FBI agent James Hosty—in Dallas—drew attention to a fresh Oswald contact with *The Worker*.

Garner: int., 1978.

263 *Note 5*: Asked by the Assassinations Committee why they had not submitted affidavits for the Warren Commission, both agents said they had not been told to do so. The other agent was Warren De Brueys.(XVII.816; affidavits entered into record at XVII.74; not asked: HSCA Report, p. 191n, 193n; and see *VF*, December 1994.)

Commission and "informant" allegation: HSCA XI.41; and see discussion in this author's book *Official and Confidential: The Secret Life of J. Edgar Hoover*, *op. cit.*, p. 320–.

Pena: XI.343, 356; XXV.671; XXVI.358; Weisberg, *op cit.*

Pena allegation about FBI: *The American Assassins*, Pt. II, CBS News, November 26, 1975.

De Brueys denied: HSCA Report, p. 193, and author's conversation with De Brueys, 1978.

Note 6: Pena was eventually beaten up by somebody—it has been suggested it was because of his allegations. Pena also alleged after the assassination that Oswald had been in his bar one night just before the fracas in the street with Bringuier and the anti-Castro Cubans. Pena, reportedly backed up by two associates, said Oswald visited the bar accompanied by a Mexican. In front of the Warren Commission, however, he vacillated and seemed to withdraw his acount. He later revived the allegation, however. His claim that Oswald had been in his bar accompanied by a man who seemed to be Mexican, may not be implausible, as the unfolding story will show (beaten: Weisberg, *Oswald in New Orleans*, p. 303; allegation: see Pena sources above).

Pena secured release: XI.358.

Note 7: Another New Orleans witness, a garage manager named Adrian Alba, alleged covert official contact with Oswald. What Alba saw, he said, occurred while Oswald worked at the William Reily Coffee company, the job he held from shortly after his arrival in New Orleans to his arrival in mid-July—just before he launched into the public phase of his pro-Castro activity. Oswald, Alba said, made frequent visits next door to chat with him—a statement substantiated by the fact that an Oswald fingerprint was found on a gun magazine Alba had kept in his office.

In a deposition to the Assassinations Committee and in an interview with the author, Alba claimed that he had seen an FBI agent pass Oswald an envelope. There are, however, serious problems with this allegation. Alba had said nothing of this in testimony to the Warren Commission years earlier. The best he could offer to explain his later supposed recall, moreover, was to say that the memory of having seen the envelope handover was triggered by seeing a TV commercial. Alba told the author he had been fearful of telling the whole story in the months after the assassination. The Committee, however, judged his information "of doubtful reliability." (int. 1978, & reported by private researcher Ian MacFarlane, December 23, 1975; *Dallas Morning News*, August 7, 1978; (fingerprint) CD 75.455–; (HSCA comments) HSCA Report, pp. 146, 193–,.)

264 Burton: interviews with Joseph Burton, 1994; *Orlando Sentinel Star*, July 4, 1976; *Tampa Tribune*, June 24, 1976; *New York*

Times, February 16 & 24, 1975; interviews with Dick Burdette, Rory O'Connor, and (re V. T. Lee) Rob Lorie, Julie Browning, 1994.

COINTELPRO, etc.: Schlesinger, *Robert F. Kennedy and His Times*, p. 641–.

265 Kaiser wrote: Kaiser, *op. cit.*, pp. 207–, 230–.

Note 8: While the FBI and the CIA stuck firmly with their denials, anomalies continued to surface. The Assassinations Committee was troubled to discover that the FBI had failed after the assassination to use the resources of its Cuban Section, the department most obviously equipped to analyze Oswald's connections in New Orleans. Was that omission, like the FBI's almost nonexistent efforts in the Mafia area, attributable to institutionalized inertia? (HSCA Report, p. 128).

17. Blind Man's Bluff in New Orleans

267 Oswald gives Quigley documents: XVII.758–762; IV.437; HSCA X.123. 544 Camp Street address on pamphlet: XXVI.783.

268 CRC at Camp Street: Report, p. 408 & this chapter.

269 Second copy of pamphlet: FBI document 97-74-67; CD 75.690–; CD 984b.

FBI investigation of "544" pamphlet: XVII.811; FBI serial 97-74-1A4 and 1A5. The most thorough study of FBI treatment of this area has been done by independent researcher Paul Hoch. And *cf.* John Newman, *op cit.*

Report suggests: Report, p. 408.

HSCA criticism of FBI: HSCA X.126, 124.

Newman inquiry: CD 75.680–; CD 1.64.

270 Further twenty: XXIV.332, 337; letter of February 7, 1968, from NARA to Paul Hoch, states that of twenty copies seized in Dallas, nine bear no address, ten bear the Camp Street address, and one bears an illegible address.

Oswald to FPCC: XX.512 (May 26, 1963); XX.514 (FPCC reply); XX.518 (Oswald reply); XX.524 (Oswald on closure).

271 Newman: FBI serial no. 89-69; CD 75.680–; CD 1.64; Secret Service reports December 3 and 9, 1963.

Rodriguez: XXIV.659; CD 4.819; Secret Service report December 1, 1963 (Rodriguez Sr.); int. of Rodriguez Jr., March 7, 1979, by Earl Golz of *Dallas Morning News*.

272 *Note 1*: As reported in *Note 7*, Chapter 16, Oswald worked for some time at the William Reily Coffee Company. The Crusade to Free Cuba Committee, was formed to raise cash and support for the CIA-backed Cuban government-in-exile, the Cuban Revolutionary Council. (Milton Brener, *The Garrison Case: A Study in the Abuse of Power*, New York: Clarkson N. Potter, 1969, p. 47.)

272 Banister: sources on Banister include HSCA X.123, Weisberg, *Oswald in New Orleans*, pp. 51, 327–, 337–, 364, 380, 391, 410; author's ints. with Banister's secretaries Delphine Roberts (1978 and 1979) and Mary Brengel (1979); Banister's brother Ross Banister (questioned by William Scott Malone, 1978); author's int. Jack Martin, former Banister investigator, 1978; int. Joe Newbrough, Banister investigator, by William Scott Malone, 1978; author's int. attorney John Lanne, 1978; author's int. Aaron Kohn, New Orleans Crime Commission, 1978; int. Sam Newman by Scott Malone, 1978.

273 Banister and Friends of Democratic Cuba: from New Orleans Court records, FODC Articles of Incorporation, May 17, 1967.

274 FBI & Banister's address: CD 75.683, report of FBI Agent Wall, November 25, 1963.

Note 2: The author Gus Russo has suggested that the physical layout of the building precluded access between the side on which the Banister office was situated and the offices on the Camp Street side. As explained to this author, however, Mancuso's restaurant on the first floor afforded access to both parts of the building. As the building has long since been demolished, there can be no certainty. Direct access or no, the two sides of the corner building were only yards apart. (Russo, *Live by the Sword*, p. 196–)

Note 3: For treatments of the Garrison investigation, see especially Patricia Lambert, *False Witness*, Landham, MD: Evans & Co., 2000, James Kirkwood, *American Grotesque*, New York: Simon and Schuster, 1970. Also Edward Epstein, *Counterplot*, New York: Viking Press, 1968; Rosemary James and Jack Wardlaw, *Plot or Politics!*, New Orleans: Pelican, 1967; Paris Flammonde, *The Kennedy Conspiracy: An Uncommissioned Report on the Jim Garrison Investigation*, New York: Meredith, 1969; Joachim Joesten, *The Garrison Enquiry*, London: Peter Dawnay Ltd., 1967 & Jim DeEugenio, *Destiny Betrayed: JFK, Cuba, and the Garrison Case*, New York: Sheridan Square Press, 1992. See too articles in *Ramparts*, January 1968 by former FBI agent William Turner, and *Playboy*, October 1967 (interview with District Attorney Garrison). Garrison himself wrote two books, *A Heritage of Stone* (New York: Putnam, 1970), and *On The Trail of the Assassins* (New York: Sheridan Square Press, 1988).

275   Banister's widow: int. Mary Banister by Andrew Sciambra (New Orleans District Attorney's Office), April 29 & 30, 1967.

Index cards and files: HSCA X.130–; and Garrison, *Heritage of Stone*, *op. cit.*, p. 98–.

Banister hire young men: HSCA X.127.

Campbell brothers: ints. June 1979.

276   *Note 4*: Allen Campbell's 1969 statements draw on a May 14, 1969, interview by the New Orleans District Attorney's Office, reported in Garrison, *op. cit.*, pp. 100, 208n59. In his 1979 conversation with the author, Allen Campbell claimed he had not actually been at 544 Camp Street in summer 1963. That time, however, is when his brother Daniel said Allen brought him into the Banister operation. Both brothers indicated they had more information to provide but were nervous about doing so.

Banister angry: HSCA X.128 (Nitschke and Roberts).

Delphine Roberts: ints. 1978, 1993; (background) *New Orleans States-Item*, December 16, 1961, November 3, 1961 & January 18, 1962; and Roberts's election manifesto, January 27, 1962; HSCA X.128–; HSCA Report, pp. 145, 146n.

279 *Note 5:* Along with other criticism of this author's work, the author Gerald Posner suggested in his 1993 book on the case (*op. cit.*) that Delphine Roberts had retracted her statements about Oswald, and implied that she had only given an interview to the author for money. Neither assertion is accurate. Roberts gave the author the information reported here spontaneously and without payment. She was subsequently paid a fee for a filmed interview in connection with a film documentary project on which the author was a consultant. It is common practice to pay such fees for television appearances, to compensate interviewees for their time and the resulting exposure, and the company concerned paid in that spirit. For her part, and after the Posner claims, Roberts confirmed in 1993 that she stood by her story as told to the author in 1978.
Delphine Roberts's daughter: int. 1978.
Ross Banister & Nitschke: HSCA X.128.
Alba: HSCA Report, p. 146.

280 FBI interview of Banister: HSCA X.126.
CIA and Banister: HSCA X.126.

281 CRC local representative (Sergio Arcacha Smith): CIA document 1363-501, Security File on Arcacha, dated October 26, 1967; CD 75.683, reports of FBI Agent Wall, November 25, 1963; int. of Mr. and Mrs. Richard Rolfe, New Orleans District Attorney's office, January 13, 1968; Arcacha's own curriculum vitae; CD 87; New Orleans Police Arrest Report, August 30, 1961 (item No. H-13903-61); HSCA X.11, 61; report of Secret Service Agents Gerrets, Vial, and Counts, December 3, 1963; HSCA X.61.
Note 6: On March 9, 1962, 544 Camp Street's owner, Sam Newman, wrote to the CRC regarding rent arrears. The letter was addressed personally to Antonio de Varona, the CRC leader who reportedly—at the initiative of Santo Trafficante played a part in the CIA-Mafia plots to murder Castro (copy of letter in files of William Scott Malone).
Caire: XXII.828; (& Oswald) XXII.831.

Bartes: HSCA Report, p. 144; & see John Newman, *op. cit.*, multiple refs.

282 Ferrie background: HSCA IX.103; HSCA X.105; CIA document 1359-503, February 7, 1968; FBI reports from New Orleans, November 26, 1963; CD 75.287–; *New Republic*, "Is Garrison Faking?" by Fred Powledge, June 17, 1967; *Ramparts*, January 1968; Arcacha letter to Eastern Airlines official Captain E. Rickenbacker, July 18, 1961; (bombing) article in *El Tiempo*, New York, March 1967.

Note 7: For detail on Ferrie, the author has drawn largely on research by Stephen Roy (writing as David Blackburst), who has specialized in studying Ferrie. (e.g. www.jfk-online.com/dbjmaadf.html).

Ferrie letter to Air Force: "Garrison's Case," *New York Review of Books*, September 14, 1967.

283 Ferrie Cuba speech: James/Wardlaw, *op. cit.*, p. 46.

"The President ought": Secret Service report by agents Wall and Viater, November 27, 1963.

"An electorate": in notes found in Ferrie's effects after his death.

Banister "bullet"/"ballot": anecdote told by Aaron Kohn, Metropolitan New Orleans Crime Commission.

Ferrie demonstration: James/Wardlaw, *op. cit.*, p. 111.

284 Ferrie and Oswald:(CAP) HSCA IX.103; VIII.14; XXII.826; (Ferrie denied *re* CRC)

HSCA X.132n; (Banister employee on Ferrie and Oswald) HSCA 1X104, *re* Jack Martin.

285 Paradis: int. 1993.

Note 8: According to Ferrie researcher Stephen Roy, Oswald joined the CAP's Moisant squadron, while Paradis was in the Lakefront squadron—which Oswald only visited. (www.jfk-online.com/dbdfcapfile.html)

Old photograph: *Frontline*, "Who Was Lee Harvey Oswald?" WGBH-TV/PBS Boston, November 1993.

Ferrie's homosexuality: see Ferrie sources *supra*.

Note 9: In August 1961, when Ferrie was arrested in connection

with an episode involving a runaway boy, Arcacha Smith—
the prominent Cuban exile who that year began using an
office at 544 Camp Street in New Orleans—intervened on
his behalf. (www.jfk-online.com/dbarcback.html)

286 Oswald homosexual?: (party) report of November 30, 1963, by
Agent Joseph Engelhardt, FBI file No. 89–69;(bars) Edward
Epstein, *op. cit.*, p. 620n3, and Gerald Posner, *op. cit.*, p. 21;
(Murray) VII.319; (Powers) interview by Robbyn Swan, 1994,
and see VIII.269.

Note 10: Jack Martin, an associate of Ferrie and of Guy Banister, claimed Ferrie once told him about a youth who had
witnessed a sex act in which Ferrie had taken part. The youth
then joined the Marine Corps and left New Orleans. The FBI
dismissed Martin's various claims as those of a disreputable
character with a grudge, but the House Assassinations Committee was less dismissive (HSCA IV.485; HSCA IX.104;
HSCA Report, p.142).

A 1967 CIA headquarters message, reported in an Assassinations
Committee staff summary, made the following bald assertion:
"Lee Harvey Oswald was a homosexual." A CIA internal critique of the Committee document, however, said this was a
distortion. According to the critique, the original document
said homosexuality was merely "a possibility" raised by the
media covering New Orleans' D.A. Jim Garrison's assassination probe. (HSCA Mexico Report, p. 237, and HSCA Box 6,
No. 7, *re* Sylvia Durán in CIA release, 1993)

"Recruiting officer": CE 1454; FBI transcript of Les Crane TV
program, New York, August 21, 1964.

Birth certificate: HSCA IX.99–; (Ferrie fakery) refer to HSCA
Ferrie analysis, *supra*, and (another example) see John Davis,
Mafia Kingfish, New York: McGraw-Hill, 1989 p. 158–, *re* Fer-
rie's role in forgery of a birth certificate for Carlos Marcello;
(Martin)www.jfk-online.com/dbjmaadf.html.

287 Oswald, Marines, and Socialism: Report, p. 383–; ("baloney")
HSCA IX.107.

288 Andrews: XI.326–, 331; XXVI.704, 732.

Note 11: Other evidence that supposedly linked Oswald to Ferrie—made much of in New Orleans District Attorney Jim Garrison's investigation and failed trial—involved the alleged sighting in Clinton, a small Louisiana town, of Oswald, Ferrie, a man who resembled Banister, and Clay Shaw. Shaw, a prominent New Orleans businessman and a former CIA contact, was to be charged by Garrison with conspiracy to assassinate President Kennedy. In early September 1963, according to witnesses Garrison produced, these men arrived in Clinton during a voter registration drive that the Congress of Racial Equality—CORE—had organized to get black citizens to vote. The witnesses included the town's registrar, its marshal, a leading member of CORE, and others—who seemed persuasive. A drive for racial equality appeared to fit Oswald's political profile, while his supposed companions—Ferrie, Banister, and Shaw—were of the opposite persuasion. The House Assassinations Committee found the sources of the Clinton story "credible and significant," and the author included the Clinton episode in earlier editions of this book. In 1998, however, the author advised readers of new research—still being prepared—that would likely cast doubt on the entire matter. That research, published in a 2000 book by author Patricia Lambert, effectively demolishes the Clinton story. It is therefore not given space in the text of this edition. The author suggests that interested readers refer to Lambert's book, *False Witness* (*op. cit.*). Other sources on Clinton have been (background: *Robert F. Kennedy* by Arthur Schlesinger, p. 303; transcripts of evidence in trial, *State of Louisiana v. Clay Shaw*, 2/6–769; ints. Edwin McGehee (barber), John Manchester (town marshal), William Dunn (CORE worker), Henry Palmer (registrar of voters), Reeves Morgan (state representative), Maxine Kemp (hospital secretary), & former police Intelligence officer Francis Frugé, 1978; HSCA Report, p. 142. See also Gerald Posner, *op. cit.*, Mailer, *Oswald's Tale*, *op. cit.*, p. 621–, *Probe* (pub. by Citizens for Truth about the Kennedy Assassination, ed. by Jim DiEugenio), June and July 1994.

Ferrie and Marcello: (as pilot) HSCA Report, p. 143n; (and Andrews) James/Wardlaw, *op. cit.*, p. 92; (Andrews and Marcello) testimony released by New Orleans grand jury, April 12, 1967; (Ferrie and Marcello case) CD 75 and HSCA X.105–; int. Joe Newbrough, former Banister investigator, by William Scott Malone, August 16, 1978.

289 Banister and Marcello: int. Mary Brengel, 1978; HSCA X.127.

290 Oswald mother/uncle links to organized crime figures: HSCA IX.93–103, 115–.

291 Clem Sehrt: HSCA IX.100.

  Note 12: Dean Andrews, another New Orleans attorney, who had links to Marcello associate David Ferrie, also said he was asked to represent Oswald after the President's murder. He named the man who called him by the pseudonym of Clay Bertrand. To reveal the true identity of his caller, he said later, would endanger his life. (XVI.331, 326, 339; (pseudonym) Epstein, *Counterplot, op. cit.*, p. 41n; (in fear of life) Weisberg, *Oswald in New Orleans, op. cit.*, p. 139.)

  Raoul Sere: HSCA IX.103.

  Termine: HSCA IX.115.

  Murret: See entry for Oswald family's connections with organized crime figures, above.

292 Helping Oswald get bail: XXV.117; CD 75.159, FBI report of November 30, 1963; *Clandestine America*, III.2, p. 7, quoting New Orleans Crime Commission Director on Bruneau; CD 6.104; VII.175; (Pecora) HSCA IX.192; HSCA Report, p. 155.

293 Schweiker: int. 1978.

18. The Cuban Conundrum

295 American University speech: Public Papers of President Kennedy (1963), p. 45.

296 "Let us, if we can": Public Papers of President Kennedy (1963), p. 606.

Alpha 66: Sen. Int. Cttee., *Performance of Intelligence Agencies*, p. 11–; raids: *Dallas Times-Herald*, March 19, 1963; *ibid.*, March 22, 1963; Albert Newman, *op. cit.*, p. 326; *Dallas Times-Herald*, March 28, 29, 30, 31 & April 1, 1963; JFK statement on raids—*JFK Public Papers*, April 1 & 12, 1963.

"Pinprick" attacks: Sen. Int. Cttee. *Assassination Plots*, pp. 172, 337; Schlesinger, *Robert F. Kennedy*, *op. cit.*, p. 543–.

297 *Note 1*: The formal title was Special Group (Augmented), an offshoot of the Special Group of the National Security Council specifically charged with the overthrow of the Castro regime. ("Note on U.S. Covert Action Programs," *Foreign Relations of the United States*, 1964–1968, XII, www.fas.org).

Note 2: The author has drawn here on 1970s interviews of Ayers and on Ayers' memoir *The War That Never Was* (New York: Bobbs-Merrill, 1976). A second book written three decades later, however, and points to sinister figures supposedly involved in the Kennedy assassination. In this author's view, it has no credibility. It is *The Zenith Secret: A CIA Insider Exposes the Secret War Against Cuba and the Plot that Killed the Kennedy Brothers* (New York: Vox Pop, 2007).

Ayers: Ayers, *War That Never Was*, *op. cit.*, p. 53; and ints. 1980, 1994, 1995.

Krulak/Kennedy: Ayers, *War That Never Was*, *op. cit.*, pp. 14, 76, 147. (In the book, Ayers called him Kartak.)

298 Exile leaders talk: AP, May 10, 1963; CRC statement, June 21, 1963.

San Roman: int. 1994. Author also drew on 1994 ints. of Ramón Font, Eugenio Martínez, Eloy Menoyo, Rafael Quintero, Segundo Borges & (courtesy of Lamar Waldron) with Enrique Ruiz-Williams.

299 *Note 3*: The document was supplied to the author by David Barrett, a political science professor at Villanova Unversity in Pennsylvania, who located it at the National Archives. (Memos of calls of August 20, 1962, Box 46, Executive Secretariat, State Department Records, NARA & see "McCone's

Telcon Gaffe" by Max Holland & David Barrett, August 22, 2012 & related citations).

Note 4: See, for example, David Kaiser's *The Road to Dallas,* p. 302, Brian Latell, *Castro's Secrets: The CIA and Cuba's Intelligence Machine.* (Latell is a former CIA analyst specializing in Latin American affairs, now with the University of Miami), p. 93–, and Gus Russo's *Live by the* Sword, p. 61–, and Seymour Hersh's *The Dark Side of Camelot* (New York: Little, Brown, 1997), pp. 3, 291–, 399n.

By contrast Arthur Schlesinger—who had been a Special Assistant to President Kennedy—devoted several pages in his Robert Kennedy biography to rebutting the notion that the Kennedys encouraged the Castro assassination plots. "No one who knew John and Robert Kennedy well," he wrote, "believed they would conceivably countenance a program of assassination." More recently, the author David Talbot argued in his book *Brothers* that there was "no compelling evidence" to support the claim that the Kennedys authorized Castro's assassination. (Schlesinger, *Robert F. Kennedy, op. cit.,* p. 488–, & David Talbot, *Brothers: The Hidden History of the Kennedy Years,* New York, Simon & Schuster, 2007, p. 93–)

Cubela: Sen. Int. Cttee. *Assassination Plots,* pp. 86– and 174–; author's int of Rolando Cubela, Havana, 1978; HSCA X.157, 162–; HSCA Report, p. 111–; and author's perusal of relevant 1994 CIA releases.

300 *Note 5:* According to interview notes taken by Assassinations Committee investigators, one of the exiles most favored by the Kennedy administration, Manuel Artime, said weeks before his own death that he "had direct contact with JFK and RFK personally. They in turn contacted the CIA . . . AMLASH [the CIA cryptonym for the Cubela operation] was proposed by JFK." (notes of HSCA investigators Al Gonzalez & Gaeton Fonzi, available in HSCA document releases of 1994 as HSCA 014584; ints. with Gonzalez, 1994.)

"traitor" thesis: refs., Latell, *op. cit.*

301 Veteran: HSCA X.65.

Veciana: ints.Veciana, 1978, 1980, 1993; HSCA X.37– and HSCA Report, p. 135–; HSCA IV.476 & ints. HSCA staff; "Dallas, the Cuban Connection," *Saturday Evening Post*, March 1976; "Who Killed President Kennedy?" article by former HSCA investigator Gaeton Fonzi, *Washingtonian*, November 1980; research by David Leigh for *Washington Post*, June–July 1980; ints. Gaeton Fonzi, 1993; Gaeton Fonzi, *The Last Investigation*, New York: Thunder's Mouth Press, 1993.

304 *Note 6*: Veciana's group Alpha 66 was to be linked to the name "Oswald" immediately after the assassination. Early on November 23, a Dallas police detective would report information from an informant that an "Oswald" had attended meetings of an anti-Castro group at an address in Dallas. Cubans had vacated the address in the last few days. It is now known that the address in question had been a local base for Alpha 66. (XIX.534, report of Deputy Sheriff B. Walthers, November 23, 1963, see also CD 1085U. There is confusion over two phonetically similar addresses, but the correct address was probably 3126 Hollandale, in the Farmers Branch area.)

Note 7: For a discussion of the Committee's debate on Veciana's claims, see HSCA volumes as indicated *supra*, and p. 330 of an earlier edition of this book (New York: Paragon, 1989) and in Chapter 24, "Hints and Deceptions."

Agents seized: Sen. Int. Cttee., *Performance of Intelligence Agencies*, p. 12–.

305 Lacombe: *ibid.*, and *New Orleans States-Item*, May 5, 1963; (Ferrie) James & Wardlaw, *op. cit.*, p. 131; (McLaney) *Washington Post*, August 1, 1963; HSCA X.185, X.72–.

Note 8: Author Gus Russo quotes three interviewees as having alluded to Ferrie's role at camps near New Orleans, and reporter Jack Wardlaw cited a *New Orleans States-Item* reference to Ferrie's role at Lacombe. (Russo, *op. cit.*, p. 187, Rosemary James and Jack Wardlaw, *Plot or Politics: The Gar-*

rison Case and Its Cast, New Orleans: Pelican, 1967, p. 131, Russo, *op. cit.*, p.187.)

Raid & McLaney: *Washington Post*, August 1, 1963, HSCA X.185, X.72–.

Note 9: Mike McLaney had owned the International Casino in Havana. In 1973, in sworn testimony to the Senate Sub-committee on Investigations, a witness stated that McLaney "represents Meyer Lansky"—the man dubbed the "finance minister of the Mob." The same witness claimed McLaney had plotted the assassination of Bahamian leader Lynden Pindling. McLaney denied the allegation, and the Assassinations Committee found no evidence that the McLaney operation in Louisiana was linked to the CIA or to the crime syndicate. (HSCA X.185)

Bringuier: memo, FBI New Orleans to HQ, May 11, 1964.

Interpen: *New York Times*, September 16, 1963.

Sturgis group financing: Fensterwald, *op. cit.*, p. 505.

Hall: (detained) Weisberg, *Oswald in New Orleans*, *op. cit.*, pp. 161, 273, 274, 276, and HSCA X.22; (Cuban detention) int. of Hall by Harold Weisberg, p. 92; Most stung by clampdown: HSCA X.13.

306   "Those individuals": Sen. Int. Cttee. *Assassination Plots*, p. 13.

"At peace": AP, July 31, 1963.

Oswald at time of "Bishop" meeting: chronology of Oswald's activities based on Warren Commission documents, by researchers Mary Ferrell & Arch Kimbrough.

Oswald at Mexican Consulate: XXIV.549, 685; XXV.17, 811. Passport: XXII.12; XXIV.509;

307   Knight: *New York Times*, March 23, 1966.

Tourist card numbers: FBI report November 30, 1963, File no. SA89-67; CD 21; CD 75; CD 88; CD 613; CD 652.

Gaudet: ints. 1977, 1978; int. by Bernard Fensterwald, 1975, by Allen Stone (WRR, Dallas), May 7, 1975; HSCA Report, p. 218–; John Newman, *op. cit.*, p. 346–, CIA Advice of Project Action 00-48-50, February 15, 1950, & 00-32-51, June 21,

1950; Asst . Dir. Ops to Chief, Inspection & Sec., January 5, 1950 & attachments, Secrecy Agreement, March 2, 1950, CIA 1993 releases.

309   *Note 10:* Gaudet said, too, that, "Another vital person is Sergio Arcacha Smith. I know he knew Oswald and knows more about the Oswald affair than he ever admitted." As the first New Orleans representative of the Cuban Revolutionary Council, Arcacha—mentioned earlier in the Notes for Chapter 17—had previously had an office at 544 Camp Street. The author knows of no link between Arcacha and Oswald.

    Gaudet saw Oswald/Banister: int. Gaudet, 1978; HSCA Report, p. 219n.

    Note 11: Interviewed after her husband's death, Gaudet's widow said he had known Banister, though not well. (int. Mrs. C. K. Gaudet, 1993)

310   "Giving some thought": Papich to Brennan, September 13, 1963, FBI 97-4196-861, www.maryferrell.org; Sen. Int. Cttee., *Performance of Intelligence Agencies,* p. 65.

    Oswald summary of achievements: Report, p. 731.

311   Oswald leaves New Orleans: XI.462–; XXIII.715; CD 170.4, 8; HSCA X.21.

312   Frontier stamp: XXV.16 and 819; XXIV.663.

IV. ENDGAME: Deception and Tragedy

19. Exits and Entrances in Mexico City

315   "Oswald's visit": AARB Report, p. 86.

    Passengers on bus: (Mumford & Winston) XI.215, ints. with both, 1993; (McFarland) XI.214.

316   *Note 1:* On the bus, Oswald sat next to a much older man who spoke with an English accent. An extensive search eventually led investigators to a person who had traveled under the name of John Bowen, but denied having sat next to Oswald. He

claimed that he was a "missionary" who traveled extensively and that his most recent trip, begun just before the Kennedy assassination, had included France and Spain. Intensive frontier checks revealed no record of entrance to either country. This man might not seem worth noting at all were it not that when tracked down he was using the name "Osborne." In New Orleans, the name Osborne had twice been used to order the printing of Fair Play for Cuba Committee material. This is likely a mere coincidence. (Bowen: XI.220; XXIV.576; XXV.42, 45, 75; Report, p. 733; "Osborne": see Notes for start of Chapter 16)

Hotel Cuba: XI.223

Note 2: A long-ago foray to a border town while on leave from a Marines base aside, the heavily documented record of Oswald's life shows no previous visits to Mexico. Guy Banister's secretary, Delphine Roberts, however, told the author in 1978 that she believed—on the basis of what Banister told her—that Oswald made more than one trip to Mexico in the summer of 1963.

Hotel Comercio: Report, p. 733; and Robbyn Swan's int. manager Guillermo García Luna, 1993.

Note 3: The Warren Commission had trouble documenting the bus travel by Oswald. Establishing how he returned to the United States remained unresolved until the production in August 1964 of a bus ticket allegedly found by Marina Oswald while working with the author Priscilla McMillan. The Warren Commission's Senator Russell was less than satisfied on this point. Oswald's re-entry to the United States was initially reported to have been by "automobile." Had that been the case, and as Oswald did not drive and had no car, questions would arise as to who might have traveled with him. Further, on its face strong, evidence that Oswald did travel to Mexico was a copy of a letter he apparently wrote on November 9— following the trip—to the Soviet Embassy in Washington, DC. Both the content of this letter and the circumstances of its writing have raised questions about its purpose and authenticity. What Lee and Marina Oswald had to say on the subject of Mexico will be reported later in this chapter. A useful research tool on the overall Mexico episode is researcher Rex Bradford's paper "Not a Shred of a Speck of Evidence for Conspiracy: Vincent Bugliosi on the Mexico City Impostor," 2007, updated, supplied to author; Nov. 9 letter: infra., Chapter 20, Jerry Rose, "Gifts from Russia: Yeltsin and Mitrokhin," *Fourth Decade*, 7.1, & HSCAVIII, 233–, 237–, 351–, 358; Marina: HSCA I.27–50, XI.150, 155,) Mexico activity: (except where indicated) Report, p. 299– and HSCA Report, pp. 121–, 248–. Oswald in Mexico: (seen with Cubans) XXVI.672; (exile haunt) Anson, *op. cit.*, p. 251.

317 Durán: ints. 1978, 1993, and other contacts; XXV.586, 634; XVI.33; XXIV.590; HSCA III.6.

Durán re. phony?: HSCA III.35, 58; int. John Newman, 1995.

318 Azcue: XXIV.570; XXIV.563; author's research in Cuba; HSCA III.127; Report, pp. 301, 734–.

319 *Note 4*: According to Cuban Intelligence defector Vladimir Rodríguez Lahera, Mirabal was—while fronting as a consular official in Mexico City—also a senior Cuban Intelligence officer. (Debriefing of AMMUG-1, April 1964, NARA 104-10183-10284)

Communist Party card: HSCA III.176, 155, 142.

Note 5: A CIA document, however, was to state that Oswald returned to the Cuban Consulate the following day—Saturday, September 28—and that Durán assisted him in telephoning the Soviet Embassy. Durán has insisted that was not so, that she did not work on Saturdays. (Helms to Rankin & attachment, January 31, 1964, NARA 104-10009-10212.)

KGB officials: ints.Valery Kostikov, Pavel Yatskov, & Oleg Nechiporenko, 1993.

CIA surveillance: HSCA report, "Oswald, the CIA, and Mexico City," by Edwin Lopez and Dan Hardway, released with redactions, 1993; David Phillips's speech to National Military

Intelligence Association, June 1976; David Phillips, *The Night Watch*, New York: Atheneum, 1977; ints. with Cuban Ministry of the Interior officials, 1978 (including Nilvio Labrada, electronics specialist).

320 *Note 6*: The Warren Report referred to this information euphemistically as having come from "sources of high reliability available to the United States in Mexico." What we now know of that will be the basis of much of this chapter. (Report, p. 305)

Surveillance: *New York Times*, September 21, 1975; *Washington Post*, November 26, 1976; Secret Service document 104; State Department telegram 1201, November 28, 1963; Assassination Information Bureau briefing document, "Oswald's Alleged Contacts with the Cuban and Soviet Embassies in Mexico City, 1978"; (with Soviets) Report, p. 734; XXVI.149, 667–; CD 1084d.5; CD 1216; and CD 347 reported in Coleman-Slawson draft.

321 *Note 7*: There was also potential for blaming the Soviets. The CIA would later note that Valery Kostikov, who told the author he met and took a gun away from Oswald, was a member of the KGB's Department Thirteen, which specialized in sabotage and murder. (See refs. in John Newman, *op. cit.*, and in Peter Dale Scott, *Deep Politics and the Death of JFK*. Berkeley: University of California Press, 1993.)

Azcue: statement, Havana public hearings on Kennedy case, July 29, 1978; Azcue testimony, HSCA, September 18, 1978; ints. Eusebio Azcue, Carmen Bilbao, Carmelle Azcue, by Robbyn Swan and Anthony Summers, 1993.

322 Oswald height: XVII.285.

Azcue description: Havana statement July 29, 1978; HSCA III.152–; (belief) HSCA III.136; ints. Azcue family, *supra*.

Mirabal: HSCA III.174.

Azcue maintained: HSCA III.139.

Note 8: Durán's former husband, Horacio Durán Navarro, said in an interview with the author that the Mexican press carried only a poor wire-photo of the Oswald under arrest after the assassination.

Durán on seeing film: ints. 1979, 1994 & corr. June 22, 1979.

323 Durán on height, etc.: HSCA III.103.

Durán on hair/ *"rubio"*: DDP, CIA to Director, November 29, 1963 & attached Mexican Police Interrogation report, November 23, 1963 (in Spanish), NARA 104-10209-10279; HSCA 111.69.

Note 9: The omission of that detail from later CIA and Mexican official reports was noted by a footnote in the Assassinations Committee Report, "Oswald, the CIA, and Mexico City," prepared by Edwin Lopez and Dan Hardway, released with redactions, 1993. (Lopez & Hardway, Mexiso City Report, *supra.*, p. 190, & notes section, p. 24n347).

Azcue "dark blond": HSCA III.136.

"Light-brown": CE 826.

Contreras: ints. 1978, 1993 & by Robbyn Swan 1993, HSCA Report, pp. 124, 125n17.

324 *Note 10:* According to Contreras, "Oswald" said he was a painter by occupation. The author failed to ask whether he understood "painter" to mean that "Oswald" had been employed as a house painter or whether he meant that he was an artist.

325 *Note 11:* The Assassinations Committee failed to reach Contreras in 1978, but the author did not. Gerald Posner attempted in his book, *Case Closed*, to cast doubt on Contreras' statements. Claiming that the author had used a translator to speak with Contreras, he wondered how—since the authentic Oswald could not speak Spanish—Contreras and Oswald could have communicated. The author did not use a translator to speak with Contreras, but Contreras did bring along an English-speaking colleague to ensure that he was completely understood. But the point is moot. The "Oswald" Contreras described could not have been the authentic Oswald, so any details about the real Oswald's Spanish-language ability are irrelevant. Posner (and subsequently author Vincent Bugliosi) have complained that, in a later interview with British TV producer Mark Redhead, Contreras said his meeting with Oswald had not been in 1963 at all. The author was a consultant to Redhead, and interviewed Contreras in the flesh twice. Contreras, who became a senior journalist, knew perfectly well that President Kennedy was assassinated in 1963, and that his meeting with an "Oswald" was shortly before the assassination. When interviewed again in 1993, his story was exactly as recounted to the author in 1978. (Posner: , p. 191–; Bugliosi: , End Notes p. 607–).

Alcaraz: int. Alcaraz, 1993; CE 2121; and multiple FBI reports collated by the Assassination Archives and Research Center, Washington, DC;

Note 12: Alcaraz named a friend, Hector Gastelo, as probably having been present with him during the restaurant encounter with Oswald. An alternative suggestion as to how the Mexico Oswald may have come to associate with students came from the Assassinations Committee. The Committee noted that Cuban consular aide Sylvia Durán recalled suggesting that "Oswald" locate a Mexican reference for his Cuban visa application. The Committee learned that the chairman of the university philosophy department sometimes held seminars at Durán's home. This, the Committee speculated, might explain why "Oswald" made contact with Contreras—who mentioned that the encounter occurred following a discussion at the philosophy department. (HSCA Report. p. 124–.)

Kennan/Keenan: ints. Steve Kennan; "The Man on the Motorcycle in Mexico City" by Bill Kelly, http://jfkcountercoup. blogspot.ie, also drawing on work by researchers Stu Wexler, Greg Parker, and Larry Hancock.

Note 13: In a further twist, the CIA reportedly ran an agent in Mexico, code-named LICOZY-3, who was a student from Philadelphia. This according to former CIA Mexico City station officer Philip Agee, who resigned from the Agency in 1968 and took refuge in Cuba.

The Kenin located in 2006 said he did not recall the Oswald encounter described by Alcaraz, and denied having had any involvement with U.S. intelligence. (Philip Agee, *Inside the Company: CIA Diary.* New York: Bantam, 1976, pp. 545, 634; Kenin: int. Steve Kennan, *Temple University News,* October 4 & November 20, 1960, *Motorcyclist* magazine, August 1963)

326 Signature, etc.: HSCA III.172; HSCA Report, p. 251.

Pictures not taken: CE 2449, 2121, p. 39.

Durán not remember: ints. Durán, 1978, 1993; HSCA III.29–39, & see HSCA III.353.

Azcue on clothing: HSCA III.143 & ints. Azcue family, 1979, 1993.

Durán in Oswald book: XVI.54.

Marina denied: see *Note 3, supra.*—also for reference to Oswald later letter to Soviet Embassy in United States, discussed infra. in Chapter 20.

Note 14: The record of Oswald's interrogations is inconsistent on the matter of whether or not he visited Mexico City. So far as the author can see, police Captain Fritz—who was in charge of questioning—made no reference to Mexico in surviving handwritten notes. Both he and FBI agent James Hosty, however, were to recall that when Oswald was asked—prompted by Hosty—whether he had ever been to Mexico City, he denied it. According to Hosty, he said his only visit to Mexico had been years earlier to the border town of Tijuana, while serving in the Marines. Postal Inspector Harry Holmes, who was present at the final questioning on November 24, stated in his Warren Commission testimony that Oswald admitted that he had been in Mexico City and that he had tried to get clearance to travel to Cuba. Holmes, however, had made no reference to such an admission in his formal memorandum on the Oswald interview—a fact that led Warren Commission attorney David Belin to ask skeptically: "Is this something that you think you might have picked up from just reading

the papers? . . ." (Fritz notes: Notes of Interrogation, www.
maryferrell.org; Fritz testimony: WC IV.210; Hosty: CE 832,
James Hosty with Thomas Hosty, *Assignment: Oswald*, NY:
Arcade, 1996, p. 25; Holmes Testimony: Testimony, April 2,
1964; Memo: CD 296).

327 "Weight": HSCA Report, p. 251.

Note 15: Edwin Lopez, one of the two Committee investigators
who concentrated most on the Mexico City episode and who
coauthored the Committee's study of that aspect of the case,
differed. He and his colleague Dan Hardway, he said in a television appearance years later, "had no choice but to conclude
that Oswald had not visited the embassies." (Lopez speaking
as sworn witness for the program *On Trial: Lee Harvey Oswald*,
Showtime, 1986)

Study: Lopez and Hardway, HSCA Mexico Report, *supra.* p. 250.

"Identified": HSCA Report, p. 249.

Hensen: Newman, *op. cit.*, p. 362–, citing Mexico City 54408
to CIA, Action: C/WH 5, July 20, 1963, NARA, JFK files,
CIA, January 1994 release (5 brown boxes) release: see Box 1,
Folder 2.

328 Standard operation: Bugliosi, *op. cit.*, End Notes, p. 600, citing
Russo int. of Gunn.

October 8 request: Cable, LADILLINGER, October 8, 1963,
NARA 104-10151-1007; & MEXI to DIR, October 9, 1963,
HSCA CIA file cited at Morley, *op. cit.*, p. 187.

CIA cable, October 10: DIR to MEXI, October 10, 1963, NARA
104-10413-10146.

329 "It is believed": CIA to FBI, et.al., October 10, 1963, CIA 201-
289248, reproduced at Newman, *op. cit.*, p. 513.

CIA on photograph: Report, p. 364; XI.469; CD 1287; CD 631;
CD 1287; CD 674. David Phillips, (, p. 141) said there was
no photograph of Oswald. See also document 948-927T, CIA
internal memorandum dated May 5, 1967.

330 CIA "did not have a known": Rocca to Houston & attachment,
May 12, 1967, CIA file no. 80T01357A, www.maryferrell.org.

Colby: int. for *The American Assassins*, Part 2, CBS-TV, November 26, 1975.

"Photographs of a certain": Scott to King, November 22, 1963, CIA file 80T01357A, www.maryferrell.org.

"Could be embarrassing": CD 1287.

Note 16: The House Assassinations Committee's Mexico Report noted that there had been one speculative identification of the photos of the man who was not Oswald. This is a reference to a CIA source—identified only as UPSTREAM—who had said the unidentified man was "a KGB type by name of 'Yuri' whom he knew in Moscow in 1964." A document suggests that "Yuri" might have been one and the same as a Soviet scientist with intelligence connections named Yuri Ivanovich Moskalev. This remains only a single, unconfirmed suggestion. (Lopez & Hardway, Mexico City Report, *supra.*, p. 179, Hopkins memorandum, April 1977, NARA 104-10428-10010).

Agency did have pictures: CD 692; CIA document 590-252, March 6, 1964 (memo to Warren Commission).

331 *Note 17*: CIA files also contained the two Oswald photos that had been taken in 1961 in the Soviet Union by American tourists visiting Minsk. The CIA claimed they were taken fortuitously, selected for reasons having nothing to do with Oswald, and that Oswald's presence in the pictures was not noticed until after the assassination. See discussion in Chapter 11. (CIA document 614-261, March 20, 1964; XX.474)

CIA and "wait out": HSCA IV.215; HSCA XI.63, 491, Rankin to McCone, February 12, 1964, NARA 104-10423-10078, Rocca to Helms, March 5, 1964, CIA 201-289248, www.maryferrell.org.

Note 18: Richard Helms, who in 1963 had been the CIA Deputy Director for Plans, told the Assassinations Committee in 1978 that the factor governing whether information could be provided to the Commission was the need "to be careful about our sources and methods." "John Scelso" (real name John Whitten), who had been chief of covert operations for Mexico and

Central America, said the CIA did not tell the Commission the origin of the photo because it was "not authorized, at first, to reveal all our [sensitive] operations." (Helms: HSCA.IV.12; Scelso/Whitten: *Washington Monthly*, December 2003; "not authorized": HSCA XI.491)

Liebeler: Epstein, *Chronicles*, *op. cit.*, p. 107, citing int. Liebeler.

CIA denied: Lopez & Hardway, HSCA Mexico Report, *supra.* pp. 9, 90–, 114–.

Cameras not used weekends: (Sov) CIA doc. *re* LILYRIC basehouse, April 30, 1964, NARA Record 104-10414-10091, (Cuban) corr. Jeff Morley, 2012, Morley, *op. cit.*, p. 179.

332 Camera broke down: Morley, *op. cit.*, p. 181, 325n, citing testimony of David Phillips.

New camera: *ibid.*, pp. 179, 324

Dozen pictures: CIA documents 929–, 939, 927A–K (CIA Document Deposition Index); (October 1) CIA document 948-927T.

Five visits: Lopez & Hardway, Mexico City Report, *supra.*, pp. 6, 91–.

Scott ms.: Winston Scott, *Foul Foe* (ms.), Chapter XXIV, p. 273, www.maryferrell.org.

Officers say CIA got Oswald photo: Rex Bradford unpub. ms, *Not a Shred . . .* , *supra.*, p. 10–, Lopez & Hardway, Mexico City Report, *supra.*, p. 97, Morley, *op. cit.*, p. 179–.

"Photographs of Oswald": HSCA Report, p. 125n.

333 AARB "CIA reports": AARB Report, p. 87–.

Colby: int for, *The American Assassins*, CBS-TV, November 26, 1975.

Agency tapped/CIA record: Lopez & Hardway, Mexico City Report, *supra.*, p. 117–, Morley, op.cit., p. 325, CD 1084d.5; CD 1084d.4–; and Ambassador Mann to Sec. State, November 28, 1963.

"Very poor Russian": Legat Mexico City to Director, November 25, 1963, NARA 104-10400-10026

"Terrible, hardly recognizable": David Slawson memo for record, NARA 104-10087-10116, HSCA Report, p. 251

334 Oswald's Russian: HSCA Report, p. 251, int. Marina Oswald, 1993.

Durán: HSCA III.114

Transcribers/"Usually": reported by Ron Kessler, *Washington Post*, November 26, 1976.

Scott: Winston Scott, *Foul Foe* (ms.), Chapter XXIV, p. 186, www.maryferrell.org.

"destroyed tape[s]: AARB Report, p. 88.

Note 19: The known comments of Mexico City CIA personnel do indicate that the *routine* was to wipe and reuse insignificant tapes. That seems to be what Station Chief Scott at least initially believed had been the fate of the Oswald recording of September 28. He reported: "Station unable compare voice as first tape erased prior to receipt of second call." David Phillips, who was running anti-Castro operations out of Mexico in 1963, told a Senate Committee that a search for the tapes on November 23 confirmed that they had been erased. (David Phillips, *The Night Watch*, New York: Atheneum, 1977, p. 125, File Summary, David Phillips, NARA 180-10143-10126, HSCA X.46, Morley, *op. cit.*, p. 209. But see Fonzi, *op. cit.*, p. 285–).

Goodpasture: Morley, *op. cit.*, p. 183.

Note 20: Author Vincent Bugliosi has suggested that Goodpasture's statements were unreliable. Only pages later, however, he relies on other Goodpasture comments to imply that her former boss Winston Scott's memory may have been "faulty" when he wrote his unpublished manuscript—or that his motive was sell books. (Bugliosi, *op. cit.*, Endnotes pp. 596, 603–).

335 Hoover memo: HSCA Report, p. 249–; Sen. Int. Cttee. *Performance of Intelligence Agencies*, p. 32; CD 87—Secret Service control no. 104 (cite uncertainly identified on document); CIA document 14, Mexico City to HQ, November 22, 1963; HSCA Report, p. 258.

"Neither the tape": Belmont to Tolson, November 23, 1963. Misc. Church Cttee. Records, NARA 157-10014-10169.

Johnson/Hoover: transcript of conversation, November 23, 1963, LBJ Tapes, LBJ Library, 1993–1994 releases.

336 *Note 21:* The available record indicates that the tape to which Hoover was referring in the exchange with President Johnson was of the Saturday, September 28 "Oswald" call from the Cuban Consulate to the Soviet Embassy—a call that, as noted earlier, seems unlikely to have been made by the authentic Oswald—if, as Sylvia Durán insisted, she had not been at the Consulate on the twenty-eighth. The HSCA's Mexico City report saw reason to believe her, and thought the intercepted call "another possible indication that an impostor may also have visited the Consulate." (Lopez & Hardway, Mexico City Report, *supra.*, esp. p. 409– , & see Newman, *op. cit.*, p. 367–)

Note 22: At 7:23 p.m. CST on November 23, Dallas Agent in Charge Shanklin had sent a new report to FBI headquarters—revising his earlier communication to Belmont and stating that only a report of the "Oswald" Mexico conversation was available—not a recording. Nevertheless, a further FBI message, sent two days later to its Mexico office—on November 25—contains a request to "include tapes previous reviewed Dallas if they were returned to you." On November 26, the Dallas office said there had apparently been "some confusion in that no tapes were taken to Dallas." Four Dallas agents who had conversed with the authentic Oswald, meanwhile, were to tell the Assassinations Committee that they had not listened to a recording of Oswald's voice after the assassination. Unaccounted for, however, is the recall of three other agents who had also conversed with Oswald—the Committee failed to contact them.

On November 26, in a conversation with CIA Director John McCone, Hoover would again allude to the matter of the photograph but not to a recording. (Shanklin November 23/ Dallas office November 26: HSCA Report, p. 250; "tapes previously reviewed": Washington to Legat Mexico, November 25, 1963, FBI 105-3702-16, www.history-matters.com; McCone:

Max Holland, *The Kennedy Assassination Tapes*, New York: Knopf, 2004, p. 106.)

Tapes flown?: Staff to Schweiker & Hart, March 5, 1976, NARA 157-10014-10168, p. 3, Belmont to Tolson, November 23, 1963, *supra.*, SA Heitman to SAC Dallas, November 22, 1963, FBI 124-10027-10345; Mexico City to Director, CIA, January 23, 1963, NARA 104-10015-10123 & see Morley, *op. cit.*, pp. 206, 330 & Rex Bradford paper cited earlier *supra.*

Note 23: The FBI agent who flew up from Mexico, future congressman Eldon Rudd, was very evidently reluctant to talk when contacted by the author in the 1970s. Questioned in the 1990s by a reporter, he said, "There were no tapes to my knowledge." ("Call on JFK Wasn't Oswald," AP, November 21, 1999)

Hoover-Johnson recording/"erased": transcript of conversation, November 23, 1963, LBJ Tapes, LBJ Library, 1993–1994 releases; Notes Relating to Audio Recording contract, January 21, 1999, www.history-matters.com; & see Bradford, "Not a Speck," *supra.*, p. 6 & see Holland, *op. cit.*, p. 69n15.

337 "false"/ "double-dealing": Brennan to Sullivan, January 15, 1964, linked to "Conspiracy—Oswald, the CIA, and Mexico City," www.pbs.org.

Three witnesses: interviews—William Coleman, 1993–1994; David Slawson, 1993; former senior CIA officer, 1993–1994, on condition of anonymity, author's memo to PBS's *Frontline* producer, 1993.

Belin: transcript, *Nightline*, ABC News, November 11, 1983 int. by Ted Koppel, cited in *Third Decade*, Vol. 4, Issue 2.

338 Note 24: The author obtained the interviews with Coleman, Slawson, and the CIA officer in 1993 for PBS's *Frontline* program. As the author gave his word that he would not publicly reveal the officer's name, and though the latter is apparently now dead, he does not reveal it now. He did at the time share the information with the relevant *Frontline* producer.

In correspondence with people other than the author,

Coleman and Slawson also referred unequivocally to having listened to Oswald tapes. Slawson, moreover, reportedly said in another interview that he listened to an Oswald tape. Jeremy Gunn, who was executive director of the Assassination Records Review Board, said in 1995 that both Coleman and Slawson told him they "heard the tape."

Much earlier in 1978, however, and in contrast to his clear recollection cited in the text, Coleman had told an Assassinations Committee interviewer that he did not have "the faintest idea" whether the CIA had explained "why it did not have an actual recording of Oswald's voice." Coleman gave a vague, hesitant answer when asked about the matter in a recorded Assassinations Committee interview. Slawson, for his part, responded to a question by a member of the Assassination Records Review Board as to whether he had heard the tapes by saying—and repeating: "I am not at liberty to discuss that." It had been very evident, even when the author interviewed the two former Warren attorneys, that they were concerned about perhaps breaching their national security undertakings.

Anne Goodpasture, the former aide to CIA Station Chief Scott cited alsewhere in this chapter, told the Review Board she thought Scott "squirreled away" a copy of the tape. For sources on the above, other information, and a back and forth on the issue between researchers, interested readers may study the End Notes for the book *Reclaiming History* by Vincent Bugliosi, who attempted—unsuccessfully in the author's view—to show that no tapes survived. For a rebuttal, see the unpublished paper supplied to the author by researcher Rex Bradford, entitled "Not a Speck of a Scintilla of Evidence for Conspiracy: Vincent Bugliosi on the Mexico City Impostor." Fresh information appeared in Jefferson Morley's 2008 book *Our Man in Mexico*. (Gunn/"heard the tape": Gunn question in AARB testimony of Anne Goodpasture, December 15, 1995, p. 27; Coleman HSCA testimony/vague: audiotape of August 2, 1978 testimony at www.history-matters.

com; Slawson/Goodpasture: "not at liberty," Bradford, "Not a Speck," *supra.*, p. 7–, 9; Bugliosi: , p. 1049– & especially End Notes, p. 592–; fresh: Morley, op. cit, pp. 7, 290).

Note 25: The most thorough document research on Mexico of recent years has been done by Jefferson Morley and John Newman. Morley is a former *Washington Post* journalist whose work has also appeared in the *New York Review of Books, Reader's Digest, Slate,* and *Salon.* He is founder of the website JFKfacts.org, which aims to improve media coverage of the assassination and press for the release of still-secret government records. Morley's biography of Station Chief Scott, with a Foreword by Scott's son Michael, was published in 2008.

John Newman was for twenty years a U.S. Army intelligence analyst and specialized in examining cable traffic. He authored *Oswald and the CIA,* published in 1995. The author, who has had extensive contact with both Morley and Newman, recommends their books as vital reading on the Mexico episode. (Jefferson Morley, *Our Man in Mexico: Winston Scott and the Hidden History of the CIA,* Lawrence, KS: University of Kansas Press, 2008; John Newman, *Oswald and the CIA,* New York: Carroll & Graf, 1995).

"Latest HDQS": Director CIA to Mexico City, November 10, 1963, CIA file no. 201-289248, www.jfk.hood.edu & see Newman, *op. cit.,* p. 512.

Agency knew/FBI copied: Morley, *op. cit.,* p. 195, Newman, *op. cit.,* pp. 348–, 392–.

339   hardly inadvertent: Morley, *op. cit.,* p. 192–.

Roman: Morley, *op. cit.,* p. 194–.

340   Phillips: Phillips, *op. cit.,* p. 142.

Phillips & FPCC/ mirror image: Newman, *op. cit.,* p. 240–, referring in greater detail to newly released CIA documents author also perused—especially memorandum from [name censored] in WH/4 Registry to Mr. Belt, and memo, Papich to Hoover, October 7, 1961, CIA box 41, folder 33, no. 3.; int. Joseph Burkholder Smith, 1994; int. & corr. Hal Verb, 1994.

Hunt on Phillips: E. Howard Hunt, HSCA testimony, Pt. II, November 3, 1978, p. 29.

Headed unit: Morley, *op. cit.*, p. 177.

"Spent several": Phillips, *op. cit.*, p. 142.

341 Committee not believe: HSCA Report, p. 125n, Lopez & Hardway, Mexico City Report, *supra.*, pp. 51, 55–, 58, 168.

"routinely": *Washington Post*, November 26, 1976.

"no question": Bugliosi, *op. cit.*, p. 1050, reporting conversations with Phillips in connection with a television mock Oswald "trial." But see, Fonzi, *op. cit.*, p. 285–.

"blip": Phillips, *op. cit.*, p. 139.

"special watch": Winston Scott, *op. cit.*, p. 269.

sworn testimony: Kaiser, *op. cit.*, pp. 288, 300.

Chilean general: memo for record, September 16, 1970, CIA cable, October 18, 1970, Report on CIA Chilean Task Force, November 18, 1970, all linked to National Security Archive Briefing Book 8, www.gwu.edu, "The Holy Grail of the JFK Story," *Salon*, November 22, 2011.

Angleton/undercover unit: Morley, *op. cit.*, pp. 113–, 162.

342 *Note 26*: Scott's widow Janet, family members have said, loathed and feared Angleton and told him to take what he wanted. According to Horton, Mrs. Scott herself asked that the material be removed. (Morley, *op. cit.*, pp. 293, 6)

Angleton/Horton turned up/flown to D.C.: Morley, pp. 2, 3, 7–, 254, 286.

Hartmann: HSCA Int. of Melbourne Hartman, October 10, 1978, p. 29–, but see Bugliosi, *op. cit.*, End Notes, p. 597.

Michael Scott/destruction: Morley, *op. cit.*, pp. 291–, 294n, 345n.

20. Facts and Appearances

345 Oswald's return to USA: XXIV.594, 569, 571.
YMCA: X.281–; XI.478; XXII.159, 207.
visits wife: XXIII.509; XXIV.702.

Book Depository job: CD 5.325; CD 3.34, 121; III.121, 212.

Note 1: The President's November 22 motorcade route, including the virtual certainty that it would pass in front of the Depository, would not start emerging in the local press until November 16. See *Dallas Morning News*, November 16, 19, 20 & 22, 1963, *Dallas Times Herald*, November 19, 1963, in CE 1022.

Renting rooms: XXIII.390; XXVI.538; VI.400–.

346   Beckley: VI.436; X.292–.

Birthday: I:53; III.40; XVII.189; McMillan, *op. cit.*, p. 379.

Supervisor: III.216.

Another job: I.68; McMillan, *op. cit.*, p. 379.

Note 2: The Warren Report did not mention the letter indicating that Oswald expected to cease working, and the IRS document did not become public until three years later. The alleged assassin's income-tax returns for 1962 long remained closed to researchers. No real clarification has yet been produced for official reticence about Oswald's income.

IRS letter: FBI Exhibit 274, reported in *Dallas Morning News*, May 1, 1977; sections 6103 and 7213 of Internal Revenue Code and 18 U.S.C. 1905, cited by Archivist of U.S.A.

Hosty: Report pp. 327, 419, 435, 437, 660, 739; analysis of Hosty involvement–Sen. Int. Cttee., *Performance of Intelligence Agencies*, Appendix A; (November 1) IV.449; I.48; III.92/96–; (November 5) I.56; II.15; Hearings on FBI Oversight before House Subcttee on Civil and Constitutional Rights, Serial 2, pt. 3, pp. 143 and 145; HSCA Report, p. 194–.

347   Women know phone number: III.43; XI.53.

Hosty and Oswald note: II.18 (Mrs. Paine); HSCA Report, p. 195–; Sen. Int. Cttee., *Performance of Intelligence Agencies*, Appendix B; (testimony of Hosty, Fenner, Shanklin, Howe, etc.) Hearings on FBI Oversight before House Subcommittee on Civil and Constitutional Rights, Serial 2, pt. 3, October 21 & December 11, 1975.

349   *Note 3*: Some have speculated that obfuscation over the note was

merely part of an effort to minimize even an innocent Bureau connection with Oswald—that Shanklin, faced with Director Hoover's fury over the failure to spot Oswald as a potential threat, tried to erase evidence of opportunities missed. Or perhaps, as suggested in earlier pages, someone at the FBI feared that full exposure of U.S. intelligence interest in Oswald would reveal elements of the case that remained hidden.

The Assassinations Committee investigated another instance of strange FBI behavior regarding Oswald and Agent Hosty. Oswald's address book, seized after his arrest, contained Hosty's name, address, telephone number, and car license number. This was not necessarily compromising, for it had quickly become known that Hosty visited Marina in search of Oswald shortly before the assassination, and Marina was to explain that she passed information about Hosty to her husband. Nevertheless, when agents typed up the address book's contents to send to the Warren Commission, the reference to Hosty was missing. Only later, following independent reports and in the light of Commission interest in Oswald's relationship with the FBI, did the Bureau confirm the existence of the Hosty notation. The Assassinations Committee investigated the omission and concluded that "one or more FBI agents sought to protect Hosty from personal embarrassment by trying . . . to exclude his name from the reporting." (HSCA Report, p. 186–; see also Report, p. 327 and CD 205, CD 385, V.112, V.242; and Malley, HSCA III.507–.)

Letter to Soviet Embassy: Report, p. 739; (on Mrs. Paine's desk) III.14–; XVI.33, 443.

Note 4: In an affidavit for the Senate Intelligence Committee and as he repeated in an interview for this book, former colleague Agent Carver Gayton quoted Hosty as having told him and colleagues that he had listed Oswald as a PSI [Potential Security Informant]. Hosty maintained, though, that he had never met him (Gayton affidavit for Senate int. Cttee, January 30, 1976, released 1994, NARA 157-10002-10267 & int. Gayton by Robbyn Swan)

350 *Note 5*: On their own initiative, Hosty and a colleague ignored the order and preserved the draft of the letter to the Soviet Embassy.

351 Hosty and "bombs": interview with Earl Golz, *Dallas Morning News*, August 30, 1978; Post-office box: XXII.717.

ACLU meeting and Paine: XI.403 and 11.408.

Oswald writes to Communist Party: XXII.70.

352 *Note 6*: The postal inspector guessed that someone might have telephoned the change-of-address to the New Orleans sub-post office—that the writing was that of a post-office clerk. There was no further investigation, just a weary comment by Warren Commission lawyer Wesley Liebeler: "Well, in any event, we will add this to the pile." The postal inspector's guess, even if it was right, changed nothing. Oswald was in Dallas and had himself already arranged for mail to be forwarded. (VII.289–308, 525–530.)

Note 7: Those who spoke of Oswald's calls in a foreign language were Mary Bledsoe, the landlady at the house in which he first stayed, Arthur C. Johnson, husband of the landlady of the second rooming house, and Hugh Slough, who also roomed there. Bledsoe and Slough believe the calls included at least one to each address by a man. (Slough mentioned this for apparently the first time in a 2006 press interview. (Bledsoe/Johnson: VI.400–; X.307; Slough: *Dallas Morning News*, March 9, 2006, & see Russo, *Live by the Sword, op. cit.*, p. 269.)

Enco manager: XXVI.250–; CE 2820.

353 Louisiana operator: CD 75.180–.

Note 8: The camp in question was at Lacombe, close to Slidell, one of a number of Cuban exile camps around Lake Pontchartrain during the period. The Lacombe property was controlled by William McClaney, who with his brother Mike, had operated out of Havana during the heyday of gambling before the Castro revolution. The House Assassinations Committee found no evidence that the 1963 McClaney operation in Lousiana was linked to the crime syndicate. For information on this camp and others see HSCA X.71–, 185, Sen. Int. Cttee., *Performance of Intelligence Agencies*, p. 11–, Russo, *Live by the Sword*, *op. cit.*, p. 183–, & 1998 edition of this book, pp. 252, 324.

354 *Note 9*: There was a report that a young man calling himself Harvey Oswald walked into the offices of the Selective Service System in Austin, Texas' capital city, on September 25. He supposedly told Mrs. Lee Dannelly, the assistant chief of the administrative division, that he had been discharged from the Marine Corps under "other than honorable conditions" and hoped to get the discharge upgraded on the basis of two years' subsequent good conduct.

The proprietor of a supermarket in Irving, the Dallas suburb where Marina Oswald lived, one Leonard Hutchinson, said that he had been asked two weeks before the assassination to cash a check for $189 made out in the name of "Harvey Oswald"—the same name reportedly used in the Austin sighting. A nearby barber, who said he cut the hair of a man who looked like Oswald, reported having seen him entering the same supermarket.

On November 9, reportedly, a man calling himself Lee Oswald visited a Dallas car showroom to discuss buying a used car, then rattled the salesman by test-driving one too fast. The account was corroborated by two of the salesman's colleagues, one of whom quoted "Oswald" as having said that in view of the high prices he might have to go "back to Russia where they treat workers like men." One salesman said "Oswald" returned to the showroom just days before the assassination.

Western Union's night manager in Dallas, a Mr. Hamblen, was sure Oswald had been a customer who collected money orders several times and—in the second week of November—sent a telegram. The customer had identified himself with a "Navy ID card and a library card." A statement by a colleague supported Hamblen's account.

On November 1, reportedly, a young man had drawn attention to himself while buying rifle ammunition at Morgan's Gunshop in Fort Worth—he boasted about having been in the Marine Corps. The three witnesses at Morgan's thought the man had looked like Oswald. Similar reports included the manager of what had previously been a gun store who recalled an early November visit by a man who resembled Oswald accompanied by a wife and two children, one an infant. The couple had conversed in a foreign language. This "Oswald" had wanted the firing pin on his rifle repaired. An anonymous caller told the police that the alleged assassin had had a rifle sighted at Irving Sports Shop. Dial Ryder, an Irving Sports employee, found a customer ticket that bore the name "Oswald". The work done had involved drilling holes for a telescopic-sight mounting.

There were reports of an "Oswald" seen at the Sports Drome Rifle Range on November 9, the day after the rifle was probably retrieved from the Irving Shop. A number of witnesses described a man who had been an excellent shot but drew attention to himself by being loud and obnoxious. Dr. Homer Wood, who was at the range that day with his young son, told the author in 1978 why he had felt obliged to report what he had seen. "On November 22, in the afternoon," Dr. Wood said, "I was watching the television at home. As soon as I saw Oswald on TV I said to my wife, 'He looks like the man who was sitting in the booth next to our son, out at the rifle range.' . . . When my son came home from school, I purposely didn't say anything to him. Well, he also looked at the television and he spoke to me quickly, saying, 'Daddy that looks just like that man we saw at the range, when we were sighting in our rifles.' " Wood's son, who had been thirteen years old in 1963, recalled the man mentioning that he was using a 6.5-mm Italian rifle with a four-power scope. Years later, after he, too, had become a doctor, the son still thought the man he saw at the range had been Oswald.

The marksman left the range, he said, accompanied by "a man in a newer-model car."

In October, when the real Oswald had just returned from Mexico, according to a teacher, she disturbed three men firing a rifle on her land near Dallas. The owner, a teacher, said one of the men had looked like Oswald, another of them "Latin, perhaps Cuban." She reportedly found a 6.5-mm Mannlicher-Carcano cartridge case on her land and handed it over to the FBI. Laboratory tests showed it had not been fired from the Carcano found in the Book Depository. The teacher said one of the men had been "Latin, perhaps Cuban." Some of the other witnesses cited above also spoke of the man they saw having been accompanied by a man they thought Latin. (Dannelly: Report, p. 732; XXIV.729–; Hutchinson: X.327; XXVI.178; Barber: X.309; car showroom: Report, pp. 320, 840; XXVI.450; X.340, 345, 347–; XXVI.430, 577, 682, 702, 703, 704, 664; Western Union: Report, 332; XI.311; X.412; XXI.774, 745, 752–; Exhibits 3005, 3006, 3015; *Dallas Times-Herald,* November 30, 1963; *Dallas Morning News,* December 1, 1963; Morgan's Gunshop: XXIV.704; previously gun store: XI.253, 262; Report, p. 317; XXII.546–; XXVI.456; Irving Sports Shop: XXIV.329–; Report, p. 315, XXII.525/531; XI.224–; (screws) I.483. Sports Drome: Report, p. 318; X.370–; X.380; X.357, 373; XXIV.304; Dr. Wood: int., 1978; X.386; XXIII.403; XXVI.368; teacher: int. Mrs. Lovell Penn by researcher Penn Jones, June 1975; and Mannlicher bullet, CD 205.182.)

354 Inspector: Sen. Int. Cttee., Performance of Intelligence Agencies, p. 91.

Note 10: Another piece of information suggests that someone other than the real Oswald used his identity in New Orleans well over two years earlier. In 1963, right after the assassination, the FBI was contacted by the manager of a New Orleans Ford Motors franchise, Oscar Deslatte. The name Oswald had struck a chord in his memory, and a check in his order files turned up a docket—which the FBI duly preserved—showing that a prospective purchaser using the name Oswald negotiated to buy Ford trucks in January 1961. Deslatte's Oswald, an American accompanied by a swarthy Cuban, tried to purchase ten trucks that month during the buildup to the Bay of Pigs invasion—a time when U.S. intelligence agents and their Cuban protégés were buying supplies and equipment for the operation.

The real Oswald had of course been on the other side of the world, in the Soviet Union, in early 1961. Oswald is a common enough name, and one would be inclined to see this episode as another red herring—were it not for the identity of the anti-Castro group that wanted to buy trucks from Deslatte. Its name, clearly legible on the docket, was "Friends of Democratic Cuba," and men at that organization link directly to the story of the authentic Oswald. A vice president of "Friends," Gerald Tujague, had employed the young Oswald as a messenger in 1955 and 1956—around the time he was a cadet in the Civil Air Patrol under David Ferrie. Guy Banister, moreover, the former FBI agent alleged to have manipulated Oswald in his Fair Play for Cuba Committee activity in summer 1963, had been on the board of directors of "Friends" in 1961.

Why Oswald's identity would have been used by anti-Castro activists at such an early date is a puzzle unless—if they had access to Oswald's identification documents and knew he was out of the country—they at that point simply thought it a useful pseudonym. In June 1960, after Oswald's departure for the Soviet Union, an FBI memo issued in Director Hoover's name warned of "a possibility that an imposter is using Oswald's birth certificate." Perhaps, in an FBI alert to the possibility that the Soviets might make use of Oswald's I.D., this reflected merely routine caution. Yet the FBI and other agencies were to resume exchanging reports referring to the birth certificate after Oswald returned from Russia. The original of his birth certificate never did turn up. As we saw earlier, meanwhile, it seems that a phony certificate had been prepared for Oswald in 1955, when he tried to join the Marine Corps while underage.

Former Warren Commission attorney David Slawson said years later that he and colleagues had been unaware of the "imposter" correspondence. It had perhaps been withheld, he thought, because of "a general CIA effort to take out everything that reflected on them." The CIA, the record shows, had known the birth certificate was missing as early as May 1960, when FBI information about it was circulated to several Agency departments. On the relevant document, the relevant passages are emphasized and the words "Oswald took his birth certificate with him" underlined. (Deslatte: CD 75.677 and int. by New Orleans District Attorney's Office, 1967; "Assassination Chronicles," Vol. 1, Issue 4, December 1995; Purchase form: FBI file no. 89-69-1A6, released 1979).

Tujague: HSCA X.134; IX.101.

Banister: articles of incorporation of FODC, filed at Louisiana Secretary of State's office, May 17, 1967.

"Imposter" warning: CD 294B; Hoover memo to State Dept. Office of Security, June 3, 1960.

other agencies: Edward Hickey to John White, March 31, 1961; XVIII.373, State Department document, July 11, 1961; see also John Newman, op. cit., pp. 143, 216, 266, 269, and VF, December 1994. Also of possible relevance are XXII.99, XVII.728, XVII.685; and FBI Director Hoover, (New York) memo May 23, 1960, FBI file no. 105-82555, unrecorded before serial 7; Slawson: New York Times, February 23, 1975; record shows: John Newman, op. cit., p. 160.

"Oswald" at DRE meeting: CD 205.646-.

355   *Note 11:* The citizen who recalled this incident was Harold Reynolds. González left Abilene soon after the assassination, and was reportedly last heard of in Venezuela. (article by Earl Golz, *Dallas Morning News*, June 10, 1979).

Note 12: De Varona stayed on November 15 at the New Orleans home of Agustín Guitart, the uncle of Silvia Odio, whose account of an encounter with a man identified as "Leon Oswald," in the company of men who said they were anti-Castro fighters, is the subject of the pages that follow. De Varona was in New Orleans to attend a meeting of the Cuban Revolutionary Council. (HSCA X.62)

Odio: interviews with author, 1978, 1979, 1993, 1994; HSCA Report, p. 137– and HSCA X.19–; also Warren XI.327, 386; XXVI.362, 472; see especially study in Meagher, *op. cit.*, p. 376–; XVI.834; CD 1553; "Dallas: The Cuban Connection," article in *Saturday Evening Post*, March 1976.

358 *Note 13:* Silvia Odio has explained that she suffered from blackouts at various periods of her life. The cause has been diagnosed medically since 1963. Her apparent shock on the day of the assassination does not, against that background, seem far-fetched. There were many, perhaps thousands, who wept openly when they heard the traumatic news of the President's assassination. With Odio's recent visitation and disturbing phone call about "Oswald," her reaction seems understandable enough. There is no doubt she did pass out, and she was hospitalized. The way the Odio incident emerged is highly complex and the result of a series of conversations for which her sister Sarita was originally responsible. In the event, the FBI became interested because of information about Jack Ruby, not Odio. (For full exposition, see HSCA X.24.) The person with whom Silvia Odio discussed the incident before the assassination was Dr. Burton Einspruch, her psychiatrist. There is no suggestion that Odio's reliability was diminished because she was visiting a psychiatrist. Dr. Einspruch explains that Odio was a young woman of wealthy birth, transferred abruptly from affluence in Cuba to hard times as an exile. She had been deserted by her husband and left with young children to raise and other family members to help. She came to him, as would so many in America, to talk out her problems. Dr. Einspruch has said, from the start, that he has "great faith in Mrs. Odio's story of having met Lee Harvey Oswald." (ints. Silvia Odio, and HSCA X.29.)

359 Letter to father: XX.690–. (Odio's own letter, sent to her father on October 27, 1963, did not survive. She clearly did write one because we have her father's reply, written at Christmas.) Slawson "has been checked": HSCA. XI.165.

Liebeler: HSCA XI.237.

360 Slawson "the most significant": *Saturday Evening Post*, March 1976.

Rankin: XXVI.834.

Hoover information on Hall: XXVI.834; collapse of Hall story: CD.1553; HSCA XI.600; Sylvia Meagher, *op. cit.*, p. 386.

Odio first conversation: CD 205.644.

361 Kaiser suggested: Kaiser, *op. cit.*, p. 257–, & corr. David Kaiser.

Oswald arriving back: Report, p. 736.

Hotel records: int. of Hilda Giser, October 8, 1964, *re* Lawnview Motel registration cards, FBI DL 100-10461, in Oswald HQ file, 105-82555, Section 222, courtesy of Jerry Shinley.

Press reported: *Dallas Morning News*, September 26, 1963.

Hall: 1967 interview for article in *National Enquirer*, September 1, 1968; Hall & HSCA: *Washington Post*, May 21, 1977; (immunized testimony) cited at HSCA X.22 and HSCA staff notes, and notes from tapes, released 1993.

362 "fabrication": HSCA Report, p. 138.

Hall career: HSCA refs. cited *supra*; Jaffe interview of Hall in author's collection, July 23, 1975; *The Village Voice*, October 3, 1977; Dick Russell, *The Man Who Knew Too Much*, New York: Carroll & Graf, 1992, pp. 480–, 777.

Intelligence training: Jaffe interview, *supra*.

Exile training: memo of researcher Scott Malone to HSCA chief investigator C. Fenton, June 3, 1977.

Trafficante: HSCA sources *supra*; Hall int. by Harold Weisberg, p. 92; HSCA X.22; & Weisberg, *op. cit.*, pp. 161, 273–; Malone memo *supra*; and memo by researcher Mark Allen to HSCA staffer Donovan Gay, June 2, 1977.

CIA "debriefing": FBI file no. 81-0351D0647, memo for Chief of Security Analysis, September 10, 1975.

Hall's son: *Dallas Morning News*, September 13, 1989.

HSCA conclusion: HSCA Report, p. 139.

"a situation that indicates": HSCA X.32.

363 HSCA speculated: HSCA Report, p. 140.

Note 14: A rider to that theory is that this was a deliberate ploy to link JURE, a left-wing exile group, with the assassination. Odio's visitors posed as JURE members, and the Odio family supported its aims. In prison in Cuba, Silvia Odio's father responded in alarm on receiving a letter from his daughter about the visit from "Leopoldo." "Tell me who this is who says he is my friend," he wrote back, "Be careful. I do not have any friend who might be here, through Dallas, so reject his friendship until you give me his name." Later, at liberty following his long imprisonment in Cuba, Señor Odio said he was sure the visitors had had no real connection to him. JURE leaders in the United States were also nonplussed. It was a fact, though, that rightist exiles thought JURE supporters little better than Communists—they were potentially targets of a setup.

Warren Commission attorneys Slawson and Coleman, who focused on possible foreign conspiracy, mulled the thought that anti-Castro Cubans "encouraged" Oswald to assassinate Kennedy, perhaps tricked him in some way. The author Jean Davison made the point that—even if the "leftist" Oswald was blamed for the assassination—his presence at the Odios' home with "Leopoldo" and "Angelo" would still leave the anti-Castro side vulnerable to suspicion. The author Vincent Bugliosi has offered a lengthy summary of possible explanations of the Odio episode. Interestingly, though usually a fierce opponent of anything that smacks of conspiracy theory, even he conceded that the Odio episode holds water evidentially and must be taken seriously. (JURE: XXVI.839; HSCA X.31; Father's letter: XX.690; HSCA X.29).

Coleman/Slawson: Coleman & Slawson to WC, June

1964, "Oswald's Foreign Activities, Summary of Evidence Which May Be Said to Show Foreign Involvement in the Assassination of President Kennedy," www.history-matters. com.

Davison: Jean Davison, *Oswald's Game*, New York: Norton, 1988, p. 192–; Bugliosi: , p.1309

"As it stands": HSCA notes *supra*, and note donated to Assassination Archives and Research Center by William Scott Malone, citing A. J. Weberman int. of Hall, 1977.

21. Countdown

364 Attwood episode: ints. William Attwood, 1978–1979 (with access to diary), Mrs. Attwood, 1994, Arthur Schlesinger, 1978; William Attwood, *The Reds and the Blacks*, New York: Harper & Row, 1967, p. 142–, William Attwood, *The Twilight Struggle: Tales of the Cold War*, New York: Harper & Row, 1987, p. 257–, Schlesinger, *Robert F. Kennedy, op. cit.*, p. 550–; Sen. Int. Cttee. *Assassination Plots*, p. 173-; HSCA Report, p. 127, Richard Tomlinson (London Weekend TV) corr. & memo of Attwood conv., January 29, 1986; "Kennedy Sought Dialogue with Cuba," National Security Archive paper & linked Attwood and White House memoranda & November 5, 1963 White House tape recording, www.gwu.edu.

365 "go-ahead": Schlesinger, *Robert F. Kennedy, op. cit.*, p. 552.

Note 1: U.S. intelligence files indicate that Lechuga had in the recent past been the lover of Sylvia Durán, the aide who in late September 1963 dealt with the Oswald visa request in Mexico City. Durán herself confirmed to the author that there had been an affair. There is no evidence in the context of the assassination story, however, that the relationship was more than a coincidence, a quirk of history. (John Newman, *op. cit.*, p. 279–, int. Durán, 1994)

Vietnam withdrawal: Schlesinger, *A Thousand Days, op. cit.*, p. 908; *JFK Public Papers*, 1963, p. 760 (for detailed study of Kennedy policy on Vietnam, see Schlesinger, *Robert F. Kennedy*, *op. cit.*, p. 712–).

CIA: Peter Dale Scott in *The Pentagon Papers* (Senator Gravel, ed.; Boston: 1971), vol. 5, p. 215–; John Newman, *JFK and Vietnam*, New York: Warner Books, 1992; *New Republic*, December 11, 1965, article by Harry Rowe Ransom.

Howard & Castro: int. Gore Vidal, 1994; unpublished 1995 ms. by William E. Kelly; Attwood memo, November 8, 1963, www.spartacus.schoolnet.co.uk.

366 Daniel: int. William Attwood, 1978; *L'Express* (Paris), December 6, 1963; *New Republic*, December 7 & 14, 1963.

367 November 5 Recording: *Guardian* [UK], November 26, 2003, citing Peter Kornbluh of the National Security Archive.

Note 2: See *supra*, end Chapter 13.

Cubela meetings/weapons: Sen. Int. Cttee., *Performance of Intelligence Agencies*, p. 16–; Sen. Int. Cttee., *Assassination Plots*, pp. 86–, 174-; HSCA Report, p. 112-; HSCA X.157–, 162–, Lattell, *op. cit.*, pp. 171–, 193–.

Note 3: When interviewed by the author in jail in 1978, Cubela insisted it had all along been the CIA—not he—who proposed assassination. Cubela was to be arrested in 1966, tried on charges of plotting against Castro, and sentenced to death. The sentence was commuted to a jail term within days, however—and the author and others were permitted access to Cubela toward the end of his imprisonment. Far from being harshly treated, the supposed traitor was allowed special privileges and released in 1979. The mild conditions of his confinement play to the credibility of the theory that Cubela was all along a double agent reporting all the CIA's approaches to Castro. (int. Cubela, Havana, 1978; Latell, p.198, *Miami News*, December 13, 1979)

368 *Note 4*: Richard Helms told the Senate Intelligence Committee that he believed he had such authority to deal with Cubela regarding a "change in government." He found it "so central to the whole theme of everything we had been trying to do, that

[I found] it totally unnecessary to ask Robert Kennedy at that point [whether] we should go ahead with this. This is obviously what he had been pushing." In his 2012 book, which covers the Cubela case extensively, former CIA analyst Brian Latell notes that Robert Kennedy and Desmond FitzGerald spoke on the phone on October 11. Case officer Sanchez has testified that he "assumed" Kennedy had been informed of progress with Cubela. (believed: Sen. Int. Cttee., *Assassination Plots*, p. 174–; spoke on phone/"assumed": Latell, *op. cit.*, p. 184)

Note 5: The information on plans for a coup using another supposed traitor has appeared in books published by authors Lamar Waldron and Thom Hartmann since 2005. Documents aside, the books drew on interviews with former U.S. officials including Secretary of State Dean Rusk and Press Secretary Pierre Salinger. It relied—most notably—on interviews with Enrique "Harry" Ruiz-Williams, a Cuban exile whom Robert Kennedy had taken into his confidence. The Waldron-Hartmann account suggests that the putative coup would have taken place on December 1, 1963. According to the coauthors, the spring 1963 clamp-down on "freelance raids was designed to placate the Soviet Union in the short term and rein in exile extremists, while planning how to replace the Castro regime with an American-style democratic form of government." The coup was to have been led by a senior army commander in Castro's inner circle, Juan Almeida Bosque. In spite of his name being published in this context in 2006, however, it is noteworthy that the Cuban regime continued to treat Almeida as an honored revolutionary hero until his death in 2009. Author Waldron has reasoned that—in the wake of Fidel Castro's own grave illness and handover of power—it was seen as pointless to pursue another national hero, the octogenarian Almeida, for alleged treachery. It is also conceivable that Almeida's status as a high-flying member of the black minority may have precluded action against him or his reputation.

In connection with this episode, this author himself interviewed Alexander Butterfield, McGeorge Bundy, William Geoghegan, Roswell Gilpatrick, Richard Goodwin, Walt Rostow, and Haynes Johnson.

The Waldron/Hartmann thesis has been faulted by other authors on the case. It "valuably fleshes out [the] portrait of RFK's secret campaign to oust Castro," wrote Jefferson Morley, but "their theory about how that ties into the assassination itself is conjectural." Gus Russo said the language of the documents cited in the Waldron/Hartmann books refers to "strikes" in Cuba, not a coup. "While their thesis is provocative," wrote David Talbot, "it is not convincing . . . there is no compelling evidence that the coup/invasion plan was as imminent as the authors contend." (coup reporting: Lamar Waldron & Thom Hartmann, *Ultimate Sacrifice*, New York: Carroll & Graf, 2005 & 2006, Lamar Waldron & Thomas Hartmann, *Legacy of Secrecy*, New York: Counterpoint, 2009, Liz Smith columns, *New York Post*, September 22, 2006 & January 6, 2009, *Daily Telegraph* (UK), September 18, 2009, Lamar Waldron int. for "Unredacted—Ultimate Sacrifice, Almeida and the Kennedys, www.maryferrell.org, author's conversations with Waldron and Hartmann & author's reporting in *VF*, December 1994; Morley: *WP*, November 27 2005; Russo: email January 5, 2006 cited at Bugliosi, *op. cit.*, Endnotes, p. 760; Talbot: cited in "Enrique Ruiz-Williams," www.spartacus.schoolnet.co.uk).

Rusk: int. Dean Rusk, 1994.

November 5 call: *Guardian*[UK], November 26, 1963, citing Peter Kornbluth of the National Security Archive.

Howard discussed: www.spartacus.schoolnet.co.uk; CIA debriefing of Howard, May 1, 1963.

369 *Note 6:* Former CIA officers and other sources confirmed to the author that calls to Cuba were monitored, along with other communications systems. (See also Sen. Int. Cttee. *Supp. Detailed Staff Reports on Intelligence Activities and the Rights of Americans*, Report, 94-755, Book III.145).

370 Farmers Branch meeting: copy of sound tape obtained by author in 1978 from retired Dallas Police Lieutenant George Butler; HSCA Report, pp. 132, 613n39; copy of tape held in files of researcher Mary Ferrell; *Dallas Morning News*, August 14, 1978.

371 Chicago and Miami threats: HSCA Report, p. 230– and notes; (Chicago) "The Plot to Kill JFK in Chicago," *Chicago Independent*, November 1975; Warren XXVI.441; Fensterwald/Ewing, *op. cit.*, p. 56; ints. retired Miami Police Intelligence Captain Charles Sapp and former Lieutenant Everett Kay (who preserved original surveillance tape of Milteer), 1978; article in *Miami News* by Bill Barry, February 2, 1967; "JFK, King: The Dade County Links," *Miami* magazine, September 1976; int. member of presidential party in Miami; CD 1347 p. 119- (which omits mention of tape-recording); (earlier Sapp warning) Sapp memo to Asst. Chief of Police Anderson, April 4, 1963; and HSCA sources as for Miami threat *supra*.

Note 7: The claim of a second Chicago plot was made by former Secret Service Agent Abraham Bolden. Although another agent has also recalled such a threat, the Assassinations Committee found no corroboration in the record. Bolden left the Secret Service under a cloud, and served time in prison for offenses allegedly committed during his government service. He said the charges were trumped up. See Abraham Bolden, *The Echo from Dealey Plaza*, New York: Broadway, 2009, which the author has not.

Note 8: See Chapter 20, *supra*.

373 Tampa alert: *Miami Herald*, November 23 & 24, 1963.
Miami speech: *JFK Public Papers*, 1963, p. 875–;

374 FitzGerald helped etc.: Sen. Int. Cttee., *Performance of Intelligence Agencies*, p. 19–.

Note 9: According to Kennedy historian Arthur Schlesinger, the speech was intended, rather, to buttress what William Attwood was saying in his conversations with the Cubans— that normal relations could be possible could Cuba break its ties to the Soviet bloc. The speech does not, however, read like an encouraging message to Castro. If that was what was intended, it was clumsy indeed—and unnecessary, as he was already receiving credible messages through the Attwood channel. (Schlesinger, *Robert F. Kennedy, op. cit.,* p. 554n, & int. Schlesinger, 1978)

Note 10: President Kennedy left Miami at 9:13 p.m., according to Dave Powers, the curator of the John F. Kennedy Library. The information in Attwood's two relevant books, and interviews with Attwood—who consulted his diary—suggests that the conversation with Havana described here occurred very late on November 18 and in the early hours of November 19. (Powers letter to author, 1979, Attwood, *The Reds and the Blacks,* p. 144, Attwood, *The Twilight Struggle,* p. 262, & ints. Attwood.)

375 Daniel: *New Republic,* November 7 & 14, 1963.

376 Echevarria: HSCA Report, pp. 134, 236; CD 87.

CIA meeting, November 22/Ruiz-Williams: See VF, December 1994, drawing on research of Lamar Waldron. Author also saw relevant interviews; Warren Hinckle & William Turner, *Deadly Secrets: The CIA-Mafia War Against Castro and the Assassination of JFK,* New York: Thunder's Mouth Press, 1992, p. 251; int. William Turner, 1994; (in RFK's confidence) see other cites in *Deadly Secrets;* Talbot, pp. 11–, 178, 183.

FitzGerald in 1964: Joseph Burkholder Smith, *Portrait of a Cold Warrior,* New York: Putnam, 1976, p. 143; int. Joe Smith, 1994.

Sanchez: CIA document 201-252234, April 13, 1966, CIA box 36, folder 29, NARA.

377 *Note 11:* Accounts differ as to whether Cubela accepted the device, rejected it outright, or took it but later threw it into the River Seine. (HSCA Report, p. 112–; Sen. Int. Cttee., *Performance of Intelligence Agencies,* p. 16–; Latell, *op. cit.,* pp. 203–, citing int. by House Assassinations Committee)

never revealed etc: Evan Thomas, *The Very Best Men: Four Who*

Dared, the Early Years of the CIA, New York: Simon & Schuster, 1995, p. 307–; Dick Russell, *op. cit.*, p. 535.

Note 12: Howard died of an overdose of sleeping pills, reportedly having been depressed following a miscarriage. The evidence indicated that she committed suicide. (*New York Times, Dallas Morning News*, July 5, 1965)

Note 13: There has been debate as to whether Kennedy said this to Johnson or Ruiz-Williams, who then repeated it to Johnson. (Haynes Johnson in *Washington Post*, April 17, 1981, November 20, 1983; int. Johnson, 1988; Talbot, *op. cit.*, pp. 10, 412n10; Deadly *Secrets*, cited *supra*, p. 273; & Richard Sprague notes of int. Johnson, 1973; VF, December 1994.)

378   McCone: Walter Sheridan Oral History, cited in Schlesinger, *Robert F. Kennedy*, *op. cit.*, p. 616.

McCone out of loop: Sen. Int. Cttee. *Assassination Plots*, p. 92; Talbot, *op. cit.*, p. 7.

"I asked him" Arthur Schlesinger, *Journals, 1952–2000*, London: Atlantic, 2008, p. 214.

Wondered: Talbot, *op. cit.*, p. 7–.

Wofford: Harris Wofford, *Of Kennedys and Kings*, New York: Farrar, Straus and Giroux, 1980, p. 415.

"National security": int. Attwood by Mark Redhead, 1986.

22. Casting the First Stone

379   Shakespeare quote: *The Rape of Lucrece*, II.939–940.

Johnson summons Warren: Earl Warren, *The Memoirs of Chief Justice Earl Warren*, New York: Doubleday, 1977, Chapter 11; Warren Commission memo by Melvin Eisenberg, February 17, 1964; Manchester, *op. cit.*, p. 730–, citing Warren int.

"a little incident": LBJ phone call, November 29, 1963, transcript at www.history-matters.com.

380   Blakey: conv. 1980 & corr. February 2013.

Hosty: James Hosty with Thomas Hosty, *Assigment Oswald*, New York: Arcade, 1996, p. 219.

DEFCON 4/3: Memo for Bromley Smith, December 4, 1963, NARA 202-10002-10180.

Cuba's position: statement by Carlos Lechuga, *Four Days, Historical Record of the Death of President Kennedy*, Rockville, MD: American Heritage Publishing Co., 1964, p. 115.

381   Daniel: *New Republic*, December 7, 1963.

Note 1: Castro was Prime Minister in 1963. He did not become President until 1976.

382   U.S. reaction: (editorials) *Dallas Morning News*, November 26, 1963; (poll) *Dallas Morning News*, December 6, 1963.

Alexander: Manchester, *op. cit.*, p. 326 & see Henry Wade testimony, June 8, 1964, V.213–. The Johnson aide who called Wade was Cliff Carter.

Warren and "Castro plot" in 1967: Sen. Int. Cttee., *Performance of Intelligence Agencies*, p. 80.

383   Smith: *New York Times*, June 25, 1976.

Note 2: Johnson had not been formally off the record during the interview with Cronkite, but insisted later that for "national security" reasons the exchange about the assassination should not be broadcast. It was transmitted only after his death. (Walter Cronkite int. of Johnson, September 1969, Lyndon Johnson Library, "The Assassination Tapes," relevant part viewable at www.youtube.com, & *Atlantic Monthly*, June 2004)

Janos: *Atlantic Monthly*, July 1973.

Marianne Means: *Sarasota Herald-Tribune*, April 25, 1975.

Note 3: Johnson also referred to his doubts about the assassination to his aide Marvin Watson—saying he felt "the CIA had something to do with this plot"—in 1967. He mentioned his suspicions of Castro to Joseph Califano and Jack Valenti, other White House aides. (Watson: Powers, *op. cit.*, p. 121; DeLoach to Tolson, April 4, 1967, FBI 44-24696; Califano/Valenti: Jeff Sheshol, *Mutual Contempt: Lyndon Johnson, Robert Kennedy and the Feud That Defined a Decade*, New York: Norton, 1997, p. 131–).

Drew Pearson account/Morgan: "The Assassination Tapes," article by Max Holland, *Atlantic Monthly*, June 2004.

384 HSCA on Roselli claims: HSCA Report, p. 114.

feedback: Sen. Int. Cttee., *Performance of Intelligence Agencies*, p. 84.

Note 4: Lyndon Johnson's biographer Robert Caro quoted the former President's friend Joe Kilgore as saying he "could believe what he wanted to believe . . . could convince himself of anything, even something that wasn't true." Others shared this impression. The weakness of the "Castro-did-it" claim, as relayed to him in 1967, was apparent to Johnson himself. He said on a White House recording of a March 2, 1967 phone call, "If you go looking at it [hard], as Abe [his friend Supreme Court Justice Abe Fortas] said, who is it that's seen Castro? Or heard from Castro? Or knows Castro . . . that's [in a position to] . . . [who] could be confirming all this? [Fortas said] that we just hear that this is what he did, but nobody points to how we hear it." (Caro: Robert Caro, *Means of Ascent*, New York: Vintage, 1991, p. 52–; (March 2, 1967 call: Max Holland, *The Kennedy Assassination Tapes*, New York: Knopf, 2004, p. 408 & see p. 396. Holland's book is masterful on this episode.)

Note 5: There is some small room for doubt as to how that remark, ominous on its face, got into the AP report. While the epithets against Kennedy appeared in the report of the same conversation by AP's rival UPI, the sentence that seemed to threaten the U.S. leadership did not. Available documentation does not clearly indicate whether both the AP's Harker and the UPI correspondent were present when Castro was speaking, or whether the UPI story was merely a pick-up from the AP story.

Fabián Escalante, a former Cuban intelligence chief who met with researchers, including this author, in 1996, did not deny the essence of the remark but said it had been distorted. He told the author that AP reporter Harker had been "reported" during an earlier stint in Havana for using his journalistic privileges "to send information unrelated to his work as a reporter." That should be taken with a sizable pinch of salt—few honest reporters long avoid the wrath of regimes whose own press is fettered. All the same, and given later revelations about the CIA's use of journalists, the Harker report—in light of its impact—deserved more investigation than it received. (AP/UPI stories: cited in CD 1135,11–, Memo for the record, November 8, 1976, CIA doc. 80T01357A; Review of Selected Items in the LHO File, April 15, 1975, NARA 104-10322-10001; distorted: Fabián Escalante, *JFK: The Cuba Files*, Melbourne, Australia, Ocean, Dick Russell in *High Times*, March 1996; "information unrelated": int. Fabian Escalante, Bahamas, 1996, *High Times*, March 1996).

Widely interpreted: e.g. CIA memo to David Belin, director of Rockefeller Commission on CIA Activities Within the United States, May 30, 1975.

Castro to HSCA: HSCA Report, p. 126–; HSCA III.216, 220 & see HSCA X.181–.

386 "Threat" remark in New Orleans: Russo, *Brothers in Arms*, New York: Bloomsbury, 2008, pp. 295, 502, citing *New Orleans Times-Picayune*, September 9, 1963.

Oswald on JFK: (under questioning) Report, p. 609; (radio debate) XXI.641; (Martello) X.60.

387 "persuasive": HSCA Report, p. 129.

Note 6: The timing of Alvarado's visit to the Embassy is important. Whether he made up the story himself or did so at the suggestion of others, he came up with it very rapidly once the fact of an Oswald visit to Mexico had become public knowledge. Although the story was slow in making news in the United States, it was in the Mexican newspaper *Excelsior* on the evening of November 24. At noon the following day, Alvarado was telling his story about Oswald at the U.S. Embassy. Until the appearance of the *Excelsior* story, the Oswald visit to Mexico was theoretically known only to Oswald's wife, Soviet and Cuban Consulate staff, and U.S. and Mexican intelligence.

The "high source" *Excelsior* quoted as the origin of its story was probably Mexican—Mexican agents worked closely with the CIA on the Embassy surveillance.

Alvarado episode: Sen. Int. Cttee., *Performance of Intelligence Agencies*, pp. 28–, 41–; Report, p. 308–; XXV.647; int. Thomas Mann, 1978, ints. former staff at U.S. Embassy in Mexico; Phillips, *op. cit.*, p. 141–; (Mann background) Schlesinger, *Robert F. Kennedy*, *op. cit.*, pp. 630–636; (Mann on Oswald's motivation, etc.) Mann cable to Secretary of State Rusk, November 28, 1963. Also see refs. in Peter Dale Scott, *Deep Politics and the Death of JFK*, Berkeley: University of California Press, 1993; ints. Laurence Keenan, 1993.

390   Nicaraguan agent: CIA memo to White House, FBI, State Department, November 26, 1963, DIR 85089.

Nicaragua: Prouty, *op. cit.*, pp. 29, 41–, 388–.

Artime: "The Curious Intrigues of Cuban Miami" by Horace Sutton, *Saturday Review/World*, September 11, 1973; "Cuba on Our Mind" by Tad Szulc, *Esquire*, February 1974; article by Szulc, *New York Times*, June 9, 1973; (camps) HSCA X.67 & see Scott, *op. cit.*, p. 91, *et al.*; (first) Hunt, *op. cit.*, p. 38.

391   *Note 7*: See Chapter 18.

Note 8: The Warren Commission noted what one member, Gerald Ford, would call "the strong personal feelings of the then U.S. Ambassador to Mexico . . . that Castro was somehow involved in a plot to assassinate President Kennedy." (HSCA II.569)

Note 9: The ancient Alvarado story was resurrected most recently in a much-trumpeted 2006 German television documentary, the thrust of which was that Castro had President Kennedy killed. The film relied on a supposed agent of today's Russian intelligence service who claimed to have found an old KGB document—dating to Oswald's time in the Soviet Union—that had suggested the Cubans might have some use for defector Oswald. The film used interviews with four supposed former Castro agents to support its thesis. A document provided by a former aide to both Kennedy and Johnson, Marty Underwood, described a purported November 22 visit to Dallas by a Cuban intelligence officer. The alleged KGB document was not produced. Underwood, for his part, would acknowledge that he had written his document as late as the 1990s. The key Cuban sources appeared in the program under pseudonyms or with their faces obscured. This author, who conducted a long interview with the film's director, Wilfried Huissman, found the documentary less than credible.

A key contributor to the Huissman documentary was Gus Russo, a journalist who has worked on the Kennedy case for many years and authored two books on the subject. In the first, *Live by the Sword*, Russo concluded that Oswald "did it for Cuba," and that leads that indicated " a possible Cuban conspiracy with Oswald" were never fully followed up at the time. The author has not had the opportunity to study the second book, *Brothers in Arms*, but it appears to credit some of the questionable elements used in the Huissman film.("Rendezvous with Death," Westdeutscher Rundfunk, January 2007, int. Wilfried Huissman, convs. Gus Russo; Underwood: AARB Report, p. 136; see also analysis in Bugliosi, *op. cit.*, Endnotes, p. 731; Russo: Gus Russo, *Live by the Sword*, Baltimore, MD: Bancroft Press, 1998—findings at p. 459 & Gus Russo & Stephen Molton, *Brothers in Arms*, New York: Bloomsbury, 2008).

Gutierrez: CD 564; Warren Commission staff memo by Coleman/Slawson, April 1, 1964; CD 566.3–; CD 663.4; CD 896.3; CD 1029; CIA documents 965–927 AK; 972–927 AR; 1179–1995.

Air Cubana: Sen. Int. Cttee., *Performance of Intelligence Agencies*, p. 30; HSCA Report, p. 117.

Note 10: Also in December, another CIA source caused a flap about the supposedly "suspicious" travels of a Cuban named Gilberto Policarpo Lopez. Lopez crossed the Texas border to Mexico the day after the assassination and flew to Havana four days later, reportedly the only person on board the flight. This story was provocative because—like Oswald—Lopez was affiliated with the Fair Play for Cuba Committee and made a stop at the Cuban Embassy before leaving. The Assassinations Committee found that he had plausible personal reasons for returning to Cuba. (HSCA Report, p. 118)

Díaz/Borrell: FBI memos—Director to Legat, Mexico, January 9, 1964, and Miami to Director, February 29, 1964, FBI file no. 105-82555; CIA memo, Curtis as originator, January 14, 1964; ints. Borrell, Señora Díaz Versón & daughter Silvia, 1993.

392   Luce: ints. Clare Boothe Luce, 1978; HSCA X.83; and int. by Earl Golz of *Dallas Morning News*, 1979; *Washington Star*, November 16, 1975; *ibid*, January 25, 1976.

393   *Note 11*: Texas Governor John Connally, who was wounded on November 22, had been Secretary of the Navy in 1961. Oswald wrote to the Secretary, asking for a reversal of the record of his undesirable discharge from the Marine Corps, when the Secretary in office was Fred Korth. As an attorney, oddly, Korth had represented the husband of Oswald's mother, Marguerite, during divorce proceedings. (XIX, Fulsom Exhibit 1, p. 61–; Oswald 201 File, Vol. 3, Attachments 1, 7, 2, Pt. 2, p. 92; & Vol. 5, Pt. 1, p. 80 www.maryferrell.org)

Note 12: Contacted by Committee investigators, Bringuier and other DRE veterans all denied having made the 1963 call to Mrs. Luce.

Note 13: In a major article on CIA manipulation of the media, Carl Bernstein reported, there was close liaison between the Agency and Time-Life, of which Mrs. Luce's husband, Henry, was publisher. In 1962, Mrs. Luce had authored a *Life* magazine story about her exile fighter protégés. (Bernstein: *Rolling Stone*, October 20, 1977; story: HSCA X.83)

Note 14: In this mosaic of apparent disinformation, a false trail about Oswald may also have been laid in Miami, the main base of CIA-backed anti-Castro activists. Before the assassination, according to a witness, one Jorge Martínez had talked about an American acquaintance named Lee who spoke Russian, was as usual a brilliant marksman and talked of President Kennedy and "shooting between the eyes." Martínez was eventually identified as an exile brought to the United States by Mike McLaney, one of the old Havana casino bosses. McLaney and his brother William appeared earlier in this book. (See Chapter 18.)

On November 26, while Alvarado the Nicaraguan was spinning his fable in Mexico, Florida's Pompano Sun-Sentinel ran an allegation that Oswald had previously been in Miami, had contacted "supporters of Fidel Castro," tried to infiltrate an anti-Castro group, passed out Fair Play for Cuba Committee leaflets, and gotten into a fight with anti-Castro militants—just as in New Orleans. Oswald had also supposedly had "telephone conversations with the Cuban government G-2 Intelligence Service." The Sun-Sentinel article named Frank Sturgis, the future Watergate burglar, as being a member of the Florida anti-Castro group Oswald had supposedly tried to infiltrate. Sturgis had once been an overseer at Havana's Tropicana casino, managed at the time by Lewis McWillie, a close friend of Oswald's executioner, Jack Ruby.

The FBI found no evidence that Oswald had ever been in Florida. Other fabrications purporting to link Oswald to Castro's Cuba were also blatantly false. The Secret Service intercepted a letter to Oswald mailed from Havana on November 28, 1963 and signed by one "Pedro Charles." "Charles" indicated in the letter that Oswald had been hired by him to carry out a mission involving "accurate shooting." Meanwhile, a letter sent to Robert Kennedy appeared to corroborate the supposed Oswald-Charles plot. "Charles" was identified as a Castro agent. Examination quickly established that the letters were mischievous—they had been written on the same typewriter. (Martínez: CD 829; CD 246; Pompano story/Sturgis: Sun Sentinel, November 26 & December 4, 1963; CD 59; CD 395; CD 1020; CD 810; L. Patrick Gray to H. R. Haldeman,

June 19, 1972 [Gray hearings, p. 47]; "Charles": XXVI.148; other letters: HSCA III.401–).

394 *Note 15*: See Chapter 19.

Mirabal: HSCA III.177.

Rodríguez: *Dallas Morning News*, September 24, 1975, reprinted from *Los Angeles Times*.

Note 16: This individual may perhaps have been Ernesto Rodríguez Cue, who in 1962 was a Cuban Embassy employee in Mexico City. He was not, apparently, one and the same as the Ernesto Rodríguez, an anti-Castro militant who operated a language school in New Orleans, mentioned in Chapter 17. (Cue: Foreign Political Matters—Cuba, memo of May 28, 1962, CIA file 80T01357A).

395 *Note 17*: Veciana's claim to have seen Oswald with "Bishop" was described earlier, in Chapter 18.

Ruiz: HSCA X.41; ints. Ruiz.

Note 18: The Assassinations Committee talked to Veciana's cousin Ruiz in Cuba, who suggested Veciana had had psychiatric problems and referred the Committee to another Veciana relative, a doctor, who—Ruiz said—would attest to Veciana's psychiatric trouble. The Committee found to the contrary that the doctor attested to Veciana's "sound mental condition." He knew, in addition, that Veciana had had to undergo vigorous tests for his work in the banking business. Another family member confirmed Veciana's mental health, and there was no evidence of any disorder of the sort implied by Ruiz. Veciana alleged that Ruiz was once approached for recruitment by the CIA, and his slandering of Veciana may have been an overkill reaction to that. (HSCA X.45)

"honesty"/ "straightest": HSCA X.42.

Note 19: In Spanish, MRP stands for Movimiento Revolucionario del Pueblo. (HSCA X.137)

396 *Note 20*: Allegations directly incriminating Castro aside, alternative versions have suggested the Cuban leader had foreknowledge but did nothing about it. Chronologically, this theme tracks back to information received from a leading member of the U.S. Communist Party, Jack Childs, who for years fed information to the FBI after meetings with Communists abroad. Following a May 1964 meeting with Castro in Havana, Childs reported to the FBI that the Cuban leader "stated that when Oswald was refused his visa at the Cuban Embassy in Mexico City, he acted like a real madman and started yelling and shouting and yelled on his way out, 'I'm going to kill that bastard. I'm going to kill Kennedy.' "

The alleged outburst has been used—most recently by Brian Latell in his 2012 book *Castro's Secrets*—to suggest that Castro knew in advance what Oswald intended. The FBI summary indicates, rather, that Castro spoke "on the basis of facts given to him by his Embassy personnel who dealt with Oswald and apparently had made a full, detailed report to Castro *after President Kennedy was assassinated* [author's emphasis]."

The Assassinations Committee also considered an allegation that surfaced late in 1964, suggesting Oswald had compromising links with Cuban Embassy staff. Mexican writer Elena Garro claimed that Oswald and two companions had attended a party at the home of a relative of Sylvia Durán, the secretary from the Consulate. Oswald and Durán, Garro said she later learned, were sexually involved with each other. The story emerged through a CIA informant named June Cobb. Author John Newman, who studied this complex story within the story, surmised that it may have been "invented to falsely implicate the Cuban government in the Kennedy assassination."

In his 2012 book, meanwhile, author Brian Latell used the statements of Cuban defectors to suggest Castro had foreknowledge. He cited one, Vladimir Rodríguez Lahera, as being convinced that Castro had lied when he said he knew nothing about Oswald before November 22. The CIA record shows that—under interrogation—Rodriguez in fact said he did not know "whether information on Oswald's visit to the

Cuban Consulate in Mexico . . . was relayed to any Cuban service." As mentioned in Chapter 19, the incoming Cuban Consul in Mexico City, Alfredo Mirabal—who was also an intelligence officer—acknowledged that he wrote a "foot-note" about the Oswald visit in his routine report to Havana. There is no evidence that this was reported to Castro before the assassination.

Latell cites a claim by a defector named Florentino Aspill-aga about an order he said he had received on November 22, about three hours before Kennedy was shot. Aspillaga, who in 1963 was a sixteen-year-old working on intercepts of covert CIA communications, said he was told to abandon routine work and listen to "all conversations" for "any small detail from Texas." "They knew," said Aspillaga, referring to his superiors, "Kennedy would be killed."

Latell draws the same inference, and that seems a stretch. So close is Cuba to Florida that far easier than tasking signal intercept operators—had Castro's people known in advance of an assassination attempt—would have been to listen to ordi-nary radio broadcasts. A high-level Cuban interest in Texas, moreover, could have reflected not so much foreknowledge of the assassination but an interest—following Kennedy's loaded "signal" speech of November 18 in Miami—in what the Presi-dent might say in Dallas, the next stop on his known schedule.

Latell also took seriously the first public emanation of supposed Castro foreknowledge of an Oswald threat against Kennedy in Mexico City—a story that was long ago exposed as fraudulent. In a 1967 *National Enquirer* article, a Brit-ish reporter named Comer Clarke claimed to have visited Havana and secured an impromptu interview with Castro. According to Clarke, Castro told him that, "Lee Oswald came to the Cuban Embassy in Mexico City twice. The first time, I was told, he wanted to work for us. He was asked to explain, but he wouldn't. He wouldn't go into details. The second time he said something like: 'Someone ought to shoot that President Kennedy.' Then Oswald said—and this was exactly how it was reported to me—'Maybe I'll try to do it.' This was less than two months before the U.S. President was assassinated. . . . Yes, I heard of Lee Harvey Oswald's plan to kill President Kennedy. It's possible I could have saved him. I might have been able to—but I didn't. I never believed the plan would be put into effect."

Castro told the Assassinations Committee that he gave no such interview. Clarke had been an inveterate purveyor of sensational and sometimes dubious stories—headlines included "British Girls as Nazi Sex Slaves" and "German Plans to Kidnap the Royal Family." Clarke's widow said in an interview that her late husband never mentioned having interviewed Castro, an event any reporter would have considered a scoop. Clarke's former assistant Nina Gadd, moreover, said *she* generated the story—without going anywhere near Cuba—drawing on claims made by a "Latin American foreign minister." (Childs: SAC, New York to Director, June 12, 1964, FBI 100-HQ-428091, Pt. 63, p. 58–; Latell used to suggest: Latell, *op. cit.*, pp. 140–, 225, 231; Garro et al.: HSCA Report, p. 124, HSCA III.285; Newman, *Oswald and the CIA, op. cit.*, p. 377–, & June Cobb refs. Robbyn Swan ints. Manuel Calvillo and Deba Galvan Debaki Garro, 1993; Rodríguez: Latell, *op. cit.*, p. 128–, Rodríguez calling card, with cover ident as AMMUG 1, NARA 104-10185-10260, Notes *re* debriefing of Cuban source on Oswald Case, May 1, 5 & 6, 1964, & Dooley to Rocca, June 19, 1964, NARA 1993.06.12.08.26.02.650000, Swenson to Rocca, May 8, 1964, NARA 104-10054-10412, Swenson to WH, May 14, 1964, NARA 104-10225-10072; Mirabal: HSCA III.176, April 1964 debriefing of Rodríguez, NARA 104-10183-10284; Aspillaga: Latell, *op. cit.*, pp. 103, 8-3; Latell took seriously: *ibid.* p. 145–; Clarke: *National Enquirer*, October 15, 1967, referring to a July interview; HSCA III.283; HSCA Report, p. 122–, ints. Mrs. Clarke and Nina Gadd by Stephen Dorril. Reporter Comer Clarke's name

is often rendered as "Clark." The author has used "Clarke,"
the spelling used on the jacket of the reporter's book *England
Under Hitler: The Shocking Plans for Britain Under Nazi Rule*,
London: New English Library, 1972.)

Kohly Jr.: int. Mario García Kohly Jr.

397 Attwood: Attwood, *op. cit.*, p. 144; int. Attwood, 1978.

Rankin remark: Epstein, *Inquest, op. cit.*, p. 105.

23. The Good Ole Boy

398 "Good Ole Boy" chapter title: This phrase is used in the South
to refer to a local "character." Detective Billy Combest of the
Dallas police, whom the author interviewed in 1978, described
Ruby thus.

"The pattern": HSCA Report, p. 156.

Note 1: The most valuable book on the Ruby case remains *Who
Was Jack Ruby?* (New York: Everest House, 1978) by the late
Washington correspondent Seth Kantor. Kantor was in Dallas
on the day of the assassination and met Ruby, whom he knew
from past journalism in Dallas, at Parkland Hospital. Goaded
by the fact that the Warren Commission said he was wrong
about seeing Ruby, Kantor spent years researching the Ruby
case. The author is indebted to him for his advice.

Ruby testified: IV.196; V.181–.

399 Hubert-Griffin: memorandum to Willens and

Rankin, May 14, 1964.

Griffin comment: Kantor, *op. cit.*, p. 159.

Hubert resignation: Kantor, *op. cit.*, p. 2.

400 Ruby request to go to Washington: V.194–.

Warren characterized: Report, p. 373.

HSCA: HSCA Report, p. 147–.

Warren: (on Ruby & organized crime) Report, p. 801; (on Cuba)
Report, p. 369.

401 Ruby youth: Report, p. 786–; Kantor, *op. cit.*, p. 96.

Capone: XXIII.423.

Chicago union episode: Report, p. 695; XXIII.433; Kantor, *op. cit.*, p. 99–.

Ruby on leaving union: V.200; (stays on) Kantor, *op. cit.*, p. 100.

402 Ignored FBI interview: CD 1306 (FBI int. of Paul Roland Jones, June 26, 1964).

Miller: int. Miller, 1978; also XXII.476 and CD 105.120, FBI report, December 17, 1963.

Kutner: Moldea, *op. cit.*, p. 167.

Jones bribe attempt: Third Interim Report, Kefauver Senate Committee, 82nd Congress, 1st Session; cited by Gus Taylor, *Organized Crime in America*, Ann Arbor, MI: University of Michigan Press, 1973, p. 337–; Report, p. 793; (Guthrie) XXII.360; (Butler) Report, p. 793; (first Butler report) XXVI.342; (records missing) XXV.514–; HSCA Report, p. 149; HSCA IX.513; (Butler) HSCA IX.153, 158; (HSCA on Jones) HSCA IX.513; (Jones and Ruby family) see *supra* and Report, p. 793; XXII.375; XXIII.203, 374; (first Dallas club—Silver Spur) XXII.302.

Note 2: The HSCA Report dates the Jones bribery scheme as 1947. It actually took place at the end of 1946 (HSCA Report, p. 149; HSCA IX.516).

Labriola & Weinberg: XXII.300; (killed) Ovid Demaris, *Captive City*, New York: Lyle Stuart, 1969, pp. 5, 17, 169–.

Nightspots: Report, p. 794–.

Escaped trouble: Report, p. 800; Kantor p. 109; XXIII.78; XXV.290; HSCA IX.128; HSCA Report, p. 156.

"Payoff man": "The Mafia, the CIA and the Kennedy Assassination" by Milton Viorst, in *Washingtonian* magazine, November 1975.

403 "Man with fix": XXIII.372.

Drug smuggling: XXIII.369.

Beard: *Dallas Morning News*, August 18, 1978; FBI document 602-982-243, June 10, 1976 & see XXVI.634—report of interview with Blaney Mack Johnson, December 1, 1963; article, "The Secret Life of Jack Ruby," by William Scott Malone, *New Times*, January 23, 1978.

McKeown: XXIII.158–; interview with author, 1978; HSCA Report, p. 152; HSCA IX.587; *New Times*, June 24, 1977; Warren Commission memo by Hubert and Griffin, March 20, 1964; (date of McKeown-Ruby encounters) *ibid.*, and notes of interview of McKeown by Sen. Int. Cttee. investigator, 1975.

Note 3: The credibility of McKeown was queried by the Assassinations Committee, due not least to his demeanor at interview. He also claimed in later years to have been visited by Lee Oswald, and that did not seem likely. His original statements about Ruby, however, are to an extent corroborated by other evidence, in particular, that of a police officer who helped a man who may have been Ruby to contact McKeown. The author found him credible on the Ruby matter.

Ruby on Cuba trip: V.200–; Report, pp. 801, 812, 370.

404 McWillie: ("closest friend") XXIII.166; V.201; ("manager") HSCA V.3; (syndicate connections) CD 689D; *Ramparts*, November 1973; (on Ruby visit) XXIII.37, 170; HSCA V.2–.

Note 4: McWillie said that he arranged to bring over to Cuba Jack Ruby and a columnist called Tony Zoppi. His hope was that Zoppi would write useful publicity for the Tropicana, and Ruby's role was to persuade Zoppi to come. In the event Zoppi could not, but Ruby, McWillie said, came anyway. As evidence to support this explanation of the Ruby trip, McWillie showed the Assassinations Committee a letter on the subject apparently written by Zoppi in 1976. Zoppi himself gave an interview to Assassinations Committee staff that threw doubt on McWillie's story. Zoppi confirmed there was a plan to go to Cuba with Ruby, but it was planned for the winter, not the summer. His statement suggests that Ruby's actual travel to Cuba was quite separate from the planned joint excursion (arranged: HSCA V.10, 26–, 167; letter: HSCA V.26; Zoppi interview: HSCA V.171; separate: HSCA IX.164, 167).

Travel record: (Havana arrival August 8) HSCA V.196–; (full month) HSCA Report, p. 151 & see HSCA IX.159–; (Labor Day) HSCA V.191, Report, p. 802; (postcard) HSCA V.195;

(exit card, September 11) HSCA V.197; (return to Cuba) HSCA V.197; (Mynier) CD 84.215–; ("numerous") CD 302.159; (in Dallas August 10) XXIII.10 (following week); HSCA V.204; (August 31) CD 302.159; HSCA V.218; (HSCA conclusion) HSCA Report, p. 151; ("courier") HSCA IX.177 and HSCA Report, p. 152.

405 Note 5: In 1959, the year he visited Cuba, Ruby had some dealings with the FBI. Between March and October, Agent Charles Flynn of the Dallas office had nine meetings with Ruby as a PCI, a Potential Criminal Informant. According to the Bureau, its interest was confined to information Ruby might pick up as a nightclub owner. It may be relevant, though, that Ruby went on an electronic shopping spree following the first FBI contact, purchasing a wristwatch with a built-in microphone, a phone bug, a wire tie-clip, and a bugged attaché case. Was the contact with the FBI somehow related to the spate of travel to Havana? Ruby's acquaintance at the New Orleans airport listened as Ruby—talking on the phone—instructed an employee not to disclose his whereabouts "unless it were to the police or some other official agency."(dealings: HSCA Report, p. 151; HSCA V.218; CD 732; electronic purchases: "Rubygate," by William Scott Malone, *New Times*, January 23, 1978, citing Secret Service and FBI reports; acquaintance listened: CD 302.159).

Note 6: In one of Ruby's notebooks, seized after he shot Oswald, police found the entry "October 29, 1963—John Wilson bond." (XIX.59, Armstrong Exhibit 5305Q). The note remains unexplained.

Note 7: Press accounts confirmed that Wilson, a sometime journalist and political activist, had indeed been detained in Cuba. In 1963, when he produced his information about Ruby and "Santos," he could not have known from public sources that Ruby had been in Cuba in 1959. Details in Wilson's account suggest that the "Santos" mentioned was indeed Santo Trafficante. The former superintendent of the detention camp was to tell the Assassinations Committee that he remembered the "English journalist" having been held in the same area as Trafficante. Two witnesses, one of them the superintendent, said Trafficante and his companions did receive special meals brought in from a Havana hotel. During his stay in Havana, Ruby stayed at the Capri Hotel, in which Trafficante had a major financial interest. (John Wilson: CIA document 206-83, November 16, 1963; FBI document 44-24016-255, November 16, 1963; CIA document 385-736, December 12, 1963; HSCA Report, p, 153, HSCA IX.175; Kantor, *op. cit.*, p. 132; (press accounts) *New York Times*, July 1, 1959; (detained with Wilson) Captain Paul Hughes, *ibid.*, and FBI document 87-8756, October 23,1959; (superintendent) HSCA V.333; (Wilson on food) FBI document 44-24016-255; (two witnesses) Loran Hall in *Village Voice*, October 3, 1977, & superintendent HSCA V.338; (Ruby at Capri) HSCA V.196; (Trafficante and Capri) *Time*, March 2, 1959).

Trafficante on meeting Ruby: HSCA V.371

HSCA on Ruby-Trafficante meeting: HSCA Report, pp. 153, 173.

Ruby-Trafficante associates:(Matthews) HSCA IX.524 and Report, p. 173; *Dallas Morning News*, April 6, 1978; CD 86.198; HSCA IX.532; int. of Harris by Alonzo Hudkins, January 3, 1978; HSCA IX.532; FBI document DL44-1639, December 13, 1963; *Miami Herald*, July 9, 1959; (own lawyer) Frank Wright, int. by researcher Larry Harris, December 28, 1977; (Dolan) HSCA Report, pp. 156, 173; HSCA IX.418–; (Todd) HSCA Report, p. 173; HSCA IX.989.

406 Ruby fearful: HSCA IX.162; and *New York Daily News*, July 18, 1976, int. Wally Weston.

Psychiatrist: "Examination of Jack Ruby," reported by Werner Tuteur, M.D.

"Temporary insanity": *Milwaukee Sentinel*, November 16, 1963.

407 Phone records: HSCA Report, p. 154; HSCA IX.188–; HSCA IV.496, 562; (HSCA finding on calls) HSCA Report, p.

156; (Matthews' wife) HSCA IX.528 and 193; (Weiner) HSCA IX.1042, 1054, 1062, 1057, and Moldea, *op. cit.*, p. 155; (Baker) HSCA Report, p. 155 and see HSCA IX.274–; XXV.247; HSCA IV.566; ("violence") Robert Kennedy, *op. cit.*, p. 60; (Miller) HSCA Report, p. 155 and HSCA IV.499 and HSCA IX.195; (Baker call) XXV.244; V.200; HSCA IV.566; HSCA Report, p. 155 and see IX.274.

Note 8: Ruby reportedly also spoke, in summer 1963 or later, with Lenny Patrick, identified by the Assassinations Committee as one of two "executioners for the Chicago Mob." The other was David Yaras, and both Patrick and Yaras had known Ruby since their youth in Chicago. Yaras was reportedly a hit man for Sam Giancana, the Chicago Mob leader prominent in CIA-Mafia plots against Castro, and had himself been involved in Havana gambling operations before the Castro revolution. Yaras, who was also close to Jimmy Hoffa, was targeted for investigation by Robert Kennedy's Justice Department team. On the eve of the assassination Yaras, like Ruby a week or so earlier, would talk by phone with the feared Barney Baker, Hoffa's aide. (See also HSCA Report, p. 150; HSCA IX.942; XIV.443–; CD 1299; *Newsweek*, October 9, 1950; Demaris, *Captive City, op. cit.*, p. 130; Moldea, *op. cit.*, p. 124; & Hoffa: see refs in Moldea, *op. cit.*, and Kantor, *op. cit.*, p. 31; call on eve of assassination: HSCA IV.567.)

Note 9: Then again, in testimony to the Assassinations Committee, Weiner reversed himself and said he had lied to the journalist and that he and Ruby had indeed discussed the union problem.

408 *Note 10:* Ruby did know a person who lived on the Pecora property, a manager in the Marcello fiefdom named Harold Tannenbaum. Tannenbaum was in regular contact with Ruby during the summer of 1963, and called Ruby an hour after the call to the Pecora number. The director of the Metropolitan New Orleans Crime Commission, Aaron Kohn, said Ruby "had girls working down on [New Orleans] Bourbon Street.

... Marcello's brother, Peter Marcello, ran one of the bigger places. ... Two other men close to the Marcello organization ran five of the biggest money-making strip joints on Bourbon Street. And Ruby would know these men, and Harold Tannenbaum managed for these men."(HSCA Report, p. 155–, HSCA IX.192, 194; & see *Clandestine America*, III.2, p. 7.)

Ruby's finances: Report, p. 797–; Kantor, *op. cit.*, p. 18; HSCA Report, p. 156; XXIII.117; (IRS) XXIII.303, 383; (safe) Kantor, *op. cit.*, p. 24; (tax lawyer) Kantor, *op. cit.*, p. 24; (bank visit) *Dallas Morning News*, October 12, 1978.

409 *Note 11:* When arrested for the murder of Oswald, Ruby would be carrying $3,000 (HSCA IX.2-).

HSCA/"knowledge": HSCA Report, p. 156.

Paul dinner: Report p. 334; HSCA IX.978–.

Campisi: HSCA Report, p. 171n9, HSCA IX.335–.

Civello: HSCA Report, p. 171; *Clandestine America*, III.2, p. 7.

Ruby morning November 22: Report, p. 334; Kantor, *op. cit.*, p. 38–; for Ruby's movements see generally HSCA IX.1080, 1101.

410 Aynesworth: FBI document DL 44-1639, report of November 25, 1963.

Ruby at hospital: Kantor, *op. cit.*, p. 41; and see HSCA V.179, Report, p. 158.

Note 12: Ruby himself denied visiting Parkland Hospital, and the Warren Commission chose to take his word for it rather than believe Kantor's statement that he saw Ruby there. Following Kantor's researches, however, the Assassinations Committee and former Warren Commission counsel Burt Griffin decided Kantor's version was more likely to be correct. Kantor, a respected correspondent, knew Ruby quite well from his working days in Dallas and had no reason to make up the story. The significance of the incident today is that Ruby denied the hospital encounter with Kantor. Why would he lie about this apparently minor detail? And what would that imply about his veracity on other points concerning his activities in those vital days? (denied: HSCA V.179; Warren took his word: Report, p. 335–; Kantor correct?: HSCA Report p. 159 and Griffin letter to Kantor, May 2, 1977, cited by Kantor, *op. cit.*, p. 202).

411 Broken up, etc.: Report, p. 337–.

Police station sightings: Report, p. 340–; analyzed by Kantor, *op. cit.*, p. 45, and by Meagher, *op. cit.*, Chapter 25.

Synagogue: Report, p. 340.

Ruby on Fair Play for Cuba Committee: Report, p. 342.

412 *Note 13*: The admission that he had had his gun with him on the Friday night made it look as though the murder of Oswald was premeditated, and Ruby later withdrew it. (CD 1252.9; HSCA V.179.)

At radio station: Report, p. 343:

Olsen: Report, p. 343.

Note 14: It may be that Ruby met with Olsen for much more than an hour. They talked in a garage, and the garage attendant's statement—coupled with the fact that Ruby omitted the episode in answers given to the FBI—may suggest that this was not a casual encounter. On the afternoon of the assassination, Olsen would be not far from the site of Officer Tippit's murder—a fact that he explained by saying he had been moonlighting, doing guard duty at a vacant estate. He could not, however, recall exactly where the estate was. Ruby was at radio station KLIF at 2:00 a.m. and at the *Dallas Times-Herald* around 4:00 a.m. (met Olsen: XV.254, 483, 532; XXIV.126, 162; XXV.228; XV.557, 566; XXVI.238; XXV.232; CD 105.325; CD 360.132; Olsen at time of Tippit shooting: XIV.264; could not recall: XXV.521, CD 1252.10, CD 1253.4 & *re* Olsen see also Shaw-Harris, *op. cit.*, p. 102; Jones, *op. cit.*, vol. I.92–; Report, p. 363)

Overnight movements: Report, p. 344.

Senior officers: Kantor, *op. cit.*, p. 53.

Ruby asked: Report, p. 346.

Ruby at 4.00 p.m.: Meagher, *op. cit.*, chapter 25; Kantor, *op. cit.*, p. 54–.

Call sequence starting 10:44 p.m.: HSCA IX.1115; CD 1138.3; XIII.247; XIV.620; XXV.251; CD 75.227, 290; CD 301.86; XXV.251; XXV.252; CD 360.132; CD 1252.12; XIV.605; XIV.620; CD 223.82–; CD 1253.6; XXV.251; Report, p. 350; (and Paul) HSCA IX.780.

413 *Note 15:* Evidence gathered by the Assassinations Committee raised questions about Ralph Paul aside from his activities during the assassination weekend. They concerned Officer Tippit. Paul had long been associated with Austin's Bar-B-Cue, where Tippit worked as a security guard for three years. He was working there in November 1963, and had been having a protracted affair with a female Bar-B-Cue employee. Like Paul, Tippit lived near the Bar-B-Cue. In view of all this, it is probable that they knew each other. Paul died in 1974. (HSCA XII.36-42, Texas Attorney General's files, 9.)

Ruby on November 24: Report, p. 353; XIII.231–.

Note 16: Senator was to behave like a man "overwhelmed with fear" for days after the shooting of Oswald, according to an associate, refused to sleep at home, and soon left Dallas altogether. (Kantor, *op. cit.*, p. 217; XXIV.164–330; XXVI.569–.)

TV technicians: Meagher, *op. cit.*, p. 449.

Minister: XII.75, 294.

Stripper call: Report, p. 353.

414 Ruby cash/gun: Kantor, *op. cit.*, p. 64–; *Texas Monthly*, November 1975.

Western Union transaction: Report, p. 219 & HSCA IV.587.

Howard: XXIV.135.

Combest: Doubleday edition of Warren Commission Report, New York, 1964 (caption to picture of Oswald shooting).

415 "intended": Kantor, p. 113.

Howard: Kantor, p. 76.

Ruby note: *Newsweek*, March 27, 1967; HSCA Report, p. 158; int. Joe Tonahill by Scott Malone, 1978.

Ruby means of entry findings: (police report) HSCA IV.578; (Warren Commission Report) Report, p. 216; Ramp witnesses: (Vaughn) XII.359; (policemen) XII.340; CE 5073; XII.287; (Flusche) *Dallas Morning News*, March 25, 1979; HSCA IV.595–; (cab driver) Tasker, XXIV.488; (journalist) McGarry, XXIV.465; HSCA Report, p. 156 & see HSCA IX.132; Meagher, *op. cit.*, Chapter 24.

416 Sorrels: HSCA IX.137; and Kantor, *op. cit.*, p. 70.

Hall: XV.64–67, HSCA IX.137.

Ruby clammed up: HSCA IX.137–; HSCA Report, p. 157n7; HSCA IV.589.

Dean report: XII.432, 439. (The report was filed on November 26, but in his Warren Commission testimony Dean said he had actually dictated that report on the preceding day.)

Note 17: The three other officers were Detective T. D. McMillon and—a week later—Detectives Barnard Clardy and Don Archer. Dean, Clardy and McMillon had known Jack Ruby for years. (XX.564; XII.412; XII.403; Archer exhibits analyzed in Meagher, *op. cit.*, p. 407–)

Griffin: Kantor, *op. cit.*, p. 144; ("damned liar") XII.329; (sure Dean lied) ints, Griffin and Dean, 1978; Warren Commission memo for files, March 30 & 31, 1964; *Dallas Times-Herald*, April 5, 1964.

417 Dean on test: HSCA Report, p. 158, and *Dallas Morning News*, March 25, 1979.

"You have to suspect": Kantor, *op. cit.*, p. 154.

Ruby and police: Meagher, *op. cit.*, p. 422–; HSCA IX.128; Kantor, *op. cit.*, pp. 148, 56; (Dean) Tyler, *Courier-Times Telegraph* undated, 1977; *Dallas Morning News*, March 25, 1979; ("hysteria") Kantor, *op. cit.*, p. 216, quoting Dallas police report of December 4, 1963.

9:00 a.m. orders: Kantor, *op. cit.*, p. 60–.

418 Harrison: (Ruby sheltering) Kantor, *op. cit.*, pp. 60, 71, 145–; XXII.81; (Miller) Kantor, *op. cit.*, p. 146–.

Note 18: Kantor said the result of Harrison's lie-detector test was "not conclusive." A supervisor in police Criminal Intelligence, Lieutenant Jack Revill appeared to say he did pass the test.

Perhaps—this was in passing in testimony—Revill meant that Harrison passed the test on the specific point of whether Harrison noticed Ruby behind him just before the shooting. (He said he did not.) Whatever about the test, Revill told the Warren Commission he had "never been satisfied" that Harrison was innocent. ("not conclusive": Kantor, *op. cit.*, p. 61; Revill: HSCA IV.589)

Butler: Meagher, *op. cit.*, p. 423–.

Note 19: In 1946, Butler had been closely involved in the probe into the Mob attempt to bribe the district attorney and sheriff of the day, referred to earlier in this chapter.

419 Dean: (and Civello) *Dallas Morning News*, March 25, 1979; HSCA Report, p. 171; CD 84.91–; (dinner) *Dallas Morning News*, March 25, 1979.

Note 20: The House Assassinations Committee, rejecting the old theory that Ruby got into the police station via the Main Street ramp, believed he could have got in through an alleyway door that opened onto the ground floor. Sergeant Dean, it turned out, had vacillated as to whether the door could be opened from the outside, claiming eventually that a maintenance man had assured him the door was secure. Two maintenance men and a porter said the opposite—that it could be opened, and without a key.

Dean refused to answer a Committee questionnaire, and it proved impossible to arrange a date for his deposition. The Committee found it improbable that "Ruby entered the police basement without assistance, even though the assistance may have been provided with no knowledge of Ruby's intentions." Dean, who said in retirement that he feared he was being "set up," maintained that his association with mafioso Civello had been in the line of duty. (HSCA on ramp/door: HSCA Report, p. 157; HSCA IX.139, 143–; HSCA IV.590; Dean *re* door: HSCA IX.144; HSCA and "assistance": HSCA Report, p. 157; HSCA IX.146; Dean "set up": HSCA IV.590).

Commission request to CIA *re* Ruby: XXVI.467–; CD 1493 *re*

Karamessines to Rankin, September 15, 1964; CD 1054 re Helms to Rankin, June 10, 1964 & see HSCA XI.286, 456.

CIA/FBI not tell re Ruby-Trafficante allegation: HSCA Report, p. 153.

"When Oswald": *Washington Post*, September 7, 1976.

420 Ruby statements: ("used for purpose") Kantor, *op. cit.*, p. 209; ("framed"/ knew) "Examination of Jack Ruby," reported by Werner Tuteur, M.D.

"The only thing": KTVT, Fort Worth, Texas, September 9, 1965 (taped in Dallas County Courthouse).

24. Hints and Deceptions

421 "Three may keep": adopted by Benjamin Franklin in *Poor Richard's Almanac*, July 1735—New Orleans Mafia boss Carlos Marcello is said to have displayed the maxim on his office door. (John Davis, *op. cit.*, p. 65).

Trafficante testimony: (1977) HSCA Executive Testimony, March 16, 1977, NARA 180-10110-10237; (immunity) HSCA immunized testimony November 14, 1977, NARA 180-10118-10137; (1978) HSCA V.375, 373, 371.

422 Audiotape: HSCA source who heard tape in int. with author, May 1989.

Note 1: The author discounts, as explained in *Note 7* to Chapter 14, a claim by one of Trafficante's lawyers, Frank Ragano, that Trafficante confessed before he died that he, Carlos Marcello and Jimmy Hoffa had orchestrated the President's assassination.

Hoffa's probable murder: *New York Times*, December 6, 1975; *Clandestine American*, II.1, p. 9, Spring 1979, Sheridan, *op. cit.*, pp. 300, 356, 408.

Giancana: *Chicago Daily News*, *Chicago Tribune*, June 20 1975, *Washington Star*, December 29, 1975, int. Joseph Shimon.

Roselli: *Washington Post*, August 5, 8, 22 & September 12, 1976.

Trafficante suspect: HSCA V.366, *New York Times*, February 25, 1977, Schlesinger, *Robert F. Kennedy*, *op. cit.*, p. 549.

"said he believed": *Washington Post*, August 22 & September 7, 1976 (Jack Anderson), March 24, 1977.

423 "means, motive": HSCA IX.61.

Marcello: (tomato salesman) HSCA IX.65; (testimony to Cttee.) transcript January 11, 1978, NARA 180-10131-10312; (recordings obtained) Assassinations Records Review Board, Transcripts of Brilab Conversations, supplied to author July 17, 1998.

424 *Note 2*: Reported by author John Davis, citing a 1988 interview with former Assassinations Committee Chief Counsel Robert Blakey. Blakey has said he was told of the episode by an Assistant Director of the FBI. The information cited does not, however, appear in a folder of surveillance material sent to this author by the Assassination Records Review Board in 1998. (visitor/Marcello: John Davis, *op. cit.*, pp. 477–, 523; Blakey told: Bugliosi, *op. cit.*, Endnotes, p. 657; not appear: Jeremy Gunn letter to author, July 17, 1998)

Record shows: Davis, *op. cit.*, p. 309.

Hauser: Davis, *op. cit.*, pp. 522–, 434, *Washington Post*, November 7, 1993.

Saia: See Chapter 17, *supra*.

425 Van Laningham: ints. Jack Van Laningham, Thomas K. Kimmel, Jr., Raymond Hult, Ronald Sievert, Van Laningham to Carl Podsiadly, letter attached to SAC San Francisco to Director, July 15, 1988, NARA 124-10193-10468, & see NARA documents 124-10356-10199, 124-10356-10198, 124-10356-10197, 124-10193-10471, 124-10193-10470, 124-10193-10465, 124-10193-10466, 124-10193-10469, 124-10193-10476, 124-10193-10475, 124-10356-10201, 124-10356-10200, Waldron & Hartmann, *Legacy of Secrecy*, *op. cit.*, pp. 46–, 750–, 862.

Note 3: The FBI document was first reported by authors Lamar Waldron and Thom Hartmann in their 2009 book *Legacy of Secrecy*, and the National Archives has provided it and its explanatory cover sheet to the author. The version obtained from the National Archives names Van Laningham as the source of the information. It shows, too, that Van Laningham gave his account to agents following his transfer to a prison at Seagoville, Texas.

Van Laningham, who claimed that he had been promised early release in exchange for his cooperation over Marcello, then wrote a series of heated letters to the FBI repeating his account of what the Mob boss had told him and—among other things—naming the other inmate who had been present as "Don Wardell." The U.S. Bureau of Prisons told the author it had no record of anyone by that name having been imprisoned at Texarkana or anywhere in the federal prison system. Interviewed in 2013, Van Laningham nevertheless maintained that the other inmate's name was Wardell, and that he had disappeared from the prison soon after Van Laningham named him to his FBI handlers as a witness to Marcello's supposed confession.

Movie rights to the confession story were purchased, with a view to a Warner Brothers movie on the assassination that would reportedly star Leonardo DiCaprio. (first reported: Waldron & Hartmann, *Legacy of Secrecy, op. cit.,* p. 754–; report: available at www.maryferrell.org; Archives version: NARA 124-10193-10465, first partially published in Waldron & Hartmann, *Legacy of Secrecy, op. cit.,* p. 835-; letters/"Wardell": NARA 124-10356-10197, 10198 & 10199, 124 -10193-10466, ints. Chris Burke (BOP), Jack Van Laningham; movie: www.legacyofsecrecy.com)

428 *Note 4:* What the prison doctor called Marcello's "senility," or mental deterioration, had certainly taken hold by 1989. Jack Van Laningham has claimed that, contrary to the recollections of FBI agents Kimmel and Hult and prosecutor Sievert, the mobster had still been mentally "sharp" in 1985, when Marcello allegedly said he had had Kennedy killed.

There are other discrepancies between the version of events as told by Van Laningham and by the FBI agents involved. Kimmel's memory was the bug in the Texarkana operation against Marcello functioned for three thirty-day periods (the periods covered by three separate court authorizations for electronic surveillance). Van Laningham said the operation lasted for more than a year. Agent Kimmel said the operation was terminated once agents concluded that Marcello was not running his criminal empire from jail and, moreover, that his mental state was such that a court would have deemed anything he said unreliable. Van Laningham claimed Marcello did indeed run his crime network from inside the prison. Attempts by the author to reach a third FBI agent involved, who went by the name "Tom Kirk" during contacts with Van Laningham, established that name was a pseudonym, The agent in question, who is retired, declined to be interviewed. ("That Kennedy": Kaiser, *op. cit.*, p. 411, Waldron and Hartmann, *Legacy of Secrecy*, *op. cit.*, p. 761, Noel Twyman, *Bloody Treason*, Rancho Santa Fe, CA: Laurel, 1997, p. 298, citing FBI, Minneapolis to Director & Dallas, 3/3/89; "senility": Bugliosi, *op. cit.*, Endnotes, p. 658-, citing multiple FBI reports available at NARA, *op. cit;* "sharp" in 1985: Waldron & Hartmann, *Legacy of Secrecy*, *op. cit.*, pp. 761, 899, citing Van Laningham letter to FBI agent Carl Podsiadly, 6-88 (more accurately identified as NARA 124-10193-10468); discrepancies: ints. Thomas Kimmel, Jr., Raymond Hult, Ronald Sievert, Jack Van Laningham.

429 Martino: ints. Florence Martino, Edward Martino, 1994.

Martino background: ints. *ibid.* & Stephanie Martino, Bill Kelly int. Frances Martino, 1994; HSCA X.161; Scott, *Deep Politics, op. cit.*, p. 115–.; Kaiser, *op. cit.*, refs.; (imprisoned) *Philadelphia Evening Bulletin*, December 16, 18 & 19, 1959; October 8, 1962; January 23, 1963; July 10, 1963.

Note 5: Martino became well known as a speaker, and published a 1963 book about his incarceration. One of his public appearances, at an anti-Castro meeting in September 1963 in Dallas—one of two visits he made to the city that month—

has especially interested researchers. He mentioned during his address that he knew Amador Odio, the father of Silvia Odio—whose encounter with a man identified as "Oswald" is thought by man to be evidence of an attempt to frame the alleged assassin. (Dallas visits: Kaiser, *op. cit.*, pp. 3, 341, 348; *re* Amador Odio: XI.380, XXVI.738; book: John Martino with Nathaniel Wehl, *I Was Castro's Prisoner*, New York: Devin-Adair, 1963)

430　"close friend": FBI document July 31, 1959, file no. 64-44828; *Miami Herald*, July 9, 1959.

Roselli/plots: HSCA notes of tapes of Loran Hall, 1977; *Village Voice*, October 3, 1977; *Human Events* (Martino article), December 1, 1963.

Robertson: int. Florence Martino, David Corn, *Blond Ghost*, Boston: Little, Brown, 1994, p. 75; Warren Hinckle and William Turner, *Deadly Secrets*, New York: Thunder's Mouth Press, 1992), pp. 67–, 84–, 107, 193.

Note 6: The operation, which became known as the Bayo-Pawley Affair, aimed to "prove" a claim that the Soviet Union still had missiles in Cuba. The raiders put ashore supposedly had the mission of bringing out two Soviet officers who had supposedly been captured by anti-Castro insurgents. A study by the historian David Kaiser, however, suggests that the operation was in fact, rather, another Castro assassination attempt. The fighters put ashore never returned, and were presumed killed. The party had motored to the Cuban coast aboard a launch owned by William Pawley, an American millionaire, who was much involved with the CIA and had previously owned the Havana bus system and an airline. He was himself on board during the ill-fated raid. For fuller coverage of the operation, see the 1998 edition of this book and the sources that follow this note. (Bayo-Pawley: *Soldier of Fortune*, Spring 1976; *The Continuing Inquiry*, June 22, 1977; (Dulles) HSCA X.83; ints. John Cummings, Ed Martino, and see Hinckle and Turner, *op. cit.*, p. 193; CIA memo for the record, May 22,

1963, released 1993—there was CIA involvement, and the CIA name for the mission was Operation TILT; see also refs. in Corn, *op. cit.*, and UPI on Bayo-Pawley, January 8, 1976; Kaiser, *op. cit.*, p. 163–).

Martino prime source: CD 1020, Secret Service Report CO234030; FBI document 105-82555-2704; CD 691.2.

Flown secretly: Branigan to Sullivan, February 27, 1964, attached to Director to SAC, New York, February 26, 1964, FBI 1-64-44828 (Martino).

Ortiz: FBI memo, "Lee Harvey Oswald, Internal SecurityCuba,"June1,1964,NARA1993.06.12.10:35:57:500000.

Cummings: ints. Cummings & Martino tapes in Cummings collection.

431 *Note 7*: As reported in the previous edition of this book, O'Connor said in an interview with the author that, though Martino's name "rang a bell," he never met Oswald at any time. The author Vincent Bugliosi, however, located a CIA document showing that Martino indeed talked with O'Connor—saying that Oswald had pro-Castro leaflets printed in Miami, and had telephoned Cuban Intelligence in Cuba. (int. James J. O'Connor by Robbyn Swan, 1994; CIA document 104-10004-10145, June 4, 1964, cited in Bugliosi, *op. cit.*, Endnotes, p. 748fn.)

Note 8: Claasen made contact with the House Assassinations Committee in 1977, stating that Martino's widow was knowledgeable (as she turned out to be when contacted by the author). Claasen at first offered his information only anonymously, but eventually spoke openly with both *Dallas Morning News* reporter Earl Golz, whose report is cited here, and with this author. (Claasen int.by Earl Golz of *Dallas Morning News*, 1978; int. Claasen, 1994; HSCA memo, Fonzi to Fenton, October 4, 1977; original draft of article by Earl Golz, 1978; HSCA memo, Lawson to Klein, August 28, 1977; & see Fonzi, *op. cit.*, p. 324).

432 *Note 9*: In her interview with the author, Mrs. Martino recalled that a young Cuban had visited their house some two months before the assassination. He had been accompanied, she said, by a tall, well-dressed man who—she thought—had been some sort of official. Reminding her of the visit after the assassination, she continued, her husband told her the Cuban had been "one of them"—meaning one of those involved in the assassination.

As of the writing of the previous edition of this book, several pages referring to Martino had been withdrawn from the National Archives at the insistence of the CIA and the FBI. As recently as 2008, according to the historian David Kaiser, the CIA had released no 201 file on Martino. (withdrawn: information supplied by attorney Daniel Alcorn; no 201: Kaiser, *op. cit.*, p. 404).

432 Martínez: (ints.) September 4, October 27 (with Robert Blakey) & October 28, 2007.

433 *Note 10*: The murdered former police chief was Rogelio Hernández Vega. The Costa Rican leader was José Figuéres. (Vega: Daniels to Walker, U.S. Dept. of State, August 6, 1948, attaching AP, July 30, 1948; Figuéres: Kaiser, *op. cit.*, p. 301)

Díaz: (CIA records) NARA 104-10169-10006 & see NARA 104-10215-10321, NARA 1993.07.31.08:55:58:710059. NARA 104-10308-10164, 104-10169-10090, 104-10102-10087 & see e.g. NARA 124-10291-10330, NARA 124-90094-10088, *et al.*; (Ruby at Trescornia) re Ruby at camp, see Chapter 23, *supra*; (press coverage) *Miami News*, *Granma* [Cuba], May 31, 1966.

434 Cuesta: *Miami News*, March 16 & May 31, 1966, *New York Times*, December 4, 1992, HSCA X.100–.

436 Escalante: "Transcript of Proceedings Between Cuban Officials and JFK Historians," December 7–9, 1995, attended by author, http://cuban-exile.com/doc_026-050/doc0027-4.html, *High Times*, March 1996; Escalante, *op. cit.*, p. 165–)

Note 11: According to Escalante, Cuesta named not only Díaz but also an exile named Eladio del Valle—who had also been linked to Trafficante—as having been involved in the assassination. Rumors about del Valle's supposed participation have circulated since publication of a *National Enquirer* story that followed his own violent death in 1967. The author has seen no good evidence, however, to support the story. Unlike Herminio Díaz, the author is unaware of him having had a track record as an assassin. (Trafficante: FBI document 105-95677, citing *Diario Las Americas*, February 25, 1967; Publication: *National Enquirer*, April 27, 1967, reprinting *El Tiempo* (New York), February 1967; & see Kaiser, *op. cit.*, p. 400–)

437 DRE: ("conceived") NARA 104-10170-10127; ($51,000) CIA memo for Cottrell, State Department, April 1963, JFK Library, supplied to author by Jefferson Morley, Moley, *op. cit.*, p. 324n; (bag) conv. Jefferson Morley, citing int. DRE's Jose Lanusa; (problem) e.g. Kaiser, *op. cit.*, p.149, Morley, *op. cit.*, p. 129–; (new case officer) Fitness Report, George Joannides, July 31, 1963, supplied to author by Jefferson Morley, Kaiser, *op. cit.*, p. 150; (blitz of calls) see Chapter 16, *supra*. & HSCA X.83–, *Miami New Times*, April 12, 2001, draft for *New York Times Magazine*, and Morley email, February 10, 2013—citing numerous newspapers that carried story.

438 Note 12: The DRE man who posed as a fellow supporter of Castro was Carlos Quiroga. See reference in Chapter 16.

Note 13: Some of the DRE's members gave testimony (Carlos Bringuier) or spoke with the FBI (Bringuier and Manuel Salvat) as witnesses with information on Oswald or Ruby. (X.32–, CD 441) "inability to find": Fonzi, *op. cit.*, p. 298. ints. Dan Hardway and Edwin Lopez.

Joannides in contact/flew New Orleans: Jefferson Morley summary from record for author, January 16, 2013.

"he could not": Robert Blakey Declaration in Morley v. U.S. Central Intelligence Agency, Civil Action 03-2545, June 2006.

Note 14: The case officer who dealt specifically with the DRE's military leader, Manuel Salvat, was as of 1962 David Morales, the covert operations chief at the CIA's secret base for anti-Castro activity in Florida. In retirement in 1973, during a drinking session in which President Kennedy was discussed, Morales said—according to his attorney, Robert Walton: "We took care of that sonofabitch, didn't we?" Some have inferred that he may have been involved in the assassination. Morales, who was not interviewed by the Assassinations Committee, died in 1978. (Salvat/Morales: NARA 104-10171-10041, (ZAMKA was the code name for Morales and AMHINT-2 the code for Salvat), corr. Jefferson Morley; operations chief: David Corn, *Blond Ghost*, New York: Simon & Schuster, 1994, p. 85; remark: ints. Robert Dorff, & see Fonzi, *op. cit.*, p. 366 & Noel Twyman, *op. cit.*, p. 450–)

Note 15: Joannides's role as DRE case officer became known in late 1998, when—following questions posed by reporter Jefferson Morley—the Assassination Records Review Board obtained some of his personnel records. Morley broke the story in *Miami New Times* in April 2001.

Outrage: ("criminal"/ "willful") *Salon*, December 17, 2003; ("The Agency") *Washington Post*, November 21, 2005; ("I no longer") int. of Robert Blakey for "Who Was Lee Harvey Oswald," Frontline, www.pbs.org; ("destroyed the integrity") Nelson cited in Jim Lesar to U.S. Archivist David Ferreiro, January 20, 2012; ("The CIA wasn't") *Miami New Times*, April 12, 2001, and see *New York Times*, October 16, 2009.

439 Fighting in courts: Morley articles, February 13, 18, & 26, 2013, www.jfkfacts.org, "JFK's Murder Secrets Test CIA, Court Procedures," www.justice-integrity.org.

No monthly reports: Morley, *op. cit.*, pp. 177, 324n.

Phillips documents remain closed: *Salon*, November 22, 2011.

Phillips background: see Chapters 16 & 19, *supra.*, (& DRE) Morley, *op. cit.*, pp. 128, 314n, & see Phillips, *op. cit.*, pp. 64, 78, 93 & see also coverage of Phillips in the Paragon paperback edition of this book, published as *Conspiracy*, (1991) and Fonzi, *op. cit.*

440 "retired officer" footnote: HSCA Report, pp. 136, 136n23; HSCA X.46.

Note 16: In a book Hunt wrote about the Bay of Pigs, he referred to his "propaganda chief" colleague—evidently Phillips—as "Knight." According to Phillips himself, in his published memoir, "Knight" had been a name used by another senior officer—evidently Richard Helms. (Crozier: referred to by HSCA as "Ron Cross," HSCA X.46– & see HSCA Report, p. 136n23; "Knight": Howard Hunt, *Give Us This Day*, cited in Phillips, *op. cit.*, p. 88fn, Thomas Powers, *The Man Who Kept the Secrets*, New York: Pocket, 1979, p. 423)

Phillips denied/Veciana "not him": HSCA Report, pp. 136, 136n23; HSCA X.46.

Note 17: A former Phillips assistant named William Kent ("Doug Gupton" in the Committee's text) said he did not recall Phillips having used the name "Maurice Bishop," and did not recall whether Hunt or Phillips used the name "Knight". A former agent named Balmes Hidalgo ("B.H." in the Committee's text) said there was a "Maurice Bishop" at the CIA, but that he had been a person other than his "personal friend" Phillips. Former Director John McCone said he had known a man named "Maurice Bishop" at the Agency, only to say later that he must have been mistaken. For more extensive coverage of the Bishop/Phillips issue, see the earliest hard and paperback editions of this book, published as *Conspiracy*. (Kent/Hidalgo/McCone: HSCA X.48–; pseudonyms used: corr. Jefferson Morley, Jerry Shinley—for whose expertise the author is indebted; earliest editions: Anthony Summers, *Conspiracy*, New York: McGraw-Hill, 1980 & *ibid.* in paperback, 1981.)

441 Veciana's secretary: at length in Anthony Summers' *Conspiracy*, 1981 paperback edition, *op. cit.*, p. 527–. Author was accompanied at Prewett int. by David Leigh of *The Washington Post*, later with *The Observer* [UK].

"suspected"/"aroused": HSCA Report, p. 136n2.

442 "perjury": Fonzi, *op. cit.*, p. 410.

"less than satisfied": int. Blakey.

Note 18: Carle is the author of *The Interrogator*, a book on his experiences during the War on Terror. The quote used here is from a February 5, 2013, letter from Carle to the author's principal colleague Robbyn Swan, who had noted that—in a book review—Carle had written: "I knew "Maurice Bishop," whose real name was David Atlee Phillips." In his letter to Swan, Carle also wrote: "Another case officer colleague—a contemporary of Phillips, now long dead—in fact the man who introduced Phillips to his second wife, also spoke to me in a way that indicated that Phillips had been "Bishop." (review: *The Interrogator*, New York: Nation Books, 2011; Carle review: *The Daily Beast*, June 10, 2012)

David Phillips: Talbot, *op. cit.*, pp. 389, 445n.

novel: as read and noted by author's attorney James Lesar. James Lesar, 1994.

443 "My private": quotation supplied to author by Kevin Walsh, May, 1979.

"had all": HSCA Report, p. 115.

444 "I feel betrayed": int. Griffin by Michael Cockerell and author for BBC "Panorama" program, January 1977.

"Consider": Griffin testimony, HSCA XI.264–.

"come close": Blakey: int. on DIR radio, New York, August 1979, transcript published by *Clandestine America*, III.3, January & February 1979; int. by Jeff Goldberg, *Inquiry*, January 7 & 21, 1980; & see Blakey Introduction, *The Final Assassinations Report*, paperback edition of HSCA Report, New York: Bantam, 1979.

Justice Dept.: *New York Times*, January 6, 1980, Justice Dept. briefing, & Summers, *Conspiracy* hardback, *op. cit.*, p. 519– & paperback edition, p. 525–.

Blakey resigned: Talbot, *op. cit.*, p. 408.

445 "Everybody": Roger Craig testimony, XVI.270.

Bibliography

Works Related to the Assassination

Anson, Robert Sam, *They've Killed the President*. New York: Bantam, 1975.

Belin, David W., *November 22, 1963: You Are the Jury*. New York: Quadrangle Books, 1973.

———, *Final Disclosure*, New York: Scribners, 1988.

Bishop, Jim, *The Day Kennedy Was Shot*. New York: Funk & Wagnalls, 1968; Bantam, 1969.

Blakey, Robert, and Richard Billings, *The Plot to Kill The President*. New York: Times Books, 1981.

Blumenthal, Sid, with Harvey Yazijian, *Government by Gunplay: Assassination Conspiracy Theories from Dallas to Today*. New York: Signet, 1976.

Bringuier, Carlos, *Red Friday: November 22, 1963*. Chicago: C. Hallberg, 1969.

Buchanan, Thomas C, *Who Killed Kennedy?* New York: Putnam, 1964; London: Seeker & Warburg, 1964; New York: MacFadden, 1965.

Bugliosi, Vincent, *Reclaiming History*. New York: Norton, 2007.

Canfield, Michael, with Alan.J. Weberman, *Coup d'Etat in America: The CIA and the Assassination of John F. Kennedy*. New York: Third Press, 1975.

Crenshaw, M. D., Charles A., with Jens Hansen and J. Gary Shaw, *JFK: Conspiracy of Silence*. New York: Signet, 1992.

Curry, Jesse, *JFK Assassination File: Retired Dallas Police Chief Jesse Curry Reveals His Personal File*. Dallas: American Poster and Publishing Co., 1969.

Cutler, Robert B., *The Flight of CE-399: Evidence of Conspiracy*. Omni-Print, 1969; Beverly, Mass: Cutler Designs, 1970.

Davis, John H., *Mafia Kingfish: Carlos Marcello and the Assassination of John F. Kennedy*. New York: McGraw-Hill, 1988.

Eddowes, Michael, *Khrushchev Killed Kennedy*. Dallas: self-published, 1975.

November 22, How They Killed Kennedy. London: Neville Spearman Ltd., 1976.

————, *The Oswald File*. New York: Clarkson N. Potter, 1977; New York: Ace, 1978.

Epstein, Edward J., *The Assassination Chronicles, Inquest, Counterplot, and Legend* (incorporating new material). New York: Carroll & Graf, 1992.

————, *Counterplot*. New York: Viking, 1969.

————, *Inquest: The Warren Commission and the Establishment of Truth*. New York: Bantam, 1966; Viking, 1969.

————, *Legend: The Secret World of Lee Harvey Oswald*. New York: McGraw-Hill, 1978; London: Hutchinson, 1978, and Arrow, 1978.

Ernest, Barry. *The Girl on the Stairs*. Gretna, LA: Pelican, 2012.

Feldman, Harold, *Fifty-one Witnesses: The Grassy Knoll*. San Francisco: Idlewild Publishers, 1965.

Fensterwald, Bernard, Jr., with Michael Ewing, *Coincidence or Conspiracy?* (for the Committee to Investigate Assassinations). New York: Zebra Books, 1977.

Flammonde, Paris, *The Kennedy Conspiracy: An Uncommissioned Report on the Jim Garrison Investigation*. New York: Meredith, 1969.

Fonzi, Gaeton, *The Last Investigation*. New York: Thunder's Mouth Press, 1993.

Ford, Gerald R., with John R. Stiles, *Portrait of the Assassin*. New York: Simon & Schuster, 1965; Ballantine, 1966.

Fox, Sylvan, *The Unanswered Questions About President Kennedy's Assassination*. New York: Award Books, 1965 and 1975.

Garrison, Jim, *A Heritage of Stone*. New York: Putnam, 1970; Berkeley, 1972.

————*On the Trail of the Assassins*. New York: Sheridan Square Press, 1988.

Groden, Robert J., and Harrison E. Livingstone, *High Treason: The Assassination of President John F. Kennedy—What Really Happened.* New York: Conservatory Press, 1989.

Hamburg, Eric (editor), *Nixon: An Oliver Stone Film.* New York: Hyperion, 1995. (*cf.* chapter by Stephen J. Rivele)

Hancock, Larry, *Someone Would Have Talked*, Southlake, TX: JFK Lancer, 2011.

Hannibal, Edward, with Robert Boris, *Blood Feud.* New York: Ballantine, 1979.

Hepburn, James (pseudonym). *Farewell America.* Liechtenstein: Frontiers Publishing Co., 1968.

Hockberg, Sandy, with James T. Vallière, *The Conspirators* (The Garrison Case). New York: special edition of *Win magazine*, February 1, 1969.

Holland, Max, *The Kennedy Assassination Tapes.* New York: Knopf, 2004.

Hurt, Henry, *Reasonable Doubt.* New York: Holt, Rinehart and Winston, 1985.

James, Rosemary, with Jack Wardlaw, *Plot or Politics? The Garrison Case and Its Cast.* New Orleans: Pelican Publishing, 1967.

Joesten, Joachim, *The Garrison Enquiry: Truth & Consequences.* London: Peter Dawnay, 1967.

———, *Marina Oswald.* London: Peter Dawnay, 1967.

———, *Oswald—Assassin or Fall-guy?* New York: Marzani and Munsell, 1964.

———, *Oswald: The Truth.* London: Peter Dawnay, 1967.

Jones, Penn, Jr., *Forgive My Grief* (Vols. I–IV). Midlothian (Texas) *Mirror*, distributed by the late Penn Jones.

Kaiser, David, *The Road to Dallas.* Cambridge, MA: Belknap Press, 2008.

Kirkwood, James, *American Grotesque: An Account of the Clay Shaw-Jim Garrison Affair in New Orleans.* New York: Simon & Schuster, 1970.

La Fontaine, Ray and Mary. *Oswald Talked: The New Evidence in the JFK Assassination.* Gretna (Louisiana): Pelican Publishing, 1996.

Lambert, Patricia, *False Witness.* New York: M. Evans, 1998.

Lane, Mark, *Rush to Judgment.* New York: Holt, Rinehart & Winston, 1996; 1966: London: Bodley Head, 1966.

———, *A Citizen's Dissent*. New York: Holt, Rinehart & Winston, 1966; Fawcett Crest, 1967; Dell, 1975.

Leek, Sybil, and Bert R. Sugar, *The Assassination Chain*. New York: Corwin Books, 1976.

Lifton, David S., *Best Evidence: Deception and Disguise in the Assassination of John F. Kennedy*. New York: Macmillan, 1981; and, with update—New York: Carroll & Graf, 1988.

Mailer, Norman, *Oswald's Tale: An American Mystery*. New York: Random House, 1995.

Manchester, William, *The Death of a President: November 20–25, 1963*. New York: Harper & Row, 1967; Popular Library, 1968.

Marcus, Raymond, *The Bastard Bullet: A Search for Legitimacy for Commission Exhibit 399*. Randall Publications, 1966.

Mayo, John B., *Bulletin from Dallas: The President Is Dead*. New York: Exposition Press, 1967.

McDonald, Hugh C, as told to Geoffrey Bocca, *Appointment in Dallas: The Final Solution to the Assassination of JFK*. New York: Zebra Books, 1975.

McDonald, Hugh, with Robin Moore, *L. B. J. and the J. F. K. Conspiracy*. Westport, Conn.: Condor, 1978.

McKinley, James, *Assassination in America*. New York: Harper & Row, 1977.

McKnight, Gerald, *Breach of Trust: How the Warren Commision Failed the Nation and Why*. Lawrence, KS: Univ. of Kansas Press, 2005.

McMillan, Priscilla Johnson, *Marina and Lee*. New York: Harper & Row, 1978.

Meagher, Sylvia, *Accessories after the Fact: The Warren Commission, the Authorities, and the Report*. New York: Bobbs-Merrill, 1967; Vintage, 1976.

———, *Subject Index to the Warren Report and Hearings and Exhibits*. New York: Scarecrow Press, 1966; Ann Arbor, Michigan: University Microfilms, 1971.

Miller, Tom, *The Assassination Please Almanac*. Chicago: Henry Regnery Co., 1977.

Model, Peter, with Robert J. Groden, *JFK: The Case for Conspiracy*. New York: Manor Books, 1976.

Morrow, Robert D., *Betrayal: A Reconstruction of Certain Clandestine Events from the Bay of Pigs to the Assassination of John F. Kennedy.* Chicago: Henry Regnery Co., 1976.

Murr, Gary, *"The Murder of Police Officer J. D. Tippit."* 1971 unpublished manuscript), Canada, 1971.

Myers, Dale. *With Malice: Lee Harvey Oswald and the Murder of Officer J.D. Tippit.* Milford, MI: Oak Cliff, 1998.

Nechiporenko, Col. Oleg Maximovich, Passport to Assassination. New York: Birch Lane Press, 1993.

Newman, Albert H., *The Assassination of John F. Kennedy: The Reasons Why.* New York: Potter, 1970.

Newman, John, *Oswald and the CIA.* New York: Carroll & Graf, 1995.

Noyes, Peter, *Legacy of Doubt.* New York: Pinnacle Books, 1973.

Oglesby, Carl, *The Yankee and Cowboy War.* Mission, Kansas: Sheed, Andrews and McMeel, 1976.

Oltmans, Willem, *Reportage Over de Moordenaars.* Utrecht, Holland: Bruna & Zoon, 1977.

Oswald, Robert L., with Myrick and Barbara Land, *Lee: A Portrait of Lee Harvey Oswald.* New York: Coward-McCann, 1967.

O'Toole, George, *The Assassination Tapes: An Electronic Probe into the Murder of John F. Kennedy and the Dallas Cover-up.* New York: Penthouse Press, 1975.

Popkin, Richard H., *The Second Oswald.* New York: Avon Books, 1966.

Posner, Gerald, *Case Closed: Lee Harvey Oswald and the Assassination of JFK.* New York: Random House, 1993.

Rand, Michael, with Howard Loxton and Len Deighton, *The Assassination of President Kennedy.* London: Jonathan Cape, 1967.

Roffman, Howard, *Presumed Guilty.* Cranbury, New Jersey: Fairleigh Dickinson Press, 1975; London: Thomas Yoselaff, 1976; New York: A. S. Barnes & Co., 1976.

Russell, Dick, *The Man Who Knew Too Much.* New York: Carroll & Graf, 1992.

Russo, Gus, *Live by the Sword.* Baltimore, MD: Bancroft Press, 1998.

_____, *Brothers In Arms.* New York: Bloomsbury, 2008.

Sauvage, Leo, *The Oswald Affair: An Examination of the Contradictions and Omissions of the Warren Report*. Cleveland: World Publishing Co., 1966.

Scheim, David, *Contract on America: The Mafia Murders of John and Robert Kennedy*. New York: Shapolsky Books, 1988.

Scott, Peter Dale, Paul L. Hoch and Russell Stetler, *The Assassinations: Dallas and Beyond—A Guide to Cover-ups and Investigations*. New York: Random House, Vintage Press, 1976.

_____, *Crime and Cover-up: The CIA, the Mafia, and the Dallas-Watergate Connection*. Berkeley, California: Westworks, 1977.

———, "The Dallas Conspiracy," unpublished manuscript.

———, *Deep Politics and the Death of JFK*. Berkeley: University of California Press, 1993.

———, *Deep Politics II* Skokie, IL: Green Archive, 1995 [not seen by author].

Shaw, J. Gary, and Larry R. Harris, *Cover-up: The Governmental Conspiracy to Conceal the Facts about the Public Execution of John Kennedy*. Cleburne, Texas, 1976 (available from its authors).

Stafford, Jean, *A Mother in History: Mrs. Marguerite Oswald*. New York: Farrar, Straus & Giroux, 1966; Bantam, 1966.

Summers, Anthony. *Conspiracy*. New York: McGraw-Hill, 1980 & paperback (revised) 1981.

_____, *Conspiracy*. New York: Paragon House, 1989.

_____, *Not In Your Lifetime*. New York: Marlowe, 1998.

Talbot, David, *Brothers, The Hidden History of the Kennedy Years. Brothers, The Hidden History of the Kennedy Years*. New York: Simon & Schuster, 2007.

Thompson, Josiah, *Six Seconds in Dallas: A Microstudy of the Kennedy Assassination*. New York: Bernard Geis Associates, 1967; (revised) Berkeley, 1976.

Thornley, Kerry, *Oswald*. Chicago: New Classics House, 1965.

Titovets, Ernst, *Oswald: Russian Episode*. Minsk: Mon Litera, 2010.

Trask, Richard B., *Pictures of the Pain: Photography and the Assassination of President Kennedy*. Danvers, Mass.; Yeoman Press, 1994.

United Press International and *American Heritage* magazine, *Four Days*. New York: American Heritage Publishing Company, 1964.

Waldron, Lamar and Hartmann, Thom, *Ultimate Sacrifice*. New York: Carroll & Graf, 2005, updated 2006.

———, *Legacy of Secrecy*. Berkeley, CA: Counterpoint, 2009.

Weisberg, Harold, *Case Open*. New York: Carroll & Graf, 1994.

———, Harold, *Oswald in New Orleans—Case for Conspiracy with the CIA*. New York: Canyon Books, 1967.

———, *Post-Mortem*. Frederick, MD: self-published, 1975.

———, *Whitewash* (Vols. I–IV). Hyattstown, MD: self-published, 1965, 1967; and (Vols I & II) New York: Dell, 1966–67.

White, Stephen, *Should We Now Believe the Warren Report?* New York: Macmillan, 1968.

Wise, Dan, with Marietta Maxfield, *The Day Kennedy Died*. San Antonio: Naylor, 1964.

(See also *The Assassination Story* [collected clippings from Dallas newspapers]. American Eagle Publishing Co., 1964)

Zelizer, Barbie, *Covering the Body, The Kennedy Assassination, the Media, and the Shaping of Collective Memory*. Chicago: Univ. of Chicago Press, 1992.

Books on Jack Ruby

Belli, Melvin, with Maurice Carroll, *Dallas Justice*. New York: David McKay, 1964.

Denson, R. B., *Destiny in Dallas*. Dallas: Denco Corporation, 1964.

Gertz, Elmer, *Moment of Madness: The People vs. Jack Ruby*. Chicago: Follett Publishing Co., 1968.

Hunter, Diana, with Alice Anderson, *Jack Ruby's Girls*. Atlanta: Hallux Inc., 1970.

Kantor, Seth, *Who Was Jack Ruby?* New York: Everest House, 1978.

Kaplan, John, with Jon R. Waltz, *The Trial of Jack Ruby: A Classic Study of Courtroom Strategies*. New York: Macmillan, 1965.

Wills, Gary, and Ovid Demaris, *Jack Ruby: The Man Who Killed the Man Who Killed Kennedy*. New York: New American Library, 1967; New American Library paperback, 1968.

Books on Forensic Science

Houts, Marshall, *Where Death Delights*. New York: Dell, 1967.

Medico-Legal Journal (Vol. 4, December 1964). Trauma. New York: Matthew Bender & Co., 1964.

Books on Intelligence

Abel, Elie, *The Missiles of October*. London: MacGibbon & Kee, 1969.

Agee, Philip, *Inside the Company: CIA Diary*. New York: Bantam, 1976.

Ashman, Charles, *The CIA-Mafia Link*. New York: Manor Books, 1975.

Barron, John, *KGB*. New York: *Reader's Digest* Press, 1974.

Bowart, Walter, Operation Mind Control. New York: Delacorte, 1977.

Corn, David, *Blond Ghost*. New York: Simon & Schuster, 1994.

Dulles, Allen, *The Craft of Intelligence*. New York: Harper & Row, 1963.

Helms, Richard, *A Look Over My Shoulder*. New York: Knopf, 2003.

Hinckle, Warren, and William Turner, *Deadly Secrets: The CIA-Mafia War Against Castro and the Assassination of JFK*. New York: Thunder's Mouth Press, 1992.

Hougan, Jim, *Spooks*. New York: William Morrow, 1978.

Kirkpatrick, Lyman B., *The Real CIA*. New York: Macmillan, 1968.

Marchetti, Victor, and John Marks, *The CIA and the Cult of Intelligence*. New York: Alfred A. Knopf, 1974; Dell, 1975.

Morley, Jefferson, *Our Man In Mexico, Winslow Scott and the Hidden History of the CIA*. Lawrence, KS: Univ. of Kansas, 2008.

New York Times, The Pentagon Papers. June 13, 14, 15, and July 1, 1971.

Phillips, David, *The Night Watch*. New York: Atheneum, 1977.

Powers, Gary, with Curt Gentry, *Operation Overflight*. New York: Holt, Rinehart & Winston, 1970; London: Hodder & Stoughton, 1970.

Powers, Thomas, *The Man Who Kept the Secrets: Richard Helms and the CIA*. New York: Pocket Books, 1979.

Prouty, L. Fletcher, *The Secret Team*. Englewood Cliffs, New Jersey: Prentice-Hall, 1973.

Rositzke, Harry, *The CIA's Secret Operations*. New York: *Reader's Digest* Press, 1977.

Smith, Joseph B., *Portrait of a Cold Warrior*. New York: Putnam, 1976.

Summers, Anthony, *Official and Confidential: The Secret Life of J. Edgar Hoover*. New York: Putnam, 1993, and (updated) Pocket, 1994.

Thomas, Evan, *The Very Best Men, Four Who Dared: The Early Years of the CIA*. New York: Simon & Schuster, 1995.

Wise, David, and Thomas B. Ross, *The Invisible Government*. New York: Random House, 1964.

_____, *The Espionage Establishment*. New York: Random House, 1967.

_____, *Molehunt*. New York: Random House, 1992.

Books related to Organized Crime

Exner, Judith, *My Story* (as told to Ovid Demaris). New York: Grove, 1977.

Kennedy, Robert F., *The Enemy Within*. New York: Harper & Row, 1960.

Kidner, John, Crimaldi, *Contract Killer*. Washington, DC: Acropolis Books, 1976.

McClellan, John, *Crime Without Punishment*. New York: Duell, Sloan & Pearce, 1962.

Messick, Hank, and Burt Goldblatt, *The Mobs and the Mafia*. New York: Ballantine, 1973.

Moldea, Dan E., *The Hoffa Wars*. New York and London: Paddington Press, 1978.

Ragano, Frank, and Selwyn Raab, *Mob Lawyer*. New York: Charles Scribner's Sons, 1994.

Reid, Ed, *The Grim Reapers*. Chicago: Henry Regnery Co., 1969; New York: Bantam, 1969.

Reid, Ed, and Ovid Demaris, *The Green Felt Jungle*. New York: Trident Press, 1963.

Sheridan, Walter, *The Fall and Rise of Jimmy Hoffa*. New York: Saturday Review Press, 1972.

Talese, Gay, *Honor Thy Father*. Cleveland and New York: World Publishing Co., 1971.

Teresa, Vincent, with Thomas C. Renner, *My Life in the Mafia*. London: Hart-Davis, McGibbon, 1973; Panther, 1974.

Other

Attwood, William, *The Reds and the Blacks*. New York: Harper & Row, 1967.

Ayers, Bradley Earl, *The War That Never Was*. New York: Bobbs-Merrill, 1976.

Eisenhower, Dwight, *The White House Years: Waging Peace, 1956–1961*. New York: Doubleday, 1965.

Goodwin, Richard N., *Remembering America—A Voice from the Sixties*. Boston: Little, Brown, 1988.

Haldeman, H. R., with Joseph Di Mona, *The Ends of Power*. New York: Times Book Co., 1978.

Hunt, E. Howard, *Give Us This Day*. New York: Arlington House, 1973.

Johnson, Haynes, *Bay of Pigs*. New York: Norton, 1964.

Kennedy, John F., (speeches), *Public Papers of the Presidents of the United States*. Washington, DC: U.S. Government Printing Office, 1962–1964.

Lasky, Victor, *It Didn't Start with Watergate*. New York: Dell, 1978.

Latell, Brian, *Castro's Secrets*. New York: Palgrave Macmillan, 2012.

Lawrence, Lincoln (pseudonym). *Were We Controlled?* New Hyde Park, New York: University Books, 1967.

Schlesinger, Arthur, *A Thousand Days: John F. Kennedy in the White House*. Boston: Houghton Mifflin Co., 1965.

———, *Robert Kennedy and His Times*. Boston: Houghton Mifflin Co., 1978.

Schorr, Daniel, *Clearing the Air*. Boston: Houghton Mifflin Co., 1977; New York: Berkeley, 1978.

Sorensen, Theodore, *The Kennedy Legacy*. New York: New American Library, 1970.

White, Theodore, *The Making of the President*. New York: Atheneum, 1965.

Official Reports

Alleged Assassination Plots Involving Foreign Leaders, Interim Report of the Select Committee to Study Governmental Operations, with Respect to Intelligence Activities, U.S. Senate. Washington D.C.: U.S. Government Printing Office, 1975 (subsequent listings are also published by U.S. Government Printing Office unless otherwise described).

Final Report of the Assassination Records Review Board, Washington, DC: U.S. Government Printing Office, 1998.

Hearings Before the Sub-Committee on Civil and Constitutional Rights of the Committee on the Judiciary, House of Representatives, on FBI Oversight (Serial No. 2, Part III), 1976.

Investigation of the Assassination of President John F. Kennedy, Book V, Final Report of the Select Committee to Study Governmental Operations, with Respect to Intelligence Activities, U.S. Senate, 1976.

Report of the President's Commission on the Assassination of President John F. Kennedy, and 26 accompanying volumes of Hearings and Exhibits, 1964; published by U.S. Government Printing Office and also Doubleday, McGraw-Hill, Bantam, Popular Library, and Associated Press (New York), 1964.

Report of the Select Committee on Assassinations, U.S. House of Representatives, and 12 accompanying volumes of *Hearings and Appendices* (on Kennedy case as opposed to Martin Luther King assassination), 1979, published by U.S. Government Printing Office; and *Report* (only) by Bantam (New York), 1979, under title *The Final Assassinations Report*.

Report to the President by the Commission on CIA Activities Within the United States. Also published by Manor Books (New York), 1976.

Texas Supplemental Report on the Assassination of President John F. Kennedy and the Serious Wounding of Governor John B. Connolly, November 22, 1963, by Texas Attorney General Waggoner Carr, Austin, Texas, 1964.

About the Author

ANTHONY SUMMERS is the author of eight acclaimed books. The most recent, *The Eleventh Day*, on the 9/11 attacks, was a Finalist for the 2012 Pulitzer Prize for History and won the Golden Dagger award for the best crime nonfiction of the year. The first edition of this book, *Not in Your Lifetime*, was also awarded the Golden Dagger.

Index

JFK inaugural address, 165
Soviet Embassy, 187, 249, 319, 338, 349
Washington Evening Star, 167, 331
Washington Post, 148, 229, 245, 331, 334
Wasp, USS, 249
Watergate, 26, 120, 202, 203, 305
WDSU station, 251, 259
Webster, Robert, 175–176
Weinberg, Jimmy, 402
Weiner, Irwin, 407
Weisburg, Willie, 226–227
Weiss, Mark, 27, 35
Wells, H. G., 187
West Berlin, 171, 172
Western Union, 414
West Germany, 151, 171, 189
White, Mrs. Roscoe, 79
White, Roscoe, 79
Williams, Bonnie Ray, 90
Willis, Rosemary, 56
Wilson, John, 405
Winston, Patricia, 315–316
Witnesses. *See also* Shots fired
Bethesda Hospital, 21
Parkland Hospital, 21
Tippit murder, 101–106
"Witting Collaborator 01 code A1," 167
Wofford, Harris, 378
Woodward, Mary, 40
The Worker (newspaper), 82, 187, 248, 262, 346
Worrell, James, 63

Wright, Frank, 106
Wrist wound, 47, 49–50

X-ray evidence, 17, 20, 23–24, 45, 53–54, 55

Yarborough, Ralph, 40, 43

Zapruder, Abraham, 24–25, 41
Zapruder film, 24–26, 33, 41, 44, 45, 47, 49, 53
Zenith Technological Services, 207

EBOOKS BY ANTHONY SUMMERS

FROM OPEN ROAD MEDIA

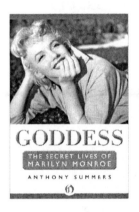
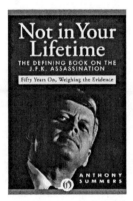
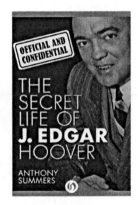

Available wherever ebooks are sold

CPSIA information can be obtained at www.ICGtesting.com
Printed in the USA
LVOW08s1520231013

358274LV00003B/596/P